TABLE OF CONTENTS

	Introduction: Starting Out on the Path	5
1	Many Are the Ancient Ones: The "Obstinate Persistence" of Polytheism	50
2	The Earth Goddess and Her Consort, Isis, Ba'al, and Mediterranean Deities	63
3	Celtic and Germanic Divinities	104
4	Slavic and Baltic Divinities	127
5	Eglė and Žaltys: A Tale of Love, Betrayal, and Metamorphosis	146
6	Basque, Romanian, Finno-Ugric, and Sámi Divinities	173
7	Veneration of Goddesses and Related Female Beings Rising to Prominence in the Middle Ages and Thereafter	180
8	Veneration of Male Divinities and Other Male Beings Rising to Prominence in the Middle Ages and Thereafter	239
9	Veneration of Fairies, Elves, and Kindred Beings	255
10	The Goodman's Brood: Demonic Beings and Practices	298
	Notes & Sources	312
	Index	323

Dedication and Acknowledgments

This book is dedicated to my husband David Hatfield Sparks, to our daughter Mariah and her husband Prado Gomez, to the memory of my maternal grandmother Maggie Lundschien, to that of my mother, Ala Mae Krause and my second mother, Lola Bell Taylor, to that of my parents-in-law Martha and Wilbur Sparks, and to that of my best friend of thirty years, Gloria Anzaldúa.

To my spiritual teachers, Mama Lola, Maggie Champagne, Angie Arrien, Tamara Diaghilev, Miriam Williams Chamani, Iroquois elder Olivier, Lazaro Pérez Moré, Roberto Carlos Hernando Ferro, and Alina Valera.

To Professors Lucia Chiavola Birnbaum and Sean Kelly, who headed my dissertation committee.

To my mewses Puck, Pyewacket, Tiresias, Lucifur, Kinkers, and Hissie.

To Diane Apostolos Cappadona, Ana Castillo, John Bowlt, Richard Bodien, Mary Broderick, Taylor Cage, Jane Caputi, Scot Casey, Ariban Chagoya, Max Dashú, Eleni Dedes, Vilius Dundzila, Arthur Evans, the Radical Faeries, Betty Sue Flowers, Marija Gimbutas, Susan Green, Kveldulf Gundarsson/ Stephan Grundy, Eahr Joan, Lisa Jones, Rhydonia Jones, Peter Limnios, Lily Litvak, James-Herbert Lundszien, John Michael Mitchell, Carol Murphy, Vickie Neubeck O'Connor, Laura Pérez, Catherine Rainwater, Marguerite Rigoglioso, Guillermo Robles, June Smith, Starhawk, Patrice Suncircle, Jonas Trinkunas, Kay Turner, John Velz, Charles Whitenberg, and Shirley Wiley.

To the staff at the Humanities Research Center at the University of Texas, the librarians at U.C. Berkeley, and librarian Susan Yach at Moraine Valley Community College.

To the spirits of Julian 'the Apostate,' Nyklot of the Wends, and the myriad pagan women, transgender persons, and men who have suffered at the hands of oppressive religious and political institutions.

Finally, I wish to thank Mogg Morgan of Mandrake for believing in my work and for publishing my manuscript; and, for inspiring the writing of this text over many years, the music of Loreena McKennitt, Fairport Convention, John Renbourn, Jethro Tull, Stevie Nicks, Sarah Brightman, and the Anonymous 4.

The Pagan Heart of the West

Embodying Ancient Beliefs and Practices from Antiquity to the Present

Vol I Deities and Kindred Beings

by

Randy P. Conner Ph.D.

Copyright © Randy P Conner 2019
First paperback Edition

All rights reserved. No part of this work may be reproduced or utilized in any form by any means electronic or mechanical, including *xerography, photocopying, microfilm,* and *recording,* or by any information storage system without permission in writing from the publishers.

Published by
Mandrake of Oxford
PO Box 250
OXFORD
OX1 1AP (UK)

Vol. 1: Deities and Kindred Beings
Vol. 2: The Veneration of Nature
Vol. 3: Rituals and Ritual Specialists
Vol. 4: Christianization
Vol. 5: The Arts and Philosophy

Introduction: Starting Out on the Path

Wherever possible, they were determined to sever Western humanity from its roots, its gods, its spirits, its memory.

—Bernard Rio, *L'Arbre Philosophal* (2001)[1]

No matter how often you talk…you will never be able to uproot our customs, but we will continue always and forever to carry on our feasts as we have hitherto. No man will ever be able to forbid us the ancient pastimes that are so dear to us.

—an angry crowd, led by Erchenwald (chief chamberlain in the Emperor's palace), attributed to St. Eligius, seventh century CE[2]

By their very nature, gods survive; otherwise, they would not be divine.

—Kelly Kamborian, "Children of the Planets: Medieval Astronomical Imagery" (1987)[3]

As you unfold the wonders of the mind … the secrets of many splendid mysteries shine forth in the light of your truth; and the wisdom of 'charmed rings,' 'blessed brambles,' and amulets and talismans, fades before the precepts of a purer faith. Yet is there no witchcraft in your philosophy?

—Walter Cooper Dendy, *The Philosophy of Mystery* (1845)[4]

Thus would a sort of polytheism return upon us…

—William James, *The Varieties of Religious Experience* (1902)[5]

Europe is never more pagan than when it searches for its roots . . .

—Jean Markale, "Aujourd'hui, l'esprit païen?" (1980)[6]

In the twelfth century CE, that is, almost a millennium ago, an anonymous Russian writer traversing the Aegean Sea defined *Iazychestvo*, which translates roughly as "paganism," as embracing the veneration of nature (the "attribution of a living soul to all natural elements"); the reverence of divinities (particularly of a Great Goddess and the thunder god Perûn [or, Parom, Perun, Perunu, Pierun, Piorun]) and of elementals; the veneration of ancestors; practices of divination and magic; the celebration of seasonal rites; rites of offering and sacrifice; and the creation of sacred arts and crafts as forms of communication with the divine. He also noted the emergence, with the arrival of Christianization, of a "dual" or hybrid (or, mixed, syncretic) sacred tradition, often referred to in Russian as *dvoeverie*.

The Russian historian and archaeologist Boris Rybakov (1908-2001), who in *Kievan Rus'* describes this medieval traveler, whose text was titled in *The Story of How the Pagan Peoples Worshipped Idols and Offered Sacrifices*, as "highly educated" and as an early writer on comparative religion, points out that this scholar was familiar not only with indigenous Slavic sacred beliefs and practices and with Orthodox Christianity but also with "the ancient Egyptian cult of Osiris" and the religions/traditions of the ancient Greeks as well as with Catholicism and Islam. Arnaldo Momigliano, in *On Pagans, Jews, and Christians* (1987), writes: "The first beginnings of a different, more historical approach to religion, and especially to polytheism, is to be found in...works of the eleventh to twelfth centuries that report on the religious situation in countries visited by...authors or their informants." Momigliano suggests that by way of "exploration and diplomacy," those who traveled far distances "accumulate[ed] new information on pagan countries" and thereby may have somewhat amended their views regarding paganism and even, as mostly Christians, their understanding of "their own pagan past."

A century prior to the Russian traveler's account, Northumbrian Christian priests in what is today northeast England and southern Scotland described 'heathenism' or 'paganism' as including the following: the veneration of Nature; the reverence of divinities ("idols") as "the worship of heathen gods"); offerings and sacrifices to pagan divinities; practices of divination and magic; and attending a pagan sanctuary. The descriptions of paganism given by the Russian traveler and the British priests are strikingly similar. The Viking Christian King Cnut (or, Canute, *c*. 985/995-1035), in the early eleventh century, forbade in his *Laws* the worship of "the Gods of the Gentiles; that is to say, the Sun, Moon, Fires, Fountains, Hills, or Trees, and Woods of any kind."

In the late thirteenth or possibly the very early fourteenth century, Auger II de Montfaucon (d. 1303/1304), then bishop of the Couserans province in southern France, appears to have presided over a book of statutes that includes a set of beliefs and practices that, taken together, constitute an extended definition of paganism that is more than a little reminiscent of the foregoing descriptions. Divination, magic, invocations, and other forbidden practices such as offering feasts to non-Christian beings were linked in the text to reverence of the goddess Diana in various manifestations. Not only were primarily pagan practices condemned, but also mixtures of pagan and Christian rites such as those involving invocations and incantations rather than only prayers.

The meaning of "paganism" and those beliefs and practices comprising it have remained rather surprisingly consistent since the Middle Ages – if not for centuries prior. Moreover, such beliefs and practices continued to exist and be performed in European regions long after official Christianization. Both these and mixed pagan-Christian beliefs and practices have been generally condemned by Church authorities.

Early twentieth-century writers – previous to the later twentieth-century's anti-comparativist agenda – continued to recognize the numerous common traits shared by pagan traditions and indicated that together these traits formed a religion rooted in nature. For example, in his 1902 study *Elder Faiths of Ireland*, the archaeologist, historian, and antiquarian W. G. Wood-Martin (1847-1917), names as elements of this "faith" a "belief in the transmigration of souls into animals, plants, and other objects…[together with] the general conception of the world as a living animal;" polytheism; veneration of ancestors; ritual specialists including wisewomen; etc.

A ritual specialist is an individual with special training and abilities who can facilitate communication between human and other-than-human realms. A ritual specialist performs many functions in a community, often including counseling; mediating disputes; performing rituals; producing medicines, often plant-based, to cure illnesses; and foretelling future events. Ritual specialists may include shamans, priests and priestesses, sacred artists (such as sandpainters, makers of icons, etc.), and others who perform such roles.

In an intriguing passage regarding the supposed earthly existence of Greek deities, Wood-Martin deploys the term "earth-born," in a way that forecasts the present-day description of certain traditions as "earth-based."

The Aim of This Text

This text focuses on beliefs, practices, and practitioners, as well as upon the arts and philosophy and, to a much lesser extent, political activism, as vessels and agents of culture, embodying and transmitting ancient and indigenous – primarily European – pagan wisdom, especially in the face of Christianization. It stresses that the West owes a great debt to its ancient, indigenous, non-Christian sacred origins and demonstrates that Christianized Western culture has not depended solely upon the personae, narratives, or symbols of Christianity for its beliefs, practices, arts, philosophies, etc., but has for millennia depended upon, and continues to appropriate, pagan images, ideas, and practices.

This text proposes that rather than insisting upon the "death of paganism" or even upon "survivals" or "traces" of paganism, although the latter two are valid concepts, we might instead entertain the notion that pagan traditions did not die simply because they were forbidden, their practitioners converted or done away with, or the material culture of their traditions destroyed, but rather that, even as Christianization progressed, pagan-rooted sacred traditions persisted and, moreover, evolved and expressed innovation.

This text contends that it is historically inaccurate, logically fallacious, and ethically irresponsible to claim the persistence and metamorphosis of these traditions for Christianity alone; we should instead understand them, depending upon the particular subject or situation we are discussing, as either pagan- or pagano-Christian (and/or pagano-Abrahamic) hybrid phenomena.

This text also contends that when we try to draw lines in the sand between "paganism/s" and "NeoPaganism/s," we are standing on very shaky ground. As with particles and waves, the nearer we approach the boundary, the more fluid it becomes.

This text infers that in the absence of the West's pagan influences, works including folk tales and ballads, many of the works of Botticelli and other visual artists, the philosophies of Ficino, Bruno, and Nietzsche, the poetry of Shelley and Yeats, the dance of Isadora Duncan, and many other works would cease to exist, would never have manifested. It also questions the supposition that most works deploying pagan figures, narratives, symbols, and so on do so mainly from a notion of ornamentation and/or a nod to the imaginative as opposed to a devotional dimension of human experience. Indeed, many pagan-inspired works of visual art, literature, music, drama, and philosophy may in fact reflect, as Gloria Kury proposes in *The Early Work of Luca Signorelli*, "sacred conversations" rather than quaint metaphors from a long-dead past. This text further infers that pagan imagery, rites, etc., may have in certain times and places served as a kind of counterdiscourse to that of the Church. This text demonstrates, moreover, that we need to question hegemonic, underlying academic assumptions that elites, scholars, and artists of various sorts did not occasionally mix with rurals or the urban poor, as, for instance, the presence of "groundlings," who celebrated seasonal rites, in attendance at Shakespeare's plays indicates.

More broadly speaking, this text demonstrates that the hegemonic narrative of Western cultural history, which basically leads from Plato to Christianity to the evolution of scientific thought and the Industrial Revolution, and for some, from there to Teilhard de Chardin, is only one way, indeed, an extremely limited way, of viewing or reading the cultural history of the West. I want to acknowledge that I understand the West to be the creation not only of ancient, indigenous, pagan traditions and cultures but also of African, Indigenous American, and other cultures and sacred traditions. My text must, however, due to constraints of time and space, remain a fragmentary account, limited to an exploration of only one web of influence, that of pagan sacred traditions.

Definitions and Descriptions

In this text, I am defining "paganism/s" as

a fluid collection of ancient, indigenous, ethnic, tribal, "traditional"), and/or earth-centered beliefs (or ideas) that together, comprise a worldview, and allied practices, typically including the basic elements given by the Russian traveler and Catholic priests, arising in antiquity and developing and transforming during the medieval period and thereafter, parallel to, in spite of, and in some cases, in reaction to, and rebellion against the onslaught of forced Christianization.

By "ancient," I refer generally to cultures predating the fourth century CE such as those of ancient Egypt, Greece, and Rome, as well as to those of the Celts, Germanics (Scandinavians), Slavs, Balts, and certain other groups like Basques and Sámi, and their European forebears, whom the Lithuanian-American archaeologist Marija Gimbutas (1921-1994). and others have referred to as "Old Europeans." These traditions were rooted in Proto-Indo-European and Indo-European cultures. They were most probably informed as well by non-Indo-European cultures such as certain ancient African cultures, including that of Egypt.

The term "indigenous" requires a bit more explanation. Charles H. Long, in "Indigenous People, Materialities, and Religion: Outline for a New Orientation to Religious Meaning" (2003), describes "indigenous" as "the basis of a new epistemological stance in the world," a way of knowing that "moves us away from the distantiated, objectified, positivistic, and rationalistic styles of knowledge" that have come to characterize Western ways of knowing.

Although the term "indigenous," as pertaining to "native" or "aboriginal," is quite old, the term "indigenous peoples," as Linda Tuhiwai Smith observes in *Decolonizing Methodologies: Research and Indigenous Peoples* (1999), is a "relatively recent term which emerged in the 1970s out of the struggles" of Native Americans/ First Nations peoples. As Shaheen Sadar Ali and Javaid Rehman observe in "Indigenous Peoples and Ethnic Minorities in Pakistan" (2001), the term "indigenous peoples" is not easy to define. Nevertheless, they cite U. N. Special Rapporteur Dr. José R. Martínez-Cobo's as a helpful, general definition: "Indigenous communities, peoples and nations are those which, having continuity with pre-invasion and pre-colonial societies..., consider themselves distinct...They form...non-dominant sectors of society and are determined to preserve, develop and transmit to future generations their ancestral...cultural patterns." For Tuhiwai Smith, the term "indigenous peoples" "share experiences as peoples who have been subjected to the colonization of their lands and cultures, and the denial of their sovereignty, by a colonizing society that has come to dominate and determine the shape and quality of their lives." Jualynne E. Dodson in *Sacred Spaces and Religious Traditions in Oriente Cuba* (2008), in writing of African-Cuban traditions, defines indigenous sacred traditions as: "those coherent sets of ritual behaviors that, over ancestral history, have developed in a land space and in conjunction with the orientation and practices of cultural groups who originally inhabited the land."

Although specific concepts and practices of various indigenous sacred traditions vary widely, certain ones appear to be found in a number of them. Semali and Kincheloe suggest, for example, that holism and an emphasis on relationality in regard to relationships among humans, animals, nature, and culture (sometimes viewed as an "ensemble of [non-literary] texts") play a significant role in a number of indigenous sacred traditions. Many of these describe, like that of the Omaha people of Nebraska and Iowa, a "mysterious life power permeating all natural forms and forces," known to the Omaha as *wakonda*. (Are you, like me, thinking at this moment of the marvelous film *Black Panther*?) Likewise, a number of them hold that "multiform appearance is an inherent potential of all animate beings."

Smith, in "An Athapaskan Way of Knowing," while focusing on the concepts and practices of the Chipewayan people of Canada, paints a portrait of a particular sacred tradition that shares much in common with other indigenous sacred traditions. For example, a number of indigenous peoples, like the Chipewayan, maintain that "[r]eality is at once material and spiritual;" that "[e]verything has a sacred aspect;" that there are "no sacred-profane, natural-supernatural, or material-spiritual dualisms;" and that there is "no body-soul antinomy." Like many other indigenous peoples, they hold that "[a]ll beings have *inkonze* [i.e., sacred force/energy];" that "both humans and animals are persons;" that "it [is] possible for humans to be transformed into animals and animals into humans;" and that "all beings, human and nonhuman, are inextricably engaged in a complex communicative interrelationship. ...Maintaining harmony requires empirical, experiential, holistic knowledge." They hold that sacred power is bestowed on "those individuals who display respectful attitudes and actions toward human and animal persons" as well as upon animals themselves, and that "medicine"/magic results from an association of human-animal communication, dreaming, and making offerings and sacrifices, "such as sprinkling tobacco on the place from which one has taken power roots." The person who practices a sacred tradition is viewed not so much as a *"believer* as a *knower."*

It is very important to bear in mind, as Dodson reminds us in *Sacred Spaces*, that "[a]ll religions are dynamic; they constantly change. Indigenous religious practices...are no different." Moreover, Dodson expands the definition of "indigenous" when she further defines the combined concepts and practices of, or sacred hybridity constructed by, Indigenous Americans and Africans brought to the Americas as "indigenous" to Cuba. Dodson states: "Our understanding is that indigenous religions evolve when there is respectful sharing of autochthonous understandings with migrant understandings, when a blending of practices evolve[s]."

I think we should be very careful when applying the term "indigenous" to European traditions and religions of the past, as the term, at present, carries a connotation of traditions of the 'developing' world – another loaded term! – that have been and continue to be damaged and/or suppressed via imperialism and colonialism and by other means. They are, like all such traditions, embedded in historical and political contexts, and these contexts differ markedly from those of ancient, medieval, and modern epochs and cultures.

I nevertheless think it might be very helpful to us to consider the concepts and traditions of European peoples prior to Christianization (and, to a much lesser extent, and only in limited areas, Islamicization) as the indigenous traditions of Europe, including the Mediterranean.

Of course, if we are to do so, we must do so with the qualification that these indigenous traditions eventually lead us back to Africa, from the place of our collective emergence.

Indeed, I think it may prove crucial that we consider pre-Christianization European traditions as such if we are ever to truly realize that "the West" means, or at least should mean, much more than "Christianized Europe," that the West also possessed – and in some places continues to possess – indigenous traditions that share/d much in common with indigenous traditions of other 'directions.'

I should note at this point that I am extremely uncomfortable with the hegemonic use of the term "pre-Christian," as if Christianity were the only norm, or as if all cultures are evolving in the direction of Christianity, and so have avoided the term herein whenever possible. I prefer to deploy the term "pre-Christianization" in such contexts.

In order to make the leap from Greek and Roman influence to Christianized Europe, the historian or other scholar must either ignore more than a millennium of the rich contributions of indigenous European sacred and cultural traditions to 'the West,' or else she or he must acknowledge their significant influence upon the construction of the West and their kinship with indigenous traditions of other parts of the world.

I should point out that some of the sacred traditions discussed herein are presently considered indigenous, including those of the Sámi and Basques, as well as some of the Indigenous American and African traditions mentioned herein.

Eglutë Trinkauskaitë (also, Trinkauske) argues in "Seeing the Swarming Dead: Of Mushrooms, Trees, and Bees" (2008) that we will not be able to comprehend Lithuanian sacred traditions in any depth if we are not able to view them as "indigenous." Rather than speaking of Lithuanian pre-Christianization sacred traditions as "pagan," "heathen," etc., Trinkauskaitë speaks in terms of "Lithuanian indigenousness," "indigenous sensibilities," and "Lithuania's indigenous religiosity." Within traditional Lithuanian "sensibilities" and "religiosity," "the material world," as in many other indigenous sacred traditions, is perceived as "religiously meaningful." Kinship with plants and animals, together with nature as a whole, comprises one of the most sacred bonds in this sacred tradition. In its notion of deep "[k]inship relations with elements other than human beings (trees,…wolves, mountains,…lakes," with "the land and all that lives in it," Trinkauskaitë compares Lithuanian indigenous sacrality to certain Indigenous American traditions which deploy the phrase "all my relations" to speak of this concept. Indeed, explains Trinkauskaitė, "The material world becomes a major resource of indigenous religions…The way that indigenous people manifest their religiosity is by *paying attention* to the material world."

As in other indigenous sacred traditions, Lithuanians venerate ancestors. Trinkauskaitė explains that "the dead are a part of everyday life" and that "a notion of reincarnation…emphasizes the cyclical and regenerative processes of life."

Trinkauskaitė acknowledges that naming traditional Lithuanian sacred tradition(s) an "indigenous religion" is problematic. In her view, "Indigenous religions as a category describes a certain religiousness, and not a particular 'religion'. Most indigenous people say that they do not have *religion* separate from life, because for them a sacred reality permeates all life." Trinkauskaitė regards descriptions of traditional sacred ideas and practices as "folklore" and as "folk religions" as even more problematic than referring to them as "religious": "In the European context scholars have been making attempts to categorize pre-Christian European religions as folk religions. …[T]hese mundane ["folk"] practices did not seem threatening [because] they were outside the purview of 'religion.'" Trinkauskaitė *does* acknowledge that "[t]hese practices and some of their accompanying attitudes survived the missionary eradicaton of indigenous religion precisely because they were not perceived as religion." She argues, however, that despite its problematic aspect, we should use the term "indigenous religion" when speaking of traditional Lithuanian sacred ideas and practices because it "develops a voice methodology for an assertive indigenous subject position." She stresses that the "category of indigenous religions not only reminds but it also legitimizes the fact that the human world is completely contingent on the natural environment." Moreover, Trinkauskaitė argues, "Because the study of indigenous traditions is not text-based, it must have a constantly open channel of communication with the current realities of the material world." Trinkauskaitė also argues that describing traditional Lithuanian sacred ideas and practices as "indigenous religion" may also assist in promoting a more ecologically sensitive, environmentalist approach to Lithuania's fauna, flora, and nature as a whole than that which Christianity has promoted (Lithuania's natural environment has been and continues to be devastated): "A possible resacralization of nature through Lithuania's indigenous religious perspect-ive may promise the renewal of values that are necessary for the future."

In the 1768 edition of his *Dictionary of the English Language*, Samuel Johnson defines "ethnick" as "Heathen; Pagan; not Jewish; not Christian," and "ethnicks" in the plural as "Heathens." This definition was echoed by the 1829 *London Encyclopaedia*, with "ethnic" referring to "Heathen, pagan," and "ethnicism" presumably to "pagan[ism]."

A century earlier, the renowned antiquarian John Aubrey (1626-1697) had noted that those converted to Christianity built "their Christian churches where their old Ethnick ones" had been. A century prior to that, the Dutch demonologist Johann Weyer (1516-1588) had used the term "*ethnique*" to refer to recalcitrant pagans. It was in this sense that the term "ethnic" was deployed in witch trials. It would appear that by the seventh century CE – and perhaps earlier – "ethnic," as *ethnos*, had come to refer to persons who continued to practice ancient, indigenous, and/or pagan traditions in largely Christianized Greece. Twelve centuries later, in 1893, in Philip Schaff's *Theological Propædeutic*, one finds: "The ethnic religions are designated by the terms idolatry, paganism, and heathenism."

In our own day, ethnic religions have been described as ones which "represent an integral element of a specific culture;" which determine membership by which culture an individual is born into; and which "tend to refrain from…proselytization" and which hence "do not disturb the larger society;" Listed frequently as examples of ethnic religions are Daoism, Judaism, Hinduism, and Shinto.

The ECER, or European Congress of Ethnic Religions (formerly the WCER, the World Council of Ethnic Religions), has recently defined an ethnic religion as a "religion, spirituality, and cosmology that is firmly grounded in a particular people's traditions." Very recently, in *America's Religions* (2008), Peter W. Williams has also defined ethnic religions as "those, like Pure Land Buddhism, which have been brought to the New World by Asian immigrants…and practiced primarily within their own communities."

Abdul Mannan Bagulia (2005) asserts that "tribal" or "traditional religions" comprise a subset of ethnic religions; these are "distinguished by their small size, their unique identity with localized culture groups…and their close ties with nature." They include animism and shamanism.

As for the terms "pagan" and "paganism," Trinkauskaitë rejects them. Alas, *mea culpa*. In the main, I am in accord with Trinkauskaitë. However, I think that in certain contexts, the term "pagan" may be a useful one, especially when considering ancient and indigenous traditions in light of their struggle with Christianization; in certain medieval and post-medieval contexts, especially those concerned with the arts and philosophy; and frankly, as a defiant reclamation of a term made derogatory by Christians, much as the terms "dyke" and "queer" and "witch" have been (re)claimed and reformulated in recent decades (as I am attempting to reformulate "the West").

"Pagan" and "paganism" – like their Germanic counterparts "heathen" and "heathenism" – are not, as some present-day academics have argued, other than being terms of opprobrium, *meaningless* terms. Their origins return us to several – not many – *not unrelated* definitions: a native to a particular place; a person who dwells in the countryside, either on a farm or in the vicinity of a heath (*haeð*); a peasant; and a civilian (typically a farmer) as opposed to a soldier. Around 1600 years ago, it commenced to be deployed to refer to persons who practiced non-Christian, non-Jewish, often indigenous religions/traditions.

I am in basic accord with Frank R. Trombley's argument for usage of the term "pagan." He writes in *Hellenic Religion and Christianization: c. 370-529*: "There is bound to be some comment about the use of the term 'pagan,' and so a brief disclaimer is necessary. The pre-Christian polytheistic religious world of the eastern Mediterranean lands was, strictly speaking, made up of many individual and localized cults of the deities of earth, sea, and sky...Be that as it may, I have discovered no good reason to avoid using the word 'pagan' in contrast to 'Christian'...as a synonym for 'polytheistic.'" He adds, "All the authorities who have recently written books on late Greek religion have used the word 'pagan' freely, and it would be pedantic to do otherwise...I fail to see any derogatory meaning in the term 'pagan.'" Anthony Winterbourne, in *When the Norns Have Spoken: Time and Fate in Germanic Paganism*, states a bit more tentatively: " [To] say with confidence that there was no such thing as paganism per se is simply too strong...[Even if there were] no unified system of belief from which pagans were converted, it does not follow from this that there could not have been beliefs held by some societies to which it would be...appropriate...to give the name paganism."

For Bertrand Lançon, in *Rome in Late Antiquity: Everyday Life and Urban Change, AD 312-609* (2000), "What Christians belatedly termed 'paganism' was in fact a mosaic of cults...Paganism...presented many faces, but was none the less coherent."

It should come as no surprise that, given the hegemonic Christocentrism of the post-medieval West, Church authorities have played an extremely significant role in the defining of "paganism." That many Christians have identified, and continue to identify, paganism/s with barbarity and evil should surprise no one. Nevertheless, even such a monster as Cotton Mather was right about one thing: he understood, as he makes clear in *The Wonders of the Invisible World* (1693), that "those forlorn *pagans*" included Canaanites; "Laplander[s]" (i.e., Sámi); "Indians" (i.e., Indigenous Americans) with their "*Powawes*" (i.e., pow-wows, rites); Nahuas (Mexica/Aztecs) with their god "Vitzlipultzli" (i.e., Huitzilopochtli, the god of war); and the (alleged) witches.

Likewise, about fifty years thereafter, the Italian philosopher, historian, and rhetorician Giambattista Vico (1668-1744) wrote in *The New Science* (3rd ed., 1744): "[I]t has been possible to find only four primary religions. The first is that of the Hebrews, whence came that of the Christians...The third is that of *the gentiles, who believe in the divinity of a plurality of gods* [italics mine]...The fourth and last is that of the Mohammedans." It is both strange and regrettable that Vico neglected to take Hinduism, Buddhism, and other religions and traditions into account. Nevertheless, especially given his extreme Christocentric bias, it is noteworthy that he names paganism as one of the four primary religions of the world and that he categorizes it as such alongside the Abrahamic faiths. Moreover, Vico deploys present, and not past, tense to refer to paganism. Further, in considering paganism to be a primary religion, he does not refer only to Greek religion, but rather of those religions and traditions that "believe in the divinity of a plurality of gods" and share certain concepts about death and immortality such as ghosts and reincarnation. Thus, he groups ancient Greco-Roman paganism with sacred beliefs and practices of the cultures of West Africans, Peruvians, Mexicans, and Indigenous North Americans of his own day. He writes: "The Greeks…had gods to the number of thirty thousand, for they made a deity of every stone, spring, brook, plant, and offshore rock. Such deities included the dryads, hamadryads, oreads, and napeads. Just so the American Indians make a god of everything."

For Johann Joseph von Görres (1776-1848), paganism referred to Egyptian religion as well as the cults of Ba'al, Dionysus/Bacchus, and Shiva, together with Germanic religion.

Almost a millennium after the Russian writer traversing the Aegean Sea defined *Iazychestvo* and thereby categorized the basic elements of paganism, I will add – thanks to numerous masterful studies of paganism as a web or network of concepts, figures, narratives, and practices, including Michael York's *Pagan Theology: Paganism as a World Religion*, Bernadette Filotas's *Pagan Survivals, Superstitions and Popular Cultures in Early Medieval Pastoral Literature*, Jordan Paper's *The Deities Are Many: A Polytheistic Theology*, and M. L. West's *Indo-European Poetry and Myth* – several other elements to the list of elements common to paganisms:

a worldview or life path that challenges the sacred/ secular, religious/ non-religious dichotomy; a conception of reality as multidimensional; ritual specialists frequently not restricted to traditionally masculine, heterosexual males but instead inclusive of women, and, in some cases, gender-diverse persons and homoerotically inclined persons; an emphasis on the local, albeit often in relationship to the ubiquitous or universal; and the theory or system of correspondences, also known as the doctrine of sympathies.

The doctrine, system, or theory of correspondences was conceived in antiquity and became extremely important in the Middle Ages and Renaissance for practitioners of magic and divination. Exemplary of this system is: "Aphrodite/ Venus – rose – myrtle – apple – shell – dove/swallow – copper – Friday – love and sexuality.' This system was also deployed by Church authorities as a tool – "weapon" might be more to the point – by which to better comprehend indigenous deities in order to convert non-Christian peoples. For example, in the early to mid-eighteenth century, in Christianizing remaining indigenous ritualists/pagans of Lithuania Minor/East Prussia, Christians drew up a list of indigenous divinities of the area in which they compared them to Graeco-Roman ones. The list included:

Bangputtis	Neptune
Jaucziû	Baubis Pan
Laima	Fortuna
Laumë	Diana Lucina
Perkûnas	Jupiter
Žemyna	Ceres

It should be noted that some pagans promoted Gnostic-like (generally speaking, flesh as evil, spirit as godly) and monotheistic beliefs and allied practices; such pagans were, however, in the minority. Moreover, perhaps in part due to the triumph of monotheism in the Abrahamic faiths and the explosion of Gnostic sects in Late Antiquity and the Middle Ages, it would appear that such beliefs and allied practices faded from the repertoires of those who continued to practice pagan-rooted traditions in Christianized Europe. Indeed, this fading of Gnostic-like and monotheistic elements from pagan-based repertoires speaks to the dynamic character of paganism. When I refer to paganism/s herein, I am not referring to the minority traditions of Gnosticism and pagan monotheism. I have also severely limited myself in regard to Hermeticism. When I discuss magical practices and traditions herein, I am referring primarily to earth-centered practices rather than to practices and traditions heavily influenced by Abrahamic faiths and Platonic philosophy, such as traditions referred to generally as "High Magic," "Ritual Magic," or "Ceremonial Magic."

I also use the terms "NeoPagans" and "NeoPaganism" herein. Alternatively, I deploy such terms as "present-day Pagans" occasionally. It is noteworthy that Gérard de Nerval (1808-1855) used the term "*néo-paganisme*" in his 1852 work *Les Illuminés* to refer to the project of Quintus Aucler to transmit the worship of the goddess Minerva to participants in the French Revolution. Certainly, the concept of NeoPaganism predates the French Revolution. I would suggest that in the Classical context, it may be traced to the efforts of the Roman Emperor Julian (Flavius Claudius Julianus, 331-363 CE) "the Apostate" to restore and in a certain sense to reinvent Greco-Roman paganism after having been raised as a Christian and then rejecting Christianity. In 980, Vladimir the Great of Kiev/Ruthenia (b. *c.* 956- d. 1015, r. 980-1015), prior to yielding to conversion, following Julian's lead, erected statues of six ancient deities on a hill near the palace at Berestove in an attempt to consolidate Slavic paganism. Other NeoPagan projects followed. Of course, these projects were undertaken when many rurals and others persisted in practicing ancient, indigenous, pagan traditions. In this light, in contrast to other writers on this general subject, I have found it exceedingly difficult to draw a line in the sand demarcating older paganism/s and NeoPaganism/s.

Jean Seznec in "The Survival of the Ancient Gods in the Middle Ages and the Renaissance," argues that "each renewal [of culture in these epochs] was accompanied by *a rise in neopaganism* (italics mine)." Even the goliards "resuscitated paganism ... in their mores." Bernadette Filotas notes that Oronzo Giordano, in *Religiosità popolare nell' alto medioevo*, maintains that "the old religion was not replaced; rather, a new layer [was] added [on] to a pre-existing religiosity."

In regard to the term "earth-centered" ("earth-based," etc.), in 1989, Judith Plant wrote of "earth-based spirituality" in "Healing the Wounds: The Promise of Ecofeminism": "The shift from the western theological tradition...to an earth-based spirituality begins the healing of the split between spirit and matter. For ecofeminist spirituality, like the traditions of...tribal peoples, sees the spiritual as alive in us, where spirit and matter, mind and body, are all part of the same living organism."

That same year, Paula Gunn Allen used the term "earth-centered" to refer to connections she made between Indigenous

American, specifically Laguna Pueblo, and an emergent woman-centered spirituality. It appears that term "earth-centered" increasingly entered academic/scholarly usage around this time, as demonstrated by Sheila Ruth in "Bodies and Souls/Sex, Sin and the Senses in Patriarchy: A Study in Applied Dualism" (1987) and by Walter L. Brenneman, Jr. in "Serpents, Cows, and Ladies: Contrasting Symbolism in Irish and Indo-European Cattle-Raiding Myths" (1989).

Although he does not use the term "earth-centered," I would suggest that folklorist Paul G. Brewster (1898-?), in speaking of a "witch master" interviewed by folklorist of the Ozarks Vance Randolph (1892-1980) in 1950, made the very connections – although in antiquated and somewhat sarcastic terms – that others would more recently make in defining "earth-centered traditions." Brewster writes: "Although he was doubtless quite unaware of this fact, this witch master…was in good (or bad) company. He was a member in good standing of that ancient and worldwide fraternity to which belong the medicine-man of the American Indians, the African witch doctor, the Lapland [i.e., Sámi] wizard, the Celtic wisewoman, [etc.]."

Since at least the early 1990s, feminist theologians and others writing on women's issues in religion as well as on ecofeminism have linked feminist spirituality and present-day Goddess reverence to "an earth-based view of the sacred." Many have been inspired by the writer, political activist, and self-proclaimed Witch Starhawk's 1990 essay "Power, Authority, and Mystery: Ecofeminism and Earth-Based Spirituality," in which she explains that "earth-based spirituality" is "rooted in three basic concepts[:]…immanence, interconnection, and community. …The Earth itself embodies spirit and…the cosmos is alive." In 1994, Eugenie Gatens-Robinson, in "Finding our Feminist Ways in Natural Philosophy and Religious Thought," linked earth-based spirituality to Goddess reverence, African traditional religions, and the sacred practices of Indigenous Americans and other indigenous peoples. In a 2000 roundtable on "feminist theology and religious diversity," Carol P. Christ, reiterates this view in describing Goddess-oriented spirituality as an "embodied earth-based spirituality."

In 2003, Jeffrey Myers, in "Other Nature: Resistance to Ecological Hegemony in Charles W. Chesnutt's *The Conjure Woman*," writing of the African-diasporic practice of Conjure, wrote, "As the practice of conjure makes manifest, this kinship [with the land] has its roots in the *Earth-based spirituality* of the slaves' African ancestors" (italics mine). Myers based his observation on Will Coleman's *Tribal Talk: Black Theology, Hermeneutics, and African/American Ways of "Telling the Story"* (2000), in which Coleman explains that in such traditions, "the line of demarcation between animate and inanimate, human and non-human, spirit and human, is…extremely fluid."

At present, the terms "earth-centered" and "earth-based" are used by many Unitarian Universalists in connection with the terms "nature-based" and "pagan;" on the official website of the Unitarian Universalist Association of Congregations, under the heading of "Paganism," one finds:

"One of the major sources of our Unitarian Universalist faith is the spiritual teachings of *earth-centered traditions* which celebrate the sacred circle of life and instruct us to live in harmony with the rhythms of nature (italics mine)."

Moreover, many present-day Pagans deploy "earth-centered" and "earth-based" to describe their belief in the sacredness of nature. Thus, since at least the 1980s, "earth-centered" and "earth-based" have been used to describe nature-venerating traditions including African and African-diasporic, Indigenous American, ecofeminist, Pagan, and Goddess-revering.

In 1983, in "The Structure of Blessedness at a Muslim Shrine in Pakistan," Richard Kurin deployed the terms "(enspirited) materiality" and "spiritually infused materiality" to speak of the material dimension of Muslim sacrality. I have found the term "enspirited materiality" useful in seeking to convey the notion that all life is imbued with sacred energy or force, and the related notion that "matter" need not be limited to that which is visible, tangible, or verifiable from a human perspective but that it may also refer to entities or beings that we tend to define as "transcendent" when they may rather be invisible. Indeed, I am beginning to prefer the term "enspirited materiality" to "spirituality," as the former underscores the embodied dimension of the sacred.

Although they do not deploy the term "enspirited materiality," I believe that one may get a sense of what I'm referring to by way of certain passages in Sara Ruddick's 1995 text *Maternal Thinking* and in Marilyn Walker's 2009 article "Spirit Matters: The Ethics of Photographing Unseen Worlds." For her part, Walker observes: "The spirit of a deceased shaman remains in *materiality* – for example, in his or her drum and dress. Likewise, the spirit of an animal would be invested in, say, a shaman's headdress made of deer antlers."

Ruddick, in speaking of childrearing, writes: "To foster growth is to nurture a child's developing spirit." Ruddick isn't completely comfortable with the term "spirit." It "may…be misleading," she thinks. "To speak paradoxically, from a maternal perspective the spirit is *material*." On the other hand, in her view, a "child's body, from its birth, is *enspirited*. …An *enspirited* body is…a source and focus of mental life." As children "name, desire, avoid, or touch" their own and others' "bodies, the bodies become resonant with 'spiritual' significance. To foster growth, then, is to sponsor or nurture a child's unfolding, expanding *material spirit* [italics mine].

I have avoided using two other terms that might be seen as resembling "enspirited materiality," namely, "spiritual materiality" and "spiritual materialism." The first of these, "spiritual materiality," has been the subject of ongoing arguments in the Abrahamic faiths regarding the materiality or immateriality of such beings as angels; more recently, it has been used in a Christian context to distinguish between the "carnal materiality" of ancient Jerusalem and the "spiritual materiality" of Christ's Kingdom on earth. It has also been recently deployed to describe the meshing of matter and "transcendence" in contemporary sculpture. "Spiritual materialism" was deployed in the

1970s by the Buddhist teacher Chögyam Trungpa Rinpoche to condemn spiritual practices linked to the accumulation of sacred objects, money, and power. Thus, neither of these terms is equivalent to "enspirited materiality" and neither seems appropriate or useful in the context of this book.

The Russian medieval traveler noted the emergence, with the arrival of Christianization, of a "dual" or hybrid (or, mixed, syncretic) sacred tradition, often referred to in Russian as *dvoeverie*. I deploy the term "sacred hybridity" to refer to this phenomenon, by which I mean a mélange of two or more sacred traditions, or elements of these traditions. It may assume several forms, ranging from a rather smooth (or at least seemingly so) synthesis, often referred to as "syncretism" or "double faith," to a looser, "messier" collage of ideas, images/symbols, narratives, and practices increasingly referred to as "spiritual eclecticism." Dodson, in *Sacred Spaces and Religious Traditions*, refers to sacred hybridity as "integrated religious plurality." Examples of more "syncretic" systems would be those of so-called "folk Catholicism," which, in one of its primary manifestations, brings together Catholic and Indigenous American/Mexican(-American) ideas and practices, and La Regla de Ocha (also known as Lucumí and Santería) and Vodou, which mix indigenous African, Indigenous American, and Catholic concepts and practices. Examples of more "eclectic" mélanges might include present-day Women's Spirituality and individual and group spiritualities mixing indigenous, Eastern (Asian, South Asian), personal symbols and rituals, and other ideas and practices.

The Emerging Field of Pagan Studies

I see this text as one among a growing number of texts relating to the emerging field of Pagan Studies. As a "self-conscious" and specific field of study, Pagan Studies is only just now emerging. Over the past several years, scholars and others involved in this field have convened at the annual convention of the American Academy of Religion and have commenced presenting papers at this and other conventions and conferences. A number have published books in recent years, some of the most notable including: Jenny Blain, Douglas Ezzy, and Graham Harvey (editors), *Researching Paganisms*; Chas S. Clifton and Graham Harvey (editors), *The Paganism Reader*; Ken Dowden, *European Paganism: The Realities of Cult from Antiquity to the Middle Ages*; Ronald Hutton, *The Triumph of the Moon: A History of Modern Pagan Witchcraft*; Prudence Jones and Nigel Pennick, *A History of Pagan Europe*; Sarah M. Pike, *Earthly Bodies, Magical Selves: Contemporary Pagans and the Search for Community*; and Michael F. Strmiska (editor), *Modern Paganism in World Cultures*. Chas Clifton and others of these scholars have also commenced publishing *The Pomegranate*, an academic journal devoted to Pagan Studies. Other scholars who and works that are forming a canon of this burgeoning field include: Pierre Chuvin, *A Chronicle of the Last Pagans*; Robin Lane Fox, *Pagans and Christians*; Joscelyn Godwin, *The Pagan Dream of the Renaissance*; Claude Lecouteux, *Les Nains et les elfes au Moyen Âge*; *Au-delà du merveilleux: des croyances du*

Moyen Âge; *Witches, Werewolves, and Fairies: Shapeshifters and Astral Doubles in the Middle Ages* (and other works); Jean Markale, *Courtly Love; The Path of Sexual Initiation*; and the works of York, Filotas, Paper mentioned above. Texts relating to pagan sacred traditions framed as studies in folklore, mythology, aesthetics, and to a certain extent, psychology – primarily Jungian, including works by Erich Neumann and James Hillman – have similarly served to impart invaluable information relating to pagan traditions while simultaneously distancing these traditions from the provenance of religion or the sacred.

The field of Pagan Studies has two primary foci: pagan sacred traditions of the past; and Modern Paganism, or, Neo-Paganism. Pagan Studies frequently overlaps with studies in Women's Spirituality, NRMs (New Religious Movements), and indigenous Spiritual Traditions. The historical background of this field of study leads, however, back to early comparative-religious and folklore studies, including such (noble, if flawed, and now often ridiculed or reviled) works as Jacob Grimm's *Teutonic Mythology*; Sir James Frazer's *The Golden Bough*; Charles Godfrey Leland's *Aradia; or the Gospel of the Witches*; Jane Harrison's *Prologomena to the Study of Greek Religion*; Margaret Murray's *The Witch-Cult in Western Europe*; and Robert Graves's *The White Goddess*. These works, despite their failings and contradictions, succeeded in describing varied dimensions of the pagan worldview in a manner that, unlike many present-day writers (particularly scientific postmodern academics), transmitted the numinous presence of ancient and indigenous European sacred traditions – as if one were opening a vial of perfume to be engulfed by their essences, or had just bitten into a madeleine. This is a rare gift to be treasured. Other early works of significance to Pagan Studies which have not been so vehemently contested are literary critical studies such as Douglas Bush's *Mythology and the Renaissance Tradition in English Poetry*. Still others, like Edward Carpenter's *Pagan and Christian Creeds*, have been virtually lost. A certain interest that simultaneously served to nurture and delay the development of Pagan Studies was that in esotericism (the occult, the supernatural, the metaphysical, etc.), which reached a pinnacle in the early 1970s. By way of focusing on the occult rather than on religion or spirituality *per se*, pagan spirituality or religiousness was often submerged in favor of a cornucopia of magical receipts, divinatory methods, and tales of UFO sightings and other "weird" experiences. Emphasis on the occult or esoteric has often led to a focus on magical practice and, in particular, on ceremonial magic and Hermeticism rather than upon paganism/s.

Among the more recent writers, while Lecouteux and Filotas concentrate on evoking a view of Nature as imbued with divine force and of reality as multi-dimensional, populated not by humans and animals alone but also by elemental spirits, Markale focuses on the way in which pagan beliefs and practices, including goddess reverence, fueled the institution of courtly love, and Godwin focuses on the role of the "pagan dream" in inspiring artistic creations. Filotas's work holds special significance for me in that I discovered it only recently, and yet found within it basically the same organizational structure that I had arrived at independently whereby to undertake my study of the pagan worldview and its elements. While Filotas's Lecouteux's, and Markale's works are generally limited to the Middle Ages, both their organizational structures and their ethnography-like approaches to pagan beliefs and practices have helped me greatly in thinking about the manifestation of these in later epochs.

In regard to York's *Pagan Theology* and Paper's *The Deities Are Many*, J. Z. Smith has observed, the term "theology" originated in a Christian context and has frequently been deployed to privilege Christianity as a (or the) superior religion and to denigrate non-Christian and, more generally speaking, non-Abrahamic religions/traditions. For this reason, the works of York and Paper are especially significant in challenging this hegemonic control of the provenance of theology; both offer extended definitions, York of "paganism," Paper of "polytheism," that resonate with the pagan worldview I will describe. Both indicate an acceptance of metanarratives, but both also recognize that these must be evidenced via historically and geographically situated and culture-specific (local, microcultural) examples. Both are versed in European as well as Asian, African-based, and indigenous and tribal religions/traditions. Paper's book is particularly useful in its careful delineation of monotheism and polytheism and in its acknowledgment of the ways in which polytheistic cultures have been pressured or coerced into accepting monotheism. York's book is particularly insightful, and indeed has aroused some controversy, in arguing for a wide embrace of paganism, stretching beyond European indigenous traditions to include African-diasporic religions/ traditions, traditional Chinese religion, and Shinto.

Contesting Absolutist Language and Mentalities

Montague Summers (1880-1948), an eccentric priest who converted from Anglicanism to Catholicism and who was profoundly interested in, or else dabbled in, Satanism, argued in *The History of Witchcraft* (1925): "[H]ere and there *lingered* various old harmless customs and festivities which had come down from pre-Christian times...the Maypole dances...and the Midsummer fires...But this is *no continuance* of a pagan cult [italics mine]."

This sort of quasi-absolutist and unconditionally absolutist language is unfortunately exceedingly common in texts regarding paganism/s and witchcraft. For example, Nicole Belmont, in "Mythic Elements in French Folklore" (1991), states: "Gallic religion, mythology, and culture left very few material *traces*...It is not our purpose here to explain the Celtic *vestiges* [italics mine]." Such quasi- ("lingered") and unconditionally ("no continuance") absolutist terminology is frequently deployed in connection with a belief that pagan traditions did not survive the onslaught of Christianization.

It is somewhat surprising, however, to find, even in the writing of present-day scholars influenced by postmodernism, who typically promote fluidity, interpenetration, and kindred concepts, "line in the sand" statements such as one finds in Ronald Hutton's *The Pagan Religions of the Ancient British Isles:Their Nature and Legacy* (1991). The British historian Ronald Hutton is without question one of the most influential writers in the emerging field of Pagan Studies. In *Pagan Religions*, Hutton argues that "the pre-Christian religions of the English were defunct by the 730s," and that after the period of the reintroduction of Germanic religion(s) during Viking invasion and settlement, these traditions vanished, around 1020, forever. Although he concedes that "paganism did bequeath an enormous legacy of superstitions, literary and artistic images and folk rituals to the culture of later ages," he maintains that "it may be concluded that the official conversion of the British Isles to Christianity left no surviving pre-Christian religions, either in remote areas or as 'underground' movements. In that sense *the victory of the new faith was born relatively swift and absolute*." He goes on to say, "What, then, after so many pages, can be said about the pagan religions of the ancient British Isles? First, that we know very little about them... [T]*he old religions of these islands perished a very long time ago, and absolutely. ...And partly because of our ignorance of them and partly because of our different needs and circumstances, they are lost to us forever* [italics mine]."

Although Hutton's arguments read very dramatically, and on the surface seem convincing, I must, with all due respect, take issue with his absolutist language. He seems extremely fond of categorical statements. Very few present-day scholars I know would dare to indulge in terms like "absolute" (even if modified by the paradoxical "relatively"), "absolutely," and "forever." It strikes me that this type of argument, this insistent belief in finality, is firmly grounded in a simplistic either/or, before/after dichotomy, in Modernist versus postmodernist, hermeneutics. It is rather ironic that Hutton accuses contemporary NeoPagans – those whom he describes as devotees of "the "earth mysteries," the "Celtic mysteries," and Wicca – of promoting movements "which build, like medieval scholasticism, upon *closed systems* of belief," relying only upon each others' works to defend their worldview(s), when he appears to be constructing a closed system of his own. Yet when many of us first read Hutton, we feel that he must be right. Paganism in England ended in 730 or 1020. Sounds reasonable...but perhaps, in truth, it was July 3, 732?! I hardly think so.

In *The Stations of the Sun: A History of the Ritual Year in Britain* (1996; reissued 2001), Hutton continues to deploy absolutist language: "Thus far in the present book two themes must be uncomfortably obvious. One is the *almost total absence of concrete evidence* concerning pre-Christian seasonal rituals in the British Isles. ...There is *no evidence* that it [Samhain/Halloween] was connected with the dead, and *no proof* that it opened the year... There is ...*absolutely no firm evidence* in the written record that the year opened on 1 November ... [italics mine]."

This notion of no "survivals" has recently

found support in a fashionable academic deprecation of the "quest for origins," no doubt, in part, a snobbish knee-jerk reaction (much more common in academia than one might think) to the widespread search for "roots" and ancestors that commenced (again) in the late 1960s and that has continued into the present. In *The Stations of the Sun*, Hutton criticizes "the view of folk customs as survivals from an archaic world," which may lead to "an obsessive quest for…origins." The notions of "no survivals" and opposition to the "quest for origins" have been especially deployed since the 1980s by many academics having a very superficial understanding of the work of the French philosopher Michel Foucault (1926-1984) in an anti-historical, anti-intellectual project, linked in some (not all) works to an obsession with the idea of *tabula rasa*, to "prove" such things as that gay/Queer people have no history and that modern-day Wicca has no historical roots (excepting Romantic fantasy and Protestantism).

In "Paganism in the Lost Centuries" (2003), when critiquing the title and allied concept of Ludo Milis's *The Pagan Middle Ages*, Hutton states: "There is no evidence of the long-term persistence of paganism as an organized religion of resistance …[P]aganism as a formal system of religion vanished from Mediterranean Europe after the sixth century."

Let's begin to unpack, to deconstruct this passage.

Firstly, Hutton does not say, "There is *little* evidence of the long-term persistence of paganism;" rather, deploying absolutist language, he insists that there "is *no evidence*."

Secondly, he states that there "is no evidence of the long-term persistence of paganism as an *organized religion*." Has Hutton demonstrated *in no uncertain terms* that paganism was or was not, constitutes or fails to constitute, an "organized religion"? As I see it, *he has not*. Indeed, at various times in his work he appears to alternate between defining paganism, as near the end of the quoted passage, as a "formal system of religion" and as ideas and practices *not* constituting such. Although numerous academics, perhaps especially those now associated with Pagan Studies and New Religious Movements, are quick to jump on the bandwagon that paganism was not an organized religion, or that paganisms did not comprise an organized religion or religions, *I for one do not think we are anywhere near settling this issue*. Indeed, we live in an epoch when the definition, the very notion, of "religion" is hotly contested. Moreover, do religions need to be "organized" to constitute "religions"? Further, is it necessary that paganism/s persisted as an "organized religion" to demonstrate that it/they persisted? If paganism was not an "organized religion" in the first place, then surely his answer to his question is that it could not have persisted as such. This is a trap I would rather not have snap down on me. It constitutes fallacious thinking.

Thirdly, Hutton goes on to state that paganism did not persist as "an organized religion *of resistance*." Again, according to his logic, it could not have persisted as an organized religion "of resistance" because it did not persist otherwise and because it may never have existed as such in the first place. By linking "organized religion" to "resistance," he effectively obscures many episodes of resistance over the millennia against Christianization.

Fourthly, and this is where it gets really interesting, he argues that paganism, again as a "formal system of religion," "*vanished* [italics mine]." Notice again his absolutist language. He does not say, "Paganism lessened considerably" or "Paganism was in the main displaced by Christianity" or even that "Paganism *all but* vanished;" no, he states emphatically that paganism "*vanished*." Although he insists that in the Mediterranean, paganism vanished with the culmination of the sixth century, he then goes on to acknowledge that it "*lingered*" into the eleventh century in various parts of Europe and among the Sámi "into the seventeenth." Again, all of this depends on defining paganism as an "organized religion." If so, then are we to think that Hutton's primary purpose here is making sure that the doors are locked, or rather that paganism 'finally' "vanished" only a little over two centuries ago?

From my perspective, however, the most intriguing remark Hutton makes within this passage is this one: "There is no evidence of the long-term persistence of paganism…[of its practitioners] meeting in secret or associated with military rebellion, once the ruling family of a particular kingdom had accepted the Christian faith and outlawed the traditional ways."

Several other brief examples of this sort of absolutism in language will have to suffice before we move on.

Alexander Murray, in "Missionaries and Magic in Dark-Age Europe" (1998), insists, "there was *no pagan survival*, as magic or anything else [italics mine]." In *The Lancashire Witches* (2002), Robert Poole argues emphatically that the "idea that early modern witchcraft was a relic of an organized pre-Christian religion…[was] long ago…*comprehensively discredited*" and that "*exhaustive research*" from witch trials "has produced *not a shred of evidence* for it…[T]he pagan hypothesis *crumbled before serious research*…[italics mine]"

Like other such pronouncements, incidentally, Poole's includes an *ad hominem*, or rather, *ad mulierum*, denigration of members of the "emergent women's and pagan movements," whom he infers have been incapable of "serious research."

I was rather surprised when I came across an article by a woman who apparently regards herself as a feminist making very similar pronouncements In "Witchcraft and Gender in Early Modern Europe" (2014), Alison Rowlands, who teaches at the University of Essex, denigrates "radical feminist inter-pretations" of witchcraft as emerging "in the context of feminist political activism outside academia" and "*thus* [italics mine] political and historically inaccurate." I must admit that I have never equated with such certainty "political" with "historically inaccurate." She goes on to repeat this notion throughout the essay: "Radical feminist writing has had a significant influence on perceptions of witchcraft outside academia." She insists that "academic historians…are dismissive of such interpretations, criticizing radical feminists for…their *ahistorical* [italics mine] use of the terms misogyny and patriarchy."

She then argues that "much of this criticism" – with which she is most obviously in accord – "is entirely justified."

Frankly, I shouldn't have been surprised, as Rowlands' article is found in Brian Levack's *Oxford Handbook of Witchcraft in Early Modern Europe and Colonial America*, which presents an extremely lopsided, skewed view of current writing on witchcraft.

Rowlands' remarks regarding the "ahistorical" usage by "radical feminists" of "the terms misogyny and patriarchy" are somewhat troubling. In regard to "patriarchy," it does seem that the emergence of a critique of patriarchy may be relatively recent, as exemplified by a remark made by the abbé Fortis in 1784 concerning women of Croatia: "Sometimes a daughter is given in marriage to the servant, or tenant, as was usual in patriarchal times; so little are the women regarded in this country." However, when it comes to "misogyny," I wonder if Professor Rowlands is aware that the term "misogyny" was clearly in usage, and its meaning understood, by at least the time of the philosopher Chrysippus (279-206 BCE) – I offer dates so as not be accused of being "ahistorical" – who utilized the Greek term *misogunia* and spoke out against misogyny; by the playwright Marcus Atilius (fl. 200 BCE), who wrote a play titled *The Misogynist* about woman-hating; and by the philosophers Antipater of Tarsus (d. 130 BCE) and Cicero (106-43 BCE), the latter of whom viewed misogyny as an illness and an outgrowth of a deep-seated fear of women. Surely anyone who has read or seen Euripides' (c. 480-c. 406 BCE) *The Trojan Women* – staged in 415 BCE – and / or his *Iphigenia in Aulis* – staged in 405 BCE – both brilliantly filmed by Mihalis Kakogiannis (Michael Cacoyannis) – realizes that these tragedies were indictments not only of war but also of misogyny, patriarchy, and slavery. Indeed, Antipater of Tarsus recognized Euripides' work as an indictment of misogyny. And so I wonder how it is that to speak of accusations of witchcraft in regard to misogyny and patriarchy might be considered "ahistorical"?

Further, since Professor Rowlands appears to self-identify as a feminist – I may be mistaken in this – I wonder what she means by "radical feminist" and why she finds it necessary to pepper her essay with denigrations of them? At first I thought she might mean that they were/are Marxists, but then I realized that she is speaking of women who believe that witches might have *actually been* witches, and/or possibly latter-day priestesses of goddesses such as Diana. Of course. As she writes, "[T]here is no evidence for the survival of organized pagan cults into the early modern period, let alone priestesses who presided over them." She is, of course, entitled to her opinion – in the absence of proving that no such evidence exists. But her characterization of feminists, "radical" or otherwise, who might believe that such women might have existed, as not relying on history but rather on politics and (illogical) emotions should not go unexamined. Her logocentrism – one might even say phallogocentrism – is rather astonishing. Let's not forget that the Greeks valued equally *logos*, *pathos*, and *mythos*.

Poole, echoing Rowlands, nails shut the

coffin he has made for them with this outrageously premature remark: "[T]his [pagan/spiritual feminist] interpretation...is passing."

Apparently neither Robert Poole nor Alison Rowlands are aware that many of those they castigate – as radical feminists who might conceivably believe in a female deity or deities, might practice Wicca or a NeoPagan spirituality or religion (why are Abrahamic feminists and other academics not disrespected or interrogated in the same manner, I wonder?) as incapable of historical research, hold Master's and/or Doctoral degrees from institutions of higher learning. Rowlands does mention Mary Daly (1928-2010) in passing, but apparently Rowlands looks upon someone who taught at Boston College for over thirty years as "outside academia."

One might also note that numerous other women whom Rowlands might have categorized as radical feminists working "outside academia" due to their beliefs – or at least open-mindedness – might have well included Marija Gimbutas (1921-1994), Ph.D., the revered archaeologist and author of the controversial yet carefully, historically documented *Goddesses and Gods of Old Europe*, who taught at Harvard and UCLA; Lucia Chiavola Birnbaum (b. 1924), Ph.D., author of *Dark Mother*, who has taught at Stanford; Elinor Gadon (1925-2018), Ph.D., author of *The Once and Future Goddess*, who taught at Harvard, Tufts, and Brandeis; Merlin Stone (1931-2011), M.F.A, the celebrated author of *When God Was a Woman*, who taught at SUNY (the State University of New York) and at UC Berkeley; Monique Wittig (1935-2003), Ph.D., author of *Les Guérillères*, *The Lesbian Body, and Lesbian Peoples,* who taught at UC Berkeley, Vassar, and the University of Arizona; Carol P. Christ (b. 1945), Ph.D., author of "Why Women Need the Goddess" and *She Who Changes*, who has taught at Pomona College, San Jose State University, Columbia, and Harvard; Kay Turner (b. 1948), Ph.D., who founded the Goddess-centered journal *Lady Unique Inclination of the Night* many years ago, and who has taught at NYU, served as the official Folklorist of Brooklyn, and been President of the American Folklore Society; Jane Caputi (b. 1953), the author of *Gossips, Gorgons, and Crones: The Fates of the Earth*, and *Goddesses and Monsters: Women, Myth, Power and Popular Culture*, and filmmaker of *Feed the Green: Feminist Voices for the Earth* (2015), who teaches at Florida Atlantic University, and who in 2016 was named Eminent Scholar of the Year by the American Culture/Popular Culture Association; and, of course, Starhawk (b. 1951), M.A., the world-renowned Witch, environmental activist, and writer of the internationally recognized *The Spiral Dance*, who has taught at Holy Names College in northern California. But perhaps these institutions do not meet Professor Rowlands' requirements for being considered "inside academia."

This absolutist language is linked to a mentality that insists that once Christianization was enforced, pagan traditions subsided dramatically or, as such writers more often insist, vanished utterly – theoretically, a very odd mix indeed of social constructivism and essentialism. (I will, for instance, never forget when a famous Mexican American folklorist branded my colleague Gloria Anzaldúa's beliefs and practices "fakelore," even though today, when both have passed, a legend has grown up that he admired her intensely.) It is also linked to an intriguing form of anti-feminism among academic women (often parading as feminism), occasionally, as in Camille Paglia's vitriol spewed at Gloria Steinem, manifesting as arrogant fury parading as academic rigor. These tendencies, moreover, are linked to another, a more generalized one, which I like to refer to as "spitting at the ancestors," a tendency which has empowered many academics over the past several decades (not infrequently granting them teaching positions and/or notoriety), from Eliot Rose to Cynthia Eller, to trash scholars including the Classicist Jane Ellen Harrison (1850-1928), the anthropologist Sir James G. Frazer (1854-1941), the writer Robert Graves (1895-1985), the mythologist Joseph Campbell (1904-1987), and, once more, the archaeologist Marija Gimbutas (1921-1994), on those few occasions when someone dares to mention them "inside the walls," which, in the minds of some academics, happily mirrors the wall our current U.S. President, Donald Trump, dreams of building.

"The West," Christocentrism, and Related Issues

In his fascinating 1991 study *The Passion of the Western Mind: Understanding the Ideas That Have Shaped Our World View*, Richard Tarnas describes his book as a "concise narrative history of the Western world view from the ancient Greek to the postmodern." He reiterates the well-worn litany of historical periods ranging from "classical Greece" and "imperial Rome" through "the rise of Christianity…and the Middle Ages, the Renaissance," to the "Reformation, and Scientific Revolution [etc.]" and once more delivers the roll-call of canonical "greats," from Plato to Paul to Augustine to Aquinas and onward, whose "personal struggles" and "epic heroism" gave birth to and reared the Western world view. "My goal," he tells us, "has been to give voice to each perspective mastered by the Western mind in the course of its evolution." This "long battle of ideas called 'the Western tradition' has been a stirring adventure whose sum and consequences we all bear within ourselves." Although perhaps deeply inspiring to some readers, and most assuredly instructive as an introduction to "the Western tradition," I must confess, although Tarnas knows that I admire him as a person, professor, and scholar of astrology, that in this instance, both his general project and his choice of words trouble me.

Firstly, I am struck by the phrases "epic heroism," "mastered by the Western mind," "in the course of its evolution," "[the] long battle of ideas," and "a stirring adventure whose sum and consequences." Taken together, these phrases paint a picture of a grand, evolutionary, teleological "battle" undertaken primarily by males exhibiting "epic heroism." Approximately twenty-five women's names appear in the book alongside hundreds of male names; all of these women's names are included in lists, in a chronological timeline, or in footnotes.

None is discussed in any depth. In the end, I find this description of the "Western mind," tradition, and worldview troubling not only because it appears to promote patriarchal and imperialistic aims and a kind of social-philosophical Darwinism but also, and more importantly, because it appears to view, rather uncritically, this "battle," this "evolution," as normative, natural, and destined.

Brenda Farnell, in *Do You See What I Mean? Plains Indian Sign Talk and the Embodiment Action* (1995), David M. Smith, in "An Athapaskan Way of Knowing" (1998), and Ladislaus Semali and Joe L. Kincheloe, in their introduction to *What is Indigenous Knowledge? Voices from the Academy* (1999), offer extremely enlightening, albeit somewhat less glowing, descriptions of "Western culture" and the "Western tradition." When we speak of "the West" in such terms, we typically refer to the "Cartesian paradigm" and/or to the "Cartesian-Newtonian model" of reality. Smith explains that within the paradigm of "Cartesian dualism… there is a strong tendency to think of ourselves as observers of an external reality and not as participants in…reality." Adding the "Newtonian model," he continues: "[A]s members of a Western literate society we are conditioned by reductionistic science to think of reality in mechanistic and materialistic terms. Reason is enthroned; intuition, emotion, and anything considered "spiritual" are often assumed to be separable, are frequently considered as secondary, or are simply regarded as irrelevant. We are used to describing reality as segmented and discrete, even though we know that from the perspective of contemporary science reality is no longer considered partitive." Smith also argues that "Cartesian dualism leads [to the belief that] humans are categorically different from, and hierarchically superior to, animals. Indeed, in the extreme Western position animals are essentially hairy, furry, scaly, feathered machines." Similarly, Farnell states of the Cartesian-Newtonian paradigm: "This bifurcation of the person into mind and body has led to a host of other dualisms: subjective versus objective, knowledge versus experience, reason versus feeling, theory versus practice, and verbal versus nonverbal."

Likewise, for Semali and Kincheloe, the Cartesian-Newtonian paradigm – which gave birth to Modernism (as opposed to postmodernism) – divides mind from matter, the knower from the known, science from faith (although they point out that at its commencement, "science was grounded on a Thomas [Aquinas]-Aristotelian synthesis of faith and reason"), "intellectual [from] experiential ways of knowing," "mental abstractions [from] passion, bodily sensations, and tactile understanding," and oral and other non-literary forms of cultural transmission from "written texts, legal codes, and academic canons." From within this paradigm, the world is viewed as a "mechanical system;" there is "no questioning the authority of the scientific method;" "the knower knows the world objectively," claiming to be "neutral" and "detached;" "knowledge production" is "hierarchical and linear;" and "truth is absolute, rather than context-dependent." Under the sway of this paradigm, "[r]ationality was deified;" "the importance of religion and spirituality" declined, with an "obsession with progress suppl[ying] new objectives and values to fill the vacuum left by the loss of religious faith;" and "commerce, industry, [and] bureaucracy" proliferated.

Noting that "Sir Francis Bacon [1561-1626]…conceptualized science as an entity that would 'bind' nature and reduce her to a slave. As a slave she could perform useful services for Europeans," Semali and Kincheloe further view the Cartesian-Newtonian, "Western" paradigm as nurturing the exploitation of nature, imperialism, colonialism, misogyny, and racism. They argue that this "dualistic way of seeing reinforced a rationalistic patriarchal expansionist social and political order welded to the desire for power and conquest. Such a way of seeing served to despiritualize and dehumanize, as it focused attention on concerns other than the sanctity of humanity." This paradigm, in the view of Semali and Kincheloe, "affected all aspects of Western life, all institutions." Moreover, since "such assumptions are seen as natural or even God-given, critics who expose their social construction and ethnocentrism are viewed as enemies of the Western "regime of truth" or of the culture itself."

As Tarnas and others have made clear, "Western" tradition, culture, and worldview are inextricably tied to the rise of Christianity. Indeed, in *The Pelican History of Mediaeval Europe* (1969), Maurice Keen identifies "western Europe" with "Christendom;" he states that these terms are "more or less analogous." Similarly, although from a more critical standpoint, D. Smith points out that the Western tradition also embraces "numerous ontologies that…[are] not primarily Cartesian; these include the Protestant fundamentalist tradition." This linkage appears to contradict the science versus faith emphasis of the Cartesian-Newtonian paradigm. This apparent contradiction may, however, be somewhat resolved in the division made by many Church authorities, especially of the past, between body and soul, immanence and transcendence, nature (here referring to non-human entities) and mankind (I use this word purposefully), men and women (Adam vs. Eve), light-skinned and dark-skinned peoples (Noah vs. Ham), and even between "rational" and dogmatic versus mystical and ecstatic aspects or traditions of Christianity. In this respect, certain branches of Christianity and the Cartesian-Newtonian paradigm promoted each other while simultaneously working in collaboration to destroy paradigms and traditions that we might today call "earth-centered" and/or "matrifocal."

Such insights into the "Western" worldview (etc.) have led Norman Davies, in his 1996 work *Europe: A History*, to observe of the notion of "the West": "For the best part of 200 years European history has been frequently confused with the heritage of 'Western civilization'. Indeed, the impression has been created that everything 'Western' is civilized, and that everything civilized is Western." Profoundly frustrated with the term "Western civilization" – Davies gives many other examples of its problematic deployment –

he writes: "From all these examples it appears that Western civilization is essentially an amalgam of intellectual constructs which were designed to further the interests of their authors. It is the product of complex exercises in ideology, of countless identity trips, of sophisticated essays in cultural propaganda."

In regard to our specific context, Davies observes of a highly influential history text, W. H. McNeill's *History of Western Civilization: A Handbook* (1986): "One sentence is awarded to pagan Scandinavia, and none to any of the other pagan lands which were later Christianized."

For years, I struggled with the notion of "the West" and with its meaning in relation to white supremacy and other matters. Then one day, my best friend, Mexican American writer and theorist Gloria Anzaldúa (to whom I shall frequently refer in this text) said to me, "Look at it this way. *I live in 'the West.' I'm a 'Western' writer.* So is Paula Gunn Allen. So is Alice Walker. You don't have to accept the definition that close-minded, racist writers and thinkers have imposed. *'The West' should embrace all of us who live in it.*" Of course, I recognize, as she did, that her and other persons of color's belonging to 'the West' came about through acts of imperialism and colonialism, but to deny such persons' cultural contributions to so-called 'Western culture' might prove even more problematic and frankly, offensive. In this way, I have, at least temporarily, made peace with my title of *The Pagan Heart of the West*.

Although many philosophers have been profoundly influenced by paganism/s, academics have tended to focus on the influence of Christianity upon their works and have, in doing so, frequently suppressed or denied their pagan sources. These academics have often stressed Neoplatonism's link to both ceremonial magic and Christianity at the expense of earth-centered pagan influence. Exemplary of such Neoplatonist/Hermeticist-focused, pagan-suppressive scholarship are two works from the early 1960s, Frances Yates's otherwise illuminating *Giordano Bruno and the Hermetic Tradition* and Paul Oskar Kristeller's *The Philosophy of Marsilio Ficino*. To interject here: while I have criticisms of Yates, I admire her work intensely. As my friends never fail to remind me, I "have issues with EVERYBODY." *Touché*.

Jay Kinney, in *The Inner West: An Introduction to the Hidden Wisdom of the West* (2004), basically defines the "inner West" as comprising Christianity; Neoplatonism; Gnosticism; Kabbalah; Sufism; Renaissance Hermeticism; individualism; and other esoteric traditions (studied primarily by male elites). Kinney's schema reflects, with the possible exception of Sufism – which has in recent decades become increasingly accepted as contributing to the Western spiritual/philosophical/esoteric canon, the same sort of bias that one finds in other, more general texts leading from Plato to St. Augustine to Teilhard de Chardin. The earth-centered traditions, including reverence of nature (other than as a poor likeness of a perfect Platonic Reality), the veneration of ancestors, and the reverence of goddesses, are ultimately erased.

Mark Booth basically constructs the same basic "map" and winds up at approximately the same destination that Jay Kinney has in his 2008 work *The Secret History of the World as Laid Down by the Secret Societies*. Booth tracks non-church (non-temple, etc.) spiritual development in the West from Plato to Neoplatonists, through Hermeticists, Rosicrucians, Swedenborgians, and culminates with (Free)Masons and Rudolf Steiner devotees.

Although in *Walkers Between the Worlds: The Western Mysteries from Shaman to Magus* (1985-6; updated 2004), Caitlín and John Matthews do not ignore earth-centered traditions, they nevertheless emphasize an "*evolutionary* search for individual consciousness [italics mine]" and proceed to map the "tree of the Mysteries" from Atlantis and Eden through Egyptian, Greek, Roman, Jewish, and Christian sacred traditions/religions to Rosicrucianism and alchemy, to culminate in Anthroposophy, Theosophy, and the Golden Dawn, thus relegating earth-centered traditions per se to a lower step on the 'evolutionary spiritual ladder' than spiritual traditions and movements that have been heavily influenced by Abrahamic faiths and intellectual elitism (as exemplified by remarks such as "These Mysteries cannot arbitrarily be open to all.").

With all due respect, I find the Matthewses frequent embrace of esoteric Abrahamic traditions, especially Christianity, troubling within the context of works on paganism. For example, they state: "Into its [i.e., 'native wisdom's'] storehouses goes every aspect of tradition, both pagan and Christian, old and new;" "Ultimately, the past is 'neither pagan nor Christian...' and we all have come from it;" and "...the Old Religion and the new religion rubbed along together." Indeed, in numerous works, they promote a comfortable ecumenism that one might say is 'easy on the' mind.

In my view, such statements, sounding more like bromides than the result of critical thinking, suggest a seamless wedding of paganism and Christianity, serving not only to minimize differences between them but also to obscure centuries of forced conversions and other forms of psychological and physical violence – they, like numerous academics, think that today's Wiccans think too much about the so-called "Burning Times" – that form a substantial aspect of the narrative of how pagan traditions were displaced by Christianity. Such statements as these are related to others, such as "The deities of the Foretime...continued to be venerated in the forms of Our Lord and Our Lady, Jesus and Mary." Firstly, I find the phrase "the Foretime" simultaneously vague, Romantic, exoticizing, and obfuscating; it is reminiscent of similar phrases – such as "noble savages" – used to infer that Indigenous Americans belong only to the past and that they are not peoples living in the twenty-first century.

Secondly, to suggest such a smooth, seamless archetypal transition from "deities of the Foretime" to "Jesus and Mary" is to further promote the simplistic, anti-historical, indeed anti-intellectual notion that "the past is 'neither pagan nor Christian.'" These statements, in turn, are linked to others that praise pagans who accepted Christianity, often forced upon them, without making trouble: "Those who remained helpful to their village...were most likely those who…were seen going to church…These descendants of Foretime belief could not afford to be rebels who stood out from the crowd or who openly opposed Christian belief." They suggest that people didn't wish to live "in mutinous hostility and resentment of Christianity," because, after all, both systems *"served the same purpose* [italics mine]."

The Matthewses do not, however, stop here. They further suggest that "if there are any successors to the tribal shamans, then the most likely candidates are the inheritors of the secret commonwealth of our native tradition;" these are not "the Wiccans of today…but those who have lived on the land, near to their roots," who just happen to be Christians – Christians who appropriate whatever non-Christian ideas and practices "reflect [their] own characteristics" in the name of "adapt[ing] to the prevailing times and customs." Nor do the Matthewses stop here. They argue that if "there seems to be an inexplicable hiatus between the Foretime's Old Religion and the modern Craft, it is either because the links are invisible or because they were never there."

Moreover, they insist – *without a shred of hard evidenc*e – not only that "The Old Religion was forced into sudden extinction" but also that "before it died, it showed its ugly side. …[T]hose with the power to heal and hurt [i.e., alleged witches and presumably other practitioners of pagan traditions] often chose to hurt out of a spirit of vengeance and retribution," thus serving to lessen, if not to pardon, the inhumane torture and execution of alleged witches and other pagans by religious, civil, and military authorities.

Finally, the Matthewses insist that present-day Pagans, Wiccans, and kin

"cannot altogether ignore the mystical cohesion of Christianity, which has preserved aspects of the native wisdom quite successfully along with imparting its own wisdom as a spiritual path. *The way back to the Foretime lies through the territory of Christian belief…*[italics mine]"

Nicole Belmont, "Mythic Elements in French Folklore" (1991), states matter-of-factly that pagan "traces" or "vestiges" didn't survive because *"the needs of the majority of the people were satisfied by the Christian system* [italics mine]." Similarly, Hutton insists in *Pagan Religions* that a "large part of the reason for Christianity's victory in places such as Ireland, where it depended solely upon its own merits, is surely that *it offered everything already given by the old cults, and added a confident promise of eternal bliss* [italics mine]."

Such assertions not only fly in the face of abundant evidence provided by Christian penitentials and confessionals that pagan-based practices persisted in much of Christianized Europe through the Middle Ages and, in some areas, well into the seventeenth and eighteenth centuries; they also, and even more disturbingly, *normatize and naturalize the process of Christianization*, support, at least indirectly, a social-Darwinist evolutionary theory of religious development, and, most troublingly – and, in my view, deeply offensively – *deny the massive violence that accompanied Christianization, from Europe, the Middle East, and Africa to the New World.*

Among the most astonishing claims made by Hutton is that persons practicing "white magic" were "devout Christians" and that "magic of any kind cannot, strictly speaking, be described as 'paganism.' It was separate from the worship of the old deities, could flourish within a Christian culture." And once more with the absolutist rhetoric: "To repeat: *no act* of magic [italics mine], however frowned upon by the Church, can be used to prove the continued existence of the old religions of the British Isles unless there is firm evidence that it involved a belief in those religions." This is amazing, in Mary Daly's meaning of that word. *Surely all acts of magic emerge from the Christian New Testament.* And yes, when Jehovah's Witnesses become upset when given Easter cards depicting colored eggs and bunnies, claiming that this imagery is "pagan," *they are correct*. I am actually surprised that this way of thinking has not led Hutton and others to claim that "white magic" is actually Islamic, since Islam followed Chritianity.

It occurs to me that unless a person were the most defiant rebel ever born (akin to Julian the Apostate) or else insane, she or he, having been made acutely aware by Church authorities of the dire consequences of declaring any other religious identity (save, in rare circumstances, Jewish or Muslim), would have, at the very least, ostensibly identified as Christian. Thus, to equate silence, in regard to the practice of pagan traditions, with an absence thereof amounts to fallacious reasoning. It also occurs to me that many Church authorities, via penitentials and other means, were only too willing to enlighten practitioners of magic as to its ancient association with paganism. Furthermore, as I have already suggested, I find Hutton's insistence on "firm evidence" of pagan belief somewhat troubling.

I am reminded of Spanish conquerors who burned the manuscripts of the Nahuas (Mexicas/Aztecs), Mayas, and others so that they could then report them as being illiterate – for a brilliant discussion of this, see Indigenous American Linda Hogan's *Dwellings: A Spiritual History of the Living World* (1996). I am also reminded of recent Christian concern that the physical remains of Jesus might have been found. Finally, I find Hutton's remark – and certainly he is not alone in his insistence on hard evidence of pagan belief – somewhat offensive in amounting to what in the '60s we referred to as "blaming the victim." If the material evidence relating to paganism has been generally destroyed by Christians, and to a much lesser extent, by adherents of other Abrahamic faiths, is it then up to the descendants of those who attempted to preserve it to prove its former existence?

I wonder how easily this argument would go down were it served to adherents of Abrahamic faiths, for example, Jews or Christians who sought to preserve their faiths in the former Soviet Union.

In a somewhat similar vein, Hutton insists that just because the "medieval world incorporated into its culture the art and letters of pagan antiquity…[or] when a modern writer compares somebody to Mars or Jove or Hercules, this is not a declaration of pagan Roman beliefs…Botticelli, Titian, [etc.] were all Christians even though they painted images of Venus." This argument rests upon superficial notions of "mythology" and "metaphor" rather than on more sophisticated descriptions of metaphor such as that given by the philosopher Mary Daly in *Pure Lust*. I would ask Hutton, following this line of argument, does such an incorporation of pagan iconography then underscore the artist's being a fine, upstanding Christian? Frankly, I think not.

Moreover, if Christianity supplied personae, narratives, symbols, and so on in such abundance, why did artists find it so compelling to draw upon the pagan "past"? Hutton, unconsciously or willfully relying upon these renditions of "myth" and "metaphor," continues, "[T]he reappearance of a pagan image in a Christian concept only demonstrates the survival of paganism itself if it can be shown to have a religious purpose, and is not being used as an analogy or for its aesthetic value."

Returning to his previous remarks concerning the practice of magic and self-identification as Christian, I would again query Hutton as to how it is that he is so comfortable in insisting emphatically that an artist's depiction of Venus is most assuredly *not* a "declaration of…pagan beliefs"? Again, I would be hesitant to make such a categorical statement, especially of artists for whom identifying as anything other than Christian might have meant imprisonment, torture, or death. I think, rather, that it is wise to put aside such absolutist remarks and to look instead, with our eyes as open as possible, and preferably not too clouded by weapon-words like "religion," "myth," and "metaphor" to try and see what truly and deeply meets our gaze, whether it be Christian, pagan, or other sacred presence.

This Christocentric, or Christocentrist, perspective becomes even more apparent when Hutton highlights, in *The Stations of the Sun*, the work of R. A. Markus, who "suggested that many phenomena in the Christianized empire which historians now recognize as 'pagan survivals' were simply taken for granted as part of the fabric of existence and of a common inherited culture. Christians were conscious of their origins but did not consider these to be very significant."

From my perspective, this statement, particularly the phrase "simply taken for granted," not only normatizes and naturalizes a series of violent acts of aggression, directly related to imperialism and colonialism, that ultimately transformed pagan Europe and the Indigenous Americas, as well as much of Africa and elsewhere, into predominantly Christian societies, but it also suggests that little resistance to this campaign occurred, that sacred hybridity occurred relatively smoothly, and that Christians did not consider the theft and cannibalizing of others' sacred traditions to be anything other than acceptable.

There are, I must note, certain times when Hutton seems to open a door to the possibility that there is more to the discussion than that "pagan survivals" were not as smoothly folded into Christianity as one might fold ingredients into a casserole, as when he notes: "It was ….the period between 1350 and 1530 [that] produced not merely a greater quantity of records of communal customs and seasonal rites, but an actual increase in both, representing a continual elaboration of religious, municipal, and courtly ritual." Hutton also acknowledges that Theo Brown may be "perfectly accurate" in describing some rites in Christianized England as "a mixture of ancient pagan belief" and Christianity. Somewhat surprisingly, however, this does not lead Hutton to consider the possibility of a pagan-based or truly pagano-Christian hybrid innovation, but rather leads him only to admit that a sacred hybridity comprised of "ancient pagan belief" and living Christianity existed or exists. What he seems somehow unable to acknowledge the possibility that this hybridity might be comprised of an ever-evolving paganism interweaving itself with certain elements of Christianity.

More recently, in "Wicca, Paganism and History" (2002), Joanne Pearson, who, like Hutton and others, not only denigrates Margaret Murray's theory of witchcraft but also like Hutton takes a Christocentrist approach, arguing that, following official Christianization, charms, spells, and folk customs that continued to be practiced should be classified as "Christian." One might also note in this context Jonathan Roper's arrogant remark in the introduction to *Charms, Charmers and Charming* (2009), in which he brags that in his anthology, "many pseudo-scholarly pitfalls – such as...excessive paganising...were successfully avoided." He does not, on the other hand, seem the least bit concerned as to whether or not the "pseudo-scholarly pitfall" of "excessive [Christian]izing" has or has not been "successfully avoided.'

It appears that the tendency in some academic studies toward Christocentrism may be mirrored by a rather vehement Anglocentrism. While I am all for pursuing the microcosmic, and one of course must focus and limit the subjects of one's studies, this is unfortunately *not* what results from a combining of Christocentrism and Anglocentrism. Instead, one imagines a dichotomy between Christianity and a few lone, or "vanished," British pagans, rather than between Christianity and a relatively common pagan worldview and allied practices that existed for millennia across vast stretches of Europe, ideas and practices that resonated in powerful ways with African, Indigenous American, and other sacred traditions. In regard to Pearson's "Wicca, Paganism and History," one cannot fail to notice her mocking – in an attempt to parody present-day Goddess-revering Witches – of the expression "the Burning Times" to refer to the period of the witchcraft trials; after all, she insists, "witches were hanged rather than burned in England." Perhaps, trapped within the prison of Anglocentrism, as she appears to be trapped within the prisons of hegemonic (patriarchal) history and Christocentrism, she remains unaware that the "Burning Times" refers to the period of the witch trials across Europe as well as in the Americas, and that although the witches of Salem were hanged, those in Mexico and in many other places were burned at the stake.

Owen Davies, who has done some very fine work in this area, is also not immune to the absolutist tendency or to Christocentrism. He argues confidently in *Grimoires: A History of Magic Books* (2009), "By the end of the [first] millennium, with

Christianity having been the sole religion across much of Europe for several centuries, paganism and its ambivalent demons of the natural world *had long ceased to be relevant* [italics mine]." This statement is troubling. It reeks of a Christocentrist, colonialist mentality, the very sort that led Christian imperialists to devastate the religions or sacred traditions of Africa and the Americas.

Having said all of this, I believe that to castigate those persons, for example, many Mexican and Eastern European Americans, who pray to the Virgin Mary and the saints as they once did to goddesses and gods, is tantamount, as I have said in another context, to "blaming the victim," and to deny the concept of a "living religion" or of "lived experience," which acknowledges that with the passing of time, together with the triumphs of imperialism and colonialism, beliefs, practices, and depictions of sacred beings may undergo change. Moreover, some of these persons approach their practices in the manner of sacred hybridity, such as that Russians have called dvoeverie, or that my friend Gloria Anzaldúa referred to as "spiritual mestizaje," or what might be termed "bireligiosity," resonating with such terms as "bisexuality" and "biracial."

Goodbye to All That

In regard to all things post-Christianization being deemed "Christian," it occurs to me – based on over twenty-five years of study of, and participation in, African-diasporic sacred traditions – that we might wish to ask, What if, in certain milieus, what was/is actually occurring is a kind of "paganization" of Christianity? In his 2001 work *L'Arbre philosophal* (*The Philosopher's Tree*), Bernard Rio relates: "Medieval accounts indicate more of a transformation than an elimination of pre-Christian religious materials. ...Although urbanization favored the new religion, the countryside submitted only in appearance. In the most isolated, least accessible regions, populations conserved their ancient customs." What is more, Rio argues, is that in certain places, "human relationships [continued to be founded on] the rule of the community. ...[T]hese peoples rejected the Christian faith. In 2005, Filotas, echoing Rio, remarks in this context, "One historian [has gone] so far as to doubt whether most supposed Christians in the early Middle Ages [can] be considered as Christian in anything but name."

It is my view that it would assist us immensely in seeking to more fully comprehend pagan sacred traditions if we were able to view them in their own light and perhaps in the light of other ancient and indigenous sacred traditions rather than to view them in a manner that relies upon Christocentrism mixed with social Darwinism as a lens or optic.

In regard to absolutist language and its allied mentality, I wish I could say that someone has found, or that one day we will find, incontrovertible proof of the secret meetings of pagans and/or witches in "fully" Christianized countries; to my knowledge, such proof remains hidden or buried. But seeing as how each year archaeologists uncover "new" ancient objects, human bones, etc., and how geneticists and others are now able to interpret that evidence, together with older materia, in innovative ways, I would most assuredly not risk making such a blanket statement as that cited above, that there "is no evidence of...meeting in secret," recognizing that some day, such evidence may be uncovered. Further, "meeting in secret" is meant to be *just that*. When no one tells, and no one asks (if one is fortunate), then "meeting in secret" remains a secret. From my perspective, the absence of evidence of meeting in secret does not prove that paganism/s did not persist but rather that in some cases, mystery remained.

I believe, as Maghan Keita, Professor of African, World, Class, and Gendered Histories at Villanova University, has wisely suggested in "The Politics of Criticism: *Not Out of Africa* and *Black Athena Revisited* (2000), that we need to be able to at least temporarily put aside notions of "absolute truth" and permit ourselves to consider "alternative ways of knowing," if we are to shed further light on this subject. Indeed, in my view, it is imperative that we shed the language of absolutism if we are to construct a fuller and more accurate portrait of European paganism/s and the sacred hybridities to which it/they have contributed.

As Richard A. Horsley remarked some thirty years ago of the so-called "decline of magic" in "Further Reflections on Witchcraft and European Folk Religion," "the general decline of magic was neither as rapid nor as thorough as [Keith] Thomas found it to be among the intellectual elite." *Thomas's tome, incidentally, was shoved at me to try to get me to shut up about pagans and witches. If certain closeted professors were upset about my being gay – one who'd been having an affair with a female student told me I should quit school, move to San Francisco, and become a waiter – they were even more upset about my interest in things witchy and paga*n.

We seriously need to avoid the pitfall of *preempting*, *short-circuiting*, *curtailin*g rather than *promoting dialogue and being open to innovative interpretations and "new" archaeological and other findings*. Several years ago, the public learned that via genetic testing, researchers discovered that the bodies of fifty-one decapitated men found at Weymouth, England – when construction workers were preparing a venue for the 2012 Olympics – were the bodies of Vikings who had lived between 890 and 1030 CE and who had been executed by recently Christianized Saxons. Who knows how this discovery might amend the history of Vikings and Saxons in that area during that epoch? According to David Score, project manager for Oxford Archaeology, "To find out that the young men executed were Vikings is a thrilling development. ...Any mass grave is a relatively rare find, but to find one on this scale, from this period of history, is extremely unusual."

Theoretical and Methodological Approaches

In conceiving and writing this text, I have been inspired by and relied upon numerous theoretical and methodological approaches.

From Marxian and related approaches, I have drawn upon the methodological practice of seeking "history from below" as well as from the Gramscian practice of exploring vernacular and subaltern histories; whenever possible, as when we shall consider Shakespearean "groundlings" of the Renaissance and peasant women revolutionaries during the French Revolution, I have sought to consider the histories of non-elites together with those of elites.

In "Notes on Italian History," the Italian philosopher and political theorist Antonio Gramsci (1891-1937) writes: "The history of subaltern groups is necessarily fragmented and episodic. There undoubtedly does exist a tendency to…unification in the historical activity of these groups, but this tendency is continually interrupted by the activity of the ruling groups…Every trace of independent initiative on the part of subaltern groups should therefore be of incalculable value for the integral historian."

It is unfortunately a fact that, for the most part, the chronicler of pagan subjectivity and the pagan worldview, like that of subaltern groups, must work with "precisely, 'fragments,' 'traces.'" What we must work with are partial or fragmentary written accounts dispersed over numerous cultures and epochs. As we do so, we cannot overemphasize the difficulty involved in this effort that has resulted from the willful destruction of pagan material culture and the silencing and erasure of pagan subjectivity by Christians.

Generally speaking, what remains in terms of literary evidence of the earth-centered pagan worldview and pagan-based traditions are Christian texts describing pagan traditions in highly mediated forms, such as medieval penitentials, which do *not* include remarks made by pagans, and, on the other hand, texts of poetry, fiction, and drama that embrace pagan figures, themes, and narratives. Where the former are concerned, such texts as penitentials might be characterized as texts composed by those in power, primarily (although not entirely) by educated, Christian, often celibate males acting in accord with the State, with their compositions representing a religious counterpart of what Professor of History Gyanendra Pandey refers to as "statist historiography."

Due to the paucity of first-hand accounts by European (and, in later times, by Euro-American) practitioners of non-Christian sacred traditions from the fourth century CE onward, until the emergence of NeoPaganism in the nineteenth and later centuries, and due to a great amount of oral rather than literary transmission, and to the suppression of pagan traditions by Christian (and, to a much lesser extent, by Jewish and Muslim) forces, we will probably never be able to reconstruct a direct account of the earth-centered pagan worldview as it existed during specific and diverse epochal and cultural contexts. Indeed, we may perhaps never succeed in reconstructing a full *indirect* account of this worldview. We must learn to read such texts as penitentials differently from the way in which the antagonistic writer intended them to be read, in order to tease out potential information regarding pagan customs or the earth-centered pagan worldview.

It should be noted that Gramsci "saw

folklore, particularly folk beliefs, as part of a system that kept subalterns trapped in a situation of powerlessness." Nevertheless, his description of the subaltern, when expanded, can be deployed to describe the condition into which pagans (adhering to so-called "folk beliefs") were forced during the campaign of Christianization; and his notion that "every trace … should therefore be of incalculable value for the integral historian" can likewise be deployed to speak of the work of those seeking to reconstruct pagan subjectivity and the earth-centered pagan worldview. If we wish to arrive at the most comprehensive description or depiction of the pagan worldview that is possible to attain under these far less than perfect circumstances, we must permit ourselves to expand the definition of "text" to include other-than-literary evidence, such as that of arts and crafts, chant, music, and dance, and pagan-based or inspired rituals.

To a certain extent, I have been inspired by comparativist and cross-cultural approaches. Comparativism in studies of the sacred commenced seriously in the late nineteenth century – ideally, as the "cross-cultural study of all forms and traditions of religious life" in which "[n]o religion would be privileged" and "[n]o religious version of history would be used as normative." The basic tenet of comparativists in this field was/is as follows: "There can be no systematic study of religion without cross-cultural perspective. Lacking this, studies of religion would amount either to separate collections of unrelated historical data, or to speculative generalizations based only on the perspective of one culture."

Among the early pioneers of comparativism in studies of the sacred were F. Max Müller (1823-1900), E. B. Tylor (1832-1917), Émile Durkheim (1858-1917), James G. Frazer (1854-1941), Sigmund Freud (1856-1939), Carl Jung (1875-1961), and Mircea Eliade (1907-1986). Unfortunately, despite lofty ideals, early comparativist studies were frequently tainted by social Darwinism, Christo-centrism, Anglocentrism, racism, and other biases, as well as a search for universals and/or a "perennial philosophy." More recently, however, comparativists have argued that a "comparative pattern can be widespread without being universal. A cross-cultural pattern does not need to appear in all cultures, but only needs to recur in relation to certain types or conditions of culture and religious systems. For example, not all religions have shamans, priests, savior figures, animal sacrifices, or scriptures. But the ones that do have certain recurrent social patterns in common."

Many present-day academics are concerned chiefly with cultural and other differences and tend to avoid comparativism whenever possible, fearing that these differences might be erased in the name of harmony or unity. To those who shun comparativism, however, comparativists insist that the "fact of the plurality of cultural worlds does not mean "that they share nothing in common; what is more, sacred narratives ("myths"), sacred space-time, periodic rites, and other things are common to many sacred traditions. Today's comparativists insist that a focus on "shared, panhuman features" must be balanced by "cultural specifics and differences." They also argue that those who insist on *not* comparing cultural, including sacred, traditions risk promoting the "false notion [that] cultures [are] hermetically sealed units isolated from one another and developing 'solely] internally, without significant influence from 'outside'."

"Cross-culturalism," like comparativism, has been shunned by many academics in recent decades. As Neil Thin points out in "Why Anthropology Can Ill Afford to Ignore Well-Being" (2009), "relativism has acted as a strong deterrent against cross-cultural" analyses. Rather surprisingly, "cross-culturalist" studies, like comparativist ones, were frequently tainted by Eurocentrism and other biases. Once, like "syncretism," "cross-culturalism" emphasized melding or fusing. "Cross-culturalism," has, however, like comparativism, continued to undergo innovation. Today "cross-culturalism" "stands for a cultural reciprocation, engagement, or negotiation" without a consequent loss of differences. In the view of Canadian Ted T. Aoki, a renowned Curriculum Studies scholar, it is vital to our educational system and our culture that, without permitting a loss of differences, we acknowledge ideas, practices, etc., that span various cultures. He refers to his 'brand' of cross-culturalism as "interculturalism," as opposed to "multiculturalism," which he finds tends to isolate cultures from each other and leads to a kind of "museumization" of these cultures. In like spirit, present-day musician Harry Aoki tells Xiaoping Li, "I make a distinction between multi-culturalism and cross-culturalism. Multiculturalism would be like you putting on a concert on Chinese music, I putting on one on Indian music. Cross-culturalism is to have erhu, pipa, sarangi, and shakuhachi play together."

Recently, Martin Japtok, in *Postcolonial Perspectives on Women Writers from Africa, the Caribbean, and the U.S.* (2003), has pointed out that a number of feminist writers are "[g]oing against recent injunctions against cross-cultural readings and skepticism about cross-cultural feminism" and insisting that the "common bond of gender," "gender-based oppression," and the "struggle against" oppression cut across "spatial setting and social structure." Also recently, Hena Maes-Jelinek, in *The Labyrinth of Universality" Wilson Harris's Visionary Art of Fiction* (2006), illuminates a kind of cross-culturalism, practiced by Harris and by Wole Soyinka, that, in Africanizing Greek mythic narratives, "point[s] to a kind of ontological cross-culturalism which subverts and dismantles Western assumptions of a superior cultural heritage." Acutely aware of present-day academic shunning of cross-culturalism, Harris and Soyinka demonstrate that "transcultural similarities ... in areas ...widely separated in both time and space" may not only be grounded in a postcolonial movement that defies Eurocentrism but also that cross-culturalism of this sort may assist in illuminating and explaining "rationally inexplicable cultural correspondences" that embrace "intuitively accessible ... essences" that speak to the "religious," the "extra-human," the "pagan."

Notably, in terms of our present context, Harris associates this "non-idealistic," non-

Platonic, non-transcendent cross-culturalism with what he, reminding us of Baudelaire's "Correspondences," describes as "convertible imageries," "transitive chords" found in an immanent, inspirited nature. In this regard, Harris associates this form of cross-culturalism with a "denial of the passivity of 'landscapes/riverscapes/skyscapes'" and with a Whitmanic embodiment of nature: "parts of ourselves are embedded everywhere – in the rock, in the tree, in the star, in the light, in the wood." Harris wisely describes this sensibility as rooted in "the pagan womb from which civilization comes…from which we all derive." Harris, as Maes-Jelinek explains, "finds a confirmation of this in 'quantum immediacy' – in the axiom in quantum physics that posits the existence of multiple, parallel, and multidimensional universes and associations between different forms of being." I have taken Harris's, Soyinka's, and Maes-Jelinek's conceptions of cross-culturalism to heart as a guide in the writing of this book.

At the same time, however, I have also sought to avoid potential dangers of comparitivism and cross-culturalism by attempting to integrate comparativism and cross-culturalism with microhistorical methodology and "thick description" herein. Of microhistory, Giovanni Levi writes: "Microhistory as a practice is essentially based on…an intensive study of …documentary material…Phenomena previously considered to be sufficiently described and understood assume…new meanings by altering the scale of observation. It is then possible to use these results to draw…wider generalizations."

Levi continues, "Despite having its roots within…historical research, many of microhistory's characteristics demonstrate …close ties…with anthropology – particularly that 'thick description' which Clifford Geertz sees as the proper perspective of anthropological work." "Thick description," coined by British philosopher Gilbert Ryle (1900-1976) and significantly deployed by Geertz (1926-2006), "seizes upon an event, performance, or other practice, and through the interrogation of its minute particulars, seeks to reveal the collective ethos of an alien culture." Not only this, however; thick description also recognizes and privileges interpretation, the relationship between the one who documents and that which or those who are the subject of that documentation. In Geertz's words, "A good interpretation …takes us into the heart of that of which it is the interpretation."

I have been deeply inspired by Carlo Ginzburg's methodological practice in his book *Ecstasies: Deciphering the Witches' Sabbath*. In *Ecstasies*, Ginzburg explains that his methodology has been inspired by the writings of the folklorists Jacob Grimm and Vladimir Propp; by Wittgenstein's reading of James Frazer's *The Golden Bough*, in which the former stresses the importance – without ignoring differences – of examining mythological, ritual, and iconographic "texts" in terms of "connections," "intermediary links," and "mutual relationships"; and by linguist Roman Jakobsen's opposition to the positing of "an extreme antithesis between synchrony and diachrony," in the face of evidence indicating that "the prehistoric antiquity of a great part of what is concealed in the [folkloric] elements that have come down to us appears convincingly attested to." Guided by these, Ginzburg reaches the conclusion that "Though only partially superimposable, these sets of myths [primarily concerning the Sabbath] are bound by a dense web of resemblances, which are probably due to the existence of a common thread." He writes of his methodology: "Figures and themes echo each other, bounce back off each other, until they compose, not merely a chain, but a sort of magnetic field – which explains how, starting from diverse viewpoints and proceeding independently, it has been possible to arrive at analogous conjectures." In *Ecstasies*, he is particularly concerned with tropes, beliefs, and practices linked to witchcraft – from "animal meta-morphoses, [and] mythical journeys to the beyond, [to] rituals and beliefs connected with the procession of the dead – and, naturally, the Sabbath… We must reknit the many threads that bound them."

From Ginzburg's and others' microhistorical and 'thick descriptive' approaches, I have appropriated the notion of focusing on certain events in rather minute detail (as in a particular "progress" in honor of Queen Elizabeth I (1533-1603)) in order to "produce [as] vivid [a] reconstruction" of an historical event as possible in order to more fully comprehend its relationship to the pagan worldview. Unfortunately, due to spatial constraints, I have not been able to deploy this methodology as often as I would have liked.

Similarly, from postmodern theory and methodological practice, I have drawn upon the notion of seeking out "*petits récits*" that challenge grand metanarratives; in the words of Jean-François Lyotard, "The grandiose theories professed by the 'priests' of philosophy and science ... are rejected in the name of a 'paganism' that recognizes no overarching authorities or truths, and contested in the name of the flows of desire that emerge in marginal groups."

On the other hand, I am troubled by academics who shun too easily and too finally what they consider to be metatheories or "grand narratives" and who denigrate or condemn scholars and writers who formulate such theories or narratives. In my view, one may gather much specific data from those who have dared to offer such theories and narratives without necessarily accepting, at least wholeheartedly, their "grand narratives."

For example, I have gleaned much information concerning ancient Lithuanian ideas and practices from Gimbutas, even if I have difficulty accepting her metatheory wholeheartedly. I also think that an open-minded approach to non- and anti-hegemonic metanarratives may work to redress the balance in regard to the patriarchal, Abrahamic, Cartesian narratives that dominate Western culture. In my estimation, absolutism in the guise of cultural relativism – such as practiced by many academics who sneer at any and all grand narratives – is an ugly costume indeed.

In regard to Gimbutas' work in particular, some academics, including feminists like Cynthia Eller in *The Myth of Matriarchal Prehistory* (2000), spend great amounts of time and pages seeking to debunk her, more than one with the goal of attaining tenure at the university where they teach, as many institutions of higher learning continue to shun study of non-hegemonic religions/traditions, particularly when they are primarily linked to women and to divination, magic, and traditional healing, and their exploration might be configured as promoting Paganism, Witchcraft, or Women's Spirituality. Despite such anti-Gimbutian diatribes, however, other scholars – primarily European ones – are presently stepping forward to acknowledge the great work that Gimbutas undertook, the great debt they owe her, and the soundness of her theories. For example, in *About Scepters, Horses, War: Sketches in Defense of the Migrational Conception of M. Gimbutas* (2007), Valentin Anisimovich Dergachev states that his own examinations of archaeological evidence from Eastern and Southeastern Europe "completely confirm the conceptual views of M. Gimbutas" including complete confirmation of the "migration concept of M. Gimbutas." Indeed, an English summary of his book concludes: "[T]he already obtained results leave no doubt in the final assessment of the rightfulness of the concept by M. Gimbutas."

From Michel Foucault I have appropriated the methodological practice of "genealogy" or "genealogical reflection," his terminology for seeking to unearth and interpret "subjugated knowledges." In "Two Lectures," Foucault describes "subjugated knowledges as primarily being "particular, local, regional," "non-centralized," "discontinuous," and "popular (*le savoir des gens*)." Foucault indicates, however, that subjugated knowledges may also include "buried knowledges of erudition."

Semali and Kincheloe, in their introduction to *What is Indigenous Knowledge?*, describe "subjugated knowledge [as knowledge that] contests dominant cultural views of reality." Because they contest hegemonic ideas and practices – such as the Church's insistence on monotheism – they tend to be viewed as threatening to hegemonic order. They exist in a "marginalized relationship to Western epistemological…power;" and as Foucault explains, their power becomes linked "to the harshness with which [they are] opposed." "[T]hese buried, subjugated knowledges," he observes, are "concerned with a historical knowledge of struggles. In the specialized areas of erudition as in the disqualified, popular knowledge there lay the memory of hostile encounters which even up to this day have been confined to the margins of knowledge."

Subjugated knowledges are dealt with by those in power in various ways. Sometimes they are devalued, denigrated, or ridiculed as being "primitive" or "naïve" and are relegated to the lowest rungs on the ladder of the "hierarchy" of knowledges. At other times, especially when they come to be viewed as "dangerous" or "demonic" because they serve the "purposes of the subjugated," they come to be branded as "pathological to other citizens" and are "erased." In this way, "social domination" is perpetuated and the subjugated remain subjugated.

Despite such potent strategies, however, fragments or traces of subjugated knowledges sometimes persist.

In "Knowledge, Belief and the

Supernatural at the Imperial Margin" (2004), Roger Luckhurst deploys Foucault's (1926-1984) term "subjugated knowledges" to speak of beliefs concerning psychic phenomena, describing them as constituting a "shadow-record of beliefs and semi-legitimate knowledges that circulated precisely because they dealt with material that failed to find sanction in orthodox channels of information."

Many pagan and pagan-inspired texts, particularly non-literary "texts" such as sacred stones, seasonal rites, and artistic evidence including chant, music, and dance, as well as Christian literary texts such as certain penitentials describing pagan practices, reflect the "particular, local, [and/or the] regional." Many have arisen from "popular" culture and wisdom (*le savoir des gens*). Others, however, are linked to "buried knowledges of erudition" such as systems of healing, divination, and magic. Taken together, they comprise "a field of entangled and confused parchments, on documents that have been scratched over and recopied many times."

While pagan and pagan-inspired texts share numerous commonalities such as veneration of nature, honoring of the seasonal cycle, and multiple manifestations of divinity, and indeed, together may constitute a pagan worldview, they remain, to a certain extent, "differential knowledge[s]," "non-centralized" sets of concepts and practices expressing particularities and associated with certain locations or regions. Steven Russell, in "Witchcraft, Genealogy, Foucault" (2001), describes his article, which examines witchcraft trials in light of these and related Foucauldian concepts, as a "genealogical reflection" on the trials. By "genealogy," Foucault, roughly speaking, means a strategy whereby one "entertain[s] the claims to attention of local, discontinuous, disqualified, illegitimate [and historically situated] knowledges against the claims of a unitary body," that is to say, in this context, against the dominant, hegemonic theology/ ideology of institutional Christianity.

Genealogy, in other words, is the active, combined search for, gathering of, and reflection upon subjugated, anti-hegemonic knowledges, which frequently, as we have noted, mix the erudite and the popular, the latter including "local memories." Indeed, subjugated knowledges investigated and analyzed in this manner are sometimes referred to as "genealogies."

Foucault argues that if we are to "establish" a kind of "historical knowledge" that constructs a more nuanced portrait than that drawn by officially sanctioned, hegemonic texts, we must practice genealogy, which he also describes as a kind of "archaeology" that promotes the (re)discovery of suppressed texts, "unsanctioned narratives," and subjugated knowledges. Such an undertaking will prove exceedingly difficult unless "the tyranny of globalizing discourses with their hierarchy and all their privileges…[is] eliminated."

Finally, Foucault suggests that a "re-emergence of…[subjugated] knowledges," a "re-appearance of this knowledge, of these local popular knowledges," a "reactivation of local knowledges – of minor knowledges, as [Gilles] Deleuze [French philosopher,

1925-1995] might call them," may climax in an "insurrection of subjugated knowledges." In our present context, we might draw from this that NeoPaganism, Wicca, Women's Spirituality, and kindred traditions and movements signify, in no small way, an "insurrection of subjugated knowledges."

As we permit ourselves to expand the definition of "text" and to undertake an "archaeology" of "subjugated knowledges" and "genealogical reflection" regarding these, we may also wish to permit ourselves, in the words of Barbara Schmidt-Haberkamp in "The Writing-Back Paradigm Revisited" (2005), to "'revisio[n]' the view of colonial history offered by the imperial centre" and risk constructing a "counter-discourse," that is, a " 'rewriting' of canonical stories" in an effort to "destabiliz[e] 'the assumption of authority, 'voice,' and control of the word' on the part of the Empire" so that we may perhaps see to data that lies past the judgments of hostile recorders and interpreters.

Stephen Morton, in a guide to the work of Gayatri Spivak, whose writings interweave Marxian, Foucauldian, postmodern, and postcolonial threads, makes a remark which I find deeply resonant with the primary subject discussed herein: "Throughout the history of western culture and thought, there are certain people, concepts, and ideas that are defined as 'Other': as monsters, aliens or savages who threaten the values of civilized society, or the stability of the rational human self." For Spivak, followed by Morton, "others" include "the foreigner, the homosexual, and the feminine." We might also add the pagan (in Abrahamic cultures) and the witch.

Inspired by Morton and others, I have come to understand pagan-inspired discourses as constituting *counterdiscourses* to that of the hegemonic discourse of the institutional Church and the State insofar as it supports the Church. Of course, pagan discourses would have once been themselves hegemonic; but with Christianization, the Church largely assumed control of discourse. Rosiska Darcy de Oliveira, in *In Praise of Difference: The Emergence of a Global Feminism*, writes: "Masculine discourse had always defined what a "normal" woman was ... [Patriarchal] ideology can then remain invisible to the extent that it is endowed with all the characteristics of an objective truth, an absolute necessity dictated by the natural order of things." However, when women began to question the "pre-established roles and norms," she continues, "when they penetrated previously forbidden spaces and produced a *counterdiscourse* [italics mine], they brought two cultures and two views of the world into confrontation."

Just as de Oliveira understands feminist discourse as representing a counter-discourse to the dominant, hegemonic, masculine discourse of Western culture, and just as Tejumola Olaniyan, in *Scars of Conquest/ Masks of Resistance*, describes Afrocentric discourse as a counterdiscourse standing in opposition to Eurocentric discourse, so I understand pagan-rooted discourse to represent a counterdiscourse contesting the Christocentric(or Christocentrist) discourse of the Church.

Moving Beyond Condemnation of the "Quest for Origins" and the "Survivals"/ "No Survivals" Dichotomy

The notion of "pagan survivals" commenced centuries ago, as evidenced by the phrase "remains of paganism" used repeatedly by the theologian Jean-Baptiste Thiers in his 1679 *Treatise on Superstitions*; it should be pointed out that the concept is Christocentric in origin and should not be viewed as an "objective," agenda-less term. It was rather unthinkingly adopted and promoted by anthropologists of more recent times, including by E. B. Tylor (1832-1917).

The concept of "survivals" has also been deployed by writers more sympathetic to ancient/indigenous/pagan traditions and in such a context has assumed a poignant, nostalgic, wistful tone, as in W. G. Wood-Martin's 1902 *Elder Faiths of Ireland*:

> Many singular customs of the Irish peasantry are but faint reflected lights of the...past, for, although the Christian missionaries did their utmost...to stamp out paganism, there remained in the hearts of the people a deeply rooted fondness for the form of worship in which they had been brought up. It was the religion of their forefathers...To the present day very distinct traces of paganism may be found in the acts of...herb- or fairy-doctors.[7]

Significantly, Wood-Martin insists, "Survivals of what we, in our pride, designate as 'pagan superstitions' are in reality religious," thus acknowledging a certain amount of respect for pagan-based traditions. Thus, although the notion of "survivals," "traces," "vestiges," etc. is of Christian origin, and as such is not judgment-free, it has, since the nineteenth century, occasionally been used to pay homage to pagan traditions.

As regards the "quest for origins," interest in ancestral roots has escalated dramatically in the early twenty-first century with the exploding popularity of organizations like ancestry.com, innovative genetic analyses, and television programs such as *Finding Your Roots*, hosted by Professor Henry Louis Gates, and *Who Do You Think You Are?* From my perspective, I think we must be extremely cautious of anti-historical, indeed, I would venture to say, anti-intellectual, views that tend to portray the "quest for...origins" as *"obsessive."* I would also say that we must be cautious of freezing pagan traditions as only "survivals from an archaic world," as this view preempts the possibility of pagan innovation. And I would then ask, *Why must it be one or the other?* Why not explore a ritual or tradition as an ornate tapestry interweaving ancient origins, current events, paganism, Christianity, and a host of other elements and influences, acknowledging that *Christianization means that paganism has been prohibited, and not that it has ceased evolving, nor, for that matter, that its deities have died.*

In regard to "survivals"/"traces"/ "vestiges" versus existing, living concepts and practices obscures, it occurs to me that this simplistic dichotomy serves to deny the possibility, as suggested by some so-called "continuity theorists," of ancient ideas and practices undergoing processes of transformation and innovation, in a state of what Marija Gimbutas has referred to as "dynamic persistence."

From at least the first decade of the twentieth century forward, some scholars, even while deploying "survivals," "traces," and kindred terms, have, in contrast to those who confine discussion to a "survivals"/living ideas and practices dichotomy and/or a "survivals"/no "survivals" dichotomy, suggested that the issue may be considerably more complex than this. For example, in his 1908 study *The Skeptics of the Italian Renaissance*, John Owen writes:

> No idea relating to the Middle Ages is more common than that which assumes the utter extinction of paganism from about 500 [CE] until its revival in the Renaissance. ...Such terms as 'revival,' 'Renaissance,' etc., are understood as if they implied a resurrection from death. This is at least a great exaggeration....There is really no period of Medieval History in which traces of pagan culture are not discernible.[8]

On the other hand, Marcu Beza (1882-1949), a Romanian writer and diplomat who served as State Correspondent of the Romanian Academy (Academiei Române), who lectured in Romanian at the University of London's School of Slavonic and East European Studies (1919-1930), and who lived during the same period as Summers, wrote in "Pagan Remnants in Roumanian Folklore" (1923):

> [I am speaking of] the festival...of a...god, be he Dionysos or any of the other deities who have not yet lost touch with us. They might have changed their names, but not their essential nature. With unimpeached desires they continue to love, and are happy to be loved by, human creatures whose ways they haunt. In the deep-green woods, near the cool fountains, in the grassy valleys and meadows, gods and goddesses still appear and sing, and dance and keep long revels...[A] boundary line hardly exists, and we can cross over and approach them.[9]

Significantly, the brilliant Russian cultural theorist Pëtr Bogatyrëv (1893-1971), in *Actes magiques, Rites et en croyances subcarpathique Russia* (1929), insists that what is occurring here is rooted in tradition but open to innovation: "Clearly, new beliefs and rites are rarely created. Only their exterior form and the objects used change with the social setting ... .Those who perform all the magical acts and rites that have appeared during our days, or rather, that are ancient practices modified and adapted, are aware of the principles that explain belief in their efficacy."

In 1961, in speaking of medieval Bosnian and Herzegovinian reverence of a Slavic goddess and two Classical heroes, Marian Wenzel not only suggested that a rather complex hybridizing process may have been at work in this sacred practice but also questioned the notion of a line dividing "pagan-before" from "Christian-after" and, in doing so, the very notion of "survivals." "A question may be raised," Wenzel suggests, "as to how far the inhabitants of these regions were Christians, if they practiced...pagan rituals." Her answer to the question she'd posed developed along these lines: "First, in so far as religion is a matter of ritual, it is clear that a person may be a devotee of several religions at the same time. There is nothing incompatible in the practice of different rituals, and in fact in ancient times people often did this, presumably on some principle of 'the more the holier.'" Secondly, she wondered "how far the uneducated…understood the dogmas of Christianity. No doubt they nodded their heads…when the Christian doctrines were explained to them. But they could scarcely be expected to believe [that] mere words would replace the well-tried ritual they knew."

Similarly, although continuing to deploy the term "survival," Hilda R. Ellis. Davidson wrote in 1970: "[A] long, cool look at these suggested survivals of the pagan world of the Vikings, the last pagan epoch in Britain, leads to the conclusion that seasonal customs are not likely to be derived from any one cult or religion, but have been associated in varying degrees with the prevailing religions since a very early period." In nascent postmodern fashion, she writes of "a number of different customs and traditions hav[ing] been superimposed and many new ideas brought in from many directions" to create a kind of "kaleidoscope" of sacred beliefs and practices. As an example of this process, which might remind one a bit of pentimento, she gives this example: "What at first sight seems to resemble a custom of the Viking Age is usually at once much older and much younger, probably based on very ancient patterns which have broken up and re-formed again."

Also in 1970, Richard and Eva Blum set forth, in *The Dangerous Hour: The Lore of Crisis and Mystery in Rural Greece*, a very illuminating argument: "Traditions are not only borrowed and practices diffused from one group to another or spontaneously generated independently in groups separated by space and/or time, but materials can be reintroduced into a culture after a considerable length of time in cultural 'cold storage.'" By 'cold storage,' they mean that things may once more emerge "after having been preserved in literature [or the arts] or museums without having been maintained as viable elements in folk culture."

To suggest that "dynamic persistence" or the innovation of tradition is not possible because ruptures have taken place is not only exceedingly simplistic, dependent on deployment of the "either/or" fallacy, but is also tremendously naïve.

Religious Studies professor Kathleen Malone O'Connor (1997) has written: "One result of the detailed and mold-breaking ethnographic work in the latter half of the twentieth century is that it has become more difficult…for scholars in anthropology…and folk religion to speak of magic or the magical arts and occult sciences as survivals of earlier unsophisticated, primitive, irrational, or illogical beliefs and practices." O'Connor sees the thinking behind the idea of survivals, especially when speaking of the esoteric, as not only judging harshly other ways of thinking and acting but moreover, as extremely binaristic, in dividing up beliefs and practices into two simplistic categories, namely, older sacred concepts that are viewed as "primitive," etc., and non-normative versus newer concepts that are deemed acceptable as normative by the orthodoxy.

Likewise, Karen Jolly, arguing in "Medieval Magic: Definitions, Beliefs, Practices" (2002) for a "contextualist approach" when dealing with this issue, stresses "shifting notions of Christian [and] pagan" by way of "dynamic interactions."

Citing Denis Byrne's article "Messages to Manila" (2003), Lynn Meskell, in *Object Worlds in Ancient Egypt* (2004), writes, "It may be more accurate to "think of ancient objects and places being constantly recycled through new systems of meaning, constantly recontextualized and 'updated' with new roles, new significance." At the same time, even the Matthewses, whose work I have briefly critiqued above, acknowledge: "Tradition is never static. It endlessly transforms, adapting itself to every generation."

Intriguingly, Nora Berend, in *Christianization and the Rise of Christian Monarchy* (2007), has gone so far as to argue that "Pagan cult evolved, with new elements appearing late in the tenth century, probably influenced by… opposition to Christianity."

In *Chicana Art: The Politics of Spiritual and Aesthetic Altarities* (2007), Laura E. Pérez draws our attention to Tomás Ybarra-Frausto's conception, in regard to the 1988 art exhibit "Ceremony of Memory: New Expressions in Spirituality among Contemporary Hispanic Artists," of the "creative reorganization of traditional religious systems" including Indigenous American sacred traditions and Catholicism. Rather than speaking in terms of "survivals," Pérez and Ybarra-Frausto point toward incessant innovation of ancient traditions as they come into contact with an increasing number of influences and as they respond to different cultural and historical contexts.

Finally, Trinkauskaitė (2008) observes: "[A]s 'paganism,' Lithuania's old religion has been considered officially dead since the fifteenth century. Yet the indigenous relationships to the landscape and to ancestral traditions could not be easily uprooted… Lithuanians [have] continued to practice the way of the ancestors into the twentieth and even the twenty-first centuries." Trinkauskaitė explains that she does not view the persistence of these traditions as "survivals," but rather as continuing "everyday practices" of persons who "inhabit the same material landscape" and who continue to relate to that environment as sacred, as they have for millennia, their religiousness or spirituality being characterized chiefly by "an ongoing religious connection to the land."[10]

Chapter 1
Many Are the Ancient Ones: The "Obstinate Persistence" of Polytheism

Not by one avenue only can we arrive at so tremendous a secret."

Quintus Aurelius Symmachus[11]

Unfortunately for pagans, the Roman statesman Quintus Aurelius Symmachus (c.340-c.402 CE), who remained resolutely pagan during a time when many were converting to Christianity, failed, in 384 CE, to convince Emperor Valentinian II (r. 375-392) of this noble truth.

It may be surprising to learn, however, that many pagan divinities continued to be revered in the West in the early medieval and later periods, especially given the hegemonic privileging of monotheism in the post-antiquity era and the tendency to equate 'the West' with Christianized nation-states. And yet it is so. One should bear in mind that many 'Western' Germanic peoples continued to practice pagan traditions until the tenth through twelfth centuries, and that Lithuanians, who, in terms of trade and in other significant arenas interacted with other 'Western' countries and regions from antiquity onward and who, in many respects, can and should be considered 'Western,' continued to practice pagan traditions until the late fourteenth century. Many others carried fragmentary bits of pagan wisdom with them in silence.

Following a brief discussion of polytheism and issues pertaining to it, we will commence our examination of divinities of ancient traditions and will then proceed to explore numerous ones that appear to have represented innovative responses to shifting historical and cultural conditions.

Polytheism and Its Elements

Polytheism is the belief in the existence of a multitude of divinities. Polytheistic religions/traditions include those of the ancient Egyptians, Greeks, Romans, Celts, Germanics/Scandinavians, Slavs, Balts, and Nahuas (Mexicas/Aztecs) as well as Indigenous American traditions, present-day religions such as Hinduism, Shinto, and the Yorùbá religion (although some Christian-influenced scholars claim it as a monotheistic faith), and Wicca and other

NeoPagan traditions.

R. J. Zwi Werblowsky, in "Polytheism" (1987), notes that polytheistic religions/traditions have suffered from "evolutionist views" of the nineteenth and early twentieth centuries that characterize early comparative-religious studies, which argue that polytheism is to monotheism as ape is to man or child to adult. Unfortunately, such 'evolutionist views' have not dissipated entirely with the arrival of the twenty-first century. A theory which seems to support an anti-evolutionary view but which represents in fact only the opposite side of the coin, and which can be traced back to early Christian writings, argued for an "Ur-Monotheism," insisting that an original Abrahamic faith constituted "the original creed of humankind and that ... polytheism developed as humans degenerated from a more innocent [monotheistic] state." In *The Deities Are Many: A Polytheistic Theology* (2005), Jordan Paper says of 'Ur-Monotheism:' "[T]here arose an early concept of ur-monotheism ... the earliest cultures were understood to have been monotheistic but lost the Truth, until it was rediscovered by the Israelites and fulfilled by Christ ... Polytheistic religions were understood not simply to be wrong; polytheism was indicative of nonhuman status."

We might posit that the pagan worldview has been defined for centuries by an unfriendly, hegemonic, dualistic Christian ideology, which, adopting an evolutionary stance, has claimed, on the one hand, that, as Paper states it, "cultures move from polytheism to monotheism to Christianity," and, on the other, adopting an anti-evolutionary stance, that polytheism represents a degeneration of an original Abrahamic faith which needs to be corrected by Christians. "Perhaps the most striking fact about polytheism," Werblowsky observes ironically, is that in contrast to evolutionary and ur-monotheistic theories, polytheism manifests "in more advanced cultures only." Generally speaking, moreover, polytheistic cultures also "practice a more sophisticated type of agriculture." Werblowsky explains that polytheism is typically associated with complex societies because in these, "the human view of the cosmos is [highly] differentiated ... there are many gods because humans experience the world in its variety and manifoldness. Hence there is also specialization among the gods."

Jan Assmann, in "Monotheism and Polytheism" (2004), defines polytheistic religions as ones which simultaneously embrace "a concept of divine unity" and "a plethora of gods." In this case, Assmann explains, unity "does not mean the exclusive worship of one god, but the structure and coherence of the divine world, which is not just an accumulation of deities, but a structured whole, a pantheon." In polytheism, "the deities are clearly differentiated and personalized by name, shape, and function." In Assmann's view, "the great achievement of polytheism is the articulation of a common semantic universe... that is, makes it possible for gods from other cultures or parts of a culture to be equated with one another ... [P]olytheistic pantheons lend themselves easily to cross-cultural translation or 'interpretation.'"

This brings up the subject of henotheism, to which polytheism is often linked. Henotheism, also called monolatry, focuses on a particular deity or similar being within a polytheistic pantheon as being most significant for a certain person or group and can also indicate that one deity may stand in for another or for many or all others. As Assmann points out, polytheism and henotheism frequently "coexist without any apparent conflict." Henotheists typically privilege one deity over another, not in order to argue that the deity they privilege, known in Greek as an *hypsistos*, is necessarily superior to another, but rather to acknowledge that it is sometimes necessary to focus on one deity rather than on multiple deities, if one is to reverence that deity profoundly. In some sacred traditions, such as the *orishá* tradition of the Yoruba, one may understand oneself to be a child or human embodiment of a particular divinity and thus may focus reverence on that deity more than others in order to strengthen this bond, acknowledging that other persons are the children or embodiments of other divinities of a pantheon.

Barbara N. Porter suggests that the stigma placed upon polytheism needs to be interrogated and that a good place to begin might be to question the dualistic dichotomy of monotheism/polytheism stressed in texts composed by monotheists. In her introduction to the anthology *One God or Many?: Concepts of Divinity in the Ancient World* (2000), Porter argues that "divinity, in all three of the monotheistic traditions in question [i.e., Judaism, Christianity, Islam] continues to be highly multiple in its forms." That is to say, there exist within so-called monotheistic religions "numinous beings," for instance, angels and demons, "who share some qualities and powers with the one God, but [they] are ... characterized as lesser spiritual beings, and not rival deities."

Paper (2005) addresses the issue of possible common features of polytheistic religions or traditions, asserting, "Given that all but a few of the vast array of religious traditions are polytheistic ... Polytheistic religions do seem to share certain features ... that contrast them with monotheistic traditions." Most importantly is that within polytheistic traditions, "ultimate truth" is not singular or monolithic. Nature is imbued with sacred energy. Divinities tend to be linked to certain natural forces and/or environments and/or locales. Ancestors are venerated. "People with differing personalities and experiences meet differing deities;" thus, a deity or similar being may manifest as male, female, transgender, as of one race or ethnicity or another, and so on. Some may manifest as royals, while others may manifest as domestics or as beings of the wild.

Reality is multidimensional, including worlds of other-than-human beings that are located on the earth (such as the fairy realm), realms of the dead, and worlds other than our own. A passage from the *Völuspá* regarding a priestess of *seiðr* reads: "She saw far, and far beyond – over every world." Likewise, a passage from Shakespeare's *Midsummer Night's Dream* (1595/1596) offers a poetic vision of this belief in a multidimensional, polytheistic reality:

For night's swift dragons cut the
clouds full fast,
And yonder shines Aurora's harbinger,
At whose approach ghosts, wand'ring
here and there,
Troop home to churchyards…[12]

The above-quoted lines from Shakespeare speak to a significant belief in many polytheistic traditions, as well as in some manifestations of Judaism and Christianity: that in ghosts. It's important to note that the idea of a multidimensional reality is an aspect of pagan consciousness in Europe but does not appear to have been banned per se during campaigns of Christianization, although beliefs in certain otherworlds and the beings thought to inhabit them were often banned. Because 'ultimate truth' is not as monolithic in polytheistic traditions as it is in monotheistic ones, concepts of the afterlife tend to be multiple or pluralistic, sometimes even within the same tradition as, for example, those in which one of multiple souls journeys to another world, another remains on earth, embodying a tree, or as a reincarnated being, and yet another becomes a ghost. The presence of ghosts indicates a parallel or lateral dimension of multidimensional reality. This vision of reality embraces both lateral and vertical dimensions; for example, the Germanic cosmos connects various vertically-positioned realities by way of a World-Tree. Fairies frequently dwell in a parallel reality reached by a special route, as described in the "Ballad of Thomas the Rhymer:" The first and second roads that Thomas and the Fairy Queen encounter lead to Heaven – "yon narrow road" that is "the path of righteousness" (ll. 45, 47) – and Hell – a broad road that is "the path of wickedness" (l. 51). The third road, however, leads to Elfland/Faerie:

And see not ye that bonny road,
Which winds about the fernie brae?
That is the road to fair Elfland,
Whe[re] you and I this night maun
gae… (ll. 53-56)[13]

Exemplary of the persistence of the notion of multidimensionality's vertical dimension in Christianized Europe is an account preserved by the English chronicler Gervase of Tilbury (c. 1150- c. 1220) in *Otia Imperialia*. This account centers on a sailor, a native of Ireland, who became lost at sea with his comrades on a voyage to Bristol. They found themselves in a strange sea floating high above the earth. The sailor dropped his knife while eating. At that same moment, the knife fell onto and stuck in the table where his wife, in Ireland, awaited his return. "Who, then, will now doubt that a sea lieth over this earth of ours, whether in the air, or above the air?" In Christianized Germany, some continued to believed in a multidimensional reality, the vertical levels of which included the plane of earth, that of the heavens, and that "between heaven and earth," where beings such as "Jack o' Lanterns," the souls of infants who had died before being baptized, hovered. On the one hand, belief in the (undeserved) punishment of unbaptized babies is clearly Christian; in my view, however, there is nothing Christian about the Jack o'Lantern or belief in it. Thus, this belief reflects a kind of sacred hybridity that embraces multidimensional reality that cannot be simply "Christian."

A related, spiritually hybrid vision of multidimensional reality appears in a nineteenth-century Italian account explaining that because witches cannot be admitted into a Christian heaven, when they die they go to live in a world usually invisible to us which lies between earth and heaven. Thanks to Vernon Lee, in her book *The Enchanted Woods* (1905), I call this aspect of multidimensional reality "invisible immanence." Indeed, one should be very careful when speaking of pagan traditions as involving "transcendence," perhaps especially when one speaks of otherworldly locations; for what may *seem* like transcendence *may in truth be invisible immanence*. Although perhaps not normally visible to human eyes, another location may appear as tangible to those residing there, that is to say, as immanent, as our dwelling place seems to us. Such a location may manifest as an otherworld, an afterlife location, or a parallel world or realm found next to or indeed *within* our own, separated from us by time, space, death, or some other factor. Grimm employs the German term *verschwinden*, "to vanish," to refer to deities, similar beings, certain persons, especially heroes, and even objects who or which are "translated" from one location to another that may not appear visible to us. In *The Viking Way: Religion and War in Late Iron Age Europe* (2002), Neil S. Price, in tracking beliefs and practices resonating with the Norse and the Sámi, discusses this notion as follows: "Sámi…spirits…[are] invisible inhabitants of a cultural landscape…The idea of the supernatural is …misleading here, because the fundamental presence of these beings [is] *entirely* 'natural' and should not be separated from the human and animal populations."

In other words, "*invisible immanence*." In a certain way, the notion of invisible immanence resonates with physicist David Bohm's concepts of the "explicate," or "manifest," "unfolded," visible "order" of nature and its "implicate," "not presently manifest(ed)," "enfolded," invisible "order," which is in turn linked to the entity of the hologram and the quality of being holographic. In *Wholeness and the Implicate Order* (1988), Bohm explains the "implicate order" in terms of a "plenum" that embraces *all* matter, the visible and the invisible, in the way that many speak today of visible versus dark matter or the presence of black holes. "[T]he implicate order," he relates, "has to be extended into a multidimensional reality…[T]he plenum…is the ground for the existence of everything, including ourselves…[The plenum might be compared to an] immense 'sea' of energy…This sea is to be under-stood in terms of a multidimensional implicate order."

As Mary Ellen Pitts points out in "The Holographic Paradigm: A New Model for the Study of Literature and Science" (1990), in the "holographic model…all things are part of an interlinked web" and, of equal significance in regard to the pagan worldview, "the notion of the 'implicate order' should not be interpreted" in Platonic, transcendentalist terms; rather, "the implicate order is seen as *underlying* the explicit, not transcending it." In "Dreams, Theory, and Culture: The Plains Vision Quest Paradigm" (1994), Lee Irwin describes the act of entering into the realm of the implicate order, into invisible immanence rather than transcendence, through gateways of dreams and visionary experiences occurring in nature; his description resonates uncannily with journeys to Otherworlds, including to afterlife realms and to "sabbats," meetings of wisewomen or witches, in pagan traditions: "[V]isionary landscapes of traditional...religions are charged with significance and power. In such a world, meaningful events are enfolded into an ecological order that is dynamically charged with the potency of dreaming." Resonating with Bohm and Pitts, Irwin writes, "[T]here is a world-process of ongoing, explicit manifestations of an implicit, emerging higher order dynamics that continues to *unfold* over the generations through a series of reorganized perceptions coupled with new interpretive perspectives." He explains that one enters "into an implicit ... order ... [an] enfolded [order]" by way of dreaming or via altering one's consciousness. "The advanced practit-ioner," he suggests, "is able to enter the visionary world at will and to unfold the implicit structure of that world in a frequently dramatic demonstration of power and ability."

In "The Detective and the Witch: Local Knowledge and the Aesthetic Pre-History of Detection" (1995), Kenneth S. Calhoun suggests that the "witch...demarcat[es] the outer limits of the interior by crossing over to the wilderness beyond" and that her entry into another realm of existence represents a "compelling view of embodied meaning in the face of the historical impulse toward transcendental disembodiment."

Of course, together with the resonance of the implicate order with realms not usually visible to ordinary eyes, or sensible to ordinary senses, the notion of a multidimensional reality inhabited by non-human beings such as elves, fairies, divinities, and so on resonates to a certain extent with the notion among many present-day physicists that numerous, if not an infinite number of, universes exist, and that, as Paul Davies explains in *How to Build a Time Machine* (2002), "each of the alternative universes is every bit as real as the others. ...[A]ll the possible quantum worlds really exist in this 'many-universes' interpretation of quantum mechanics, there is an infinity of parallel universes." Davies stresses that when he asserts that "[e]very possible universe will be there somewhere," by "there," he means somewhere " 'alongside' our space and time."

In regard to divinities, they may abide by differing sets of ethics; for example, those of Hermes as trickster differ from those of Demeter the compassionate mother and from those of Baubo, who delights her with a bawdy dance.

In polytheism, as in monotheism, divine beings can manifest in a human form, as in the cases of messiahs, avatars, *bodhisattvas*, often as teachers or saviors. Because most of us tend to think of the Greek gods as fictive figures of mythology, we forget that those who revere(d) Demeter and Dionysus believe(d) that they had "walk[ed] on [the] earth." In *The Homeric Hymn to Demeter: Translation, Commentary, and Interpretive Essays*, Helene P. Foley reminds us that "the [Eleusinian] Mysteries are a result of Demeter's encounter with mortals and mortality ... . [T]he Mysteries are offered to mortals because of her stay in their realm." Likewise, in Augustine of Hippo's (354-430 CE) *City of God*, one finds, "In those times, Dionysus, who was also called Father Liber, and was esteemed as a god after death, is said to have shown the vine to his host in Attica." Germanic and Lithuanian deities that continued to be revered during the Middle Ages, including Odin, Thor, and Perkûnas, were likewise believed to walk among and bestow gifts upon humanity. Their journeying on the earth was often signified by a road or street, like those of the god Freyr and the goddess Holda.

Polytheistic traditions or religions, like others, place great emphasis on communication with the divine. They tend to embrace multiple forms of communication, reflecting their 'poly-' sensibility. Some of these forms exist in monotheistic faiths, such as prayer. Others, such as various kinds of divination and magic, are explicitly forbidden. Others may be undertaken only by ritual specialists or religious authorities. The creation of altars, making offerings and sacrifices, dance, and so-called 'possession' or embodiment of a divinity, are among the many forms of communication in polytheistic traditions/religions. Certain forms of communication, such as magical practice and possession/embodiment, further reflect the 'poly' consciousness of practitioners by way of embracing metamorphosis or shapeshifting.

Deities of diverse regions have often been compared to each other. For example, Saxo Grammaticus (*c.* 1150-*c.* 1220) compares Thor to Jupiter, Odin to Hades/Pluto, and Hel to Persephone/Proserpina. Likewise, Snorri Sturleson (1178-1241) identifies Freyr with Saturn. Elsewhere, Odin is compared to Hermes/Mercury. Although polytheistic religions/traditions are not, generally speaking, universalizing religions/traditions in the sense that Christianity is, their "articulation of a common semantic universe" permits the translatability of deities and nurtures correspondences, sometimes leading to a mentality like that of Late Antique Hellenism, which envisions a "common religion" of numerous peoples simultaneously embracing a kind of unity together with great diversity and emphasis on local expression. Such a mentality often leads to spiritual/religious hybridity. In some cases, it should be noted, a type of "masking" occurs, by which devotees continue to worship the same divinities but agree to, or else pretend to, call them by other names. Generally speaking, although traditions or religions possessing multiple divinities, or else "faces" of divinity, cannot be reduced to accumulation and amalgamation, practitioners of such frequently appreciate and practice hybridity or symbiosis, two or more religions/traditions practiced simultaneously yet not necessarily mixed. Present-day terms for such practices include "bricolage," "add-on," and "assemblage;" this spiritual notion is, incidentally, often reflected in eclectic altars.

Polytheistic hybridity is nurtured by the theory of correspondences, also called the "doctrine of sympathies." This theory, applied for millennia by shamans, priestesses, priests, and practitioners of magic, indicates that certain divinities correspond to certain times of the day, days of the week, colors, aromas, flora and fauna, personality traits, cities, and so on. For example, one finds that "Apollo and Minerva presided over Athens, Bacchus and Hercules over Boetian Thebes, Juno over Carthage, Venus over Cyprus and Paphos, Apollo over Rhodes; Mars was the tutelary god of Rome, as Neptune of Taenarus; Diana presided over Crete."

Such a mentality sometimes leads to the "practice of 'hyphenating' gods," e.g., the conflation of Egyptian and Greco-Roman deities, such as that we have just seen in the case of the cult of Melkart-Herakles-Hercules at Cadiz.

In speaking of the peoples who were conquered by the Romans, John North notes that because, other than the Jewish people and early Christians, the overwhelming majority were polytheists, they "were willing enough to accept the mutual identity of their gods and goddesses ... . [T]hose who moved from one area to another found beliefs and rituals they could understand; it could be assumed that 'the gods' were the patrons of all the peoples of the empire, although called by different names in different areas."

This phenomenon is linked to that of *myrionime* (as the Greeks called it), indicating a deity who has a myriad names, such as Apuleius' Isis. This phenomenon was often depicted artistically as *signa panthea*, as with statues of Hera/Juno crowned with smaller representations of numerous other deities, such as of Athena/Minerva, Aphrodite/Venus, and Artemis/Diana; indeed, it appears that the notion of 'pantheism' commenced not as the God-as-Nature conception of Spinoza and others but rather as a conception of myriad deities corresponding to a single deity toward which one's focus is directed, at the same time that one acknowledges the presence of other deities. In polytheistic traditions, divinities are, generally speaking, born, undergo various experiences including amorous relationships, die, and are reborn, often in forms other than those in which they first appeared.

In acknowledging the persistence of divinities revered in the Middle Ages and in more recent epochs, we contest the survivals/no survivals dualistic mentality that presently governs pagan historiography; we illuminate an alternate Western worldview that embraces a significant pantheon of non-Abrahamic, non-Christian divinities; and we demonstrate that the pagan worldview and its contents developed alongside the hegemonic, primarily Christocentric, Abrahamic worldview that has dominated the West since the 'triumph' of Christianization.

This type of hybridity is demonstrated by the sacred system of the Iberian Peninsula prior to the triumph of Christianity. In *The Ancient Spaniards*, Gérard Nicocini speaks of "traces of a highly developed pantheon among the Iberians who soon accepted Oriental and Semitic deities, and later assimilated them to the gods of Greece and Rome." Somewhere between 1100 and 800 BCE, Phoenicians began settling in present-day southern Spain. The Phoenicians brought to Iberia not only their pantheon but also their alphabet, ceramic pottery, incense and perfumes, amulets, and funerary rites. Phocaean Greeks sojourned and settled in Spain, perhaps from as early as 800 BCE and peaking around 550 BCE. Celts settling in the northwest of the Iberian peninsula also contributed to sacred traditions. Nicocini continues, "This [hybridity] was the case ... with the cult of Melkart-Herakles-Hercules at Cadiz, which spread widely throughout Lower Andalusia and along the coast as far as Cartagena." José M. Blázquez, in *Religiones en la España Antigua*, observes that an omnipotent, indigenous goddess came to be hybridized with the Phoenician Astarte and the Greco-Roman Aphrodite/Venus. Although Astarte's cult, emerging around 400 BCE, was widespread, including at Jaén, Granada, Salamanca, and Pozo Moro, she was especially revered at Seville; Nina Consuelo Epton reports in *Spanish Fiestas* that a "small image of her was discovered [there] as recently as 1960." Similarly, a chief male deity who may have been honored with human sacrifice came at some point to be identified with the Phoenician Ba'al Hammon and the Greco-Roman Kronos/Saturn. An indigenous solar deity appears to have merged with Apollo and with the Celtic god Lug(h). Nicocini notes, "The cult of the Carthaginian goddess Tanit-Caelestis was [also] widespread. She was assimilated to Hera-Demeter-Juno, with a variety of functions, including the safeguarding of human fertility and that of the land."

It has also been suggested that Tanit and/or an unnamed indigenous goddess linked to the reverence of deer and the hunt merged at some point with Artemis and Diana. According to Blázquez, the celebrated fifth- or fourth-century BCE masterpiece known as the "Lady of Elche" is probably an image of Tanit. Seville, Epton reports, was especially known for its temple to Salammbo, divinized priestess of Tanit, immortalized by Flaubert; two young Christian converts, Justa and Rufina, who later became the patron saints of Seville, were martyred there in 303 CE when they refused to take part in a procession honoring the Goddess and her priestess. Blázquez observes that a maiden goddess of night, death, the afterlife, and destructive magic, associated with the color black and with goats, came to be identified with Persephone/Proserpina and with the Celtic goddess Ataecina. A male deity, possibly named Saur, a warrior god and a patron of bulls and perhaps also of bullfights, came to be fused with the Greco-Roman Ares/Mars. Epton suggests that the Roman goddess Cybele and her male consort Attis may have also come to be linked to Saur and to Ares/Mars, by way of the sacrifice of bulls and baptism in the blood of the bull practiced in the cult of Attis and Cybele; she writes: "Cybele and Attis ... appealed to Andalusian emotions ... to [a] deep-seated need for a traumatic transition between wild grief and ecstatic joy ... [as well as to] a belief that the malevolent forces of winter must be overcome, that [the] blood [of the bull] must be spilled in the fields to ensure the prosperity of the crops." Epton further suggests that the roots of Spanish devotion to the Virgin Mary and Jesus may be traced to ancient devotion to Cybele and Attis, and that present-day Seville's "great bull-cycle of the *corridas* [, which] begins at Easter" and which includes bullfighting, may lie in the festival of the Hilaria of Attis and Cybele's cult, which included bull sacrifice.

The Persistence of the Gods

If indeed the ancient gods survived Christianization, or have survived it, then what has rendered this possible?

Perhaps because many did not see, or have not seen, themselves, their bodies, their psyches, reflected in an aggressive, warlike, patriarchal, ascetic, elderly, typically light-skinned, male deity, or else in his compassionate, self-sacrificing son, or in the son's mother, a virgin forsaking eroticism? Or perhaps because they did not grasp the connection of Biblical divinities with nature, with the seasonal cycles, with the particular landscapes they held dear and farmed? Or because they valued the sanctity of the body more than guilt and shame? Or perhaps because they could not, or were forbidden to, communicate with Biblical divinities through ancient tools of divination and magic (although Christian divination and magic most assuredly were practiced, they were also frequently condemned)? Due to the more than millennium-long campaign against peoples who practiced pagan traditions, we may never know.

In 392 CE, as Demetrios Constantelos points out in "Byzantine and Ancient Greek Religiosity," "Hera and Zeus, Demeter and Poseidon, Hermes and Athena, Apollo and Aphrodite and several other Olympian deities were officially pronounced dead." They were *not* pronounced "dead" as they might have been by pagans, who in saying so also would have inferred their imminent rebirth, but rather by Christians who meant that the pagan gods were *finally* dead – *forever*. If one believes in, or acknowledges the reality of, the ancient goddesses and gods, this pronouncement may strike one as absurd, perhaps even as hubristic and offensive – certainly as offensive as it was for many Christians when Nietzsche proclaimed the death of the Biblical God. Whether one does or does not, however, acknowledge the reality of the ancient divinities, this doesn't change the fact that the Christians who pronounced it so were in error, were badly mistaken. Perhaps they meant to undertake a preemptive strike. Or perhaps their giddy hubris got the better of them, managed to convince them that what they *wished* to be true would *be so*. If they wanted Hera and the others to die, *they'd better be prepared to commit deicide*.

One of the final official attempts of the Classical world to protect and promote paganism against Christianization was the reorganization of the Platonic Academy, founded in or near 385 BCE, in 410 CE by Plutarch the Great (*c*. 350-430). One of his successors, Proclus Diadochas (410-485 CE), held ceremonies for the Magna Mater (or Cybele), Pan, Asclepios, and other deities. After almost a thousand years in existence, the Academy was closed by the Roman Emperor and Christian zealot Justinian "the Great" (482/483-565 CE) in 529 CE. Thankfully, some members of the Academy found sanctuary at the court of Khosru I (Chosroes Anushirvan, d. 579), the Zoroastrian king of Persia.

The Earth Goddess (of many names), Isis, Apollo, Diana, Mercury, Mithra, and many other deities were worshipped in Late Antiquity in temples in England, France and elsewhere in Europe. Some persons of Greek heritage continued, in spite of Christianization, to worship Artemis, Asclepios, and Janus in the fifth and sixth centuries CE.

Vulfolaic (or, Valfroy, Walfroy, Wulfilaïc, Wulfilaich, Wulflaik), the bishop of the town of Yvois-Carignan, later made a saint, boasted to Gregory of Tours (c. 539-594) of his convincing the people of Trier (in present-day Germany, near Luxembourg, Belgium) to destroy a great statue of the goddess Diana. This may in fact have been a statue of the synthesized Celtic-Roman goddess Diana Arduinna-Diana – the worship of whom, incidentally, was established at Rome circa 82 CE, with the Cisalpine Celts carrying her worship to Italy – and the site may have alternatively been Villers-devant-Orval in Belgium. Arduinna" is variously spelled Ardoinne, Ardoinna, and Arduinne; while "Diana-Arduinna" is also spelled "Deane Arduinna. "I kept telling them that Diana was powerless, that her statues were useless, and that the rites which they practiced there were vain and empty." Finally, after continuously praying for its destruction, Vulfolaic rejoiced as a "great crowd of people" assembled at "Diana's statue" with ropes in hand. The statue is believed to have represented her as dressed in a short tunic and carrying her bow and arrows. Although the statue proved difficult to pull down, it finally "crashed to the ground." "I had it broken to pieces with iron hammers and then reduced to dust."

Some deities persisted into the early period of the Christianization of Britain, France, Belgium, and elsewhere, including Orcus/Dis Pater, Ares/Mars, and Cybele. In the seventh century, practitioners of earth-based traditions continued to visit temples to Mercury, Jupiter, and Apollo at Rouen. According to St. Eligius, Orcus, an avatar of Hades/Pluto, a.k.a. Dis Pater, god of the underworld and of treasures, continued to be revered in seventh-century France, receiving offerings and animal sacrifices. A Spanish penitential indicates that Orcus continued to be revered there, or else celebrated as the carnivalesque spouse of the goddess Maia, into the ninth or tenth century. In medieval Germany, he metamorphosed into Orke (or, Lorke), also the mate of the deity or similar being of May (sometimes locally called Holzmuoia).

The canons of the Council in Trullo, held in 691/692, indicate that many persons of Greek heritage continued to worship certain of their goddesses and gods, including Dionysus and Pan, in the late seventh century.

According to Frank R. Trombley in *Hellenic Religion and Christianization*, "The cults of female deities, like Artemis, Cybele, and Ge [Gaia], ... are still occasionally [reported as existing] in the eighth and the ninth [centuries CE]." Many Greek shepherds, as well as descendants of ancient Spartans and Laconians and persons dwelling on the Mani Peninsula (in the past called Maina) continued to worship the ancient gods into the ninth century.

The tenth-century Greek compilation *Geoponika* indicates that Zeus continued to exert some power during that time, as demonstrated by a charm which states that if persons enjoying wine wish to keep from becoming drunk, they should recite a line from the *Iliad* (Book 8, 170) of Homer that reads: "Thrice Jupiter thundered from Ida's heights." The *Geoponika* also indicates that tenth-century agriculturalists may have continued or reclaimed an ancient practice of ridding a field of the parasitic herbaceous plant osproleon (commonly known as broomrape) by sketching, with chalk or white pigment, five shells with the image of "Hercules suffocating the lion" and planting them in the four corners and center of the field. Apparently, invoking Hercules might not be the worst idea to suggest to farmers of our own day; according to Larry W. Mitich, an expert in this field, damage of crops by broomrape continues to result in "great economic losses in southern Europe."

In 988, only eight years after establishing what might be called a NeoPagan system of worship, reminiscent of that the Roman emperor Julian sought to establish, Vladimir, the ruler of Kievan Rus,' unlike Julian 'the Apostate,' converted to Christianity, primarily in order to gain greater power. That same year, he agreed to ban indigenous, earth-centered traditions, collectively called *pohanstvo*, throughout Kievan Rus'. In *A Cultural History of Russia*, Joel Carmichael observes, "The Russian conversion to Christianity was bound to be basically no more than nominal after all; it would have been too much to expect, even of the higher clergy, any real grounding in Christian dogma. ...[Thus,] paganism was not touched, to be sure, for a very long time to come." George P. Fedotov, in *The Russian Religious Mind: Kievan Christianity* (1946), argues that although some historians date the "true" Christianization of Russia to the late fifteenth century, "exact dating has no meaning because even in the nineteenth century [pagan] survivals were still deeply rooted."

In eleventh-century Belgium, the prince-bishop of Liège condemned persons in the region of the Forest of Ardennes who continued to revere the goddess Diana. In the twelfth century, many Europeans continued to believe in and make offerings to the Fates, whom they frequently associated with fairies. In the early thirteenth century, Alexandre de Villedieu (*c*. 1175-1250), the Christian grammarian, mathematician, and canon of Avranches, France "complained that the old gods were being worshipped in Orléans, that Venus, Bacchus, and Faunus had their altars and their festivals there: the path to Paradise was lost."

Two ancient, divinized heroes, the Hyperborean warriors Hyperochus and Amadocus, may have been venerated in Bosnia and Herzegovina from the second century CE into the fourteenth century. Hyperochus and Amadocus were honored for having assisted Achilles and the Delphians in their battle with the Gauls/Celts. Evidence including carvings and tombstones documented by Marian Wenzel indicates that they were represented as twin horsemen and formed a triad or trinity with a goddess who was probably identified with the Slavic sun goddess Jelena or else (the) Vila.

During the Middle Ages and the Renaissance, the prophet known as the Cumaean Sibyl was bestowed with even greater supernatural status when she transformed from mortal prophet to Fairy Queen.

For much of 1522, a plague ravaged Rome. Although many prayed to Jesus Christ, the Virgin Mary, St. Sebastian, and St. Roch, their prayers went unanswered. The prayers of Pope Adrian VI (1459-1523; pope, 1522-1523) equally went unanswered. Thus, many Romans turned elsewhere. One of those to whom they turned was a well known practitioner of magic known as Demetrios of Sparta. He was convinced that only by sacrificing to the ancient deities of Rome would the plague come to an end. In April, 1522 he led a great crowd of Romans, together with a tame ox or bull held by a silken thread and decorated with garlands to the Coliseum, where the animal was sacrificed. Unfortunately, because Christian sources translate the name of the deity or deities to "the Devil" and "devils," it is difficult to know for which of the gods the sacrifice was meant. However, seeing that it was an ox or a bull, the sacrifice was probably made to Jupiter, Phoebus Apollo, Cybele, Neptune, or a combination of these. As the sacrifice occurred in April, it may well have been for Cybele/Mater. The pope and other Church authorities appear to have condoned this pagan rite, only to pretend shock and repulsion after it failed to rapidly end the plague. Raymond Crawford, in *Plague and Pestilence in Literature and Art* (1914), relates: "As soon as the clergy realized the enormity of the sacrilege they had condoned_they instituted a penitential procession, which marched through the city, scourging themselves to bleeding and crying Misericordia."

In 1536, the god of fire and metallurgy, Vulcan, appeared to a Spanish merchant who was traveling by night through a forest in Sicily. The god was leading an entourage of Cyclops. This apparition was succeeded by an eruption of Mount Aetna. In the late seventeenth century, French theologian Jean-Baptiste Thiers (1626-1703) condemned the persistent practice of invoking Jupiter prior to drinking alcohol in order to prevent drunkenness. In the eighteenth century, on Mont Saint-Bernard in France, persons may have continued to honor the god Jupiter, under the name of Jou, at the site of an ancient temple of Jupiter.

Needless to say, the ancient divinities do not seem to have been pleased with Christianization, although cynics might say that if they were displeased, they were nevertheless conquered. Moreover, it is possible, granting their existence, that, as pagans were increasingly Christianized and disrespected and deserted the elder deities, at least some of them may have punished former pagans for submitting to the new faith. In his 1902 work *Elder Faiths of Ireland*, Wood-Martin considers this intriguing possibility: "It is ... highly probable that the Irish goddesses ... were not originally ... malevolent, but when Christianity invaded and captured their territories, their disposition...changed, and they...wreak[ed] vengeance [on their former worshippers] for their change of faith."[14]

Chapter 2
The Earth Goddess and Her Consort,
Isis, Ba'al, and Mediterranean Divinities

The first thing we ought to preach is reverence towards the gods.
from "Letter to a Priest," Flavius Claudius Julianus (331/332-363 CE)[15]

In the chapters that follow, we will devote ourselves to the existence of the Earth Goddess and various other deities, with an emphasis on their persistence and metamorphosis in an increasingly Christianized Europe. This chapter will focus on the continuing reverence of the ubiquitous Earth Goddess, on Isis and Ba'al, and on Greek and Roman sacred beings.

The Earth Goddess

In Lithuania Minor/East Prussia, incidentally, the home of my maternal grandfather's ancestors, the Earth Goddess Žemyna was honored by pouring beer from a sacred vessel upon the earth and then sharing the remaining beer with the celebrants. She was honored similarly during funeral rites, when devotees chanted, "Be joyful, Žemynele, receive this soul and guard it well." It appears that at some point, various local goddesses and gods merged with Žemyna/Žemynele so that she acquired the ancient status of a ubiquitous Great Goddess. After Christianization, the prayer to Žemynele underwent hybridization: "Dear Earth-Goddess, you who makes all things bloom, let our fields bring forth rye, wheat, barley, and other grains. Kindly Goddess, send your holy angel to us. Send the evil one away, that he may not mock us."

Many persons in the region continued, however, to offer black suckling pigs to Žemyna into the seventeenth century. The grandmother of the family would offer a portion of the cooked pig to the Goddess, while the remainder was eaten by the family. Marija Gimbutas notes that as recently as the eighteenth century, Lithuanians offered gifts to Žemyna upon the birth of a child. Earth was to be kissed in the morning and in the evening. Offerings to the might of the earth — ale, bread, grains, herbs, or a sheaf of rye — were interred, laid in front of stones, attached to trees or thrown into

the sea, rivers, lakes and springs.
While the plant desires
Its mother-earth's embrace, who longs for it,
And she most soft, beneath the yielding Earth
Lies waiting, grant her increase.
Columella, On Agriculture[16]

One can only imagine what the "young ladies" of the late eighteenth and early nineteenth centuries to whom William Butler addressed his *Chronological, Biographical, Historical and Miscellaneous Exercises: Designed For the Daily Use of Young Ladies* (1st ed., 1799; twelfth ed., 1846), might have thought as they encountered Astraea, Ceres, Diana, Flora, Fornax (baking), Freyja, Hygeia, Isis, Juno, Maia, Minerva, Strenua (strength), Venus, Vesta, and other goddesses in the pages of his guide to what young women should know. What might they have thought when they realized that in the past, many women and men had worshipped goddesses alongside male gods? Could they have imagined that in some places, they continued to do so?

The Roman scholar, orator, and consul Cornelius Tacitus (*c.* 56 CE – after 117 CE), in *Germania* (98 CE), wrote of certain tribes of Germanic peoples including the Angles, tribes from northern and eastern Germany, and perhaps tribes from Sweden (and possibly also of certain West Slav/Wendish tribes in the vicinity of the Elbe River): "None of these tribes have any noteworthy feature, except their common worship of Ertha, or Mother-Earth, [or Nerthus] and their belief that she interposes in human affairs, and visits the nations in her…chariot." The priest of the Goddess, who "can perceive the presence of the goddess in this sacred recess…walks by her side with the utmost reverence as she is drawn along by heifers." He and others of her worshippers ceremonially bathe her statue, including the vestments, and even her chariot in a "secret lake." Whenever she visits, it is a "season of rejoicing, and festivity," and peace reigns, with every weapon being kept "under lock."

During the first years of the twentieth century, the banker, writer, and early anthropologist Edward Clodd wrote in *Magic in Names and Other Things* (1920), "From time immemorial to the present day … the worship of the Earth-Mother – Goddess of many names "in every clime adored" – has been accompanied by sacrifices to her." Eleanor Hull echoed in *Folklore of the British Isles* (1928): "The worship of Mother Earth is perhaps the most widespread … of all forms of ancient worship … . Thus, some of the most ancient invocations and some of the earliest charms are addressed to the Earth Mother." In our own time, scholars such as the Lithuanian-American archaeologist Marija Gimbutas, concerned with matristic or matrifocal traditions, often cite ancient objects of art as evidence of a ubiquitous Earth Goddess. This metanarrative of "the Goddess" has inspired much controversy. Among the most recent works to address this controversy is Richard G. Lesure's *Interpreting Ancient Figurines* (2011); therein he critiques what he deems the "increasing grandiosity" of Gimbutas' claims in constructing a worldview in which woman- and Goddess-centered cultures succumbed to patriarchal ones. It is important to note that his critique of Gimbutas' work is attached to a broader critique of metanarratives, which he rejects as privileging similarities over differences and which he views as reflecting "manifestations of an underlying essence." He links metanarratives, and especially the "Goddess" metanarrative, to both "theoretical" and "analytical essentialism."

In stark contrast to Lesure, numerous Late Antique Roman male writers promulgated the theory that matrifocal cultures preceded patriarchy. For example, in the third book of *On Agriculture*, Varro (116-27 BCE) makes an intriguing remark concerning the few persons who survived a great flood that had brought an end to the Golden Age. These survivors were the children of Ceres and Saturn, the first of whom they looked upon as a creator deity and as the mother of the earth and to whom they appear to have offered primary homage. They were also thought to have spoken a language older than persons born after the flood. Varro refers to those born after the flood as the children of Neptune. Lucius Junius Moderatus Columella (fl. first century CE), a writer on agriculture, natural history, and veterinary medicine, likewise alludes to pre- and post-flood mortals; like Varro, he speaks of the intimate bond shared by the Earth Goddess and the civilization prior to the flood. The only real difference in his version is that the male deity coupled with the Earth Goddess is Prometheus rather than Saturn. "Earth," he relates in *De Re Rustica*, "is called the common mother of all things – because she has always brought forth all things and is destined to bring them forth continuously." Even those Roman writers influenced by patriarchal theology or ideology acknowledged the significance of the Great Goddess and praised her, as does the Emperor Julian (331/332-363 CE) in his "Hymn to the Mother of the Gods": "Who then is the Mother of the Gods? She is the source of the intellectual and creative gods ... . [S]he is in control of every form of life, and the cause of all generation ... . [W]e must pick the fairest fruits from the earth ... and offer them to the goddess." Julian is grateful to the Goddess above all, he writes, "that she did not disregard me when I wandered as it were in darkness," that is, when he identified for a time as a Christian.

Among Slavic peoples, the Goddess of Earth appears to have been known since time immemorial. The Slavic Wends revered the Goddess and created many images of her in clay and stone. In *The Russian Religious Mind* (1946), George P. Fedotov writes: "At every step in studying Russian popular religion one meets the constant longing for a great divine female power ... the cult of the Great Goddess who once reigned upon the immense Russian plains ... in Mother Earth, who remains the core of Russian religion." In the worship of the Goddess "converge the most secret and deep religious feelings of the folk. Beneath the beautiful veil of grass and flowers, the people venerate with awe the black moist depths, the source of all fertilizing powers, the nourishing breast of nature, and their own last resting place." In a Russian folksong, "Mother Earth, the Humid" ... alludes to the womb ... of the Earth ... . Earth is the Russian ... mother ... fertile ... [and] black." Likewise, in *The World of the Russian Fairy*

Tale (1987), Maria Kravchenko relates that in common "with many agricultural peoples, the ancient Slavs had a particular veneration for the earth as the nurturer, creator and source of all living things ... frequent prayers were addressed to the earth ... all [being] preceded by three low bows." When pagan Russians passed away, they returned to the "universal Mother Earth," who takes the deceased "into her bowels." For traditional Russians, the "custom of bathing the deceased and putting on clean linen ... contains the ancient desire not to stain the purity of the earth." Likewise, Joanna Hubbs, in *Mother Russia: The Feminine Myth in Russian Culture*, resounds, "The land was called Mother ... in the peasant tradition ... all things are borne by the earth and derive from her fertility. The soil is the great *baba*." Similarly, in relation to the earth, the Don and Dnieper Rivers were called the "little mothers." Furthermore, notes Hobbs, Mother Earth was eventually historicized and politicized as Mother Russia, and signified by the Matrioshka doll.

The Slavic Earth Goddess Mat' Syra Zemlia was revered into the early twentieth century, especially in her hypostasis as Tat'yana on May 10. To know if crops would flourish, a woman would grind a stick into the ground. If she then put her ear to the ground, she could hear the Goddess' response. If she heard the sound of a "well-filled sleigh gliding over the snow," then good crops would follow. Also into the early twentieth century, the ancient custom of swearing oaths by the earth persisted until well into the nineteenth century; and "if plague or cholera struck a village, at midnight the old women" and virgins would gather, "with the widows clutching skulls and the virgins scythes." They then "ploughed a furrow round the village to let out the earth-spirit so that it might destroy the illness."

The Earth Goddess was revered in the Middle Ages and, in some cases, thereafter, by various names, including the Germanic Erce, Erda, Erde, Fjorgyn(s), Frau Gaue, Harke, Hertha, Hlodyn, Hludana, Holda, Iörð, Nerthus and Rinda; the Basque Ama Lur; the Slavic Mat' Syra Zemlia and Tat'yana; the Lithuanian Žemyna; the Estonian Ma-Emma; the Finnish Etelä; and the Sámi Mader-akka ("The Old Woman of the Earth"). Richard North, in *Heathen Gods in Old English Literature*, suggests that the goddesses Rheda and Eostre, documented by Bede, might also be included in this list.

In "Gunnlöð and the precious mead (*Hávamál*)," Svava Jakobsdóttir posits that a rite may have been undertaken in the Middle Ages in Germanic indigenous spirituality/ensprited materiality in honor of the Earth-Goddess Jorð (Jarðar) and other deities, semi-divine beings, and rulers. Traces of this rite, she suggests, are metaphorically recorded in *Hávamál*, a poem of the *Poetic Edda*. In this poem, the giantess Gunnlöð appears to take on the roles of both the Earth-Goddess Jarðar and her mortal representative, a priestess, perhaps a practitioner of *seiðr* divination and magic. From her "golden throne," she offers Odin "a drink of the precious mead," which is called miaðar or Odrerir. As Gunnlöð assumes the role of goddess and priestess, so Odin appears to take on the role of initiate, here called Loddfafnir, perhaps a warrior or ruler. If Jakobsdóttir is correct, this rite of offering mead to an initiate may have formed part of a cycle of initiation rites. This cycle of rites appears to have included: (1) a ritual, symbolic sacrifice, death, and/or dismemberment, as in shamanistic traditions, of the initiate; (2) an intimate coupling with a representative of the Earth-Goddess; (3) the receiving of counsel regarding ethics and perhaps also a narrative of one's destiny; and (4) lessons in material-sacred practice, including instruction in runes, magic spellcasting, and invocations, offerings, and sacrifices. In Jakobsdóttir's view, the rite involving the Earth-Goddess's representative must have taken place in a shrine dedicated to her, vé Jarðar ("Earth's shrine"). She continues: "Belief in [the Earth-Goddess] is connected with the earth in the most literal terms. It is not unlikely that the religious ceremonies [of ancient Scandinavians] derived from belief in the earth and in rebirth took place in specially prepared hills or caves." Jakobsdóttir further suggests that within the context of this rite, a chain of associations linked the Earth-Goddess not only to Gunnloð and to other mead-serving giantesses but also to the goddess Freyja, to the Valkyries, and by extension, to the *huldrefolk* – elves and fairies. This rite may have conferred or confirmed rebirth, reincarnation, or immortality upon the initiate. Moreover, it may have been linked to a rite of foster- or blood-brotherhood, wherein two kinsmen bound themselves to each other and to the earth. This rite of mead and *hieros gamos* also appears to have had a Celtic parallel, with the goddess Medb, whose name suggests "intoxicated via drinking mead" and who later transmogrified into Queen Maeve and the Fairy Queen Mab, presiding over the rite. In Celtic tradition, the rite was referred to as the *banais rígi*. Perhaps most significantly in our present context, Jakobsdóttir argues that the rite of mead and embracing the Goddess may have imparted to the initiate *jarðleger skilningr*, "earthly wisdom," the wisdom of earth-based traditions.

In certain locales, the Earth-Goddess may have represented an amalgam of various Celtic, Germanic, Roman, and other goddesses. An eleventh-century protective spell reads: "Take earth, throw it with your right hand under your right foot and say:/ 'I catch it under my foot, I have found it./ Lo, earth has power against all creatures.'"

Peter Dronke suggests that the medieval philosopher and astrologer Bernard Silvestris (*c.* 1085-*c.* 1150) *invented* the goddess Natura, which he, Dronke, opposes to the Earth Goddess. This opposition is *greatly exaggerated*, and the "invention" of Natura incorrect; it would be much better to say that "Natura" represents an example of pagan-centered response to cultural developments in regard to vocabulary and classification, such as seen in shifts from "Negro" to "Black" to "African American." Nevertheless, Dronke's work can assist us in our exploration of this goddess.

Medieval herbal handbooks frequently speak of the Goddess of Earth or Nature. Her presence is evidenced by seemingly trivial names such as that given to *Galium verum*, a plant with "slender, ascending stems, whorled or cruciate leaves, and small clustered flowers," Christianized in England as "Our Lady's Bedstraw" but in German called *Muttergottesbettstroh*, "the Mother Goddess's Bedstraw." Her presence is also evidenced by her appearance in herbal handbook illustrations. In one such handbook, the goddess Sancta Tellus, referring to the Roman Earth Goddess, is depicted as "dressed in classical robes. She is placed in front of a large herb at the base of which a large serpent coils. She holds a cornucopia indicating her importance as an earth deity who presides specifically over the fate and efficacy of medicinal herbs and plants." Her presence is further evidenced by an invocation in a twelfth-century herbal:

> Earth, divine goddess, Mother Nature, who generatest all things ... ; Guardian of sky and sea and of all gods and powers ... [W]hen the soul departs, to thee we return. Thou indeed art called Great Mother of the Gods ... thou art the source of the strength of nations and of gods, without thee nothing can be brought to perfection or be born; thou art great, queen of the gods. Goddess! I adore thee as divine, I call upon thy name ... i give thanks to thee, goddess ... Now I make intercession to you, all ye powers and herbs, and to your majesty ... this I pray and beseech you, be present with your virtues .[17]

A thirteenth-century Italian manuscript depicts Tellus similarly. Dronke writes of this illustration and the accompanying text: "She is the Magna Mater of gods and men. The suppliant goes on to implore her to give healing power to the herbs he is about to use." Dronke further points out that another such prayer, one concerned with gathering wild cucumber to heal gout, is directed to the goddess Hygia, but that she is in turn addressed as a daughter or descendant of Tellus, the Earth Goddess.

To a certain extent, Christian writers and authorities sought to appropriate this Goddess for the Church. According to Dronke, this process escalated dramatically in the ninth century and climaxed in the twelfth century. Ninth-century manuscripts depict Her as a "womanly, numinous being, a nimbus round her head and vine-tendrils growing out of her mouth" and as "opening her mouth and swallowing [a] stream spewed by [a] dragon." Later manuscripts, particularly Italian ones, continue to portray her as wearing a "splendid full-length robe [and] a flowering headdress." In both illustration and text, Her breasts were often emphasized as a multivalent sign of nurturance, intimacy, mystery, and – especially significant in our context – "matter's latent divinity."

Needless to say, Christians insisted that nature was the creation of God. Still, a kind of religious hybridity developed wherein, for example, a twelfth-century prayer might commence with an invocation of Jesus but culminate with one to "Terra Mater, creator of herbs." In an Anglo-Saxon prayer of the twelfth century, the practitioner pleading for fertility of the fields prays to the Christian God, the Virgin Mary, and "Earth, mother of men"; She is depicted as the Bride of God, as the Church is the Bride of Christ, as a secondary deity who is the recipient of His bounty: "Erce, Erce, Erce, mother of earth,/ may the omnipotent, eternal Lord grant you/ fields growing and thriving." In another Christianized or hybrid spell to heal a wound, this instruction is given: "Sing also this many times, 'May earth bear on thee with all her might and main.'" Not surprisingly, the Earth or Nature was often conflated with, or subsumed by, the Virgin Mary. The Goddess' iconography, which frequently associates her with a reptile, must have also contributed to the iconography of St. Martha. As Ecclesia, She even came to represent the Church itself! Indeed, Tellus was occasionally invoked as herself in medieval Italy during the celebration of Easter, as is evidenced by a southern Italian Exultet Roll. This type of appropriation was not, however, always sanctioned. To offer "cakes to the Queen of Heaven" was, for example, condemned by some Church councils as early as the seventh century.

Even within the context of a culture thought to be completely Christianized, Mother Nature or the Earth Goddess sometimes appeared to be capable of standing on her own, that is, as a first principle, as in the curse "May the earth destroy you with/ all her might and main." When the Earth or Nature stood her ground, Church authorities became deeply troubled. Dronke suggests that they sought to distinguish a Christian Natura from an indigenous Earth Goddess, whom he names Terra. "There can be no doubt," he writes, "that Terra ... began life as a goddess, not a personification, and that this was never wholly forgotten." When this Christian severing of Earth and Nature failed, they sought to eradicate the divinity. Ernst Robert Curtius writes, "Natura is a cosmic power ... she possesses an inexhaustible vitality ... her power over men's souls is proved by the Christian polemic against her ... . The pagan Natura never entirely vanishes from consciousness."

In later centuries, in England and elsewhere, the Earth Goddess came to be identified with – some would say "demoted," but, beyond obvious patriarchalization and Christianization, I prefer to think of it as primarily a transformation meeting the needs of votaries of a certain time and place – the Harvest Queen, who was often represented by a grain 'dolly,' a variety of which, conical and spiraling in shape, was referred to as the 'Mother Earth' dolly.

Although it is difficult to know when – or even if – reverence of the Basque goddess of the earth, Ama Lur, ceased, the well-known witch trial focused on the alleged witches of Zugarramurdi, taken together with other evidence, suggests that she may have been revered at least into the early seventeenth century. Indeed, Luis Araquistáin (1945) suggests that the meetings at Zugarramurdi on Saturday evenings may have persisted into the late nineteenth or early twentieth century. Although Christianization of the Basques commenced quite early, in the fourth century, and climaxed in the eleventh century, many Basques continued to practice earth-centered traditions in the sixteenth through nineteenth centuries. In his brilliant 2007 study of Basque mythology and religion, Andrés Ortiz-Osés states: "[T]he Earth is a maternal or matriarchal deity, as such, feminine and not masculine ... earth is Woman ... this radically feminine character of Mother Earth is reinforced by the presence, among the Basques, of the Sun and the Moon ... [who are Earth's children." Ama Lur, the primordial womb, is both giver and taker of life. She exists as the perfect embodiment of the site at which matter, *berezko*, and spirit, *aideko*, converge. Among her attributes are the laurel, the oak, salt, and certain minerals and precious stones. Menhirs, dolmens, and cromlechs mark sites sacred to her. She is assisted by a male divinity called Maide, who aids in the building of dolmens and cromlechs. In ancient times, a cult to her stressed the art of healing. "Earth is the Great Mother," Gimbutas states in *The Balts*; "All life comes from her: humans, plants, animals. In Lettish she is called Zemes mate, "Mother Earth," in Lithuanian Žemyna, or Žemynele, from *žemò*, "earth." Her anthropomorphic image is vague; she is the Earth holding the mystery of eternal life."

In Baltic regions, the Earth Goddess Žemyna and other Earth- and/or Mother Goddesses were revered into the seventeenth and later centuries. Paul Einhorn, a Livonian/ Latvian who served as a Lutheran minister from 1621 until his death in 1655, and author of *Historia Lettica* (1649), was unhappy to report that many Livonians/ Latvians continued to revere the mother goddesses, or *mates*, in the mid-seventeenth century. Whereas among the Lithuanians, the Earth or Mother Goddess was typically described in the singular, as Žemyna, among the Livonians/Latvians, divine motherhood and nurturance of the earth were typically envisioned as plural. Among these were Juras Mate, Mother of the Sea; Lauke Mate, Mother of the Fields; Meza Mate, Mother of the Forests; Cela Mate, Mother of the Road; and Darza Mate, Mother of the Garden. These *mates* were especially honored in late autumn. Paul Einhorn was also deeply disturbed by the high status of women in the region, by the erotic elements of their songs and rites, and by Latvians' continued reliance upon "soothsayers, augurs, and priests of the idols." Profoundly related to Žemyna and mirroring the Latvian Mates are the Deives, or "goddesses;" they are "guardians of grain and cattle." They were represented or embodied by "big flat stones" that were housed in granaries, placed in holes dug in the earth and covered with straw. Normally, no one dared touch them; if they did, they might well be injured or worse. Deives were sometimes identified with or associated with *laumës*, fairy-like divinities. Numerous lesser divinities ruled by Žemyna, called *žemepacios*, assisted in promoting fertility of the earth Vaitkevicius notes, "In the sources of the sixteenth to seventeenth centuries," that is, in Christianized Lithuania, "gods and goddesses, such as ... Žemynele had defined spheres of sacredness. They were guardians of the farm, the people who live there, their property, personal happiness and work." Gimbutas relates in *The Balts*: "According to seventeenth century records, there were no festivals in villages during which the earth deity, Žemyna, was not venerated."

In more recent times, some Finns continued to perform a rite involving the sacred marriage, or *hieros gamos*, of a human male with the Earth goddess with the intention of "curing infertility in one part of the soil by transferring it to soil from a fertile field." Mary MacLeod Banks relates:

"A man comes out dressed as a bridegroom in a procession with bell-ringing and wedding songs. At night they drive out in wagons and make their way in silence to a certain fertile field. The oldest man addresses the earth and the bridegroom bows repeatedly to the ground. Shovelsful of the soil are thrown into the wagons ... On their return to their home village they" – the couple, consisting of the human "bridegroom" and the Earth Goddess – "are greeted with clapping of hands and cries of delight. The bridegroom visits his own and every other wagon carrying his spade in his hand, as if welcoming his bride." The "bridegroom" then distributes the fertile soil among all the participants in the rite.

Duotheism, the Divine Couple

Ronald Hutton asserts that ancient paganism is primarily polytheistic, whereas "Modern Paganism (and especially Wicca ...) is mainly duotheistic, recognizing a pairing of a goddess and god who between them represent the cosmos." Some traditions of ancient paganism appear to reflect, however, a duotheism that resonates with that of present-day Wicca. These religions/traditions include Egyptian paganism, with its divine couples including Isis and Osiris (later, Serapis) and Horus and Set. In ancient Greek religion, Artemis and her brother Apollo were often worshipped as a divine pair. The works of Marcus Porcius Cato (234-149 BCE), Marcus Terentius Varro (116-27 BCE), and Lucius Junius Moderatus Columella (fl. first cent. CE) on agriculture, *De Agri Cultura*, *Rerum Rusticarum*, and *De Re Rustica*, respectively, address a duotheism linked to Roman paganism that resonates with that of Wicca/Witchcraft. Their works emphasize deities revered and rites practiced by agrarian peoples of Roman Late Antiquity. At the outset, Varro, a scholar, the first librarian of the public library at Rome, and a devotee of the earth goddess Tellus, explains that his text concerns how one "ought to proceed in farming." Farming, like other industries, is rooted in the sacred and thus commences with homage to the Divine: "And since we are told [that] the gods help those who call upon them, I will first invoke them." Varro is careful to point out, however, that he "do[es] not mean those urban gods, whose images stand around the forum," but rather "those twelve gods who are the special patrons of husbandmen." These twelve deities are especially significant in that they simultaneously speak to polytheism, the reverence of many deities, and to duotheism, the reverence of a divine couple. Yet all but one of the six pairs of deities invoked by Varro are comprised of a "goddess and a god": "First, ... I invoke Jupiter [/Zeus] and Tellus [/the Earth Mother/Gaia/Rhea/Cybele], who, by means of the sky and the earth, embrace all the fruits of agriculture; and hence, as we are told that they are the universal parents, Jupiter is called "the Father," Tellus is called "Mother Earth." And second, Sol [/the Sun/Phoebus Apollo] and Luna [/ the Moon/Artemis/Diana/Selene], whose courses are watched in all matters of planting and harvesting." Varro continues to invoke Demeter/Ceres and Dionysus/Bacchus/Liber as a couple, "because their fruits are most necessary for life; for it is by their favor that food and drink come from the farm." He then invokes the couple Robigus and Flora, "for when they are propitious the rust will not harm the grain and the trees, and they will not fail to bloom in their season." He then invokes the couple Lympha, goddess of the healing power of water, and Bonus Eventus, a god of good fortune and success in business, "since without moisture all tilling of the ground is parched and barren, and without success and 'good issue,' it is not tillage but vexation.

One same-sex couple invoked by Varro is that of "Minerva and Venus, of whom one protects the olive yard and the other the garden; and in her [i.e., Venus's] honor, the rustic Vinalia has been established [on August 19th]." Incidentally, same-sex pairs are often twins, such as Castor and Pollux, or relatives, such as Horus and Set, astrologically manifesting as Gemini. In regard to Horus and Set, here we have a clear example of a same-sex pair linked to a heterosexual pair, Isis and Osiris. Due to the ordering of deities in this listing, it appears that Minerva may in some sense correspond to the masculine, and Venus to the feminine, within this same gender couple. Noteworthy is that in the Renaissance, as we shall see, Minerva and Venus frequently join Juno to form a triad or trinity of goddesses. This list suggests that in rural areas of Europe where Roman influence was profound, reverence of these deities, due to their significant association with agriculture, may have outlasted that of other deities whose connection with rural life was not as deeply felt. Cato adds another divine couple to this list: Jupiter Dapalis ("of the feast") and Vesta. This couple is honored at feasts held for agricultural workers prior to the planting of "millet, panic grass, garlic, and lentils." The significant stress on divine couples, particularly that of a female deity associated with the earth, the moon, grain, and flowers, and a male deity associated with the heavens, the sun, and wine may have also been remembered for a long time in areas influenced by rural Roman traditions. Like Cato and Varro, Columella tends to speak of divine male-female couples; among these he counts Venus and Cupid (or Bacchus), Oceanus and Tethys, Neptune and Amphitrite, and the celestial Jupiter and "Mother Earth." Vertumnus, a god of seasons and the ripening of plants, and Pomona, a goddess of fruit, were also revered as a divine couple. Stephen J. Yeates, in *A Dreaming for the Witches*, observes that "there was a…divine couple amongst the tribes of north-west Europe, who are generally referred to as Celts." With the arrival of Romans in these areas, the "divine couple consisted of a male divinity, represented in the guise of a Roman god, alongside a female divinity, in native guise and usually with a local name."

Sometimes, however, both divinities comprising the couple shared Celtic or Roman names. Among such divine couples are: Rosmerta and Mercury; Mater and Mercury; Sirona and Apollo; Nemetona and Mars; Inciona and Veraudinus; Bricta and Luxovius; Bergusia and Ucuetis; and Nantosuelta and Sucellus. Beyond the Greeks and Celts/Gauls, many others have revered divine couples; as we have seen,

Lithuanians, in revering Žemyna and Žemepatis and Saulė and Menulis, also revered divine couples.

This ancient goddess and god couple continue to appear in medieval and post-medieval accounts of groups of alleged witches, in descriptions including mention of the Lord of the Animals, or Lord of the Forest, as, for example, in medieval and Renaissance Italian cults in which, as Maurizio Bertolotti, in "The Ox's Bones and the Ox's Hide: A Popular Myth, Part Hagiography and Part Witchcraft," has documented, the "Lord of the Animals" presided, together with Diana, as "the Lady," at ceremonies including the resurrection of oxen, as well as in Pierre de Lancre's (1553-1631) descriptions of the Lord of the Forest in *On the Inconstancy of Witches*. In 1597, the male witch Andro Man of Aberdeen spoke of encountering a heterosexual couple of leaders, the Quene of Elphen and Christsonday. In 1823, Anne Joseph Eusèbe Bacconnière-Salverte spoke of the reigning deities of medieval and Renaissance witchcraft as being Diana (or Dame Abunde/Habundia) and Pan. Together, among other roles, this divine couple embodied "ideas of fertility and prosperity" and creation/creativity.

Thus, it would appear that some traditions of paganism – from antiquity through the late sixteenth century – reflect a duotheism that indeed resonates with that of present-day Wicca.

The Lithuanian Žemyna was often coupled with a spouse or brother named Žemepatis (also, Žemininkas, Žemòpatis, Žiemiennik). Reverence of Žemepatis persisted into at least the mid-to-late sixteenth century, as documented by the Polish-Lithuanian historian Maciej Stryjkowski (*c.* 1547-*c.* 1593). He was especially revered by the peasants of Žemaitija. He was celebrated at the end of October, following the harvest, with offerings and sacrifices, including animals of both sexes (the meat of which was consumed by participants), breads, and beer. Devotees prayed to him, "To thee, O Žemininkas, our god, we make an offering and thank thee/ for keeping us healthy and wealthy last year, for corn and all the goods you gave us,/ for your kind protection against the fire, plague, and enemies of all kinds." Likewise, Menulis, god of the moon, often forms a couple with the sun goddess Saulė. Another divine Baltic couple, Curche and Gurcho, protects crops and promotes fertility of the land and animals.

The Anglican priest John James Blunt (1794-1855), in *Vestiges of Ancient Manners and Customs Discoverable in Modern Italy and Sicily* (1823), argues that the duotheistic tendency in polytheism, which, as we have seen, may include same-sex couples/pairs, was transferred from paganism to Christianity, as evidenced by churches dedicated to "Sts. Marcellinus and Peter, to Jesus and Maria ... &c." Not to mention the well-known fairy couple of the Fairy Queen and Fairy King; as the Reverend Edward Smedley noted in 1855: "The notion of a fairy king and queen was as old as the time of Chaucer, who speaks [in]…the ' Merchant's Tale,' ... [of]— 'Proserpina, and all her fayrie;' and, again,— 'Pluto, that is king of fayrie.'"

Isis

Lucius: Blessed Queen of Heaven, whether you are pleased to be known as Ceres, the original harvest mother who in joy at the finding of your lost daughter Proserpina abolished the rude acorn diet of our forefathers and gave them bread raised from the fertile soil of Eleusis; or whether as celestial Venus ... or whether as Artemis ... or whether as dread Proserpina ... I beseech you, by whatever name, in whatever aspect ... have mercy on me...

Isis: I am Nature, the universal Mother, mistress of all the elements ... sovereign of all things spiritual ... the primeval Phrygians call me Pessinuntica, Mother of the gods; the Athenians ... call me Cecropian Artemis; for the islanders of Cyprus I am Paphian Aphrodite ... for the Eleusinians their ancient Mother of Corn. - Apuleius, *The Golden Ass*[18]

The reverence of Isis (in France, Ysis) commenced in Egypt. She is a goddess of "immense magical power," the sister and/or spouse of the god Osiris, the mother of the god Horus, and the deity who confers kingship upon pharaohs. The need or desire to embrace this African goddess was so powerful that her cult spread to Rome and from there to many other locations in Europe and elsewhere. Apuleius (b. *c.* 124 CE) wrote of the goddess Isis in *The Golden Ass*, "Nature, the universal Mother, mistress of all the elements ... [whose] nod governs the shining heights of Heaven, the wholesome sea-breezes." She was "worshipped in many aspects," was "known by countless names," including Aphrodite, Proserpina, Bellona, Hecate, and Demeter, the "ancient Mother of Corn," and was venerated by the "whole round earth." Isis possessed centers of worship in Austria: Noreia; Belgium; England: Brougham Castle, London, Silchester, York; France: Arles, in the Aquitaine, Autun, Besançon, Boulogne [Haute-Garonne], Fréjus, Langres, Languedoc, Lyons, Manduel [Gard], Marseille, Nîmes, Paris, Provence, Riez [Basses-Alpes], Soissons; Germany: Augsbourg, Cologne, Trêves; Greece: Athens; Hungary; Sicily; and Switzerland.

The cult of Isis persisted in Egypt, especially in Alexandria, into at least the early sixth century CE in spite of the vehement efforts of Christians, who finally succeeded in incinerating her temple in the 480s, to destroy any evidence of her reverence. Some Egyptian practitioners of divination and magic, as well as some "Coptic villagers," appear to have continued to worship her as well as Horus and Nepthys "through the eighth century."

Christians appropriated numerous images, beliefs, and practices from the cult of Isis, including the image of the Virgin Mary, the wearing of "black cassock[s] and white surplice[s]," the "use of the *crotalus*, or rattle, ... [referencing] Isis'...*sistrum*," and perhaps even the cross, as an abbreviated version of the ankh. R. E. Witt remarks, "To hold that the Egyptian goddess Isis was the forerunner of Catholicism's Mary, Mother of God, is to raise the question of the uniqueness of Christianity." In part for this reason, Church authorities despised and were determined to destroy the cult of Isis. Witt notes that Clement of Alexandria, in citing the *Gospel*

According to the Egyptians, was convinced that one of Jesus's main objectives was to "destroy the works of the female," particularly the worship of Isis, "the Queen of the South."

In Roman times, one of Isis' Parisian temples stood "at the western limits of the city, on the marshy left bank of the Seine, later the site of the famous abbey and church of St. Germain-des-Prés and of St. Sulpice." The sixteenth-century historian Lemaire de Belge(s) recounted the myth that Isis had once traversed the Seine, visiting Paris to see its ruler, Lugdus. Destroyed by Christians, its ruins were visible through the early sixth century (and perhaps for a longer period of time). Isis also appears to have possessed a temple at the present-day site of the Cathedral of Notre-Dame de Paris. The Goddess was officially worshipped until the conversion of Clovis I in or near 498 CE, and most probably for many years after that in secret. The Frankish kings Clovis I (known as Chlodowig prior to conversion to Christianity, *c.* 466- 511) and his son Childebert I (*c.* 498- *c.* 558) were largely responsible for the destruction of the cult of Isis and her temple in Paris. St. Geneviève displaced Isis as patron of Paris.

In the mid-sixth century CE., the Church of Saint-Germain-des-Prés (called that of Saint Vincent until the ninth century) began to be built on the ruins of her temple. Nevertheless, many remained convinced that the term "Paris" might refer to the "grove" or "barque of Isis;" that the name of nearby Issy was named after her; that, as the monk Abbon (*c.* 850-*c.* 922) of Saint-Germain-des-Prés documented in his poem *Histoire du siège de Paris par les Normands* (*History of the Siege of Paris by the Normans*, *c.* 887/897), she was the tutelary deity of Paris; and that as a goddess of mariners she was honored each January 3.

The bishop's throne at Aix-la-Chapelle (or, Aachen), a spa city in westernmost Germany, was ornamented with an Alexandrian ivory portrait of Isis as a patron of mariners and Horus in her barque. That this image was seen as a sacred equivalent to Christian ones is suggested by the fact that it was placed parallel to a "plaque of Jesus in the company of the evangelists."

At Aix-la-Chapelle, moreover, the March 5 festival of the Navigium Isidis (this was the traditional Roman date of her festival), the promenading of the vessel of Isis, is thought to have been celebrated at least as late as 1132/1133. Astoundingly, from locations mentioned by the Benedictine abbot, musician, and chronicler Rudolf of St. Trond (*c.* 1070-1138), this promenade may have tracked between one hundred and fifty and four hundred miles (depending upon what routes it took between Aachen, Germany and Utrecht, Belgium and if it was a one-way or round trip). Rudolf describes the Navigium Isidis as centering on a boat on wheels with many sails and decorated with flags that was "pulled from city to city," surrounded by musicians, singers, and "semi-naked" dancers. It is noteworthy that while the boat of Isis was associated, as one would expect, with water, it was also associated with the moon (as was that of Osiris), especially as a horned crescent, and was envisioned as a "boat of heaven," crossing the celestial "ocean" during the night just as the boat of the sun god Ra (Re) crossed it during the day. In this connection, Isis may have corresponded or lent attributes to goddesses including Juno, Freyja, and Wanne Thekla as well as to St. Ursula.

In the Basilica Sanctae Mariae de Ara Coeli (Basilica of St. Mary of the Altar of Heaven) in Rome, for centuries "there was an altar dedicated to Isis by someone who had returned safely from a perilous journey." According to the respected Italian archaeologist Rodolfo Amadeo Lanciani (1845-1929) in the late nineteenth century, this altar "bore the conventional emblem of two footprints, which were believed by the Christians to be the footprints of the angel seen by [Pope] Gregory the Great on the summit of [the pagan emperor] Hadrian's tomb."

From the medieval period through at least the eighteenth century, numerous Egyptian artifacts related to the cult of Isis were discovered at Rome. These included an obelisk, sphinxes of green and red granite – the head of the former being that of the female pharaoh Hatshepsut – , images of the goddess Hathor in bovine form, a relief of a procession of bald-headed priests of Isis, and a capital carved with "papyrus leaves and lotus flowers." All were discovered in the vicinity of the Church of Santa Maria sopra Minerva. Such artifacts are known to have inspired medieval and later works of art such as the sphinxes at the gate of the Church of Saint Anthony on the Esquiline sculpted in the twelfth century by Pietro Vassalletto (fl. 1170); it is not inconceivable that they also inspired rites.

It would appear that the cult of Isis persisted in Germany for a very long time, or at least that her image continued to appear, even when it was conflated with the persona of the Virgin Mary or a female saint. She appears to have also been conflated with the local goddess Ciza, no doubt in part due to the similarity of their names. Jean le Maire, in 1512 CE, wrote of "the time when Isis, Queen of Egypt, visited Germany and showed its primitive people how to use flour to make bread." Johannes Turmair-Aventin, near 1522 CE, claimed that "it was from Fraw Eysen (or, Eisen), that iron (German *eisen*) took its name, adding an account of her cult." so that we read of Fraw (or Frau) Eysen as "Lady Isis" or "Lady Iron." Her name may (or may not) be recalled by place-names including Isenheim in northeastern Germany and Isenburg, (in the past) located in southwestern Germany. Fraw Eysen was celebrated annually in the twelfth century and perhaps thereafter.

In Paris, when the church of Saint-Germain-des-Prés was dedicated to St. Vincent, a statue of Isis was tossed into a corner of the church, allegedly to demonstrate the Christ's victory over the goddess. The statue appears to have survived into the eleventh century, however, when an abbot set the statue in a niche in the church, perhaps believing that it was, or hoping others might assume it was, an image of the Virgin Mary. That this image was made of black stone or plaster painted black is significant in that it speaks to an ancient association of the Goddess with dark-skinned women of African heritage as well as to the emergence of Black Madonnas during the medieval period. It was not simply "dirty" or "soiled," as some who deny the blackness of black Madonnas are quick to claim. It is significant in that it indicates that certain Europeans were not averse to worshipping deities thought to originate in Africa.

The statuette was venerated until 1514 – that is to say, for approximately five hundred years – by women of the neighborhood who made offerings, including candles, to her, women who may well have been aware of her original identity. At this time, the secretary of the church assured Abbot Briçonnet that he had found a woman praying and making offerings to the statue. He insisted that she was lying when she claimed she had thought it was a statue of Mary, that she knew it was Isis. Perhaps she viewed it, as many practitioners of sacred hybridity do, as both.

It is difficult to imagine, however, how anyone could have perceived the statue as representing Mary – not because of her dark or black skin, but due to the other features of the statue. The writer and printer Gilles Corrozet (1510-1568), who was in Paris when the statue was destroyed, described it as *"maigre, haute, droite et noire…nue, sinon avec quelque figure de linge, enlacée autour de ses members,"* that is, "thin, tall, straight and black … naked, if not for some linen entwined around its arms and legs." Hardly a typical representation of the Blessed Virgin.

Paul-Yves Sébillot, in *Folklore et Curiosités du Vieux Paris* (2002), speaks of this local reverence of Isis as a "persistent cult, more or less clandestine," a "tradition that was perpetuated in secret." The statuette was destroyed by order of Briçonnet. It was ground to powder, and the powder was cast into the Seine. Where Isis had stood, a large red crucifix now loomed.

The goddess-revering women, however, moved on. Theodore Child (1888), citing a document from the early seventeenth century, relates, "the old women of Paris were tenacious in their heathen ways, and…transferred their [ritualizing from the statuette of Isis] to a statue of Ceres" which had been discovered in the faubourg St. Jacques.

Isis came to be displaced by or else conflated or identified with the Virgin Mary – perhaps including La Vierge au Lys, Our Lady of the Lily (or Lililes), celebrated each February 8 in Melun (once called Iseos or Isia), France, where a temple to Isis once stood. As a goddess of water and the sea and a patron of mariners, Isis was eventually conflated with, or displaced by, the Virgin Mary in the latter's depiction as Stella Maris, the Star of the Sea. Intriguingly, this suggests that there might be a correspondence between the Egypto-African Isis and the West African Yorùbá *orishá* of motherhood and the sea, Yemonja/Yemayá, who is also conflated with Stella Maris. Indeed, a correspondence may also exist among Isis, the Yorùbá *orishá* of fresh water, eros, and the arts, Oshún, and the Virgin of Caridad del Cobre, all of whom have been depicted as protecting three men in a boat.

Isis also came to be identified with various female saints, including Ursula and Géneviève. Arthur Weigall notes in *The Paganism in Our Christianity* that "in the church of St. Ursula at Cologne, a statue of Isis was adapted in the Middle Ages for one of the capitals of the pillars." So significant was the conflation of Isis with St.

Géneviève that "[w]hen Jean Louis Verger, the assassin-priest, was brandishing his Catalonian knife near the fallen Archbishop of Paris [in 1857], in the church of St. Etienne du Hont, he raised...an extremely characteristic Parisian cry, ..."Down with the Génévièvians! Down with the goddesses!"

The cult of Isis was to emerge again during the Enlightenment and the French Revolution, a subject to which we shall return later. In the late nineteenth century, in a village church on the Danube, not far from Linz, "pious Catholics pay[ed] their devotions" to a "statue of Isis, made of black basalt,... regarding it as an image of the Virgin Mary."

It is possible that the Holy Thursday Easter festival held at Champs-Golot, Epinal, in the region of Lorraine, France, since medieval times into the present, in which children lead a parade of small boats, originated in the Navigium Isidis. In *Isis in the Ancient World*, in which he notes that references to Isis have been located in the Church of Ara Coeli in Rome and in the "pagan remains beneath St. Peter's," Reginald Witt relates this intriguing observation he made in 1965 in the Church of St. John the Divine on Ios: "[I] examined the stele...behind the iconostasis [a wall of icons] and saw for [myself] that in this building, where the priest had just invoked the Panagia [i.e., the Virgin Mary] as 'Mistress of the World,' Isis still stood hidden but obstinately alive, uttering her own praises to prying eyes."

In 1904, William Jasper Nicolls wrote in *A Dreamer in Paris*:

What is this subtle fascination that permeates the air of Paris, and insinuates itself into one's inmost soul? What mysterious and occult sources are at work in our unknown surroundings, in the movement of which the pagan goddess Isis seems to rule? Isis, "the universal mother nature, mistress of all elements, first-born of the ages, supreme of goddesses, queen of names, ruler of the gods, sole manifestation of all gods and goddesses, whose glance makes awful silence in the shining heights of heaven, in the depths of the sea, and of the world beneath, whose unchanging being is worshipped under many forms, with many rites, and under various names, as mother of the gods, as the Cecropian Minerva, Paphian Venus, Dictynnian Diana, Stygian Proserpina, the ancient goddess Ceres, as Juno, Bellona, Hecate, Rhammesia"—but whose true name is Queen Isis.

With arms extended across a stone parapet I hold fast to the solid earth while my soul takes wing and soars to the feet of Isis. " I am that which is, has been, and shall be. My veil no one has listed. The fruit I bore was the sun."
Beneath me the dark waters of the Seine slow silently through the city, the city of Julian who here erected an altar to Isis,— the favorite goddess of the Parisians. The twinkling stars of the dark firmament above me meet the thousands of the city's lights and are lost in numbers. I can imagine the sacred ship of Isis, launched from the shore of the Île de la Cité in memory of the goddess who sought in the sea the body of her spouse. In the arms of Paris, and in old carvings

is the ship of Isis. "Pagan Paris believed in Isis, Christian Paris continued to believe in her even after her temple had been razed to the ground to make way for the cathedral of Notre Dame: for as late as the reign of Louis XIII a statue of Isis was worshipped by the old women in the church of Saint Germain des Prés … For the moment I am at the feet of Isis. I eagerly inhale the breeze that fills my lungs with the mystery, the witchery, the fascination of Pagan Paris. Beneath my feet flows the treacherous river whose lurking depths conceal the unknown. Above, are the stars, the everlasting stars, and beyond are the lights of the city. Perhaps the spirit of Isis still moves on the surface of this dangerous river, still hovers over and mingles with those eternal stars and the midnight lights. Perhaps that is the mystery, the secret, the inscrutable charm, that envelops Paris, Pagan Paris, the midnight Paris of today.

For Isis was the goddess above all others who represented the feminine, and whether for good or evil it is the feminine that rules Paris. In the service of Isis there must have been a peculiar attractiveness, a lofty and religious enthusiasm …Through expiations and purifications it promised to lead its votaries to sanctification of life, and to a truer perception of the life divine. Hail! O Isis!—the goddess of the receptive and producing principle in Nature, the goddess of procreation and birth, the goddess who called to herself her select circle of worshipers in a dream—the goddess of the dreamers in Paris.

…

Lazily extended in the shade of some widespreading tree, my head [rests] upon the lap of Mother Earth—of Isis …[19]

Ba'al

Ba'al, whose name means "prince" or "lord of the earth," is revered "throughout almost all of the ancient Near East, as far as Egypt and Jerusalem." He is a god of rain, thunder, storms, fecundity, prosperity, sacrifice, and death/rebirth (he dies and is reborn annually). He is often depicted as a young bull or as a man possessing or crowned with bull horns; thus, a horned god linked iconographically to Cernunnos and other horned deities. He is typically paired with a goddess, either Anat or Ishtar/Astarte or Shapash. He is identified or associated with numerous ancient gods including Bel-Marduk, Set, and Adonis. His name may also be linked to the British god Bel/Belenus, for whom the festival of Beltane is named. In medieval magic, he is sometimes, as Ba'al Zebub (see 2nd Kings 1.2-6, 16), associated with Beelzebub or Belphegor. Although the fifteenth-century grimoire *The Book of Angels* is primarily a work of ceremonial or ritual magic, it contains themes and references to materials that are commonly linked to earth-centered pagan traditions, such as fertility and blood. In *Angels*, which contains pagan references such as directing the practitioner to chant, "O gods, by the virtue of this figure show me this…in my dreams," Ba'al is invoked as a "lord" of "demons" who is linked, by way of correspondences, to Wednesday and the planet Mercury (and thus indirectly to the gods Hermes and Odin/Woden). Ba'al is invoked, by way of a waxen image of a man that is ritually fed with water, the blood of a black cock, and dove's blood, in expectation that in this image and rite will provide the practitioner with power over demons and with wisdom.

Greek and Roman Divinities
Aphrodite/Venus

Aphrodite, the Greek goddess "born of the foam of the sea," is a goddess of sensuous love, fertility, beauty, the arts, and both war and peace, attributes as well of her Roman counterpart Venus. The pagan emperor Hadrian (76-138 CE; r. 117-138 CE) infuriated early Christians when he had architects build a temple to Venus on the site in Jerusalem where Christians believed Jesus had risen from the dead. Hadrian also defiantly had a temple built to Adonis in Bethlehem on the site where Jesus was believed to have been born. When the Council of Nicaea convened in 325 CE, members ordered the destruction of the temple of Venus. The following year, Empress Helena (c.?250 CE – c.?330 CE), the Christian mother of Constantine the Great (c. 272 CE-337 CE; r. 306 CE-337 CE), oversaw the destruction of the temple and the construction of the Church of the Holy Sepulchre, claiming that the tomb of Jesus rested there.

Helena and the Council of Nicaea were not altogether successful in seeking to destroy the memory of, or belief in, Aphrodite/Venus. Pagans, often drawn to sacred hybridity, explained Christian events with pagan astrological imagery, including that "Jesus died on the day of Venus, lay in his grave on the day of Saturn, and arose from the dead on the day of Helios." Coptic magical texts of the sixth and seventh centuries invoked Aphrodite together with other Greek, Egyptian, Christian, and Gnostic divinities. Aphrodite/Venus continued to be worshipped in seventh-century Rouen, France. The early ninth-century *Epistola Canonica sub Carolo Magno* (*c.* 814) "chastises priests for giving communion to people who had disregarded multiple admonitions against observing ... Friday (Venus' day)." This was considered a "lucky day for marriages," as Venus is the goddess of love. Also in regard to the medieval and Renaissance European manifestations of the doctrine of empathies or correspondences, eroticism, courtesanship, and prostitution were all governed by Venus.

In the mid-eleventh century, a tale surfaced, however, that placed Venus between a groom and his bride. It is not clear whether or not this tale was considered factual; whatever the case, it enjoyed widespread popularity in the Middle Ages, appearing in numerous, including English, Scottish, French, and German variants. A young nobleman was married at Rome. While engaging in a ball game during the wedding festivities, he placed his wedding ring on a nearby statue of Venus so that it would not be damaged during the game. When the game was over, and he attempted to retrieve the ring, it wouldn't budge. He heard a voice whisper in a commanding tone: "Embrace me. I am Venus, whom you have wedded. I will never return this ring." Only after the intercession of a Catholic priest did the statue, embodied by the Goddess, relinquish the ring.

A prayer to Venus from the *Picatrix* of the eleventh- or twelfth-century, a divinatory and magical text translated from Arabic into Latin and becoming extremely popular in Spain, France and other parts of Europe, is a praise-hymn invocation. The writer-ritualist greets the goddess as "sovereign and fortunate ... and beautiful, perfumed and ornamented [with] ... gold and silver; you who delight in love, joy ... and pleasantries ... chants and musical instruments string and wind, songs accompanied by flutes ... games ... repose, and love." By naming her many attributes, he is seeking love.

As we have learned above, Alexandre de Villedieu claimed that Venus continued to be worshipped at Orléans in the early thirteenth century. A thirteenth-century document, Vincent de Beauvais' (*c.* 1190-*c.* 1267) *Speculum naturale*, resonating with the *Picatrix*, describes her vividly: "[S]he loves clothes, bands of gold and silver, songs, pleasures of the senses and games ... [H]er speech is soft, she has beautiful eyes and eyebrows, she is concerned with making herself beautiful, she has a light body and beautiful skin, and a medium waist."

She was frequently called 'Dame Venus' in the Middle Ages. In Italy, she was conflated with a (or *the* Cumaean) Sibyl as well as with the Fairy Queen. She was invoked by alchemists, astrologers, and magicians.

In Germany, Venus was conflated with the Germanic goddesses Holda and Freyja as well as with the Fairy Queen. As such, she possesses an entourage of elves who dance with her. Also in Germany, she came to be called Frau Minne. A cavern inside the Venusberg/Mount of Venus emerged as her dwelling-place. From the fourteenth century onward, numerous sites, especially in Germany, were claimed as the Venusberg. One of these sites was the Hörselberg, situated between Eisenach and Gotha in Thuringia. Her connection with Freyja or Frigga and with the Hörselberg is enhanced by her connection with the mandrake; in a medieval manuscript we find: "Friday is a holy day and Mistress Venus' own day in the Hörselberg where the mandrakes live." Inhabitants of the area imparted that it was there, deep within a cavern, that "Venus, the pagan goddess of love, held her court in all the pomp and revelry of heathendom."

Other German "mounts of Venus" were located in Swabia, near Waldsee, and in Saxony, near Freiburg. Great celebrations of song and dance were thought to be held on the Venusberg and in its cavern palace. The minstrel Tannhäuser is believed to sojourn with her there.

In *Les Enfants de Vénus: Art et Astrologie à la Renaissance* (1993), Gwendolyn Trottein relates that during the Middle Ages and Renaissance, Venus, as simultaneously a "feminine power," a "goddess," and a "cosmological force" (planet possessing astrological significance), exerted a tremendous influence on the people, especially the artists, of the time, particularly in the areas of "sensuality ... pleasure ... [and] fertility." "She is at once the legendary lover, mythological goddess, and planet;" "At once both planet and mythological goddess, [she] intervenes directly in the lives of mortals." Others in the Middle Ages and Renaissance envisaged Venus in euhemeristic terms, as Christine de Pizan (1364-1430) viewed her, or as a kind of messiah, avatar or *bodhisattva*; in Boccaccio's (1313-1375) words, as a "celestial woman sent to earth." According to Trottein, Venus served as a "source of Dionysian inspiration, promoting a 'pagan' cult of beauty, pleasure, and liberation."

Venus was thought, as were other deities, especially planetary ones, to have spiritual children, for whom she was deific mother, guardian, and patron (Greek, *poliouchos* or *polias*); this notion is reminiscent of a belief among practitioners of African-diasporic religions/traditions that initiates, priests, and priestesses are children of certain *orishás* (deities). Venus, via astrological associations, considers as her special offspring persons born under the signs of Taurus and Libra, as well as those who are (at least partly due to affiliation with these signs)

> Musicians, Gamesters, Silk-men, Mercers, Linen-Drapers, Painters, Jewelers, Players, Lapidaries, Embroiderers, Women-tailors, Wives, Mothers, Virgins, Choristers, Fiddlers, Pipers, ... singers, Perfumers, ... picture-drawers, Gravers, Upholsterers, Limners, Glovers, all such as fell those Commodities which adorn Women either, in Body (as Clothes) or in Face, (as complexion-waters).[20]

Beyond these professions, as previously noted, she patrons lovers.

Enea Silvio Piccolomini (1405-1464), who ultimately became Pope Pius II (pope, 1458-1464), was once asked by a doctor of the king of Saxony if he knew of an Italian 'mount of Venus' where the magical arts were taught. He replied that he knew of only one mountain that was dedicated to the goddess Venus, that being Mt. Eryx of Sicily. His reply indicates that at least some persons of the Renaissance were familiar with the reverence of the goddess Venus Erycina in ancient Sicily and perhaps in later times. Enea may or may not have known that prior to its association with Venus, Eryx was home to Tanit and Astarte. With Roman occupation, the former goddesses were hybridized with Venus Erycina (or V. Erucina). Her temple stood for centuries. During the medieval period, the Normans built Venus Castle on its ruins. Enea did not seem to know if the magical arts were taught at Eryx. He did, however, inform the doctor that he had heard that instruction in necromancy could be obtained at Norcia, located in southeastern Umbria, Italy. Indeed, it would appear that during the Middle Ages and the Renaissance, Norcia became so linked to necromancy that *norcino* became a synonym for "necromancer." The writer and scientist Johann Wolfgang von Goethe (1749-1832) utilized the term in *Faust*, and it continued to be used into at least the late nineteenth century. Norcia lies near the Monte della Sibilla (or Monti Sibillini) as well as the Lago di Pilato, the Lake of Pontius Pilate. The lake received its name from its water becoming blood-red on certain occasions. It gained the reputation of possessing magical powers. Practitioners of magic were believed to travel long distances to consecrate their grimoires on an islet in the middle of the lake. Prominent Italians who are thought to have performed this rite (or had it performed for them) include the poet Luigi Pulci (1432-1484) and the sculptor, metal smith, and writer Benevenuto Cellini (1500-1571).

Pierre de Lancre, who persecuted alleged Basque witches in the Labourde region of France, wrote in his *Tableau de l'inconstance des mauvais anges et demons* (*Treatise on the Inconstancy of Evil Angels and Demons*, 1612, recently translated as *On the Inconstancy of Witches*) of Venus in the early seventeenth century. This passage may be read metaphorically or spiritually; we might immediately assume the former to be correct were it not for his descriptions elsewhere in the text of Hecate, Medea, Circe, and others as having actually lived. In a passage concerning Basque women of the Labourdin region of France that is at its outset reminiscent of descriptions of Avalon, that is sensuous and indeed beautifully written, De Lancre writes: "[T]his is a land of apples. Women eat only apples and drink nothing but apple juice ... . This is the sea that once gave birth to Venus out of its foam, Venus who is reborn many times among this seafaring people." In sensuous terms ill-befitting a monstrous Inquisitor – and yet utterly unsurprising, de Lancre continues, "This mixture of grown girls and young fishermen can be seen at the coast ... . Wet all over, they can go and dry off in the neighboring chamber of love, which Venus seems to have provided for this singular occasion on the seashore."

Aphrodite/Venus was Catholicized as, or hybridized with, the Virgin Mary as well as St. Afra of Augsburg, the latter of whom, like Aphrodite, was believed to have been born on Cyprus. In her association with St. Afra, Aphrodite/Venus may have also become linked to the Slavic goddess Ciza.

In 1907, Mary Hamilton observed that in Cyprus, the "summer festival, a fair on the water, [was] popularly called the festival of Aphrodite," due to the "long-standing tradition of the island's chief cult."

Apollo/Helios/Sol

Phoebus Apollo, also called Helios and Sol, is the Greco-Roman god of the "eternal light of the sun, as well as a deity of music, gymnastics, poetry, oracles, and male beauty. He continued to be revered in Roman England in the late second century; at that time, one of his chief temples was destroyed by Christians. In the late third century, however, the church they built on the ruins of his temple was destroyed by the Emperor Diocletian [(245-313, r. 284-305)], who briefly restored Apollo's reverence. At this time, "the inhabitants of ... Westminster, were offering incense to Apollo." In the sixth century, that is to say, during the early Middle Ages, Apollo continued to be worshipped at Monte Cassino, Italy. By the early seventh century, Christianity once more prevailed over the reverence of Apollo in Britain, and where he had been revered, a church that eventually became Westminster Abbey was founded. Also in the seventh century, a Coptic magical text invoked Apollo together with other Greek and Egyptian divinities.

During the ninth century, the god, as Apollo Medicus, together with Asclepius and the Earth Goddess, continued to be invoked by healers seeking to heal tumors, as evidenced by manuals of herbal medicine. In the tenth-century *Geoponika*, which continued to be read and used in the Renaissance and thereafter, agriculturalists learned that because laurel is sacred to Apollo and "has a great deal of fire in it," it will keep away demonic spirits who might damage crops. Also because laurel is sacred to Apollo, it can assist "when performing acts of divination."

In the second decade of the fifteenth century, San Bernardino of Siena (1380-1444) became livid on learning that at the same time he was ministering to the people of Abrezzo, in Tuscany, Italy, a goodly number of the town's inhabitants were continuing to make offerings at a font near a spring, within a grove, at the foot of the hill of Putigliano which was sacred to Apollo. Although it is unclear how much of the font remained at the time, or what condition it was in, it is likely that at least some of the pagan monument remained in place because of the recorded destruction of it that followed. In 1425, many persons continued to visit the font, called Fonte Tenta, to make offerings in order to be healed of various illnesses; it "was the resort of enchanters and witches, who gave out that the water had miraculous healing powers." According to Johann Joseph von Görres (1776-1848), certain persons also continued to consult an oracle of Apollo there at the font in the fifteenth century. When Bernardino first tried to destroy the site in 1425, so many protested that he was "expelled from Arezzo with every circumstance of indignity, and forbidden to return to the city." However, after three years, with a new, more zealously Christian government in place, Bernardino was welcomed back to Arezzo. A short time after Easter, 1428, he and his flock stormed Fonte Tenta, destroyed it, and set up a cross where the font to Apollo had been. Ultimately, the Church of Santa Maria delle Grazie would be built on its ruins.

Although typically regarded as mere poetic device, it would rather seem that certain references to Apollo in the correspondence of Thomas Jefferson Hogg (1792-1862) and other early nineteenth-century writers may in fact, as Patricia Merivale suggests in *Pan the Goat-God: His Myth in Modern Times* (1969), speak to the emergence of a private, NeoPagan cult. This cult, as Merivale's title indicates, centered on Pan, but it appears that Dionysus and Apollo may have also been revered by members. Reference to "Dithyrambic," a dithyramb being a hymn to Dionysus/Bacchus, in the context of speaking of rites "consecrated to the only true gods" may indicate reverence of this god. In a June 15, 1821 letter to Percy Bysshe Shelley (1792-1822), Hogg wrote of a walk he had recently taken with Thomas Love Peacock (1785-1866), "I need hardly add that we propitiated the far-darting King by a garland and an inscription, in Bisham Wood, which we hope to show you some day. SMINTHEEI." Merivale points out that both the "far-darting King" and "SMINTHEEI" refer to Apollo, with the former being an epithet for him and the latter referring to Smythia, a "town in the Troad sacred to Apollo." Shelley, in response, wrote to Hogg on October 21, 1821: "How much I envy your walks ... i am glad to hear that you do not neglect the rites of the true religion."

Artemis/Diana

Artemis, like her Roman counterpart Diana, is a goddess of the moon – typically the waxing, crescent moon – and of hunting, the protection of animals, midwifery, witchcraft, and the love of women for each other. "The cult of Artemis," Frank R. Trombley relates, "proved exceptionally difficult to eradicate." Diana continued to be revered in the Middle Ages in places in Europe influenced by Romans. In some cases, it is difficult to say whether Church authorities were troubled by the cult of Diana or of a local goddess who reminded them of her.

The Church's tendency to discuss the reverence of Diana (or, alternatively, a local goddess the Church found synonymous with, or identified as, Diana) in connection with "witchcraft" – whether to compare or contrast them – appears to have commenced sometime between the fourth and the early tenth century CE.

St. Taurinus (d. 412 CE?) allegedly Christianized the inhabitants of Evreux in Normandy, France. At that time, Diana, whom Taurinus called "Satan," allegedly vacated her temple in the form of an "Ethiopian, dark as soot, with a long beard, and fire issuing from his mouth." Nineteenth-century inhabitants of Evreux continued to claim to see this black hypostasis of Diana/Satan, whom they called "the Goblin." Around the same time, one of the earliest descriptions of witches in non-Classical Europe is found in a tale concerning St. Germanus of Auxerre (a.k.a. St. Germain, d. 448). One night in France, after he'd finished dining and was about to retire, he noticed that servants were busily preparing another table. When he asked who would be dining so late, the servants responded, "the good women that walk by night." Later, he watched as many persons arrived and sat down to eat. He learned, however, that this was a gathering of spirits or what we might at present call "astral bodies," as it happened that at the same hour he witnessed the guests dining, they were, in terms of their physical bodies, asleep (or perhaps in trance) in their beds.

During the sixth century in what is now France, Caesarius of Arles (d. 543) complained that many peasants continued to worship Diana; unsurprisingly, he referred to her as the "demon Dianum." She was especially revered at that time by women seeking successful childbirth. Offerings to her included "sandals, headband[s], a scented lock of hair, [and] belt[s]." Also in the sixth century, Gregory of Tours (*c.* 539-594) bemoaned the fact that many persons persisted in worshipping Diana in Trier, on the banks of the Moselle River in Germany. A shrine to her there was destroyed by St. Wulfilaich (d. *c.* 594). St. Samson (d. 565), the bishop of Dol, Brittany, witnessed a troop of women, led by a hirsute sorceress holding a hunting spear – undoubtedly a reference to Diana – who seemed to be flying through a forest.

St. Eligius, the seventh-century bishop of Noyon, continued to struggle against paganism; "[of] his supposed surviving homilies, one is especially notable for his warnings against pagan superstitions [such as worshipping] Diana." Like Caesarius of Arles, he referred to her as a "demon." Eligius was deeply troubled by women worshipping Diana who convened in the woods. Among continental Germanic peoples, the Alemannic laws of the early seventh century "forbade the burning of *strigae*"; at this time, "*striga*" was a multivalent term embracing female human followers of Diana as well as vampiric supernatural beings who devoured human males. The burning of *strigae* was prohibited because to burn them meant that they were believed to actually exist, and according to the authors of Alemannic law, they did not. To believe in them constituted a form of heresy. This belief, and the consequent determination to prohibit the burning of *strigae* was seconded by Rothari (*c.* 606-652), King of the Lombards, in 643. As Wolfgang Behringer explains in *Witches and Witch-Hunts: A Global History*, "Christians must not believe that women devour a human being from the inside...and therefore supposed witches (*strigae*) must not be killed." Also in the seventh century, a Coptic magical text invoked Artemis together with other Greek and Egyptian divinities. As the seventh century drew to a close, the missionary bishop St. Kilian (d. *c.* 689) was greatly troubled to find that "Diana was the chief goddess of Würzburg" in what is now Germany; he was martyred as he tried to convert the east Franks "from their worship of Diana," who insisted that they would continue to worship the gods of their ancestors.

According to Geneviève Saint-Martin in *L'Auvergne: Des Monstres, des sorciers, et des dieux* (2001), Diana continued to be worshipped in the late eighth or early ninth century CE in the Auvergne region of France, especially in the vicinity of the Cantal Mountains and the Santoire Valley. The village of Dienne appears to have been named after the goddess. In the vicinity of the village is the Rocher Laqueille, a temple of Diana is believed to have stood until the reign of Charlemagne (768-814), when he ordered its destruction. Similarly, in the Ardèche department, in the Vivarais region of southeastern France, the village of Desaignes appears to have been named after Diana, from Disannia, a "deformation of the name of the goddess of the hunt, Diana." We will return to Artemis/Diana when we discuss her cult in the context of witchcraft.

Ares/Mars

Ares is the Greek god of war, as is his Roman counterpart, Mars. Especially as Mars, he seems to have also been associated with male fertility. Reverence of Ares/Mars persisted in Roman Britain into Late Antiquity. The *Canons* of the Council of Trullo, held in Constantinople in 691/692 CE, suggest that Mars, the god of war, may have still been revered in Greece and Asia Minor into the late seventh century, that is, into the Early Middle Ages. Canon 62 states: "We have determined that ... the festival celebrated on the first of March [is] to be removed completely from the life of the faithful." This was a Roman festival which celebrated several deities including Mars. As Richard Trexler notes in *Public Life in Renaissance Florence* (1980), "the statue of Mars was wreathed and laurelled in [Florence] in the fourteenth century." He stresses that this statue was considered a "pagan image" and not a pagan "idol;" while 'idols' were envisaged as being "without spirit, without efficacy," 'images' were, like that of Mars, considered as possessing "participatory intelligence."

Athena/Minerva

Athena is a Greek goddess of virginity, war, and wisdom, and was the patron of the city of Athens. Minerva, her Roman counterpart, shares certain traits in common with her but differs from her in numerous ways. They share being goddesses of wisdom; unlike Athena, however, Minerva is neither a goddess of war nor a supporter of patriarchy. Minerva is, other than a goddess of wisdom, primarily associated with commerce, crafts, and mathematics. Over the centuries, however, Athena and Minerva became increasingly meshed in regard to their personae and attributes.

From around the first through fourth centuries, a grand temple to Minerva, whom the Romans identified with the Gallic goddess Sulis, stood at Bath, England; the temple complex included the famed thermal baths. Unfortunately, the complex was destroyed by Christians, probably in the fourth century. The head of the statue of Minerva was severed from its body, perhaps in an effort to destroy its "demonic" power. Temple facades were used as paving-stones, and the site of the temple became a garbage dump. The baths, however, continued to be used, experiencing periods of refurbishment and decline. Stephen J. Yeates, in *The Tribe of the Witches: The Religion of the Dobunni and Hwicce* (2008), notes that "Nennius, AD 796 to 820, referred to the hot springs in the kingdom of the *Hwicce* as the third wonder of Britain, thus indicating their continued veneration into the ninth century AD."

In the sixth century, Isidore of Seville (*c.* 560-636) referred to Minerva as a goddess of weaving, and Martin of Braga (*c.* 515/520-580) denounced women weavers' invocations of the goddess: "The fact that women invoke Minerva at their looms ... what is this if not evil worshipping?" St. Eligius, the bishop of Noyon, continued to struggle against paganism in seventh-century France: "Let no woman dare to name Minerva ... while weaving or dyeing or doing any other work, but let them wish to be in the grace of Christ in all their work." At this time, the Goddess continued to receive offerings and sacrifices. The *Canons* of the Council of Trullo, held in Constantinople in 691/692 CE, suggest that Minerva may have still been revered in Greece and Asia Minor in the late seventh century. Canon 62 forbids celebration of a March 1 festival honoring several deities including Minerva. Also in the seventh century, a Coptic magical text invoked Athena together with other Greek and Egyptian divinities.

In the *Geoponika*, a tenth-century collection of agricultural lore that remained popular throughout the Renaissance, an ancient cure for headache continued to be recommended: "The inscribing of the word *Athena* on the leaf of the olive, and fixing the leaf on the head with a thread, has indeed been useful, and it has, as a charm, cured the headache."

Moreover, Minerva's archetypal status may have been enriched when Saxons brought not only their brand of Christianity but also tales of, and perhaps cult practice of, certain Germanic goddesses of weaving with them to the British Isles. As a result of cross-pollination of Celtic, Greco-Roman, and Germanic traditions that may have been occurring since the sixth century or so – as well as, perhaps, the influence of Byzantine Christian iconography – as evidenced by bracteates, Minerva may have become linked to the Classical Parcae, the Celtic goddesses Sulis and Brigid, and to various Germanic goddesses associated with weaving, including Freyja, Frigga, Holda, Horn, and the Norns, as well as others whose names have been lost. Moreover, these associations may have in turn become linked to female seers, perhaps practitioners of *seiðr* divination and magic, and to Valkyries. Warnings, typically more indirect with the passage of time, against reverence of Minerva, especially among female weavers, continued into the eleventh century.

This persistent association of Minerva and weaving returns us to medieval Bath. Bath experienced a renascence when it was purchased by the physician and churchman John of Tours (d. 1122). Bath became recognized as a center of the fabric trade and became a popular venue for fairs; among products displayed there, "Bath Beaver," a thick wool fabric with a shaggy nap, used on caps and coats, became as popular as the fairs themselves. Meanwhile, medieval writers including Hugh of St. Victor (*c.* 1078-1141), Ranulf Higdon (*c.* 1280-1363), John of Trevisa (*c.* 1326-*c.* 1402), and John Lydgate (c. 1371-1449) kept the memory of Minerva, especially as a goddess of dyeing, spinning, and weaving, alive.

In the mid-twelfth century, the philosopher and astrologer Bernard Silvestris (*c.* 1085-*c.* 1178) penned his *Cosmographia*. Although his work appears to acknowledge the Biblical God – it is not altogether clear whom he refers to as God, although he does identify the highest deity as male – he focuses on several goddesses who oversee the creation of the universe. Silvestris describes these goddesses as follows: "I call 'gods' those beings whose presence is ever attendant upon God." One of these goddesses who works directly with the high, male god is Minerva. A handful of scholars including Dermot Moran (1998) and Mark Kauntze (2009) have argued that this work is Christian rather than pagan, their evidence is not impressive. Moran describes this work as "allegorical," in an effort to argue that the work is Christian; it is not written, however, very differently from the Biblical book of Genesis, yet I doubt that Moran would describe that narrative as "allegorical." He clearly deploys the term to dissuade us from recognizing Silvestris' account as an alternative spiritual or religious text explaining creation that contrasts considerably with the Abrahamic narrative. The account is actually much more reminiscent of a Gnostic pagan or Gnostic pagano-Christian narrative than to the Biblical one. Early in the text, Silvestris identifies Minerva with a goddess named Noys and addresses her as "supreme image of unfailing life, God born of God, substance of truth, issue of eternal deliberation, my true Minerva." A bit later, Silvestris has one of the other goddesses,

Silva (also called Nature), make a suggestion to Minerva in regard to the task of creating the universe. Immediately after doing so, Silva apologizes, saying: "It is for the universe that I, Nature, appeal; it is enough for me if I may behold the birth of the universe and its creatures, I seek no more…I blush to have sought to instruct [you,] Minerva."

Also during the mid-twelfth century, the translators Hermann of Carinthia, who was a Slav, and Robert of Ketton, who translated the *Qur'an* and Arabic works on astrology, astronomy, and other subjects from Arabic into Latin, sojourned at Beziers and Toulouse. In Roman times, both of these cities were associated with Minerva. A great temple to Minerva stood in Toulouse. According to some, the basilica of Notre-Dame-de-la-Daurade in Toulouse was erected over the site of a temple to Apollo; others, however, maintain that in the late fourth or early fifth century CE, Bishop, now Saint, Exuperius (d. 410 CE) transformed the temple of Minerva at Toulouse to a church honoring the Virgin Mary the "Golden." The Black Madonna of la Daurade, by far the most popular icon of the basilica, may refer in part to Minerva/Athena, and particularly to her alleged African origins. To return to Hermann of Carinthia and Robert of Ketton, while we might consider their conversation in Hermann's *De Essentiis* (*The Essences*) merely poetic, I think this may be, to some extent, a reductive interpretation. For two men who seem to have taken themselves, and to have been taken, quite seriously, and given the locales in which they were sojourning, and the astrological texts to which they devoted a great amount of time, it may be that when Hermann records Robert as saying to him, "Now, since the divine hand itself has restored you in answer to my prayer, do not doubt the presence of the goddesses!," we are meant to take him at his word. The "goddesses" appear to refer to Minerva and to the Atlantides, or, Hesperides, the daughters of Atlas (Aegle, Erytheia, Hestia, Arethusa, and occasionally, Hespera), who guard the "golden apples Hera received from Gaea at her marriage to Zeus."

In this conversation, Hermann is concerned that he may be punished for revealing certain mysteries. He remarks: "While we went forth from our inner sanctuaries into the public festival of Minerva, the multitude of people milling around were gaping at us…[at what] our most earnest labor had acquired for us from the depths of the treasures of the Arabs."

Robert responds, "I certainly do not fear what case there might be against you as long as you are in the hands of the goddesses." This response no doubt helped Hermann to feel more secure about revealing certain mysteries, but it was a dream vision of the goddess that convinced him of the value of his and Robert's work. While he slept, the "lofty goddess approached from on high and touched [his] head with her right hand." "The sight of her," he relates, "like the Sun suddenly blazing forth, at first made me completely dumbfounded, and only gradually did I then become accustomed to it. She said to him, "Wake up,…and look around." He tells us: "When I had recognized her, I fell before the feet of the goddess and said, 'O Queen of all divine spirits, show me what your foster-child can do!' 'Arise,' she said, 'and follow me.' "

Hermann expresses his concern to Minerva that, in his estimation, between the two of them, Robert is her more intimate spiritual son, but she disagrees, insisting that she has created the pair of them to be "one man." She then bestows Hermann with "a counting-board and a rod, then scales, and finally a certain light-giving lamp penetrating everything." These tools may represent, respectively, mathematics, graphic arts (or possibly designating ceremonial space), music, and astrology/astronomy. Minerva then instructs him to write down and publish the mysteries that are known to him: "Take up these things, I charge you with this duty: do not give them out bit by bit...but distribute what has been given to you with a liberal hand – without any hesitation. For our wealth increases when it is given freely."

Hermann then tells Robert that when the latter reads what he has written, he will realize that he has been led to do so by the goddess: "When you have inspected [this text], you will realize that I have not lacked the help of the goddesses."

In 1203, at Constantinople, a thirty-foot tall bronze statue of Athena was destroyed by a Byzantine mob due to the sacred power it was still thought to possess. Prior to this event, many commoners had accepted the statue as a goddess or symbol of the earth.

Minerva's memory also survived in the late-thirteenth-century construction of the Church of Santa Maria sopra Minerva at Rome, a name clearly meant to suggest that the Virgin of Christianity both corresponded to and had triumphed over the ancient goddess.

When Hermann (above) speaks of participating in the "public festival of Minerva," he may be referring to a celebration in her honor that was documented in the fourteenth century but a form of which may have also occurred during his own. We know that in 1323 and 1325, *jeux floraux*, "floral games," were held on the first of May in honor of either the Virgin Mary, Minerva, or both, and that poets who won poetry competitions at this festival were honored with images of violets or eglantine fashioned from gold or silver and/or gold or silver images of Minerva. In the mid-sixteenth century, the poet Pierre de Ronsard (1524-1585) won the competition and received a statue of Minerva. Some time later, the poet François Maynard (1582-1646) won the competition, but when he failed to receive his statue of the goddess, wrote "On a Minerva of Silver, Promised but Not Given."

Quite possibly by way of the web of associations linking the goddess to Celtic and Germanic goddesses, Minerva, commencing around the twelfth century, came to be linked, together with Diana and Herodias, to alleged witches and their concepts and practices. Both the French demonologist Jean Bodin (1529-1596) and the scholar Reginald Scot (*c*. 1538-1599) connected the cult of Minerva to that of Diana, fairies, and witches, with Scot writing of women who were thought to "fly away," or who believed that they did so, to meet and dance with "Diana and Minerva;" "to dance with the fairies ... to banquet or dance with Minerva."

Chaucer (1342-1400) evokes this web of associations in the *Canterbury Tales* (1386), in the figure of the Wife of Bath. Like Minerva, she is a weaver: "In making cloth she showed so great a bent/ She bettered those of Ypres and of Ghent." And like Minerva, she is fiercely independent, a sort of warrior, with "a hat/ As broad as a buckler or a shield," ending her tale with a wish that women be sent "husbands meek and young and fresh in bed" and cursing men "who won't be governed by their wives." Moreover, she is, like the latter-day Minerva, linked to witchcraft. She regrets the passing of "fairy folk" and disdains the "holy friars [who] seem to have purged the air." She is a crone who practices amatory magic: "And knew the remedies for love's mischances/ An art in which she knew the oldest dances." In "Chaucer's Weaving Wife," Thomas Jay Garbáty expands this web of associations to include not only the characters of literary works – La Vieille in the *Roman de la Rose*, the practitioner of amatory magic in *Tristan and Isolde*, and Dame Houdée in *Pamphile et Galatée* – but also of another goddess linked to witchcraft: Holda. Speaking of the bawdy aspect of the Wife's persona, Garbáty writes: "the ancestor of the bawd, in the old romances, was the benign sorceress who was in the confidence of the girl and her lover and who taught her protégée the arts of love ... . The old woman had to know all the occult tricks of her amorous trade."

In 1576, John Stow reported in his 1598 *Survey of London*, an unexpected treasure was discovered when workers were digging for clay to make bricks in Lollesworth Field, or Spitalfield, in Bishopsgate Ward in London. They discovered, buried in the field, many Roman clay pots, cups, dishes, coins, and oil lamps, but perhaps the most intriguing find was a sculpture of Pallas Athena/Minerva. Such discoveries may have inspired Renaissance idealization of Pallas Athena/Minerva as the ideal hero: with virgin-like purity, one sacrifices one's life for the 'good fight.' She differs from the goddess Venus in centering her life on labor and battle rather than on love. While Minerva shares the month of March with Mars, she differs from him in resorting to violence only when absolutely necessary. Indeed, to a certain extent, she exemplifies the adage that 'the pen is mightier than the sword,' in being envisioned as a patron of writers. Especially in relationship to the Medici family, she became symbolic of wise governance, with Medicean Florence coming to be viewed as the "New Athens." As such, she was regarded as the patron of jurists.

Veneration of Minerva emerged once more during the Enlightenment and French Revolution.

Cybele

Figurines of a goddess flanked by lions suggest that the worship of Cybele, or Kybele (Kubela, or Kubele, in Greece), the "Mother of the Gods," may have originated as early as 6,000 BCE, but was, with greater certainty, worshipped by Phrygians in the eighth century BCE. Trombley relates that the worship of Cybele "was deeply rooted and was still practiced in the isolated mountain districts of eighth-century Caria" in southwestern Anatolia (present-day Turkey). Her cult was brought to Greece near the sixth century BCE, to Rome circa 204 BCE, and to Spain by the Romans, where her worship was grafted onto the worship of an indigenous goddess. Cybele is a goddess of the "regenerative forces of nature, of animals as well as vegetation." She is also associated with ecstatic dance and is a patron of transgender male-to-female persons, who served as her *gallae* priestesses. She, like Venus, has a male consort named Attis, who bears resemblance to Adonis, the consort of Venus.

In Spain, with Christianization, Cybele was hybridized with Santa Eulalia de Boveda, a patron saint of prophecy and of birds, especially of geese, who is fêted on February 12th. The saint's church in Allariz, Spain was built on the ruins of Cybele's temple. Still later, Cybele/Santa Eulalia became a religio-carnivalesque figure, represented in carnival form by a woman or large figure wearing a crown, dressed in pink with a blue and red cape, and holding a lyre.

An ancient charm to stop field-mice from damaging crops that was made known to, and assumedly practiced by, farmers in the tenth and later centuries, thanks to the extremely popular medieval compilation *Geoponika*, read: "I adjure you mice that are found here…I give you such-and-such a piece of land…But if I find you here again, I will take the Mother of the Gods with me and will cut you into seven pieces."

For centuries, an altar in the Church of San Michele (St. Michael) in Borgo in Pisa, Italy, unproblematically displayed images of the narrative of Cybele and her consort Attis.

In *The Mother Goddess in Italian Renaissance Art*, Edith Balas states that Cybele "experienced a brief but important revival during the Renaissance" and that documents concerning her cult "preserved in the Medici library, the Vatican library, and private manuscript collections" played a significant part in the development of Humanism. Cybele's iconography, she asserts, influenced Michelangelo, Pinturicchio, Andrea Riccio, Giulio Romano, Pirro Ligorio, and other painers and sculptors of the Renaissance. She also notes that Cybele and other pagan deities wielded an influence on Renaissance astrology. Cybele was associated with the earth, while her beloved Attis was linked to the moon. Moreover, both Cybele and Jupiter were patrons of the sign of Leo. Balas also asserts that Cybele and Venus were both frequently equated in the Renaissance with the Virgin Mary.

Cristiano Grottanelli, in "Archaic Forms of Rebellion and Their Religious Background," suggests that the memory of Cybele and her *gallae* priestesses persisted in the actions of certain radical groups, including laborers of the fifteenth through nineteenth centuries who stole "deer from manorial forests (1451)," sacked "a ship full grain that was to be exported in spite of a grain crisis (1629)," destroyed "field boundaries (1760-1779)," and demolished "weaving machines (1812)." Grottanelli explains that some of the men involved in these actions "dressed in women's clothes" and that some even dressed as "fairies."

Demeter/Ceres

Demeter is a goddess of the earth and of agriculture, specifically, of the cultivation of grains. She is also a patron of the mother-daughter relationship. She and her daughter, Persephone/Proserpina) are the subject of both a myth and a Mystery religion. While a maiden, Persephone was abducted to the Underworld by the god Hades when he lusted after her. There, he married her and made her his queen. Her mother, devastated, bargained with Hades to let her daughter return to the earth for half of the year, while remaining with him the remainder of the year, with their narrative becoming a seasonal myth. From this mythic narrative, the Eleusinian Mysteries emerged. The Roman Ceres – hence, "cereal" – is likewise a goddess of agriculture and specifically of grains.

The goddess Demeter/Ceres appears in John Langley's 1546 combined translation of and commentary on the Renaissance bestseller, *De Rerum Inventoribus* (1499), by Polydore Vergil. This work demonstrates Renaissance acknowledgement of the earth-centered roots of folk figures and seasonal rural festivals: "And our midsummer bonfires may seem to have come of the sacrifices of Ceres, Goddess of corn, that men did solemnize with fires, trusting thereby to have more plenty and abundance of corn." About fifty years later, Paul Hentzner, a German traveler, sojourning at Windsor in the summer of 1598, described, in *A Journey into England in the Year 1598*, a harvest rite he observed there which included "an image richly dressed, by which perhaps they would signify Ceres." In this hypostasis as Harvest Queen, Ceres became synonymous with the Earth Goddess. There is no reason to believe that Vergil and Hentzner did not share the connection they made with Ceres with persons celebrating the rites – *they were not privy to Star Trek's "prime directive"* – thus suggesting that persons dwelling in the sixteenth century may have been made aware by Vergil, Hentzner, or others of the ancient name of the Goddess they were celebrating, if they had not already learned this on their own.

In the early seventeenth century, Pierre de Lancre wrote of the maritime industries of the Labourdins: "Now in the Labour almost all the people throw themselves into the inconstant work of the sea .... And although nature has given the earth as nursemaid to all mankind, they prefer ... the cares of the thunderous seas to those of the sweet and serene goddess Ceres."

Although we might read this passage as metaphoric – and certainly, de Lancre's insistence that women who claim to worship Diana cannot be doing so because there is only one God seems to lend support to this interpretation – his equal and somewhat contradictory insistence case that Venus, Hecate, Medea, Circe, and other female deities and legendary women actually existed indicates that he may mean us to read the passage concerning Ceres as indicating actual reverence.

In sixteenth-century Paris, after the destruction of a statue of Isis at Saint-Germain-des-Prés, certain women who had been performing rites at the statue "transferred," as we noted above, their ritualizing to a statue of Ceres found in the faubourg St. Jacques. This statue was housed at the church of the convent of the

Carmelites on the rue d'Enfer in Paris until 1790. The nuns insisted that the statue represented St. Michael the Archangel, and that the iron spikes crowning its head did not signify sheaves of wheat but were simply there to keep birds away. Nonetheless, the statue in fact appears to have represented Demeter/Ceres, and it is thought that her rites continued to be observed by the nuns until the destruction of the church. This data suggests that for over two centuries, and perhaps for a great deal longer, women honored the goddess at the convent.

In 1801, under the auspices of Lord Elgin (Thomas Bruce, 7th Earl of Elgin, 1766-1841), the mineralogist and travel writer Edward Daniel Clarke (1769-1822) and his companion John Marten Cripps (d. 1853), both of Jesus College, Cambridge, carried off, among other treasures, a statue of Demeter at Eleusis, which they deposited in the Fitzwilliam Museum at Cambridge. This might be just one more stolen work of sacred art, save for one thing. Several travelers documented the anxiety experienced by the people of Eleusis upon the removal of the statue. This anxiety arose not simply because Clarke and Cripps were robbing them of one of their most treasured possessions but also because, according to the documents, revered the Goddess and the sacred or magical potency of her marble image. Sir William Gell (1777-1836), a highly respected archaeologist and early Egyptologist, also of Jesus College, wrote of this statue in 1801: "The inhabitants have retained some notion of the gifts of this Goddess, for they affirm that the fertility of the land will cease if the statue be taken away." The statue was taken away less than three months later. George Jones (1800-1870), an American Episcopalian chaplain known for his proselytizing, his sojourn in Japan and other journeys, and his book *Sketches of Naval Life* (1829), also wrote (some years later) of this statue and event – with a pronounced disdain for the people of Eleusis. "I have met with no people whose superstition is so childish and absurd." He describes men who were hired to carry this statue and others to the ship that would carry them to England dropping the statues, running away, and crying out that the "marble was complaining of its removal." "Dr. Clarke," he adds, "had great difficulty in procuring the Cambridge Ceres [note the terminology, the 'Cambridge Ceres'], at Eleusis, from a superstitious regard [for] the statue." Intriguingly, Jones notes that one man of Eleusis was "greatly alarmed" because he saw "tears ... flowing down the face" of a statue of St. Demetrius, "who must be unwilling to part with it," presumably referring to the statue of the Goddess after whom the saint was named.

During the Greek revolt against the Ottoman Turks in the early nineteenth century, a secret society called the Philike Hetairia, the Society of Friends, was founded to play a part in the struggle. Although some have doubted the seriousness of its members in regard to ancient beliefs and practices, members of one of the highest initiatory levels of the society were linked to Demeter by way of being named the "Priests of Eleusis."

Dionysus/Bacchus

Dionysus (or, Dionysos) is a god of wine, theatre, male fertility, and the cycle of "growth, death, and rebirth." He is also associated with bisexuality and effeminacy, or what we might today term "genderqueer" or "nonbinary" behavior or identity. Edward Tripp relates, "His rites involved a mystical communion in which, during moments of religious frenzy induced with the aid of wine, music, and dancing, his worshipers became identified with the god," with this altered or entheogenic state of consciousness being referred to as *entheos*. The richness of Dionysus's persona is perhaps best expressed by Euripides (d. 406 BCE) in his tragedy *The Bacchae* (or, *Bakkhai*).

Augustine of Hippo, in *The City of God*, relates that the god Dionysus was "said to have shown the vine to his host in Attica," that is, to have walked among humankind as a teacher of wine-making. The *Canons* of the Council of Trullo suggest that Dionysus/Bacchus may have still been revered in Greece and Asia Minor in the late seventh century CE, particularly during the Brumalia. Canon 62 states: "[O]ne is not permitted to ... invoke the name of the abhorrent Dionysus" when "they squeeze out the wine in the presses." "Brumalia" (or, Bromalia, Broumalla, Bruma; also, Ambrosia) like "Hiemalia," signifies the "winter feast" and refers to the winter solstice. The Brumalia lasted from about November 24 til December 25. Although it referred primarily to winter, the Brumalia was also held on February 18 and August 15 and/or September 18. John Lemprière offers this description of the Brumalia in his *Bibliotheca Classica; or, Classical Dictionary* (1792):

> The Brumalia or Bacchanalia were feasts in honour of Bacchus...These were feasts of great importance, but were attended by great licentiousness and other excesses. Their form and solemnity were first introduced into Greece from Egypt by a certain Melampus...The worshippers imitated in their dress and actions...Bacchus. They clothed themselves in fawns' skins, fine linen, and mitres; they carried thyrsi, drums, pipes, and flutes, and crowned themselves with garlands of ivy, vine, fir... Some imitated Silenus, Pan, and the Satyrs, by the uncouth manner of their dress, and their fantastical motions. Some rode upon asses, and others drove the goats to slaughter for the sacrifice. ...[B]oth sexes joined in the solemnity, and ran about the hills and country, nodding their heads, dancing ...and...crying aloud, *Evoe Bacche! Io ! Io! Evoe! Iacche ! Io Bacche! Evohe !*...[T]here followed a number of persons carrying sacred vessels...After these came a select number of noble virgins, carrying little baskets of gold filled with all sorts of fruits. Serpents were sometimes put in the baskets...After the virgins, followed a company of men carrying poles, at the end of which were fastened phalloi. The heads of these men, who were called *phallophoroi*, were crowned with ivy and violets, and their faces covered with other herbs. They marched singing songs upon the occasion of the festivals, called *phallica asmata*. Next to the *phallophoroi*

followed the *ithyphalloi* in women's apparel, with white striped garments reaching to the ground; their heads were decked with garlands, and on their hands they wore gloves composed of flowers. …Among the Romans both sexes promiscuously joined in the celebration during the darkness of night.[21]

Thus, the reverence of Dionysus/Bacchus persisted into the late seventh century and, as we shall see, beyond it, in spite of Christianization.

Although one must of course be suspicious of hostile, here, Christian, sources, the narratives of two brothers who briefly came to rule the Byzantine Empire in the early tenth century suggest that they may have – perhaps as a secret family tradition – worshipped Dionysus. While the Brumalia had, to a certain extent, undergone secularization, Leo VI's (b. 866-d. 912; r. 886-912) celebration of it did not go unnoticed. A ceremony within the fête appears to have been a sensuous ritual bath including flowers floating on the water, and the emperor proudly celebrated it in the magnificent bath he had had built. It seems that Leo's brother and successor, Alexander (b. 870-d. 913; r. 912-913), may have performed a ritual to Dionysus and other deities and ancestors shortly before he died, probably in late February 913, perhaps in a belated attempt to ask that his cancer be healed. He is said to have made offerings to Dionysus and others by way of dressing bronze statues of them and celebrating by torchlight a private form of the Anthesteria. This festival honored Dionysus, the dead, and the maturing of wine from the previous harvest.

In the tenth-century *Geoponika*, vintners were told to wear, in honor of Bacchus, crowns of ivy when they were pruning grapevines. Likewise, they were told not to plant cabbages near grapevines because they remind Dionysus of his enemy Lykurgos. In *Observations on the Popular Antiquities of Great Britain* (1849), we learn that the Vinalia, honoring Dionysus/Bacchus in early November, was appropriated by the Church and transformed into Martinmas (November 11), honoring St. Martin. It remained, however, a day of feasting and of drinking. In the early thirteenth century, Alexandre de Villedieu reported that Dionysus/Bacchus continued to be worshipped at Orléans.

A group of seventeenth-century artists, the Bentveughels, appear to have founded a cult to Bacchus. An early eighteenth-century poem from *The Compleat Vintner* that speaks of love, marriage, Bacchus, and wine reads:

What priest can join two lovers' hands,
But wine must seal the marriage-bands?
As if celestial wine was thought
Essential to the sacred knot,
And that each bridegroom and his bride
Believ'd they were not firmly ty'd
Till Bacchus, with his bleeding tun,
Had finished what the priest begun.[22]

On October 9, 1703 a scholar walking in Enghien (since 1850, Enghien-les-Bains), a suburb of Paris, noticed that workers in a vineyard there, when entering the *pressoir* (here referring to a large room containing a device used to extract juice from crushed grapes during winemaking), performed a "genuflexion in front of a statuette of Bacchus that was sitting atop a barrel." This would appear to echo the rite banned by the Council of Trullo in the late seventh century,"[O]ne is not permitted to … invoke the name of the abhorrent Dionysus" when "they squeeze out the wine in the presses."

On October 7, 1730, Abbé Jean Lebeuf (1687-1760) witnessed a rite at Vitry-sur-Seine in Paris, in which seven local vintners held a great fête to celebrate the wine harvest and Bacchus. The number seven was significant because it was his sacred number and he was thought to have six close companions. It is conceivable that these rites represented a continuation as well as an innovation of the ancient celebration of the Oschophoria (also called the Ramalia in ancient Rome), when grapevines "were carried in honour of Bacchus or…Ariadne…in Autumn when the grapes were ripe." In some places, the rites were probably masked as rites honoring St. Dionysius/St. Denis.

The Bacchic rite continued to be held at Vitry into the nineteenth century. In 1856, Jacques-Antoine Dulaure and Camille Leynadier, in *Histoire physique, civile et morale de Paris depuis les premiers temps historiques*, reported that this ceremony was also being performed at Bacharach, a town on the Rhine in western Germany.

According to Charles Magne in "Les divinités païennes sur la Rive Gauche de l'ancienne Lutèce" (1902), vintners in the Loire Valley practiced a similar rite into his day. Near 1906, Mary Hamilton reported that vintners of Naxos continued to describe the wine they made as the "wine of Dionysos."

Hera/Juno

Hera is a goddess of marriage, jealousy, and the cycle of life, death, and rebirth, as well as a "patroness of the fertility of the earth," Also sometimes a goddess of storms, she has been called the "Queen of Heaven."

The *Canons* of the Council of Trullo, held in Constantinople in 691/692 CE, suggest that Hera/Juno may have continued to be revered in Greece and Asia Minor in the late seventh century, as Canon 62 refers to the persistence of a March 1 festival in her honor, especially in her hypostasis as Juno Lucina, a goddess of pregnancy, childbearing, and motherhood. (Lucina was, of course, also linked to the goddess Artemis/Diana.) For this reason, the festival was called the Matronalia. It is notable that her Roman hypostasis as Juno Sospita, or Savior Juno, bears a rather uncanny resemblance to the figure of a shaman, speaks to wild nature and also to warriorhood in a way that other manifestations do not, at least not as dramatically, and suggests possible correspondences with both Artemis/Diana and Athena/Minerva, as well as, perhaps, to Pan/Faunus and Heracles/Hercules. As Juno Sospes, she is depicted as "clad in a goatskin, with the animal's head and horns drawn over her head to form a helmet." She wears elfin shoes "turned up at the toes" and is "armed with spear and shield."

Hera/Juno continued to be revered in the Middle Ages and into the Renaissance. In various parts of medieval Europe, the figure of Hera appears to have become hybridized with female divinities of Germanic origins, possibly including Freyja, Erde, and Hertha (possibly originating in Nerthus). During the Middle Ages or Renaissance, Hera also came to be associated with a group of goddesses including Holda, Perchta, and others. Indeed, her name may have contributed to the emergence of one of them: Tante Arie.

Many persons, it seems, came to envision Hera or this amalgam of goddesses as cross between Santa Claus and Mother Goose; as Gobelinus Persona (1358-1421), a monk of Paderborn, Germany, recounted, each winter she flew over the countryside "between Christmas and Twelfth-day, dispensing earthly goods in abundance." Germans named her Vrö Here. This may account for the place-name of Eresberg, later changed to Stadtberg. It is conceivable that a connection between Hera/Juno and St. Nicholas (who would morph into Santa Claus) commenced to develop in or around the tenth century, when legends about the saint were transcribed and when columns from the ruins of the temple of Juno Sospita were incorporated into the Church of San Nicola in Carcere at Rome.

Hermes/Mercury

Hermes, like his Roman counterpart Mercury, performs several roles; he is perhaps best known as the messenger of the gods, an intercessory between deities and humans. This role links him to two others: "guide of travelers" and psychopomp or "guide of souls," whereby he carries the souls of the deceased to the afterlife. A trickster and "patron of merchants, thieves, and rogues," he is also a god of "athletic contests and games" and, some say, of astronomy. He is, moreover, a masterful magician, carrying not a caduceus *per se* but rather a magical, wealth-bringing staff.

His worship persisted into the seventh century in France and Germany, perhaps especially in the Alsace-Lorraine region; also at this time, pagans continued to visit temples to Mercury, Jupiter, and Apollo at Rouen. Eight centuries later, an Italian, a rural peasant named Giovanni (surname unknown), who sojourned with his wife and children in France for a time, especially at Lyon, healed many people and met King Louis XI (r. 1461-1483), to whom he gave a magic sword, a magic shield, and a magic mirror. Giovanni did not claim, as more than a few did, to be a manifestation of the Son of (the Biblical) God; rather, he claimed to be an incarnation of the god Mercury. He also believed himself to have been, in another incarnation, a disciple of the magus Apollonius of Tyana, and "like him, he wore an iron chain around his neck." After sojourning in France for awhile, he vanished from sight.

The Moirai, or Fates

The Moirai (or, Moerae, Moirae), or Fates, have been revered in Greece for over 2,500 years. The Romans named them the Fata or Parcae. When three in number, their names were Clotho, Lachesis, and Atropos, three goddesses who prophesy destiny, who spin, measure, and finally cut the thread of life. As James Rennell Rodd (1892) explains, although the Moirai are typically thought to number three, on the island of Zakynthos (or, Zante), they number twelve. The Moirai are usually depicted as black-garmented crones.

In some places, with Christianization, the three Moirai transformed into Jesus Christ, the Virgin Mary, and John the Baptist. Elsewhere, they were collapsed into a single angel, including a hypostasis as the Angel of Death.

The Reverend William Jones (1755-1821), educated at Oxford, in his "Reflections on the Growth of Heathenism among Modern Christians," was quite troubled by the presence, at the end of the eighteenth century, by a statue, in a church in the village of Wharton, near Kettering, in Northamptonshire, of the Fates. He observed that while the baptistry was all but hidden, the statue of three "elegant figures as large as…life, of the three Fates, Clotho, Lachesis, and Atropos, spinning and clipping the thread of a…man's life," was featured prominently in the church, suggesting, in his view, that paganism was overtaking Christianity.

Women of eighteenth- and nineteenth-century Greece traditionally offered the Moirai "cakes made of honey," depositing them in caves believed inhabited by them, "with a view to hastening marriage." They also performed this rite "in the rock chambers under the Museum Hill at Athens" until they were prevented from doing so; Rennell Rodd (1892) notes that although Edward Dodd, author of *A Classical and Topographical Tour through Greece* (1819), had witnessed this "offering of cakes" in the rock chambers in the first years of the nineteenth century, by his own day, "these female votaries [were] perforce excluded."

In the not too distant past, they were believed to visit a child on the third or fifth night after she or he was born. At this time, the family left the door unlatched, kept a lamp burning, and in the child's room placed a low table with three stools or cushions.

Rodd relates that the Moirai would then appear and commence "writing" the narrative of the child's destiny upon his or her forehead. After they did so, they were treated to a feast. "On the table are set out such dainties as the Fates love," John Cuthbert Lawson (1910) relates, "including always honey…three white almonds, [cakes,] a loaf of bread, … water … and…presents from which the goddesses may choose what they will…such as jewelry and even money [gold in Corfu]."

In *The Dangerous Hour: The Lore of Crisis and Mystery in Rural Greece* (1970), Richard and Eva Blum discovered that the Moirai continued to be revered into the mid-twentieth century. When a baby was born, women visited a site sacred to the Moirai, offered them a banquet of desserts, and prayed that they would bless the child.

Charles Stewart, in *Demons and the Devil: Moral Imagination in Modern Greek Culture* (1991), points out that belief in the Moirai persisted into the late twentieth century. Like the Blums, he notes, drawing attention to studies conducted from the 1950s through the 1980s, that the Moirai were thought during this period to "bear good tidings, as well as evil." He writes, "One should leave milk and honey out for the *moíres* [i.e., the Moirai] when they visit the house to decide an infant's fate three days after its birth." Needless to say, the Fates are also involved in death as an aspect of one's destiny; a lyric sung by "the widow of a beloved café owner who was killed [in a] car" accident indicates that his death was in part brought about by the Moirai, with the place he died having the uncanny name of Mavromoíres, the "Black Fates."

Noctiluca

Noctiluca, the "sovereign queen of the night," is the "Goddess of Nocturnal Light." Her name can also mean "Night Shiner," "Glowworm" or "Firefly," and she has given her name to bioluminescent creatures. Noctiluca is a goddess of life, death, fertility, bodies of water, night, and the moon. Noctiluca is conceived as an avatar of the goddess Diana akin to the Greek Selene and the Roman Luna; a temple to her as Diana Noctiluca stood on the Palatine in ancient Rome. She was invoked at the Secular Games and was celebrated in May or June with a ritual that has been compared to the Eleusinian Mysteries of Demeter and Persephone/Proserpina that culminated with the chant, "The Goddess of Night becomes Light!" She was also celebrated at a Feast of the Sun and Moon on August 28th and possibly on March 31st.

In Iberia/Spain, she became conflated with an indigenous Iberian goddess whose name has been lost, in part because Iberians typically kept the names of their deities secret, as well as with the Phoenician Tanit and/or the Semitic Astarte, who had earlier been conflated with the indigenous Iberian goddess. Noctiluca's cult was centered in the vicinity of Málaga, a port city in Andalusia in southern Spain. Its name signifies "the Queen," which some believe refers to Noctiluca. However, the goddess also appears to have been honored with ceremonial dances in the northwest of the country. Rincón de la Victoria, a fishing town just east of Málaga, is known for its limestone marine caves, some with Paleolithic and Neolithic paintings. Legend has it that medieval Arabs protected their gold in the caves and hence named them Las Cuevas del Tesoro (once known as El Higuerón or El Suizo). One of the caves is believed to have served as a sanctuary of Noctiluca. In the mid-twentieth century, Professor Manuel Laza Palacio (1909-1988) discovered a betyl that he believed had once served as a representation of the Goddess, together, he determined, with a bicorn altar. Is it possible that this altar-stone represented a horned animal companion or horned male consort? Others, however, have seen the "bicorn altar" as breasts. Surrounding the Goddess figure and/or altar were found remains of sacrificed animals.

In the mid-twelfth century, John of Salisbury named Noctiluca in conjunction with Herodias and Hecate as a goddess of witches. It is conceivable that alleged Spanish witches did indeed revere Noctiluca as their forebears had done. John of Salisbury's acknowledgment suggests, however, that Noctiluca may have possessed a wider following than that of Spain alone. Thus, it is possible that the reverence of Noctiluca persisted into the High Middle Ages. By the eighteenth century, she was linked not only to Diana but also to Herodias and Bensozia, in the context of the witches' sabbat. In Spain, evidence from the vicinity of Málaga suggests that she may have eventually been, due to her associations with both water and light shining in the darkness, Catholicized as both Nuestra Señora del Carmen and Nuestra Señora de la Candelaria.

Poseidon/Neptune and Amphitrite

Poseidon/Neptune, a god of the sea and earthquakes, and his wife Amphitrite, a Nereid or an Oceanid, and goddess of the sea, continued to be revered in the Middle Ages in France and elsewhere. The *Homilia de sacrilegiis* of the late eighth century condemned rites in honor of Neptune performed at brooks and springs; and it would appear that certain medieval Europeans continued to celebrate a version of the Roman Neptunalia on July 23.

In 1082, the scholar John Italus was condemned by the Orthodox Church, but not before he had, through his writings and teachings, gathered around him a number of followers, including a man named Serblias. As Kenneth M. Setton recounts, Serblias "went out in the dead of night to the end of a promontory overlooking the sea. Standing there for awhile, like the devotee of some ancient pagan cult, he suddenly threw himself into the water, screaming as loud as he could, 'Receive me, Poseidon!'"

For many centuries, mariners participated in the ceremony of "Crossing the Line." This ceremony was held on December 3 and was derived from a Roman celebration in honor of Neptune. The ceremony focused on "passing from north to south latitude, or vice versa. The custom, in some form or other, is believed to be very ancient, and to have been originally instituted on the occasion of ships passing out of the Mediterranean into the Atlantic, beyond the 'Pillars of Hercules.'" In the ceremony, two of the men performed the roles of, or else embodied, Neptune and Amphitrite. This phenomenon of contesting the border between ritual and dramatic performance is frequent in enactments of the pagan worldview, as it is in the Christian tradition of miracle and morality plays. A report from the mid-seventeenth century was given by Captain Edward Hall (fl. 1644-1652):

> The best executed of these ceremonies I ever saw, was on board a ship of the line, of which I was lieutenant, bound to the West Indies. On crossing the line, a voice, as if at a distance, and at the surface of the water, cried: "Ho, ship ahoy! I shall come on board!" This was from a person slung over the bows, near the water, speaking through his hands. Presently two men of large stature came over the bows. They had hideous masks on. One represented Neptune. He was naked to the waist, crowned with the head of a large wet swab, the end of which reached to his loins, to represent flowing locks; a piece of tarpaulin, vandyked, encircled the head of the swab and his brows as a diadem; his right hand wielded a boarding-pike, manufactured into a trident; and his body was smeared with red ochre, to represent fish-scales. The other sailor represented Amphitrite, having locks formed of swabs, a petticoat of the same material, with a girdle of red bunting; and in her hand a comb and

looking-glass. They were followed by about twenty fellows, naked to the waist, with red ochre scales, as Tritons.[23]

Neptune and Amphitrite and their entourage were greeted with great fanfare. They were paraded around the ship. At some point, Neptune remarked that one or more of the young men had not yet been initiated. A young male apprentice known as a 'Johnny Raw' was then rubbed with shaving soap and dowsed with soapy water that had been used in shaving. If he took it well, he was permitted to join in soaping up and dowsing other initiates.

Priapus

Priapus is a lord of phallic sexuality; he is also a protector of farms and livestock. He appears to have been invoked at least twice in medieval Scotland. In the *Chronicle of Lanercost*, one finds that in 1268, in the district of Lothian, a pestilence was killing many cattle. To counteract this epidemic, a lay Cistercian brother – apparently deciding that the Biblical God was not answering their prayers – erected a statue of Priapus, gathered with peasants to make a bonfire, and sprinkled the cattle with water that had been touched by a dog's testicles. The cattle stopped dying until the man performing these rites was reprimanded and told to cease such ritualizing. Fourteen years later, at Eastertime, John, a priest of Inverkeithing, "revived the profane rites of Priapus, collecting young girls from the village and compelling them to dance in circles in honour of Father Liber [i.e., Bacchus]." After the priest had gathered "these females in a troop, out of sheer wantonness he led the dance, carrying in front on a pole a representation of the human organs of reproduction, and singing and dancing himself, like a mime, he ... stirred them to lust."

* * *

In 392 CE, as Demetrios Constantelos points out in "Byzantine and Ancient Greek Religiosity," "Hera and Zeus, Demeter and Poseidon, Hermes and Athena, Apollo and Aphrodite and several other Olympian deities were officially pronounced dead." If one believes in, or acknowledges the reality of, the ancient goddesses and gods, this pronouncement may strike one as absurd, perhaps even as hubristic and offensive – certainly as offensive as many Christians have found Nietzsche's proclamation of the death of the Biblical God. Whether one does or does not, however, acknowledge the reality of the ancient divinities, this doesn't change the fact that the Christians who pronounced it so were in error, were badly mistaken, as we have seen. With Christianization, many Egyptian, Greek, Roman, and other Mediterranean and Near Eastern divinities survived and were displaced by, or in some cases, joined by, by way of masking, deploying the theory of correspondences, or by other means, images of the Biblical God, Jesus, the Virgin Mary, or the saints. For example, Isis, besides being displaced by Mary, also transmogrified into Saint Anne, Saint Géneviève, and Saint Ursula. Similarly, the legendary high priest Calchas lingered on as St. Michael; while Romulus and Remus, the legendary founders of Rome, became Sts. Cosmas and Damian; and Antinous, the handsome young man loved by Emperor Hadrian, who, in sacrificing his life for that of the emperor, came to be deified, was Catholicized as St. John the Baptist. Theseus slaying the Minotaur was remembered in Christian churches, by way of labyrinths, such as that of Santa Maria Trastevere in Rome, with Christians retracing the hero's steps as they traversed "meandering paths on their knees, murmuring prayers in memory of the passion of the Lord." In 1853, Octavian Blewitt, in Murray's *Handbook for Travellers in Southern Italy*, noted that the Church of San Giovanni Maggiore was built on the ruins of a temple to Antinous. In the late nineteenth century, the archaeologist Rodolfo Amadeo Lanciani described a statue of St. John he observed at Rome that was "obviously modelled on...Antinous, with the same abundance of hair, the same profile and characteristic eyebrows."

According to Greek Law No. 1672/39, present-day Greeks were forbidden until quite recently to worship their ancient goddesses and gods. Father Eustathios Kollas, head of the community of Greek priests, recently said of those who wish to do so: "They are a handful of miserable resuscitators of a degenerate dead religion who wish to return to the monstrous dark delusions of the past." Recently, however, an Athenian court ordered a lifting of this ban. Still, pagan Greeks face a difficult struggle in the homeland of Demeter, Dionysus, and democracy.[24]

Chapter 3
Celtic and Germanic Divinities

In comparison with many other European cultures, Christianization of the Celtic world commenced very early, near the early fifth century, and proceeded at fever pitch during the seventh. Some ancient Celtic deities were displaced early on by, or became conflated with, manifestations of the Virgin Mary or saints. Goddess-to-Saint Brigid, patron of the arts and poetry, keeper of the sacred fire, is a prime example.

I want to stress that while I am, as a student of paganism, far from infallible, I have found surprisingly little, especially in view of Wicca's heavy reliance upon Celtic traditions, in the way of the persistence of Celtic deities in Christianized regions inhabited in antiquity by the Celts. One finds fragmentary and often controversial data here and there: a Christian church, bearing the name of Templebrian, in the parish of Kilgariff, seems to have assisted in preserving the memory of the Jason-like hero Brian, son of the goddess Brigid. A controversial source relates that in 1613, the missionary Michel Le Nobletz (1577-1652) was shocked upon learning of three women who, living on the Ile-de-Sein in Brittany, were believed to carry on the traditions of the Druids, serving as priestesses to a mysterious solar deity, Doué-Tad; etc. This may be one of the reasons why Hutton and other academics focusing on the British Isles have been led to proclaim the early and final demise of paganism and its lack of historical connection to present-day NeoPaganism.

The apparent fading of many Celtic deities does not, however, indicate that the allied worldview did not persist in other ways in areas once occupied by Celts. Certainly, in terms of the veneration of nature, the celebration of the seasonal cycle, and practices of divination and magic, the earth-centered worldview of the Celts has held on quite tenaciously. Moreover, if deities haven't fared so well, related beings have. In certain cases, as with the Tuatha Dé Danaan, it appears that deities (were) transformed into other beings, including fairies, in Christianized Celtic areas.

Moreover, it is in the end extremely difficult to say definitively whether reverence of a particular deity survived Christianization or not. I am acutely aware – as I think others should be but sadly, quite often seem not to be – that just because something hasn't been "discovered" or, more accurately, *recovered*, as of yet, *this does not mean that such a thing did not occur*. In my view, all one need do is think about the impact of the "discovery" of the *Dead Sea Scrolls* and the *Gospels of Thomas* and *Judas* upon Christianity and that upon Judaism and Christianity to acknowledge that this may well also be the case with certain earth-centered traditions and their practices.

When considering this subject, I think we also need to complicate and contest a present-day academic stance that pits folklore against an energetic and persistent belief in archetypal forces and that ultimately characterizes folklore as groupings of figures, narratives, and such that are no longer believed in but simply thought to be quaint recollections of obsolete concepts and practices now emptied of sacred or archetypal presence or force. This permits some present-day academics to argue that Modern- or NeoPaganism in general and Wicca in particular share no vital connection with past paganisms because they rely too much on folklore, which, without ever actually saying so and indeed pretending to the contrary, these academics portray as a *dead thing*. Intriguingly, moreover, to criticize Wiccans and NeoPagans for drawing too much upon folklore is in a way to blame the victim, to deprecate those who are seeking to reconstruct that which Christianization has torn asunder. Not to mention that Christianity, in its construction, relied heavily on folklore. In contrast to a number of present-day academics who write in the field of Pagan Studies, I would argue that "folkloric" figures and performances *do not necessarily equal a lack of belief* in the divine or archetypal force that may lie behind concepts and practices that have responded to innovation.

Furthermore, if goddesses and gods *are in fact living entities*, as, for instance, Christians believe Jesus to be – and I am well aware that this may be interpreted by academics as a radical hypothesis – then they hold the power of metamorphosis and may themselves choose to transform; for example, Cernunnos may choose to morph from Cernunnos "proper" into the Lord of animals or another avatar or hypostasis. Further still, they may further hold the power to influence the ways in which we communicate with and about them in various cultural milieus and epochs.

Danu and Àine

In Celtic tradition, the goddess Dôn (Welsh) or Danu (or Anu; Dana, Irish) is the mother of the Tuatha Dé Danaan, a family of divinities, some of whom eventually metamorphosed, or else were demoted, into fairies. In the view of Edward Clodd (1840-1930), a banker, writer, and anthropologist, the goddesses. Danu and Àine are the same entity. Danu/ Àine is the moon-goddess or "Queen of Heaven" who is propitiated at the summer and winter solstices. Her name refers to a "ring" or "circle" and signifies the moon. She is a patron of literature who weeps when bards and scholars die and then serves as a psychopomp to lead "them into fairy realms." Deploying the theory of correspondences, the antiquarian writer Nicholas O'Kearney linked Àine to numerous other goddesses including Anna Perenna, Athena, Diana, Isis, and Luna, as well as to the Bean-sidhe (or banshee), the fairy-divinity who announces the death of a loved one.

After Christianization, many of the attributes of Àine were appropriated by the Church for St. Ann(e). Typical of appropriation, in one of its more perverse forms, she was alternately transformed into the daughter of a pagan king who ran off to become a Christian, with St. Patrick as mentor. Her memory also persisted (as documented in 1942) in the form of a folk figure named Àine or Àine O'Corra, portrayed as a human woman abducted by the fairies. Also in more recent times, her name has sometimes been given as "Hannah." Nevertheless, it appears that Àine continued to be honored as such into the eighteenth and nineteenth centuries, especially, it seems, in the field of medicine, more, particularly, in the practice of bloodletting. O'Kearney explains that "herb-doctors and charm-mongers believed she [i.e., Àine] had unlimited influence over the human frame." As such, she controlled the vital spark within the human body, which circuited the body every twenty-four hours. If a patient's vein were opened at a time not favorable to Àine, that patient would likely die; as Wood-Martin notes, "Blood-letters would decline to operate on a day devoted to Aynia [i.e., Àine], for the efflux would carry away the 'vital spark.'" When O'Kearney was a young boy, an elderly woman healer named Maire Ruadh-ni-Hararan (b. *c.* 1720), whom the family frequently called upon for counsel, observed as the family doctor commenced to perform bloodletting on young O'Kearney. He notes that the woman had learned to heal from her mother. He recalls that just as the doctor was about to make the cut, she cried out, recognizing that this was not a time favorable to Àine and insisting that if the child's vein were punctured, he would most assuredly die. Needless to say, O'Kearney recovered and remained grateful to Ruadh-ni-Hararan. O'Kearney, in 1852, and W. G. Wood-Martin, in 1902, suggested that veneration of Àine may have persisted into their own time. It should be noted that O'Kearney was not above telling tall tales, but I find nothing to indicate that he did so when speaking of Àine; and since he was recognized by colleagues as possessing this tendency, I do not think Wood-Martin would have reiterated his account had he considered it to be a fabrication. In particular, it appears that some elderly people of the nineteenth century continued to believe that Àine held particular sway over certain days of the year, as, for example, the three days following the early August festival of Lughnasa (or, Lughnasadh, Lugnasa, *Lúnasa*, aka Lammas)). I tend to believe that this claim is valid, as I do not think Máire MacNeill would have reiterated it in the brilliant study *The Festival of Lughnasa* (1962) if it had seemed to MacNeill to be just a tall tale. Memory of the Goddess has persisted in the form of names of sacred stones and sites. Àine's memory is linked to sacred stones like that called the "chair of Àine," near Dunany in County Louth in northeastern Ireland, which is associated with lunacy. Wood-Martin notes that "Aynia [i.e., Àine] occurs as a personal name on the Ballymorereigh Ogham stone, in the county Kerry." The parish of Lissan in northern Ireland is named after the goddess: Lios Àine means "Àine's Fort." In the vicinity are Tobar Àine, "Àine's Well," and Croc Àine, "Àine's Hill." In County Tyrone, at Knockmany, one finds a group of sacred stones consecrated to her, Annia's Cove, decorated with spirals, zigzags, and circles signifying her presence; in the nineteenth century, peasants told others that this site belonged to Àine the Fairy Queen. On a personal note, Àine is considered to be the patron banshee of my father's paternal ancestors, the O'Con(n)ors.

Belenus

Belenus, the "Shining One," is a Gaulish solar god of healing comparable to Apollo who carries the sun in a horse-drawn chariot. Peter Berresford Ellis explains that "he was regarded as having gained victory over the powers of darkness by bringing people within sight of another harvest." A god of life and death, he transports souls of the dead across the waters to the Otherworld.

His name may derive from a word meaning "apple;" his sacred tree appears to be the oak; and certain plants thought to be gifts of Belenus, particularly henbane (*belisa*; in German, *bilsen-kraut*). Burchard of Worms condemned the continuing earth-centered ritualizing, in the eleventh century, of the gathering of *bilsen-kraut* by a young, naked girl. It is significant that in Germany, henbane came also to be known as Devil's Eye, suggesting that "the Devil" of the witch trials may have perhaps been inspired in part by the god Belenus. Belenus' name appears in many place names including Billingsgate (Belenus' Gate) in London; Munsterbilsen in Belgium; Billum in Denmark; and "many places named Bel-Air throughout France [and Brittany]."

Belenus is typically considered to be the consort of the goddess Danu. In Britain, however, the goddess Minerva also came to be coupled with Belenus, and as such was called Belisa, the "Very Brilliant One"; this is perhaps due in part to the fact that at Bath, England, "at her altar there flamed a perpetual fire." According to Ellis, "Belenus was venerated in Gaul for many centuries after the Roman conquest." He continues to be acknowledged and celebrated during the festival named for him: Beltane.

Brigid

Brigid (or Breedh, Brida, Bride, Bridgit, Brighit), whose name signifies "bright arrow" or "exalted one," is a Triple Goddess comprised of three sisters, one a healer, one a bard, and one a smith or metallurgist.

Brigid is also a goddess of fire, crafts, and prophecy. Oaks, wheat, oats, sheep (particularly ewes and lambs), and cattle are especially sacred to her. She has been compared to various other goddesses including Minerva and Vesta.

From around the sixth century onward, it is exceedingly difficult to distinguish the goddess from St. Brigid (*c.* 451-525), who assumed her name and her primary attributes as well as the date of her festival (we will return to Brigid briefly in our exploration of seasonal rites). Miceal Ross, writing in the journal *Folklore* in 1998, in "Anchors in a Three-Decker World" (1998), points out that "The foundation of the influential Abbey of Kildare is attributed to St. Brigid, but reference to the presence of a perpetual fire guarded by the nuns near the oak grove suggests that it was preceded by a pagan shrine to the powerful Celtic goddess Brigid. Kildare means 'Church at the Oak.'"

Cernunnos

The god Cernunnos is a Celtic deity whose origin may more specifically be Gaulish, referring to Celts primarily of France, Luxembourg, and Belgium. Typically depicted with stag horns, he is a patron of animals – called the "Lord of Animals" – and a god of wealth, abundance, sacrifice, and the underworld. From a stela from Reims, Marne, France, where, as he sits in a yoga-like position, a bag full of coins falls from his throne-like seat, we may deduce that like Hades/Pluto or Dis Pater, he was also worshipped as a god of wealth and abundance.

I have found no continuing worship of Cernunnos *per se*, at least not by this name; *this does not mean that there was none, and to argue this would be both preemptive and arrogant*. Certainly, horned deities, such as the "Lord of the Forest," continued to be revered, some of whom may have been synonymous with Cernunnos.

It is conceivable, although somewhat controversial, that Cernunnos metamorphosed over time into figures including the Lord of the Forest, the Green Man, Puck, Herne the Hunter, the Man of the Oak, the Green Man, Jack-in-the-Green. If we say that Cernunnos may have contributed to the custom of dressing as a stag or bull on the Kalends of January, a custom that persisted tenaciously in many places in medieval Europe, and as a stag in the Abbots Bromley dance, which continues to be performed in England and the United States in our own time, with his contribution to these ritual performances suggested by his depiction as being flanked by a stag and a bull on an altarpiece from Rheims, France, this most certainly does *not* indicate that Cernunnos was no longer conceived of as a divine presence by those who costumed themselves as bulls or stags at the New Year or danced in Abbots Bromley near year's end.

As has been the fate of many Pagan gods and goddesses, an altar to Cernunnos was appropriated by Christians to build an altar at Notre-Dame in Paris.

Lugh

Lugh, (Lleu in Wales; Lugus in England and France), whose name may mean "the Shining One," is a god of the sun, arts (including music [the harp] and poetry) and crafts (including metallurgy), games (that of Irish *fidchell*, *gwyddbwyll* in Welsh, a predecessor of chess), war (he possesses a magical spear), weather (especially thunder and rain), male beauty, and sorcery. He is the father of the Irish hero Cú Chulainn. Lugh was compared by the Romans to Mercury.

Lugh's reverence has remained primarily in the celebration of Lughnasa/Lammas), typically held on August 1 or 2nd, which we will discuss later in regard to calendrical festivals.

Lugh has been both diminished – as from deity to fairy – and sanctified. In folklore, Lugh transformed into Lleu Llaw Gyffes, then into the leprechaun (from "Luchorpain"), and much later, into John Barleycorn.

It seems that he has also been remembered in regard to certain place-names, such as the ancient Luguvalium (now Carlisle in Cumbria), as well as London and Lyon.

He appears to have been Christianized as St. Molua (or, Mo Lua, Lua; also known as St. Mulvay). The feast day of St. Molua (sixth century), an Irish abbot who lived in a monastery near Belfast, is August 4. His birth name was Lughaidh (pronounced "Lua"), clearly demonstrating his linkage to Lugh. Indeed, Molua was sometimes called Saint Lughaidh.

The Matres and Other Goddesses

Fragmentary evidence concerning the Matres — a Roman name for a triad of Celtic Mother Goddesses — suggests that in Alsace and Franche-Compté, a cult dedicated to the Matres may have persisted into the nineteenth century. It is more likely, however, that, as Edward Anwyl (1866-1914) and others have suggested, the Matres transformed into fairies. Anwyl notes that "in some parts of Wales, Y Mamau ("the mothers") is the name for the fairies." The war-goddess Badb, whose name suggests "rage" or "fury," who is associated with the battle-goddesses Neman, Macha, Mórrigan, and who is linked to the crow and raven as birds of omen, was so demonized and denigrated with Christianization that by the early years of the twentieth century, her name, as "Bav," came to be "applied ... in the South of Ireland to a scolding woman or virago; goddess and witch have finally degenerated into common shrews."

Môn

Môn appears to be both a mother-goddess and a moon goddess (hence her name); she also appears to be associated with pigs. In *The Journey Through Wales*, Gerald of Wales (*c*. 1145-1223) suggests that even if reverence of the goddess Môn/Mona had faded — she may well have been revered until at least the mid-tenth century — her memory remained in the late twelfth century:

> The island of Anglesey is an arid stony land ... this island produces far more grain than any other part of Wales. In the Welsh language it has always been called 'Môn mam Cymru,' which means 'Mona the Mother of Wales'. When crops have failed in all other regions, this island, from the richness of its soil and its abundant produce, has been able to supply all Wales.[25]

Segeta

Segeta, whose name means "harvest," was known as the "Fecund One." She is a Gallic, or Gaulish, Celtic goddess of the Segusiavi people, the "people of the goddess Segeta." Segeta, over time, was conflated with certain other Gaulish and Greco-Roman goddesses, including Seia, the Roman goddess of sowing, and Sirona, a Celto-Roman goddess of healing, especially associated with thermal springs, of fertility, as linked with eggs, and of stars; Diana; Ceres; and Copia, a goddess of abundance, so that she became a Gallo-Roman goddess. She is a patron of agriculture, especially of grain crops and the harvest, and of healing springs, as of Aquae Segetae (now called Sceaux-du-Gatinais [Loiret]).

As Seia, she continued to be invoked, sometimes in alliance with the Biblical God, by practitioners of herbal medicine from the ninth through the fourteenth or fifteenth centuries.

Near the end of the fifteenth century, the *précenteur* (choir master) Jacques d'Amoncourt became deeply troubled when he became aware that some women of the church were making offerings to and invocations before a certain statue in the church of Saint Etienne at Lyons, France, primarily, it would appear, at the end of December, when the saint's feast was held. This statue was supposed to represent the Virgin but was in fact an ancient statue representing Segeta of the Segusavi. It is not clear whether the women accepted that the statue represented the Virgin, but this is rather doubtful, as the statue (which no longer exists) is described as having reminded one of "Diana of Ephesus or of the Goddess of the Earth." It may have been the case that they were practicing a form of sacred hybridity. Or they may have simply been worshipping the ancient goddess. D'Amoncourt seems to have thought it was the last of these, as he broke the statue into pieces in an effort to put the women's devotions to a stop.

Germanic Divinities

Of St. Eligius's seventh-century "supposed surviving homilies, one is especially notable for his condemnation of keeping Thursday holy in honour of Jupiter (Thor...)." Also in the early seventh century, St. Gall (d. *c.* 630) commanded that inhabitants of what is now Austria abandon their worship of three deities who appear to have been Odin, Thor, and Freyr, or else local variants of these. Likewise, in seventh-century England, King Edwin (584-632/ 633, r. 616-632/ 633) commanded that his Northumbrian subjects (of far northeastern England), abandon the worship of Woden (comparable to Odin); on the other hand, Penda (d. 654, r. 632-654) of Mercia continued to worship the old gods. Eorcenberht (r. 640-664) "ordered the destruction of Kentish idols." In the eighth century, Pope Gregory III (pope, 731-741) commanded Boniface (Winfred) (*c.* 675—754) to baptize any pagans who had previously been formally initiated into a pagan cult, such as that to Thor (identified with Jupiter), or who had been baptized by a pagan ritual specialist pretending to be Christian. The Carolingian *Indiculus* (c. 750) condemned the worship of Thor (identified as Jupiter) and Odin/Wotan (identified as Mercury). Charlemagne insisted that the Saxons abandon worship of the Germanic deities, on pain of death. Pagans were "asked" (as evidenced by a document of 743 CE and as increasing in deployment dramatically near 790):

Do you renounce the Devil?
Do you renounce all that is diabolical?
Do you renounce all of the Devil's words and works?
Do you forsake Tunaer [i.e., Thor] and Wodan [/Odin] [and Saxnote, {mythical
forefather of Saxons and god of battle comparable to Tyr}]?
Do you renounce all the demons who are their comrades?[26]

I find it extremely significant that these questions were basically replicated in the eighteenth century – that is, a thousand years later – when Catholic authorities were Christianizing the Indigenous Americans, the Coahuiltecas (now extinct) and others, of what is now San Antonio, Texas, with, of course, the names of divinities being changed. Following the interrogation, Saxon pagans were made to recite: "I forsake all the works and words of the devils, Thunaer [i.e., Thor] and Woden [i.e., Odin] and Saxnote and all the fiends that are their companions."

In the late ninth century, King Alfred of Wessex (849—899, r. 871-899) continued to insist that inhabitants of England abandon pagan deities. Burchard condemned, in the late tenth or early eleventh century, German reverence of Thor (identified as Jupiter) and the Norns (identified as the Fates), as well as the veneration of fairies, elves, dwarves, and kindred beings. What is highly significant here is that persons were now forbidden even to believe in the existence of the Fates, fairies, Wild Women, and werewolves; to acknowledge their existence was itself viewed as anti-Christian. In eleventh-century Sweden, Church authorities condemned persisting reverence of Germanic divinities.

The Dísir and the Norns

Germanic mother goddesses or maternal divinities, the Dísir were associated with the dead, prophecy (as oracles they were called Spâdîsir and were comparable to the Moirae, Parcae, and Norns), and wisdom and were offered sacrifices called *dísablót*. They appear to have been revered by both women and men, including male skalds and priestesses who were perhaps called *Veleda*. They also appear to have been linked to "individual families" and more specifically to the female ancestors of these. They were revered "not only in certain cult centers" but also on family farms. They were worshipped in Sweden at least through the early eleventh century. In or near 1019, the Icelandic skald Sigvatr Thórðarson, perhaps because he was a Christian, was "refused entry into several farms because the *dísablot* was being held then.

The Norns appeared at the births of children and offered them gifts and predicted their destinies. Although the Norns are complex divinities who are somewhat difficult to define, it is generally held that Urðr is the crone who remembers and diagnoses the past; she is sometimes considered a death-bringer. Verðandi, the mother, focuses on the present. And Skuld, the maiden, sees into the future. In certain depictions, two are seen as possessing beneficence, while the third is portrayed as evil. They were frequently associated with the Valkyries. Although the Norns appear to have been revered as such during the Middle Ages, they were also frequently conflated with fairies. As such, they may be the ancestors of the fairies of "Sleeping Beauty." In texts written by Christians, the Norns were often referred to as the 'Fates.' Burchard of Worms (d. 1025), in his eleventh-century *Corrector*, queries persons suspected of non-Christian concepts and practices: "Hast thou believed ... either that those who are commonly called the Fates exist, or that they can do that which they are believed to do? That is, that while any person is being born, they are able to then determine his life to what they wish ... ?"

They also came to be known as the Fatal, Wayfaring, Wayward, or Weird (or Wyrd) Sisters, and in this way became associated with witches, as in the legend of Macbeth. In *The Beauty and the Hag* (1993), Lotte Motz provides evidence, in the form of a charm, indicating that the Norns continued to be revered in eighteenth-century Norway. The charm invokes three women; "the first could spin a golden thread;/ the second could fix [bind] a woman's womb;/ the third could put it in its proper place." Motz writes of this charm: "These women are obviously women's goddesses – working a woman's craft, and treating a woman's disease. The charm is one of several variants, all showing three young women, who either wander or are seated, and who are able to cure ailments peculiar to women."

Freyja

Freyja "was probably the most widely worshipped of the Norse goddesses." Although perceived as a Great Goddess, her primary concerns appear to have been agriculture, eroticism, and magic. Freyja loves gold, and weeps tears of gold. Ferns (*freyjuhár*) are sacred to her, as are moss and yarrow. She is sometimes described as Queen of the Valkyries and the dead, particularly of unbaptized (and hence Pagan) infants. As a goddess of eroticism, Freyja is believed to have enjoyed pleasure with many divine and semi-divine beings, including her brother Freyr and the dwarfs who fashioned Brisingamen, her magic necklace or torque. A foremother of the fairy tale witch, Freyja rides upon a cat or a wagon drawn by cats.

That her worship was linked to, or preserved elements of, shamanism is inferred by her garment of falcon or hawk feathers, which she uses to 'fare forth' into other worlds, and by the type of magic she practices and teaches to others, which incorporates a shamanistic or altered state of consciousness. That her worship was matrifocal in character is indicated by the fact that this type of magic, *seiðr*, was practiced primarily by women and gender-diverse persons and was in later times branded 'feminine magic.' It was contrasted with *galdr*, or runic magic, the runes being a sacred and divinatory alphabet; *galdr* was 'masculine magic.'

In later centuries, Freyja, like other originally peaceful deities, became a goddess of battle, having the responsibility of overseeing the spirits of fallen warriors; this shift indicates a kind of "evolution" – or perhaps devolution – of the earth-centered worldview. The *Indiculus superstitionem et paganiarum* (*Index of Superstitions and Paganism*) suggests that worship of Freyja remained widespread among Germanic peoples other than in Scandinavia during the eighth century. Katherine Morris, in *Sorceress or Witch?: The Image of Gender in Medieval Iceland and Northern Europe* (1991), notes that in 999 CE, a year before Iceland's government decided to make Christianity its official religion, the Christian Hjalti Skeggjason voiced the new characterization of the goddess Freyja when he referred to her derogatorily as a "bitch" at the Althing, Iceland's governing body that met annually.

Nevertheless, in remote areas of the north, Freyja was still being worshipped in the twelfth century. Alfred Maury suggests that Freyja became conflated with the goddess Eostre, mentioned by Bede in connection with Easter, and in later centuries with Holda and with witchcraft. In *Witchcraft and Magic in the Nordic Middle Ages* (2011), Stephen A. Mitchell argues: "The connection between Freyja's more frightening attributes and subsequent constructions of the witch figure is readily made, as are the transfer of her positive aspects to the Virgin Mary."

I would complicate this remark a bit to suggest that among those who continued to revere Freyja in a post-Christianization context, both positive and negative aspects would probably have remained with the goddess.

In this regard, she may have, like the goddess Frigga, become known, especially in Belgium, as Vrouw Vreke and with the mythical St. Vreke(n). She may also, like the goddesses Isis, Holda, and Hörsel, have become hybridized with St. Ursula. Following another train of associations, she may have also become Catholicized as St. Verena, allegedly an Egyptian woman who journeyed to Rhaetia (present-day Switzerland). Other than her origin and her settling in Switzerland, next to nothing is known of this controversial saint's life. Links of the saint to the Goddess are suggested by associations with cats, corn, the linden tree, eroticism, love, and marriage. In the late nineteenth century, Lina Eckenstein recounted that

[a]ccording to folk-custom in districts between the Aar and the Rhine, girls who have secured husbands sacrifice their little maiden caps to Verena. At Zurzach married couples make pilgrimages to the Verenastift in order to secure offspring … . Her day [Sept. 1], which comes at the harvest festival, was a time of unrestrained license in Zurzach, a fact on which the *Acta Sanctorum* cast no doubt.[27]

The syncretic Freyja-St. Verena may have come to be called Fru (or Frau) Frene. Moreover, this syncretic figure was further associated with Venus.

In his poem "Freya [/Frouwa] and the Goddesses of Love," Gustav Thormod Legis (1806-1867) links Freyja to the goddess Holda. Herein, Freyja is she who "holds the power;" "to grant pleasure is [her] nature." "You're still revered in all lands," the poet writes, "Where love is at the heart of being,/ Love, your magic power!"

In recent decades, as a combined result of the emergence of the feminist and contemporary Pagan/Heathen movements, Freyja's worship has experienced a revival. As Gundarsson explains, "Freyja is particularly called upon today by women who wish to regain the strength which Christian culture has denied them for so long."

Freyr

Freyr is one of the Vanir deities, who are believed to have preceded the Aesir in regard to the Germanic pantheon. The Vanir are broadly considered to be more resonant with earth-centered and matrifocal traditions, whereas the Aesir are considered more resonant with patriarchal and transcendent religions/traditions. In comparison to studies devoted to Thor and Odin, the persistence of Freyr in the medieval world has perhaps not been given its fair share, except perhaps by Richard North in *Heathen Gods in Old English Literature*. Therein, he argues that "[t]o heathen kings and subjects alike there were more powerful *numina* [i.e., gods, than Odin/ Woden] to propitiate – the natural phenomena and farming activities on which they relied for spring growth, autumn harvest and their winter lives." "Instead," he continues, "it is likely that Germanic practitioners of earth-based traditions on the Continent and in Britain" were more attuned to "an older era" in which earth-gods like Freyr predominated.

In the seventh century, North notes, Freyr was depicted in Christian texts as the "god of this age" or the "god of this world." North believes that earth-centered beliefs and rites, including those linked to Ingui/ Freyr, continued in England, especially among peasants, following early efforts at Christianization, to be promoted once more with Viking hegemony in the ninth century: "The peasants are rarely mentioned in the sources, but it can be assumed that some of their old ways continued within Christianity until these ways were given a new lease of life by the Vikings in the ninth-century Danelaw." He believes that the cult of Ingvi/Freyr may have constituted one of the most significant forms of worship in the late ninth century. It is noteworthy that the Ynglingar, one of the royal families of Sweden, traced its origins to Freyr.

North cites a fourteenth-century Christian text, the *Flateyjarbók*, as recounting that in the early eleventh century, "It was the peasants' belief that Freyr was alive, as in some ways it seemed he was, and they thought he would need to have marital relations with his wife." North suggests that in the local hypostasis of Ingui, Freyr – for North, an avatar of Nerthus, whom, he argues, is a male deity – and an earth-goddess – possibly Skaði, and/ or in later times, Frigga – may have joined, via mortal representatives, in a *hieros gamos*, possibly as late as the ninth century. He further suggests that with Christianization, this union morphed into that of Christ and the "Bride of Christ," i.e., the Church. Freyr was revered into at least the late tenth century in Iceland and into the early twelfth in other Scandinavian countries.

Frigga

Frigga, whose name means "beautiful" or "loveable," is the spouse of Odin. She may have originated in the ancient goddess Nerthus. By the common people of Lower Saxony she was called Fru Freke. A "Mother Goddess" and the "queen of heaven," she is also a solar deity, presiding over love, beauty, marriage, and destiny. She may also be a patron of trees. In this connection, one of her sacred plants is white satyrion of the orchid family (*Orchis odoratissima*; *Satyrium albidum*), "from which love-potions are brewed." Another is the strawberry, a symbol of eros. In this regard, Frigga becomes linked to elves and dwarves, who love strawberries. Also in this regard, Frigga accompanies children who go berry-picking at Midsummer.

She gave her name not only to Friday but also to Freefolk, Hampshire, in England, its older name being Frigfolc, as well as to Froyle and Frobury, also in Hampshire, as well as, possibly, Freckenhorst in North Rhine-Westphalia, Germany (it may have also or alternatively been named after Freyr/Fricco). Frigga's association with Friday may have led to the belief that Christians should not speak of fairies on Fridays because on that day, as on Wednesday, they can "be present while still invisible." In an English charter of 959 CE, one finds "thence to Friday" and "thence along the road to Friday's (i.e., Frig[ga]'s) tree." Eleanor Hull asserts that Frigga's "worship ... continued in England up to the thirteenth century," that is, into the High Middle Ages. In Christian lore, Frigga was sanctified as the non-existent St. Vreke(n). On the other hand, she came to be called the Devil's Grandmother. Frigga's memory also persisted into the nineteenth century as a carnivalesque figure: "In the neighborhood of Dent in Yorkshire the country people, at certain seasons, particularly in autumn, have a procession, and perform old dances, one of which they call the giants' dance. The principal giant they call Woden [Odin], and his wife Frigga."

Nehalennia

Although Nehalennia is in fact a hybrid Celtic-Roman-Germanic goddess, I have listed her here because she is most often associated with Germanic and "Northern" goddesses. Nehalennia is a goddess of fertility, seafaring, trade, and the afterlife. She is often depicted wearing a hooded cap (sometimes winged like that of Hermes), holding a basket of fruit, standing on a ship, and companioned by a dog. Her major cult centers included Cologne, Germany and the island of Walcheren in the Netherlands. During the early-to mid-eighth century CE, statues and shrines of Nehalennia, who continued to be worshipped at that time, were destroyed. Over the next several centuries, Nehalennia may have transmogrified into Wanne Thekla. In the twelfth century, it appears that celebrating Nehalennia, perhaps in connection with Wanne Thekla, Isis, and/or the Virgin Mary, reemerged noticeably, as demonstrated by a procession in which the divinity was carried in a ship drawn over land. Commencing around 1600 and continuing throughout the nineteenth century, artworks belonging to the cult of the goddess were unearthed or otherwise revealed (for example, by a violent storm in 1647), recalling, and providing evidence for, the cult of Nehalennia.

Odin/Woden

Odin, whose name signifies "fury," "wildness," and "inspiration," is primarily a god of "battle, death, and spiritual wisdom." He often wears a mask or hood; in this hypostasis, he is nicknamed Grim(r). He also often wears a hat or cloak that possesses magical powers. He is typically identified with Mercury in writings by Christians. As a battle god, he is the leader of a band comprised of the souls of fallen warriors. The approach of this band, nicknamed 'the Wild Hunt,' often signals death. Odin is also the master of Valhalla, the paradise of warriors. And he is the lord of dwarves.

As a diviner whose cult appears, like those of Freyja and Freyr, to have been inspired by shamanism, Odin is master of the runes and a necromancer who divines the future by way of communicating with a skull. That his worship is linked to shamanism is indicated by the manner in which he acquires the knowledge of the runes – by hanging himself on a sacred ash tree, by his possession of the eight-legged horse Sleipnir (the horse being an archetypal shamanic vehicle), and by his avian companions, the ravens Huginn and Muninn, who function as all-seeing eyes. Like many shamanic figures, Odin is often depicted as one-eyed, another sacrifice to gnosis. He is, like many shamans, a wounded healer. In this respect, he resembles the blind Greek prophet Tiresias as well as the Yorùbá god of medicine, Osanyin. As a magician, Odin is the owner of a ring and a spear possessing supernatural powers. He is also a patron of games, particularly of dice.

In terms of gender diversity, Odin is said to have donned feminine attire on various occasions. Moreover, one of his aspects or nicknames is Jalkr, which means "gelding." Gundarsson suggests that this appellation may refer to "Odinn's initiation into the art of *seiðr*-magic .... [To] assume the feminine powers of vision and understanding or to give himself up totally to the feminine principle, a man had to be capable of giving up his masculine identity, even to the point of dressing and living as a woman for a time."

Odin, as Woden, was the chief Germanic god worshipped by the Anglo-Saxons "in Kent, Essex, Hampshire, Wiltshire, Somerset, Staffordshire, Bedfordshire, and Derbyshire." His importance among Thuringians is evidenced by his being toasted prior to the toasting of Thor, presumably other divinities, deceased heroes and possibly ancestors, and living loved ones.

The royal family of England once traced its ancestry to Woden [Odin]. In a chart given in Grimm's *Teutonic Mythology*, we find that Ethelbert (r. 560-616) of Kent, Raedwald (d. *c*. 625, r. 599-*c*.625) and Earpwald (r. *c*. 616-628) of East Anglia, Penda (d. 654, r. 632-654) of Mercia, and other early English kings were all considered descendants of Woden. Eighth-century worship of Woden and consecration of Wednesday to him is indicated by *Indiculus superstitionem et paganiarum* (*Index of Superstitions and Paganism*). In Scandinavia, Odin was worshipped into (at least) the eleventh and twelfth centuries. Frisians are said to have worshipped Odin into the fourteenth century.

Mindy Macleod and Bernard Mees, in *Runic Amulets and Magic Objects*, note that Odin was among the gods invoked by Icelandic magicians of the sixteenth and seventeenth centuries. In the *Galdrabók*, for example, Odin was invoked to assist the practitioner in learning the identity of a thief. Due to Christianization, however, Odin was sometimes referred to by practitioners of magic as the "greatest of fiends" rather than as a god.

Stephen Mitchell relates that in October 1484, at a trial held in Stockholm, Ragvald Odinskarl not only confessed to pilfering several Christian churches but also to having served Odin for seven years. Although we do not know what happened to Odinskarl, it would appear that his partner in crime, Joan Landh, was executed during the following March. Mitchell argues that despite other possibilities, the evidence suggests that Odinskarl was "someone who worshipped, or was somehow subject to, Odin." Similarly, in June 1492, at another trial held in Stockholm, Erick Clauesson was convicted of worshipping Odin. Since Clauesson was said to have made nine trips on Thursday evenings to ritualize in a cemetery to Odin in order to attain money; thus, his case spelled out certain associations with Odinic reverence during this period, including: the number nine (the number of nights Odin sacrificed himself by hanging on a tree); the day Thursday (it would appear that Thursday, once sacred to Thor, also became sacred to Odin during the Middle Ages); the location of the cemetery; dancing widdershins (*widerthagit*); and the goal of obtaining money. Although he does not say so directly, it is possible to draw from Mitchell's evidence that at least literate persons, if not also others by way of oral transmission of written texts, may have been aware that correspondences had been established by the fourteenth century between Odin and the Roman god Mercury as well as the planet of that name. Mitchell draws our attention to a runestick from the late fourteenth century which includes an invocation of Odin, albeit as the "greatest among devils," in order to magically determine the identity of a thief. Mitchell also notes that pagan and Christian elements had already begun to mix in fourteenth-century texts and rites seeking Odin's aid; he wisely compares this kind of sacred mélange to that one finds in African-diasporic religions such as Vodou and La Regla de Ocha (Lucumí, Santería). Although Mitchell doubts the continuing existence of a bona fide cult of Odin in the late Middle Ages, he does believe that Odin continued to be "understood as a potential source of power...wealth...and happiness" and a "source of power within Nordic ... charm magic" into at least the late fifteenth century.

Grimm, in *Teutonic Mythology*, relates that Swedish reports documented reverence of Odin from the sixteenth into the seventeenth century. Likewise, Mitchell points out that "Odin continued to be named in a variety of well-documented practices and beliefs" in later centuries, such as with the "Christmas sheaf" (*julkärve*) in winter festivals. In the early seventeenth century, a man named Jöns from Småland was condemned for having 'given himself up' to Odin, allegedly in seeking to obtain wealth, and for sharing the knowledge of the spell to obtain wealth with another man, Christman I Svenhult. The latter, in a rite similar to that we have already encountered, was to go "to a crossroads on a Thursday night, surrender himself to Odin," and invoke the god three times: "Odin come, Odin come, Odin come...I want to serve you." In the final years of the seventeenth century, Peter Rudebeck reported that numerous persons in Småland 'invited Odin as a guest' if they desired prosperity. Additional elements – together with the number nine, Thursday, etc. – were added to Odinic beliefs and practices at that time, including black horses and occasionally a black coach drawn by black horses, alluding to Odin's relationship to the Wild Hunt.

A mysterious event took place in eighteenth-century Sweden. A barrow was discovered in Småland, in a place referred to after the rise of Christianity as Hell's Mount. When the vault was opened, "there burst forth a wondrous fire, like a flash of lightning." Some were convinced that this was the tomb of Odin.

Long after the Germanic peoples were Christianized, Odin's/Wodin's memory survived in place-names including: Odense, Wednesbury (Woden's Fortress), Wednesfield (Woden's Plain, above the headwaters of the River Thames), Wôdenesberg, Wodnes beorh, Wodnes denu (Woden's Valley, in the bounds of West Overton), and Wodnesfield. Wistman's Wood in Cornwall may have once been a sacred grove of oaks honoring Odin/Woden.

In the nineteenth century, in Yorkshire, England, "the country people... in autumn, have a procession, and perform old dances, one of which they call the giants' dance. The principal giant they call Woden, and his wife Frigga." Also in the nineteenth century, Odin's head (*Ceann Odair*) was thought by many living on the island of North Uist in the Outer Hebrides, Scotland, to be buried on Griminish Farm, with "Grim" being a nickname of Odin. The nearby promontory fort of Caistel Odair is also named after Odin. In this same area, horse races, *An Odaidh*, were held into the nineteenth century that at least some persons linked to reverence of Odin. As the Reverend Archibald Macdonald related in 1894, "There can be little doubt that this [horse race] was the survival of a pagan festival in honour of...Odin, who was so much connected with the district....[M]any still living remember it."

In the Swedish province of Bleking in the nineteenth century, a sheaf of grain continued to be left on the harvested field for Odin's horse Sleipnir. Also in nineteenth-century Sweden, a people who had not sacrificed humans to Odin for centuries, performed a symbolic human sacrifice by blackening the faces of young men, dressing them in animal skins, and symbolically sacrificing them. Moreover, Macleod and Mees note, Odin's, as well as the trickster god Loki's, "memory may have survived into the late nineteenth century in a Lincolnshire [, England] sickness charm, usually thought to be of Nordic origin." This hybrid pagano-Christian charm reads in part:

Father, Son and Holy Ghost,
Nail the devil to this post –
With this mell (i.e., hammer) I thrice to knock
One for God and one for Wod (i.e., Woden/Odin) and one for Lok (i.e., Loki).[28]

Fogel suggests that the German-American representation of St. Niklas (St. Nicholas), nicknamed locally Belznikel, at Christmastime may have been inspired by Odin. He further suggested that behind the superstition of ravens and crows bringing bad luck might be traced back to Odin who, in the company of ravens, led dead heroes to Valhalla; and that, on the other hand, the horseshoe was thought to bring good luck because the horse was the steed of Odin.

Odin/Woden, like Holda and other female divinities, became associated in the Middle Ages with the Wild Hunt, Furious Host, or Herlething. In this role of the Wild Huntsman, Odin/Woden, according to William Henderson, came to be identified or synonymous with the Erl-King; although one might alternatively suggest that the Erl-King and the other personae signify peculiarly medieval (and post-medieval) manifestations of an Odin-like entity. Certain times and places were especially associated with the Wild Hunt, including nights of the full moon and the vicinity of the River Wye. The English monk Orderic Vitalis (1075-1142/ 1143) reported that in or near January 1091, a priest named Gualchem, associated with the Church of St. Albin in Bonneville, France, observed, in the vicinity of Angers (once the Celtic town of Juliomagus), the Wild Hunt. He was returning to Bonneville from administering last rites to a man known to him when he encountered an enormous crowd, some walking and others riding on horseback, including knights, clerics, and many other men as well as women. He realized that they were the spirits of the recently deceased, the *manes mortuorum*. Perhaps because of his predominantly Christian perspective, he imagined them to be undergoing a purgatorial experience. Of his vision, he remarked, "This is doubtless the troop of Herlechin, of which I have often heard but never believed." Walter Map (*c.* 1140/1159-*c.* 1210), in *De Nugis Curialium (Courtiers' Trifles, c.* 1181-1193), associates the Wild Hunt with the legendary British King Herla. Herla and his courtiers were said to have sojourned two hundred years with gnomes or fairies underground. Upon returning to ground level, the King and his courtiers realized that, should they dismount from their horses, they would immediately turn to dust; thus, they returned to the otherworldly realm. Eventually, however, they manifested as the Wild Hunt, transporting the souls of the dead to the Otherworld. In Map's view, the Wild Hunt also included erotic encounters between mortals and spirits. Occasionally mortals stole horses ridden by riders of the Wild Hunt; but such an act often cost them their lives. It is not difficult to understand why many persons did not wish to encounter the Wild Hunt, as it might result in death.

Map claims that the last time numerous persons observed the Wild Hunt in England was on December 19, 1154, that is, near the occasion of the winter solstice, during the first year of the reign of Henry II (1133-1189, r. 1154-1189). However, in 1180 and again in 1182, others living in France witnessed the Wild Hunt. Gulielmus Alvernus (Guillaume d'Auvergne, William of Auvergne, William of Paris, fl. 1218-d. 1249), Bishop of Paris, reported that certain persons continued to believe that they saw the Wild Hunt storming by on mountain roads in the early-to-mid thirteenth century. Also in the thirteenth century, Gervase of Tilbury documented the Hunt. Tales of the Wild Huntsmen becoming thieves and outlaws were appended to the original conception of the Hunt in the Middle Ages.

In the sixteenth-century, we find evidence of the Wild Hunt allegedly occurring in the vicinity of Lucerne,

Switzerland. The so-called "Army of God," the Guottisheer, replacing the earlier Wuottisheer, "Wotan's Army," many experienced seeing the dead pass by in a great group of dancers. It was considered an honor to be asked to join them, and it was thought that as a temporary participant in their festival, the honored participant would afterward be blessed with good fortune. In sixteenth-century Lower Saxony, the tale of the Wild Hunt experienced a significant metamorphosis. When, after being involved in a hunting accident, Hans von Hackelnberg, Chief Master of the Hounds to the Duke of Brunswick, lay upon his deathbed, the parson stood at the bedside praying for him. Defying the parson and his God, von Hackelnberg shouted, "The Lord may keep His Heaven, so He leave me my hunting!" The man of God, infuriated, cursed him: "Hunt then till the Day of Judgment!" Thus, the leader of the Wild Hunt was transformed in Lower Saxony into the person of Hans von Hackelnberg. Within a Christianized milieu, the leader of the Wild Hunt was occasionally, in the region of the Harz Mountains, also identified anti-Semitically with the Wandering Jew.

In the seventeenth century, de Lancre reported that in some places, the Wild Hunt was then being referred to as the "Hunt of King Arthur."

The Wild Hunt continued to occur in nineteenth-century France (in the forest of Fontainebleau), Sweden, and Germany (as the Wüthendes Heer). In Sweden, the chambers of ill persons were sometimes left open so that, if they wished, the sick and dying might join the ranks of the Wild Hunt. In nineteenth-century Germany, the Wild Hunt could best be observed by standing at a crossroad at midnight on Christmas Eve. In the forest of Grünewald, on the island of Möen, the leader of the Wild Hunt was thought to be headless and to hunt on horseback, carrying his head; this depiction may have inspired Washington Irving's figure of the Headless Horseman in "The Legend of Sleepy Hollow." Nineteenth-century Scottish Highlanders envisioned the Wild Hunt as the Sluagh, or "spirit multitude," an army of the dead whose blood fell upon the rocks, forming red lichen nicknamed Fuil nan Sluagh, "Blood of the Hosts."

In the early twentieth century, peasants of Carinthia (now divided between Austria and Slovenia) placed wooden bowls of meat in front of their homes to propitiate the leader of the Wild Hunt.

Unfortunately, during the twentieth century, many Nazis and other right-wing and fascist zealots reconstructed the reverence of Wotan and appropriated his figure to promote ultranationalism, white supremacy, virulent anti-Semitism, and right-wing totalitarianism. As Mattias Gardell amply demonstrates in *Gods of the Blood: The Pagan Revival and White Separatism* (2003), this tendency has continued into the present. Of course, other divine figures have been appropriated and perverted by other groups and individuals, as, for instance, has happened with Jesus Christ at the hands of right-wing Fundamentalist, "born again" Protestants like the minister Jerry Falwell and evangelical/charismatic Catholics like the actor Mel Gibson. Moreover, as Diana L. Paxson points out in

"Sex, Status, and *Seidh*" (1997), many present-day Pagans who revere Wotan/Odin and other Germanic divinities struggle against rightist values.

Sif

Sif is primarily known as the wife of the god Thor. She is also known for her beautiful, flowing, golden hair. After the trickster god Loki cut off her hair when she was sleeping, he was punished by having to make her an exquisite wig made of spun gold. Due to her beautiful hair, Sif's sacred plant is Golden Maidenhair (*Polytrichum aureum*), called *Sifjar-haddar*.

Otherwise, Sif's identity and roles remain somewhat mysterious and controversial. She may, like Jorð and Hloðyn, have been an earth-goddess associated with rites involving the drinking of mead (such as those described above); in the *Hymiskviða*, she is linked to a cauldron in which mead is brewed and to casks of mead. She may have also been a goddess of rain as well as of love and/or eroticism and possibly of cooking.

Evidence suggests that the reputation or cult of this goddess, usually (as in the opinion of Rudolf Simek) viewed as of very minor importance, may have risen significantly in medieval southern Germany. Sometime during this period, moreover, she was Catholicized as, or hybridized with, the Virgin Mary, as Mariasif and/or Mariahilf, the latter appellation suggesting a linkage of Sif with the goddesses Holda and Pharaildis, who are also called Hilda.

Thor

Thor, whose name means "Thunderer" or "Boldness," is, in a nutshell, a storm god and the Germanic Hercules. A burly, wild-eyed, red-haired man wearing iron gloves, Thor rides in a chariot drawn by goats. According to Richard Perkins in *Thor the Wind-Raiser and the Eyrarland Image* (2001), "Thor appears to 'play' his beard like a wind-instrument;" "Thor was thought capable of producing a wind by blowing into his [red] beard." Edgar C. Polomé observes that as a "thunder god, Thor was the protector of the peasant class, which depends on the weather for its crops" Thor's most well known attribute is his hammer, Mjöllnir, which signifies the thunderbolt and which is considered a being in its own right. Grimm notes that "brides and the bodies of the dead were [once] consecrated with it." Kveldulf Gundarsson, in *Teutonic Magic: The Magical and Spiritual Practices of the Germanic Peoples* (1990), also suggests that Thor is a god of eroticism, his hammer being a phallic symbol. Due to the tendency of Christian writers to employ Greek and Roman names for Classical, Celtic, and Germanic deities, it is frequently difficult to tell when they are referring to the reverence of the Roman Jupiter, the Germanic Thor, or the Celtic Taranis. However, we may assume that a majority of references to Thursday as a sacred day refer to Thor. Reverence of Thor or of an amalgam of Thor and kindred gods is evidenced by numerous penitentials which prohibit and condemn the "observ[ing of] Thursday in honor of Jupiter." In the seventh century, St. Eligius condemned keeping "Thursday holy in honour of

Jupiter;" he was especially concerned with a festival to Thor-Jupiter that occurred (and which persisted for centuries) on the first of May, a date that coincides with the Celtic celebration of Beltane and the Roman festival of Floralia. It also appears that another festival honoring Thor at the winter solstice was, with Christianization, displaced by Christmas.

St. Eligius also condemned the "render[ing of] any devotion to the gods of the trivium, where three roads meet." He might have been referring, as mentioned above, to sacrifices made to the goddess Hecate; but it is also possible that he referred rather to a well-known trinity of Germanic deities, namely Odin, Freyr or Frigga, and Thor. In the eighth century, many were continuing to revere the sacred tree/pillar Irminsul, which has been linked to the reverence of Thor. Eighth-century reverence of Thor, as well as consecration of Thursday to him, is also indicated by *Indiculus superstitionem et paganiarum* (*Index of Superstitions and Paganism*), as it is by the Anglo-Saxon *Penitential* "tentatively ascribed by Albers to Bede:" "Do not ... celebrate Thursday in honor of Jupiter ... according to pagan tradition." The *Homilia de sacrilegiis* of the late eighth century castigated those who "honor[ed] the day called Jupiter's [i.e., Thursday] because of Jupiter and [who did] no work on that day." In the eleventh century, Burchard of Worms (d. 1025) continued to find it necessary to warn against pagan practices on Thursdays.

With Christianization, the god of thunder became identified with Jesus Christ, with minstrels describing the latter as the "lord of thunder." William A. Chaney points out that in the late ninth century, the Christian god is either paired or identified with Thor as he "who thunders and rules," and a "land-grant of King Edward the Elder in A.D. 901...opens 'In the name of the High Thunderer, Creator of the world.'" However, Thor also came, paradoxically, to be identified with the Devil. It appears that in Christianized Germany, he became the object of a rite in which his effigy was brought to a church and then stoned and burned by a group of boys.

However, in the tenth century, it appears that a cult focusing on Thor may have arisen among defiant pagans in Scandinavia and in the British Isles. Audrey L. Meaney, in *Anglo-Saxon Amulets and Curing Stones* (1981), states: "Thor's hammers began to be worn commonly in Scandinavia in the tenth century, perhaps in emulation of the crosses worn by Christians. Could the English models have originated from the same cause – a desire by pagans to imitate and even counteract the wearing of a cross?"

A copper amulet of the eleventh century, probably worn "as a pendant," portraying a fish and perhaps belonging to a fisher folk, includes the protective spell, "May Thor protect him with that hammer which came out of the sea. A rune-stave from the close of the twelfth century calls for protection of its bearer: "Hail to you and (be) in good spirits!/ May Thor receive you./ May Odin own you."

A temple to Thor was still standing at Dublin in the final years of the tenth century. Likewise, a temple to him in Sweden was standing in 1125, that is, in the High Middle Ages, when it was destroyed and its sacred hammers stolen by Magnus Nilsson.

With Christianization, many came to demonize Thor. In spite of this – or, alternatively, in part due to this – shift, it appears that some practitioners of magic called on Thor as a demonic spirit who could assist them with their spells. In *Runic Amulets and Magic Objects* (2006), Mindy Mcleod and Bernard Mees note, "Some of the spells recorded in Scandinavian spell books…call on old Germanic deities such as Odin and Thor…often in the company of Satan or Beelzebub." One spell from the late eleventh century, "recorded in a manuscript from Canterbury," invokes Thor as the "lord of ogres." In late sixteenth-century France, Thursday was thought to be a special time for witches to congregate – perhaps an association with Thor or Jupiter.

Richard Perkins observes, following Oscar Montelius, in *Thor the Wind-Raiser and the Eyrarland Image* (2001), that as "late as the seventeenth century, Thor was being held responsible for rain in Småland in Sweden." Also at this time, Thursday also continued to be considered sacred in Sweden, where, according to Grimm, "[r]elapses into paganism [then called *launblôt*] were frequent." Sacrifices continued to be made to Thor at Närke (or Nerike), in Orebro County, in the seventeenth century. Moreover, some persons continued to swear by Thor, as "Thore-Gud."

A mysterious event occurred in the eighteenth century when a group of Swedish sailors working for the Dutch, whaling near Greenland, became lost in a tempest. Noticing the light of a distant fire, they finally reached the shore where it blazed. There, they encountered an old man who was warming himself at the fire. When he asked them where they'd come from, they at first answered from Holland; when he asked a second time, they explained that they were working for the Dutch, but that their home was Bohuslän. He then asked them if they knew where Thorsby was. When they responded affirmatively, he asked them if they were familiar with the collection of "great stones and the earthmounds" there. When they again responded affirmatively, he asked if they would beseech the people there to preserve the site and protect it from destruction. If they promised to do so, they would be rewarded with a "good wind." How would this old man ensure their gaining a fair wind? "My name is Thorer Brack," the old man told them; he was the spirit of, or an avatar of, the god of thunder, banished by the Church. "My habitation is there; but I am now a fugitive. In the great mound by the Ulfvesberg my whole race lies buried, and at Glosshed's altar we performed our worship to the gods." The sailors "then parted from the old man and had a fair wind home."

In the late eighteenth century, in the Harz region of Germany, "before cows are taken out to pasture for the first time in spring, they are made to step over an ax and a fire steel, wrapped in a blue apron. Thórr's 'belt of might' appears in Norse folklore as a 'blue band.' It may thus be seen that the blue color, as well as the blue flame, symbolized this deity."

In nineteenth-century Holstein, anyone who could do so would abstain from labor on Thursdays, particularly women from spinning, fearing that if they spun, they would be struck by lightning. In Bavaria, as a storm approached, the windows of houses would be thrown open in order to let the thunderbolt be able to pass freely through the houses and then return to its owner.

According to William Shepard Walsh in *Curiosities of Popular Customs* (1898), numerous persons continued to employ Thor's hammers in nineteenth-century Iceland in the hope that they would protect them from dangerous storms. In the early twentieth century, sheeps' bones that resembled Thor's Hammer were worn by seamen sailing in the North Sea.

In Germany, where Thor eventually became identified with the Devil, he came to be called Hammer or Meister Hämmerlein; his hammer came to be associated with certain pieces of rock and belemnites called "thunderstones" (my maternal ancestors from Lithuania Minor/East Prussia referred to them as "*Perkuhnsteine*," "stones of the [Baltic] god Perkûnas"). Likewise, nineteenth- and early twentieth-century Danes continued to keep thunderstones in their houses to protect against storm damage. Similarly, houseleek and stonecrop, two plants corresponding to Thor, both nicknamed "Donnerbart" (i.e., "Thunderbeard") in German, continued to be planted on roofs of houses in nineteenth-century Germany, France, and England to protect against lightning. In regard to plants, Thor is also associated with aconite, basil, chamomile, nettle, thistle, and vervain, which also protect against damage by thunder and lightning.

Thor's memory, like Odin's, also lingered on in place-names. Isaac Taylor, in *Words and Places; or, Typological Illustrations of History, Ethnology, and Geography* (1902), observes:

> We find traces of the worship of this deity in the names of Thundersfield in Surrey, two places called Thundersleigh in Essex and one in Hants, as well as Thundridge in Herts and Thunderhill in Surrey. To the name of Thor we may assign Thursley in Surrey, Thurleigh in Bedfordshire, Kirby Thore in Westmoreland, Thurscross in Yorkshire, Thurston in Suffolk, Thurstable and Thurlov in Essex, Thursfield in Staffordshire, Thursford in Norfolk, Tursdale in Durham, Thurshelton in Devon, Thursby in Cumberland, Thurso in Caithness, Torness in Shetland, and Thorigny in Normandy, all of which, as we have seen, are in regions settled more or less by Scandinavian colonists.[29]

In late 1905, C. J. Tabor reported receiving a "Thar-Cake" (or, Tharf cake, Therf cake, Thor cake, Thurd cake), also known as a "Parken [or, Parkin, Perkin] cake," from a Miss Berry who lived in Oldham, Lancashire, England. Similar to gingerbread, with ingredients including ginger, candied peel, almonds, and treacle, it is typically served on November 5th, Bonfire Night (or, Guy Fawkes Night). Tabor writes: "According to local authorities this date coincides with an old feast in honor of the Scandinavian god Thor." Others, however, named the cake a "Har-Cake" and claimed that it was sacred to Woden/Odin, one of his names being Har. These cakes may have also honored the dead and been offered to ancestors.

Edwin Miller Fogel (1874-1949) suggests, in *Beliefs and Superstitions of the Pennsylvania Germans* (1915), that among Pennsylvania Germans of the nineteenth and early twentieth centuries, various customs and superstitions might be traced to the reverence of Thor (also called Donar). These include: the placing of a stone, the *Donarkeil*, thought to be produced by thunder and lightning, under one's pillow to alleviate insomnia; eating greens on Thursday; driving cattle to pasture on Thursday; expecting a thunderstorm to occur on a certain Thursday; and the significant use of the color red, corresponding to Thor, as in wearing "red flannel underwear … to prevent rheumatism and in" tying red wool or string "about the finger to stop nosebleed;" Red was, however, due to the influence of Christianity, contradictorily viewed as a sign of trickery or evil; having once been sacred to Thor, the color was now transferred by some to the Devil. For this reason, reddish horses and red-haired persons were not to be trusted. Intriguingly, the early twentieth-century sociologist and folklorist Newbell Niles Puckett believed that in the United States, West African and Germanic sacred semiotics may have 'infiltrated' each other so that concepts concerning red were hybridized in Southern, including New Orleans', manifestations of Vodou; red is traditionally a chief color used in sacred arts and attire of Vodouisants.

Þrúðr

Although it is not clear whether or not she possessed a cult with followers, it is worthy of note that Þrúðr, or, Trude, is the name of Thor's daughter. The word Þrúðr which appears to have possessed multivalent signification, signified not only strength, power, and fortitude, but also truth, maidenhood, and virginity. Thor's daughter, an unmarried Valkyrie, was apparently so significant a figure at one point that her name was taken by many women including, it appears, Saints Gertrude and Hiltrude. On the other hand, during the medieval period, perhaps due to her and their reputation as practitioners of magic and/or as Valkyries, her name also became synonymous with "witch." Her name may also be etymologically linked to "troth" and "truth."

The Valkyries

The Valkyries, whose name signifies "to choose" (*kiosa*), relates to the choosing of which side will win a battle as well as the choosing of those who will live or die in battle, and those among "the carnage of the battlefield" (*valr*) who will be taken to Valhalla, the paradisal afterlife of warriors, and honored as ancestral heroes. There are said to be nine Valkyries; the most well known is Brunhilde. Grimm describes them as beautiful Amazon-like women, "their lances, helmets and shields glitter[ing]," riding into battle on magnificent horses." "Rooted in their being is an irresistible longing for this warlike occupation." However, they are also patrons of spinners, weavers, embroiderers, painters, and writers. The Valkyries eventually came to be associated with the Roman goddesses Bellona and Minerva, with Germanic goddesses including the Dísir and the later Holda and Perchta, with the divinities or elementals known as the Wild Women of the Woods, and with bees (as "stingers"). In the Christianized Anglo-Saxon charms, probably of the tenth or eleventh centuries, the Valkyries are acknowledged as "Victory Dames" (*sigewîf*) but are also demonized as "evil spirits possessing...swarming insects." In the early eleventh century, the Valkyries became increasingly identified with *wicce*, witches. Anna-Leena Siikala notes that "[c]eiling frescoes dated 1300 in the Cathedral of Schleswig, Northern Germany ... depict a "Valkyria" [as] a female witch aside a broomstick." During the witchcraft trial of Ragnhild Tregagås at Bergen in 1324, a spell intended to "dissolve the marriage of her former lover, Bárd," surfaced; herein, she invoked the spirit of the Valkyries: "May the first bite you in the back./ May the second bite you in the breast./ May the third turn hate and envy upon you." Thus, we may acknowledge that veneration of the Valkyries persisted into the Late Middle Ages.[30]

Chapter 4
Slavic and Baltic Divinities

Slavic Divinities

In 980 CE, Vladimir the Great, a Christian convert, forfeited his allegiance to the Church to lead a pagan resistance movement against Christianization. He had a great statue of Perun, the god of thunder and lightning, built, and commenced worshiping in a sacred grove. In the manner of Julian the Apostate, he "erected new idols" on a hill near the palace at Berestove; seeking to stabilize and synthesize a Slavic pantheon, he emphasized reverence of and sacrifice to the gods Perun, Khors, Dazhbog, Stribog, and Simargl, and the goddess Mokosh. One might describe this attempt as an early NeoPagan experiment. Simultaneously, he commenced turning Kievan Rus' "into one of the most powerful states in Eastern Europe." Not long after, however, Vladimir once more yielded to Christian conversion and shortly thereafter insisted upon the forced Christianization of his subjects. Following official Christianization, at the end of the tenth century, numerous deities, particularly goddesses, came to be associated with witches and witchcraft, including Baba Yaga (Russian; in Wendish, Jaga-Baba), N'ed'el'a (Ukrainian; or Nedolya, Russian), and Pjatnica (Russian and Serbian), goddesses of night and the dead; and Kolyada (Russian) and Pehtra Baba (Slovenian).

Ciza

Ciza, whose name signifies "alive" or "breast," the latter signifying "nurturer," is a great goddess of the Wends, Czechs, Serbs, Poles, and others. She might also have been discussed under Germanic divinities, as she appears to have also been worshipped by the Suevi. She has been associated with goddesses including Isis (especially as Eysen), Aphrodite/Venus, Artemis/Diana, Demeter/Ceres, Nerthus, Sif, Holda, and Dziewanna; like Artemis/Diana, she carries a javelin, is accompanied by hounds, and dwells in the forest. At some point, Ciza became conflated with Bensozia, as Bena Ziza, the "good Ziza," and with fairies.

Often depicted as naked and as crowned with grape leaves, and as holding apples and grapes, she is a goddess of earth, of the sun, moon, stars (the *Siebengestirn*, i.e., the Pleiades), and fresh water (especially of lakes). She is a guardian of forests and wild animals; and she encourages the growth of plants and crops. She also brings happiness, beauty, good fortune, and peace and is a patron of marriages, children, and midwives.

Grains and eggs were offered to her. Three of her major cult centers were at Augsburg (formerly called Cisara or Zisaris), Rostock, and Racibórz, Germany. A wooden temple appears to have been built for her at Augsburg. The cathedral at Racibórz is believed to have been built over the ruins of her temple there. She was celebrated on what is now Shrove Tuesday as well as on September 29. On the former holiday, raised donuts or fritters dipped in honey, now called *fastnachts* by Germans and German-Americans, were offered to her and ceremonially eaten. Long after official Christianization, some persisted in thinking that Ash Wednesday signified returning to Ciza as Mother Earth. At the September festival, in the nineteenth century taking the form of the Schnitterin, she was celebrated as the Kornmutter, the Corn Mother, as well as the Messerweible, the Sickle-Woman. Her worship was officially banned around 965; her cult, however, persisted later into the Middle Ages.

The poet Küchlin (1373-1391?/ fl. 1437?), who lived at Augsburg, wrote:

> They built a great temple therein,
> To the honour of Zise the heathen goddess
> Whom they after heathen customs
> Worshipped at that time;
> The city was named Zisaris
> After the heathen goddess, [who] was its glory.
> The temple long stood entire
> Until its fall .[31]

Both Morena and Ciza have, due in large part to Christianization and popular resistance to it, been transformed into carnivalesque figures.

Dazhbog

Dazhbog is a benevolent sun god, a giver of wealth and bountiful harvests, and a special protector of the dead. He is depicted as having a silver head and a golden moustache. He lives in the far east, in a golden palace, in a land of eternal summer. He is born every morning, as a young man rides in a chariot drawn by fire-breathing white horses, becomes a mature king at noon, and dies as an old man each evening. On the summer solstice, he weds the moon goddess. He rules over twelve kingdoms, which signify the twelve signs of the zodiac. His children are the stars.

Jelena, the Vila, Hyperochus and Amadocus

It appears that either the sun goddess Jelena or (the) Vila, or a multiple manifestation of this divinity, may have been revered in Bosnia and Herzegovina from ancient times into the fourteenth century and thereafter. (The) Vila is a beautiful, "fair-skinned winged woman with glistening garments and golden hair falling to her feet," a goddess of forests, flowers, herbs, and bodies of water. A guardian of animals possessing the power of metamorphosis, she may transform into a "snake, swan, falcon, horse, or whirlwind." A goddess of prophecy and healing, she is also associated with the fairies.

In an expression of Late Antique or medieval hybridity, she formed a triad or trinity with the Hyperborean heroes Hyperochus and Amadocus. The goddess and the heroes were venerated in the vicinity of the cave of Vjetrenica, near the village of Zavala, in Herzegovina. This cave, once inhabited by cave bears and leopards, was known to persons of the Middle Ages as a place where fairies sang and danced. Moreover, from the sounds of wind blowing in the cave, diviners predicted the future. Marian Wenzel observes: "The ritual involving the Goddess and the [divinized heroes] is still [in the mid-twentieth century] into a purification ceremony in the event of plague. It is performed both for cattle and for people."

The Vila sometimes manifested as plural female beings. As such, they were known to shoot arrows, often fatal, at those who intruded upon their rites. Those who made offerings to them, however, like Bulgarians who tied colorful rags to trees and cast cakes into the water, or who offered them sprigs of thyme, oregano, and burning-bush (or, false dittany), plants used in traditional medicine, were welcomed.

Their dances were believed to produce crop circles, *vilino kolo*.

In the late nineteenth century, votaries continued to make offerings to the Vila(s). These were primarily young women living on the Croatian Littoral on the coast of the Adriatic Sea who would place, on sacred stones and in grottoes, flowers, fruits, and silk belts. As they did so, they would chant, "Take, O Vila, that which you desire."

The Serbian writer, archaeologist, teacher, and editor Milan Đ. Miliéeviæ (1831-1908), shared an account of a traveler who, asking the name of a church in Niš, Serbia, built in the eleventh century, was told that it was called "Holy Mother of God Rusalia (or, Rusalija)." The traveler remarked, "But Rusalia is not the name of the Holy Mother." "Well, then," the peasant replied, "Let it be the Holy Trinity Rusalia."

Khors, Simargl, Stribog

Little is known of Khors, Simargl, or Stribog. Possibly of Persian/Iranian origin, Khors is a god of the sun and moon, health and hunting, bountiful harvests, fair weather, destiny, righteousness, and creativity. Devotees appear to have been addressed prayers to him at dawn while facing eastward. Simargl appears to have originated as a fabulous creature of ancient Persia/Iran, bearing resemblance to a griffin; at some point, he evolved into a god of bountiful crops and later into the legendary Firebird. Simargl was celebrated at the summer solstice and eventually Christianized as the Holy Trinity. Stribog is a god of the air and especially of cold weather as well as a distributor of wealth. The cults of Dazhbog, Khors, Simargl, and Stribog appear to have both climaxed and, for the most part, culminated in the final years of the tenth century.

Lada

Lada is a Wendish as well as a pan-Slavic and Baltic goddess of beauty, fertility, and marriage who is depicted holding a ring in her right hand. Lada's favorite beverage is mead. She is associated with the planet Jupiter and celebrated in springtime. Her cult is thought to have originated in the Neolithic. She may have been worshipped by the Celts, and she corresponds to the Germanic goddesses Freyja and Lofn, the latter of whom is the patron of non-marital love. Carved figures of her may have stood in meadows, typically within birch forests, and may have been decorated with guelder-roses, rue, garden lovage, and evergreens.

Her cult appears to have persisted into the fifteenth or sixteenth century.

Plants sacred to Lada continue to decorate the heads of young Ukrainian women attending traditional weddings. When young women throw these head-wreaths into streams, they divine their prospects for marriage depending on how the wreath is carried by the water. A Ukranian praise-song which includes the lines, "Blessed are you, O Mother Lada, you who calls in spring and dismisses winter, also suggests that her reverence continued into the nineteenth and perhaps also the twentieth century. In the *Encyclopedia of Ukraine*, we find: "Some colloquial expressions allude to the cult of Lada: in Volhynia *laduvaty* means to conduct a wedding, and in Transcarpathia ... *ladkanky* [or *ladkanie*] are wedding songs, and *ladkaty* is to sing wedding songs."

Morena

Morena (or, Marena, Marzaniok, Mór, Mora, Morana), the goddess of winter as well as of death and regeneration, whose name signifies "to freeze" as well as the month of March, was most probably revered until the mid-to-late tenth century, when Poles were being converted to Christianity. Some, however, continued to revere her into (at least) the nineteenth century, offering her grain at harvest-time. She came to be linked to other figures: Poles linked her to Jagusia, Baœka, or Zoœka, while Russians linked her to Alkonost. As a goddess or similar being of death, she is patron of the cemetery. She is also a shapeshifter who can "take on a variety of shapes, such as a black cat, a white crow, [a] goose, a stone figure of the Blessed Mother, and even a [Catholic] priest." She announces herself by knocking on a door or window three nights in a row or else is announced by the howling of a dog, the hooting of an owl, the screeching of a magpie, or a broom or picture falling for no apparent reason.

Mokosh

Wends and other Slavs also revered the great goddess Mokosh. Her name alternately signifies "damp" (*mokryi*) – as in "Damp Mother Earth" – "to plait," and "Mother of the cat" (*maty kota*). Further, it has been suggested that her name is related to or derived from the Greek *malakia*, transformed into *mok-oši*, which connotatively signifies both gender diversity, typically "effeminacy," and moistness brought about by erotic activity; if this is the case, then it is possible that she might be associated with self-pleasuring, same-sex eroticism, and transgender behavior or identity. She is occasionally associated with the Slavic goddesses Ciza and Morena. She is sometimes compared to Hecate and Aphrodite and to Freyja, Holda, and Percht, as well as to the Persian divinities Anahita and Ardvi. She is typically depicted as holding a cornucopia. She presides over birth, death, and destiny. A goddess of moistness and fertility, Mokosh is described as a deity of both water and earth and was invoked to bring rain. Like Diana, she protects animals and is a patron of cats. She presides over the growing of hemp, the raising and shearing of sheep, the making of wool, and spinning. She is a special patron of women, especially spinners. She sometimes embodies stones, especially menhirs and breast-shaped stones, and blind and disabled persons offered wool and sacrificed sheep to these stones to receive her healing power. She is also a goddess of divination and magic. Friday is her sacred day, and October 28th her feast-day; at this time, grain and sacrificial animals were offered to her. On the eve of Christianization of Kievan Rus', she was the only female deity in Vladimir the Great's pantheon prior to his conversion. She continued, however, to be revered into the sixteenth century. In the centuries that followed, much of her cult was appropriated for Saint Paraskeva (or, Parasceve, Paraskeviia, "Saint Friday"). However, Mokosh also became the archetypal witch. Her memory was preserved into the nineteenth and twentieth centuries in folktales and in Russian embroidery, which depicts her as a woman raising her hands in supplication and flanked by horsemen (reminiscent of the great goddess of the Scythians). In certain places, Mokosh continued to be venerated as a patron of the household.

Perûn

Perûn was one of the most widely worshipped deities of the Slavs; he is generally synonymous with the widely worshipped Baltic deity Perkûnas and also shares many attributes with the Germanic Thor. The sharing of these attributes with Thor is not surprising, as one of his chief centers of worship was at Novgorod, where Slavs intermixed with Germanics. He is a god of thunder, lightning, and rain, the ruler of the heavens, lord of harvest and, later, a god of war. He is typically depicted with a silver head and golden moustache and as riding in a fiery chariot. Among his attributes are the oak, the Perûnik flower (*Iris germanica*), the rooster, the six-spoked wheel, and Thursday. Offerings and sacrifices, such as of cocks, were made to him beneath oaks, and a sacred fire of oak wood was kept eternally burning for him. The penalty for letting the fire die was death. A rainmaking rite to Perûn included "naked flower-decked maiden[s] whirling ecstatically;" and whenever oaths were sworn, they were sworn in his name. His festival took place on July 20.

During the reign of the Kievan Prince White Igor Rurikovich, specifically, in 944 or 945 CE, Igor signed a peace treaty with the Byzantine Christians, whereby pagans and Christians were to dwell together in peace, with pagans swearing to Perûn and Christians swearing to Christ. The treaty appears to have succeeded for a number of years. As in other such cases, this tolerance on the part of a pagan ruler led, rather rapidly, to the 'triumph' of Christianity and the formal banning of earth-centered, indigenous traditions.

In 980, Vladimir the Great had a great statue of Perûn built, and he commenced worshiping the god in a sacred grove, together with the deities Khors, Dazhbog, Stribog, and Simargl, and Mokosh. Simultaneously, he commenced turning Kievan Rus' "into one of the most powerful states in Eastern Europe." In December 987, however, Vladimir reconverted to Christianity. He appears to have concluded that his conversion and the region's Christianization would "strengthen the state and increase its prestige among his Christian neighbors," that "a monotheistic religion would consolidate his power, as Christianity and Islam had done for neighboring rulers." More specifically, his conversion allowed him to marry Anna, the sister of Basil, then ruler of the Byzantine Empire; and relations with Bulgaria, Germany, and Poland improved dramatically. He had the statues of the pagan deities destroyed. He commanded that the statue of Perûn (which the Catholic historian Jan Dlugosz [1415-1480] describes as "wonderful") be dragged by a horse and thrown into the Dnieper River. As he did so, "men and women began to cry ... . Perûn ... toppled over with a resounding crash. Harnessed bulls pulled him over dung while soldiers bastinadoed him."

Vladimir then founded the Church of St. Vasily (St. Basil) on its ruins, following which he took the Christian name of Vasily. He allotted a tenth of all property under his control to the Church as an act of tithing. On August 1, 988, he commanded that all persons of Kiev be baptized in the Dnieper River by the Bishop of Korsun and numerous Greek Orthodox priests. Any who disobeyed had their goods confiscated. In the thirteenth century, Vladimir/Vasily was canonized for his role in Christianizing the region.

In the twelfth century, however, in *The Story of How the Pagan Peoples Worshipped Idols and Offered Sacrifices*, an anonymous Russian scholar complained, "[E]ven today, those living in the outskirts worship the god Perûn and other pagan gods." Many sermons of the twelfth and later centuries continued to condemn the persistent reverence of Perûn; in the twelfth century, one frustrated priest bemoaned, "Even now, in remote places, they pray to him, the cursed god, Perûn." In 1274, Church authorities in Kiev found it necessary to once more ban reverence of Perûn.

Baron Sigismund von Herberstein (1486-1566), an ethnographer who sojourned in Russia as a diplomat in 1517 and 1526, noted in *Rerum Moscoviticarum Commentarii* (*Notes on Muscovite Affairs*, pub. 1549), that when the statue of Perûn was destroyed during the late tenth century, a rope appeared on the bridge near where the statue had been cast into the water and, just as a pagan was undergoing baptism, the god Perûn said of the rope, "This is for you, O inhabitants of Novogorod, in memory of me." The rope was meant to be a sign of punishment awaiting those who had betrayed their ancient god. "From that time forward," von Herberstein noted, "for a period of over five hundred years, whenever the Novogorodians heard the voice of Perun, they would lash each other with ropes for having betrayed their god ... . Such a tumult arises therefrom that all the efforts of the Governor can scarcely assuage it."

Boris Rybakov observes that in the vicinity of Novgorod, in defiance of Christianity, devotees of Perûn continued to keep 'eternal' fires burning for Perûn into the seventeenth century. Perûn is remembered in place-names like Perunovo in Belarus. Some Slavs continue to call Thursday *Perendan* (Perûn's Day).

According to W. E. S. Ralston in *The Songs of the Russian People* (1872), although Christians fairly successfully appropriated the traits of Perûn for St. Elijah, the god's memory persisted into the nineteenth and early twentieth centuries, when Croatians took note of him when gathering fern blossoms on Midsummer Eve, and among certain Ukrainians, "May Perûn strike you dead" persisted as the most terrible curse.

Perperuna

Perperuna is the spouse or female counterpart of Perun. Unfortunately, little is now known about her. Her name is thought to be a feminization of Perûn, with her original name probably having "been lost at an early date." She was invoked by those desiring rain, with virgins typically assuming central roles in these rites.

Pripoldnica

More is known of others whose reverence faded during the High Middle Ages, for instance, that of the cult of Pripoldnica (or, Poludnica, Poludniowka, Poludnitsa, Prezpoldnica, Prezpolnica, Pripolnica, Przypoludnica, Pschesponiza, Pschiponiza, Psezpolnica, Pshespolniza). The Wends may well have venerated Pripoldnica, the 'Midday Spirit' or 'Midday Witch.' A crone, she is described as airy and white, as having red eyes and a long red tongue, and as wearing a crown of weeds. She carries a whip or sickle and rides on gusts of wind or on a flying wheel. Reminiscent of Hecate, she is sometimes accompanied by seven black dogs. She, or a spirit resembling her, appears to have been known to the ancient Israelites, as suggested by Psalms 91:6, where we read of "the destruction that wasteth at noonday;" and she appears to have been known to sixth-century CE Parisians, as is suggested by Gregory of Tours in The History of the Franks, where a woman who prophesied an imminent conflagration was mocked as being "possessed by the noontide demon." She is also highly reminiscent of the Irish banshee and the Spanish/Mexican hybrid pagan-Catholic personae la Llorona and Santissima Muerte. She frequently attacks agricultural labors who work during noontime when they should be resting. She also brings storms, illness, and death (including decapitation) to those who anger or neglect her by not speaking with her. On the other hand, she can be of great assistance to agricultural workers, espec-ially those who respect her and engage her in conversation. To these, she brings abundant harvests. She was acknowledged and venerated by some into (at least) the late nineteenth century.

Rod

Rod, a god of destiny who shares a bond with the Rozhanytsi, may also have served as high god of the Eastern Slavs; as such, he is symbolized by a six-petalled rose inside a circle (called *gromovoi znak*), which continued to be carved on roofs in the early twentieth century in order to protect one's dwelling from lightning.

The Rozhanytsi

The Rozhanytsi (or, Rožanicas, Rozanice) are Slavic goddesses of destiny. Their name derives from *pryoda*, "nature," and *roditi*, or *rodyty*, "to give birth;" they are also known as the Orisnicas (Bulgarian, from the Greek oriza, "to determine," bearing a rather uncanny resemblance to the Yòrubá term for "divinity," *orishá*), Sudnice (Czech), and Sreca (Serbian). Although their worship was explicitly forbidden in the twelfth century, the goddesses of destiny persisted into the early twentieth century. Candles were lit for them, and they were offered salt, bread, cheese, honey, and wine, especially by Croatians and Slovenians, when children were born. Comparable to the Fates or Norns, the Rozhanytsi have pale skin and wear white garments, white scarves on their heads, and necklaces of gold and silver.

When they appear at midnight as a triad, upon the birth of a child, they divide the pronouncement of the child's destiny amongst themselves. The third that each pronounces differs depending on locale. In some places, the first and second foretell different positive aspects of that child's life, while the third foretells negative experiences. In another, the first pronounces the destiny; the second modifies it, either by "intensifying or softening" it; and the third finalizes it. In yet another, the first foretells the number of years of life and on occasion the type of death; the second foretells occupation; and the third, marriage and other significant events. The Rozhanytsi also offer the infant gifts. Sometimes these are tangible presents, but more often they are attributes; for example, the first may offer intellect; the second, health, beauty, or eloquence; and the third, a successful career or prosperity. Offerings to the Rozhanytsi include bread, salt, grits, wine, candles, gold, and silver coins, upon a child's birth and on September 9th. When Slavs were being Christianized, one of the main questions they were "asked" in the twelfth century was: "Have you offered, at the time of someone's birth, bread, cheese, and honey to the Rozhanytsi?," thus signifying their importance in Slavic life. Then they were told, "The faithful should serve God and not the Rozhanytsi." Indeed, so significant were the Rozhanytsi in the late thirteenth century that on one of the occasions when the Bible was translated, the passage from Isaiah (65: 11) which reads, "But ye are they that forsake the Lord, that forget my holy mountain, that prepare a table for that troop, and that furnish the drink offering unto that number," was translated as, "You have abandoned me and prepared a table for the Rozhanytsi."

Svantovit, Triglav, Porenut, and Rugevit

Wends also revered the gods Svantovit, Triglav, Porenut, and Rugevit. Like some Hindu deities, they possess multiple heads.

Svantovit (or, Svantevit, Svetovit, Sviatovyt, Svyatovit, Swiatowid), the "holy one," is a god of war, the sun, and agriculture. Like Svarog, he was sometimes identified as or with Radegast. He is depicted as a handsome, beardless man, with very curly hair; as naked or as wearing armor (when depicted as such, a silver sword hangs from his belt); as having four heads, perhaps representing the seasons; and as holding a bow in his left hand and a metal drinking horn in his right. A magnificent saddle and bridle were placed next to his statue. Birds, oxen, and horses are sacred to him. His beautiful white horse was utilized in divination: a step forward with its right foot meant good fortune, while one with its left foot betokened disaster. Svantovit was honored annually with a harvest feast that drew great crowds; he was offered honey cakes, wine was poured into his drinking horn, and cattle were sacrificed to him. At this feast, the high priest divined the future by way of analyzing the filled drinking horn and by way of hippomancy, divination deploying horses. In or near 1135, King Eric II (r. 1134-1137) of Denmark set out for Slavic lands. He seized the town of Arkona on the island of Rügen, where the Rans Wends lived and had a great temple. Eric and his men besieged the fortress in which the temple to Svantovit, with its crimson curtains, stood. Eric first cut off drinking water to those who refused to convert. Then, after some desperate for water converted, he gave the populace one more chance. This time, all who refused to convert were killed; the others were baptized. Not long after he left Arkona, however, Eric learned that those who had converted had returned to paganism. Svantovit was, however, eventually Catholicized as St. Vitus.

Triglav's three heads represent the lower, middle, and upper worlds. His black horse was used in divinatory rites. It is possible that he commenced as a goddess, Trigla, or that he became a goddess, or that his feminine counterpart or spouse was Trigla. In the eleventh century, Otto (1060/1061-1139) equated Triglav with a demonic spirit and claimed to exorcize him from a female devotee. In 1150, however, many were still revering Triglav. Thus, upon the death of the Christian prince Pribislav-Henry, his wife Petrissa, also Christian, surrendered his domain to the Germans because she feared that if she didn't, the Wends would remain pagan. Triglav was eventually Catholicized as St. Ethelbert or St. Peter.

Porenut is depicted with five heads, one for each direction, plus a fifth on his chest. He is sometimes shown holding a trident and rising from the sea. He is a god of justice and marriage and a patron of mariners, reminiscent of Poseidon.

Rugevit, the "god of Rügen," is depicted with seven heads and with seven swords hanging from his belt and an eighth in his hand, indicating his role as a war god. He is also a god of springtime and fertility. The oak, the color red, and the swallow are sacred to him; the first two of these suggest that he shares traits with Perun as well as with the Germanic Thor and the Baltic Perkûnas.

In 1168, the Wendish princes Tetislav and Jaromir were forced to open the temples of Porenut and Rugevit to Christian forces. These temples, located in the town of Garz, harbored great wealth, including gold and silver, exquisite purple silk, and weapons. The Christians plundered the temples and chopped and burned the statues of the gods. Despite this tragic occurrence, it is nonetheless significant that Svantovit, Triglav, Porenut, and Rugevit were all revered into the High Middle Ages.

Svarog

The cults of other divinities persisted into later centuries. Svarog, a Russian and Wendish deity, is the "bright" god, the embodiment of the creative power of nature. He is a god of the sky (from the Sanskrit *swarga*, "sky"), the sun, fire, and thunder. His name is also related to *svara* and *svarka*, which signify "conflict," "dispute," and "war;" thus, he probably also hails as a god of war. He is the father of the gods Dazhbog and Svarogich. He shares numerous traits with the Slavic god Perûn. His worship probably commenced at the onset of the Iron Age. He is mentioned by Procopius of Caesarea (fl. 530; d. after 562), and John Malalas (*c.* 491-578) identifies him with the Greek god Hephaestus, perhaps because it is said that he created the sun from glowing metal. His cult proliferated during the eleventh and twelfth centuries. The Church found it necessary to ban worship of Svarog and of fire in the fourteenth century, that is, in the Late Middle Ages, two hundred years after his worship had been banned among the Wends and over three hundred years in what is now Russia and the Ukraine.

Veles

Veles, sometimes depicted with the head of a bear, at other times as a serpent that dwells in the water, or else as a dragon, is a god of the forest as well as of cattle, wealth, commerce, and trade. As with Perûn, persons concluding treaties swore an oath to Veles. The god was celebrated during the winter solstice and the spring equinox; and although he was Christianized as Saint Vlas (Vlasii, or St. Blaize), in south Russia, during the harvest festival, the last sheaf, plaited into a knot, was called the " 'beard' of Veles" into the nineteenth century.

Yarilo

The god Yarilo (or, Erilo, Iarilo, Jarilo, Jarylo, Yarylo; also, Gerovit) is represented by a young man "adorned with flowers and carrying jingle-bells, with his face painted red and white." He is also depicted as barefoot, wearing a white cape and a crown of wheat and wildflowers, holding ears of wheat in one hand, and riding a garlanded, white stallion. His name suggests "corn sown in springtime;" young women led the dance in his honor at the time of spring sowing. Linguists have also noted that *yar* is used widely in the Ukrainian language to evoke "light, warmth, or strength." His name also signifies "ardent" or "passionate;" reminiscent of Dionysus and Eros, he is a god of erotic love and fecundity. He provides abundance of rye and wheat. In spring, probably at equinox, was a festival for him celebrating fecundity. At a rite called Semik, on June 4th, or at the summer solstice, his funeral took place; at this time, he returns to the heavens. The most beautiful maiden of the village was chosen to play the part of Yarilo. Condemned by Christians, Yarilo's festival continued to be celebrated in 1121, when around 4,000 "men and women, who had gathered together from all over Rus," gathered to honor Yarilo with "erotic dancing" and "shrieks of delight." Eighteenth-century Russians at Voronezh continued, in springtime or early summer, to celebrate the god; at this time, his festival was called a "satanic game" by Church authorities. Gimbutas notes that in "Kostroma, until 1771, people buried an idol [of Yarilo] with exaggerated attributes" as part of a ceremonial rite in honor of the god; "[t]he burial of a phallic idol typifies the year god's cycle." At this time, the Church, via bishop St. Tikhon Zadonskij, once more officially banned the festival. Although Yarilo eventually became hybridized with St. Elias and/or St. George, it is, in my view, significant that he continued to be revered into the late eighteenth century. In 1913, Yarilo was evoked by Igor Stravinsky in *The Rite of Spring*.

Other Slavic Divinities

Numerous other cults of Slavic divinities probably (although not certainly) faded or vanished during the tenth through twelfth centuries with Christianization, including those of Bielibog, the "white" god of beneficence, typically depicted as an old man dressed in white, with a long, flowing beard, and his opponent, Czernabog (or, Èerny Bog, Chernabog, Cornu boh, Czarnobog, Zcernoboch), the "black" god of misfortune, the underworld, and the waning year, is depicted as a warrior holding a bloody spear and a shield portraying a wolf's head, the inspiration for the "Devil" of the "Night on Bald Mountain" sequence in Disney's *Fantasia*. It must've been Christians or unbelievers who named Chernobyl, the "forest of Czernobog," after him.

Baltic Divinities

Cardinal Oliver Scholasticus, Bishop of Paderborn, in his description of the Holy Land written about 1220, refers to Baltic heathens as follows: "They honour forest nymphs, forest goddesses, mountain spirits, low-lands, waters, field spirits and forest spirits. They expected divine assistance from virgin forests, wherein they worshipped springs and trees, mounds and hills, steep stones and mountains slopes."

Just prior to Christianization, there was an attempt in Lithuania to construct a state religion with three primary deities, the most important being Perkûnas, the most important site being Romuva. This move resembles that taken by Vladimir in Kievan Rus'; and both of these recall the attempt by Julian the Apostate to construct a synthetic Greco-Roman religion. Thus, the Lithuanian and Rus'ian material-sacred systems may be viewed, like Julian's system, as representing early experiments in NeoPaganism. These movements suggest a kind of 'evolution' of paganism.

Another piece of information relating to pagan innovation may be alternatively interpreted as signifying an emphasis on locality in regard to earth-centered traditions or as a shifting of places in an increasingly hierarchical pantheon. This data indicates that in 1258, the primary Lithuanian deities revered may have included Diveriksas (a god of hares, probably linking him to Medeina and probably a manifestation of Perkûnas), Nunadievis (the "first god," a patron of justice), Medeina, and Teliavelis. Several years later, Medeina (as Zvoruna), Teliavelis, and Diveriksas, now as Perkûnas, may have kept their key places in the pantheon, while Nunadievis may have been displaced by Andaja. Andajas appears to have emerged later than many other Baltic gods and appears to have appropriated traits from the Greek god

Asclepius, of whom Balts must have learned at some point in their history. In an effort to "withstand the pressure of warlike neighbors and the influence of Christianity," Duke Gediminas (r. 1316-1341) sought to focus Lithuanian reverence on Perkûnas and to create a state religion around him, as it was hoped this deity would be able to stave off enemies. Teliavelis continued to be revered in the fifteenth century.

Jaan Puhvel, in "The Baltic Pantheon" (1973), observes, "[T]he Lithuanians were Christianized, and merely officially and from the top, only in the late fourteenth and early fifteenth centuries, and ... the ecclesiastical authorities in East Prussia had their hands full stamping out heathen practices in the full sixteenth century."

In Lithuania Minor/East Prussia, many persons continued to practice earth-centered traditions in the mid-sixteenth century. According to Georg Sabinus (1508-1560), rector of the University of Königsberg, practices included venerating snakes, worshipping numerous ancient deities, and sacrifices of rams.

Cults of numerous Baltic deities persisted into the Christianized period. Those that persisted until at least the final years of the fourteenth century most probably included: Autrimpus, an Old Prussian god of lakes and the sea; Lytuvonis, a deity of rain ("Lithuania" is a "land of rain"); Ežernim, a god of lakes (*ežerai* are lakes in Lithuanian); Warpintas, a deity of the harvest associated with sacred serpents, whose statue, said to stand in the sacred oak grove of Romuva, was offered a vessel of milk and flowers; Occopirmus, an Old Prussian god of stars and the night sky, sometimes as god of heavens and earth; Suaixtix, a Prussian god of light and stars; Giltine, a goddess of death, souls, ancestors, and regeneration; and Patrimpas (or, Potrimpo, Potrimpus, Potrumppo, Potrympus), a Prussian god of lakes, springs, rivers, as well as of prosperity (*"trymp"* signifies "satisfied"), divination, magic, communication, and the cycle of life, death, and regeneration, associated with the grass snake and depicted as a ruddy, fat, laughing man.

Numerous deities continued to be revered into the fifteenth and sixteenth centuries, especially in southwestern Lithuania and in Lithuania Minor/East Prussia, including: Pilwite, an Old Prussian god of grains, abundance and rich harvests; Auschauts, an Old Prussian god of illness and healing; and Žemepatis.

Reverence of a number of Baltic deities, including Vejopatis, Picollos, Velnias, Cerekling, the Pagirniai, Saulë, and Menulis persisted into the seventeenth and eighteenth centuries. Vejopatis, a god of wind and storms, has, like Janus, two faces. He is also depicted with a rooster sitting on his head. He holds a barrel in his right arm, which is raised, and a fish in his left, which is lowered. In seventeenth-century Lithuania Minor, fisher folk continued to honor him with effigies and offerings. One fisherman who did so was referred to by a local Catholic priest as a "real old Prussian heathen."

Not surprisingly, several deities of night, death, and the afterlife, including the Old Prussian Picollos, who was also a deity of air, and the Lithuanian Velnias, suffered demonization and became equated by Christians with the Greek god Hades and with Satan. Evidence suggests that these deities may have, where pagans are concerned, risen in status during the period of Christianization, when sacrifices of cows and horses to them were recorded, perhaps due to an attitude of defiance among certain seventeenth-century pagans who might have come to view these particular deities as Lucifer-like rebels.

Cerekling also continued to be revered in the seventeenth and perhaps eighteenth centuries, often manifesting as a divine couple, Curche and Gurcho. Patrons of farms, they protect crops and promote fertility of the land and animals; at Heiligenbeil and elsewhere, they were offered beer, milk, corn, honey, and other gifts. Latvians held feasts with singing and dancing in their honor.

Laima

Laima is a goddess of fate or destiny. Her name, from *laimò*, signifies "happiness" or "fortune." Much like the Norns, she dispenses good fortune, misfortune, and length of life. She also blesses births and marriages and curses those who offend her. She is a patron of pregnant women and infants. She is also a guardian of plants – the linden is her sacred tree – and domestic animals. Laima may assume the form of a linden tree, snake, swan, cow, lamb, or cuckoo. Dainius Sirutis notes, "Zoomorphically, Laima appears as a cuckoo, which also represented Laima in ancient statuary. In the form of a bird, she specifically warns people of misfortune and announces fate to people." Sometimes she appears in the plural, as three or seven *laimës*. Sometimes Laima "takes up residence in the human body" as a kind of archetypal presence attracting good fortune; this presence has been termed the *Laimë-dalia*. For Laima, fate is intimately connected to spinning and weaving, two industries of which she is patron. Mary Kilbourne Matossian observes in "Vestiges of the Cult of the Mother Goddess in Baltic Folklore" (1973): "Spinning and weaving are her most characteristic activities. They symbolize the creation of matter, especially of human flesh...The umbilical cord is also a 'thread of life.'...In the process of creation living flesh is 'wound around' the spindle of the body, or spine. Death is a process of unwinding this thread from the body: the Greeks today say, when someone dies, "His spindle is wound full." Two types of divination are associated with her: young women perform amatory divination at midsummer while invoking her aid; and the colors of her rainbow sash predict fortunate and unfortunate years, 'blue' and 'red' years, respectively. In Christianized Lithuania, Laima's role was generally appropriated by the Virgin Mary. However, Laima appears to have been revered as the owner of the linden tree into the nineteenth century, about thirty miles from my maternal ancestors' home.

Medeina/ Zvoruna

Somewhat more significantly, cults of the goddesses Medeina and Laima, together with that of the god Perkûnas, appear to have persisted into the nineteenth century. Goddess of the forest, Medeina's name (or

Medein, Meideine, Mejdejn, Modeina) derives from the Lithuanian *medis*, signifying "tree," "wood," or "grove." I imagine that Medeina (or, a local variant of her name) must have been an important deity in the lives of my maternal ancestors, as the place to which they moved in the Kaliningradskaya Oblast was very near the Ibenhorst (or, Pjatihatka) Forest. Medeina is sometimes identified with Zvoruna (or, Þevërûna, Þevrûna, Þvërûna Þvërûna, Þvorûna, Þvorûne), and occasionally as the hybrid goddess Zvoruna-Medeina. Zvoruna's name is derived from *þvëris*, which means "beast." Medeina, or Medeina-Zvoruna, is reminiscent of Artemis/Diana: she is single, amazonian, and a protector of animals. Gimbutas (1999) explains that Medeina signifies the "incarnation of the powers or fecundity of wild nature." In *Lithuania: Guiding Facts for Tourists* (1930), we learn that Medeina "was a giantess, and during the happy days when Lithuania was covered by woods, used to wander through the forest, clad in a bearskin, with a bow on her shoulders and a quiver at her side, singing gaily. And her song was as lovely as the nightingale's." Her entourage includes hares, wolves and greyhounds. Gimbutas (1999) explains that the hare "helped the goddess to protect her forests, especially by leading hunters astray. The sight of a hare in Medeina's forests created fear." Occasionally, she assumes the form of a she-wolf. The linden tree is sacred to her, and she "may have possessed the oak prior to Perkûnas." Her primary residence is believed to be on Medþiokalnis Hill near Kraþiai. According to Vaitkevicius, in "A New Outlook for Þvërûna-Medeina" (2005), she was worshipped primarily by nobles, warriors, hunters, and beekeepers. Somewhat surprisingly, however, one of her functions was to prevent hunters from killing; perhaps this indicates preventing them from over-killing. Vaitkevicius points out that a special kind of bond of friendship existed in Lithuania between beekeepers who lived in the woods and who shared bees. Although little is known about the rites of her cult, Vaitkevicius suggests that the first animals slain in the hunt may have been sacrificed to her, and that she may have also been given offerings to protect domestic animals from wolves. Her cult is indicated by sites referred to as Hare Churches (*Kiškio bažnyèia*) and Wolf-footprints (*Vilkpede*); the former are sacred stones, mounds, or groves connected to her worship, while the latter are stones that appear to be engraved with wolf tracks. These were found primarily in the vicinity of castles and estates of nobles, which appear to have been constructed near them in order to acknowledge or draw upon their power. Her worship was especially prevalent in eastern and also south-central Lithuania, near present-day Alytus. She became increasingly eminent with the formation of the centralized, possibly NeoPagan religion in the thirteenth century and was considered a special patron of the family of King Mindaugas (r. 1236-1263). Out of respect for the Goddess, he would not hunt in the forest if he caught sight of Medeina's hare. Mary Kilbourne Matossian notes that during this period, Lithuanians dedicated linden trees to her. Her reverence diminished only as the forests of Lithuania were devastated. Even so, as Gimbutas points out, in the nineteenth century, some persons continue to revere Medeina as "the Lady of the Forests" or "the Lady of the Trees" and envisioned her as dwelling in a "huge mansion [where she was] assisted by strong young priestesses."

Menulis

Menulis, the moon god, wears a "gown of starry night" and rides in a chariot drawn by magical grey horses. He grants light, health, beauty, and prosperity. He also serves as a guardian of the dead. He is a passionate lover who falls in love with the sun goddess Saulė but later abandons her for Aušra (corresponding to Venus as a goddess of dawn), an action which angers Perkûnas, the god of thunder. Some Lithuanian farmers continued to revere Menulis and to make offerings to him in the early eighteenth century. His memory lingered in customs of planting by the moon, which my family, like many others, followed. My mother told me that moon signs were carved inside the eaves of the roof of my grandparents' house in Texas to remind them of when to sow and reap. An invocation to Menulis reads: "Young man, young man,/ Prince of the heavens,/ Grant me a bit of luck."

Pagirniai

During these centuries, Lithuanian women also continued to honor the Pagirniai or Numejai, household deities whose altar was kept in a corner of the house under the quern (a simple stone mill used for grinding grain by hand). Parts of meals as well as hens were sacrificed to the Pagirniai. When a mother's "death was approaching, she entrusted the wife of the younger son" to continue her practice of honoring the Pagirniai.

Perkûnas and Perkûne

Near my ancestors' home, what is more, was a village named Perkuhnen, one of numerous villages of that name. The name honored the god of lightning and thunder, Perkûnas, synonymous with the Slavic Perûn. His name means "striker." He is depicted as a hunter or warrior, with a thick black, copper, red, or silver beard. He sometimes wears a crown, or else a wreath of flames. In one of his hands he holds, like Zeus and Thor, an axe, one of his chief attributes. Gimbutas writes of his axe: "The stone axes dropped by Perkûnas possess a peculiar power of fecundity. They are still called "the bullets of Perkûnas." Stone or bronze axes, "battle-axes," were frequently ornamented in prehistory by zig-zags, the symbol of lightning, and by circles, the sun symbols. Miniature axes of bronze were worn as amulets [until the end of the fourteenth century]." Two of his other chief attributes are the oak and the perpetual fire, both of which signify his presence. He dwells in a castle on a high hill in the heavens. Storms begin brewing when he traverses the heavens in his fiery chariot drawn by a goat. When thunder is heard, a proverb says, "God is coming — the wheels are striking fire." Some say that Perkûnas was born as a human and before death was transformed into a god. He occasionally returns to earth when he finds it necessary. He grants rain and thereby purifies the earth and nurtures fertility. He assists in exorcizing winter and heralds springtime.

He protects and heals suffering and illness – "especially the toothache, fever and fright" – through the medium of trees and stones that he has touched. He was envisioned as both a nobleman and a warrior, a political as well as a sacred role model. He is "very just, but restless and impatient; he is the great enemy of ... unjust or evil men. He throws his axe at evil people or tosses lightning bolts at their homes. He does not tolerate liars, thieves, or selfish and vain persons." Some say there are nine Perkûnases; each rules one year in a nine-year cycle.

A *daina*, or sacred song, sung to Perkûnas – and warning of his destructive potential – includes:

Perkûnas struck the oak
with nine flashes.
Three flashes split the trunk.
Six split the treetop.[32]

And an invocation to him reads: "O Divine Perkûnas, Have mercy on us, push away the darkness, and we shall be obedient to you until the end of the world."

Offerings to Perkûnas included goats and, as a *daina* (sacred song) records, barrels of rye, barley, and hops. Perkûnas' cult seems to have climaxed in thirteenth century. In the early fifteenth century, Hieronymus Pragensis (Jerome of Prague, d. 1416) observed that some Lithuanians were continuing to worship Perkûnas and/or the smith-god Teliavelis in the form of an "iron hammer of rare size." The Synod at Riga, Latvia condemned the persistent worship of Pçrkons in 1428. In 1583, Jesuits complained that numerous Þemaitijans and other Lithuanians and tribal peoples inhabiting the area were continuing to revere Perkûnas, including at Vilnius, with sacred fires. Offerings of rye, barley, and hops continued to be made to him in 1604. Persistent worship of Pçrkons, including animal sacrifices to him, among Letts/Latvians was once more condemned in 1610. In the 1718-1719 Vilnius Academic College logbook of pastoral activities, we find that some Lithuanian farmers continued to revere and make offerings to Perkûnas. The *Annals* of the Jesuits for 1734 condemned persistent worship of Pçrkons in the vicinity of Daugavpils, Latvia. At this time, some Letts/Latvians continued to pray to him to pass over them when he arrived in storms, to do "no harm to their houses or fields." In Lithuania Minor/East Prussia, Perkûnas' power continued to be respected in the seventeenth and eighteenth centuries by way of ritual actions undertaken when a thunderstorm commenced. Recalling the steeds of the god, persons would make the sound of the *poppysmus*, the "clucking of the tongue." This sound appears to have calmed the god so that he would not wreak havoc on the person's property or do other harm. This particular response to a thunderstorm is particularly intriguing as regards our text because it was also expressed in the same context thousands of years earlier by ancient Greeks and Romans, as documented by Aristophanes and Pliny. Incidentally, in Classical connotation, *poppysmus* also referred to the sound made by the coming into contact of sexual organs during intercourse, possibly suggesting an association of the noise of the thunderclap, rain, and fertility.

Returning to Lithuania Minor/East Prussia, during this period, an approaching thunderstorm was sometimes also accompanied by animal sacrifice in honor of Perkûnas, of a sheep, pig, black rooster, or hen, as well as an offering of beer. In the nineteenth century in Lithuania Minor/East Prussia, his memory persisted not only by way of the village name of Perkuhnen (near my ancestral home) but also by way of a rite employing an axe. When storms were approaching, householders would place a finger in an axe-head with a hole bored though it and twirl the axe-head around three times before hurling it at the door, to prevent the house "from being struck by lightning." Also in the nineteenth century, many continued to offer the deity, although now having exchanged his name for that of "God," bacon, in hope that he might protect them during dangerous storms. When it commenced thundering, the devotee would put a side of bacon on his or her shoulder, would walk "with head uncovered" into the field, and would say, "O God, fall not upon my fields, and I will give thee this flitch [of bacon]." When the storm ended, the devotee would take "the bacon home, and consum[e] it with [the] household as a sacrifice."

It seems likely, seeing that his mother was transformed by the Church into a manifestation of the Virgin Mary, that he and his attributes may have contributed to a Baltic/Slavic conception of Christ – those aspects of his persona and those attributes, needless to say, which were not appropriated by the Church to enhance its depiction of the Devil. Evidence indicates that Perkûnas was likewise appropriated by the Church in constructing a portrait of St. Elijah (Elias, Ilya) and St. Stanislaus.

Perkûne is the mother, spouse, or female counterpart of Perkûnas. As with the Slavic Perper?na, little about her has been recorded, and her name, a feminization of Perkûnas, appears to have displaced an older name probably predating that of Perkûnas and granting her a much more significant place in the Baltic pantheon. Perkûne has been Christianized as Panna Maria Percûnatele (a. k. a. Presvyataya Mariya Gromnitsa), the Very Holy Mary the Thunderer, with a festival held for her on February 2 (Candlemas).

Saulë

Giver of "light, warmth, and food," the sun goddess Saulë, like Apollo and other solar deities, journeys across the heavens each day. She travels in a "chariot with copper wheels drawn by fiery steeds." Each evening, she bathes her horses in the sea and reclines beneath an apple tree. In *The Balts*, Gimbutas relates, "The farmer's life was regularly patterned by prayers to Saulë at sunrise and at sunset, for all fieldwork was entirely dependent on the sun's beneficence." Prior to Christianization, Saulë was celebrated at the summer solstice with bonfires. "Adorned with a wreath of braided red-fern blossoms," Gimbutas notes, she "danced on the silver hill wearing silver shoes." In winter candles were lit for her when she felt weak. In the logbook of pastoral activities of Vilnius Academic College for 1718-1719, it was observed that certain Lithuanian farmers were continuing to revere and make offerings to the sun goddess Saulë at that time.

Veïu Mâte, Gabija, and Gawenis

Three deities whose reverence may have continued well into Christianized times include the Latvian goddess of death, Veïu Mâte, and the Lithuanian deities of the hearth, Gabija and Gawenis. As the "Mother of the Spirits," Veïu Mâte receives the dead in the cemetery and serves as a psychopomp, assisting them on their journey to the afterlife; she commences by burning their old clothes. She is clad in a white woolen cloak. She is said to live in "the world behind" our world; it is called Vinsaule. By all accounts, she has withstood Christianization. She is offered honey and honey-cakes. The goddess Gabija is the goddess of fire and the hearth in earth-centered Lithuanian tradition. She is thought to dwell in the hearth and, alternatively, in the barn. Vaitkevicius speaks of reverence of Gabija in the sixteenth and seventeenth centuries, and Norbertas Vëlius, in *The World Outlook of the Ancient Balts*, notes, "[T]he 1718-1719 logbook of Vilnius Academic College explains that "in a certain locality visited by them 'the lips of the farmers still pronounce the names of five gods ... [including that of the] Fire'," that is to say, the goddess Gabija; they continued at this time – over three hundred years following official Christianization – to envision her as a goddess and to make offerings to her. Her festival occurs in late August, when she is offered loaves of bread and devotees pray to her, "Holy Gabija, stay quiet in your place. Live with us in peace, Holy Gabija. Holy Gabija, live happily with us."

In the nineteenth century, Rugiu Boba, the Lithuanian "Old Woman of the Rye," a crone patron of the harvest, came to be associated with Gabija. In this form, she was offered a cake at the annual harvest festival; yet some Lithuanians continued to revere the goddess as Gabija. As Jonas Balys notes of late-nineteenth and early twentieth-century Lithuanian women: "Every evening the housewife puts the glimmering coals and ashes together in the fireplace and prays: 'Dear fire, little Gabija, do not burn, if not intentionally fired; you are nicely covered, then sleep, please, and do not walk in this house.'"

Gabija sometimes has a male spouse or consort, Gawenis (or, Gavanas, Gavenas, Gavenis; he was presumably revered until at least the latter half of the fourteenth century. He is generally of lesser importance than Gabija. His name means "dirty." He dwells in the furnace. A trickster, he is often depicted as a soot-covered man wearing a sieve on his head. He is a shapeshifter, sometimes metamorphosing into a woman or rabbit. His special time is 2-3 p.m. (synonymous with the time of day associated with Pan). He gives gifts to children. He represents winter ritually expelled in spring; in this role, he is chased by participants holding scourges and switches who throw water at him. "Gawenis is sharpening his knife" means that the sun is being drawn into a mirror for magical purposes. This reverence persisted as veneration of fire into the mid-twentieth century among Lithuanian-Americans.

Other Baltic Divinities

Reverence of a number of Baltic divinities

persisted into the nineteenth century, including: Audros or Audra, a god or goddess of the sea, lakes and rivers, storms, and tempests, who continued to be offered sacrifices of bread and pigs in the nineteenth century; Pergrubryus, an Old Prussian god of plants and springtime who continued to be toasted with beer and invoked to take the winter away and make the fields fertile and green; Puschkaytus, an Old Prussian and Latvian deity, depicted as hirsute, with disheveled hair, a god of earth, fertility, fruits and grains, trees (especially the elder and pine) and sacred groves, underground kingdoms, and dreams and divination, comparable to the Greek god Pan and to Roman Silvanus, who continued to be offered beer and bread and honored at a festival of thanksgiving at harvest time; and Perdoytus, an Old Prussian god of fishing and sailing and a patron of seafarers, who continued to be offered tuna on bread to calm the seas and to provide abundant fish.

Christians who studied the ancient traditions of Lithuania and elsewhere deployed the theory of correspondences. For example, in the early sixteenth century, when many continued to revere ancient deities in Baltic areas, the *Constitutiones Synodales* of 1530 compares Ausschauts to Asclepius (or, Aesculapius); Autrympus to Neptune; Occopirmus to Saturn; Parcuns (Perkûnas) to Jupiter; Pecols/Pocols (Picollos) to Pluto (Hades) and the Furies; Piluuytus (Pilwit) to Ceres; and Suaixtix to the Sun (Phoebus Apollo). I think we need to contemplate the possibility that some persons who persisted in practicing Baltic traditions may have been inspired to consider their local traditions in light of these correspondences (to assume that all who persisted in practicing Baltic traditions were illiterate or could not have otherwise learned of these correspondences is naïve and, moreover, characteristic of stereotyping). In the eighteenth century, Jakob Brodowski and Philipp Ruhig suggested such comparisons as: Laima corresponds to Fortuna; Perkûnas to Jupiter; and Žemyna to Ceres.[33]

Chapter 5
Eglë and Žaltys: A Tale of Love, Betrayal, and Metamorphosis

The old Lithuanian obdurately retained his mode of life and his heathen idolatry. The tree, the duck, the cuckoo, the hill, the wind – all these he deified and worshipped ... Animals, plants and numerous phenomena are represented as in a close relation with human beings. — Clarence A. Manning, *The Daina*[34]

Since time immemorial, figures of pagan deities and "idol[s] made of dough," "rags," and wood have been revered and/or deployed in magical rites, have sometimes been ceremonially "carr[ied] through the fields," because they have been thought to be filled with "divine life." Sometimes they have been said to be able to speak or to move about. Images of the Germanic gods Thor and Freyr have, for example, been described as possessing these abilities. In the past, many of these objects were made of perishable materials. Many were destroyed by Christians. This is, needless to say, tragic for students of material religion. Nevertheless, many present-day objects reflect and continue to transmit ancient wisdom.

Zenon Elyjiw, in "Ukrainian *Pysanky*: Easter Eggs as Talismans," explains that a "properly decorated egg," a *pysanka* (in Lithuanian, *marguciai*) "was considered a universal talisman." By "writing" eggs with certain symbols, the already envisioned power of eggs to promote fertility and to protect from evil was enhanced. "To give the *pysanka* the magic power of a talisman," however, "it was supposed to be decorated at a proper time, following certain procedures, and using proper ornamental motifs." Elyjiw also relates that the "talismanic power of the *pysanka* was enhanced by beeswax," which was "considered a magical, wonder-working substance," and by the plant dyes used to color the eggs, most of which were "used in folk medicine" and "supposed to have supernatural powers." Likewise, Orysia Tracz, in "Tradition in Ukrainian Life," explains that designs on eggs such as those signifying the sun and other symbols are meant to magically beckon the spring, to "bring good fortune and turn away evil." "The basic solar ornaments on the *pysanka* are the swastika (*lamanyi hrest*)...and the rosette-star (*zirka*) ... .From the Neolithic time comes the *bezkonechnyk* – the ... meander." Yet another symbol is a serpentine line; these are called *tsyhansk'ki dorohy*, "gypsy roads." They are meant to confuse and thus drive away evil spirits. Lithuanian *marguciai* embrace symbols including the sun, moon, grass-snakes, rue, and stars. In "Confessions of a Pysanka Nut," Tracz relates: "I enjoy writing *pysanky* ... .Often I think about the women of the deep, deep past for whom this was not a hobby, but a necessary ritual for the continuation, for the rebirth, of nature each spring ... .When I sit writing them, often very late into the night, I feel a strong tie with our antiquity."

The art of "writing" eggs is indeed an ancient one, predating Christian Easter eggs by more than a millennium, perhaps many more. Archaeological digs have uncovered sacred eggs, at least one of which was painted yellow-green, perhaps to signify springtime growth, made of clay and bone in the Ukraine, Lithuania, and elsewhere. Egg writing makes use of the theory of correspondences. Red, often achieved by dying eggs in beet juice, signifies the sun and perhaps also erotic love; in Slavic paganism, it signifies the goddess Lada. In Ukrainian egg writing, white signifies purity, yellow, wisdom, green, springtime, orange, power, and black, the night.

Marija Gimbutas writes in *Ancient Symbolism in Lithuanian Folk Art* of finding a host of pagan symbols in her homeland's arts, often in Christianized contexts, including on Easter eggs, roofed poles, dowry chests, distaffs, and sashes. More recently, other Lithuanian scholars have added to her treasure-trove of data. Toads and snakes serve as signs of the life-force; together with trees, they also signify ancestral spirits. The axe, goat, and horse signify the god Perkûnas and protect one from storms, enemies, and imprisonment. Of solar symbolism, which corresponds to the sun-goddess Saulë (a rather uncanny parallel with Amaterasu of Japanese Shinto), Gimbutas relates in *The Balts*: "[T]he sun is depicted as a ring, a wheel, a circle, a circle with rays, a rosette or a daisy (in Lithuanian called *saulutò*, "little sun," or *ratilas*, "wheel"), the flower of the Sun." For Balts, the sun signified "dynamic vigor" and "verdant life." In *The World Outlook of the Ancient Balts*, Norbertas Vëlius takes note of these and other symbols, including that of the crescent moon and the World Tree, on objects of everyday as well as ceremonial use. He also reminds us that animal masks worn in present-day carnivals trace their origins to pagan artists of vernacular culture.

So many objects embody and transmit ancient wisdom, from Russian *matrioshka* dolls observed by Joanna Hubbs in *Mother Russia: The Feminine Myth in Russian Culture* to exquisite embroideries discussed by Mary B. Kelly in *Goddess Embroideries of Eastern Europe* to masterfully decorated breads presented by Nikolay Nikov in *Holidays of the Bulgarians in Myths and Legends*.

The Tale of Eglë and Žaltys

Long ago, a father and mother had twelve sons and three daughters. Their youngest daughter was named Eglë. One summer evening, the three daughters went bathing in the lake. When they finished bathing, they lay down on the bank to dry themselves. Eglë noticed that a snake was lying in the sleeve of her blouse. The eldest sister got a branch and hit it and tried to chase it away. The snake looked up at Eglë and said, "I will return to my home if you'll give me your word that you'll marry me." Eglë looked at the snake and, beginning to cry, asked, "How can I marry you? I'm a girl. Please return to your home." But the snake wouldn't take "no" for an answer. What was Eglė to do? She agreed to marry him.

Three days later, the parents saw a troupe of serpents approaching their yard. These were the *pirsliai*, the marriage-proposers. When Eglė's family saw the serpents, they hid their daughter. They dressed up various animals— a sow, a cow, a goose, a sheep – in Eglė's clothes, and presented them one by one to the snakes. At first, the snakes were fooled, but each time, the cuckoo told them, "That animal is not the girl! Cuckoo! Cuckoo! They've cheated you!" after which they returned to Eglė's home. Finally, Eglė's parents accepted the snakes' proposal. The snakes led Eglė to the edge of the sea. There they encountered a handsome young man who told Eglė that he was Žaltys (pronounced Zhal-TEES), the same being as the snake who'd been lying in the sleeve of her blouse.

Eglė, Žaltys, and the snakes then journeyed to the bottom of the sea. There lay a magnificent palace with serpentine decor. There they celebrated their marriage. For three weeks, they drank and danced. In the palace, Eglė came to know every amusement, and there seemed to be ample freedom. Eglė grew happier and happier, until she almost completely forgot her former life.

Nine years passed. During that time, Eglė gave birth to three sons, Ažuolas, Uosis, and Beržas, and finally to a daughter, Drebulė. One day, when the eldest son had finished playing, he asked Eglė, "Mother, where do your parents live? Why don't we go and visit them?" His question prompted Eglė to recall her other life. She wondered how her parents, sisters, and brothers were doing. Were they all in good health? Were they all still alive? She began to miss them, and asked Žaltys if she could go with their children to visit her family. He was opposed to the idea. But he said, "Fine. But first I want you to spin the wool on this distaff. She set up a spinning wheel, and began to spin. She spun day and night, but the wool on the distaff never diminished. Eglė realized that this was a trick Žaltys had played on her, to keep her from going, that the distaff was enchanted. So she decided to pay a visit to an elderly woman, a *piniuonė* or magician – others say it was a *ragana*, a sorceress; still others, that it was Žaltys' mother. "Please tell me how to spin this, good mother." "Throw it in the fire; otherwise, you'll never finish." So Eglė threw the wool in the oven. Suddenly, a large toad appeared in the flames, with spun threads coming out of its mouth. In this way, Eglė finished her spinning. She went once more to Žaltys, who agreed that she should visit her parents, as soon as she finished wearing out a pair of iron shoes that he presented to her. She walked and walked and even pitched them against rocks, but alas, nothing would wear them down. So she once more visited the old woman. "Throw them into the fire." So once more she threw the charmed objects into the flames, this time into a forge. Within three days, the shoes were worn down. Eglė again went to her husband. "Yes," said Žaltys, "you may go, once you have baked a loaf of bread to give as a gift to your family." Then Žaltys had his servants remove all the cookware except for a sieve from the palace. How can I, Eglė wondered, draw water without a bucket, and knead the dough without a pot? Once more Eglė visited the old woman, and the woman told her, "Take the leavening and coat the bottom of the sieve with it, and gather water in this, and then knead the dough in the sieve." So Eglė coated the sieve with the leavening, kneaded the dough, cooked the bread, and presented it to Žaltys.

Her husband then accompanied her and her

children to the shore of her homeland, where he said to her, "Make sure that you return home within three days' time. When you're ready to return, you and the children come to the shore, without the rest of your family, and sing to me, 'Žilvinas, if you are alive, show me milky foam; if you are dead, show me bloody foam.' And if you see milky foam, you'll know that I'm alive; but if you see bloody foam, then you'll know that I've been slain. And you, my children, remember not to share this song with anyone else." And Žaltys took leave of them.

Eglë's trip proved to be a joyous one. Her family fed her all her favorite foods. They and her old friends and neighbors wanted to hear all about her life among the serpents. They told her she shouldn't return, that she and her children should stay with her family. She was enjoying her stay so much that even after nine days passed, she failed to notice.

During her stay, her brothers decided they were going to kill the serpent. But first they had to learn how to find him. They took the eldest son, Ažuolas, into the forest, and hitting him with birch canes, they demanded that he tell them how to find Žaltys, but he would say nothing. The next day, they did the same thing with Uosis, but he also would say nothing. The next day, with Berpas, to no avail. Finally, on the fourth day, they took Drebulë into the forest. When they began to beat her with birch canes, she told them everything. Going to the shore, they called out, "Žilvinas, Žilvinas." As soon as Žaltys appeared – he did so in serpent form – they beat him and chopped him into pieces, casting the pieces into the water. Then they returned home, saying nothing to their sister Eglë.

Nine more days passed before Eglë realized how long she'd been gone. She went with her children to the water's edge, where she called out, "Þilvinas, Þilvinas." The sea stirred, and with the waves appeared bloody foam. Eglë heard the voice of her beloved, "Your twelve brothers have chopped me into pieces with a scythe; our best-loved child, Drebulë, told them how to call me." Eglë began to cry, and turning toward her children, declared:

"May you, Drebulë, tremble always,
May you tremble day and night.
May the rain wash your mouth
And the winds comb your hair.
And you, my sons,
may you become robust trees.
And I, your mother,
shall become a fir tree."[35]

More than thirty-five years ago, I sat with my maternal grandmother, Margaret "Maggie" Lundschien, a Texan farmer and midwife, one summer afternoon in her wild garden, when she pointed toward a rose bush and said, "One day, after I'm gone, I'll come back to you as that butterfly on the bush." In winter, playing dominoes in her icy hallway in the early hours of morning, she told me, on visiting the "bone yard," that if you ventured into a cemetery late at night, you could hear the dead whispering among the trees. My grand-mother's tales of spirits, her fascination with divination (including astrology, Tarot, and table-rapping which terrified my mother when she was a child), her motherly care for animals, and her deep-seated belief in reincarnation, wedded to my early delight in fairy and folk tales, nurtured my attraction to "pagan" (or, revived/reconstructed pagan) spiritual traditions. These interests, however, became more closely tied to Lithuanian traditions per se after I encountered, in the 1980s, the writings of the Lithuanian-American archaeologist Marija Gimbutas. My later meeting with her, at a 1989 conference at the Jung Institute in San Francisco, inspired the realization that my love of my grandmother's folk wisdom and tales, on the one hand, and my academic interest in folklore, mythology, and religious studies, on the other, were rooted in the same soil. This meeting with Gimbutas, who bore an uncanny resemblance to my grandmother, save that one was an intellectual, the other a farmer, also inspired me to try to learn more about my grandmother's ancestors. In doing so, I learned, over the course of fifteen years, thanks in large part to genealogist Patsy Hand and a young man who is undoubtedly a distant relative, James-Herbert Lundszien, who lives in Germany, as well as, more recently, historian Vilius Peteraitis, that my grandmother's insistence that we were not Germans was, at least on her father's side, rooted in fact. While my grandmother's maternal ancestors may have lived in Germany and were, it appears from fragmentary records, Jewish (her mother was orphaned at an early age; she may have been reared as Christian, although my grandmother recalled visiting synagogues as a child), her father's people were western Lithuanians who moved in the early eighteenth century or thereabouts to the region that is now known as the Kaliningradskaya Oblast, has been previously known as East Prussia and Lithuania Minor, and is controlled by Russia. The Lunczyns, or Lunc(z)ynas family, a name probably meaning "to bind or tie together," mostly farmers, lived in the village of Ackmenischken (later renamed Dünen by occupying Nazi forces), perhaps signifying a "place of sacred stones (*akmuo*)," and in neighboring villages. My great-great grandfather left Ackmenischken in 1853 for Texas. Other family members remained until World War II, when the Nazis and then the Soviets devastated their land and forced them to emigrate, as Gimbutas' family was forced to do. My increasing interest in the beliefs and practices of ancient Lithuanians has led me most recently to Romuva, an international group of practitioners of traditional Lithuanian spirituality; conversations with Romuva elder Rudra (Audrius) Vilius Dundzila have been particularly inspiring.

Some years ago, I discovered the story of "Eglë and Žaltys" when I decided to check out a book edited by Irina Zheleznova titled *Tales of the Amber Sea: Fairy Tales of the Peoples of Estonia, Latvia and Lithuania*. The tale immediately intrigued me. On the one hand, it reminded me of "Beauty and the Beast" and "The Little Mermaid," on the other, of the myth of Persephone's abduction by Hades. I soon learned that the tale of the "Queen of the Serpents" is among the most popular of Lithuanian folktales. I became increasingly captivated by the tale as I read Ada Martinkus's illuminating analysis, *Eglé, la reine des serpents: Un conte lithuanien*. In that analysis, which might be described as poststructuralist with a typically heavy emphasis on linguistics, Martinkus provides over sixty variants of the tale. Her references to pagan archetypal figures, motifs, and concepts have provided the basic foundation for my own essay, in which I will seek to analyze the folktale —

more commonly known as "Eglë, Queen of the Serpents" or "Eglë, Queen of the Grass-Snakes," or, in the original Lithuanian, "Eglë Þalèiø Karaliene" – in terms of its possible pagan spiritual significance.

It is my belief that this tale – or at least parts of the tale, such as Eglë's marriage to Žaltys and the transformation into trees – may predate the introduction of Christianity. However, those parts of the narrative concerning the family's attempt to deceive the serpents and the brothers' ultimate slaying of Žaltys do not conform to the pagan Lithuanian reverence of snakes and rather strongly suggest Christian influence. Clearly, the tale has metamorphosed over the centuries. Although I might have considered it earlier in this text, I have decided to place it here, as its telling reached a kind of pinnacle in the late nineteenth and early twentieth centuries. Told within a Christian context, in the culturally accepted, non-threatening form of the folktale, the tale of "Eglë and Žaltys" continues to transmit pagan motifs and concepts which challenge the historical practices of Church authorities in Lithuania and provide, via the persona of Eglë, a model or archetype of pagan sensibility and resistance to the destruction of the pagan worldview.

Eglë

In "Vestiges of the Cult of the Mother Goddess in Baltic Folklore," Mary Kilbourne Matossian relates that "the Lithuanians would bring food offerings to a wooden female figure hung on a pine or fir tree." Although it is not made clear in Matossian's article, it is conceivable that this figure represented Eglë. By way of both her name – meaning "spruce" or "fir" – and her narrative, the folkloric figure of Eglë evokes numerous divine feminine beings of pagan Lithuanian spirituality; indeed, she may signify a mixture or fusion of figures including a primordial snake-goddess, Saulë, Laima and the *laumës*, Aušrine/ Wakarine, Gabija, Žemyna, Medeina, Giltinë, and Ragana.

It is possible that as the "Queen of Serpents," Eglë's origin returns us to the reverence of a serpentine goddess in Neolithic Europe, as is depicted in ritual art of the Vinca culture (in the vicinity of Belgrade). Marija Gimbutas, in *The Living Goddesses*, describes the "classic image of the snake goddess" of Old Europe as one portraying her "sitting yogi-like or squatting, with snake-shaped limbs. Her head appears either as human, snake-like, or masked and perhaps crowned." This goddess is also typically depicted with exaggeratedly round eyes and long mouth. She is associated with certain symbols including the coil, spiral, zigzag, wave, and dotted or diamond band. The goddess was revered in the form of a serpent in part because snakes' "periodic molting reinforced their role as symbols of renewal" and because they "were also thought to embody deceased ancestors." It appears that in numerous ancient cultures, including but not limited to those of Egypt and Crete, an original serpentine goddess later divided into an anthropomorphic deity possessing a serpent as a consort or sacred animal.

It is this separate yet bonded relationship which may link Eglë to the sun-goddess

Saulė. As Eglė bathes with her sisters in the evening, so Saulė washes her horses in the sea at day's end. As Eglė traverses various realms, so Saulė traverses the heavens each day, and dwells in a castle "beyond the abode of the dead." In terms of the tasks Eglė undertakes in order to return to her parents' home, that of spinning links her to Saulė, who "oversees her daughters' spinning and weaving." Both Saulė and Eglė correspond to sacred trees: Saulė to the birch (one of Eglė's sons is Beržas, the birch), and Eglė to the spruce or fir. Both may assume the form of birds. Perhaps most importantly, however, both cherish snakes. Prudence Jones and Nigel Pennick, in *A History of Pagan Europe*, relate that "Saulė is also the hearth fire, and the house-snake, Žaltys, which lives by the fire, is said to be beloved of her"; and Gimbutas reminds us, "It is of course a crime to kill it [i.e., the snake, *žaltys*], and a proverb says: 'Do not leave a dead *žaltys* on a field. Bury it.' The sight of a dead *žaltys* would cause the sun [goddess Saulė] to cry."

Her bond with the serpent, her transformation into a tree, and the task of spinning link Eglė to the goddess Laima and to the *laumės*, fairy-like spinning spirits. Matossian observes: "Spinning and weaving are her [i.e., the Goddess's, specifically Laima's] most characteristic activities. They symbolize the creation of matter...Hence the common metaphor, 'the thread of life' ... Death is a process of unwinding this thread."

Like Eglė, Laima may assume the form of a tree, the latter's being the linden. She may also assume the form of, or embody, a snake – thus linking her to the Old European snake-goddess and to Eglė in her role as the "Queen of Serpents"; a cow – in some variants of the tale, Eglė's family dresses up a cow as Eglė in an absurd attempt to deceive the serpents; or a cuckoo – a bird who assists Žaltys and into which Eglė metamorphoses in those variants in which she does not transform into a tree. As a cuckoo, which also represented Laima in ancient statuary, she predicts destinies. It should be noted that occasionally the cuckoo is also associated with the goddess Medeina and with the gods Velnias and Perkûnas, and at times is perceived as a separate divinity, Gegutė. Gegutė or the cuckoo corresponds to the season of spring and especially the month of May (Gegužis), weddings, the gift of prophecy, the power of metamorphosis, and melancholy. Clarence Manning relates in *The Daina: An Anthology of Lithuanian and Latvian Folk-Songs*, "The cuckoo carries in itself the soul of the dead. Very appropriately, then, his song is doleful as no other bird's is. The verb 'to cuckoo' (Lith. *kukuoti*) signifies 'to lament.' The cuckoo is nearly always likened to a woman, and very rarely to a man."

The bovine episode in the tale of Eglė links her not only to Laima but also to Aušrine/Wakarine, the goddess of the planet Venus, who "possesses a troupe of cows that she metamorphoses into young women – her sisters – called to play the role of *laumės*, the three fates of Lithuanian mythology. The eminent place that the cow occupies makes her a valuable representative for the young spouse."

The task of baking, undertaken prior to setting out for her parents' home, links

Eglė to Gabija, goddess of the hearth-fire. So significant is Gabija in Lithuanian spiritual culture, Gimbutas notes, that as "late as the first decades of the twentieth century in Lithuania, the mother of the family, while baking bread, first prepared a little loaf for Gabija, marking it with a fingerprint." The task of baking also links Eglė to the earth-goddess Žemyna, who was offered bread at harvest-time and on other occasions; in later times, she often appeared as Rugiu Boba, the Old Woman of the Rye. Like Gabija, Žemyna, despite Christian attempts to bury her memory, survived; as Gimbutas relates, "Offerings of bread to Žemyna continued through the early twentieth century. A loaf or piece of bread was left in a rye, wheat, or barley field at the first spring plowing to ensure a fertile year, or at harvest's end to secure abundance for the next year." Eglė also shares with Žemyna a special bond with trees; indeed, Žemyna is associated not only with the oak and linden but also with the *eglė*, the fir or spruce; offerings to Þemyna were often tied to the branches of trees. Another absurd attempt by Eglė's parents to deceive the serpents by dressing up a sow as Eglė further links our heroine to Žemyna, to whom sows were sacrificed.

By way of her transformation of herself and her children into trees, Eglė resonates with Medeina, goddess of the forest, Lady of the Trees. In *Lithuania: Guiding Facts for Tourists*, we learn that Medeina, resembling the Greco-Roman Artemis-Diana, "was a giantess, and during the happy days when Lithuania was covered by woods, used to wander through the forest, clad in a bearskin, with a bow on her shoulders and a quiver at her side, singing gaily. And her song was as lovely as the nightingale's." Gimbutas observes that she was an "incarnation of the powers or fecundity of wild nature. Her sacred animal was a hare ... Folk beliefs relate that this alert, quick little animal helped the goddess to protect her forests, especially by leading hunters astray." Matossian notes that in the "thirteenth century the Lithuanians dedicated sacred lindens to a forest Goddess, Medeina"; her reverence diminished only as the forests of Lithuania were devastated. Even so, she continued to be remembered in nineteenth-century folklore as "the lady of the forests" who lived in a "huge mansion and [who was] assisted by strong young priestesses."

Although the tale of "Eglė and Žaltys" does not explain fully the method by which Eglė transformed her children and herself into trees, it is possible that Eglė may have in some way taken her own life and those of her children in order to transmit their souls or spirits into trees, as occurs in Greek myths such as those of Venus and Adonis, Cybele and Attis, Apollo and Hyacinthus, Apollo and Cyparissus, and numerous others. In this context, she may be related to Giltinė and Ragana, two goddesses associated with death and regeneration and with protean metamorphosis. Of Ragana in particular, Gimbutas notes, "Ragana also carried the energy of a snake: if a *ragana*" – here referring to a priestess or embodiment of the goddess, in later times considered a witch – "died, you might see her hair curl, like a Gorgon's, into snakes, and little snakes crawl out of her mouth." Thus, we return to the "Queen of the Serpents."

The tasks undertaken by Eglë, which, as Martinkus astutely observes, correspond symbolically to maiden (spinning), bride (wearing iron shoes), and mother (baking). If we add to this list Eglë's dwelling underwater (akin to dwelling in the underworld) and her final task of transforming herself and her children into trees, which we may compare to the "crone" – in Lithuania, signified by Giltinë or Ragana – then we may complete the narrative of the life cycle of woman or the goddess. As Martinkus demonstrates in this regard, the tale of "Eglë and Žaltys" bears resemblance to the myth of Persephone; Persephone the maiden may be compared to the young Eglë; Persephone as Hades's bride to Eglë as the bride of Žaltys; Demeter to Eglë as mother; and Hecate or Persephone as Queen of the Underworld to Eglë as Queen of the Serpents. In this comparative reading, Hades and Žaltys occupy a similar position as chthonic spouses.

By way of wearing iron shoes, Eglë may also be associated with a male divinity, Velnias, the "great blacksmith of Lithuanian mythology" prior to the arrival of Perkûnas; as we will see, Velnias is himself associated with Žaltys.

Following the methodology of Ginzburg in *Ecstasies*, I would suggest that the numerous correspondences linking Eglë to the deities of pagan Lithuania form, in his terminology, a "dense web of resemblances" that "compose, not merely a chain, but a sort of magnetic field." These "correspondences" and the "web of resemblances" operate, to borrow Everson's linguistic analogy, as "phrases" and "sentences" to compose a "grammar of spirituality." Taken together, they infer an archetypal construction of greater significance than, it would seem, of any of the separate manifestations of feminine divinity described above, suggesting that we are meant to view Eglë as a folkloric representation of a Great or Mother Goddess rather than as a particular manifestation of divine feminine energy. The "magnetic field" which these would appear to "compose" may be described as that *pasaulëpiûra* or worldview of pagan Lithuania, which consists primarily of the reverence of divinity in embodied and natural forms, frequently related to femininity and chthonian identity. More particularly, this *pasaulëpiûra* acknowledges the natural cycle of birth, life, death, and regeneration – in Everson's (following Gimbutas) archaeomythological terms, "a labyrinth of conceptually-related symbols emphasizing a dialectic of formation, destruction, and reformation." The culturally accepted form of the folktale permits the transmission of, in Marina Warner's terms, this "elaborate code" of pagan, goddess-centered images and concepts to audiences (of recent centuries) inhabiting a Christian cultural milieu; in this subtle, often unacknowledged way, "Eglë and Žaltys" may serve to impart, again in Warner's terms, "heterodox knowledge" challenging the dominant paradigm of patriarchal Christianity.

Christians, needless to say, were deeply disturbed on discovering the reverence of goddesses and feminine spirits in medieval Lithuania; and they encountered great resistance in their campaign to convert Lithuanians to Christianity. Indeed,

Lithuania was one of the last countries in Europe to be introduced to Christianity, and the last to accept it as the dominant religion of the nation. Officially Christianized in 1387, Church authorities were continuing to demand in the late seventeenth century that "All ungodly chapels [and] holy bushes ... must be completely destroyed and demolished" and that "peasants [should] renounce and abandon their paganism." As in other European countries, traditional spiritual beliefs and practices survived the longest among the *pagoniškas*, the "pagans" or "heathens," the rural peasants (*valstietija*). If Christianity was to "triumph" in Lithuania, it was imperative that Saulė, Žemyna, Laima, Aušrinė, Gabija, Medeina, and other goddesses be dethroned and banished.

So powerful was the reverence of divine feminine beings, however, that Church authorities appropriated certain elements in composing a Balticized manifestation of the Virgin Mary; this is perhaps evidenced most clearly in the Basilica of Our Lady of Aglona in Latvia. "Aglona" derives, not surprisingly, from "*aglojs*" or "*aglaine*," the Latvian equivalent of "*eglė*." The church, built in 1699 by Dominican monks from Vilnius, Lithuania, lies in the vicinity of Lake Eglė and the castle mound of Egli. The painting of Our Lady was executed in or around 1700; this manifestation of Mary is linked to Our Lady of Trakai, Our Lady of Czestochowa, and to the Black Madonna of Ostra Brama. Each August, approximately 100,000 pilgrims arrive from Lithuania, Belorussia, and Russia to pay homage to Our Lady of Aglona. Beyond possible Christian appropriation of the figure of Eglė, her name and those of other pagan goddesses continue to be spoken each day as Lithuanians speak of the fir tree, the sun, the earth.

Žaltys

Žaltys lends his name, or else receives his name, from the grass-snake called in Latin either *natrix natrix* or *natrix tripodontus*. Žaltys is alternately described as a "mystically endowed creature," the "sentinel of the gods," and a deity in his own right. While Žaltys is his folkloric name, his theonym is Žilvinas. The form Žeminas brings the earth-goddess Žemyna to mind. According to Prane Dundulienė in *Þalèiai Lietuvio Pasaulėjautoje ir Dailėje*, the term *žaltys* simultaneously implies "snake, life, vitality, [and] vital capacity."

In order to better understand the reverence of snakes or serpents in pagan Lithuania, it may be helpful to briefly examine their reverence in other ancient and premodern cultures. Jacob Grimm, in *Teutonic Mythology*, observes that in many such cultures, Snakes, by the beauty of their shape and the terror of their bite, seem above all animals to command awe and reverence." He observes (as does Gimbutas) that they are revered as symbols of the cycle of birth, death, and regeneration. Perhaps this is why they were perceived as "lords of life" – like D. H. Lawrence's "Snake" – and are often depicted wearing crowns – also suggested by the "hoods" of certain snakes. Their crowns, as well as jewel-like eyes, link them in turn to wealth; they are frequently thought, like dragons, to guard treasures. Their crown-like "hoods" were alternately perceived as helmets; thus, they became linked to war, with helmets bearing serpent figures being worn by warriors from ancient through medieval times. They were also believed to possess healing powers, with medicines being prepared from their venom.

In ancient Egypt, the *kneph*-snake was sacred; in the Hellenistic period, it continued to be honored as the *agathodaemon*; Romans knew this snake as the *anguis*. Especially in the form of the caduceus, the serpent assisted numerous deities – Hermes in communication and magic, Asclepius in healing – or was otherwise associated with them, as with Hecate. At the Parthenon in Athens, the sacred serpent of Athena was fed a honey-cake each day; while in many Greek homes, snakes were offered milk. Greeks held that if a snake licked one's ears, that individual, by way of venom, might be bestowed with the gift of prophecy, as in the myths of Melampus and Cassandra.

Archaeological evidence suggests, as mentioned above, that the reverence of a serpentine goddess occurred in Neolithic Old Europe. Millennia later, in Teutonic religion and mythology, the serpent Miðgarðs-ormr, or Iörmungandr, lay coiled about the base of the cosmic world-tree Yggdrasil, an image also known to ancient Balts. The god Odin possessed several nicknames alluding to serpents, including Ofnir and Svâfnir. Warrior heroes descended from Odin were sometimes described as possessing snake-eyes, and Teutonic helmets, shields, and swords were embellished with serpents. Some Germanic peoples believed that the King and Queen of Snakes wore crowns on their heads. They revered snakes as the Greeks and others had done, by offering them milk; in return, milkmaids and others were often rewarded with health and prosperity. According to Grimm, "In some districts they say every house has two snakes, a male and a female, but they never show themselves till the master or mistress of the house dies, and then they undergo the same fate."

To kill a snake, especially the king or queen, would result in devastation. Lombards revered both trees and serpents, bringing to mind this combined association in the tale of "Eglë and Žaltys". Pomeranians of northeastern Europe revered certain snakes and told of snakes who, when offered milk, would offer their crowns to humans, especially to infants, for whom they demonstrated particular affection. They believed that to kill a snake while it lay near an infant – in truth, it was guarding the child – would result in the premature death of the infant. One tale told of a woman who, while sleeping, was impregnated by a snake after it entered her open mouth. After the child (a were-snake?) was born, the snake who was its father "never left the baby's side, it lay in bed with it, and ate out of its bowl, without doing it any harm." Other peoples of Germanic, Slavic, and Baltic heritage also revered snakes, with names resonating with names like Zmij, Zmiye, and Zmek, reminding us of Žeminas, an alternate theonym of Žaltys. Prussians offered milk to a particular serpent perceived as the sacred animal or embodiment of the god Patrimpas. Rimvydas Sliazas, in "Elements of Old Prussian Mythology in Günter

Grass's *Dog Years*," observes: "To the Balts, the sacred snakes were the protectors of good health. [They] prayed to them for children. The souls of the departed were believed to continue living in snakes. [They] welcomed the dwelling of snakes in their homes as a good omen and fed milk to them. Letts, ancient Latvians, recognized in certain snakes their goddess Brekhina; these snakes, called *peena mahtes*, "milk mothers," were honored in homes and fed milk.

Many Lithuanians revered and fed snakes called *giviotis*, "living ones," in their homes. The place where the serpent resided in the house was called the *krikštas* or *kertė*. This place often contained a millstone on which, or else a chest or clay jar in which, the snake could rest. This site was considered an altar. This tradition continued beyond the fifteenth century CE, when the Christian missionary Jeronym Jan Prazsky observed that Lithuanians continued to keep snakes in their houses, to feed them, and to honor them with other offerings. At Vilnius, sacred serpents remained beneath the altar after the temple of Perkûnas was converted to a cathedral. Stasys Samalavicius, in *An Outline of Lithuanian History*, notes, "[T]he greatest honor was bestowed on the grass-snake. As a rule people used to keep grass-snakes in their homes too...If such a grass-snake was accidentally killed it was considered a sign of a great misfortune to the whole family." In *Ancient Symbolism in Lithuanian Folk Art*, Gimbutas observes: "In folk beliefs..., the *žaltys* is associated with sexual life...Encountering a snake prophesied either marriage or birth ... it used to be considered a blessing to have a *žaltys* in one's home ... The *žaltys* was said to bring happiness and prosperity." Moreover, this "mystical and gift-bestowing creature is known to Lithuanian folklore as 'the sentinel of the gods' (*Dievu siuntinelis*)." Gimbutas explains that traditional Lithuanians would "never harm a *žaltys*. If, while mowing a field, they noticed one lying in the grass, they refrained from mowing that particular spot...It is of course a crime to kill it, and a proverb says: 'Do not leave a dead *žaltys* on a field. Bury it.' The sight of a dead *žaltys* would cause the sun [goddess Saulė] to cry." She also points out that in the 1950s, it was not uncommon to see a Lithuanian house's crossbeams "topped with carvings of reptilian shape, to ensure the well-being of the family." In *The Living Goddesses*, she relates: "Up to the mid-twentieth century, harmless green snakes often shared the house with people. They occupied the place of honor, the sacred corner of the house, and were fed milk in addition to their regular diet. The snake protected the family, or more exactly, symbolized its life force."

Ancient Lithuanians held that the *žaltys* served as an intermediary or intercessory between the realms of the living, the dead, and the deities and spirits. Moreover, they believed that the souls of deceased humans might enter into the bodies of snakes. The healing power of serpents remained in vernacular belief through the twentieth century. Irene Luksis Goddard recalls that when she was a young woman in Lithuania, a panacea called *Gyvatine* including whiskey, vodka, and a small snake was sold at the outdoor market in her hometown. Nor has the role of the *žaltys* as intermediary been forgotten. The exquisite gates of the Žaltes Valley in Alytus remind the visitor of that time when the people held that the soul or spirit of the dead might enter the body of the *žaltys*.

Ophidian reverence played a special role in the traditional Lithuanian calendar, especially between the first of the year and the summer solstice. Kirmelinë, held on January 25, celebrated the awakening of snakes from hibernation. Gimbutas notes that into the early twentieth century, Lithuanian "peasants celebrated *kirmiu diena* [or Kirmelinë]...when snakes symbolically awakened and abandoned the forests for the houses. This special day marked the beginning of everything, the awakening of nature." Algirdas J. Greimas, in *Of Gods and Men*, translates a portion of a Latin Christian text which reads: "Honoring them [i.e, the snakes] as deities, *at a certain time of the year* they invite them to the table with a seer's prayers. Crawling out (from out of their sleep) they lie down on the clean cloth ... and make themselves comfortable on the table. There, *pakrikstine* (= having tasted a little of) every dish, they slither [away]." Only after the serpents have tasted the food and peacefully departed may the family eat.

At Lygë, the spring equinox, the *žaltys* was honored as one member of a dueling dyad, the other member of which was a bird (often a stork); their struggle, like other symbolic struggles ritualized at this time, signified, among other things, the shift from winter to spring. During this springtime celebration, special breads made of mixed grains, pastries containing hemp, and vodka seasoned with herbs were served. Vernacular belief held that at this time, one might discover prosperity in the form of the golden crown of the Snake King. On the occasion of a related spring festival, Velykos – its traditions appropriated by Christians for Easter – serpents numbered among the motifs found on *marguciai*, "many-colored" eggs given as offerings and gifts as tokens of rebirth or regeneration. Motifs of serpents were often placed between those of sun and moon. Of the connection of snakes and eggs, Dundulienë notes, "Lithuanians considered reptiles and birds to be demiurges (world creators), often emerging from a cosmic egg ... these totems guard people from various misfortunes, [and] lead to welfare and happiness." At Rasa, the summer solstice, many believed that, as at the spring equinox, one might discover the Snake King's crown.

Žaltys, like Eglë, is a folkloric figure; but also like her, beneath his folkloric identity lies divinity. As Martinkus explains, Žaltys is a deity or spirit of water, is "King of the lake." As such, he is capable of "provoking all sorts of maladies, of sending to earth great plagues, drought, famine, flood" but he is also the "master of the healing waters." Also associated with magical metamorphosis, he may take the form of a grass-snake, an aquatic snake, and a human. Žaltys, like Eglë, appears to also herald a complex chain of divine or supernatural associations. He is perhaps most importantly the consort of Saulë, this aspect of the sun-goddess being assumed by Eglë in the tale. We are reminded once more of the proverb, "Do not leave a dead *žaltys* on a field. Bury it. The sight of a dead *žaltys* would cause the sun [goddess Saulë] to cry." Particularly if Martinkus is correct, he may also be related to – or perhaps even the son of – the crone- or "witch"-goddess Ragana, who, as Gimbutas explains, "carried the energy of a snake. If Ragana died, you might see her hair curl, like a Gorgon's [or Medusa's] into snakes, and little snakes would crawl out of her mouth."

Beyond these associations with goddesses, it appears that Žaltys may bear an association with the Old Prussian deity Patrimpas, also depicted as serpentine or ophidian and as a god of the waters. Sliazas notes that "Traditions preserved in Lithuania show that the god [Patrimpas] and the waters he ruled were believed to possess curing and rejuvenating qualities." Samalavièius adds, "Patrimpas was the guardian of warmth, plants and fruits. Ancient Lithuanians used to give him offerings of wax, amber, sheaves of corn." Similarly, Žaltys may also be related to Andojas, a Lithuanian deity of water who heals, shapeshifts, and serves as an intermediary or intercessory between the worlds.

From the variants of the tale of "Eglë and Žaltys" collected by Martinkus, it is evident that he may also correspond to the god Velnias. In *Chthoniðkasis lietuvio mitologijos pasaulis*, Norbertas Vëlius refers to Velnias as "the main mythological being belonging to the chthonic world," noting that "he has more than 200 names and appears in the shape of various animals, birds, reptiles, and people of different age groups and professions." Vëlius continues: "The greatest attention in Lithuanian folklore is given to [the god Velnias, who is a]...patron of animals[;]...a deity of the "erotic sphere" who is "attractive to women, who seeks their love and even marries them; [a god] ... "of the dead;" …[a guardian "of wealth" [;] [a] mediator between the two worlds [; and]…a patron of the people who maintain[n] ties with both these worlds, i.e. wizards and sorcerers." Dwelling at the base of the World-Tree, he is comparable to the serpent Žaltys. Vëlius also makes the intriguing observation that Velnias – and thus possibly also Žaltys – may be among the eldest deities revered by the Lithuanians as well as one especially cherished by commoners. This observation would seem to support Gimbutas's and others' assertions of extremely ancient and deep-seated reverence of serpents among Balts and neighboring peoples. Vëlius argues that the worship of Velnias and the veneration of serpents correspond primarily to pre (or non-)-Indo-European – Gimbutas's Old European – culture and to vernacular culture, as opposed to the worship of sky-gods like Perkûnas and Dievs, which corresponds to Indo-European and elite culture. Two chthonic types of beings related to Velnias and perhaps indirectly to Žaltys, as Martinkus indicates, are the *kaukai* and what we might term the Lithuanian "green man." Gimbutas explains that the *kaukai* are typically "bearded gnomes" who are "believed to help people by increasing grain and hay" as well as by bestowing other types of prosperity. Their "chthonian origin" is implied by their name, which refers to a "dry or frozen clod or lump of earth." They dwell underground and are vegetarians, associated especially with mandrake root and mushrooms. "Their patron divinity is the god Puskaitis, who lives under the elder bush" and whose sacred animal is the boar; he is a chthonic deity who serves as an intermediary between the realms of the living and the dead. Where the "green man" is concerned, Martinkus points out that the names Žaltys and Žilvinas are related to numerous words signifying "green" and "tree." For example, *žalias*, *žalsvas*, *žalsvumas*, and *žalumynai* refer to "green," "greenish," "greenishness," and "greens" (or "verdure"), respectively; while *želti* signifies "to germinate," *želvi* a "young tree," and *žilvitis* a "willow tree." In this context, Martinkus notes that trees and the grass-snake, beyond the obvious "green" connection, share a special connection in the realm of soul: while animals are believed to have "icy" or "frozen" souls, trees and other plants are thought to possess "watery" souls. This suggests that Eglë may have been at least partially motivated to transform her children into trees instead of into other entities because, not being able to return to the serpentine realm following the murder of her husband and their father, she and her were-snake children might nevertheless continue to share a spiritual connection to Žaltys by way of assuming another embodiment in the "green," "watery" cosmos.

One cannot overemphasize, incidentally, the symbolic significance of water – the abode of Žaltys and that element connecting serpents and trees – in pagan Baltic spirituality. Baltic deities of water include the goddess Juras Mate and the gods Andojas, Bangputys, Patrimpas, Upinis, and Velnias. Vykintas Vaitkevicius, in *Senosios Lietuvos Đventvietës: Žemaitija*, observes:

"[Bodies of water] were considered sacred ... Water is the world of the dead, the abode of the souls ... .Water is also a sphere of gods and deities...Legends say that springs, lakes and swamps contained submerged houses and churches, sometimes [even] people [and] deities."

It is conceivable that the tale of "Eglë and Žaltys" commences at the time of the summer solstice, that is, at Rasa, when "girls used to go swimming ... because they believed that 'on that night, water possessed magic power to restore freshness and good looks." Water also serves a ritual function in the traditional Lithuanian wedding: according to the Žemaitian wedding customs a deep ditch symbolizing a water obstacle is dug out across the road when the bride is brought to her husband's home for the first time; in the tale of Eglë, this journey across water to the husband's home is magically extended to include a voyage to an underwater kingdom. The "watery" site of the sauna also served an important ritual function during both weddings and birthing rites.

As with Eglë's correspondences to numerous divinities, so Žaltys's correspondences to various divinities and spirits suggest a "web of resemblances" contributing to the composition of that "grammar of spirituality" or "magnetic field" we have identified as the pagan *pasaulëpiûra* (worldview), which emphasizes the reverence of divinity in embodied, natural forms and which acknowledges the cycle of birth, life, death, and regeneration, witnessed so vividly in the molting of serpents.

The struggle between the chthonic and

celestial divine beings referred to above may have begun – at least in part – in ancient India, as the Indian folkltale of "The River Snake" suggests. The latter part of this tale bears an uncanny resemblance to that of "Eglë and Žaltys". We know that the Hindu relationship to serpents is a complex one, with sacred serpents including the royal *nagas* and the *kundalini*; and there appears to be, as elsewhere, a profound connection in ancient Indian spirituality of the serpent to the divine feminine. In "The River Snake," a serpent ferries a young woman across a flooded river in return for her future firstborn child. As in the fairy tale "Rumplestiltskin," time passes, the woman bears a child, having forgotten her promise to the serpent. When the snake reappears, the woman, under duress, gives her daughter to him. The daughter departs with the snake to dwell beneath the water. It would appear that they learn to love each other. Eventually, the young woman gives birth to four sons. One day, the woman returns to her mother's home with her children. Her brothers express interest in meeting their ophidian brother-in-law. They are, of course, lying. They get him drunk and proceed to chop off his head.

This folktale infers that the struggle between the serpent, who signifies the chthonic divine, and the celestial divine, here signified by the brothers, evidently predates the emergence of Christianity. If somehow this tale traveled circuitously to the Baltic lands, perhaps at a very early date, then the struggle already imbedded within it may have encountered a parallel struggle between Old European and Indo-European cultural motifs, narratives, and values, that is, between chthonic beings like the Snake Goddess Gimbutas describes and /or Velnias/Žaltys on the one hand and celestial deities like Perkûnas on the other. This struggle would of course have both shifted and intensified dramatically with the emergence of Christianity, whose authorities and practitioners appropriated what they considered to be beneficent aspects of the celestial deities and spirits for the Christian divine family, while employing attributes of the chthonic deities and spirits to Balticize the Christian Devil and his supposed – especially female – followers.

Despite the serpentine staff of Moses, Christ's advice to his followers to "Be ye therefore wise as serpents" (Matthew 10: 16), and the Gnostic Ophites sect, Christians, primarily associating the serpent with Satan, were horrified upon encountering ophidian reverence among Germanic, Slavic, and Baltic peoples (not to mention their parallel horror on finding such veneration in the Americas).

As Grimm observes, pagan religious practitioners "worshipped kind, beneficent snakes, while in Christian opinion, the notion of snakes being malignant and diabolic predominates." Nevertheless, they acknowledged the power of the serpent. For instance, the *Vita Barbati* tells of how a serpent fashioned from gold by a Germanic Lombard artisan was "melted down and reformed into Christian chalice and plate, in recognition of the sacredness of the gold snake." In the fifteenth century, Jeronym Jan Prazsky was shocked to find Lithuanians worshipping snakes. Two centuries later, a

Jesuit missionary condemned them for continuing this practice. In the eighteenth century, determined to put an end to this practice, Jesuit authorities confiscated many domesticated serpents and alternately cast them into fires or drowned them in lakes – suggesting an uncanny resonance with the drowning and burning of cats during the Inquisition, the promoters of which linked cats to witches. The *žaltys* was demonized, and, not surprisingly, Velnias, the deity perhaps most closely identified with Žaltys, was transformed into the Baltic version of Satan.

In terms of the relationship of serpent and woman, the "triumph" of Christianity over pagan spirituality could not have produced a more shocking transformation. Following thousands – perhaps even hundreds of thousands – of years of the associated veneration of serpents and divine feminine beings, the serpent became a symbol of evil, associated on one hand with Eve's sin and with feminine destructive magic and, on the other, with the Virgin Mary's triumph over evil, illustrated by her stepping on the serpent's crown. In spite of the odious campaign against the reverence of domesticated serpents, however, such reverence continued into the twentieth century; and despite the attempt to vilify the ancient bond of serpent and woman / goddess, the memory of the *žaltys*/ Zaltys / Žilvinas and of woman's/ the goddess's bond with the snake has survived in the poignant tale of Eglë.

Trees

Alfonsas Kazitenas, in "Amid Trees," writes of the presence of trees in Lithuania: "In the past our land was famous for its huge, impassable forests. There were coniferous trees – pines, firs, and junipers, and there were nearly twenty sorts of deciduous trees ... [including] oaks, ashes, maples ... limes ... birch-trees, asps, alder-trees, willows, cherries, guelder roses and rowans." Gimbutas echoes, "The rich natural environment absorbed the Lithuanian soul, sustaining in it a profound veneration for the living land with its deciduous and coniferous trees."

Like many pagan European cultures, the ancient Balts, including the Lithuanians, revered trees and worshipped in sacred groves. Grimm observes that "there were many such sacred groves in ... Prussia and Lithuania." Vaitkevicius notes that sacred forests and trees are "often referred to in ancient written sources" pertaining to Lithuania, and that these literary documents, together with orally transmitted folkloric traditions, acknowledge that the "forest is considered as ... a different world, or a way leading there. The trees of such a forest are regarded as untouchable. They are the abodes of the gods or of the dead and the places of their revelation. The tree is regarded as alive, it has blood as a human being."

Jonas Balys, in "Lithuanian Mythology," writes, "Some trees were regarded as living beings who feel pain; blood was said to flow from them." Trees, with their roots in the earth and their branches reaching toward the heavens, symbolized the linking of the chthonic, earthly, and celestial realms. Many Lithuanians "revered remarkable oaks and other great shady trees, from which they received oracular responses." Trees were especially associated with rites of healing, "sacrifice and magic." Certain trees were thought to possess healing powers. Balys notes that trees "which have a cavity through the trunk, are worshipped and it is good for a man to crawl through and be healed of a disease." Rita Balkutë observes that the bark of certain pine trees was believed to heal various illnesses, and that a particular oak tree growing in East Prussia was visited by Lithuanians hoping to heal afflicted eyes, hands, legs and feet. Vëlius adds, "Offerings were usually made under firs and pines to cure lameness." Those desiring healing would circle around the oak tree or press their bodies to its body, afterward leaving offerings in its branches. Balkutë also notes that "sterile or ill women tied beautifully embroidered aprons on special trees asking for children and health." It was also believed that one could, in certain situations, offer one's illness to a tree or else shut it up inside a tree. "People suffering from epilepsy or from many warts, tied many knots on strings, went to the woods, drilled a hole in a large tree, stuffed the knotted string into the hole and closed the hole with a cork and ran away, not looking back, with the hope of getting well."

Those who held trees sacred believed that "even to break a twig would [be] a sin. They thought that he who cut a bough in such a grove either died suddenly or was crippled in one of his limbs." Once Christianity became Lithuania's dominant religion, "people's gatherings" in sacred forests and groves were "characterized as relics of the old faith." Nevertheless, many persons continued to venerate trees and to resist Christian intolerance of the ancient rites. Pagan Lithuanians frequently compared loved ones to trees: "When we grew at our father's [house] ... like two oak trees"; "Oh, my linden, linden, you are my mother, your roots are her feet, your branches are her arms and these green leaves are her kind words." "The oak, the linden," the *daina* goes, "stand by the road together./ Branches incline with each other." Their interweaving reveals the interwoven nature of humans and trees in the pagan Lithuanian psyche.

According to Gimbutas, Lithuanian belief in the "oneness of human and plant life stems from the belief that the life force, or soul, is the same in [all beings] and from the belief in metempsychosis. The soul is immortal." Lithuanians traditionally believed that upon death, the soul, or part of the soul, of a person that is called the *siela* might well reincarnate as an animal or tree. In Martinkus's words, "The destiny of mortals is, as one can see, linked to that of trees."

Lithuanians associated certain trees with femininity and were thought to house the souls of women; these included linden (or, lime), spruce (or fir), pine, aspen, apple, pear, and cherry. Other trees, such as the oak, maple, ash, juniper, and birch were linked to masculinity and thought to harbor the souls of men. Traditionally, when an infant celebrated his or her first birthday, the *apgelai* ritual was undertaken. This female-led rite included cutting a tuft of the child's hair, planting a "masculine" tree for a male infant and a "feminine" tree for a female infant, and placing the tuft of hair beneath the tree in the soil. Particular trees were further associated with age groups and family roles. For example, the linden often signified a mature woman or mother, while the cornel (-cherry) or dogwood often signified a young woman or daughter; similarly, the oak or juniper often signified a mature male or father, while the maple often represented a male youth or son. Trees may have also suggested either opposing forces or complementary elements forming a symbiotic dyad or triad; for example, while the linden was typically associated with the compassionate and creative aspects of the divine feminine, the pine corresponded to the destructive aspect of the divine feminine. Trees also appear to have been associated with certain locations: for instance, the birch was frequently planted at the entrance to a farm, while the ash and the maple were planted nearer the house. The oak, on the other hand, was most often considered a wild tree of the forest.

Trees, as Vaitkevicius, Gimbutas and others have observed, are frequently associated with death and rebirth (regeneration, reincarnation). Martinkus notes that it was commonly held that if many old trees were destroyed by a storm or by being cut down, many elderly people in the vicinity would die shortly thereafter; similarly, if younger trees were destroyed, the same fate awaited young people. Moreover, if an individual chopped down a tree unnecessarily which had been planted by his or her parents or grandparents, that individual would die shortly thereafter. If he or she dared to chop down more than a single tree unnecessarily, then he or she would take with him or her into death another family member. J. Kudirka, in *The Lithuanians*, reports that funeral paths were often strewn with twigs of fir; similarly, in Estonia, spruce twigs were thrown at the funeral procession. Coffins for women tended to be fashioned from "feminine" trees, those for men from "masculine" trees. A *daina* relates that the "coffin of [one's] father" was made from oak, while the coffin for one's mother was made from "the linden." Moreover, as Martinkus notes, "into the nineteenth century, funerary monuments for men were made of oak, ash, or birch, while those for women were made of fir, aspen, or linden."

Gimbutas, as mentioned above, maintains that an aspect of the soul (or one of multiple souls), the *siela*, may take up residence in a tree (or other plant) or animal. In Vaitkevicius's view, trees are "the abodes ... of the dead ... It is often believed that after death, souls do their penance in the trees ... the soul's life in the trees [is a kind of] a purgatory." Martinkus explains that it was held by many pagan Lithuanians that the goddess Laima allots each mortal soul a certain number of years of life. If by chance that individual dies before reaching that number – through violence, death in childbearing, or devastating illness – then her or his *siela*-soul may inhabit a tree until the original number bestowed by Laima is attained, at which time the soul will probably be reincarnated in another mortal. When a tree squeaks, Vėlius relates, "people say, 'Here is a soul weeping.'" The belief that souls reside in trees permits an orphan, Graþina Krivickas observes in "Relations Between the Living and the Dead in Lithuanian Folklore," to beseech a linden to serve as his or her mother, or an oak to serve as his or her father. Krivickas also draws our attention to a *daina* which suggests that the soul of a deceased young woman has taken refuge in, or been reincarnated in, a birch tree (usually associated with male souls) as well as in the grass, flowers, and water of a spring: "Oh, my true father, do not chop down the birch tree by the roadside,/…The birch by the road, I am."

A *daina* collected by Antanas Juska in the nineteenth century, also illustrates the concept of trees harboring the souls of the dead, depicting a person or persons who has/have died and have transformed into trees, including a linden. an oak, a maple, and a dogwood. "The green trees bend," the *daina* culminates, "My family weeps for me."

Occasionally, a soul's inhabiting of a tree results from a transformation effected by a negative intention or spell directed against an individual. For instance, in one *daina*, a mother, wondering why her son has been transformed into an oak tree, learns that he has been cursed by a young woman. Another *daina* focuses on a young mother whose sinister mother-in-law transforms her into a linden while her husband is away at war.

When the young woman's husband returns, his mother insists that he chop down the linden prior to seeing his wife. Although we cannot be certain, it is possible, if not probable, that these last two *daina* were composed during the Christian period. It is difficult to imagine that a young man's transformation into an oak, or a young woman's transformation into a linden, would have been perceived as the result of a curse in pagan Lithuania, considering the respect accorded to these trees. Moreover, during the pagan period, the felling of a linden may well have been perceived as a sacrilege and hence might not have been undertaken by a son, no matter how respectful he might have been toward his mother. However, it is possible that the last *daina* dates from the transitional period, since the stepmother's insistence that her son chop down the linden is clearly depicted as a destructive desire.

Trees were frequently thought to be guarded (or particularly dear to) or inhabited by deities. The best known association of a deity and a tree in Lithuanian mythology is probably that of the celestial Perkûnas and the oak. Perhaps the most sacred tree in the region stood in a forest at Romuva in Lithuania Minor, East Prussia. This was a holy oak, decorated with fabric, which appears to have been dedicated to the reverence of Perkûnas. According to Grimm, "No unconsecrated person was allowed to set foot in the forest, no tree to be felled, not a bough to be injured, not a beast [in the forest] to be slain." Numerous other deities are likewise linked to trees. The god of fruits and grains, Puskaitis, lived beneath the elder, a tree "associated with fertility and the underworld." The linden was cherished by the goddess Laima. Velnias, with links to Žaltys, was associated with the fir tree, or *eglë*. Beyond these associations, we know of Girátis, a youthful male deity of the woods, and of Medeina, who also loved the linden and who may have possessed the oak prior to Perkûnas.

In the tale of "Eglë and Žaltys," Eglë ultimately transforms her children and herself into trees. In most variants, it seems, she begins with her eldest son and ends with her youngest child and only daughter. In the case of individual trees, it may occasionally help to mention their symbolic significance in other European cultures extending beyond the Baltic region. As mentioned above, although it is rarely if ever stated directly in the tale, it is evident, from what we know of pagan beliefs concerning trees as housing the souls or spirits of the deceased, that in transforming herself and her children into trees, Eglë is taking their lives; at the very least, she is transferring their souls or spirits from one form of life to another. In this light, Eglë's action may bring to mind the Greek sorceress Medea, who, legend has it, slew her children as an act of vengeance.

Eglë turns her eldest son Ažuolas into an oak. In Lithuanian pagan religion and mythology, the oak was sacred to Perkûnas, the lord of thunder. Martinkus observes that Perkûnas's name "is linked etymologically, to the oak (Lith. *perku-*, Latin *quercu-*)." She also points out that the "oak symbolizes authority; representing the pater familias or, in his absence, the elder son ... it occupies one of the highest (or the highest) place among sacred trees." In a well-known myth, Perkûnas chops an oak tree in half; when he does so, blood flows from it, demonstrating, Manning explains, that "sacred trees have been endowed not only with a personal spirit, but also with human physical characteristics." Perkûnas's symbol of authority is a twisted oak branch; this branch, fashioned into a scepter called the *krivulë*, became in pagan Lithuania symbolic of spiritual and political leadership. The oak was sometimes also associated with the god Velnias, whom, as we have seen, has been linked to Žaltys. By way of the notion that cuckoos were thought to dwell in oaks, the tree is also linked to the goddesses Gegutë and Laima. Like the ash, the oak may represent the cosmic "world-tree." In the pagan psyche, the oak and the ash formed a symbiotic dyad, with the oak being perceived as "active" and the ash as "yielding" or "receptive." The oak also signifies longevity and divine messages; in terms of the latter, pieces of oak were used in divination among Germanic and possibly also among Baltic peoples. Vernacular belief held that if, during a time of pestilence, people walked through the smoke of oak and ash ritually burned together, they would survive the plague. Many believed that oaks should remain in the wild and should not be planted on family property: "those who do so will die when the trunk reaches the size of the planter's arm." Offerings and holy images were frequently deposited in hollow places in oaks. Oaks were also thought to "summon brides," which, in terms of our tale, may link Ažuolas to a more joyous time, the occasion of his parents' marriage.

Eglë transforms her middle son, Uosis, into an ash tree. This tree is sacred to the aquatic deity Andojas, who serves as a god of justice as well as a guide between the realms of the living and the dead. As the latter, Andojas may be associated with Žaltys. The ash, even more than the oak, is considered representative of the world-tree, which, like Andojas, links various realms of being. At the world-tree's base we find a sacred spring as well as a sacred snake; in terms of our tale, the snake corresponds to Žaltys and the spring to his dwelling-place. Among Germanic and Baltic peoples, as well as among the British, it was considered dangerous to break a bough from the ash. However, at the time of the summer solstice, branches of ash were hung on doors as protection against malefic spirits.

The form of the birch awaits Eglë's youngest son, Beržas. Like the oak and the ash, the birch may stand for the world-tree. Most often, however, it corresponds to the youngest male member of the family and to springtime, the summer solstice, and joyous intimate relationships. Birch trees were linked to divination, especially concerning love and marriage. At spring and summer festivals, a refreshing beverage made of birch was consumed; cows, symbolic of fertility, were decorated with birch leaves; and girls made wreaths which they threw up over their heads onto a birch tree to see who would marry first. In terms of our tale, these associations of the birch may link Beržas to the joy his mother experienced as a maiden. The birch is also linked to the god Velnias (with connections to Žaltys), to the goddesses Laima and Medeina (with connections to Eglë), and to *laumës* (fairies). As Marija Kuncaitis, following Danute Bindokiene, relates, "With great sorrow and thundering anger Eglë turned to her [daughter] Drebulë," who had betrayed her under duress, and uttered:

May you turn into a willow,
May you shiver day and night,
May the rain cleanse your mouth,
May the wind comb your hair![36]

In pagan European cultures, the willow was often linked to psychic powers and creativity, but it was most known for its association with sadness, grieving, death, and the underworld or afterlife. In Greek religion and mythology, Jane Gifford relates in *The Wisdom of Trees*, "Persephone, Queen of the Underworld, had a sacred willow grove. The Greek sorceress Circe had a riverside cemetery planted with willows that was dedicated to Hecate ... [who] haunted crossroads and tombs."

Of these, Persephone parallels Eglë in certain respects. Elsewhere in Europe, the willow is "associated with funerals. Garlands for mourning were traditionally woven from willow branches and willows were once planted on graves to ease the passage of the soul at death." Rimvydas Sliazas notes that the "willow is considered a cursed tree in Germany, for Judas hanged himself from a willow. In East Prussia there is a belief that the branches of the willow turn into snakes," an association which might link the willow to Žaltys. While the sentiment behind Eglë's statement – which reads in part like a curse – remains the same, the tree most often associated with her daughter is the not the willow but the aspen, a member of the poplar family. While the aspen is sometimes linked to Laima, it is most frequently linked to deities and spirits linked to death and the afterlife, including Velnias, who is in turn linked to Žaltys. In Slavic mythology, an aspen bridge built over a fiery river leads mortals to the afterlife. In Greek myth, the aspen or poplar is associated with Persephone. In the Celtic world, where the tree was also associated with death, wands of aspen were "used to measure bodies and graves, and people feared a baleful charm should they be struck with it." Moreover, incense of aspen or poplar was burned during the Celtic festival of Samhain to protect individuals from malefic spirits. Vëlius notes that in pagan Lithuania, the aspen was sometimes associated with evil. According to other variants of the tale, Eglë transformed Drebulë into a cornel-cherry or dogwood.

Eglë at last transforms herself into a spruce or fir tree, an *eglë*. The fir, traditionally a feminine tree, was known as the "daughter of the forest" and, like the oak, was not considered a domesticated tree. The fir was regarded as superior to all other feminine trees; she was the mother and protector of plants, animals, and humans – especially during storms. It's said that once a tiny bird hurt its wing, and could not continue with his family on their migratory journey. Among the trees, only Eglë offered to shelter him. Thus, the god Vejas declared that henceforth, she would remain evergreen while other trees lost their leaves in autumn and winter. Fir and spruce trees were also thought to possess great healing power; Vëlius notes that "offerings were usually made under firs and pines to cure lameness." At traditional Lithuanian marriage ceremonies, an *eglë* was sometimes suspended from the ceiling to symbolize the "ever-green" union of bride and groom. Fir and spruce trees were also frequently linked to death and regeneration. Vernacular belief held that while if one dreamed of an oak, a man would die, if one dreamed of a fir, a woman would die.

Funeral paths were strewn with fir or spruce branches. Vëlius recounts that "fir timber was used to make grave monuments to women." The fir or spruce is also associated with sacrifice; in ancient *dainos*, the fir sometimes stood for a small goat which was to be offered to a deity. The tree was further linked to numerous feminine deities and spirits, including Žemyna and *laumës*; according to Matossian, as noted above, Lithuanians often brought food offerings to a wooden female figure hung on a pine or fir tree. An interesting parallel to the association of the *eglë* tree and Eglë with goddesses and female spirits may be found in the Germanic reverence of Frau Fichte (Mother Spruce), to whom offerings are made and who is especially celebrated in springtime, with decorated boughs which are carried in procession, including to barns, which, by way of the power of Frau Fichte, are believed to promote fertility and to protect animals from harm. Among the few male divinities or spirits with whom the fir or spruce is associated, its connection with Velnias (who, again, bears association with Žaltys) is perhaps the strongest. Finally, according to Vëlius, this tree corresponds to western Lithuania, that region most linked to early goddess reverence and to the veneration of serpents.

Trees, which possess profound spiritual significance and associations with divinities, also represent a "web of resemblances" and assist, together with Eglë's and Žaltys's correspondences to various divinities and spirits, in composing the "grammar of spirituality" or "magnetic field" we have identified as the pagan Lithuanian *pasaulëpiûra*.

Ancient forests and sacred groves suffered as Christianity spread throughout Europe. In the words of Robin Lane Fox in *Pagans and Christians*, "The triumph of Christianity was accompanied by the sound of the axe on age-old arboreta." As early as the fourth century, St. Martin of Tours chopped down a holy tree revered by Gauls. The fifth-century bishop St. Patrick, renowned for ridding Ireland of snakes – held sacred by the pagan population – was responsible for the destruction of the Druid grove of Fochloch. John of Ephesus, in the sixth century, "made several assaults" on trees sacred to Artemis. In the eighth century, as part of an effort to Christianize the Saxon pagans of northern Germany, Charlemagne destroyed a hallowed tree regarded as the embodiment of the cosmic tree Yggdrasil. During the same epoch, St. Boniface chopped down the sacred oak of the god Thor (or, Donar) on the peak of Mount Gudenberg at Geismar in Germany. In the following century, the Italian churchman and anti-pope Guibert (or, Wilbert) of Ravenna rooted up a sacred grove which appears to have been dedicated to the Slavic solar deity Radegast. Eleventh-century Saxon and Frisian pagans watched as their sacred groves were destroyed by order of archbishop Unwan of Hamburg-Bremen, and as the Basilica of St. Vitus was constructed from the wood of one of the groves. Later that same century, the Christian Polish prince Brzetislav burnt to the ground the sacred groves and forests (*rok*, or *uroczysko*) of the Bohemians.

In Lithuania, destruction of trees and sacred groves did not commence immediately. The thirteenth-century King Mindaugas, even after converting to Christianity under pressure, continued to worship in a sacred grove. In the late fourteenth century, however, the Christian ruler Wladyslaw Jogaila (married to the Christian queen Jadwiga) began to destroy the sacred groves of Lithuania as well as to destroy the sacred serpents revered by the people. Also during this period, the Christian missionary Jeronym Jan Prazsky (Jerome of Prague) demanded that the Lithuanian ruler Vytautus destroy the sacred groves (*šventa giria*). A massive protest resulted: "A multitude of women besought [Vytautus] to stop him [i.e., Jerome], saying that with the woods he was destroying the house of god from which they had been wont to get rain and sunshine."

Although Jerome had already begun felling the sacred groves, his work remained unfinished, as Vytautus expelled him from the country. Christian destruction of sacred groves and forests in Lithuania continued, however, as in 1618, when a group of "Jesuits cut down a sacred oak, devoted to Perkûnas, in Kraziai"; in 1725, when another group of Jesuits chopped down and burned two more oaks sacred to Perkûnas (and called "the oak gods"); and in 1746, when sacred spruce trees were chopped down at Berzoras in order to build a church dedicated to St. Stanislavas. Pagan defiance of the Christian repression of tree reverence nevertheless continued in certain areas, as among sixteenth-century Žemaitians who continued to venerate a sacred juniper, and early twentieth-century Žemaitians who continued to make offerings to a sacred pine in the vicinity of Vieksniai.

One cannot stress too much the

devastating blow dealt to the spiritual consciousness of the pagan cultures of Europe – as well as to the biosphere – via the destruction of pagan groves and forests by Christians. Jacques Brosse, in *Mythologie des arbres* (*The Mythology of Trees*, 1989): writes: "Thus, after the triumph of the Church, ...[all] cultic worship of trees was prohibited; and one can imagine the zeal which led the missionaries to destroy the trees.

There was a certain hill, Medžiokalnis, which was named for the goddess Medeina; it lay in the vicinity of Kražiai and was once graced by a sacred forest: "[N]ow completely denuded, it was once covered by a dense oak grove which was the home of Medeina ... As more and more of the Lithuanian forests were laid low, she used to appear to the woodcutters, ... wailing ... "Lithuania is a forest land! Fell the trees, but when you have felled them, Lithuania will cease to be!"

The destruction of forests initiated by Christians escalated in Lithuania with the rise of industrialization and continual warfare. In 1850, forests occupied 50% of the country; by 1905, only 30%; and by 1920, only 17%. Even more forests were destroyed during World War II. Thanks to an emerging ecological movement in Lithuania in recent years, forests now cover approximately 28% of the land.

Weaving the Threads Together

From our exploration of three primary elements of the tale of "Eglë and Žaltys" – there remain many others – we may determine that, by way of the figures of Eglë and Žaltys and the motifs of serpents and trees, the tale, weaves a "dense web of [correspondences and] resemblances " which nurtures the construction of a "grammar of spirituality" or a "magnetic field" signifying the *pasaulëpiûra* of pagan Lithuania, with its emphasis on the cyclic process of birth, life, death, and regeneration and its reverence of divine energy in embodied, natural, frequently feminine and chthonic forms.

Pagan Lithuanians, like many other peoples, revered trees and serpents as sacred entities and as housing human or divine spirits or souls. Except for certain ritual sacrifices and on certain necessary occasions, they regarded the killing of serpents and the destruction of trees and forests as dangerous, criminal, sacrilegious, heinous. Church authorities were repulsed by the pagan reverence of feminine and chthonic divinities, trees, and serpents and viewed their vanquishing as a necessary task in completing the Christianization of Lithuania.

In light of this evidence, it seems that no deep-seated pagan motivation exists for the murder of Žaltys in the tale, other than perhaps a dim memory of an ancient struggle between the chthonic and celestial deities of the early Indo-European cosmos. If we admit the possibility of this memory, which seems to have almost entirely vanished from premodern, pagan Lithuania, then it would seem that its return must have been nurtured by the profound hostility of Christianity toward the reverence of embodied – and ensouled – Nature and toward feminine and chthonic divinities. It occurs to me that Eglë's brothers, who sometimes number twelve, may stand for Christianity; if this is the case, then their slaying of Žaltys becomes comprehensible. It is as if during Eglë's sojourn with Žaltys beneath the water, the world above, already in transition – as demonstrated by the family's attempt to deceive the serpents – altogether changes. She and her wereserpent children return to a world that has utterly ceased to revere snakes as embodiments of divine energy; the serpent, now perceived as evil, must be destroyed.

We might expect Eglë's character to accept this fate, yield to this destiny, to transform into an icon of the Virgin Mary stepping on the serpent that is now identified with Satan; but she does not do so. Instead, she rages against her brothers, parents, and even against her only daughter, who, under duress, has betrayed Žaltys and her. It is abundantly clear that Eglë cherishes Žaltys more than life itself. Her rage, grief and love suggest, in my view, resistance against an emerging *pasaulëpiûra* which demonizes not only the serpent but the reverence of Nature as a whole, as well as feminine divinities who resist assimilation to the image of the Virgin. Eglë's final act consists of transforming her children and herself into trees. As mentioned above, this act of transformation may involve the taking of their lives and hers. In this linking of magical activity to the taking of life, we return to the image of the (sometimes serpentine) crone Ragana, and also perhaps to that of "Lithuanian pagan priests and priestesses [who] drowned themselves rather than see the victory of Christianity." In a completely pagan context, Eglë's transformation of herself and her children into trees would most likely have been perceived as a magical action transferring the life-spirit from one honored form into another. It is conceivable that such a tale, one disentangled from the slaying of Žaltys, might have been told in pagan Lithuania. In a context of transition from "paganism" to Christianity, or in the context of Christian domination, Eglë's magical action might suggest defiance against the Christian campaign against the reverence of trees. I have already suggested that the telling of "Eglë and Žaltys" may permit, in a Christian cultural context, the subtle transmission of, in Marina Warner's terms, an "elaborate code" of pagan images and concepts to audiences and thus the imparting, again in Warner's terms, "heterodox knowledge" which challenges the dominant paradigm of Christianity. However, I would suggest that above and beyond this transmission and imparting of "heterodox knowledge," the telling of the tale of Eglë's marriage to Žaltys and grief upon his death, combined with her consequential transformation of her children and herself into trees, might accrue, in a Christian context, an aspect of defiance against the devaluation of the *pasaulëpiûra* of pagan Lithuania.

In *The Language of the Goddess*, Marija Gimbutas, in referring in particular to the Inquisition and more generally to the "triumph" of Christianity over "paganism," asserts that pagan traditions remain in Lithuanian "sacred…rivers and springs … [in] gnarled trees brimming with vitality … [and] in beliefs and fairy stories."

The tale of "Eglë and Žaltys" has inspired works of art including poetry by Salomeja

Neris, musical works by M. K. Èiurlionis and Mikas Petrauskas, a ballet by Eduardas Balsys, and a film by Vitautas Grivitskas. Figurines of "Eglë and Žaltys" have been sold at the fair of Lithuania's Saint Casimir held on March 4; here, she appears as a joyful, crowned young woman embracing, and embraced by, her beloved, also crowned, Žaltys. Dundulienë observes of Þaltys and the *žaltys* that the serpentine form appears on *marguciai* (eggs), woven sashes, dowry chests, roof adornments, and many other objects. "All these totems," she notes, "guard people from various misfortunes, [and] lead to welfare and happiness." When Ada Martinkus's parents asked a Lithuanian gardener to kill a snake in the garden, he replied, "I hope it isn't a *žaltys*."

I would suggest that "Eglë and Žaltys"/ "Egle Zalciu Karaliene," by way of transmitting, in the form of the folktale, abundant data relating to pagan spiritual beliefs and practices, may serve not only to inspire spiritual questioning but also perhaps, by way of revivifying ancient archetypes of divinities and spirits inhabiting an embodied and inspirited cosmos where the reverence of trees and serpents is taken for granted, inspire a more balanced hybridity or symbiosis (what Gimbutas once referred to as the "double faith") of pagan beliefs and practices with Christianity, or, among the more radically-minded, resistance against the dominant religion and its worldview in favor of a self-conscious, postcolonial return "to our most ancient human roots." In "Bypassing Rue Descartes," a poem centered in Paris, written in Berkeley, California and recalling the pagan spiritual concerns of his motherland, Lithuanian-born poet Czeslaw Milosz (1911-2004) acknowledges as one of his "heavy sins," that of pushing a "rock down onto a water snake coiled in the grass." The poem ends, "And what I have met with in life was the just punishment/ Which reaches, sooner or later, the breaker of a taboo."[37]

Chapter 6
Basque, Romanian, Finno-Ugric, and Sámi Divinities

Basque Deities

The Basques (in Spanish, *vascos*, also, Euskalunak) have inhabited the region of the Pyrenees, in northern Spain and southern France, since remote antiquity. While some scholars categorize them as a Celtic or at least Indo-European people, others believe that they may have been a non-Indo-European.

Christianization of the Basques commenced in the fourth century. Many Basques, however, appear to have resisted the new religion; thus, efforts to Christianize them were reinforced during the High Middle Ages. Evidence provided by Pierre de Lancre and others suggests, however, that, despite the fact that many Basques became zealous Christians, earth-centered traditions persisted at least into the seventeenth century, and possibly thereafter.

Beyond the earth goddess Ama Lur, together with her daughters Eguzki, the Sun, and Ilargi, the Moon, – who, like certain other lunar deities, is envisioned as guardian of the dead and patroness of souls – the reverence of several other deities appears to have tenaciously persisted into at least the seventeenth century: Mari, Jaungoikoa, Atarrabi, Mikelats, and Aker.

Aker

The primary male deity that the goddess Mari (see below), over time, came to be associated with, however, was neither her spouse nor her sons, but instead the god Aker, who came to be seen as her male consort. A phallic god, often, like Jaungoikoa or Basajaun, Aker is depicted as being black-skinned, and he corresponds to Dionysus. The association of Mari and Aker appears to have climaxed at the time of the Basque witch trials in the seventeenth century. Perhaps because Aker is accompanied by or may manifest as a goat, the place where Basque witches met came to be known as the *akelarre*, the "field of the goat." For the Basques, a gathering of those called witches represented a coming together of the priestesses of Mari and the priests of Aker. Although named *brujas* and *brujos* or *hechiceras* and *hechiceros* by Spanish Christians, votaries of Mari and Aker appear to have referred to themselves as *sorguiñas* and *sorgins*. These gatherings appear to have been heavily erotic; in *Los mitos vascos: Aproximación hermenéutica* (2007), André Ortiz-Osés writes, "[I]n paganism, sexuality obtains a sacred character ... [It] signifies the fountain of life ... the fertility of vegetable and animal life [and] the fertility of woman ... denoting abundance and riches."

The gatherings also included the sacrifice of a goat, representing the sacrifice of Aker. The blood of the goat was believed to fructify the earth; its flesh was cooked and shared by participants, imbuing them with its lifeforce, in this case, male lifeforce, known as *indar* (female lifeforce is *adur*). Christian Inquisitors, not surprisingly, misinterpreted these gatherings as demonic; Ortiz-Osés refers to this as a "cultural struggle between a nature-centered and a spirit-centered [by this he means "transcendent"] religion."

Jaungoikoa

Jaungoikoa is considered by some to be the husband of the goddess Mari (see below; others grant Sugaar, a storm-god, this role). His name appears to mean "lord (*jaun*) of the moon (*goikoa*)." Although not much is now known about him, some believe him to be one with Basajaun, the Lord of the Forest (*basa* can mean "forest," "desert," or "wilderness"), who is depicted as a "man of Nature, a farmer, miller, a blacksmith, or a shepherd." It is conceivable that in some times and places he became conflated with Aker. It may be that in his *Tableau de l'inconstance des mauvais anges et demons*, Pierre de Lancre, writing of earth-centered traditions among the Basques of the late sixteenth and early seventeenth centuries, was speaking of either Jaungoikoa or Basajaun when he spoke of persisting belief among alleged witches in the Lord of the Forest. Araquistáin (1945) suggests that Jaungoikoa and/or Basajaun may have been revered, or at the very least remembered, in the early twentieth century.

Mari

Mari (or, Amari, Amaya, Maya) is depicted in multiple local hypostases, including La Bruja, La Dama de Aketegui, La Dama de Amboto (or, Anboto), La Dama de Muru, La Señora, and the "Saint" of the Cave. She is typically depicted as a beautiful woman, finely dressed and surrounded by wealth. She is the Queen of Nature and mortals; in some accounts, she is also a maiden who metamorphoses into the Queen of the Underworld, comparable to Persephone. She sometimes travels through the air surrounded by flames, reminiscent of the fiery mandorla of the Virgin of Guadalupe. A shapeshifter, she occasion-ally manifests – as she has into the twentieth century – as a fiery tree, a ball of fire, a cloud, a raven, a vulture, or a sickle; at other times, she is seen combing threads of gold or winding skeins of golden thread around the horns of a ram, or else riding on a horse or driving a chariot pulled by four horses. She has two sons: Atarrabi and Mikelats. Her sacred sites include various mountains, caves, grottoes, and dolmens. As a mountain-dwelling divinity, she is "believed to inhabit the highest peaks of mountains like Amboto, Aizkorri, and Muru." Offerings to her placed at entrances to caves, include candles, money, sacred stones, sheep and goats, and entrails of cows. In return for honoring her, practition-ers are rewarded with protection from illness, fertility of crops, and other gifts. She rewards her devotees by changing coal into gold and punishes those who disrespect or abandon her by changing gold into coal. She is a special patron of goatherds and shepherds. As a patron of wisewomen or witches, she is known as "*la Señora de las brujas*," the Lady of the Witches. Her female faithful sometimes gathered in meeting places called *eperrlandas*, 'places of partridges,' these birds being sacred to her and "propitious to witches."

Not surprisingly, Christians condemned Mari as La Maligna, the "Malicious" or "Wicked One." According to Julio Caro Baroja, many elderly people continued to observe and pay homage to Mari in the mid-twentieth century. Devotees of Mari have been said to drink *patxaran* (or, *pacharán*) made from the sloe berries of blackthorn and flavored with anise, vanilla, and coffee beans, to attain altered states of consciousness in which to communicate with her.

In a poignant, tragic poem, "The Basque Witches" (alternatively titled "The Basque Brujas"), the Mexican American poet Gloria Anzaldúa evokes the reverence of Mari in writing of two women who love each other who suffer at the hands of the Inquisition.

Romanian Divinities
Ileana Sânziana

Numerous divinities might be mentioned here, but I shall confine myself to brief discussion of two: Ileana Sânziana and Kalojan.

The name of the goddess Ileana Sânziana appears to have emerged from Roman reverence in Romania of the goddess Diana. Besides being identified with Diana, Ileana Sânziana, as a goddess of the moon, has also been identified with the goddesses Selene and Bendis. She is described primarily as a beautiful maiden who is sister to the sun. She dwells at the opposite end of the cosmos from her brother. It appears that at some time, in some places, Ileana Sânziana became conflated with another goddess, Cosânzeana, a goddess of earth and flowers, comparable to Flora. In this light, she is called the "queen of flowers," particularly of carnations. With the Christianization of Romania (primarily in the sixth-seventh centuries CE), the goddess came to be known as Sancta Diana (or, "Saint Diana"), or Sânziana. She also came to be associated with St. John the Baptist and in this regard came to be called Ileana Sânziana, deriving from "Ioana," the feminine form of "John." Rather surprisingly, in this hybrid manifestation, she is said to be the only being other than the sun – presumably identified with Christ or the Biblical God – who "stands at the gates of paradise." Ileana Sânziana also came to be identified as the Queen of Fairies, Zâna Sânziana.

She is a goddess of healing, agriculture, beauty, love, marriage, and fertility. Plants sacred to her include St. John's wort, from which garlands worn by young women seeking partners are made, and the mandrake, which also pertains to loving relationships, as well as to healing.

It is not clear when or even if reverence of the Romanian goddess ever truly vanished from Romanian spirituality/enspirited materiality. Unquestionably, since Christianization, she has been venerated alongside St. John the Baptist and the Virgin Mary, but they have not managed to displace or eradicate her in the way that they have been able to do so elsewhere. It also appears that her reverence was generally hidden during the Communist period. While in the past she was honored both at the winter solstice and at midsummer, nowadays, she is primarily celebrated during the summer solstice. In 2008, Romanians living in the vicinity of Sirnea were invited to attend the Vespers of St. John the Baptist, to be followed by the Sânziane celebration of Ileana Sânziana.

Kalojan

Marcu Beza, in *Paganism in Roumanian Folklore* (1928), describes a harvest tradition that persisted in early twentieth-century Romania. The male deity honored at this time, that is, between August 8th and 15th, was Kalojan (or, Caloian), which means "Good John," "Handsome John," or "Beautiful John" and which may have been derived from "*kalos Adonis*" ("beautiful Adonis)."). Beza compares the rite performed by young women for Kalojan to that performed by women for Adonis in Mediterranean antiquity; indeed, he argues, "Kalojan is a direct survival of the ancient Adonis ritual." He describes the role of Kalojan in Romanian earth-centered tradition as one of a god that dies and is reborn annually. It might be argued that Beza is simply reiterating the Frazerian 'dying and rising god' theory of his time, but the evidence that he offers in terms of descriptions of rites and sacred songs sung to him attests to the validity of this interpretation where Kalojan is concerned. For example, he reports that groups of maidens make from clay the figure of a youth, which they place in a small coffin. A pall is thrown over it, and flowers and various aromatic plants such as basil, mint ... Then they slowly raise the coffin – one of the girls personifying the priest ... .[With] loud singing, with tears, with burning of incense and lighted candles, they go in procession to a secluded spot under poplars or under thorn bushes, where they bury the Kalojan.[38]

One of the songs to him goes:

Jan, Kalojan,
Your mother sought you,
Broken-hearted,
Through deep woods
And through the glades;
Jan, Kalojan,
With burning tears
Your mother weeps for you![39]

When the image of Kalojan is unearthed, he, like Adonis, Osiris, Jesus, and others, is said to have risen from the dead; the young women chant or sing, "Kalojan is not dead! Kalojan has risen from the grave!"

Finno-Ugric Divinities

The Magyars, a Finno-Ugric people of Hungary, practiced a paganism that embraced many elements of shamanism. They were animists, pantheists, and acknowledged numerous divinities. Because so much was destroyed with Christianization, which culminated in the mid-eleventh century, our knowledge of Magyar shamano-paganism remains extremely fragmentary.

They appear to have worshipped a primary male god, Isten, a creator, warrior, and source of wisdom, who lived in the heavens, and a primary goddess who possessed numerous titles or hypostases. She was known as Nagy Asszony, "Great Queen" or "Great Lady," Boldog Asszony (or Boldogaszony), "Beautiful, Glad Queen," and "Baba." An earth-goddess, she presides over marriage, childbirth, and agriculture. Her chief celebration occurred at the winter solstice. Her special day was Tuesday. She was kept in Hungarian Christianity as the grandmother of Christ. She has seven daughters who distribute gifts to humanity.

Magyars, incidentally, also possessed runes called *rovás* that some are convinced formed a written tongue that was suppressed and its literary evidence destroyed. The Christianization of Finland took about six hundred years, beginning in the twelfth century in southern Finland and culminating in the eighteenth in Karelia. Anna-Leena Siikala, *Mythic Images and Shamanism: A Perspective on Kalevala Poetry*, states that "efforts of the clergy in the seventeenth and eighteenth centuries led to the widespread eradication ... of the ethnic religious tradition which had survived the Middle Ages." Siikala notes that in the "eighteenth century, sacrificial groves were felled in Savo and North Karelia."

Many divinities continued to be revered into the sixteenth century, as Mikael Agricola (*c.* 1510-1557) reported in his *Psalter* of 1551 and as Siikala reiterates. Some Finns, however, despite enforced Christianization, continued to practice earth-centered traditions into the eighteenth century, still others, into the twentieth.

Deities who appear to have been revered into later centuries include: Luonnotar, a goddess of nature; Maan Tyttö and Manuen Neiti, goddesses of earth; Tapio, lord of the forest and animals; Mielliki, Tapio's spouse and goddess of the forest; Nyyrikki, son of Tapio and a guide to travelers; Tellervo, daughter or handmaid of Mielliki and Tapio, goddess of honey and music of the flute; Vellamo, goddess of water and patron of fishermen and mariners (who was offered flaxen shirts); Ahto, her male counterpart; Ututyttö, the goddess of the "mist," who resides in the highest heavens; Kuutar, goddess of the moon, Päivätär, goddess of the sun, and Tähetär, goddess of the North Star, all of whom are associated with spinning, weaving, and the dyeing of fabric; Otavatar, god or similar being of the Great Bear constellation; the crone-goddess Louhi; and the thunder-god Ukko.

Louhi

Louhi, the crone-goddess, is comparable to Hecate, Badb, and Baba-Yaga. She is mistress of the dead and the underworld, Tuonela (also, Manala). As such, she is the wife of Tuoni, the god of death. They have a daughter, Tuonetar (also, Loviatar), and a son. She is also associated with iron and is said to spin iron thread. She is often depicted as having claws and is said to transform herself into a bird, typically a raven, at will. Not surprisingly, Louhi is also associated with wolves. Certain sacred songs also suggest that her powers include transgender metamorphosis, or else that she is considered to be a "masculine" woman, as she is described as donning a "man's long shirt" and/or as fashioning wings from a man's shirt. Thus, transgenderism and theriomorphic metamorphosis appear to intersect in her persona. These combined elements also indicate an association of Louhi with shamanism and with the figure of the Finnish tietäjä. Moreover, Louhi carries or creates a tail for herself from a sauna whisk. Anna-Leena Siikala suggests that this may be one of the reasons why with Christianization, the figure of Louhi was demonized into that of the destructive witch.

Tapio, Mielliki, and Nyyrikki

Tapio, known as the "king of the forest" and the "gray-bearded old man of the forest with [a] fir-sprig hat [and a] furry coat of lichens," protects not only wild but also domesticated animals such as cattle. Hunters were expected to honor him with prayers and offerings before hunting wild animals – Tapio rewarded those who revered him with abundant game – while farmers prayed to him to protect their livestock and to guide them home should they wander and become lost. According to Siikala, "Tapio was ... venerated until the twentieth century."

Mielliki, a beautiful goddess who wears a blue mantle and exquisite jewelry, is the "gracious gamekeeper of the forest." Like Tapio, she rewards those who honor her with abundant game, but what is more, she shows them where to find silver and gold.

Nyyrikki, the son of Tapio, wears "a red high peaked hat" and "cut[s] blazes through the countryside, make[s] guide signs leading to the hills," so that the devotee "will see how to go ... will know the way." Not only is Nyyrikki reminiscent of the Greek god Hermes but his name also bears an uncanny resemblance to "nierika," the Huichol entrance to the Otherworld, and his attributes bear an uncanny resemblance to those of the Yorùbá orishá Eleggúa.

Ukko

Ukko, the lord of thunder, calls to mind Zeus, Thor, Perun, and Perkûnas. As Siikala relates, "there was thought to be none superior to Ukko, the god of thunder who could rend even cliffs asunder." He is also a god of creation and the heavens and is patron of farmers who grow corn. He is companioned by a dog, as is depicted on a shaman's drum. As a god of heavens and a creator-god, he came to be conflated, during the period of Christianization, with the Biblical God. A mid-nineteenth century incantation of a Finnish shaman, or *tietäjä*, reveals that although the Christian God had generally been assimilated by this period, Ukko continued to be revered as a "beneficent god" and as the "true guardian of the clouds." In other cases, Ukko appears to have been identified with Jesus Christ, as in the prayer/incantation "Oh Ukko, Supreme Jesus ... belt me with belts of protection."

Sámi Divinities

Olaus Magnus, in the *Description of the Northern People* (1555), wrote of the Sámi (derogatorily called Lapps or Laplanders) of northernmost Europe: "Much has been said about the idolaters and their superstitious rites in this most northerly region of the world, and how there is hope that one day they will hear our preaching of the divine word and not be slow to enter the communion of believers in Christ."

As with Finno-Ugric and other peoples, Christianizing the Sámi took several centuries, culminating as recently as the eighteenth century. Generally speaking, Sámi men worshipped gods, while Sámi women worshipped goddesses; there were, however, notable exceptions.

The Mother Goddess, Máttaráhkká (or, Mader-akka, Madder Akka), is "the Old Woman of the Earth." She has three daughters: Sáráhkká, (or, Sar-akka, Sarag-Akka, Sarakha, Zar-akka, Zarakka), Jouksáhkká (or, Juksakka, Juks-akka), and Uksáhkká (or, Ukssakka, Uks-akka). Together, they are envisioned as both the goddesses of birth and as the three Fates.

Sáráhkká was considered "the most important of all the deities" by many Sámi. Her name refers to a female creator or else to threads, as in the threads spun by the Fates. A patron of women, home, and family, she was worshipped by both women and men, with her altar being near the hearth. Sáráhkká is responsible for clothing a soul in a body. She assists in the birth of humans and domestic animals. She was offered porridge, beverages, and "roosters, hens, reindeer calves," and other animals, some of the meat of which women would share in a feast to the Goddess. She was conflated with, and her traits appropriated by the Church for, the Virgin Mary. Jouksáhkká, "the Woman of the Bow" and later also identified with Stäuk-edne, "The Gun Mother," is not only a goddess of hunting; she is also responsible for transforming some of female fetuses into males (a power sometimes attributed to Uksáhkká), serves as a midwife, and protects children from harming themselves. Uksáhkká, "the Door Woman," is a protector of the home, thought to dwell under the door. Food was sacrificed to her at each meal. Máttaráhkká and her daughters were offered spinning wheels, animal sacrifices, and a special porridge. This porridge was also eaten by pregnant women in their honor shortly before giving birth.

Baiwe, the sun goddess, promotes growth and protects against illness. She was celebrated at midsummer, when a special porridge was offered to her, white animals were sacrificed to her, and devotees prayed to her for abundant milk and reindeer. Ruonaneid is a goddess of springtime and the growth of plants, especially grass and herbs.

The goddess Jouksáhkká is sometimes seen as forming a duality – possibly antagonistic one – with the god Leaibolmmái (or, Leib Olmai). The latter is a god of trees, especially the alder ("*leib*" refers to "alder"), and hunting and is a patron of forest animals. In relation to Jouksáhkká, however, he, like she in certain manifestations, is envisioned as gender-diverse or transgender; in this regard, he is referred to as the "man of menstrual blood."

Other male deities include Radien, a father, creator, and king whose identity may reflect Christian influence; and Horagalles (or, Horagales; also, Atkakatj), the thunder god, whose name probably means "Thunder-Hero," who is known to some Sámi as Pajan, which means "Blacksmith;" and who is comparable to Ukko, Thor, Perûn, Perkûnas, etc.

Horagalles continued to be worshipped in the mid-eighteenth century, when reindeer were sacrificed to him; this sacrifice, which included burying the reindeer so that only its antlers appeared above the ground, was called the *tjekku* sacrifice. No female reindeer was sacrificed to him, and only men could partake in his feast. Kiase Olmai (or, Gjase-Almai, Kiöse-Almai, Tjatse olmai) is the god of fish and patron of those who live by fishing. Biegga Olmai (or, Bieg-Olmai, Biegga Galles, Bjeg Olmai) (from *pjegg*, "weather" and *olmai*, "man") is a god of "weather and wind, water and sea." The drum of the elderly Sámi *noaide* Anders Paulsen (or, Poulsen, Pouelsen), which the Church confiscated, offered evidence that he continued to revere Biegga Olmai, together with other divinities, in 1692. Junkare (or, Stor-Junkare, Storjunkare, meaning "Big Junkare"), a god of earth and hunting, continued to be worshipped in 1738. At this time, a figurine of him, probably carved from birch wood, was confiscated at Kaitum, Sweden. The man who carved it "confessed before the district court that he had bowed and knelt in worship before [it]."[40]

Chapter 7
Veneration of Goddesses and Related Female Beings Rising to Prominence in the Middle Ages and Thereafter

> They are sinners ... who leave food for Perchta [o]n her hallowed night – Perchtennacht. And Christians are earnestly admonished to cease believing in Frawn Percht[a] or Frawn Hold[a], Herodyasis [i.e., Herodias], or Dyana [i.e., Diana], the heathen goddess.
>
> Stephanus Lanzkrana's *Die Hymelstrass* (1494)[41]

During and after the Middle Ages, a host of divinities and kindred beings appeared on the radar of Europe, noticeably in regions that had long before been officially Christianized. Some had been known since antiquity – Aphrodite/Venus, Artemis/Diana, Athena/Minerva, Hera/Juno, Pan/Faunus, as well as the seemingly Biblical Herodias – while others – Bensozia, Biel, Habundia, Holda, Mourie, Puck/Robin Goodfellow, Satia, Shony, and others, who are frequently discussed in a group (in Italy, for example, as the Signore Notturne, the "Lady/Ladies of the Night" (also used to describe fairies) – seem to emerge at this time. In some cases, these latter divinities may represent ancient deities given new names, like new bottles containing old wine. I would argue, however, that the veneration of these beings undoubtedly responded to particular medieval and post-medieval European needs, hopes, dreams, and so on. This is to say, earth-centered beliefs, practices, personae, and narratives persisted, and, moreover, underwent innovation as cultural and epochal shifts occurred. This possibility of new divinities coming into existence is, of course, in keeping with ancient polytheistic and henotheistic traditions. This phenomenon, in a nutshell, represents one of those occasions when the notion of "pagan survivals" fails to express the dynamic character of pagan sacred traditions alongside of, and in spite of, Christianization.

A prime example of an updating of ancient divinities may be found in philosopher and astrologer Bernard Silvestris' twelfth-century *Cosmographia*, which we have previously discussed in relation to Minerva. In this work, an alternative narrative, or counter-narrative, to that given in the Biblical account in Genesis, several goddesses undertake the task of creating the universe. Together with Minerva (who is linked to or identiiied with Noys), Silva (also called Nature), Hyle, and Endelechia – all known to ancients but not in the same collective way that Silvestris presents them – create the universe and the beings within it, (possibly) with the assistance of a high, male god. Minerva/Noys, we may recall, is addressed as "supreme image of unfailing life, God born of God, substance of truth...true Minerva," while Silva/Nature is described as primordial chaos, a primeval sea. Silvestris suggests the latter's evolution and his updating when he writes of her, "Behold, oldest of things as she is, Silva yearns to be born again, and to be defined in her new birth." Hyle is described as "Nature's most ancient manifestation, the inexhaustible womb of generation," while Endelechia, thought by some to be a sun goddess, the spouse of Apollo, and the mother of Psyche. Silvestris describes Endelechia as follows: "From the very source...of this our life and light, there issued forth by a sort of emanation, the life, illumination, and soul of creation, Enelechia. She was like a sphere, of vast size...Her shining substance appeared just like a steadily flowing fountain...[like the] firmament and the stars."

Numerous scholars have suggested that such personae, beliefs, and practices enjoyed relative tolerance for several centuries preceding the twelfth. By the twelfth century, however, Christian church authorities had become all too aware of the rise of the popularity of such divinities or beings and of the seriousness of their devotees; as Massimo Centini relates in *Le Schiavi di Diana: Stregoneria e sciamanismo tra superstizione e demonizzazione* [*The Slaves of Diana: Witchcraft and Shamanism between Superstition and Demonization*, 1994], at this time the Church commenced aggressively combating these dramatically increasing non-Christian and pagano-Christian hybrid traditions, especially those promoting Goddess reverence. As Claudia and Luigi Manciocco relate in *L'Incanto e l'arcano: Per una antropologia della Befana* (2006), during the thirteenth century, persecution of these beliefs and practices escalated dramatically. The Renaissance, much more than the Middle Ages, would become the "Dark Ages" for those, especially women, who neglected to put aside traditional beliefs and practices.

"Winter Goddesses"

Of a number of the goddesses/beings emerging or re-emerging in the Middle Ages and thereafter, Lotte Motz observes in *The Beauty and the Hag*: "Though many names are encountered, the creatures show such strong resemblances to one another that we may be sure of one basic configuration; she is a spirit of the woodland, a visitor to human dwellings in the winter season." She stresses that the "religious status of the Ladies is affirmed by the anger of the Church" which refers to those who revere these goddesses or spirits as "sinners."

In "The Winter Goddess: Percht, Holda, and Related Figures" (1984), Motz emphasizes that these "female forces ... are indeed divinities," that they "belong to a widely diffused type," and that the 'type' is the Great Goddess in her role as "Lady of Wild Beasts."

Before proceeding, I want to very briefly mention an article by John B. Smith that focuses on one of the female beings discussed herein: "Perchta the Belly-Slitter and Her Kin" (2004). Although I appreciate his seeking to balance, by bringing forth her sinister traits, the portrait of Perchta promoted by Romantic and present-day Wiccan literature, Smith is incorrect when he argues that describing Perchta or numerous others of the beings discussed herein as "goddesses" is a product of Romanticism and the Brothers Grimm; to the contrary, Perchta and kindred beings were frequently described as goddesses or otherworldly beings centuries before the advent of Romanticism and the Grimms. Indeed, their status as goddesses rather than fanciful folkloric figures was typically established by linking them to the pagan goddess Diana.

For example, in their works of 1726, 1766, and 1774, Bernard de Montfaucon, Pierre Carpentier and Charles Du Fresne Du Cange linked the goddess Diana to Bensozia, Habundia, Hera, Herodias, Holda, and Noctiluca, clearly indicating that all of these, like Diana, were considered goddesses, and, moreover, held so much in common that they were frequently identified with one another. Many of these divinities or beings have been associated with the giving of gifts including material abundance and fertility. Many have also been associated with witches and witchcraft, such as Baba Yaga and Ragana. In 1781, for example, Johann Georg Krünitz not only linked Erde, Freyja, Hertha, Holle (Hulda), Lamia, Lilith, and Saga (goddess of history) to the goddess Diana but also further linked these goddesses to witches (*Hexen*, etc.).

On the other hand, it appears that at least some of these beings were seen as fairies or kindred beings, typically, as the rulers of these. For instance, in 1606, Strozzio Cicogna, in speaking of fairies, noted that Habundia is their Queen. In my view, it is conceivable that some persons have seen them as fairies, whereas others have seen them as goddesses; whereas still others may have perceived them as ancestral spirits. Yet others may have perceived them as all of these at once.

To "affirm the claim of divine stature (i.e. that people had faith in these figures)," Motz points out that great powers such as creating snow were attributed to them; that they mostly appeared during "a sacred period of the year," i.e., the winter solstice, when divinities are honored; that offerings were made to them; and that the Church found it necessary to prohibit reverence of them. These goddesses are typically unmarried and, like Diana, not interested in marriage or male companionship. Also like Diana, they are typically hunters who feel most at home in the wild, but they are also spinners and nurturers and instructors of young women. As John Mitchel Kemble noted in 1849, "Spinning and weaving are the constant occupation of Teutonic goddesses and heroines: Holda and Bertha spin ... the fairies [spin] ... the [Valkyries] ... also weave..." As Lina Eckenstein notes, the tasks of spinning and weaving were appropriated by numerous female Christian saints, including Lufthildis, Lucie of Sampigny, Walburg, Gertrud, and Genovefa of Brabant.

Motz notes that these goddesses frequently "appear as leaders of the so-called Wild Hunt, which is described in legends as the ride of terrifying creatures moving in sound and fury through the sky." At least one of the possible origins of the association of such goddesses with the Wild Hunt lies in the cult of the Celto-Roman goddess Epona. Epona, not only the "Mistress of Horses" but also a patron of the dead, was celebrated in Late Antiquity in what is now Germany at the time of the winter solstice. Wolfgang Behringer, following Carlo Ginzburg, suggests that through a connection with Diana and other goddesses, Epona survived in the popular memory for centuries, ultimately lending her role as leader of the cavalry and guardian of the dead to medieval goddesses of the Wild Hunt. Frau Gode, or Wode, suggesting a female counterpart of, or spouse of, Odin/ Woden, also led the Wild Hunt. The image of goddesses leading the Wild Hunt contributed in no small way toward the depiction of witches riding to sabbats.

In *L'incanto e l'arcano*, Claudia and Luigi Manciocco, in viewing these goddesses collectively as reflecting "the Lady of the Beasts," emphasize the connection between these goddesses, their devotees, and equines and birds. They suggest that this connection is rooted in the hunting culture of the Paleolithic and its reverence of a "Mistress of animals and forests." They consider this connection in light of the early belief that the souls of the dead transform into "migratory birds." They consider this connection in terms of shamanistic practices. They also consider this connection in light of the great importance of equines, especially asses, as well as oxen, in early agricultural societies. They point out that in numerous ancient rites, oxen were sacrificed only to be rejuvenated miraculously, asses were honored as steeds of the gods – including of Dionysus and Cybele – and participants wore animal masks, frequently representing birds or equines. They demonstrate that traditions reflecting this connection persisted for many centuries in the January Kalends – in 567, Maximus, Bishop of Turin snapped at the people of Turin, "How can you honor the Epiphany of the Lord, you who are so devoted to the celebration of the Kalends?"; and the feast was still being condemned 600 years later – and that they have continued to manifest into our own day in celebrations of La Befana and kindred female beings. In this light, I recall the thrill I experienced as a child when I first learned of the winged horse Pegasus. Given this chain of associations, it is not difficult to imagine how the notion of witches riding on brooms (a connection with hobby-horses?) might have come into being.

Herodias

Herodias (or, Herodiade), "la Dame présidente de la nuit" ("Lady President of the Night") appears in numerous documents of the Middle Ages. In the tenth century, Ratherius (*c.* 887-974), who became bishop of Verona, complained that as many as a third of the world's population were worshipping Herodias as a goddess. Her cult was condemned as a demonic delusion by the Council of Trèves in 1310, and evidence suggests that it persisted into at least the fifteenth century.

Common knowledge imparts that Herodias is a figure of Christian lore, specifically, the wife of King Herod, who came to be conflated with their daughter, Salome, who allegedly danced in order to obtain the head of John the Baptist.

It is conceivable, however, that Herodias' origins may be more complex than previously thought; to insist that she possesses Christian roots only may be shortsighted.

Her name, for example, may derive from Latin: *ara dea*, *era dea*, and *ero dea*, respectively, mean "altar of the Goddess," "Mistress Goddess," and "I will be a goddess."

Heurodis, the spelling of Eurydice's name in the medieval ballad of *Orfeo and Heurodis*, may represent an alternative spelling of Herodias, conceivably indicating a relationship between Herodias and Eurydice. One should bear in mind that in centuries past, differently spelled variants of names abounded (within my own family, my maternal grandmother's surname is spelled at least a dozen different ways). A medieval association of Herodias and Eurydice makes sense, as during this period, Eurydice and Orpheus came to be associated, as evidenced by the just-mentioned ballad, with fairy lore, which was in turn associated with the lore of witchcraft. In the ancient tale, Orpheus, by way of playing melancholy music on his lyre, convinces Persephone/Proserpina and Hades to release the newly deceased Eurydice; in the medieval account, Orfeo must convince the Fairy Queen and King to release Heurodis.

I have recently learned of a name that bears great resemblance to Herodias: Herodicê. In present-day Italian, "Erodice" may stand for both Herodicê and Eurydice. Herodicê is mentioned in the *Deipnosophists*, the 'After-Dinner Philosophers' of Athenaeus (*c.* 170-230 CE) (for those of you who have not yet delved into Athenaeus, it is a treasure trove of ancient information! In it we learn that it was Sappho the "courtesan from Eresus," and not the Lesbian poet, who "loved the handsome Phaon," as in it we learn that the candle-laden birthday cake most probably originated in the *amphiphôn*, the "shining-all-round" cake that was offered to Artemis and Hecate.) According to Athenaeus, the ancient writer Nicias, in a work now lost, relates that Herodicê was the wife of the legendary Arcadian king Cypselus. Cypselus' ancestors included Zeus and Callisto. As both his name and that of Herodicê appear in a complex genealogy of divine beings, it is likely, although I have not as yet been able to account for her ancestry, that she, too, possessed divine ancestors. I am led to believe this more strongly because the daughter of Herodicê and Cypselus, Merope, married Cresphontes, whose ancestry included Heracles. I am also led to believe that Herodicê may have possessed such ancestry because of certain things we learn about her in Athenaeus and in light of a key we possess about her daughter Merope. Athenaeus, paraphrasing Nicias, relates that Cypselus founded a certain city (Basilis?) in Arcadia. The goddess Demeter became the patron deity of this city. In the Goddess' honor Cypselus instituted a beauty pageant. Herodicê won the first pageant and became famous for her beauty. Thus, a relationship exists between Demeter and Herodicê. This relationship may be indirectly supported by the name given to her daughter, Merope. This name signifies a "bee mask" or honey, and Demeter's association with bees is well known, including her possession of "bee" priestesses. Another goddess, however, is equally associated with bees and bee priestesses: Artemis/Diana. In this regard, Athenaeus noted that this beauty contest continued to be held in his own time, that is, in the third century CE. The women who competed in the beauty pageant came to be called the Chrysophoroi, the "bearers" or "wearers" of gold. An honorary inscription found at Ephesus, the center of the worship of Artemis, honors a woman named Aurelia Metrodora as being a member of the *synhedrion* (or, *synedrion*, the "board") of Artemis'/Diana's Chryso-phoroi. Thus, a complex relationship appears to exist among Herodicê, her daughter Merope, the women who participated in the pageant (the Chrysophoroi), bees and honey, gold, and the goddess Artemis/Diana. As has become abundantly clear, Diana has been associated with witchcraft since the Early Middle Ages, indeed, since antiquity. It is hence fairly evident from this albeit complex evidence that we are meant to associate Herodicê with Goddess reverence, as well as with beauty, bees, honey, gold; and it is conceivable that she may have stood as an earthly representative or reminder of Eurydice (/Persephone?), Demeter, or Artemis, or perhaps a complex relationship shared by these three divine women.

Gobelinus Decanus Bilefeldensis (d. 1418), among others, suggested that the name "Herodias" represented a combining of the names of the goddesses Hera and Diana; the variant "Herodiana" strongly suggests this possibility. As such, Herodias may have also become linked to, or identified with, the goddess Juno. Further, she may have come to be linked to, or envisioned as accompanied by, a troop of male aerial beings, as well as *pilosi*, hairy goblins (called *panitae* in Greek), who themselves eventually came to be identified with incubi. She may have also come to be linked to *strigae* and other female beings and witches taking the forms of "nightbirds." Also in her hypostasis as a *noctiluca*, she appears to have become conflated with the goddess Noctiluca as well as Hecate and as such to have become a patron of witches.

The French scholar Bernard de Montfaucon (1655-1741) linked Herodias to Diana, Hecate, Noctiluca, Bensozia, and "enchantresses" who, into the thirteenth century, rode to gatherings on horseback. Later on, she was identified with Perchta and La Befana. Several nineteenth-century German scholars suggested that the little known Germanic goddess Hruoda, whom they linked to Ostara, might have also contributed to the depiction of Herodias. As such, they linked her to certain healing plants including rue and Lady's Slipper (also associated with Aphrodite/Venus). She has in this light also been linked, perhaps in part due to her name, to roses and thus to love.

Herodias, like other of the divinities discussed here, was thought to be especially active on the eve of Epiphany, or Twelfth Night. At this time, she delivered gifts to those who honored her. Moreover, her devotees, under her guidance, were believed to drive away evil, to heal the sick – especially pregnant women and infants, and to divine the future during this festival.

In the fourteenth century, Herodias was associated with pythonesses, oracles or mediums. In 1423, Bernardino of Padua condemned these women as witches who had converted from Christianity to the worship of Satan. Almost a century and a half later, in 1569, such women were condemned as witches and as practitioners of *pythonissarum* by the Council of Salzburg.

In recent centuries, Christian(ized) farmers in what is now Croatia would shoot arrows into clouds to ward off tempests; as they did so, they might either pray to St. Barbara to spare them or curse the storm-clouds, shouting, "Begone, Irudica (i.e., Herodias)! Your mother was a pagan (*poganica*)!"

It is possible that Herodias persisted as, or else morphed into, or was reformulated as, Aradia in the nineteenth century.

Habundia, Bensozia, and Others

Reverence of Habundia, whose name indicates "fullness of blessing," appears to have risen dramatically during the Middle Ages.

Her origins most probably lie, as Gulielmus Alvernus (fl. 1218), bishop of Paris, has suggested, in the Roman goddess Abundantia, also called Copia – hence, "cornucopia." The connection of Habundia with Abundantia is supported by the existence in France of numerous statuettes of the latter.

She may, however, also represent a conflation of Abundantia with the Roman goddesses Ceres, Diana (a Catholic priest of the late nineteenth century remarks, "The Lady Abundia is distinctly identified with Diana's crew, nay, herself represents that goddess"), Ops, Fecunditas, Fortuna, and the Fates/Parcae; the Gallo-Roman goddesses Rosmerta, a goddess of abundance who sometimes holds a cornucopia who may have been viewed as the spouse of the horned god Cernunnos, Abnoba, a goddess of forests, rivers, and the hunt, linked to Diana and worshipped in the Black Forest and elsewhere in Germany, and the Matres; and to the Germanic divinity Fulla, the handmaiden of Frigga (or Freyja) and a goddess of wealth, also called "Die Üppige," the "Luxurious" or "Abundant."

Habundia is a dispenser of abundance and destiny as well as a guardian of pregnant women and infants.

She may, drawing on the description of the Roman Abundantia, have been depicted as wearing a garment of green and gold and a crown of flowers, perhaps as holding a cornucopia, and as holding or surrounded by flowers, fruits, and grains. Like Fulla, she may have been depicted wearing a golden belt.

Guillaume d'Auvergne reported that certain persons believed that Habundia/Domina Abundia/Satia visited their houses in the early-to-mid-thirteenth century. In the late thirteenth-century epic poem *Roman de la Rose* (*The Romance of the Rose*, c. 1270), Guillaume de Loris and Jean de Meun, castigating people who believe in Habundia, insist, as in the *Canon Episcopi*, that they only imagine that they "go roaming with Lady Abundance [*dame abonde*]." The poets claim that in their own time, every third child born becomes a worshipper of Habundia/Dame Abonde.

The belief that a third of the world was devoted to Habundia and/or kindred female divinities became increasingly common in the Middle Ages. The most astonishing suggestion here, however, it seems to me, concerns the sacred or genetic origin of Goddess reverence and the enormous number of persons born with such a predisposition. Beyond this, it is significant that at least some of the practitioners described here do not believe that they are traveling in the flesh to convene with the Goddess, but rather that hers are gatherings of spirits or souls, accomplished by means not unlike those undertaken by shamans. On the other hand, others may have envisioned themselves as traveling in the flesh to celebrate rites in caves where the goddess or goddesses resided.

Habundia, who was identified with Satia, was also sometimes identified with Bensozia. Although the name "Bensozia" is usually interpreted to mean "the Good Society," it may actually possess a mixed etymology, deriving in part from the Thracian moon goddess Bendis, whom the Greeks identified with Artemis. This possible partial derivation of the name is especially intriguing in that not only is she akin in attributes to goddesses of the moon, who are often associated with witchcraft, but when one observes her portrait, as she stands holding a spear and wearing a hooded Phrygian mantle, it is not difficult to understand how this image might have been translated into that of the witch holding the broom and wearing a hooded cape or conical hat. Bensozia is occasionally depicted as a nude woman with serpents emerging from her vagina and encircling her body, reminiscent of both the *pythonissa* and the caduceus. Moreover, Bensozia is associated with fairies and sometimes said to be their queen. In 1280, the Council at Couserans, a province of France located in the Pyrenees, condemned her veneration.

Numerous persons residing in various parts of Europe continued in the late Middle Ages, as recorded by the Polish theologian Nicolaus Magni de Jawor (*c*. 1355-1435), to leave vessels of food for Habundia and Bensozia, particularly during the last week of December and the first week of January. Offerings included bread, cheese, milk, meat, eggs, wine, and salt. In return, the goddess or goddesses would bestow families who were generous with gifts and with abundance and prosperity; if, however, households were selfish and did not prepare a feast, they would be punished with ill fortune.

The cults of these goddesses eventually became assimilated into that of the fairies, and the feasts held for them were in some places displaced by the Christian feasts of Christmas and the Epiphany. Habundia was also displaced to a certain extent by the male Saint Abundius/Abonde and by the female Saint Abondance/Abundantia, the latter of whom is fêted on December 26th, and perhaps most significantly, by the Virgin

Mary as Nostra Signora dell' Abbondanza.

Moreover, as Francis Douce notes in *Illustrations of Shakespeare, and of Ancient Manners* (1839), veneration of Habundia became linked both to fairies and witches: "Dame Habunde (or, Abunde) has been classed among the names given to the president of the witches ... she appears to have been the genuine queen of fairies ... bestowing happiness and abundance on all her votaries." Douce's remark is seconded by Charlotte Touati in "Des Striges antiques au sorcières médiévales" ("From Ancient Striges to Medieval Sorceresses," 2003); she notes that devotees of Habundia eventually came to be called an *estries*, a vernacular form of *stryx*, or "witch."

Sheela-na-gig

Sheela-na-gigs are a type of sculpture portraying a nude female which are found in and on churches and Christian sacred sites in Ireland and England; they appear to have been carved primarily from the eighth through sixteenth centuries. For Church authorities, they may have represented "graphic warnings of the danger of female seductiveness that leads to hell."

It is well known that such images are found worldwide; indeed, the resemblance of the Sheela-na-gig to a "terrifying witch" portrayed on a warrior's shield from the Trobriand Islands is uncanny. Over the centuries, many have felt that Sheela-na-gig must have been, or must be, a goddess if traced to her origins. She may have emerged from a conflation of the Celtic goddesses Aine, Badb, Danu, and Nemain; the Classical divinities of terror and bawdiness, the Gorgon and Baubo, respectively; and an Etruscan female "genius of death." In Gimbutas' view, "with her round eyes and large vulva, [Sheela] is none other than the ancient frog or toad goddess, the birth giver and regeneratrix from the Neolithic." Anne Ross has described her as a fertility figure as well as an apotropaic one. Recently, in a very impressive study, Barbara Freitag has suggested that Sheela-na-gig was a folk divinity thought to assist in childbirth.

We may perhaps decipher more about her by considering Sheela in light of St. Gobonet, a legendary Celtic saint whose historicity is extremely doubtful and who has been associated with Sheela for centuries. Gobonet is depicted as very reminiscent of the Virgin Mary; this might remind some readers of the way in which Nahua (Mexica/Aztec) goddesses were desexualized to construct the image of the Virgin of Guadalupe. Gobonet's, thus perhaps also Sheela's, functions include: assisting in childbirth; cultivating and healing with herbs; protecting humans and cattle from illness and epidemics; protecting the military; and transforming other entities by means of magic.

Perhaps by conjuring St. Gobonet, Church authorities, on realizing that the populace was not going to accept the official view of Sheela, were able to provide an affirmative, however subtle, portrait of the goddess not by linking her to sin but instead by linking her to a female saint and connecting her attributes to the saint. One might consider this process one of appropriation only; it occurs to me, however, that this medieval and postmedieval interweaving of goddess and saint might also rather vividly demonstrate the process of pagan innovation, here taking the form of an alleged Christian saint undergoing paganization by devotees.

Due to Gobonet's profound association with Sheela, coupled with the lack of hard evidence regarding the saint's historicity, I have chosen to take the liberty of deploying "Sheela/Gobonet" (and v.v.) to proceed with discussion of the goddess/saint.

Sacred stones attributed to Sheela/Gobonet include megalithic stones thought to enhance fertility and charm-stones that were in later centuries called "evil eye stones." The River Shannon and certain healing wells have been considered sacred to Gobonet/Sheela. Where flora are concerned, apples, the ash tree (symbolic of the life-force and the mystery of death/rebirth), and gorse (or, furze), an evergreen shrub with yellow, scented flowers that grows especially in winter (symbolic of fertility and the sun), may be attributed to Gobonet/Sheela. Where animals and insects are concerned, bees (sweetness of life, healing, metamorphosis), cattle (fertility), eels (success in battle, metamorphosis), and salmon (great wisdom, regeneration, immortality) have been attributed to Gobonet/Sheela.

Occasionally Gobonet is depicted as standing on a crossed wheel; it is conceivable that this wheel represents the sun and/or the directions or the cycles of the seasons or of life, in this way speaking to the attribution of a divinity of life, death, and regeneration. As a saint/goddess of healing, especially of ambulatory disabilities, Gobonet/Sheela arches over healing wells.

As such, pilgrims seeking healing typically offered her colorful handkerchiefs, swatches of clothing, or rags, as well as, perhaps, small cakes.

Gobonet/Sheela's primary celebration falls on Whitsuntide (a moveable feast that typically occurs between May 15 and June 15, depending on when Easter falls). She has also been celebrated on February 11 and on May Eve (Beltane). In County Kerry, my father's ancestral home, the Whitsuntide celebration included fishing for eel and salmon, both thought to bring good fortune from Gobonet/Sheela. In County Cork, near Loch a Dereen, at Whitsuntide and Beltane, celebrants danced around a "clump of furze" deemed sacred to her. A primary rite in her festivals included dancing around a pole topped by a cake and decorated with flowers or apples, reminiscent of a Maypole and possibly signifying sexual intercourse; the couple who continued dancing after everyone else had exhausted themselves received the cake.

Patricia Monaghan, in *The Red-Haired Girl from the Bog* (2003), serves up a marvelous portrait of Sheela-na-gig: "Sheela – a world-class contortionist – reaches hands around legs to stretch her vulva into a circle the size of her head. ...[S]he grins hugely. ...Call it a stance of power or a posture of sexual invitation; call it yoni yoga or vulva vaudeville ...Sheela-na-gig is one old woman who does more than just wear purple."

Gruagach

We have noted belief in the existence of *gruagach* in the plural above. However, it appears that during or after the Middle Ages, many persons in Scotland began to think of the Gruagach as a "benign female spirit that was believed to look after the cattle." She commenced to be envisioned as the "fair-haired daughter of the Sun" (possibly named Grannus) and as a "sun-goddess," also carrying the name Griannan, signifying her long golden tresses. She is described as "good-humored, sportive, placable" and "moderate in [regard to] demands." Believed to be able to manifest in many places, or to embody many sites, particularly stones, at once, the Gruagach was revered on St. Kilda and elsewhere into the eighteenth century with libations of milk – in some places "once in summer or autumn," in others, each Sunday, in still others, daily – and offered thanks and praise, especially in regard to the welfare of cattle. In her name, when cattle were moved from one pasture to another, "they were sanctified with salt, water, and fire." It has been suggested that the practice of magic "spells" also occurred at sites sacred to her. Some believed the Gruagach to be the mother of the Cailleach.

The Cailleach

The Cailleach Beara, while meaning "the Maiden," is known primarily as the "Old Woman." She is sometimes considered a member of the family of the Tuatha Dé Danaan deities. The Cailleach is linked to Muireartach, a sea goddess or similar being who is herself reminiscent of the Inuit goddess Sedna. Muireartach has shaggy hair, one terrifying eye, and some features reminiscent of a mackerel.

When taken together, the evidence concerning her suggests that at some early time, the Cailleach was most probably regarded as a "great goddess," as she is described as being both a giver and taker of life, as a deity presiding over nature, the seasons, and the stages of human life, and as a patron of numerous persons and pursuits.

As a creator, the Cailleach is especially associated with mountains – in this aspect, she is thought to reign over the four corners of the world – and bodies of water. As a goddess of seas, the Cailleach is called Cailleach Uisge; as a goddess of rivers, she is Cailleach na h-Abhann. As a goddess of nature, the Cailleach is a mother of both flora and fauna. Plants sacred to her include gorse, holly, marsh reeds, and water plants. She has been compared to Artemis as a patron of animals, and she often shapeshifts into the forms of animals. Animals sacred to her, and into which she metamorphoses, include the cormorant, deer, eagle, gull, heron, pig, and wolf. She possesses a herd of magical deer. Sometimes she is depicted as riding on a pig or wolf. She also possesses a cow that gives "great quantities of milk." A patron of fishers, she occasionally appears as a giant woman cleaning fish. As a patron of animals, the Cailleach is associated with Mala Liath, "Grey Eyebrows," a crone-goddess or similar being who patrons boars and pigs.

As a goddess of the seasons, the Cailleach appears to proceed through the stages of life. During the spring and summer months, she is envisioned as a "fair young woman" who bestows "luck and plenty" to her devotees. In winter she becomes a crone who wears a cloak or hooded cape. It is typically grey in color, sometimes grey plaid. She is said to wash her great cape each winter in the whirlpool of Corryvrechan, between the islands of ura and Scarba, off the western coast of Scotland. In this association, she is identified with the Germanic merwoman/goddess Mar Gyga. As a goddess of winter in particular, she is depicted as a controller of the weather. As a brewer of storms, she was, probably around the eighteenth century, nicknamed "the Old Wife of Thunder." Eleanor Hull recounts: "When an unusually heavy storm is coming on, the people say, – 'The Cailleach is going to tramp her blankets to-night.'" From late January through mid-February, she often stirs up storms and brings frost; this is the time of the so-called "wolf month," Faoilleach. Perhaps for this reason, in the hope that she might protect those who honored her, she may have been fêted in late January or early February (as well as at harvest-time). It appears that she was in her death-wielding and perhaps also lusty, "wolfish" aspect sometimes called Gobag; as such, she is depicted as a wolf, beaked bird, snake, or she-goat. If she was not venerated at this time, she would "kill the sheep and the lambs."

Like the Classical Zeus/Jupiter, the Germanic Thor, the Slavic Perun, and the Baltic Perkûnas, as a deity linked to thunder and lightning, the Cailleach carries a *slachdan* (or, *farachan*), a hammer that also serves as a wand. When winter gives way to spring, Hull relates that the rurals used to say, " 'The Cailleach has thrown her mallet under the holly,' for the heavy pounding of the hammer has ceased and vegetation will revive again."

The Cailleach is often depicted as having one eye, which, as in the case of the Greek seer Tiresias and the Vodou Bawon Samndi, suggests the ability to simultaneously see the worlds of the living and the dead, thus speaking to her role as death-wielder. Her name, which roughly translates as "knife-wielding veiled one," also suggests a death-wielding goddess, as well as warrior, priestess, and crone. As a death-wielder, she is linked to a tale of a child born from the ashes of burnt bones. The child was named Gille Dubh Mac nan Cnàmh, "Black Lad, Son of the Bones;" despite, or perhaps due to, his strange birth, he was considered the child of "Bones" herself, the Cailleach. The manner in which he is born (reborn?) recalls the ritual associated with persistent cults which was referred to as the "miracle of the bones," in which the bones of a sacrificed animal miraculously reassemble themselves, phoenix-like, into a living, reborn animal. Presumably, the son is black because he is born from the ashes of burnt bones; but this may be too simplistic a presumption.

The Cailleach's cult appears to have been centered in the vicinity of Dingle in County Kerry in Ireland and in the Lochaber area of Scotland, near Ben Nevis, the highest mountain in the British Isles. "Hags' beds" linked to the Cailleach were visited by women wishing to become pregnant, while the figure representing the Cailleach, was, as Queen of the Harvest, toasted in recent centuries with whiskey by farm laborers, who repeated, "Here's to the one that has helped us with the harvest."

Eventually, for many, the Cailleach became associated with fairies; as with them, it came to be thought by some that she was not immortal but did live a life much longer than humans and, resonating with the cat's nine lives, it came to be thought that she experienced seven cycles of life before dying. She was sometimes depicted as the Fairy Queen. She also came to be envisioned as an ogress or giantess. As fairy or ogress she came to be called "Gentle Annie" or "Black Annis." It is conceivable that the "loathly hag" of the "Wife of Bath's Tale" in Chaucer's *Canterbury Tales* represents a hypostasis of the Cailleach. Prior to and lasting into the late nineteenth century, some envisioned her as a banshee, particularly of certain "Leinster and Meath families." Christians dealt with her in the three main ways typical of Christianization: she was carnivalized, demonized, and conflated with a saint. As a demonic spirit, she was said to be Moreover, some of her attributes may have been appropriated by St. Berach, who died in 595 CE and whose feast is celebrated in February, typically on the 11th or 15th. Donald Mackenzie is correct in suggesting, however, that it is not possible to draw a line in the sand as to when or where – or if – the Cailleach ceased to be regarded as a goddess and commenced to be envisioned as other or lesser beings. Indeed, it is possible that at some times and in some places, she was regarded as simultaneously being all of the above.

Her memory has also persisted in the form of "hags' beds" stone sites; in the form of a doll or effigy called the Cailleach or "Maiden;" and in place-names. In County Armagh, on the mountain of Slieve Gullion, one finds both the Cairn and the Lake of Cailleach Beara. In County Sligo, the stone monument on Slieve Daeane near Loch-da-ghedh is called the House of Cailleach Beara. The Falls of Lora at the mouth of Loch Etive (which means "Little Ugly One" and which refers to the Cailleach), the Ardnamurchan peninsula, and the village of Benderloch are other Scottish sites sacred to her. As part of the Lughnasa) festival of early August, Bilberry, or Blackberry, Sunday, although presently primarily celebrated in a Christianized form, in Dublin and elsewhere, many persons of earlier centuries celebrated the Cailleach by picking berries on a hill in County Armagh and taking turns sitting in a stone "throne" there called "Cailleach Beara's Chair." The Cailleach has also been celebrated with a ritual dance, the Cailleach an Dùdain, which includes the use of a wand and appears to mimic the cycle of life, death, and regeneration.

In the late nineteenth century, in the Aran Islands off the west coast of Ireland, the term "*cailleach*" referred to a wisewoman, typically an elderly woman, who counted among her powers that of transferring an illness from one person to another.

Gyre-Carline, Grýla, Gói

In Scotland, Gyre-Carline was known as the "mother-witch of Scotland." She appears to have emerged in the sixteenth century (perhaps earlier). Her name may have multiple origins, and like many divinities of premodern Europe, her persona reflects the interweaving of numerous cultural traditions. Her persona may have interwoven, or simultaneously reflected, both the Germanic Valkyries, the Greek goddess Hecate, and the Roman goddess of battle, Bellona.

"Gyre" signifies "falcon" or "vulture," which may speak to the *fylgia* or animal-soul and perhaps to the act of flying; as derived from Old Norse *gýgr*, an "ogress," "giantess," "troll-woman," or "witch." "Gyre" may also be etymologically connected to "Valkyrie."

"Carline," deriving from Old Norse/Middle English (*källing, kärring, kerling*), signifies an elderly woman, particularly a peasant woman, "crone," or "witch" (as "carl" or "karl" designates a man, typically a peasant).

Perhaps the most well known place-name of this type is Carline's Loup, shortened to Carlops, near the River Esk, not far from Edinburgh. Here, two witches, Mause and Jenny Barry, were said to have lived, at the foot of the hill, near two conical rocks, between which they would enjoy "bounding and frisking" on their brooms late at night.

In "Scandinavian Folklore in Britain," Hilda R. Ellis Davidson finds a connection between *gýgr* and "Gyro Night," a holiday that is linked to a being called Grýla (or, Gygr, Gyro). Davidson notes that "the pursuit of the word *gýgr* leads us [down] strange paths," including towards "Gyro Night" and towards "Gyre Carline, who has been claimed as the Hecate or Mother Witch of the Scottish peasants." Thus, we may conceivably gain insight into the persona of Gyre-Carline by briefly turning toward the Goddess, giantess, or similar being Grýla, who appeared on the scene around the thirteenth century (perhaps as early as the eleventh). She is known in Iceland and in the Faroe Islands, the Orkney Islands, and Shetland, and possibly also in parts of Germany.

Grýla is thought to speak in a strange voice, alternately described as masculine or animal-like; she is also occasionally said to speak in reverse (although this sounds like it might reflect Christian prejudice linking her to the Devil). As a being of the "outside," the *utangards*, she is thought to live in the mountains, probably within a cave. A rather monstrous being, Grýla is thought to have a son or male children, the Jólasveinar; she might in this light be compared to Grendel's mother of *Beowulf* and possibly also to Caliban's mother Sycorax of Shakespeare's *Tempest*. Grýla is depicted as riding a black horse with fifteen tails (to a certain extent, reminiscent of Odin's eight-legged horse, Sleipnir), with fifteen children seated upon each tail; it is conceivable that these children represent the souls of deceased children, which might link Grýla and, ultimately, Gyre-Carline, with the Wild Hunt. Her strong connection with animals has linked her to the *fylgia* or *varden*, the animal-soul. Grýla is sometimes envisioned as plural, as the Grýlur. For Lotte Motz, in *The Beauty and the Hag*, Grýla in turn corresponds to Gói, the giantess daughter of the giant Thorri, who himself personifies winter and lent his name to the Germanic month stretching from January 14 to February 13. According to Motz, Gói is said to rule the following month (although it seems more likely that Thorri and she shared the month ending on February 13). After Gói was abducted by the giant Hrólfr, evoking Persephone's abduction by Hades, her "family went in search of the young woman, and her father instituted a festival in her name: the Gói-blót. After she was found she stayed with her husband in the mountain and became the ancestress of many rulers of the land." Gói is described as wearing a coat of fur. She is generally a patron of winter and especially of snow. Motz relates: "It is ... claimed that snow falls on earth when she lifts her skirts for her needs, or when she shakes her feather pillows. And when she is diligent in the latter task (when it snows in February) men, fields, and beasts will prosper in the coming year."

In Motz's view, Gói not only corresponds to Grýla but also to "Frû Go or Frû Gode in northern Germany."

Returning to Grýla, her representatives or devotees, including men, are thought to have worn masks and animal skins and horns and/or to have dressed in seaweed and to have "visited farms ... during the winter period to demand offerings." She also appears to have been honored in February, possibly on the first full moon of the month, which would be roughly equivalent to the Celtic Imbolc or the Catholic Candlemas. In this light, Grýla has been compared to the Cailleach, to the goddess Brigid, and to St. Brigid. The giantess Gói, described above, was also honored in February with the Gói-blót. Grýla's celebration appears to have also included a dance performed by the men in disguise and women they encountered on their procession, as well as feasting. It is possible that the festival also centered on fertility, with a representative of Grýla carrying a large wooden phallus or phallic staff by which to confer fertility upon women. In more recent centuries, her persona, in regard to these visits, has been transformed into a combination of Santa Claus and the Witch of "Hansel and Gretel;" she is said to collect children who have behaved badly during the year into a sack and to carry them home with her to eat. The celebration of "Gyro Night" last took place in February 1914 until it was revived several years ago. Davidson relates, "[I]n the Orkneys, two older boys used to dress up as terrifying old women in masks, and chase the smaller boys with ropes." The giantess Gói continued to be remembered into the twentieth century; Motz relates: "Even in modern times the women of Iceland appear, lightly dressed, before their houses, to welcome Gói at the time of her festival.

Gyre-Carline is nicknamed the "Gay Old Wife." She has also been described as wearing a grey mantle and as carrying a wand or staff, reminiscent of a *seiðr* priestess or perhaps a Celtic priestess. In regard to certain descriptions of witchcraft, "grey witches" are those who perform both beneficial and destructive acts. She carries an iron club. A shapeshifter, she sometimes transforms into a sow. It is possible that Gyre-Carline is a goddess or similar being of the waters or sea, as suggested by the nautical terms "gyre," referring to a circular ocean current, and "carline," timber used to support the deck of a wooden ship. She holds the power to transform "water into rocks and sea into solid land." The center of her cult appears to have been in southeastern Scotland, in the vicinity of Fife. Women of Fife were especially concerned that they finish spinning all the flax by the last evening of the year so that they not incur the wrath of Gyre-Carline.

If we pick up the breadcrumbs we have found scattered on the "strange paths" that Davidson describes, weave the various threads together, we end up with a tapestry-like portrait that may conceivably give us a more in-depth understanding of the persona of Gyre-Carline. She appears to have emerged in the Middle Ages or Renaissance from a cross-pollination of Celtic and Germanic origins. She is a giantess or goddess who is sometimes terrifying in appearance; may, in regard to speech and other features, display gender variance or diversity; dwells in the mountains, probably within a cave; has a deep connection with animals, especially, perhaps, the falcon, the vulture, and the horse, and perhaps also fish, with this connection displayed in attire and possibly linked to theriomorphic transformation and magical flight; punishes children who misbehave and women who do not complete the task of spinning; confers fertility and prosperity on her devotees; holds the power to transform elements into each other; visits mortals in winter and is celebrated in winter, primarily in February.

To indicate her association with heresy, and perhaps also with Herodias, Christians dubbed Gyre-Carline the "wife of Mohammed" and the "Queen of the Jews." She was also demonized as a cannibalistic being called Raw Head and Bloody Bones, tales of whom were told to frighten children.

Nicneven

Nicneven, like Gyre-Carline, hails from Scotland. Her existence and cult are controversial. Some say she is only a figure of satire – she is depicted in a satirical poem, "The Flyting of Montgomerie and Polwart" (*c.* 1580) – while others are convinced of her veneration and her cult.

The fact that an alleged witch named Nicneven was burned in May, 1569 at St. Andrews suggests, however, that by the time of the satire's publication, the name or persona of Nicneven had already come to be associated with witches and witchcraft. Further, this fact may also indicate that wisewomen may have taken this name as a kind of cultic title, with "Nic-" signifying "daughter of" in Scottish Gaelic; thus, possibly, "Daughter of Neven." Indeed, it has been suggested that we do not really know the surname of the witch who was burned but rather only her cultic name.

Her name may also signify "Bone Woman," signifying her role as a death-wielding divinity; and/or from "*nic*," an old Germanic term for "washing" which forms a part of the god Odin's hypostasis as Hnickar (or, Hold Nickar, Old Nikkar) as a powerful patron of the waters and which gives rise to water beings called "nickers" (or, knickers, *nicksas, nixas, nixen,* nixies, *nykrs*), who love to sing; who foretell the future; who bring rain and fertility; who bring prosperity to brides and assist women in labor; and who, by way of *Jungbrunnen,* springs of rejuvenation, may rejuvenate elderly people.

Like other European female divinities, Nicneven may have mixed ancestry. Her name may derive in part from Nemain, a Celtic battle-goddess who, together with

Badb and Macha, comprise the triad of goddesses, or the triune Goddess, known as the Mórrigan. Nemain suggests "frenzy," an altered state of consciousness which seems to have frequently inspired warriors in ancient and medieval battles, such as the Germanic *berserkrs* and *ulfserkrs*. It seems that Nemain could terrify her devotees' enemies so gravely that they sometimes died from intense fear rather than from being wounded. In later centuries, in Ireland, Nemain contributed to the persona of the banshee. She has also been linked to the Iceni war-goddess Andraste.

Nicneven has been called the "Elfe Queene" and spouse of the "King of Pharie;" in 1808, John Jamieson named her "the Scottish Hecate or mother-witch." She is depicted as wearing a "long gray mantle, and carrying a wand, which, like the miraculous rod of Moses, could convert water into rocks."

If in fact a cult to Nicneven existed, it may have been centered in or near Fortrose (also called Channery, Chanonry, or Chanrie) in Ross-shire in northeastern Scotland, northeast of Inverness. To the southeast, Fortrose is bordered by Moray Firth, a roughly triangular inlet of the North Sea. Moray Firth is known for its grampuses, or Rosso's dolphins (*Grampus griseus*). In the *Notes* to Richard Franck's *Northern Memoirs, Calculated for the Meridian of Scotland*, we learn that several hundred years ago, Fortrose/Channery "came to be peculiarly renowned for sorcery." It is perhaps most famous for the burning to death – possibly actual, possibly legendary – within a spiked barrel of a mysterious man nicknamed "the Brahan seer," a second-sighted man who may have lived during the sixteenth or seventeenth century. Regarding primarily female witches, however, Fortrose/Channery was associated with Nicneven. The "witches of Chanrie" were said to possess the "power of compelling grampuses [i.e., Risso's dolphins] to come ashore," a power which would "have been of great use to [the] town-folks." Among those accused of witchcraft at Fortrose/Channery was Janet McGillichoan, whose trial took place in August, 1630. In my view, the occult location of the area in which Fortrose lies needs to be further explored; within ten or fifteen miles, one finds not only sites pertaining to *Macbeth*, such as Cawdor and the heath in Hardmuir where the Weird Sisters are alleged to have appeared, but also the village of Auldearn, known for the trial of the alleged witch Isobel Gowdie, as well as the peninsula of Tarbat Ness, allegedly the "site of a Roman fort which was later used as a meeting place for a witches' coven."

A rather unusual garment linked to Nicneven as well as Gyre-Carline suggests that men may have numbered among devotees of the goddess. This seventeenth-century garment, variously named "warlock fecket," "warlock weeds," and "weird coat," was a jacket made of snakeskin, possibly from water snakes, that was dried for nine months and a day, and coated, allegedly, with fat from a wolf and other materials; it was thought to be impenetrable against many weapons, and to have been a special garment worn, primarily by men, to gatherings of witches that were said to take place during the full moon in March.

Other than possibly near the spring

equinox, Nicneven appears to have been feasted primarily at Samhain.

Senach, the Seven Daughters of the Sea, the Mither o' the Sea, and Mother Carey

Turning toward more localized divinities, in eighth-century Ireland, a Christian abbot of Westmeath recorded non-Christian reverence of a group of goddesses or female spirits he referred to as the Seven Daughters of the Sea. The reverence of these beings was linked to that of a deity named Senach, who her-/himself was in turn associated with fairies. It appears that reverence of the Seven Daughters came to be hybridized with Christian concepts and practices, as suggested by this invocation:

I invoke the seven Daughters
of the Sea
Who fashion the threads of the sons of long life.
:
I invoke Senach of the seven periods
of time,
Whom fairy-women have reared on the breasts of plenty,
:
May the grace of the Holy Spirit be upon me![42]

Belief in the Mither o' the Sea (or, De Midder o' de Sea, Mother of the Sea) appears to have been centered in the Shetland and Orkney Islands of northern Scotland. In the former islands, she "came to be regarded as a sea deity who could be invoked by fishermen for protection against the Devil," while in the latter, she was envisioned as the "benign spirit of the summer, who stilled the storms, brought warmth to the ocean, and filled the seas with teeming life." It is, on the other hand, possible that is someone offended her, then she might seek to harm them. For example, in the early seventeenth century, alleged witch Katherine Carey sought to heal a man who was being troubled by the "spirit of the sea," conceivably the Mither o' the Sea, but perhaps it was another marine spirit. It is said that fishermen of Lunnasting, Shetland continued to invoke her in the early twentieth century, in order that she might fill their nets with fish. Belief in the Mither o' the Sea appears to have been linked to belief in a male deity of winter named Teran and to a myth embracing the seasonal cycle. The Mither ruled from the spring equinox until the fall equinox, while Teran ruled the remainder of the year. Their reigns were marked by battles, the *vore tullye* (also, *bogel ree*) of spring and the *gore vellye* of autumn, as evidenced by gales, tempests, and such.

The phrase "Mother Carey's Chickens" refers to the stormy petrel (or, storm-petrel, *Procellaria pelagica*), a small seabird of the order of *Procellariiformes* (with *procella* meaning "storm") in the *Hydrobatidae* family. Many observations of stormy petrels have been documented from the eighteenth century onward, including in waters of the coasts of the Isles of Scilly, St. Kilda, the Orkney and Shetland Islands, Portugal, the Cape of Good Hope, Alaska, California, Florida, the Bahamas, Cuba, and elsewhere. They are called "stormy" because they tend to gather during storms in order to collect food that rises to the surface of the water;

indeed, they are sometimes described as harbingers of storms. In 1817, in "An Account of the Stormy Petrel," it is observed that

> no person has traversed the ocean, without taking notice of the flocks of Stormy Petrels, or Mother Carey or Kerry's Chickens flitting past his vessel, like swallows, or following in her wake, and gleaning their pittance of food from the surface of the water. Feathered in black, with some portion of white, and usually making their appearance in greater numbers previous to or during a storm...[43]

By the last decade of the eighteenth century, the phrase "Mother Carey's Chickens" was being deployed to refer to the Jacobins of the French Revolution, "because their appearance was the foreboding of woe, the heralding of a tumult and political stormy weather," as well as to certain supporters of Thomas Jefferson who were deemed "Jacobins." By the commencement of the nineteenth, on the other hand, fine ships were being compared to Mother Carey: "The old ship, sir, was a fine seaboat; she rode like a Mother Carey, and wouldn't allow any water to board her. She was as comfortable a craft in a storm, as ever floated."

Mother Carey and her "chickens" may possess both Christian and pagan associations. In regard to Christian ones, some writers have argued that "Mother Carey" is derived from Mater Cara, "Dear Mother," and refers to the Virgin Mary, especially in her manifestation as Stella Maris, the "Star of the Sea," which, intriguingly, constitutes a representation of the sea goddess Yemayá in the Yorùbá diasporic religion of La Regla de Ocha (Lucumí, Santería). In this regard, petrels are called, in French, oiseaux de Notre Dame, and in Italian, uccelli pescatori di Santa Maria. Not to mention that the term "petrel" derives from Saint Peter. On the other hand, given their ominous aspect, petrels have been said to belong to the Devil as the "Prince of the Air" and have been deemed the "Devil's Birds." Some sailors and others have "believ[ed]... that each [petrel] contains the soul of some shipwrecked mariner. And as they are always in motion, never resting, they are sometimes called by the French "Ames damnées ["damned souls"]" – which, needless to say, is a Christian rather than a pagan notion.

Anna Drury, writing in 1860, suggests that the figure of Mother Carey, like that of Davy Jones, possesses pagan associations. The surname "Carey" may not be altogether insignificant, as synchronistic as this may be. "Carey" derives from Ó Ciardha, meaning "descendant of Ciardha." *Ciardha* is a Gaelic term signifying "dark" or "black." This surname may conceivably possess ethnic designations; it may also, if the members of the Carey Heritage and Society are correct, in being translated as "Children of the Dark," possess shamanistic and pagan associations.

As for the color black, together with an association that we shall discover shortly, that of petrels with omens, and the possibility, however remote, that the surname might be linked in some way to the Greek "Ker" (possibly by way of the proto-

Indo-European *kar/ker*, "rock," or, more probably, via the Egyptian *k-l* or *k-3*, "soul," transposed into Greek as *k-r*, thus, *keiro*, "to cut," as to cut the soul from the body, or *keres*, the "souls of the dead"), in 1912, we find: "Mediterranean sailors regard them as ill-omened, and Mother Carey is probably a modern form of the Greek Ker (*kare*), the black goddess of fate and death." The Keres are often described in the plural, as referring to death-bringing goddesses, daughters of the goddess Nyx.

The surname "Carey" might also be linked in some way to the Old Norse *kari*, "wind, gust, squall," and/or to *afkárr*, "wild," perhaps by way of the mélange of Germanic and Celtic cultures in the British Isles. In Germanic tradition, Kára is a Valkyrie who protects Helgi Haddingjasði (and is tragically, mistakenly slain by him) and who takes the form of a swan.

Mother Carey has also been linked to the Germanic goddess Holda. As with Holda, when Mother Carey shakes out her feather pillows and mattress, it snows on the earth, thus linking birds, snow, and female divinities. In 1865, Wheeler relates (as William Walsh will reiterate in 1913): "When it is snowing, Mother Carey is said by the sailors to be plucking her goose...[A] myth of the old German mythology ...described the snow as the feathers falling from the bed of the goddess Holda, when she shook it in making it."

In 1882, folklorist W. S. Lach-Szyrma asks, "Old Mother Cary, who picks her chickens in Devonshire when the snow falls?" This association, however, brings encounter with another seabird, the great black petrel, or, fulmar, nicknamed "Mother Carey's Goose." In an 1889 article, we find:

> As these small birds are known as "Mother Carey's Chickens" it is but a natural consequence that the great black petrel, belong- I ing to the same family, frequent in the Pacific Ocean, and a ravenous feeder upon dead whales, should be called "Mother Carey's Goose;" and when it snows the sailors say " Mother Carey is plucking her goose," [it is] supposed to be [an] interpretation of the old German legend that described the snow as the feathers falling from the bed of the benignant goddess Hulda, when she shook it up in making it.[44]

By adding the goose to our chain of associations, one might speculate that Mother Carey might be linked in some way to Mother Goose.

According to Drury, Mother Carey is an "obscure sea-divinity, chiefly celebrated for her 'chickens,' as Juno ashore for her peacocks." This "sea-divinity" might be Ino/Leucothea. In the *Odyssey* (5: 333-365), Ino/Leucothea (the "White Goddess"), seeking to assist Odysseus, offers him her veil, to protect him from the fury of Poseidon. Upon doing so, she transforms into a petrel (or gull) and dives to the depths of the sea, where has dwelt since she, as Ino, in fleeing her husband, drowned herself and her child. Dionysus, whom she has helped to raise and who loves her, transforms the dying Ino into the sea goddess Leucothea. Or the "sea-divinity" might be the Greek goddess Amphitrite, or Thalassa, or Thetis.

Or she might be the Germanic Valkyrie Róta, who sends sleet and storms, is associated with petrels, and appears to have been acknowledged in the Orkney and Shetland Islands. Further afield, Mother Carey might also share attributes with the Inuit sea goddess Sedna, who is associated with petrels. Most often, however, petrels and Mother Carey have been associated with witches and witchcraft.

Although its first usage remains mysterious, we know that the phrase "Mother Carey's Chickens" was deployed in the mid-eighteenth century to denote stormy petrels by sailors under the command of Captain Philip Carteret (1733-1796) of the British Navy. Writers on the subject have suggested that by that time, Mother Carey was already a "celebrated ideal hag." By 1817, petrels had themselves gained the nickname of "witches."

Mother Carey was considered a witch, one rather like Prospero, who brews tempests, or else an ancestral or goddess-like being resembling a witch (such as Circe), who is the keeper of storms, not unlike the *orishá* Oyá in the Yorùbá religion. As a mortal witch, Mother Carey was, in 1837, "understood to have been a hag who caused an immense number of shipwrecks in the days of the belief in witchcraft, not only by her supposed influence with the " Prince of the Power of the Air," but by lighting false watchfires on the heights, as used often to be done upon those coasts where the infamous system existed." As Ariel assists Prospero, or as Puck assists Titania and Oberon, so petrels are the "feathered attendants" of the "ocean witch" Mother Carey, "just as the more amiable Mother Venus had her doves." Indeed, this "sea witch['s]…presence [is] made visible by her feathered attendants."

Mother Carey has sometimes been compared to Mother Shipton (possibly Ursula Southeil, *c*. 1488-1561), a "witch and prophetess who is alleged to have lived in Tudor times: "Mother Carey is supposed to be a kind of ocean witch, a supernatural Mother Shipton, who rides the blast." Let's recall, incidentally, as Ryoji Tsurumi (1990) reminds us, that the terms "Mother" and "Old Mother," when placed before a surname, frequently connoted in the medieval, Renaissance, and later periods, not only a poor woman and/or a crone but also "an intermediary between the everyday world and the world of the supernatural."

It is difficult to tell when a tale surfaced that connected a ship named the Tiger to a certain female passenger who reminded mariners of Mother Carey and linked her to seabirds and witchcraft. According to the tale, which may represent an interweaving of a couple or several historical events, belief in divinities or otherworldly beings, and fiction, an "Indiaman" ship (large merchant ship used on trade routes to India) named the *Tiger* was significantly damaged by a series of violent storms as it neared the Cape of Good Hope.

> Here, however, the winds and waves seemed bent on her destruction; in the midst of the storm, flocks of strange looking birds were seen hovering and wheeling in the air around the devoted ship, and one of the passengers, a woman called "Mother Carey," was observed by the glare of the lightning to laugh and

smile when she looked at these foul-weather visitants; on which, she was not only set down as a witch, but it was also thought that they were her familiars, whom she had invoked from the Red Sea; and "all hands" were seriously considering on the propriety of getting rid of the old beldam, (as is usual in such cases,) by setting her afloat, when she saved them the trouble, and at that moment jumped overboard, surrounded by flames; on which the birds vanished, the storm cleared away, and the tempest-tossed Tiger went peacefully on her course![45]

The *Tiger* "Indiaman" and the storms it encountered on nearing the Cape of Good Hope are documented, historical facts. The *Tiger*, owned by Sir Edward Michelbourne and captained by John Davis (1543-1605), set out for the Cape of Good Hope and elsewhere on December 5, 1604. As they were approaching the Cape on May 7, 1605, a terrific storm arose which continued on May 9th. We read in Clements R. Markham's *Life of John Davis* (1889): "Rounding the Cape of Good Hope on the 7th, they encountered a furious gale of wind on the 9th, which lasted for two days with rain and thunder." Thus, ship, storms, and dates are established. It is also factual that "strange looking" petrels inhabit the area and that they were and continue to be observed by mariners. But what are we to make of "Mother Carey" and the "flames" surrounding her?

The mysterious flames were in fact reported: "In the full fury of the storm, flickering flames, like candles, appeared on the Tiger's mast-heads. Spanish mariners would have believed that these St. Elmo lights were indications of the presence of their guardian saint."

These flames appear to have been a manifestation of "St. Elmo's Fire." This unusual electrical phenomenon, wherein flames appear to manifest on mast-heads or else as balls of fire floating through the air or auras of fire circling people's heads, is named after St. Elmo, or rather, St. Erasmus of Formiae, the patron saint of sailors. In ancient Greece, these flames were thought to be sent by the Dioscuri, Castor and Pollux, as a sign that the ship and its crew would survive a dangerous storm. Its other names, together with kindred phenomena, include corpse candle, fetch light, *feu follet*, *igniis fatuus*, jack-o'-lantern, and will-o'-the-wisp. Two others bring us nearer to Mother Carey and the tale of the *Tiger*: Davy Jones – Mother Carey's spouse – and Witch's Fire.

Can we, however, come any closer?

Shakespeare provides an intriguing hint. In *Macbeth*, the First Witch complains that once, when she was hungry and observed a woman eating a large amount of chestnuts, and she asked the woman of she might have some, the stingy, gluttonous woman refused to give her any. The Witch notes that the woman's husband is the "master o' the *Tiger*" and that he's "to Aleppo gone." Now, the Witch intends to punish the greedy woman by creating a storm at sea that will damage her husband's ship: "Though his bark cannot be lost,/ Yet shall it be tempest-toss'd." Of course, it is quite possible that the Witch and her curse are entirely fictional. Yet the cursing of ships via sinister sorcery appears to have been rather commonplace; moreover, on seeing *Macbeth*, King James must have been reminded of the North Berwick witches, who were tried in 1590 for attempting to kill the King and his Queen by way of destroying the royal ship with the royal couple aboard.

Shakespeare may have taken the liberty of blending a couple of or several historical events in this passage. The (or a ship named) *Tiger* sailed to Aleppo or the vicinity in 1583 and 1587. It is the Tiger's voyage of 1604-1605, just prior to the completion of the writing of *Macbeth*, however, that most clearly interweaves the damaging storm at sea with a witch and sinister magic. Thus, if the "master o' the *Tiger*" and his wife refer to any historical persons, then they most probably refer to John Davis and his wife, Faith Fulford (1561-1604).

In this context, we might bear in mind that John Davis was a colleague of the Elizabethan court astrologer John Dee. He was also no stranger to pagan-rooted or inspired feasts:

> On this occasion our *Baas*, for so a Dutch captain is called, appointed a Master of Misrule, named the *Kesar*, the authority of which disorderly officer lay in riot, as after dinner he would neither salute his friends, nor understand the laws of reason, those who ought to have been most respectful being both lawless and witless. We spent three days in this dissolute manner, and then shaped our course for the Cape of Good Hope, sailing towards the coast of Bacchus, to whom this idolatrous sacrifice was made, as appeared afterwards.[46]

Although it is not possible to say whether a curse was indeed performed upon Davis and his wife, it is intriguing that his wife died in 1604, at 43, with the reputation of being an adulteress who had an affair with a counterfeiter and who sought to end her marriage by bringing false charges against her husband, while in 1605, Davis himself, as "master o' the *Tiger*," was brutally slain by Japanese pirates. *It is not too difficult to imagine that they were cursed.* It is most likely mere coincidence that Faith Fulford's sister Elizabeth married Thomas Carey, becoming Elizabeth Carey. Yet, seeing as the Fulford family was very well known, it is not inconceivable that Shakespeare may have taken advantage of this coincidence. And it is not inconceivable that groundlings and others who saw *Macbeth* "connected the dots" as he and we have done.

I think that, in regard to the tale told above, of "Mother Carey" as a witch on the *Tiger*, we might consider the possibility that just as some of those on board observe an incident of "St. Elmo's Fire" or "Witch's Fire," while others probably did not, so some, perhaps not all, might have noticed "Mother Carey" on board. That is to say, "Mother Carey" might, like many other alleged witches and otherworldly beings (as Ariel, Puck), have possessed the power of traveling "in spirit," embodiment/ "possession," rapid flight, and/or bilocation.

In my view, it is likely that the alleged witch Katherine Carey, who was tried for witchcraft in Scotland in June, 1616, may have also contributed to the development of the mythos of Mother Carey, her petrels, witchcraft, and the sea. What little we know of Carey, other than her encountering and being instructed by fairies, concerns her attempt to heal a "patient [who] was troubled with the spirit of the sea." This "spirit of the sea," who would "not let him bide in peace and quiet," led Carey to attempt to heal him with sacred stones. While the relationship here between Carey and the "spirit of the sea" appears to be antagonistic, it is conceivable that the two became merged in the popular psyche due to widespread knowledge of this event, and/or that Carey, in wishing to heal the ill man, made offerings or sacrifices to the "spirit" and in this way became linked to them.

By 1817, some thought Mother Carey to "have been a New England witch, who used to ride her broomstick between Rhode Island and the Bermudas." (One cannot help but think of the mysterious Bermuda Triangle.)

In the 1830s, Mother Carey made appearances primarily as a folkloric character: "the Witch" in a pantomime, *Davy Jones; or, Harlequin and Mother Carey's Chickens* (1830), in James Fenimore Cooper's *The Water Witch; or, the Skimmer of the Seas* (1834); and Allan Cunningham's *Lord Roldan: A Romance* (1836), in which a character remarks, "She mayn't be such a witch as Mother Carey...but damme if I feel any inclination to cross her!" She has also made appearances in George Melville Baker's play *Among the Breakers* (1872), and Rudyard Kipling's "The Children of the Zodiac" (1891), as well as in John Masefield's "Mother Carey" (1915), in which "She's the mother o' the witches" (l. 1) and Davy Jones is "her man" (l.6) and much more recently, in Barbara G. Walker's *Feminist Fairy Tales* (1996). Of course, one must not neglect Kate Douglas Wiggins' 1911 novel *Mother Carey's Chickens*, made into a delightful Disney film with Hayley Mills, *Summer Magic*. In my view, one of the most marvelous descriptions of Mother Carey is found in Charles Kingsley's *The Water-Babies* (1864):

> In the centre of this sea is a circular marble throne, whose base has three hundred and sixty divisions, from which meridian lines run out and span the great world; and from its centre rises a pole of electric light reaching upward into the heavens to the constellation of the Southern Cross. On this throne sits Mother Carey, the fashioner and maker of millions upon millions of new creations of more varied shapes, colors, qualities, and functions than any but little children ever dreamed of. She sits quite still with her chin upon her hand, looking down into the sea with two great, grand blue eyes, as blue as the sea itself. Her hair is as white as the snow, for she is very, very old— in fact, as old as any thing which you are likely to come across, except the difference between right and wrong.[47]

Wanne Thekla

Sometime during the Middle Ages, a cult to Wanne Thekla is thought to have emerged in the Netherlands and Belgium. She may have originated in the goddess Nehalennia. Wanne Thekla has also been compared to Freyja, Frigga, Hertha, Holda, Isis (as Isa), Nerthus, Perchta/Berchta, and Terra Mater/Cybele. As Wanne Thekla, however, this deity surfaced in the medieval period. She is a goddess of winds, navigation, the cultivation of flax, spinning, and weaving. She is also a goddess of weather, especially of tempests. When a storm approaches, it is said that Wanne Thekla is coming. Known as a "witch-queen," she is the queen of the witches and elves, and generally speaking, of the spirits of air."

"At night she descends to the earth, accompanied by an entourage of companions," we are told; as she arrives on the earth, the goddess and her court are met by a "large female entourage." She appears to have been celebrated during the winter and again in early May. Her ship, a "cloudship" or *Vindflot*, cannot be seen by everyone, particularly when there's fog or heavy rain; or else it appears as a ghost ship. It is in connection with her ship and a procession of devotees alongside the ship (a representation thereof) that Wanne Thekla becomes linked to the other goddesses to whom she corresponds. Maximilian J. Rudwin writes in *The Origin of the German Carnival Comedy* (1920):

> The ship-procession was probably also a part of the worship of Nerthus. Tacitus also speaks of the procession in a *vehiadum* [i.e., conveyance]of the image of Nerthus, the Earth-Mother, amongst the Ingaevonic tribes, who lived about the mouth of the river Elbe and who beyond doubt are the progenitors of the so-called Anglo-Saxon race. This *vehiadum* of Nerthus, who, as will be shown forthwith, probably is identical with the goddess Tacitus found worshipped by the Suevi in a ship procession, was a ship-cart, a *terrae navis*, as was the ship of Isis, which traveled on land and water, and also the Skiðbladnir, the ship of Freyr, which sailed in the air and on the water. The theory that the *vehiculum* of Nerthus was a ship-cart finds further support in the fact that the procession set out from her sacred grove in an island of the ocean. …There is no doubt that Nerthus is the same as Freya… Nerthus-Freya, moreover, is identical with Wanne Thekla, who also comes and goes in her ship.[48]

The procession with the ship of Thekla included older women dressing a young maiden to represent or embody Thekla with ribbons and flowers. The young woman then rode about in a cart, ornamented to represent the ship, in a parade with the women. The women appear to have marched in the nude, "skyclad," or else wearing very little clothing, probably draped with flowers. Onlookers bestowed the goddess's representative and the others with coins as they processed. At some point, the goddess's devotees made offerings to her. Following the parade and the making of offerings, "they dance[d] and jump[ed] and [drank] at Pottelberg where a gallows once stood. On the Leye River, flowing through the city of Cortryk, [Thekla] sail[ed] in her beautiful ship with her company; when their night festival…ended, she command[ed] the four winds to carry her ship away."

Derk Buddingh (1844) connects Thekla to the *nechsen*, water beings, comparable to mermaids, and contrasts her with *hexen*, "witches," whom he views as sorceresses who perform acts of destructive magic. One is led to wonder whether Buddingh might be inferring the existence of two cults, one "benign," rather like the cult of Fairy spoken of elsewhere, the other, sinister, with the *nechsen* referring to beneficent "witches"? Goethe (1749-1832) indicates a similar dualism in his oppositional pairing of *nixen* and *hexen* in his poem "Was wir bringen. Forstezung. Halle," wherein it's pondered: "*Hexen-Nixe? Nixen-Hexe?*" which is typically translated as "Witch-Mermaid? Mermaid-Witch?" but which may indicate a bit more than this, as "witch" and "mermaid" differ somewhat in terms of classes of beings to which they belong. Certainly, more research needs to be undertaken in regard to the pairing of *nechsen/hexen* as well as its possible relationship to Thekla, other goddesses, and sacred specialists.

Ultimately, reverence of the goddess Thekla in the form of the ship procession transformed in the region into a celebration of the May Queen. Other rites of Thekla's festival metamorphosed into a great fair and feast that continued to be celebrated in the nineteenth century. Wanne Thekla also came to be Christianized as the Virgin Mary (as Stella Maris, to whom, in La Regla de Ocha (Lucumí, Santería), the *orishá* Yemayá, goddess of the sea, corresponds) as well as St. Ursula, St. Gertrude, St. Pinnosa, and St. Thecla.

Vénus de Quinipily

In Brittany, at Baud, in Morbihan, reverence of a goddess who came to be called the Vénus de Quinipily, persisted into at least the late seventeenth century, probably well into the nineteenth century, and perhaps even into our own time. It has most assuredly reemerged in the present. Professor of history and Egyptology Sylvie Caroff has recently argued that the history of the well known statue of the "Venus of Quinipily" may be traced to Isaic and Gallic origins and to Roman occupation of this area of Brittany. I have, however, decided to speak of her here because of the ambiguity surrounding her ancient cult coupled with the apparently dramatic rise of her cult in or near the seventeenth century CE.

It is probable that in remote antiquity, a Gaulish Great, Mother, or Earth Goddess was worshipped in this area. When the Romans arrived, they brought with them the cult of Isis, Serapis, and Harpocrates. It appears that the indigenous goddess eventually came to be conflated with Isis as exemplary of Gallo-Roman mixing. She may have also become linked to the Celtic-Gallic goddesses Belisama, Brigid, Litavis/Llydaw, and Sulis, and to the Roman Minerva and Venus in a complex system of sacred hybridity. Although some Christians renamed her, or displaced her with, St. Anne, the patron saint of Brittany, and/or as regional manifestations of the Virgin Mary, Notre Dame de la Clarté and Notre Dame de la Couarde, most of those who wrote about her in the seventeenth century and thereafter referred to her as the "Venus of Quinipily," while most of her devotees appear to have called her Groach Hoart (or,

Groah Goard, La Gward), the "Elder Female Guardian," or Ar Groareg (or, Grouech-Houarn), the "Woman of Iron." She appears to have been associated with the powers of earth (abundant crops), water (especially rivers and rain), and fire and with healing and metallurgy.

Devotees would gather around her granite statue of six-and-a-half feet to pray, make petitions, give offerings, and celebrate. The statue represents the goddess as wearing a long stole that covers her genitalia. Otherwise, she is nude. It is possible that at one time, she was shown with her genitalia uncovered, resonating with the goddess Baubo. She has rather short hair – a sort of page-boy haircut – and wears a headband, fillet, or crown. Her face and gaze, together with the positioning of her legs, are highly reminiscent of Egyptian statuary. Male devotees would often touch the statue in asking the goddess to relieve rheumatism and sinusitis. Women often prayed to find intimate partners, become fertile, or to bear children. Women may have ritually masturbated against the statue in order to beckon, celebrate, or placate the goddess. At some point, the statue was transferred from Castannec on the River Blavet to Quinipily.

During the later seventeenth century, between 1660 and 1672, various attempts were made by Church authorities to rid Baud of the statue and to destroy it in an effort to force the cult of the goddess to disband, including one occasion when the statue was cast into the Blavet (it took several oxen to drag it there) and another when the statue was partially if not almost entirely mutilated. Then, during the final years of the seventeenth century and the first years of the eighteenth – in part due to violent peasant rebellion in defiance of the ban – the statue was either reclaimed from the water and placed upon a pedestal on an estate at Quinipily, or else a copy of it was made and placed there (no one seems quite certain which of these occurred). The statue became linked to a *cuve-jardin*, a stone tub typically meant for small gardens, into which offerings including coins were placed. Those desiring fertility or hoping to be healed sometimes ritually bathed in the tub. In the eighteenth century, inscriptions were carved into the sides of the pedestal, stating that the statue represented Venus and had been venerated since the arrival of the Romans. By the early nineteenth century, it was argued that the statue did not represent Venus but rather Isis. Although the estate did not survive, the statue did, as well as, it would seem, the cult; well known writers including Prosper Mérimée (1803-1870) and Gustave Flaubert (1821-1880) observed and wrote of it and acknowledged continuing rites. In 1877, Katharine S. Macquoid offered a rather lurid description of the statue in *Through Brittany*: "It looks a fit emblem of dark pagan worship. ...The idol loomed through the trees in gigantic weirdness. ...through the veil of apple-trees before us loomed the gray pagan idol with its misshapen limbs, its mocking smile seeming to assert sway over the wilderness." In 1883, however, a less judgmental, less sensationalist J. G. R. Forlong noted that since the statue of the goddess had been restored in the early eighteenth century, "she has continued ever since...[to be] piously worshipped."

Persistent and/or NeoPagans continue to, or once more, revere the goddess today.

Esterelle

Esterelle might have been included in our discussion of fairies, as she is frequently referred to as the "fairy Esterelle," but I have decided to include her here because she is referred to as a goddess rather than a fairy in several texts including the *Dictionnaire encyclopèdique de la France* (1842) and "Estérel (1876) by the Abbé Guigou; and because the latter explains how she came to be called a fairy. After Christians documented and condemned her cult in the early fourteenth century (or thereabouts), Guigou relates, those who persisted in revering her began to refer to her as a fairy or nymph rather than as a goddess.

Although Esterelle may have originated in Ostara/Eostre, it is more likely that she originated in or emerged from Diana, as she was sometimes called Diane Estérelle, or else Diana's Celtic counterpart Arduinna (or all of the above). It is, however, as Esterelle that she came to be revered as a goddess in the Middle Ages, possibly a goddess of fertility and the hunt as well of the stars and moon.

Her cult was centered in Provence, near Cannes. The Esterel Massif mountain range, of volcanic origin, is thought to be named after her.

Women made offerings to her in order to promote fertility and pregnancy. In exchange, she or a woman or priestess embodying or representing her gave the women a magical beverage to enhance fertility. Fishermen, hunters, and woodcutters, some of whom were alleged to have encountered her, may have also made offerings to her (tales are told of men who, never having seen such a beautiful being, never left the forest where they encountered her).

Some of the offerings made to her were placed at the sacred stone called the *Lanza de la Fada*, the "Fairy's Lance" or "Fairy's Stone." This dolmen "is one of the largest in Provence, about sixty tons and two meters high." It may have been a Megalithic burial site. It caught the attention of Nostradamus (1503-1566). Offerings were especially made to Esterelle on December 31.

It is thought that a temple or shrine may have been built to her. Her devotees also maintained a sacred grove to her, including pine, cork, and chestnut trees. Anyone who chopped down a tree in the grove risked being put to death. Unfortunately, the grove was devastated by fire in 1835.

To a certain extent, Esterelle was displaced by the Virgin Mary, as Notre Dame de l'Esterel, with a monastery being built on her sacred grounds. Troubadours, however, are said to have sung her praises; and many others continued to believe in the existence of and perhaps continued to make offerings to Esterelle in the nineteenth century.

La Guenne

Alternately revered and feared in France and Brittany, we might have spoken of La Guenne in our discussion of fairies or of sinister nocturnal beings. I include her here, however, because she is thought to have been a medieval localized manifestation of the goddess Diana. In the eyes of the Christianized, she is viewed as a "rapacious variety of *lutin*…who appears as a goat."

Tante Arie

In the French Alps, Tante Arie may have originated in Hera/Juno as a goddess associated with the element of air and of gift-giving in winter – from Hera to Herie or Harie to Arie. Others, like those at the Musée du Jouet de Moirans en Montagne, in Jura, maintain that Tante Arie "does not seem to have descended from [an earlier] divinity" but rather seems to have emerged in the medieval period. She is said to be a friend of the goddess Perchta. She has also been connected to Holda and La Befana

She is thought to live in a little chalet in the French Alps. She is much loved and very generous; she is a protector of women and children; she is a giver of gifts in wintertime; and very few things upset her other as much as laziness and disorder in the household. However, she punishes criminals by setting fire to their houses. She is especially concerned with education, encouraging young people to study, and with alleviating the poverty and oppression of rural peasants. She is also a patron of bakers and innkeepers. Tante Arie is offered bread, milk, and mistletoe. In the past, during her winter celebration, young men and women impersonating her would offer children apples and nuts. In return, the children would offer them beverages – in recent times, coffee and mineral water – in the hope that this would cause them to unmask themselves. Since the nineteenth century, Tante Arie has increasingly been described as a fairy rather than as a divinity and has been increasingly displaced by Father Christmas. A "Chanson de la Tante Airie," probably from the vicinity of Montbéliard in eastern France, celebrates her arrival: "Dressed like a peasant/ With her pretty bonnet/ She travels the country/ On her little grey donkey." The refrain goes: "Do you know Tante Arie,/ The good fairy of this land?/ All the children dream of her."

Brava Part

Brava Part, often identified as a "witch," hails from the Italian Alps. Her origins – which appear to be Ladin(o) – are mysterious. She is thought to dwell within a cave near the Cavallo River not far from Folgaria. She prefers solitude over community, and if bothered, she often responds with fury. On the whole, however, she is a kind and generous being. In the twenty-first century, she continues to be fêted during the final days of August. From the fair that is held each year in her honor, which includes healing products and sessions, it is possible to deduce that she is a patron of the healing arts. The many crafts displayed at her fair by master craftspersons suggests that she is also a patron of crafts. She is also honored with floats, walks in nature (sometimes to her alleged residence), and a "witches' dance."

Richella

In 1457, Nicholas of Cusa (1401-1464), Bishop of Bressanone, questioned two women from the Val di Fassa, in the far north of Italy, in the province of Trentino, in the Dolomites region of the Alps, who claimed to revere a "good mistress," Bona Domina Richella. Richella appears to have shared traits with the Classical Diana and Fortuna as well as the Germanic Holda. Richella is described as a well-dressed woman who wears very large ornaments on each side of head, similar to those worn by the famed Dama of Elche, except that Richella's appear to have been semi-circles, perhaps crescent moons. Somewhat strange are her hairy hands, possibly suggesting theriomorphic transformation. Like Artemis, Richella is a "mistress of the animals" and may be associated with the *salvani*, hairy human-like beings who dwell in caves but who enjoy the company of humans and who sometimes visit their houses in the hope that a kind person will offer them something to eat. More specifically, Richella may be associated with Silvana, Queen of the *salvani* and "protectress of wild animals." The testimony of the women who were questioned indicates that Richella was celebrated during the four Ember weeks, that is, roughly speaking, at the time of thee equinoxes and solstices.

The name "Richella" is an intriguing one. In the Renaissance, the term *richella*, together with its variant forms *ricella* and *ritichella*, referred to lace and lace-work, perhaps especially in the context of weddings and brides, with richella/lace being used to ornament pillows and curtains of the marriage bed. Considering the fact that a number of the goddesses or similar beings herein are associated with spinning and weaving, it hardly seems surprising that, with the escalation of lacemaking in the fifteenth and sixteenth centuries, a divinity of women might come to be associated with, or perhaps come to be seen as the patron of, lacemakers. In our own time, women living in the Val di Fassa, including at Canazei, and in the Dolomites, including in Predol and Selva di Val Gardena, are known for their beautiful lace embroidery on pillows and other items. It is conceivable that Richella is also a patron of lacemakers.

The women who were questioned by Nicholas of Cusa appear to have been of Ladin(o) heritage. Ladin(o) is a Rhaeto-Romance language spoken in the region with an allied, rich culture, both emerging from the Roman colonists who settled the area in ancient times. It is quite possible that the women were lacemakers. The cultural or ethnic heritage of these women suggests that the goddess Richella may have, at least to a certain extent, been a Renaissance avatar of the ancient Rhaetian goddess Reitia (also known as Loudera, comparable to Libera, a Dionysus-like goddess). Reitia is primarily a goddess of earth, fertility, healing, and writing. She was linked by the Romans to Juno but she has also been compared to Cybele, Gaia, Inanna, and the Spartan goddess Ortia. It appears that certain traits of Richella, and perhaps also of Reitia, were appropriated by the Church for Santa Giuliana. Adriano Vanin suggests that a fifteenth-century May celebration in honor of Santa Giuliana, with sacrifices and feasting, may have its origins in a feast to Reitia and her male partner, in Etruscan named Tinia, as indicated by a priest's song including the term "Tinarez," a possible combination of Tinia and Reitia.

La Signora della Montagna

La Signora della Montagna, the Lady of the Mountain, is another goddess or goddess-like figure of the Ladin(o) region of the Italian Alps. Her present-day characterization suggests that she may originally have been perceived as a Dea-Madre, a Mother Goddess. She is depicted as a woman who possesses an exquisite jewel that resembles blue ice; and she leads an entourage of the souls of deceased children, suggesting her role as a death-wielder, psychopomp, or patron of the dead.

Madona Oriente

As for Italy, Madona Oriente, a fairy-goddess, was revered in vicinity of Milan in the late fourteenth century. Her followers were called *bona gens* ("good people"), or "fairies." She has sometimes been identified with Diana and also Cybele; Manciocco and Manciocco suggest that her name "Oriente" may have pointed toward Asia Minor as the supposed place of her origins. She has also been identified with Herodias. And she may have also been nicknamed "Lady of the Good Game," La Signora del Bon Zogo (or, Domina Ludi, La Donna del Bon Zogo, La Signora del Zuogo) and/or the "Lady of the Course," as in running in a circle on a track (Domina Cursus). By way of note, gatherings of an earth-centered sort, which would ultimately be branded "sabbats," were often called "games;" in this context, the word "game" takes on a sense of festive ritualizing. Oriente's cult appears to have emphasized herbal medicine. In 1380, an Inquisitorial trial at Milan condemned the *bona gens*, the "fairies," in this case signifying devotees, of Madona Horiente as witches, and in 1384/1390, also at Milan, Petrina Bugatis of Bripio and Sibillia Zanni were similarly condemned. Petrina was quoted as having confessed that she "believe[d] that Lady Horiens, Mistress of her society, [was] like Christ, who is Lord of the World." Indeed, it was "forbidden to utter the name of Jesus during the meetings." Petrina, who commenced attending gatherings devoted to Madona Oriente when she was sixteen, explained that when devotees went to these gatherings, they often traveled in the guise or forms of animals, particularly donkeys and foxes, indicating a practice akin to shamanism and/or to Germanic "faring forth" by way of the *haminja* or *fylgia*. When they arrived, they greeted the Mistress, probably embodied by or represented by a priestess, with the greeting "May you fare well, Lady Horiens." The priestess, like the Goddess, may have held an apple in her hand as she welcomed devotees. They then participated in various rites, including animal sacrifice and the subsequent revivification of the animals, especially oxen, and feasting at homes of the faithful or their allies. On other occasions, they were instructed in the arts of healing, divination, and magic. Matteo Duni, in *Under the Devil's Spell*, stresses that these accounts "were quickly interpreted by judges as forms of devil-worship, in which Satan had presented himself under various guises to deceive incautious women."

Zobiana

The origins of Zobiana (or, Giubiana, Iobiana) are mysterious and probably multiple. Now an Italian carnivalesque figure, she was apparently a significant "witch-goddess" in the later medieval period and in the Renaissance, perhaps especially during the early fifteenth century, when she was mentioned by Bernardino of Siena (1380-1444). The name appears in Late Antiquity on Roman epitaphs as Iobiana, e.g. "Rest in peace, Iobiana"; ironically, it is associated in this context with early Christians. Some have suggested that her name is linked to Jupiter/Jove and to Thursday, in Italian, *giovedì*, Jove's Day. Beyond Roman origins, she may also possess Celtic roots, as her cult was apparently most prominent, and her present-day carnivalesque appearances most common, in Piedmont and Lombardy and other areas once inhabited by Celts; moreover, several of the other figures appearing with her in her carnivalesque manifestation may be traced to Celtic lore, such as the marine fairy-goddess Ancamna, whose name in Italy is Anguana. From her current depiction as a crone, as well as from her association with winter, one might also surmise that one of her ancestors may be a divinity or similar being resonating with the Celtic Cailleach Beara. It is further conceivable that Zobiana possesses Germanic ancestry, as she manifests in Lombardy, which was also settled by the Lombards, a Germanic people. In this light, especially as she is said to periodically transform herself into a feline, and as she practices a form of magic that might be akin to *seiðr*, she may also be linked to the goddess Freyja. As linked to winter and snow, she may also share a relationship with Holda.

Moreover, if one attempts to disentangle data regarding Zobiana/Giubiana/Iobiana from narratives subjected to demonization and carnivalization, tales that make of her an ugly sorceress who lives in the forest, reminiscent of Baba Yaga and the Witch of "Hansel and Gretel," one may deduce that she, rather more like Artemis/Diana, is fiercely independent, dwells in the wild, and has animals as close companions. One may also deduce that she was most probably fêted on certain Thursdays and in winter, perhaps in late January or early February, and – from a "Hansel and Gretel"-like demonizing legend in which she is seduced by delicious food so that she will not eat a child – that she may, at least in later days, have been offered risotto with saffron and luganega sausage.

It is not surprising that this divinity with mysterious and multiple origins came to be linked to witches. As such, she was considered a mask of the Devil, and her followers, it would appear, were persecuted. Eventually, however, as happened in so many cases, demonization metamorphosed into carnivalization. At present, Zobiana/Giubiana manifests as a gaunt crone wearing long, red stockings and carrying a broom.

Red stockings are significant here; they embrace not only legs but also a great deal of cultural, including sacred and mythical, symbolism. In the Middle Ages, Fsumptuary laws prevented many persons, including Jews and peasants – the latter with which Zobiana resonates – from wearing red stockings, which were generally reserved for noblemen and Church officials (particularly bishops). Troubadours sometimes dared to wear them. When the lusty Wife of Bath dons them in Chaucer's *Canterbury Tales*, they suggest the scarlet of passion, as they will centuries later when John Gay's Blouzelinda, a shepherdess in *The Shepherd's Week*, includes them in her attire. Red stockings may have been worn by the Wife to magically protect her from venereal disease, as they were worn by a "shop girl" in 1908 to prevent her legs from giving out or causing her great pain as she stood and waited on customers all day. Spiritually and mythologically speaking, red stockings are primarily the property of divinities and divinized heroes, like Hercules (shown wearing them in a tapestry), and of Christian angels, as in the early fifteenth-century Italian Festival of the Ascension. In medieval and post-medieval European earth-centered traditions, red stockings are donned by such beings as (the) Strömkarl, a water being who plays a harp or fiddle to seduce young women, and Wodna Zona, the Wendish Lady of the Water. Most recently, they have been worn by the Devil and Dracula.

An effigy of Zobiana/Giubiana is burned at her festival on the last Thursday of January, signifying the death of winter and the coming of spring. She is nowadays compared to La Befana.

Aïa

Aïa (also, Ambriane, Caieta) hails from Gaeta (in antiquity, Caieta), a city in Lazio, central Italy. She may have originated in an ancient goddess, thus we might have discussed her as such. She seems to have been known to Virgil (70-19 BCE) as the wetnurse of Aeneas (whose tomb continued to be shown to travelers in 1721 but the location of which was lost by 1854). Others have linked her to Amas, the wetnurse of Diana, or to Cybele, who was nicknamed "Ammas," which became "Emma," as the wet-nurse of humankind. It is as a medieval and post-medieval, reincarnated or newly manifesting goddess or fairy, however, that Aïa is primarily remembered. Beyond Gaeta, she was revered in much of what is now Italy. Her name may refer to "a woman who governs," although others claim it represents a shortening of "Gaia." She is a tall, beautiful woman dressed in a long, white gown and wearing a white veil. She protects, blesses, and nurtures infants. When one hears cradles or other furniture inexplicably rocking, it may be that Aïa has come to visit. When a mother is too weary, Aïa may lull her infant to sleep.

La Befana

La Befana is a crone who holds the power to bless or punish families, especially children, and who visits mortals during the winter, typically at Epiphany or Twelfth Night (January 6), in Italy. Befana's name derives from the Greek term *epiphaneia*, signifying a visible manifestation of a deity.

Befana is traditionally depicted as an elderly, black-skinned woman with thick lips and red eyes. Today, she is often depicted as a light-skinned woman. She is contradictorily described as toothless and as having sharp teeth of threatening appearance. She is now frequently depicted as a witch riding on a broom. She traditionally wears flowing black garments; nowadays, she may dress in gold, purple, green, or other colors. She alternately holds a lantern, a spindle and distaff, and/or gifts.

She is traditionally represented by a large doll, puppet, mannequin, or statuette made of wood and/or rags and dressed in her customary attire, as well as by those who celebrate her, who dress likewise and who blacken their faces. Fruits sometimes adorn her images' breasts and hips. Representations of her are often held up to lighted windows during her celebration, when they are not being paraded in the streets.

Befana can be cruel – she has been compared to a killer whale – or kind, depending on whether or not those who believe in her behave well or badly during the year; most often, however, even when she punishes, she later shows compassion.

She is said to dwell in the land of Befania, to which she opens the gates at Epiphany. She is sometimes said to dwell within a cave.

Befana has primarily been revered, it would appear, since the Renaissance, and perhaps since the Middle Ages. She may, however, represent a post-antiquity, post-Christianization hypostasis or avatar of a more ancient goddess, or else may represent the coming together of the archetypal energies of several goddesses as well as, perhaps, some Christian personae. Befana has, for example, been described as an avatar of the Great Goddess or Mother Nature. According to Massimo Centini in *Le schiavi di Diana* (1994), one of Befana's alternate names, Marantega, refers to the Mater Antigua, the Ancient Mother. Moreover, she dies as the Crone of Winter to be reborn as the Maiden of Spring, thus representing the ancient triadic relationship of the Maiden, Mother, and Crone.

Indeed, her origins may lie in a form of European shamanism, in which she manifested as a so-called "Bone Mother" or goddess of death-rebirth. Befana has also been linked to the Magna Mater, that is, to the Roman goddess Cybele as well as to Juno and Diana, especially as Diana Epiphanes, that is, as Diana appearing in visible, physical form.

During medieval and post-medieval periods, Befana also came to be identified as "the daughter of Herodias," i.e., Salome, and thereby became linked with another goddess associated with witches and witchcraft. In Venice, by the eighteenth century or perhaps earlier, Befana had come to be called Radòdese, identifying her with Herodias.

Befana is alternately considered a goddess, fairy, or demon – sometimes all at once. As a fairy, she holds "the same place [in Italy] as the queen of the fairies formerly did in England." In a song sung to her, she is described as a "fairy whom many here love." As a demon, she is associated with Lamia and with "she-goblin[s]" and as such is sometimes called Befanaccia.

In more recent times, she sometimes has a husband named Befano or a male consort named Befanino. She is assisted by elf-like beings called Befanotti.

She is believed to manifest as an "epiphany" in the presence of her celebrants; a popular song to her goes:

A fairy whom many here love
Who comes every year to find you
She has come to us, La Befana

Every heart is full of joy
From valleys, villages, countryside
Our Befana
has arrived
…
And as La Befana departs
She wishes all great happiness.[49]

Song lyrics suggest, moreover, that some of her devotees understand themselves as having an intimate relationship with her, much as initiates of Vodou share intimate relationships with certain *lwas* (deities): "Befana Befana/ you are my lady/ you are my wife."

Not surprisingly, Italian Christians have not always depicted Befana in a positive light. She has, as mentioned above, been identified as Salome, the daughter of Herodias. As such, she is said to have watched from her window as the Magi journeyed toward Bethlehem. Moreover, Befana has alternatively been associated with "Herod's grandmother, …the maid of the High Priest who accused St. Peter of belonging to Jesus of Nazareth, …[and] an aunt of Barabbas."

On the other hand, Befana has also been linked to the Magi as a giver of gifts (they are particularly linked by way of the gift of a gilded pine cone). Having missed out on the birth of Jesus, as she annually searches to find him, she brings gifts to children.

She has also been linked to saints, including St. Anthony (as a guardian of animals) and the fictitious Christian Saint Eustachio (Eustace), who appropriated attributes from Diana, especially her stag. Indeed, Befana has even been linked to a manifestation of the Virgin Mary, Santa Maria Aracoeli (St. Mary of the Altar in the Air), who displaced the goddess Juno. In this light, Gaetano Moroni (1840) describes a tribute which, until 1802, "used to be made to the Pope on Epiphany morning by the Collegio de' Novantanove Scrittori Apostolici, consisting of a hundred ducats contained in a silver chalice, and which was called the Befana."

Despite certain Christian associations, celebrations for Befana as a goddess or fairy have continued. Her festival signifies the dying of the old year and the birth of the new, the metamorphosis of the Crone into the Maiden. Celebrations typically include a torchlit procession of the image of Befana through the streets; masked and costumed figures, primarily representing Befana and her entourage, with ceremonial cross-dressing or mixed gender attire and blackening of faces, engaging in playing music (drums, cymbals, trumpets), singing, dancing, feasting, making offerings to Befana (dark bread, ricotta, pecorino, wine), ritually sacrificing (by fire or water) images of Befana, and distributing gifts; and a fair with stalls selling fruits, cookies, and other items.

Following the public celebration, Befana, like Santa Claus, descends into homes via the chimney. Traditionally, she places gifts, including chestnuts, fruits (oranges, apples, pears), candies, and trinkets in stockings attached to the fireplace. Befana's gifts represent "seeds" to encourage growth in the New Year of joy and abundance and likewise signify rebirth. If children are especially naughty, they are given pieces of coal, or else ashes or dust. However, they are often later given gifts. Not to say that coal only represents the negative in regard to Befana; rather, it also "traditionally symbolizes the 'latent energy in the earth,' the 'hidden fire.'" One item which serves as both an offering to and a gift from Befana is the Pefanino, a cookie made in the shape of Befana.

Although many living in the late nineteenth century felt very anxious about "the sweeping away of old customs," in 1885, May Cheney (1862-1942), founder of Cheney's Pacific Coast Bureau of Education in San Francisco, described, in Bret Harte's *Overland Monthly*, her experience of a very much alive Feast of Befana:

> The Eve of Befana was welcomed at Rome with a prodigious beating of tin cans and a deafening noise of tin trumpets. ...The streets were filled to overflowing with a gay crowd of pleasure-seekers, all laughing, talking, and pushing each other along in the direction of the Piazza Navona. Before the afterglow had fairly faded from the sky, torches began to appear in the narrow streets leading out of the Corso, and the blast of trumpets was heard from the piazza.
>
> As the giving of presents, which in England and America takes place on Christmas day, is postponed in Rome until Epiphany, the peasants always hold a fair on the evening preceding. The Piazza Navona has been for years the scene of the display, and thus became the center of the Befana festivities. ... A row of brilliantly-lighted booths enclosed the square, which was filled with a noisy crowd of people, shouting and blowing trumpets in each other's ears. Torches went flying about in every direction. ...
>
> [T]he booths...were filled with knick-knacks of every description. There were carved and painted wooden boxes, brackets, and shelves, gay scarves, cheap jewelry, pins carved out of lava, and, in particular, quantities of coral, a bit of which is worn by every Italian, man, woman and child, as a protection against the baleful influences of the "evil eye"... Some of the booths were given up to small shows. The fronts of these were placarded with pictures of the beauties or monstrosities to be seen within. ...
>
> By far the greater number of the booths, however, were devoted to displays of toys; for this festival is par excellence the children's feast. ...
>
> By nine o'clock the noise and confusion in the piazza became unbearable. For the sons and daughters of the Campagna, hardened by long custom, the fun was just beginning.[50]

In 1982, Stanley Gee, in "Some Notes on Italian Folk Customs," made a remark that I find especially intriguing in our present context; in regard to the great significance of Befana in Italy and her triumph over male gift-giving figures like St. Nicholas, he states: "This is not surprising because the lifestyle of Italy is based on a Matriarchal Society, and even the principal Christian devotions are addressed to the female figure of the Madonna." Gee also recorded a song that celebrates La Befana: When upon "the mountain the snow is falling," Befana arrives, bringing gifts for all. "Friends we shall remain/ And as La Befana departs/ She wishes all great happiness."

Fru Gaue and Fru Herke

Turning toward Germany, Fru Gaue (Frau Gaude; also, Frau/Fru Gaüa, Gaue, Gauden, Go, Goda, Gode, Goden, Godmor, Goeya, Goia, Gol, Gwodan; also, F. Wagen, Waud, Wauf, Wode) is a female parallel to "Godan," a variation on "Odin," with "Wode," etc. referring to "Woden" – is a goddess of the harvest, especially of grain crops, in particular, of rye. "*Fru*" is an intriguing term; in Latin it signifies "corn," while in Norwegian it signifies a "married woman." So it is with "Gaude; "*gauden*" signifies "delight." Gaue (etc.) is sometimes said to be the mother of Thor, also called Eorðe or Godmor. She is sometimes depicted as a crone, typically with thick, unkempt hair and a long nose – although this may be a Christian depiction. As a sometimes sinister divinity, she was euphemistically called "Gode the Good," fearing that to call her "Gode the Goblin" would fuel her wrath. The center of her cult was at Hörselberg. Her "furious ride across the fields of Grabow," accompanied by hounds, in Mecklenburg-Western Pomerania, Germany was thought to promote their fertility. Not surprisingly, Gaue's ride came to be associated or identified with the Wild Hunt of Odin. Gaue continued to be revered in nineteenth-century Mecklenburg at harvest time; a farmers' song to her included, "Fru Gaue, hold your fodder/ this year on the wagon,/ the next year on the cart." We shall have occasion to speak further about this divinity, or one of her close relatives, possessing the kindred name of Godo, when we consider harvest rites.

Fru Herke (also, Arke, Erka, Freen, Freke, Frick, Fricke, Fuik, Häksche, Harf, Harfe, Harke, Harre, Herche, Here), a related goddess or similar being, may have been hybridized with Frigga, Hera, Freyja, and/or Erde at some point. As a latter incarnation of Erce/Erde, she may have been seen as a more generalized Earth-Goddess. She has been called "Lady Rake" or "Lady Knife." She has been demoted, demonized, and folklorized as Pumpernelle, spouse of Pumpernick ("Fart of the Devil") and linked to Pumpernickel bread.

Especially as Häksche, she is associated with witches and witchcraft; in some parts of northern Germany, into the nineteenth century, she was known as "*Die Hexe, de olle Häksche*," that is, "the Witch, Old Häksche."

Beyond teaching women to spin, – into the last years of the nineteenth century, many young German women continued to acknowledge the presence of Herke as they hurried to finish spinning flax before she arrived near the winter solstice– it is Herke who "introduced the cultivation of the turnip." In Saxony-Anhalt, Germany, Herke, traversing the heavens at Christmastime, "flies through the air in the shape of a dove, makes the fields fruitful, carries a stool to sit on." She resides inside the mountain Frau-Harkenberg in Germany.

Holda/Holle

Holda/Frau Holle has been "considered a divinity of much importance." The cult of this divinity appears to have escalated dramatically in the Middle Ages.

Her name may have meant "lovely, kind[,] sweet," or "gracious" prior to Christianization, if this name was in fact used prior to Christianization; its usage by pagans not yet experiencing conversion remains controversial. If, however, this goddess was called "Holda" prior to Christianization, her name, as signifying "gracious," may link her to Freyja, as this is one of the latter's appellations. "The gracious" may have also spoken to her being a goddess or "benign night spirit" embodying the fear of [and/or respect for] the dead."

Christians may, however, have given this name to an ancient goddess and interpreted it to mean one of two things:

(1) an identification with the Biblical persona Hulda the prophetess (d. c. 620 BCE, 2 Kings 22: 14), a descendant of Joshua who lived in Jerusalem during the time of Jeremiah. The Huldah Gates of the southern wall of the Temple Mount are named for her. In Hebrew, her name means "weasel." Although weasels were considered unclean animals, they were also thought to possess psychic insight;

or (2) "Mother Hell." In this interpretation, Holda becomes the spouse, mother, or more often, the grandmother of the Devil. We have much more evidence for this interpretation than for the first. If this is the case, then "Holda" is a derogatory name, tantamount to changing the name of an ancient male, or at times a female, deity to "the Devil" or "Satan" or the name of a beneficent being to a "demon" or "demonic spirit." Aron Gurevitch, in *Medieval Popular Culture: Problems of Belief and Perception*, observes that Church officials considered Holda to be demonic.

In *Dives and Pauper*, an early fifteenth-century encyclopedic commentary on the Ten Commandments which also refers to medieval customs, she is named "Al-holde." Priscilla Heath Barnum, in her explanatory notes on *Dives and Pauper*, suggests that the (possibly mixed) etymology of her name speaks to her identity: "The etymology of the word 'holde' is double-sided, having meanings associated with kindness and fear; in Middle English, 'hold' can mean 'kind' or 'gracious' but in Old English can also mean 'carcass' or 'dead body'."

In his *Corrector*, Burchard (d. 1025) identifies Holda with Diana. We know that the worship of Diana was carried into the region by the Roman legions. For example, in the manner of "*interpretatio Romana*," the cult of an indigenous forest goddess who had at some point been identified with the Gaulish goddess Abnoba now transformed into the hybrid goddess Diana Abnoba, who came to reign over the Black Forest, as evidenced by an altar at the Baths at Badenweiler. In centuries past, commoners and Church authorities alike acknowledged that Holda was a Germanic manifestation of Diana. In this regard, they associated Holda with statues of Diana and with hunting. A statue that, according to legend, was fought over by the inhabitants of Pottendorf and Gera-Untermhaus, which looks most like a statue of Ops, Abundantia, or possibly Cybele, was in past centuries claimed by these people to be a statue of Diana. However, they also insisted that it represented their divinity Holla. The statue was later identified as the Virgin Mary. As such, it appears to have been claimed by and then later discarded and abandoned (in or near 1882?) by Church authorities in Gera-Untermhaus. In brief, it is conceivable that – at least in some places, perhaps especially the Black Forest region of Germany – Holda is identical to Diana Abnoba and that she reflects a Gallo-Roman goddess given a derogatory Christian name.

Burchard, however, also identifies Holda with the Roman Parcae (in German, Parzen). This triad of female divinities of destiny may indicate that Holda may represent a manifestation of the Celtic Matrae, the Germanic Norns or *Disir*, the Greco-Roman Parcae/Moirai/Fates, or a hybrid being drawing upon a couple or all of these.

In her appellation of Frigaholda, she also becomes linked to the Germanic goddess Frigg. She may also correspond to the Anglo-Germanic Hertha. Her nickname "Königin Saligfraulein," roughly, "Blessed Queen," may link her with the goddess Saelde. Holda may have also represented in some sense a metamorphosis of the ancient priestess (or type of priestess,) Veleda. In 1833, Georg Liebusch suggested that Holda might in fact be the goddess Ciwa, worshipped by the Wends in Germany.

Some Christians referred to her as "Holda the Pagan" or as *Strigaholda* ("Witch-Holda") and to her followers as *Strigaholden*.

It is evident that in some times and places in Christianized Germany, devotees of the goddess named "Holda" commenced – perhaps in the mid-ninth century? – honoring her by that name. It has even been suggested that some time later on, some accepted the nickname of "the Devil's Grandmother" (hypernym) and continued to pay her homage as such. This (at least) surface acceptance of names might imply simple masking or more complex hybridizing. Together with the fact that many sacred sites deploying the name "Holda" sprang up, alongside names like "Holdemme," signifying "the nurse/nurturer Holda," it would seem that this acceptance of names might also indicate pagan accommodation and/or resistance, not unlike the present-day acceptance and revision by same-gender-loving persons of the term "Queer." In 1839, Ludwig Wilhelm Schrader went so far as to suggest that the so-called "Witches' Sabbat" did not celebrate the Devil, at least not primarily, but rather Holda as his grandmother – "*seiner Großmutter*!"

Holda is well known for her black hair, alternately depicted as beautiful and flowing, as unkempt, or as matted (perhaps styled in this way). She combs her hair "in the midday sun." She customarily wears gleaming white garments but may also wear green, as the fairies also often do. When she is depicted as having "bristling, matted hair," she resembles the Inuit goddess or similar being Sedna. Of a person who has shaggy hair, it's said, "He has been riding with Holle." The "ugly" Holda may, however, at least in the main, represent a Christian revision of her depiction meant to denigrate, ridicule, and demonize her. Holda is typically "kind and helpful."

Indeed, she is rarely angry or hostile. Several situations, however, can stir her fury, including disorder in household affairs;" disrespect towards her by farmers and others; and abuse of women by men.

When she determines that she and/or her faithful have been slighted or abused, she is thought to be capable of sinister behavior. In this aspect, she is said to instruct practitioners of magic in the arts of stealing milk from farmers' cows and depriving men of virility. In this aspect, she is associated with imps.

Occasionally, Holda is considered as being plural. As such, the 'Holdas' appear as the Brunnenholden, female beings of springs, the Wasserholden, female water beings, or as the Huldre, the "hidden folk." Related to this plurality, Holda is sometimes intimately connected to the *Saligen*, "blessed" female nature beings or fairies who live in the mountains of Austria, Bavaria, and Switzerland; in this connection, Holda is seen as the Fairy Queen.

Holda is sometimes said to dwell within a mountain, particularly within – as is the case with Hörsel – the Hörselberg. As a goddess of springs, she is also said to dwell in wells and in lakes and fountains/wells"}; she likes to "bathe in the midday sun."

As a creator-goddess, she is described as combining "the form of a lovely woman with the trunk of a tree ... a legend of Hesse describes her as being a beautiful woman in front, while behind she resembles a tree." In this regard, trees sacred to her are called Frau Hullibaum; a pond sacred to her, Frau Holles Badeplatz; and a stone sacred to her, Frau Hullistein. She is frequently associated with the rose and is in this regard linked to Frau Rose.

Where animals are concerned, Holda is a guardian of cats, linking her to the goddess Freyja; if a young woman neglects her cat, Holda makes it rain on the night of her wedding. When not riding in a celestial chariot, she is said to ride on a "splendid roan horse" decorated with silver bells that produce a beautiful sound and announce the arrival of the goddess. She is also associated with ladybugs.

As a celestial goddess, she "directs the aerial phenomena;" she is "a being of the sky, begirdling the earth" and a goddess of the moon. She rides in a boat (or a black chariot) amongst the stars, and for this reason, "Holda's street" is another name for the Milky Way. We might recall that Isis also rides in a celestial boat, as do the Egyptian goddesses Hathor and Ma'at, and the Sumerian goddess Inanna, perhaps indicating a relationship between these divinities.

Perhaps the most well known description of Holda, however, is that of a goddess of snow; "when it snows, she is making her bed, and the feathers of it fly." Farmers and rural peasants, into the nineteenth century, would also say when it snowed, "Frau Holle is plucking her geese!" In this capacity, Holda became known as the Lady of the Snow. As such, however, she is a kindly being, unlike the cruel snow queens of Hans Christian Andersen and C. S. Lewis.

A goddess of farming, Holda "imparts fruitfulness to the earth," especially when she "walks around the ploughed land." In this aspect, the ladybug, who must be respected, else she will damage crops, and the cow are two of her sacred attributes. The ladybug is also sometimes seen as the chariot of Holda (or Perchta): "There is a legend of a peasant maiden who was fond of ladybugs, and who was taken to Holda's realm in a carriage drawn by the insects, to be protected during an approaching war, and who, at its close, was sent home with an outfit of fine linen."

Holda is also a patron of vintners. She is especially a patron of women. A guardian of pregnant women and a nurturer of infants, she heals women when they are ill, promotes their fertility, and assists them with childbearing and childrearing. She also instructs them in domestic responsibilities. She takes care of infants who die prior to baptism, the *holden*, who are considered pagans (this suggests, intriguingly, that one is naturally "pagan," that one must be "made" Christian). Her train of followers includes "the souls of the dead, including the souls of children and of babies who have died unbaptized." In this regard, she is a goddess of death and the afterlife or otherworld. Drowning children and adults alike find their way to her joyful home; in her beautiful garden, watered by a celestial river (or, alternatively, in her submarine, paradisal home and garden), abundant with fragrant flowers and delicious fruits, where the stars sparkle, Holda receives the "souls of the deceased" and eventually sends them back to the earth to be reborn as children. She offers those she cares for "flowers, fruit, cakes, and the produce of her incomparable garden." In this aspect as a goddess of the cycle of death/rebirth, Holda's sacred bird is the stork, who carries souls of those to be reborn to expectant mothers.

Those who sojourn with Holda/Holle do not always experience death/rebirth while in her care. For example, a tale is told that a girl who loved to play in the forest was swept up by Holda during a war and was cared for by her until the war's end several years later, when Holda returned the young woman to earth to be married.

She also presides over the cultivation of flax and spinning, rewarding women who spin well and punishing those who exhibit laziness when spinning. She prohibited spinning during her winter festival; at this time young women were supposed to rest. Catherine Rager, in *Dictionnaire des Fées et du peuple invisible dans l'occident païen.* (2003), suggests that this notion may have partly inspired the tale of "Sleeping Beauty." When Holda is displeased with women because they either do not spin when they should or do when they shouldn't, she is likely to pull down their bed sheets when they're sleeping.

Holda also serves as a dispenser of destiny and as Queen of elves and dwarves. When travelers are lost in the forest, she provides illumination and guides them home or to their destination. She is a goddess of healing; she is believed to care for the ill and disabled in her mountain cave. She also blesses new houses and households.

Like other divinities, Holda is associated with certain sacred sites. One of the most significant of these is Externsteine (or. Egesterensteyn, Eggesterstein, Eghesterenstene), a natural rock formation of five limestone (others claim sandstone) pillars in the Teutoburg Forest (Teutoburger Wald) in northwestern Germany. Rituals may have commenced there as early as the Paleolithic. They appear to have focused on revering deities and on tracking solar, lunar, and other celestial movements. Holda – together with Mithra, Odin, and Ostara/Eostre – is thought to have been worshipped there. Nature – stones, trees, and snakes – appears to have also been venerated there. The worship of Holda and other pagan deities was forbidden there from about 772 CE onward. In the ninth century, it commenced to be occupied by Christian monks. Its pagan use was acknowledged seven centuries later by Hermann Hamelmann. Unfortunately, its reputation was somewhat marred by Nazi veneration of the site; archaeologist Wilhelm Teudt (1860-1942) and others desired to resacralize it as a sacred grove. Today, however, it has become a "sacred destination" for Pagan pilgrims.

Another sacred site of Holda was Hollenteich, or Holle's Pond, in what is now Naturpark Meissner-Kaufunger Wald, on the Hohe Meissner Mountain, in Hesse, Germany. Here, the goddess sometimes manifested as a beautiful woman bathing. Into the nineteenth century, women "seek[ing] health and fecundity" would gather there. They would pray for fertility and to become pregnant. Newborns were taken there to be blessed. Cattle were taken there to be purified. It was thought that Holda/Holle's paradise lay at the bottom of Hollenteich. Roman coins found in the pond suggest that the site has been used for rituals since ancient times, perhaps to a Roman goddess. Nearby is a strange volcanic formation called Kitzkammer; it is formed from volcanic rock, specifically, columns of basalt. Its shape has been compared to a vagina, it is associated with cats, and it is thought to be another entrance into the realm of Holle. Yet another nearby site is Hollenstein, the largest cave in Hesse, also thought to be a gateway into Holle's realm. Offerings of apples, elderberries, and oak branches continue to be brought to Hollenstein.

Holda is also thought to have been patron of the town of Baldenburg/Biały Bór, in West Pomerania, Poland.

Holda was/is especially revered in late winter or in early spring. When she awakens from a winter nap, and spring is emerging, it is vital that not only that humans arise but that plants be awake to receive and honor her; "Tree, wake up! Frau Holla comes! (*"Baumelten wach auf, Frau Holla kommt!"*), "Tree, sleep not, Frau Holla comes! (*"Bäumchen schlaf nicht, Frau Holla kommt!"*), farmers would chant as they shook fruit trees. Otherwise, Holda would not shower the trees with her blessings.

She was/is also remembered in late autumn near Halloween, and during the winter solstice. At these times, she was/is offered flowers, fruits, fruitcakes and apple pies, meats, and other foods. One of the most popular dishes associated with her is *Schmalnudeln*, a sort of beignet or doughnut (without a hole), often filled with cheese. Some say that in the past, sacrifices of pigs and oxen were made to her; after these sacrifices, Holda sheltered the spirits of the animals, who sometimes appeared as ghosts in the mountains. Processions and dances are held in her honor.

Near Halloween, Holda leads the Wild Hunt and troops of witches. During the Middle Ages, Holda came to be associated with, and occasionally identified with, Abundia, Herodias, and other divinities linked to witchcraft.

Indeed, she appears to have been the central divinity of a cult of wisewomen/

witches. During and after the eleventh century, Holda, particularly as Striga Holda, became increasingly linked to witches. In this more sinister guise, she may appear as a horned goddess, and she is accompanied by bats and crows. Holda and witches are linked geographically by way of her appearances in the vicinity of Hexenlinde (the Witches' Linden Tree) and Hexentanzplatz (Witches' Dancing Place), which are located near Mount Hohenzollern in southern Germany; and by way of an old saying of inhabitants of Wildemann in the Harz mountains regarding snowfall, Holda, and witches: "The old witch is in the Brocken."

During the last days of December and the first days of January, she travels about in a wagon over the earth, dressed in calfskin, holding a magic wand, and bringing prosperity and gifts. It is thought that gifts offered to her are turned into, and returned as, gold to those who have faithfully and lovingly offered them. During the last days of the year, women as well as men dressed in feminine attire, all carrying brooms, would, in Holda's name, travel from house to house, blessing families and distributing gifts. Oftentimes, a particular woman would represent or embody the goddess; clad in a white robe, cap, and veil, she would distribute gifts including apples and nuts. It has been suggested that decorating fir trees originated as a rite honoring Holda.

Holda appears to have been honored into (at least) the nineteenth century. In the sixteenth century, the Christian zealot Martin Luther (1483-1546) raged against the reverence of Frau Holda, remarking on her fiddle-playing and her 'tremendous' nose. In Christian lore, Holda, not surprisingly, was transformed into a demonic spirit, mistress of witches; if Grimm is correct in this, however, it took several centuries, possibly until the Renaissance, for the Church to succeed in its metamorphosis of Holda and her followers into the Devil and his minions. Paradoxically, Holda was also Christianized as the Virgin Mary in her aspect of Our Lady of the Snows (probably around or after the fourteenth century; Notre-Dame-aux-Neiges, at Aurillac, France [also known as Notre-Dame de la Conception et Notre-Dame d' Aureinques and bearing likeness to Notre-Dame du Puy] is a well-known Black Madonna), primarily because of associations with snow and with nurturing children; Holda has also been Catholicized as well as, according to some, St. Ursula, St. Martha, and St. Agnes. In some places, her festival was displaced by that of St. Thomas, as "Thomasnacht;" in others, by the Nativity of Christ.

In 1630, a German man accused of witchcraft confessed to having ridden with Frau Holle in the Wild Hunt. At this time, the goddess was said to have been attended by a pagan priest or priestess. The historian Johann Georg von Eckhart (1664/1674-1730), in his preface to Gottfried Wilhelm Leibniz's *Collectanea Etymologia* (1717), observes that German peasants living in the vicinity of Meissen (the home of Dresden china) in Saxony continued to pay homage to Holda (as Fraueholde or Fraue Faute [Lady Fate]) at that time. Sometime during the eighteenth century, or so it was told, a drunken man became lost as he was rambling through the woods in Bavaria. When the goddess attempted to guide him with her light, he yelled, "Go away, you scumbag, you witch! Did I ask you to shine on me?!" The light ceased. Somehow, he made his way to an inn. A man escorted him home. He suddenly fell ill with a high temperature and died before dawn.

In the nineteenth century, she began to be displaced – very unfortunately, in the eyes of some – by Christkind/Santa Claus. In spite of a certain degree of Christian denigration, demonization, and carnivalization of her character, however, she continued to be celebrated "in Thuringian and Hessian, as well as in Markish and Frankish tradition." In 1819, G. Reimar wrote, "She is a pleasant and friendly goddess, but she can also be forbidding and terrifying ... at Christmas ... she goes out into the world, rewards and punishes ... she is the great mother of the mountains, an earth goddess."

Rural feasts continued to be celebrated in her honor. Certain farmers in Hesse, Germany, continued to believe that Holda/Holle paid an annual visit to farms, rewarding those who remained faithful to her with abundant crops, and destroying the crops of those who neglected her or turned against her.

During this period, Holda/Holle also transformed into the fairy tale character Frau Holle/Mother Holle. The Grimm's' tale "Mother Holle," also titled "Old Mother Frost," preserves and transmits significant information concerning Holda. It stresses the themes of Holda as a goddess of snow, domestic work, and abundance; her paradisal home beneath the water; her associations with apples, birds and feathers, and snow; and her insistence that women spin, bake bread, gather fruits, and perform other tasks if they wish to be rewarded (with "roast and baked meat every day" and with gold) rather than punished. "What are you afraid of, my child?" Holle asks a young woman who has discovered her cottage; "Stop with me: if you will put all things in order in my house, then shall all go well with you; only you must take care that you make my bed well, and shake it tremendously, so that the feathers fly; then it snows upon earth. I am 'Old Mother Frost.'"

Several German films have treated the narrative of Holda. In 1964, *The Twilight Zone*, in an episode titled "The Bewitchin' Pool," paid tribute – unknowingly? or had Serling done his homework?) to Holda in the figure of Aunt T, a kindly, elderly wisewoman whose home can be reached by abused and neglected children by way of a swimming pool or, presumably, another body of water. In her paradise home, children are set to enjoyable tasks and delight in delicious desserts.

In 2004, a statue honoring the goddess, carved from wood by Viktor Donhauser and his son Ilya, was erected in the vicinity of Hollenteich. In 2006, Dennis and Wolfgang Dovidat founded the Consulate of Frau Holle Land, which holds festivals and tours. In 2007, Christianity and the reverence of Holda came together as a rite, including a festive celebration as well as a mass for women executed as witches and a formal apology from a Christian priest, was held at the foot of the Hohe Meissner.

Perchta/Bertha

Perchta, also known as Bertha, shares much in common with Holda and has been compared to Hecate. She has also been linked to Isis, Diana, Habundia (Abonde), Phinzen, Sack Semper, and Satia. Her cult appears to have emerged in the Middle Ages, especially in Alsace, Austria, Bavaria, Bohemia, Moravia, Swabia, and Switzerland. Germanics, most probably the Winnili/Lombards, carried her cult to Italy.

Her name means "the shining one," "bright, luminous, glorious;" as such, she is depicted as wearing "snow-white garments" (she is sometimes clad in half black, half white attire, which may signify life and death). This depiction, together with her role as mother of dwarves and/or trolls may have partly inspired the tale of "Snow White." Alternatively, she wears a blue dress.

As a beautiful woman, she is called Schönpercht.

She is alternatively portrayed as Ugly Percht (Schiachpercht), having shaggy hair and a tail. Sometimes she is depicted with a long, beaklike nose, as a kind of avian goddess. In her related hypostasis as Schnabelpercht, with a beaklike nose and swan- or goose-like feet, she may be – together with other divinities including Hera, Aphrodite, and Diana, who was in Toulouse called the "Queen with the Goose Foot" – an ancestress of Mother Goose. Unsurprisingly, Christians preferred to depict her as "Ugly Percht" or even as Teufelsmutter, the "Devil's Mother."

She sometimes wears green or yellow shoes and carries keys (like Hecate), flowers, or a spinning wheel. As Wild Perchta, she lives in the forest, sometimes within a cave, or on a mountain; she prefers these environments to those of farm or household.

She is a goddess of earth who promotes fertility of the land. Her sacred flowers are the daisy, the forget-me-not, associated with blue eyes and with treasures, and the primrose. M. D. Conway (1870) relates:

> Bertha [/Perchta] entices some favored child by exquisite primroses to a doorway overgrown with flowers. This is the door to an enchanted castle. When the key-flower [i.e., the primrose, *Schlüsselblume*] touches it, the door gently opens, and the favored mortal passes to a room with vessels covered over with primroses, in which are treasures of gold or jewels.[51]

The goat is her sacred animal, and she sometimes transforms into or embodies a goat. However, breads or cakes offered to her in the form of deer antlers, *Hirzehörnli* or *Perchisbrod*, suggest that the deer may also be especially sacred to her.

Like Holda, Perchta is a patron of spinners and presides over all work in the home. She will stamp on those who spin during her festival, hence her nickname "Frau Stempe" (or, Stampa) – which might also refer to a type of dance emulating this action. She is also, however, considered a patron and ancestress of royal families.

She is a goddess of night; Claude Lecouteux notes: "Percht is ... a personification of *giberahta na[c]ht*, Old High German for 'transfigured night.'" She is Queen of the elementals, or alternatively, the souls of unborn (or deceased, not yet reborn) children, known as *Heimchen*. She also watches over children; in this capacity, she is called Kinderfrau, "Nanny."

One of those occasions on which she appears is at the time of death; thus, she is, like Holda, a goddess of death and rebirth. In this hypostasis, she is often called the White Lady; as such, Perchta bears likeness to the Irish banshee or the Mexican la Llorona or Santissima Muerte; she "appears in many houses, when a member of the family is about to die." She also appears at crossroads and elsewhere to travelers and hikers who are destined to die. She has been known to appear when German rulers are near death; a nineteenth-century account reads:

> The dusk of evening has fallen over Berlin. A great yet silent crowd is rapidly moving through the chief street towards the royal palace, and every now and then a low whisper is heard, in which can be distinguished the words: " The King is very ill." In the palace itself yet greater silence reigns. The King's guardsmen stand motionless, the servants' steps are inaudible on the carpets of the corridors and the rooms. Now the tower clock strikes midnight; all at once a door opens, and through it glides a ghostly woman, tall of stature, queenly of bearing.
>
> She is dressed in a trailing white garment, a white veil covers her head, below which her long flaxen hair hangs, twisted with strings of pearls; her face is deathly pale as that of a corpse. In her right hand she carries a bunch of keys, in her left a nosegay of Mayflowers. She walks solemnly down the long corridor. The tall guardsmen present arms, pages and lackeys give way before her, the guards who have just relieved their comrades open their ranks ; the figure passes through them, and goes through a folding door into the royal ante-room.
>
> "It is the White Lady; the King is about to die," whispers the officer of the watch, brushing a tear from his eye.
>
> "The White Lady has appeared," is whispered through the crowd, and all know what that portends.
>
> At noon the King's death was known to all. "Yes," said Master Schneckenburger, " he has been gathered to his fathers. Mistress Berchta has once more announced what was going to happen, for she can foretell everything, both bad and good. She was seen before the misfortunes of 1806, and again before the battle of BelleAlliance. She has a key with which to open the door of life and happiness. He to whom she gives a cowslip will succeed in whatever he undertakes."
>
> Schneckenburger was right. It was Bertha, or Berchta, who made known the King's approaching death...[52]

Perchta is primarily fêted during late autumn and winter. She takes part in the Wild Hunt, and during the last days of the old year and/or the first ones of the new, she drives about in a wagon over the earth, inspecting households for order and cleanliness and distributing gifts. As she drives over the earth, gold chips fall from her wagon. Likewise, when a human repairs her chariot, he or she is paid in gold.

During her winter celebration, typically held from around December 30 until its culmination on January 5 or 6 (as Bechtelistag, Berchtetag, Berchtoldstag, Perchtentag, or Pertennacht), she is often impersonated by young men dressed in her costume, in the past sometimes over three hundred young men, roving the streets. This attire may include wearing calfskin and cowbells (or they may be accompanied by cowbells), suggesting her bovine manifestation.

Feasting the goddess Perchta rose dramatically from the thirteenth through fifteenth centuries and continued, on a lesser scale, into at least the early twentieth century. In 1350 and again in 1468, Church authorities condemned feasts held for Perchta. Motz notes that "a sermon of the fifteenth century censures those who still believe that Diana, 'commonly known as Fraw Percht,' is wont to wander through the darkness with her throng." In certain places in the Alps those devoted to Perchta continued to leave offerings of crepes for her on the evening of January 5 and lit candles to guide her to their homes in the late nineteenth and early twentieth centuries.

Traditionally speaking, women spend a great deal of time preparing her feast. She is offered fish (typically herring or carp) and porridge. The special porridge, covered with a layer of honey, is called *Bachlkoch*; all members of a household including servants taste it in her honor. She is also offered wine, bread, cheese, meats, eggs, dumplings or noodles, and cakes or doughnuts. Lotte Motz notes that in the past, "fried cakes would be placed on the roofs of Tyrolean houses, milk and dumplings held in readiness for her and her 'children.'" Milk of which she tastes that remains after she has drunk of it is called *Perschtmilch* and is considered to have the power to heal, and thus is fed to poultry and cattle.

Perchta was increasingly denigrated, demonized, and carnivalized by Christians. On the other hand, some of her traits were appropriated for St. Margaret and St. Nicholas.

For a very long time, the French, who also revered her, would speak of the 'good old days' when "Berthe spun," "*au temps que la pure Berthe filait.*"

Hörsel

Hörsel appears to have been revered by Thuringians of central Germany and others from the early Middle Ages onward. Her name may have come from the mountain where she resides, the Hörselberg, situated between Eisenach and Gotha in Thuringia, as it has been variously suggested that it derives from *Ursa*, signifying a bear; from a word meaning "grazing," speaking of the goddess' connection to the earth, grains, and/or agriculture; from a word meaning "hearing," referring to mysterious sounds that have been heard coming from the mountain; or from a Sanskrit root meaning "burning" or "bright," referring to her own luminescence or else uncanny lights that have been observed on the mountain. Some said that at night, one could hear weird wailing or else demonic laughter emanating from the Hörselberg. In 1398, an incident which today might be interpreted as a 'close encounter,' involved "three great fires in the air, which presently ran together into one globe of flame;" these objects then "parted again and finally sank into the Hörselberg."

Hörsel is typically depicted as a beautiful, fair-skinned woman of small stature wearing a cap like that worn by ancient Phrygians. She is a goddess of the moon who sails the celestial seas in a ship, accompanied by her handmaidens, the stars.

Among her attributes are the mandrake and the owl, suggesting that her concerns may have included fertility, wisdom, and magic, and perhaps also the mystery of death/rebirth. She sometimes takes the form of Tutosel, "the magical Night-owl who leads her wild company of Valkyries through the air at night." As such, she may have also been linked to battle and fate. She also appears to have been linked to comets, as she is can manifest as "fires in the air." She "helps heavily-loaded wagons up the hills and brings fruitfulness and blessings to young and old." With some who are faithful to her, she grants treasures that she stores in the mountain. She is said to welcome the souls of the dead. Offerings have been made to her near or in a mountain spring or in the River Hörsel, a tributary of the River Werra, which may in turn link Hörsel to the divinity Frau Werra.

Hörsel has been linked to goddesses including Isis, Venus, Freyja, Frigga, Holda, and Fru Gaue. Like Isis, Venus, Holda, and several other goddesses, Hörsel's Catholic guise is that of St. Ursula. As St. Ursula, her handmaidens, the stars, and/or her "wild company of Valkyries" is transformed into a entourage of 11,000 virgins, suggesting that Hörsel may have been a special patron of women.

She has also transmogrified into a folkloric figure, "Old Urschel." In this manifestation, she is sometimes seen as a less powerful figure who has been cursed by an evil magician deploying the so-called *Seventh Book of Moses* and who must be assisted by a young male hero.

During the period of the witch trials, the Hörselberg became known not only as a gathering place of sinister witches and the very home of the Devil.

Phinzen, Sack Semper, and Rupfa

Phinzen was venerated in southern Germany, including Bavaria, and in Austria. She is a patron of women and of spinning. Her name derives from a Greek term meaning "fifth day," and she is thus patron of Thursday; in Bavaria, Thursday is named after her. Her devotees were sometimes known as the Donnerstagsfrauen, the "Thursday women." They were also known as Pfinzdaweibli, which may be translated as "Phinzen's women." Over time, she became linked to a female figure called Sack Semper. She may have been celebrated several times a year, including in January – in this regard, she came to be linked to the Germanic goddess Perchta – and in late winter or early spring, near what is now Carnival-time. During Phinzen's festival in late winter or early spring, people acknowledged her great power over all things, suggesting that she may have originally been a "great" or earth goddess. Also during her festival, women seem to have "ruled the roost."

Sack Semper appears to have multiple roots; like many goddesses of the medieval and later periods, she is of mixed heritage. She may have emerged as a transformed, local variant of the Germanic goddess Frigga. She has been compared to other goddesses emerging in the Middle Ages including Habundia, Holda, and Perchta/Berchta. Beyond these comparisons, she may have been associated with light. In a Christianized milieu, her persona became conflated with that of Saint Simpert of Augsburg (750-818); it may indeed have been his name that was appropriated for her rather than the other way around, suggesting that her original name had perhaps been lost. It is possible that her name is derived from an appropriation of the Christian concept of "saint" combined with the goddess Perchta/Berchta ("Sankt Berchta") and the Christian Saint Simpert, thus transmogrifying from "Sanktbert" to "Sankt-Sempert" to "Sack Semper." She was celebrated in early January and, likely due to her identification with St. Simpert, on October 13th.

Like Phinzen, Rupfa was a goddess or similar being of women and spinning, with her main attribute being the *spinnrocken*, or distaff. She was venerated in Germany, especially in Bavaria, and in Austria. Also like Phinzen, she was fêted primarily in late winter or early spring and thus in Christianized times with Carnival. During her festival, women respected her by ceasing their spinning.

Frau Rose

Frau Rose is also known as Mutter Rose ("Mother Rose") and Alte Mutter Rose ("Old Mother Rose"), as well as Möder Taersche. As the last, she dwindled into a figure in a game played by girls in the nineteenth century.

Some have seen her as a medieval manifestation of the goddess Freyja. She has also been likened to or identified with Holda. She may have further corresponded to other divinities including Aphrodite/Venus, Krasopanj, Lada, and Simerzla, and with attributes of love, beauty, fertility, and the dawn. Not surprisingly, her sacred flower is the rose. By way of the rose, She may have also been linked to Herodias. Her association with the rose also links her to a number of fairy tales including "Sleeping Beauty" (or, "Briar-Rose") and "The Beauty and the Beast." She has been Catholicized as the Virgin Mary, particularly as Mary the Mother of God or the Mater Dolorosa (the Grieving Mother).

Jecha and Bil

The existence of a cult of Jecha among Thuringians is controversial. Those who favor her existence and cult describe her as a goddess of the wilderness and the hunt, with her name sometimes being related to *Jagd*, "hunt." Others, including Ludwig Ettmüller, have linked her name to *jaehe*, suggesting rapidity, and/or to *jehen* (Middle High German), suggesting discoursing. In "Das Thüringer Königreich" (2001), Rüdiger Gebser describes Jecha as a goddess of the hunt as well as of poetry; in his view, Thuringians transformed the ancient cult of Diana into that of Jecha. Some, however, have seen her as a latter-day embodiment of the ancient Germanic priestess, or type of priestess, Veleda. Numerous place-names including Jecha and Jechaburg, two of several villages comprising the district town of Sondershausen in Thuringia, lend support to the existence of a cult of Jecha.

In regard to Bil, the novelist, dramatist, and librarian Christian August Vulpius (1762-1827), whose sister was married to the writer Johann Wolfgang von Goethe (1749-1832), lists Bil together with other divinities revered in Germany, which suggests that she was not considered merely a folk figure. She, together with her brother Hjúki, assists Máni, the Moon, on his nightly journey. Bil is sometimes associated with the goddess of history, wisdom, Sága, at other times with Iðun, the goddess of immortality, with "Bil-Iðun's Way" being a Germanic name for the Milky Way. Just as Hjúki controls the waxing moon, so Bil controls the waning moon. Some believe that the myth of Bil and Hjúki gave rise to the nursery rhyme of "Jack and Jill."

Eostre/Ostara

Although the goddess Eostre/Ostara may have been worshipped in antiquity, her cult appears to have reemerged or escalated dramatically during the Middle Ages, particularly in Germany and in England among Anglo-Saxons. Most of the information – and it is exceedingly scant – that we have concerning Eostre derives from Bede in the eighth century CE: "Eosturmonath has a name which is now translated 'Paschal month,' and which was once called after a goddess of theirs named Eostre, in whose honour feasts were celebrated in that month. Now they designate that Paschal season by her name, calling the joys of the new rite by the time-honoured name of the old observance."

R. T. Hampson, in *Medii aevi Kalendarium; or, Dates, Charters, and Customs of the Middle Ages, with Kalendars from the Tenth to the Fifteenth Century* (1841), relying on Bede, notes, "The name of Easter is clearly traced to that of Eostre, a goddess to whom the Saxons and other northern nations sacrificed." Some view her existence as controversial; indeed, some have accused Bede of *inventing* her. Beyond the rather obvious question as to *why a Christian scholar would want to invent a pagan goddess* – if not simply to demonize a female divinity or to cannibalize pagan Goddess reverence as Barbara Newman has done – Henleigh Wedgwood and John Christopher Atkinson, in discussing Bede's suggestion that the Church might have appropriated the goddess Eostre's name and festival for Christianity, state in *A Dictionary of English Etymology* (1872):

> The reasons for doubting the authority of Bede upon such a point are very slight, the main objection instanced by Adelung being the unlikelihood that the name of a pagan deity should be transferred to a Christian feast. But the same thing seems to have taken place with the term Yule, which from designating the midwinter feast of the pagans was transferred to the Christian feast of the Nativity.[53]

Her name may be derived from Old Norse *ast*, "love," and she may thus be associated with Freyja. However, it may also be derived from terms signifying the east and the dawn. In this regard, she may be somehow linked to Ushas and Aurora, the beautiful Vedic and Roman goddesses of dawn, as well as to Ashtaroth/Astarte. She has also been seen as either akin to or identical to Holda. She is described not only as a goddess of dawn and springtime but also as a ruler of earth and the moon, and a goddess of love as well as of war and peace. Her festival was in March or April (or both), hence the month's Anglo-Saxon name Ostermonat. Eostre's cult appears to have been connected not only with sacred stones but also with plants including the beech tree.

Elements of the festival may have including dancing, lovemaking, and foolishness. Offerings to her include gingerbread cakes.

Place-names including Ostenholz, Osterhagen, Osterrode, and Osterwald in Lower Saxony, and Esterberg, Osterberg, Osterhöfen, Osternohe, the brook of Osterbach, and the Osterloch cave in Bavaria strongly lend support to her cult's existence. Moreover, the Externsteine has been considered a sacred site of Ostara's/Eostre's cult.

Theologian and scholar of early archaeology Karl Wilhelmi (1786-1857) suggested that her cult was served by wisewomen or witches who were later demonized and became, thanks to the Church's efforts, evil women who attended services for the Devil.

In *Asgard and the Gods* (1902), returning to the Externsteine stones, which we have previously noted in regard to the reverence of Holda, we read:

There are no legends about the goddess of spring. One monument alone, and that a newly discovered one, remains of the old worship, the Extern-stones [i.e., Externsteine], which are to be found in the Teutoburg Forest at the northern end of the wooded hills. It is stated in the chronicle of a neighbouring village, dating from last [i.e., nineteenth] century, that the ignorant peasantry were guilty of many misdemeanours there when doing honour to the heathen goddess Ostara/Eostre. Had the clergyman only told us whether there were processions, dances, feasts, scattering of flowers, or any other kind of sacrifice, a clear light might have been shed over the manner in which the goddess was worshipped. Still, this fact proves that not only the name, but also the worship of Ostara was kept in the memories of the people for hundreds, perhaps thousands, of years, and shows how deeply rooted it was. The rocks may perhaps have been called Eastern or Eoestern-stones, and may have been dedicated to Ostara. There, as elsewhere, the priests and priestesses of the goddess probably assembled in heathen times, scattered Mayflowers, lighted bonfires, slaughtered the creatures sacrificed to her, and went in procession on the first night of May, which was dedicated to her. Very much the same as this used to be done at Gambach, in Upper Hesse, where, as late as thirty years ago even [i.e., circa 1870], the young people went to the Easter-stones on the top of a hill, every Easter, and danced and held sports. Edicts were published in the eighth century forbidding these practices ; but in vain, the people would not give up their old faith and customs. Afterwards the priestesses were declared to be witches, the bonfires, which cast their light to great distances, were said to be of infernal origin, and the festival of May was looked upon as the witches' sabbath.[54]

Unfortunately, during the twentieth century, the name of Ostara was marred by extreme nationalists and Nazis. In 1919, a NeoPagan cult naming itself "Ostara" advocated not only nudity – which would have been fine in and of itself – but also excessive nationalism, racism, and classism. The Nazis named one of their anti-Semitic journals after her. It strikes me as tremendously unjust, however, that Ostara should be condemned or brushed aside because the Nazis appropriated her and contaminated her sacrality, as they appropriated and contaminated so many sacred personae, symbols, and rites.

Pharaildis/Vronelde and Anne Marie Jacqueline

Pharaildis is a goddess or similar being native to Belgium and the Netherlands as well as the patron saint of Belgium. She has been compared to Holda. She is associated with a cult of sacred stones, and the goose appears to be her sacred animal. She may be a patron of birds as well as of women and children and of healers. She is linked to both the harvest and with winter, the latter suggested by her saint's day, January 4th. In the Netherlands, the Milky Way has been described as the "street of Vrouelde," Vroueldenstraat. It is difficult to tell when the identities of the Goddess or similar being and saint began to merge, although a date of around 1100 CE has been suggested. Pharaildis may, like Perchta and others, also be an ancestress of Mother Goose.

In Belgium, Anne Marie Jacqueline appears to have been an eighteenth-nineteenth local manifestation of a divinity of earth, winter, fertility, abundance, and gift-giving resembling several other divinities including Holda, Fru Gaude, and Befana. She also appears to have been associated with a children's nursery rhyme game called in English "the Lady of the Land."

Saelde and Chlungeri

A Germanic, predominantly Swiss, goddess or similar being of destiny and/or fortune, Saelde, like the Roman goddess Fortuna, possesses or rides on a wheel. Saelde appears to have emerged during the medieval period, probably sometime between the fifth and eighth centuries. Her name probably means "blessed." Like the Norns, she attends births and blesses infants. She not only possesses the gift of prophecy but also those of telepathy, protecting soldiers from harm, and "transporting herself whither she will." Grimm writes of her: "Saelde ... bends her face toward her favorites, hearkens to them (as a god hears prayer) ... is kind and obliging, but can be cross; those ... she forgets, shuns ... she [like other gods and goddesses, has] a road." She 'clothes' people in their destinies, making them garments of "sorrow and high courage."

The cult of Saelde appears to have been largely appropriated by Christians, who, sometime around 800 CE, would seem to have transformed her from a goddess into a concept signifying the Biblical God's blessing of certain faithful persons with health, good fortune, and love, as exemplified by Ottfrid's *Evangelienbuch* of the mid-ninth century and Walther von der Vogelweide's poetry of the late twelfth and early thirteenth centuries. Moreover, her name continued to be invoked during baptismal rites. Motz, notes, however, that a "woman was exiled from the town of Bern [in Switzerland] in the sixteenth century after she had admitted to having ridden with Frow Selden in the *Wüttisheer* [i.e., the Wild Hunt]."

Another predominantly Swiss goddess or similar being is Chlungeri. She appears to have been a crone-goddess. Her cult appears to have been centered in the vicinity of Zurich. She is, like so many others, a patron of spinning, and was, like others, fêted during the winter solstice. At this time, women ceased spinning to honor her; if they did not do so, Chlungeri punished them. Like many other goddesses, she has suffered demonization and carnivalization over the centuries, nowadays being depicted as a hunchbacked old woman with a large nose and claw-like fingernails.

Zlota Baba, Frau Werra, Pehtra Baba, Dodola

Several Slavic female divinities appear to have emerged during the medieval or later periods. Zlota Baba, "the Golden Crone," is a goddess of travelers and a guardian of grandchildren. Zlota Baba is depicted as an elderly woman holding two babies, or, alternatively, one infant thought to be her granddaughter. The finest reindeer were sacrificed to her. Although some, like Sigismund von Herberstein (1486-1566), have seen her cult as legendary rather than factual, it is mentioned in the narrative of the Russian monk Stefan (St. Stephen of Perm, 1340-1396) in the *Nikonian Chronicle* as one of the cults he was determined to destroy. Russian scholars of the late nineteenth century stated that "[a]ll her temples were destroyed by Stephen the preacher of Christianity in 1389." Her cult, however, appears to have continued into the sixteenth century, as documented by Olaus Magnus in his *Description of the Northern People* (1555): "[A] statue has been set up by the public highway ... [of] Zlota Baba ... 'the little old woman of gold'. Individual travelers seek to propitiate it with certain small presents, even if they are worth a mere trifle. Otherwise, they imagine they will have no safety in the journey they have undertaken." Some years later, Alessandro Guagnino (fl. 1560), an Italian officer from Verona in the military service of Poland, observed: "And in this region of Obdoria [roughly, Siberia] to the mouth of the River Obba is an ancient idol carved of stone, Zolota Baba, that is to say, 'the Old Woman of Gold,' as the Muscovites refer to it." In 1803, François Joseph Michel Noël wrote of her and her cult:

> The Slavs looked at this goddess as the mother of the gods. Her temple was in a meadow near the river Obigo. Her statue

was of gold, or at least gilded; she held in her arms a child, one believed to be her granddaughter: she was surrounded by very noisy musical instruments; she delivered oracles…by way of her priests. No one dared to approach her without bringing her a present; and, [if one had no gift to offer,] then one removed one's garments and deposited them at her feet as an offering, while bowing to the earth, and trying thus to obtain her favor.[55]

Offerings to Zlota Baba not only included garments but also clippings of hair. Christian August Vulpius suggested in 1827 that the statue might have been engineered to produce certain trumpet-like sounds meant to strike awe in the hearts of devotees. She is said to be the mother of the gods Bielibog and Czernabog. From the description given by Noël, it would seem that her cult dissipated sometime between 1600 and 1800.

Wends, together with others living in what is now Germany, especially in the Voightland of Saxony, may have also venerated Frau Werra, a patron of flax and spinning and of baking. Her name may connote someone who lives near a fence, which resonates with the concept of the witch as a "fence-sitter" or "hedge-rider," a haegtesse; and ultimately, Werra became synonymous with "witch." The Werra River in Thuringia, Germany may be named after her. It appears that she was sometimes nicknamed "the Devil's Grandmother" (hypernym).

From a persistent rite involving "tossing [a] little spade for scraping [a] ploughshare into the air" around the time of the spring equinox "and then sticking it in the earth at the spot where it [falls]," it might be fairly safely deduced that Pehtra Baba (also, Šalobarda) was originally a Slovenian earth-goddess. Over time, she became linked to or synonymous with Zlota Baba. She also became linked to, and appropriated some of the traits and attributes of, Perchta/Berchta. She also came to be nicknamed Bela Gospa, the "White Lady," and as such, became Queen of the White Ladies, i.e., the Fairy Queen. She was Christianized as St. Lucia.

Finally, let us not forget Dodola. A divinity of rain, she may conceivably be related to the thunder goddesses Perperuna, the spouse of Perun, and Perkûne, the spouse of Perkûnas. She is invoked by those desiring rain. "When there was a drought," a group of young women "would go dancing from house to house, singing as they went songs" which included invocations to Dodola, such as "Oi, Dodo, Dodole," and "prayers for rain." One of the young women, a 'green woman' dressed in a skirt of leaves, embodied Dodola. Dodola's rainmaking ceremony is remembered today in the *dodola* dance of Serbia and similar dances in other Slavic regions.

Ragana and Baba Yaga

The cult of Ragana, a goddess, as Gimbutas observes, of "death and regeneration," may be ancient, but she is primarily a post-Christianization figure, probably revered from at least as early as the ninth until the final years of the fourteenth century and perhaps thereafter. Her name derives from *regeti*, "to see" or "to foresee," and/or from *ragas*, "horns," suggesting the crescent moon. She is sometimes depicted as a beautiful nude woman combing flowing, golden hair. Like Diana and Hecate, she is a lunar goddess (a trait she shares with the god Menulis), especially of the dark moon and lunar eclipses. She is also, like Diana and the Lithuanian Medeina, a goddess of the forest, dwelling within its depths. The birch tree is sacred to her; sometimes she rides upon a stick of birch. She likes to bathe in frozen lakes. When angered because disrespected, she damages crops, makes couples infertile, and turns bridegrooms into werewolves (reminiscent of Angela Carter's "The Company of Wolves"). She frequently shapeshifts, becoming a bird (including a crows, magpie, quail, or swallow), fish (especially carp or pike), snake, toad, butterfly, moth, dog, hedgehog, mare, or sow. She holds the power to resuscitate the dead. She is a diviner and magician, and sometimes manifests in the plural as *raganas*, bands of witches who travel at night, often in the guise of crows.

Andreas Johns (2004) explains that as a crone, Baba Yaga is often depicted as "an unmarried old woman…a mother without being a wife."

She is the "mother of winds," a war goddess, and a psychopomp: a guide of souls. Johns writes, "Baba Yaga is the guardian who lives at the gateway to the land of the dead." It is perhaps because she is a psychopomp that she, like Tiresias and other liminal beings, is sometimes depicted as being partially or wholly blind. Also like certain liminal beings, she is sometimes portrayed as physically impaired in regard to mobility.

She is "the mother and mistress of the beasts" and shares a special relationship with birds. As such, she sometimes transforms into a bird or snake. She "lives in nocturnal darkness, deep in the woods;" and her house is composed partly of human skeletons and supported on bird's legs.

At some as yet undefined point, she appears to have been the focus of an initiatory cult that involved a purification by fire. With increasing Christianization and her demonization, this rite "was turned on its head" into a fairy tale narrative of a male hero throwing the "old witch" into the fire, reminding one of "Hansel and Gretel." As such, she continued to appear in carnivals, wearing a terrifying horned mask and holding fire-tongs.

Perhaps for these reasons and others, George Liebusch, in 1833, linked Baba Yaga to moon goddesses, Medea, healers, shamans (*Schamanen*), and witches (*Hexen*).

On the other hand, she came to be seen as a life-affirming figure, a localized manifestation of the Old Woman of the Harvest. As such, she became increasingly linked to agriculture as well as spinning and weaving.

She appears to have been revered from some point after the ninth and into the fourteenth or fifteenth century. Johns has suggested that she may represent a latter-day incarnation of the goddess Mokosh: "A parallel to Yaga can also be found in the ancient Slavic pagan religion[:] …Mokosh… Mokosh clearly belongs to the high cult, while Baba Yaga would have belonged to the low cult." She has also been said to correspond to Pripoldnica.

Among Christianized Slavs, Baba Yaga was, on the one hand, turned into a witch, demonic spirit, or Carnival figure, while on the other, she may have been Catholicized as St. Margaret as well as St. Paraskeva.

Drãgaica, Precesta, Baba Dochia: Maiden, Mother, Crone

Drãgaica is the Maiden Goddess of Romania. She might, like numerous of the beings discussed here, have been described in our discussion of fairies; she is alternately referred to as a goddess or fairy, or indeed, a fairy-goddess. I have chosen, however, to discuss her here, based on particularly admirable and very recent studies by Madalina Rucsanda (2009) of the Department of Music at Transylvania University of Braºov and Daniela Baciu (2010). Drãgaica appears to be a post-medieval avatar or hypostasis of the Romanian goddess Ileana Sânziana (see above), who herself is thought to have emerged from Roman reverence in Romania of the goddess Diana.

Rucsanda refers to Drãgaica as the "protective agrarian divinity of the…cornfields, cattle and married women." She also points out that in the plural, Drãgaica "is a special name given to …female aerial spirits, dressed in white and appearing at night to bewitch men."

Baciu describes as a "divinity synonymous with Sânziana" who is celebrated in the regions of Transylvania, Moldavia, and Wallachia. Sânziana has, like Drãgaica, been described as either a fairy or goddess or as a fairy-goddess. As Rucsanda explains, the name of Sânziana derives from Sancta Diana, a name which remains "common nowadays in Transylvania."

According to Baciu, Drãgaica "is a patron divinity of wheat. Her celebration coincides with the day of the birth of St. John the Baptist (June 24) and she manifests through the dance of a group of 5-10 unmarried young women, of whom only one, the prettiest, is chosen to represent the figure of the goddess of agriculture." She notes that all "of the young women are dressed in white and their faces are hidden by veils. Only Drãgaica is adorned with sheaves of wheat. The young women go from house to house, singing of the wealth of the crops of their hosts as they perform a joyful dance with jumping movements that create a cross." She also notes – significantly in our context – that "Drãgaica may be identified with the goddesses Diana and Juno of Roman mythology and with the goddesses Hera and Artemis of Greek mythology." Rucsanda, following Demetrie Cantemir (1673-1723), and in agreement with Baciu and Ghinoiu, relates that Drãgaica corresponds to both Demeter/Ceres and Artemis/Diana. Further, Rucsanda maintains that the "customs, beliefs and…folklore of Drãgaica trace back to a Neolithic goddess, a lunar, equinoctial and agrarian divinity." She is also associated with the witch-goddess Herodias. Nicknames include the Bride, the Elder Sister, the Mistress of the Sisters, the Empress, and the Queen of Grain.

Drãgaica appears to be associated with the Pleiades, known to Romanians as the Hen constellation, and her celebration also acknowledges their visibility at midsummer.

Although women are the primary participants in her celebration, men also take part. As Rucsanda relates, the "country or mountainous feasts to celebrate the agrarian goddess have become opportunities for young people to meet each other in view of marriage." Her festival's jumping dance, accompanied by the song "Come Drãgaica, jump, jump, jump," is meant to promote fertility and pregnancy.

The goddess' sacred plant, which bears her names – Drãgaica as well as Sânziana, and is called in Christian lore "Our Lady's Bedstraw," is *Galium verum*, a perennial herb with small, yellow tubular flowers that blossom at the summer solstice. Let's recall that *Galium verum* also belongs to the Goddess of Earth or Nature, and that in German the herb is called *Muttergottesbettstroh*, "the Mother Goddess's Bedstraw." Stems with the flowers are pinned on the veils of the young women taking part in the goddess' celebration; and the young woman "who performs the role of the divinity" wears a wreath of the plant on her head. The young women also carry a banner that is decorated with garlic, ears of wheat, wormwood, colored ribbons, and bedstraw blossoms. Yellow bedstraw gathered at midsummer and "kept in a white silk sachet" is believed to possess "magical properties;" "if the flower is pinned in their hair by virgins or young wives, they will become [more] attractive and lovable." Moreover, the young women make bedstraw wreaths to hang "on gates, doors, windows, sheds, beehives and even on vegetable beds or thrown over houses and leant against eaves; people believe that they will protect their house and household against evil forces, and they will also bring good luck, health and wealth to people, animals and crops." Further, bedstraw and bedstraw wreaths are deployed in divination in various ways, "considered by the young girls a way to find their predestined husband and the time they are supposed to marry. The men's cross-shaped wreaths and the girls' circle-shaped wreaths are thrown over their houses. If they get stuck on the roof, this is a sign of a wedding." Another divinatory method involves looking through the wreath in order to have a vision of the man a young woman will marry. Thirdly, if a young woman puts untwined bedstraw under her pillow at night, she will dream of her future spouse.

Drãgaica's celebration continues to be held in present-day Romania.

The Mother Goddess of Romania, Precesta reigns, according to the culture's pagan calendar, together with Drãgaica, from the summer solstice to the autumn equinox and then reigns alone to the winter solstice, or else reigns from the autumn equinox to the winter solstice. Although she may be considered as a hypostasis of an ancient Great Goddess, her own existence is only known from the late seventeenth/early eighteenth century, primarily in connection with Baba Dochia and Drãgaica.

Baba Dochia, Old Woman Dochia, is the Crone Goddess of Romania who, according to the pagan calendar, reigns from the winter solstice until the vernal equinox. She is the "personification of the Old Year." Her primary festival, which commences on March 1 and culminates on March 9, the traditional date of the spring equinox in Romania, honors the dying of the old year and the (re)birth of the new. These days are called the "Days of Old Women." Baba Dochia possesses six "bad" and six "good" coats to wear at this time, depending upon whether the weather is "bad" or "good."

Baba Dochia, like numerous other figures discussed herein, represents a process of Christianization and re-paganization. At some unknown point during the campaign of Christianization in Romania, an indigenous, perhaps Great, Mother, or Earth Goddess, as well as perhaps a Roman goddess such as Ceres or Diana – I would guess Hecate or Proserpina – was displaced by Saint Evdokia. Evdokia (*c*. 98-117 CE) was a courtesan or prostitute who converted to Christianity and became a nun. As a result of pagan persecution of Christians, she was beheaded and thereby became a martyr and thereafter a saint. Over the course of centuries, the ancient goddess and the saint hybridized, or else the saint served to mask the goddess, until at some point, the goddess or hybrid being was re-paganized, as Baba Dochia. Her name, [Ev]dochia, like that of the saint, signifies "benevolence," "kindness," "delight," and "desire."

Baba Dochia is a goddess of fate or destiny and a patron of mountains, farmers and grains, shepherds and sheep, and strawberries.

A very special item of ritual art is associated with Baba Dochia: the Martisor (pl., Martisorul). Martisorul are intertwined red and white cords, reminiscent of peppermint candy canes, usually looped into figure eights, like the symbol of infinity. White signifies the Crone, males, winter, and cheese, while red signifies the Maiden, maidens, spring, and red wine. martisorul serve as amulets or talismans that protect the wearer and promote health, loving relationships, and abundance.[56]

Chapter 8
Veneration of Male Divinities and Other Male Beings Rising to Prominence in the Middle Ages and Thereafter

[O]ne of the parish comes to me and says, "Sir, this is a busy day with us, we cannot hear you; it is Robin Hood's day. The parish are gone abroad to gather for Robin Hood…"

Hugh Latimer (*c.* 1485/1490-1555),
The Sixth Sermon preached before King Edward, April twelfth, 1549[57]

One understands how certain academics might come to the conclusion that present-day Witchcraft/Wicca is an entirely new religious movement when one peruses such works as Janet and Stewart Farrar's *The Witches' God: Lord of the Dance* (1989). In an attempt to portray the title figure of this text, the Farrars have, rather than focusing on indigenous European, Mediterranean, and Egyptian or African divinities that might have *actually* contributed to the emergence of a premodern European god revered by alleged witches, instead drawn rather uncritically upon Shiva, Polynesian fertility gods, Brazilian and Chinese deities, and so on in sketching their portrait of the "Witches' God." Indeed, they have far outdone Margaret Murray in casting a net for sources that are highly doubtful in terms of contributing to the portrait of a premodern European god. But perhaps this was not their intention in the first place; perhaps they rather intended to emphasize, as Hutton and other academics have, that Wicca is a twentieth-century creation. On the other hand, one can empathize with the Farrars in their seeking afar, as, in contrast to what Church authorities rattling on about the Devil on the one hand and Murray on the other would have us believe, either the male deity or deities associated with medieval and later European traditions did not play as prominent a role as did female divinities in association with alleged witches, or else data concerning them is far more paltry than that concerning female divinities who were revered during medieval and later periods by many including those considered alleged witches. Indeed, the Farrars themselves indicate as much, in statements such as: "As for England and Scotland, we have...only folklore, the evidence of artifacts such as hill-cut figures...Which brings us to the surprising fact that we cannot be certain of the actual original name of the Celtic Horned God. All we have is the Herne of British folklore."

On the other hand, numerous ancient African (including Egyptian), Mediterranean, and European deities may have contributed to the construction of medieval and post-medieval deities revered by alleged witches. As I have noted previously, I have found no continuing worship of Cernunnos, at least not by this name; as I have said, in my view, that does not mean that there was none, and to argue this would be both preemptive and presumptuous.

Lords of the Forest and of Animals

Among Saxons and Thuringians, Biel was a god of the forest, perhaps especially of oak trees, and possibly, although highly unlikely, a god of the sun. Place-names such as Bielstein, Dornenbiel, Eichenbiel, Espenbiel, Heiligenbiel, and Steinbiel, towns in Germany; Bielshöhle, a cave in the Harz mountains; and Bienne, a town in Switzerland, indicate that Biel was once revered.

Maurizio Bertolotti, in "The Ox's Bones and the Ox's Hide: A Popular Myth, Part Hagiography and Part Witchcraft" (1979, 1991), offers evidence that the "Lord of the Animals" presided, together with Diana, as "the Lady," at ceremonies of feasting on, and the resurrection of, oxen occurring in medieval and Renaissance Italy. Bertolotti describes this deity as "an ambivalent divinity to whom hunters ... attributed the power of overseeing the fortunes of hunting activities." He argues that although the significance of this deity faded with the "decline of the hunting economies," "the most characteristic of his attributes" were appropriated by "divinities coming after him," including non-Christian and Christian subjects of reverence.

Certainly, horned deities, such as the "Lord of the Forest," continued to be revered, some of whom may have been synonymous with Cernunnos. It is conceivable, although somewhat controversial, that the god Cernunnos, as a patron of animals and a god of wealth, abundance, sacrifice, and the underworld, metamorphosed over time into figures including the Lord of Animals or Lord of the Forest, the Green Man, Puck, Herne the Hunter, the Man of the Oak, the Green Man, Jack-in-the-Green. His memory may have also subtly lingered in celebrations of the Kalends, especially in stag and bull costumes, in the Abbots Bromley dance, and in other celebratory rites.

The Lord of the Forest was certainly known in the Middle Ages, as evidenced by the *Mabinogion*, in which he appears as a "great black man" who "carries an iron spear" and who "is keeper of the forest," with "a thousand wild animals graz[ing] about him." The animals bow their heads and worshi[p] him as obedient men do their lord." What is more, the wizard Merlin has been identified as the Lord of the Forest.

In Russia, the Leshy is Lord of the Forest; in Christianized Russia, Leshy came to be called Déduško, the Devil.

The Forest Lord's presence is also

evidenced by persistent reverence into at least the seventeenth century, and possibly into the twentieth, of the Basque divinities Jaungoikoa and Basajaun, the Lord of the Forest (*basa* can mean "forest," "desert," or "wilderness"), who is depicted as a "man of Nature, a farmer, miller, a blacksmith, or a shepherd." Both were said to be revered by alleged witches.

A god possibly pictured as possessing bull horns is the mysterious Mourie (or, Maree). In Scotland, the mysterious Mourie, Christianized as St. Maelrubha, is thought to be an avatar of an ancient Celtic or Germanic deity. Mourie continued to be revered at the Isle of Maree (or, Innis Maree), a small island in Loch Maree during the seventeenth century. Mourie was honored on August 25th as well as at Samhain/Halloween. Bulls were sacrificed to him to encourage fertility of livestock. During the eighteenth century, a grove of "oak, ash, willow, wicken, birch, fir, hazel, and enormous hollies" sacred to the god was documented on the island; at present, mostly oaks, and not nearly as numerous, remain. A sacred burial ground was also reported. Arthur Mitchell (a self-identified Christian writer), in speaking of the cult of Mourie and other related practices on the Isle of Maree, wrote in 1881 in *The Past in the Present: What is Civilization?*:

> We are told there that there were monuments of idolatry in the island, and stones which were consulted as to future events; that the people gave adoration to wells, and poured milk upon the hills as oblations; and that there were certain 'poor ones,' called 'Mourie['s] … devilans' … who received the sacrifices offered to him.[58]

In the late nineteenth century, some locals still spoke of Mourie as "the God Mourie."

Pan is the goat-footed Greek god of shepherds, groves, lustiness, and the music of flutes and pipes. The *Canons* of the Council of Trullo indicate that, despite his legendary death, Pan continued to be revered in Greece and Asia Minor – despite his legendary death – into the late seventh century, especially in connection with the Bota, a festival in his honor. Canon 62 states: "We have determined that … the Bota … [is] to be removed completely from the life of the faithful." Five centuries later, the twelfth-century Byzantine/Orthodox canonists Zonaras (d. 1159?) and Balsamon (d. 1195) likewise condemned this festival, which persisted in Greece and which they viewed as a pagan, "Hellenic" custom, continued to be celebrated by peasants. Thus, we may say that Pan was revered far beyond his alleged death, into the High Middle Ages.

Although Pan was primarily perceived in symbolic terms during the Renaissance, this shift toward the symbolic did not result in a lack of belief in the sacred energy or force that he signified. As the "pan-," the "all," he was thought to embrace the cosmos and all within it. The seven pipes of his panpipes came to represent the seven celestial spheres, and his playing their harmonious relationship. His curved shepherd's crook, together with his horns (when they did not promote his demonization), suggested the spiraling movement of the cosmos, progress combined with the cycles of the seasons and other significant cycles. His crook also came to represent wisdom, and crook and panpipes together came to signify the relationship of philosophy and music. As a god of both nature and philosophy and as a mirror of the *Anima Mundi*, Pan came to be seen as embodying a nature-based philosophy such as pantheism or (proto-) animism. Thus, Pan came to embody an earth-centered consciousness and worldview rooted in an immanentist celebration of spiritually imbued matter. The Renaissance Neoplatonist Giovanni Pico della Mirandola (1463-1494) insisted in his *Orphic Conclusions*, "He who has not attracted Pan will approach nature in vain." Pan was considered a tutelary deity of both the very wealthy Medici family and peasants of the countryside; as the latter, he was associated with the paradisal environment of Arcadia. Pan was also increasingly considered an iconic source for Satan and as the god of witches.

An early seventeenth-century text, *Robin Goodfellow, His Mad Prankes, and merry Jests*, leaves no doubt that Pan and Puck/Robin were eventually conflated and came to represent the patron deity of persons persisting in celebrations and /or for witches. Its well-known illustration depicts a gigantic Puck/Pan as a hybrid human-goat Horned God dancing in the midst of a circle of ritual participants. He has goat horns, large ears, longish hair, a full beard, an erection, and lifts his right leg. He holds a broom in his left hand and a torch in his right. His horn is strapped over his shoulders. A musician plays a horn to his left and the left of the circle. Vessels outside the circle suggest offerings and/or feasting. Birds fly overhead. We see eleven dancers in the circle, but if we measure the space each occupies, it is likely that the god's form hides two more dancing behind him; this brings the number of dancers to thirteen, suggesting a coven.

Needless to say, although a few compared Pan and Christ as shepherds of their respective flocks, most Christian writers – not to mention Church authorities – were less than thrilled with Pan's persistence and kept insisting on his death. Henry More (1614-1687), for instance, longed for a day when the sabbat would be no more, when the goddess Rhea and Pan would no longer be celebrated (an intriguing forecasting of the Goddess and God of present-day Wicca), and "Pan's pipes shall then be mute." Elizabeth Barrett Browning (1806-1861), a Christian zealot whose poem "Goblin Market" has turned her reputation on its head, denounced the god and rejoiced in his passing in "The Dead Pan." We have previously encountered, when treating Apollo, evidence of a NeoPagan cult whose members may have included Leigh Hunt (1784-1859), Thomas Love Peacock (1785-1866), Percy Bysshe Shelley (1792-1822), Thomas Jefferson Hogg (1792-1862), and other early nineteenth-century writers. Patricia Merivale, as we have mentioned, offers evidence of this cult in *Pan the Goat-God: His Myth in Modern Times* (1969). Considering that both Hunt and Shelley used the term "Universal Pan" in poems, it is possible that this was the chief title by which they revered the god. This cult appears to have possessed a geographical center: Marlow Bridge, Bisham Wood in Maidenhead, England. Merivale draws our attention to a letter written by Peacock to Hogg on September 7, 1818, which the former signs, "In the name of Pan, yours most sincerely. Elsewhere in the letter, Peacock writes, "I hope I shall see your Homeric physiognomy in this gelid valley which we have consecrated to the only true gods, to whom I hope you continue to pour Libations and sing Dithyrambics." In November of that same year, Peacock wrote to Shelley, "And were I not fearful of the risk of such a malediction, I would say, 'May Pan never be propitious to me if I be not in all coming fortnights as regular as the dial.'" On October 12, 1821, Shelley wrote to Hogg of an "altar [he had "raised"] to the mountain-walking Pan (Pan Oreibateis)."

Thanks to Shakespeare, Robin Goodfellow a.k.a. Puck is perhaps the most renowned earth elemental. Belief in Robin Goodfellow or Puck arose in the Middle Ages and continued into the twentieth century. (Please bear in mind that he might also be considered under the rubrics of elves, fairies, and elemental beings whose cults flowered during the Middle Ages and thereafter.) Puck's ancestors are probably Greek – Pan; Roman – Faunus; Celtic – *phuka* or *puca* (Irish) and *pwcca* (Welsh), as well as, perhaps, Manannan, son of the Celtic god Lir; and Germanic – *pûki* (Old Norse, Icelandic) and *pook* (German). In this regard, it is important to point out that in regions with Germanic pantheons, beliefs in *landvættir*, elementals of the land, *genii loci*, have persisted for many centuries. Also called Hobgoblin and Robin Goodfellow, he was thought to be the son of a male fairy and a mortal woman, and he is primarily linked to playing pranks and shapeshifting. Some "Pennsylvania Dutch" Germans living in Pennsylvania and New York circa 1895 continued to believe in his existence. Helen Sewell Johnson, in "November Eve Beliefs and Customs in Irish Life and Literature," notes that the "Irish countryman of the twentieth century [her article is dated 1968] – in spite of time, Christianization, and a famine – still believes that the fruit and the blackberries must be harvested before November 1, because on Halloween the *puca* goes about spitting on them and making them inedible."

Lady Alice Kyteler was alleged to have headed a band of heretical sorcerers, to have practiced magic, concocted potions, and sacrificed animals at crossroads (a practice common to Africans, ancient Greeks, and others). She was also thought to have conjured a male being named "Robin (or, Robert), son of (the) Art" or Robin Artisson (or, Robert A.). He may have been synonymous with Robin Goodfellow, or Puck. This spirit sometimes took the form of "a Negro [or Ethiopian]. [As such,] Alice received him as her incubus and allowed him to copulate with her. In return, he gave her wealth." He was said to carry an iron staff, which enhances his association with Africa. He was said to be accompanied by two other black men, who also carried iron staffs that appeared to serve as magic wands.

Lords of the Sea

Shony is a god of the sea who brings both fertility and death and who may thus be related to Cernunnos as well as to Odin,

Neptune, Nickar, and possibly Oceanus, who is occasionally depicted as having horns. The occasional indirect linking of horned gods with the sea recalls the Greek deities Poseidon Taureios, to whom black bulls were sacrificed, and Dionysos as the "Bull-Horned," to whom the Elian women chanted, "Come hither, Dionysus, to thy holy temple…by the sea…O goodly Bull!"

Shony appears to have manifested occasionally as a water-horse. His cult appears to have arisen sometime prior to 1695 (when he appears in Martin Martin's [d. 1719] *Description of the Western Isles of Scotland*) and continued, even though prohibited by the Church, into at least the nineteenth century. Shony's name may suggest "sacrifice" or Samhain/Halloween. He may have been, to a certain extent, identified with St. Mulvay (who may have lived in the sixth century or who may have been legendary). He was honored in Scotland, especially on the isle of Lewis, at Eoropie. The isle of Lewis was a center of Germanic material-sacred activity; its name, from *Ljót-ulf*, signifies a "fierce wolf." Shony also appears to have been revered in the area of Moray Firth, well known for the persistence of pagan traditions. In *Primitive Beliefs in the North East of Scotland* (1929), Joseph M. McPherson recounts that in the late nineteenth century, "Moray Firth fishermen, when at sea, would never mention such words as Church or manse or minister. Any utterance suggestive of the new faith would be displeasing to the ancient god of the ocean, and might bring disaster upon the boat."

At Candlemas (Feb. 2) Shony was offered milk and porridge, and at Samhain/Halloween, he was toasted with ale. Shony's association with these festivals may indicate a link with alleged witches. Milk, porridge, and ale were offered at the seashore, probably at Stoth Bay, so that the god would provide the people with plenty of fish as well as seaweed with which to fertilize their fields: "Shony, I give you this cup of ale, hoping that you'll be so kind as to send us plenty of seaware for enriching our ground for the ensuing year." Some have alleged that Shony and/or Maree required human sacrifice. In the nineteenth century, fishermen would sometimes say, "The sea maun its nummer!" Morag Skene explains that in earlier times, "no effort would have been made to save a drowning man or indeed bring ashore a drowned man or even to touch the corpse of a drowned man. It was believed that bad luck would befall those who attempted the rescue….[The] Sea God…had to be constantly appeased by human sacrifice."

This association persisted and metamorphosed into the folkloric figure and sinister spirit of Davy Jones, the "Devil" of the sea. François Joseph Michel Noël (1756-1841) relates in the *Dictionnaire de la fable* (1803), he may appear as a creature with enormous eyes, sharp teeth, a huge tail, and nostrils from which spout "bluish fire," as a giant column of water, or as a hurricane. One might classify Davy Jones as merely a folkloric figure or a persona of popular culture, were it not for his being considered an entity of the sea comparable to Old Nick, Nix, and the nickers, who ruled "all the harmful spirits of the sea." His "locker" lies at the bottom of the sea, and while a treasure is to be found there, death by drowning may also be found there.

Other Male Beings
Hjúki
Hjúki is one of two divine children, the other being his sister Bil, who – either willfully or by force – assist Máni, a god of the moon, on his nightly journey. The Germanic Hjúki controls the waxing moon, while his sister controls the waning moon. Some believe that the tale of Hjúki and Bil gave rise to the nursery rhyme of "Jack and Jill." In my view, research needs to be done regarding possible connections of "Hjúki," "Hwicke," and "Wike" on the one hand to "Hwicce," "Wicce," and "Wicca" on the other. It may be – if Amalia Schoppe (1832) was correct in linking "Hviki" to "Fülle" – that these terms turn out to be related by way of the attribute of abundance and perhaps the goddess Habundia.

Stuffo
The statue and cult of Stuffo are said to have been destroyed by Boniface in the eighth century. Very little is known about Stuffo. He may have been a Germanic god of drink and festivity comparable to Bacchus (in that aspect), perhaps portrayed as holding a goblet or stein, and/or perhaps a divinity of vegetation or the forest, as he appears to have been transformed in Christianized, folkloric milieus – especially at Oberdorla and Niederdorla, Germany – into a Green Man, a *Laubmann*. He is recalled by various place-names including Staufenberg, Mount Stuffenberg (now called Hülfensberg), and a cave called Stuffensloch which, according to legend, the god Stuffo concealed himself after Boniface destroyed his image.

Krodo
The Germanic cult of Krodo may have been centered at Sollstedt, a municipality in Nordhausen, Thuringia, as well as near Goslar in the Harz Mountains, particularly on the Rammelsberg. He has been compared to Saturn, in part because he is thought to have been depicted "as an old man with long hair and a flowing beard." Krodo is also thought to have been portrayed as holding a basket of fruit and flowers in his right hand and a wheel, possibly a spinning wheel, in his left. This may or may not indicate gender diversity or the mixing of traditionally feminine and masculine attributes. He is further said to have been depicted as standing on a giant perch. A place-name associated with Krodo, Krötensumpf, also suggests that he may have been linked to toads and swamps. His cult was allegedly eradicated around 920 CE through the efforts of Henry I the Fowler (876-936).

Püsterich
The name of the god Püsterich is derived from *pust*, meaning "to blow," or *puster*, "bellows." According to the Slovak archaeologist, poet, and politician Ján Kollár (1793-1852), Püsterich is a Wendish deity. He was perhaps a god of weather, especially winds and storms, possibly corresponding to the Germanic Thor, the Slavic Perun, or the Baltic Perkûnas. He may have also been a phallic deity comparable to Priapus. A figure of the god

was found in an excavation of the fifteenth or sixteenth century; by 1546 (or 1646, according to others), it had made its way to the castle of Rottembourg in Sondershausen, Germany, an area allegedly maintained in the past by heathen priests. In the 1860s, the figure was housed in the Cabinet of Antiquities at Sondershausen. It appears that a similar figure was discovered in the late eighteenth century in a chapel in the Kyffhäuser hills in Thuringia. The former figure stood between two and four feet tall and weighed sixty-two pounds. It was possibly made of brass, although even after its left arm was broken (and ultimately lost) in trying to decipher what metal it was made from, tests proved inconclusive. The figure leaned on one knee and appears to have touched his head with his right hand and his huge, erect phallus with his left. The head and mouth had holes from which water and other liquids emerged when the figure, in truth a sort of humanoid teakettle, was heated. As an aeolipile/eolipile, it was based on heating devices going back to Roman times, became popular during the seventeenth century, and anticipated the steam engine.

Here is a description borrowed from Elias Schedius' *De dis Germanis* (1648) which appears in Katharine Burton's description from *Our Summer in the Harz Forest* (1865):

> The face is ugly, and looks like a rude boy, who out of malice distorts his features; the right hand lies on the head, the fingers of the left upon the left knee; the left arm from the elbow to the hand is wanting, by reason of the trial made, as above; on the crown of the head there is a hole, almost big enough to admit a man's finger, and instead of a mouth there is such another; the belly is two feet six inches round; the inside of the image is hollow, and holds about a pail-full of water; both the feet are lost; it kneels with the right leg, and the left is erect. When this image is filled with water, all the holes being stopped close, and put upon the fire, it sweats to such a degree that it falls down in large drops; and when the heat increases, the pegs fly out and give a report as if it thundered; whereupon from the two holes in the head, come forth flames of fire thirty feet vertically, and as many horizontally, during fifteen minutes; which experiment being tried one day in the kitchen by a captain, in the count's absence, the castle was set on fire, which, with much difficulty, was extinguished. Some are of opinion that these flames do not come from that image by natural means, but that the pagan priests effected it by their magic.[59]

And this from Thomas Ewbank's *Descriptive and Historical Account of Hydraulic and Other Machines for Raising Water* (1842):

> ...the ire of the god was expressed by sweat (steam) oozing from all parts of his body; and if the people still remained obdurate, his fury became terrible: murmurs, bellowings, and even thunderbolts (the wooden plugs) burst from him; flashes or streams of fire rushed from his mouth and head, and presently he was enveloped in clouds of smoke; when the people, horror stricken,

consented to comply with the requisitions.[60]

Moreover, Ewbank adds, "It further appears that the monks in the middle ages made use of this idol, and found it not the least effectual of their wonder-working machines. It was in fact in this manner chiefly that the great body of ecclesiastics then maintained their influence over the multitude."

It appears that such vessels became rather popular in the Middle Ages, both in Europe and in the Islamic world (where they often took the form of animals rather than that of humans). In our particular context, it would seem that several figures or copies of the Püsterich *per se* image found their way to England sometime prior to 1725, perhaps as early as the Anglo-Saxon period. At least one was discovered around 1592. One was recovered during a dig at a canal at Basingstoke near 1790 (housed in the Museum of the Society of Antiquaries in 1851) and another at Essington in South Staffordshire. Over time, these figures came to be called by the sobriquet "Jack of Hilton." Erect phalli were covered over with metal (?) leaves. In the seventeenth century, it became a Christmas tradition that "Jack" performed his magic. Unfortunately, this magic included great cruelty to a goose that was basically cooked alive by the object. Thus, a god was mocked, an animal abused, and a pagan rite which had already been Christianized was now carnivalized and trivialized.

The Pied Piper

In 1284, a piper believed to be skilled at luring away mice from towns and villages was hired by the town of Hamelin, in Lower Saxony, northwestern Germany to rid the town of its mice. Although he miraculously accomplished this feat, the town's leaders refused to pay him for his efforts. Thus, on June 26, 1284, at 7 a.m., the "Pied Piper," so called because of the variegated garment he wore, playing his flute, led 130 of Hamelin's children and young adults out of the town, past the cemetery, on a road called Unterkoppen, toward the north. One of the older youth was the daughter of the mayor of Hamelin, who was preparing to marry. The children and young adults never returned. Some said they perished, while others insisted that the piper had led them into another world (that of fairies, elves, or dwarves?) inside a hill. The street on which they had departed was later renamed Bürgerlosestrasse, "the street without citizens." No music or dancing was permitted thereafter on that street. The stained glass windows of the main church of Hamelin memorialized the event. Apparently these windows were still in existence in the sixteenth century. Also in the sixteenth century, "the senior magistrate [continued to] customarily sign his public documents with two dates: the 'Year of Our Lord – ,' and the 'Year of the Departure of the Children – .'"

Robin Hood

Robin Hood is a legendary (anti-) hero, dressed in green, whose historicity remains unproven but who may have lived in

England during the Middle Ages. He led an outlaw band of "merry men" who dwelt in the forest.

Timothy J. Lundgren argues that one of the chief reasons for Robin Hood's rapid rise to venerable figure to be honored in seasonal rites concerns his yeoman status; "yeoman" in this context refers to a commoner who is a "lesser freeholder," classed just below the gentry, who cultivates his own land.

What is significant here, in my view, is that a countercultural hero embraces celebration of an earth-centered worldview as well as resistant to hegemonic political and religious institutions. It is also significant that his appeal brought together various economic and social classes and that his persona and those of his companions were fêted in rituals as well as in the performing arts and in occasions mixing these.

Robin Hood most probably became associated with Maid Marian due to a bricolage of his legend with two (at least apparently) other folk figures, a young farmer named Robin (alternatively, Robechon) and his beloved, a shepherdess named Marian (or, Marion; alternatively, Marote, Marotele). The couple Robin/Robechon and Marian/Marote/Marotele is known to us primarily from medieval ballads and songs and from a musical play by Adam de la Halle (fl. 1260), *Le jeu de Robin et Marion* (*The Game/ Play of R. and M.*), which appears to have been composed for the court of Naples around 1280. The couple and their döppelgangers came to be associated with the rites of May/Beltane and to a lesser extent in hunting rites, demonstrating a popularization of the pagan concept of duotheism.

Robin the farmer's kinship with Robin Hood is suggested by the anonymous French lyric "L'autre jour" (c. 1300), in which Marian links him to the forest and to jovial activity, singing, "I love him more than any other/ creature; he has gone into the forest/ under the green leaves to play." Based on similar songs such as "Ce fu(t) en Mai," it seems likely that Robin and Marian are celebrating the rites of May in "He, Marote" (anonymous French song, c. 1300). In this song, Robin pleads: "Come play/ in the woods; I'll make you/ a garland of gladiolas." When he attempts to make love to Marotele (Marion) in a meadow filled with irises, and she cries out that she is a virgin and must remain so, Robin ceases his attempt; he embraces her gently, and tells her, "I'll always be at your disposal." "L'autre jour" also probably speaks to the rites of May or a kindred rite of spring; when Robin returns from the forest, he and Marian and "all the shepherds of the area [gather] in a valley, on a meadow" to sing, play "fife and drum," and dance. Robin is determined, "for the sake of his beloved, to look good" as he, with hat and staff, dances the "Aatie." Their association with May is explicit in yet another anonymous French song (c. 1300), "Mout me fu grief: Robins m'aime," as is their association with paganism (in this song, Robin exclaims, "ye Gods!," whereas in other similar songs, the Virgin Mary and other Christian figures are addressed). Herein, Robin, as tokens of his affection, gives Marian "a belt and a silk purse" (in *Le jeu*, he buys her a dress "of scarlet silk") and sings: "When shall I see you again,/ precious lady as red as a rose/ In May!"

Adam de la Halle's *pastorelle* focuses on Marian's struggle with a knight desirous of her and her eventual reunion with Robin. The play climaxes in a dance. One of the most intriguing aspects of the dance is that it includes an element of ceremonial cross-dressing or mixed gender attire, with Robin and Marian exchanging garments: Robin puts on Marian's "little cap," while she dons his money pouch and jacket. Following the dance is a feast, which is mirrored by a feast for the audience, as well as, possibly, a dance, games, and amorous rites. This mixing of performative and lived realms is typical of dramatic performances of the Middle Ages, Renaissance, and seventeenth century.

The green-hooded (anti-) hero continued to play a role in non-Christian and pagano-Christian rites in the Renaissance, including in the rites of May and in Martinmas, with celebrants including commoners and kings, among the latter, Henry VIII. During this period, Robin Hood appears to have acquired other well-known attributes and narratives with which later epochs have associated him, including "his being part of the Saxon resistance to the Norman Conquest, [and] his habit of robbing from the rich to give to the poor." He also increasingly took on the roles of patron of the forest and its creatures and of patron of banquets. Shakespeare (as we shall see) further linked Robin Hood and the forest of Arden to the winter rite of the hunting and sacrifice of a stag. Bishop Hugh Latimer (1470-1555), a zealous Protestant, wrote in his *Sixth Sermon before Edward VI* (1537-1553, r. 1547-1553) of the honoring of Robin Hood:

> I came once myself to a place, riding on a journey homeward from London, and I sent word over night into the town that I would preach there in the morning, because it was holiday; and methought it was an holiday's work. The church stood in my way, and I took my horse and my company, and went thither. I thought I should have found a great company in the church, and when I came there the church door was fast locked. I tarried there half an hour and more: at last the key was found, and one of the parish comes to me and says, "Sir, this is a busy day with us, we cannot hear you; it is Robin Hood's day. The parish are gone abroad to gather for Robin Hood: I pray you let them not." I was fain there to give place to Robin Hood: I thought my rochet should have been regarded, though I were not; but it would not serve, it was fain to give place to Robin Hood's men. It is no laughing matter, my friends, it is a weeping matter, a heavy matter; a heavy matter, under the pretence of gathering for Robin Hood, a traitor and a thief, to put out a preacher, to have his office less esteemed; to prefer Robin Hood before the ministration of God's word and all this hath come of unpreaching prelates.[61]

Christsonday

A very intriguing male being emerging in the Renaissance appears to reflect both pagan innovation and pagano-Christian hybridity: Christsonday. This being appears to have manifested primarily in the last years of the sixteenth century in Scotland, particularly to alleged witches Andro Man, Jonet Wischert, Marion Grant, and Christen Reid. Christsonday appears to have represented the male half of a heterosexual couple, with the Quene of Elphen (Queen of Elfland, Fairy Queen) being the female (and dominant) partner. A shapeshifter, his primary hypostases appear to have been as a man, a young horse (*staig*, which does not mean "stag"), and an angel garmented in white. He appears to have been considered by alleged witches to be "God's godson" and a fourth member of the "trinity" of Christianity, invoked on occasion by the phrase "Father, Son, Holy Ghost, and Christsonday." He was associated with Ruidday (or, Rood Day), a harvest feast occurring on or near September 14th, with Samhain/Halloween, and with Martinmas on November 11th. He also appears to have been associated with the third finger of the right hand, as his devotees were allegedly ritually cut on this finger. Alleged witches danced with him and may have shared erotic relations with him (possibly including the men). Church authorities appear to have understood Christsonday to be Satan in his particular manifestation as the Antichrist.

The Metal Man

One of the most intriguing beings in Ireland long after Christianization and was dependent upon industrialization. In 1823, Lloyd's of London erected, at Tramore Bay, an iron figure, called the Metal Man, to warn ships away from dangerous waters and treacherous rocks. Thus far, there is no particular reason to include the Metal Man here. However, sometime after the Metal Man was erected, as O'Farrell relates in *Superstitions of the Irish*, young women birthed a tradition of dancing around the figure, which stands upon a high pillar, just as women have done for thousands of years at sacred stones, in the belief that by doing so, they would find themselves married within a year. In my view, this rite serves as evidence of pagan innovation as well as of the paganization of things not originally pagan (Very proto-Steampunk!).

Robert the Jackis and Others

We know very little about certain male beings evoked by alleged witches in the sixteenth and seventeenth centuries. Nevertheless, their names reflect significant examples of pagan-based, non-Christian innovation; with some appearing in Pitcairn's *Ancient Criminal Trials* and Potts' *Wonderfull Discoverie*, they include: Fancie, Laing, Mak Hector, Read Reiver, Robert the Jackis, Robert the Rule, Rorie, Roring Lyon, Swein (Swain?), Thief of Hell, and Thomas a Faerie. *Martinelli* were male beings who assumed the form of goats in order to serve as steeds to transport women to ceremonial gatherings. It seems likely that the Roberts among them, and perhaps others as well, shared common traits with Robin Goodfellow or Puck. Most share in common the wearing of green and yellow garments. Into the sixteenth century, these colors were worn in Scottish ceremonies on Beltane and at other times by celebrants; indeed, citizens were told by authorities to wear these colors. Green and yellow were also associated in the Middle Ages with fairies and elves (thus they might also be treated under the rubrics of elves or fairies), as well as sometimes signifying effeminacy and homoeroticism.

Transgender, Trans-species Beings

Before proceeding, I should make it clear that in comparing transgender processes to other sorts of metamorphosis or the uncovering and revealing of one's core identity, I am not seeking to offend persons who identify as transgender. However, the literature on pagan traditions indicates that in the past, transitioning from one sex or gender to another was frequently viewed in tandem with theriomorphic and other modes of "shapeshifting."

Scrat, or 'the scrat,' was venerated in the seventh and later centuries by some Germanic and Anglo-Saxon groups. Scrat is related to the Germanic practitioner of *seiðr* magic, a magical practice associated with transgenderism, while also carrying the meanings of "monster," "hermaphrodite," "eunuch," and "prostitute." Apparently Scrat was envisioned as an archetypal 'hairy androgyne' (far from the Greek conception of the beautiful androgyne). Scrat is a shapeshifter; s/he may also appear as an infant, a giant, a bear, a horse, a butterfly, or a red-capped dwarf resembling Rumplestiltskin. His/her nickname Katzaus may suggest a linkage to the sacred cat and to the cult of Freyja. S*kratta* and *seið-skratti* were also employed interchangeably to refer to a practitioner of *seiðr*. S*kratta* was also synonymous with *seið-læti*, the term describing the strange noises made by *seiðr* practitioners during rituals. This appellation may also indicate an association with *katzenmusik*, another name for charivari, a chaotic musical performance. Scrat was honored with gifts of food, often placed in houses or at forest shrines. If remembered, s/he would, like the fairy tale elf, perform tasks for the faithful. Scrat's cult may have survived into the sixteenth century. Places sacred to him/her include Scrathawe, Strathawe, Scrachawe, Scratta Wood on the border of Derbyshire, and other sites in England and elsewhere. Eventually, s/he became identified with the Devil, taking the nickname of Old Scrat or Scratch.

Another, more mysterious, being who may reflect transgenderism and hybridic animal status (like the werewolf and mermaid) is the Hynd Knight, one of the beings revered by the alleged witch Andro Man in the final years of the sixteenth century. Although little to nothing is known about the Hynd Knight, the name suggests "female deer" (hind) + "knight." It is possible that no masculinity is indicated by the name. I would speculate, however, that since "dame" was often deployed as the female equivalent to "knight," the word "knight" may indicate masculinity or maleness in this context, thus suggesting a transgender being. Since we know that Diana was remembered in the Middle Ages and Renaissance, it is conceivable that she may in some way be linked to the female deer, her sacred animal, in the name of "Hynd Knight." Thus, it is conceivable that the Hynd Knight is a transgender female-to-male, were-being related to Diana, who was, as we have seen, intimately tied to witchcraft during the Middle Ages and Renaissance.

"Satisfied by the Christian System"?

As we have seen, numerous non-Christian divinities were reclaimed, reconstructed, or emerged in the Middle Ages and thereafter. A majority of these were female. Why might this be? Those who have studied the interrelationship of women and Christianity during this period will recall that it was at this time that the cult of the Virgin Mary escalated dramatically. This was the period when such awe-inspiring women as Hildegard von Bingen (1098-1179) and St. Joan of Arc (Jeanne d'Arc, 1412-1431) manifested profoundly Catholic religiosity, when the adoration of women saints proliferated.

Let us recall what Ronald Hutton and Nicole Belmont have written of this period: Belmont, in "Mythic Elements in French Folklore" (1991), states matter-of-factly that pagan "traces" or "vestiges" didn't survive because "the needs of the majority of the people were satisfied by the Christian system;" while Hutton insists in *Pagan Religions* that a "large part of the reason for Christianity's victory in places such as Ireland, where it depended solely upon its own merits, is surely that it offered everything already given by the old cults, and added a confident promise of eternal bliss." We might ask, why then were so many women attracted to heretical movements or traditions like those of the Waldensians and Cathars?

Why then, besides the names of the Blessed Virgin, St. Anne, and so many other female saints, do we find the names of Diana, Minerva, and Herodias, together with a host of others reflecting pagan origin and innovation – Aïa, Baba Dochia, Baba Yaga, La Befana, Bensozia, Brava Part, the Cailleach, Chlungeri, Dodola, Domina Satia, Dragaica, Eostre, Esterelle, Frau Rose, Frau Werra, Fru Gaue, La Guenne, Gyre-Carline, Habundia, Fru Herke, Holda, Hörsel, Madona Oriente, the Mither o' the Sea, Mother Carey, Nicneven, Pehtra Baba, Perchta, Pharaildis, Phinzen, Precesta, Ragana, Richella, Rupfa, Sack Semper, Saelde, the Seven Daughters o' the Sea, La Signora della Montagna, Tante Arie, Vénus de Quinipily, Wanne Thekla, Zlota Baba, and Zobiana, among others?

It would appear that Hutton, Belmont, and others (primarily following Hutton's lead) have indulged in reductionist and perhaps fallacious thinking when they insist that "the needs of the majority of the people were satisfied by the Christian system;" or that a "Christianity ... surely...offered everything already given by the old cults, and added a confident promise of eternal bliss."

Why, then, were so many women, and some men, drawn to heretical sects and to cults of non-Christian divinities?

Jennifer Ward, in *Women in Medieval Europe* (2002), suggests that many women were drawn to heretical sects because in this way they might simultaneously escape patriarchal marriage, housewifery, and the dogma of the Catholic Church (the last of which they would not escape as Catholic nuns). "In Languedoc," she writes, "the Cathars offered the best opportunity to live an ascetic life." She continues, "The Perfect [i.e., male or female monks] in Languedoc included women from leading noble families."

As to why many women's and some

men's needs and desires appear to have been met neither by Christianity (nor other Abrahamic faiths that might have occasionally been available to them) nor by heretical sects, but rather by the reverence of Holda and other such beings, Ward provides us with a clue: although some heretical sects like the Lollards included working-class women as devotees, many women who joined heretical groups were elites, as were many men who joined. She mentions, for example, the fourteenth-century couple Beatrice de Planissoles and her husband, the Lord of Montaillou, both of whom are believed to have been or been influenced by the Cathars.

Thus, many working-class and poor women and men whose needs and desires might not have been met either by the Church or by heresies attracting elites may have been drawn to cults of female and, perhaps to a lesser extent, to cults of male divinities and of couples. This is not to say, however, that elites were not also drawn to the reverence of female divinities. Indeed, much more study needs to be undertaken in regard to the possible mixing of economic classes that might have occurred in such settings. From those divinities we have encountered herein, I would suggest that many persons dwelling in officially Christianized Europe hoped and prayed that pagan divinities, particularly goddesses or female otherworldly beings, might meet needs and desires that both Christianity and heresies such as Catharism, at least in their view, failed to meet. Although I would not wish to impose a present-day attitude and pursuit in regard to choosing one's belief system, it does seem, given the hegemony of the Church in medieval and post-medieval Europe, that to follow female diviities might have involved some sense of determination either, from a conservative position, to keep to ancient traditions, or from a resistant one, to defy the Church's hegemony, or perhaps a combination of both.

It is conceivable that as some women experienced greater independence in the Middle Ages and the Renaissance (although probably to a lesser extent in the latter), they played a role in determining their spiritual belief system, perhaps even when they knew that in doing so, they might trouble or anger Church authorities.

These needs and desires included, not surprisingly, the special and far-ranging concerns of women, from physical beauty to motherhood to work to making one's way in the world as a single, unmarried woman (Diana, Holda). Such needs and desires might have been met to a certain extent by the Late Antique and early medieval Church by way of certain images of the Virgin Mary that promoted motherhood and that emphasized the body as the temple of the soul; or by way of images and narratives of female saints that, while stressing asceticism, nevertheless promoted conceptions of women as possessors of great moral fortitude and occasionally of physical prowess.

Increasingly, however, especially between the thirteenth and sixteenth centuries, images of the Virgin promoted by the Church focused more and more on transcendence of the body than on its participation in the incarnation of the sacred. In regard to women in general,

Donna Spivey Ellington (1995) points out that this period witnessed a widespread "growing suspicion of the body and of women's bodies specifically, in European society as a whole." This tendency increased exponentially with the emergence of the witch hunts.

It seems plausible that many women might have felt more than a little alienated from such images of women, and that this alienation might have led them to seek out, or else keep to, other images and narratives, beliefs and practices that spoke to women who did not lead ascetic lives but who lived in this world as lovers, wives, mothers, laborers, and so on. This yearning must have grown even more profound as emergent Protestantism sought to eliminate "the Virgin and other female saints from their prominent place in religious life," leaving "worshipers with only masculine images for devotional inspiration." Indeed, it occurs to me that whether or not the path that certain women took toward the sacred during the Middle Ages and Renaissance was fully self-conscious, in the way that "choosing" a religion might be or at least seem today, their journeys may have in some sense reflected a privileging of the need or desire for embodied experience of the sacred over that for a largely disembodied, transcendent experience of the sacred. This appears somewhat evidenced by the reasons for which they looked toward female divinities who bore much greater resemblance to those of indigenous and ancient pagan traditions than to the Virgin Mary or female saints.

Let us recall that many ancient female divinities appear to have been reverenced into the Middle Ages and thereafter, albeit sometimes in a masked manner, including Isis, Demeter, Cybele, Minerva, the Cailleach, and a host of Germanic, Basque, Cuman, Slavic, Romanian, Baltic, Finno-Ugric, and Sámi divinities, together with many manifestations of the Earth Goddess. A number of these, like Isis, Demeter, and Earth Goddesses were perceived as "Great Goddesses" to whom one might look for all things.

However, together with some men, women also looked to female divinities to assist them in their everyday occupations, including spinning, weaving, and sewing (Gyre-Carline, Fru Herke, Holda, Perchta, Phinzen, Richella, Rupfa, Wanne Thekla, Frau Werra); baking (Frau Werra); farming and raising of livestock (Baba Dochia, Drăgaica, Fru Gaue, Gruagach, Habundia, Fru Herke, Holda, Vénus de Quinipily); hunting (Diana, Esterelle, Holda, Jecha); fishing and navigation (the Cailleach, Dodola, Esterelle, Mother Carey, Seven Daughters o' the Sea, Wanne Thekla); and healing (Brava Part, Herodias, Holda, Madona Oriente, Vénus de Quinipily). Perhaps especially because many of them were working-class or poor, they also looked to these divinities to provide their children and themselves with a few special gifts beyond the bare necessities (Anne Marie Jacqueline, Tante Arie, La Befana, Perchta). They also looked to female divinities to assist them in matters of love and marriage (Baba Dochia, Drăgaica, Eostre/Ostara, Frau Rose, Herodias, Vénus de Quinipily), childbirth, and childrearing (Aïa, Esterelle, Frau Rose, Grýla, Habundia, Herodias, Holda, Saelde, Sheela-na-gig,

Tante Arie, Vénus de Quinipily).

Those devoted to female divinities also appear to have needed or desired to honor Nature as sacred in and of itself and not merely as a male "God's handiwork." They continued to venerate the Earth and its waters (Baba Dochia, the Cailleach, Eostre/Ostara, Holda, Mither o' the Sea, Mother Carey, Pehtra Baba, Seven Daughters o' the Sea, Vénus de Quinipily), Moon (Diana, Eostre/Ostara, Holda, Hörsel, Vénus de Quinipily), Sun (Grugach), and stars (Holda, Hörsel, Vénus de Quinipily, Wanne Thekla); and they continued to celebrated the pagan-based seasonal cycle (the Cailleach, Eostre/Ostara) which was, unsurprisingly, appropriated wholesale by the Church. They depended on female divinities to assist them in learning of their fates (Baba Dochia, Habundia, Holda, Hörsel, Saelde) by way of divination (Drãgaica, Herodias, Madona Oriente, Saelde, Zlota Baba), and to assist them in working magic (the Cailleach, Drãgaica, Gyre-Carline, Hörsel, Madona Oriente) to influence, to possibly transform, their fates, and even occasionally, to avenge themselves when wronged by those who held greater power.

Perhaps most significantly in terms of Belmont's and Hutton's view that Christianity was sufficient to meet the needs and desires of Europeans, especially in light of Christianity's "confident promise of eternal bliss," many of those devoted to female divinities depended upon them to assist them in the dying process (the Cailleach, Mother Carey, Nicneven, Perchta), to care for their souls and especially for those of their offspring who died as infants (Holda), to guide them into the afterlife (Holda, Hörsel), and to assist them in the process of rebirth (the Cailleach, Holda, Nicneven).

As for the veneration of male divinities and beings – Puck, Shony, local and/or folkloric manifestations of the Devil, etc. – it would appear that images and narratives of the Biblical God and his Son failed to meet the needs or desires of many women and men, leading them to seek masculine divine personae elsewhere.[62]

Chapter 9
Veneration of Fairies, Elves, and Kindred Beings

The converted Barbarians of Europe could not wholly give up their belief in helpful spirits, and Christianity classed them ... as devils.

Henry Charles Lea, *A History of the Inquisition of the Middle Ages* (1901)[63]

You must understand, that after they have delicately banqueted with the ... lady of the Fairies ... nothing is missed of all this in the morning. For the Lady Sibylla, Minerva, or Diana with a golden rod striketh the vessel[s] ... and they are fully replenished again.

Reginald Scot, *The Discoverie of Witchcraft* (1584)[64]

Evidence indicates that a cult devoted to the fairies was widespread in the Middle Ages and Renaissance and in some places persisted for a long time thereafter. A. D. Hope, in *A Midsummer Eve's Dream: Variations on a Theme by William Dunbar* (1970), states: "[T]here was a common belief in the later sixteenth and the seventeenth centuries that certain initiates in human society were accustomed to visit the fairy kingdom, that there was in fact an active fairy cult."

In the fourteenth century, Chaucer depicts fairies as having vanished long before; in the sixteenth, Reginald Scot suggests that people no longer fear them; yet in 1846, Kenelm Henry Digby, in *Mores Catholici*, observes:

> The late author of *Letters on Demonology* [Sir Walter Scott] thinks that Chaucer could not be serious in averring, that the fairy superstitions were obsolete in his day, since they were found current three centuries afterwards. Had he reflected upon the councils, the bulls of sovereign pontiffs, the exertions of the monks and friars, to whom Chaucer expressly ascribes the expulsion, at an early period, from the land of all such spirits, he would never have used such an argument.[65]

Iscanus's twelfth-century *Penitential* insisted that the English abandon the veneration of fairies. In the mid-thirteenth century, Berthold of Ratisbonne/Regensburg (*c.* 1210-1272 CE) condemned the offering by Germans and particularly by Bavarians of banquets to fairies and other beings, insisting that they were "all demons." "O ye village folk," he wrote, "many of you would go to heaven but for ... believ[ing] ... in divination and seeresses and in cunning women and in night-ladies and ... in Robin Goodfellow."

The Problem with Purkiss

One of the most intriguing present-day writers on fairies is Diane Purkiss. I find her work simultaneously seductive and troubling. Moreover, I find it exemplary of much of the scholarly writing being published at present by scholars of Pagan Studies and related fields; in certain important ways, her work resonates with that of Cynthia Eller and Ronald Hutton. In *At the Bottom of the Garden: A Dark History of Fairies, Hobgoblins, and Other Troublesome Things* (2000), Diane Purkiss observes that in the past, fairies were often considered "pagan gods, reduced in stature ... . This used to be a very popular way of understanding fairies. Because they were linked to nature ... it was possible to see in them reduced, tamed, Christianized forms of important deities." She then rather cavalierly dismisses this theory, insisting that "[i]t is not helpful to argue that fairies used to be pagan gods if that is no longer what they were by the eleventh century, and they were not. To say that fairies were once gods is helpful in the sense that it is helpful to say that cars were once ox-carts." On the surface, this sounds wise.

Yet when one begins to ponder her argument, and one commences to try it out with terms other than "fairies" and "gods" – as, for example, "It is not helpful to argue that gay people "used to be" sexual inverts "if that is no longer what they were by" the mid-twentieth century, or, more appropriately in our present context, " 'To say that' transgender persons in pagan Scandinavia 'were once' ritual specialists if that is no longer what they were in Christianized Scandinavia, 'and they were not,' is 'helpful [only] in the sense that it is helpful to say that cars were once ox-carts'" – one commences to sense a problem with this argument. This same type of argument is, by way of note, advanced by Owen Davies in *Cunning-Folk: Popular Magic in English History* (2003). Such arguments not only indicate a kind of historical disinterest on the part of historians but also suggest a rather defiant anti-historical, perhaps even anti-intellectual, stance.

To the contrary, I believe that it might be *extremely helpful* to "say that fairies were once gods." Why? Because it opens our eyes to the process and campaign of Christianization, to one of its most successful tactics, indeed, a two-pronged or two-part one: (1) to transform pagan deities and similar beings into diminutive, irritating but not very powerful beings; (2) to transform pagan deities and similar beings into demonic beings, frequently avatars of Satan. Purkiss's argument suggests to me that she is not terribly interested in confronting this tactic or the effects of the broader campaign of Christianization upon pre-conversion Europe. I would guess that she is probably equally disinterested in, if not hostile toward, theories that speak to the patriarchalization of European religions/traditions.

Purkiss also argues in *At the Bottom* that we should be "suspicious of any text in which the name Diana occurs [such as the *Canon Episcopi*] ... the goddess may be tacked on by the learned Christian." She follows a very popular current argument that rightly insists that the name of Diana may signify a Christian interpretation of a local deity or similar being, but that prematurely or wrongly insists that this *must* be the case. This argument unfortunately neglects to mention that in numerous places where Diana's name is mentioned in medieval and Renaissance texts, she had been worshipped *as Diana*, thanks to Roman imperialism, in Late Antiquity and indeed into the Middle Ages, including in Italy, England, France, and Germany, and thus it is conceivable that her name survived among persons other than "learned Christians."

This argument also errs in assuming little or no contact between "learned Christians" and the remainder of the population. It is also, in my view, somewhat presumptuous (and extremely reductionist) for Purkiss and others who follow this argument to insist upon a rather radical dualism of "learned Christians" and others. This argument also rests upon a solid partition between elite and popular culture. In Purkiss's case in particular, this argument comes into conflict with a bold and much wiser statement she herself makes earlier, that "popular culture has always been a mixture of high and low," that "[p]eople take stories from various places and retell them," and that "[h]igh culture does not trickle down but flows." She notes that "Shakespeare knew this," as demonstrated by his elite-popular braiding of fairy lore, and even goes so far as to almost directly contradict her later statement by calling to mind the Scottish witch Alison Peirsoun, who "put fairies together with Hermes Trismegistus."

Deities into Fairies

The transformation of deities into fairies emerged in a time of crisis for the pagan worldview, as Christianization was becoming ever fiercer. The deities who had been revered for millennia could no longer be revered openly. Christians equated them with demons, ultimately with Satan himself. Many Europeans, however, were unwilling to accept such demonization. It was thus necessary to find an archetypal vessel in which to pour their reverence for these beings. They located that vessel in the notion of elemental beings, fairies and kindred beings whom they most likely hoped would not threaten the Church in the way that reverence of other goddesses and gods most certainly would, and did. This is not to say that elementals like fairies did not exist prior to the transformation of deities into fairies, etc. We know, of course, that they did – dryads, nymphs, etc. Rather, it was in the Middle Ages that beings earlier acknowledged as deities joined them, often as their rulers, so that, for example, Diana, as Titania, became the Fairy Queen. This metamorphosis of deity into fairy was not, however, as we have seen, ubiquitous; in many places, resistance to Christianization insisted that gods remain gods. This process, however, denotes an innovation or evolution in the pagan worldview, or perhaps a devolution; however one views it, it indicates dynamism rather than stasis.

Hera/Juno; Aphrodite/Venus; the Fates (Greek Moirae, Roman Parcae); Nereids; Nymphs; Dryads; the Celtic goddess Danu (or, Anu, Dana), Mother of the Tuatha Dé Danaan, the deities of Ireland who were demoted or transformed into fairies; the

Celtic goddess Maeve (or, Medb), who was demoted or transformed into the Fairy Queen Mab; the Celtic Mórrígán, who was demoted or transformed into Morgan Le Fay; the Germanic Norns – these are some of the goddesses who appear to have transformed into fairies.

Where the Mórrígán is concerned, Gerald Cambrensis (c. 1146- c. 1223), when referring to Morgan La Fay's removal of King Arthur's body to the Isle of Avalon, acknowledges that she originated as a goddess (*Dea*). Intriguingly, Lewis Thorpe, either unconsciously or willfully, in a well-known translation of Gerald's work on Wales, mistranslates *Dea* – a very simple term to translate – as "sorceress."

These divinities appear, generally speaking, to have undergone a process of cultural amalgamation, hybridization, and/or conflation, to emerge in the Middle Ages as the rather distinct collection of beings known as fairies; this indicates once more the transformative power of paganism in spite of Christianization. At this time, moreover, they became linked to goddesses and female beings like Habundia, Holda, Perchta, and Satia, whose cults, as we've seen, emerged or rose dramatically in popularity during the Middle Ages.

It is simplistic to suggest, as the terms "pagan" and "heathen" suggest, that all rural folk clung to earth-centered beliefs much longer than urbanites; it does, however, appear that non-elite rurals wielded greater influence on the earth-centered worldview than they had, for example, in the halcyon days of the Greek and Roman Empires, as many beings of the Middle Ages and thereafter were increasingly depicted as more concerned with the daily tasks of rural life, increasingly portrayed as beings dwelling close by, perhaps even behind the stove. This process of shifting from an emphasis on not-necessarily-rural (e.g., Zeus, Athena) to often primarily rural deities and similar beings, from ruling deities and similar beings to farm-laboring ones, from elites to non-elites, also indicates a transformation of the earth-centered worldview. These shifts, it needs to be underscored, were responses to very 'real' shifting historical and spatial/local conditions. The transition from deity to fairy, and the emphasis on beings nearer the hearth, so to speak, were fueled by Christianization and the needs of persons traumatized by and resistant toward its leviathan campaign to discover ways in which to protect the reverence and memory of divine ones they treasured.

Possible Persian/Iranian Influence

Present-day scholarship increasingly indicates that the emergence and conception of European fairies was inspired or influenced by Persian/Iranian belief in the *parî* (or, *peri*), from which the English "fairy" and the French *péri* may have been wholly or partly derived. The term *parî* originated in Sanskrit as a term for "mountain" or "mountain stream" and eventually came to refer to elementals of these places and to form a part of the name and characteristics of the Hindu goddess Parvati. Secondarily, European fairies may have also been influenced by the *devis*, ancient Hindu goddesses.

Apparently, the *devis* and the *parîs* and made their way from India to Persia. In ancient Persia, the *devis* manifested as the *daçvas* (or, *daiva*, *dçv*), the "Shining Ones" and in Persia included both male and female divinities, including goddesses of water known as the Apas.

Zoroaster (eleventh-tenth century BCE?) and his followers, including Xerxes (486-465 BCE) and Kirder (third century CE), opposing ancient pagan concepts and practices and promoting patriarchal dualism, condemned reverence of the *daevas*, whom they characterized as amoral and evil, predominantly male, demons called *drug* (or *drauga*, as opposed to *ahuras*, *yazatas*, and *amesha spentas*, whom they characterized as beneficial).

During the Sasanian Empire (224 BCE-c. 640 CE), "images [of pre-Zoroastrian goddesses – apparently excepting those of Anahita, who was assimilated into Zoroastrianism as Aredvi Sura Anahita – and other divinities and beings] were destroyed and the lurking places of the *devs* [or, *daevas*] [were] demolished." Zoroastrian "iconoclasts held" that such "cult statues...were inhabited by *devs*" and that many persons were continuing to venerate them and place "offering[s]...before them;" thus, they must be eradicated. In spite of the efforts of Zoroastrians, worship of the *daevas* appears to have continued in Persia, Southern Uzbekistan, and Western Tajikistan into at least the eighth century. I believe that sometime during or after the eighth century, especially with the emergence of Islam, certain attributes of the *daevas* were transferred to the *parîs*.

Although *parîs* could be male, they were most often conceived of as female, typically as beautiful (excepting, on occasion, having hairy legs and animal hooves), seductive beings who alternatively made human men their slaves; shared consensual, loving relationships with mortals, sometimes giving birth to 'mixed-race' children; or served humans magically. *Parîs* were celebrated with feasts in Persian pagan or hybrid pagano-Islamic ritual. As with familiars, Persian and possibly also Indian influence on the conception of fairies may have resulted from cross-pollination between Europeans, Persians, and Indians during the Middle Ages and Renaissance.

Names and Kinds of Fairies

In the mid-ninth century CE, in the Netherlands and elsewhere, persons reported the existence of fairies, whom they referred to as the 'White Ladies' (an appellation which also surfaced as White Nymphs and Witte Wyven [or W. Wivven]). In or near 1601, Martin Del Rio (1551-1608) described these *Nymphae albae* ("White Nymphs") as young and/or matronly women clad in white who often appeared bearing candles, which may suggest priestesses of a cult of fairy rather than the stereotypical evil witch at the Satanic sabbat. These women were sometimes described as wearing black and white checkered attire.

Over the centuries, fairies acquired numerous names, including: the *Bona res* ("Good Ones" or "Good Things," linked to the goddesses Diana and Habundia and eventually with witches), *Dominae bonae* ("Good Ladies"), or *Bonnes Dames* ("Good Women"); the "Kindly Ones" (in French, *Bienveillantes*; in German, *Hulden*); the "Blessed Ones" or "Blessed Souls" (in

German, *die Saligen, Selige Seelen*, or *Seligen*); the "Joyful Women" (in Latin, *Felices Dominae*); "Women of the Night" (in Latin, *Dominae nocturnae*; in German, *naht vrowen*); the "Night Owls" (in French, *Noctambules*); and the "Malevolent Ones" (in French, *Malveillantes*; in German, *Unhulden*). In Ireland, where they were often considered the children of the goddess Danu, or else the votaries of the goddess or Fairy Queen Aine, they were called the "Mother's blessing," acknowledging the goddess as mother, or, alternatively, the "Gentry," the "Good People," or the "Others."

The fairies are thought to be led by a queen, and sometimes also a king. Maeve, or Mab, a local and/or diminutive hypostasis of the goddess Medb, and Titania, an avatar of Diana, both acknowledged by Shakespeare, in *Romeo and Juliet* and *Midsummer Night's Dream*, respectively. The fairy king Oberon, who appears in Huon of Bordeaux, also plays a significant part in *Midsummer Night's Dream*.

Fairies have often been thought to be three in number. As such, they were often referred to as the "Mothers," evoking associations with the Germanic Dísir and the Romano-Celtic Matronae. As a triad, Fairy Queens, like the Norns, possess individual names, the most well known of the triad being Morgue, Arsile, and Magloire, the last one comparable to the evil fairy of fairy tales. Magloire may also, incidentally, correspond to the mandrake as a magical plant. In the Disney film of *Sleeping Beauty*, there are three good fairies: Flora, Fauna, and Merriweather, reflecting an animist sensibility; and one evil one: the fabulous Maleficent. In pagano-Christian contexts, the three fairies came to be conflated with the "three Marys."

Other fairy-like beings include the Slavic *vily* and the Baltic *laumës*. 'The' Vila is sometimes viewed as a goddess, and sometimes, especially in plural manifestation, as a fairy. *Vily* were connected with the souls of the dead, deriving their name from *vel*, "to perish." As such, they often danced on or near graves. They remain eternally youthful, typically possessing pale skin, golden hair, and wings. They dress in white garments. Shapeshifters, they sometimes metamorphose into falcons, swans, snakes, horses, or whirlwinds. They once lived among humans, but mostly dwell deep in the forest, in caves, on mountains, in bodies of water, or in clouds. Guardians of flora and fauna, they practice herbal medicine and love to ride horses and stags. They possess the gift of prophecy. They love children, sometimes giving birth to infants, at other times abducting human children; they nurture their own and human children primarily with honey and instruct them in divinatory, magical, and healing arts. The *vily* were celebrated with song, dance, and offerings of flowers, fruit, cakes, and silk ribbons into the twentieth century in Bulgaria, Croatia, and elsewhere. Patricia Monaghan (1981) relates, "Should a human wish to learn her skills, blood-sisterhood was forged with the Vila. The applicant appeared in the woods before sunrise on a Sunday of the full moon. Drawing a circle with a birch twig or broom, she placed several horsehairs, a hoof, and some manure inside the circle, then stood with her right foot on the hoof calling to the Vila."

Gimbutas (1963) describes *laumës* as "naked women with long hair and long breasts [who] dwelt in forests, near expanses of water and stones. They were constantly mingling with humans and, yearning for motherhood, frequently used to kidnap infants or small children."

The presence of, and concepts and practices centering on, elves, dwarves, fairies, *vily*, *laumës*, and kindred entities indicate an evolution or metamorphosis of, or innovation in, pagan traditions. They also suggest, in my view, that the fairies may have simultaneously reflected demotions of goddesses and spiritual responses to the shifting needs, desires, and mentalities of medieval and post-medieval cultures.

Mélusine

Mélusine is said to be the daughter of a fairy named Pressia and King Elinas of Albany/Scotland. Her name suggests that she may be linked in some way to the hybrid goddess Diana Lucina. Mélusine seems to be immortal. However, she is cursed to live as a hybrid female-serpent. The curse can be partially removed, however, if she weds a man who loves her. Nevertheless, every Saturday, she reverts to her hybrid form; thus, she asks that her husband not disturb her on Saturdays. According to legend, one of her husbands, Raymond of Poitiers (Raimon[din] de Poitiers, 1099-1149; r. as prince of Antioch, 1136-1149), a member of the noble family of Lusignan of Poitou, a province of western France, decides to spy on her on a Saturday and discovers her secret as she is taking a bath. Mélusine, both infuriated and humiliated, flees Raymond. She does, however, leave two children behind. Since the twelfth or thirteenth century, the Lusignan family has claimed Mélusine as an ancestress. It has not, however, been alone in doing so; other families, including the Meddygyon Myddfai family of Wales has, for instance, have also claimed Mélusine as an ancestor, as have certain noble families including the "Luxembourg, Rohan [of Brittany], [and] Sassenaye."This should remind us of the Connollys, Lees, MacCodrums, MacHennessys and Flahertys, Irish and Scottish families who count mermaids and selkies as ancestors. Each year, at the May Fair held near Lusignan, near Poitiers, France, "Mélusines," gingerbread cakes bearing her image, commemorate her tale.

Sibylia

During the Middle Ages and the Renaissance, the prophet known as the Cumaean Sibyl was conflated with the goddess Venus and with the Fairy Queen, or else she transformed into her; as such, she was frequently called "the Lady Sibylla" or "the fairy Sibylia" and was invoked in magical rites. Some said that in Late Antiquity or the Middle Ages, she moved her residence from Cuma to Monte della Sibilla, near Norcia, in the Apennines, in southeastern Umbria, Italy.

Within *La Salade* (1438-1442), a mélange of diverse subjects, which Antoine de la Sale (*c.* 1388-*c.* 1462), a Provençal writer who lived in Italy, wrote for the young prince Jean d'Anjou, duc de Calabre (1426-1471), whom he tutored, was a piece titled "Du monte de la Sibylle et de son lac et des choses que j'y ai vues et ouï dire aux gens du pays" ("Of the Mount of the Sibyl and her lake and the things that I saw there and what is said of the people of that country"). This text followed from an expedition to the summit of Monte della Sibilla, near Norcia, in the Apennines, in southeastern Umbria, which de la Sale had commenced in May or June 1420. He had heard tales of this mountain since he was a child. When he arrived at the summit, he discovered an entrance to a cavern, but fear, apparently, caused him not to enter. He learned that previous to his attempt, five young men of a neighboring village had reached the entrance to the cavern, but fear, too, nourished by moaning winds, had driven them back. However, he also learned that a priest, Don Anton Fumato, had claimed to discover the entrance to the cavern and to have dared to enter it. He had made his way across a steep bridge over an abyss, which led to a road guarded by a couple of animated statues of dragons. The priest had, however, decided not to proceed. Just beyond the dragon statues, he had learned from some adventurous Germans, stood a great metal door.

A German knight, it was said, had once made his way past the metal doors and had arrived at a great crystalline door. Beyond this door lay a wonderful country inhabited by beautiful beings dressed in rich attire, primarily engaged in playing music, dancing, and feasting. While they shared a *langue maternelle*, a 'mother-tongue,' they also communicated with each other telepathically. Upon meeting their queen, the Sibyl, he asked her, "And when the world ends, Madame, what will become of you?" She replied, "We shall become that which has been ordained; don't try to understand." She suggested that he remain with them eight days and depart on the ninth. Days turned into years; he loved the life he led within the mountain. One day, however, he discovered, by way of spying, that the beautiful women of that country transformed into serpents once a week and then returned to anthropomorphic form. He was horrified. He suddenly recalled he was a Christian and decided to escape. He did so, and proceed to plead with three popes, Pope Innocent VI (pope, 1352-1362), Pope Urban V (pope, 1362-1370), and Pope Urban VI (pope, 1378-1389), to absolve him of having spent so much time in the company of beings indulging in worldly pleasures. All three popes refused to absolve him. The knight decided he had no other choice but to return to Monte della Sibilla. Although the third pope underwent a change of heart, decided to absolve him, and sent men after him, it was too late. The knight was never seen again in this realm. In 1497, seventy-seven years after De la Sale's attempt to find the magical realm within the mountain, Arnold de Harff of Cologne, Germany once more made the attempt. In my view, De la Sale's "Du monte de la Sibylle" and related accounts are significant in conveying the interpenetration of belief and legend in premodern Europe.

Weyer reports sixteenth-century German belief in a group of Sibyls, whom he equates with the dead, echoing a common association of the dead and fairies: "[P]ublic dances of ghosts (we called them white women or white Sibyls in the vernacular) were said to have been celebrated here and there."

Sibylia, as "Sib," was known to ritual magicians, wisewomen, and wisemen. When Sibylia is depicted outside the realm of ceremonial magic, as in *The Life of Robin Goodfellow*, the element of cajoling her to do another's bidding is removed. Instead, she appears, like Titania, as the Queen of Fairies, who visits the homes of mortals, punishing those who do not keep house well and rewarding those who do.

It is worth noting that in the sixteenth century, Sibylia was linked in chains of cross-cultural correspondences to the Fates, the Valkyries, Habundia, and other goddesses and beings.

Fairy Characteristics

In one of the best-known studies of the realm of fairies and kindred beings, Robert Kirk's (1641?-1692) *The Secret Commonwealth of Elves, Fauns and Fairies*, fairies are described as "intelligent, studious spirits [who possess] light, changeable bodies (like those called astral), somewhat of the nature of a condensed cloud, and best seen in twilight ... their bodies of congealed air are sometimes carried aloft ... their chameleon-like bodies swim in the air near the earth."

Fairies are often said, not surprisingly, to wear green, the color most associated with nature.

Probably for this reason, one tribe of fairies is known as the Dames Vertes, the "Green Ladies;" they are also called *sylphides*. They are sometimes thought to have originated in the Celtic goddess Arduinna. They are described as having light skin, blonde hair, and blue eyes. The Dames Vertes primarily inhabit the vineyards and orchards of Burgundy, France. They also dwell in caves laden with precious stones. They are often observed braiding floral head wreaths, often of daisies. They spend evenings dancing beneath the moon. They sometimes take human males as lovers.

Other fairies also inhabit caves, speak in an unknown tongue, play mysterious music, travel at night, and entertain certain humans while harassing others who interfere with their activities. They frequently shapeshift, often into the form of deer. Fairies live within hills, or in large houses, lit by ever-burning lamps. They have many books, "nothing of the Bible" but instead, magical texts of "charms and countercharms." Sometimes they visit mortal fairs and marketplaces. In the nineteenth century, fairies were believed to "attend the markets at Milford Haven and at Laugharne" in Pembrokeshire. Fairies believe that time is cyclic and is signified by the seasonal cycle and by the course of the planets around the sun: "every Thing goes in a circle ... and is renewed and refreshed in its revolutions." They journey from their homes in caravans called "raids," especially on the pagan festivals of the solstices, equinoxes, and Beltane and Halloween. They possess psychic abilities, including the gift of prophecy; and they are most often seen by those possessing the ability of clairvoyance, or "second sight." These persons notice their presence especially at funerals and banquets. In the sixteenth century, Joan Tyrry of Somerset testified that fairies assisted her in recognizing when others had been bewitched by practitioners of sinister magic. Some fairies, like those of the Scottish Highlands, travel in whirlwinds; not only this, but they use whirlwinds to transport humans as well as food and other things they desire from the human realm to their own realms.

William Camden (1551-1623), in his magnum opus, *Britannia, or a Geographical Description of Great Britain and Ireland, Together with Adjacent Islands* (1588, translated into English 1610, 1637), focuses on negative actions taken by mischievous and angry fairies and elves; considering his association with the Protestant royalty of England, this is not surprising. He speaks of those using "fairy arrows" or "elf-shot" to wound cattle with a devastating disease and humans with a kindred illness. He does, however, speak respectfully of a wisewoman who seeks to heal the human victim by invoking beings "from the east, west, south, and north, from the groves, woods, rivers, marshes" : "fairies white, red, black."

The notion of fairies doing harm is as much documented as their beneficent acts. In Ireland, for instance, "fairy blasts" could bring about depression or even death.

Although fairies were occasionally associated with the Virgin Mary and were sometimes appropriated by Christians, they also served as signifiers of pagan resistance to Christianity. Some say that the fairies so despise the Virgin Mary that they consider her special day, Saturday, to be an evil day. On the other hand, Robert Kirk (1644-1692), a minister of the Church of Scotland, in *The Secret Commonwealth of Elves, Fauns, and Fairies*, insisted that fairies and Christians were not the enemies that some supposed them to be.

Fairies and the Dead

Fairies are thought to have originated in the west and to return to the west; this signifies a connection with the ancestral dead. As for the fairy lifespan, "They live much longer than we; yet die at last, or [at] least vanish from [their present] State." Some say that they, like the cat, live nine lives.

Fairies were frequently associated with the dead, or with ancestral beings, in the Middle Ages and thereafter. In the late twelfth century, Walter Map (*c.* 1140/1159-*c.* 1210), in *De Nugis Curialium* (*Courtiers' Trifles*), recounts a tale of a knight of Brittany whose wife died young. The knight was devastated by her loss. One evening on his way home, he saw a large group of women and fairies dancing in a circle. He could not believe it when he saw his late wife dancing with the troop. Convinced that this was fairy magic, he retrieved her from the circle and took her home. They remained happily married for many years and had several children together. According to Map, in his day the children were referred to as "the sons of the dead mother." Here we also have hints of parallel worlds and multidimensional reality, porous boundaries between the worlds of the living and the dead, together with the association of faeries and the dead.

As Wolfgang Behringer points out in *Shaman of Oberstdorf*, fairies, the ancestral dead, parallel worlds, and multidimensional reality may have been further linked to the notion of a "peasant utopia." Noting that Alpine fairies were sometimes referred to as the *Säligen Lütt*, the "Blessed Dead," he explains that the *Saligen* were "enchanted ... peaceful people [of] the mountains who helped human beings, spoke with animals, rewarded the good and sometimes punished the bad, and ... possessed the gift of flight." They typically dressed in white, lived within mountains, and loved to sing in the evening. Behringer continues: "Peasant utopias were connected to the existence of the *Saligen*. They helped in gathering berries and in spinning flax...They spun threads that had no ends, baked bread that never got smaller, no matter how much one cut off." Those whom the *Saligen* looked upon kindly were fortunate indeed. Occasionally, marriages occurred between humans and *Saligen*.

Mortal-Fairy Encounters

The English chronicler Gervase of Tilbury (*c.* 1150- *c.* 1220) wrote of a mountain, Cavagum, in Catalonia, Spain, a cavern of which was thought to be inhabited by fairy-like mountain elementals. Due to their presence, both gold and silver were found in abundance in that region. Among humans encountering the fairies of the mountain was a young woman who spent seven years in their company. Among the most intriguing reports concerning time spent among fairies is that related by Gerald of Wales (Giraldus Cambrensis, b. *c.* 1145—d. 1223) in his *Journey Through Wales* (1188) regarding the Tylwyth Teg (pronounced *terlooeth teig*), the "fair family" or fairies of Wales.

A Christian priest named Elidyr (or, Elidorus, probably b. *c.* 1080/ 1100—d. before 1176), who was known to Gerald's uncle, David FitzGerald (d. 1176), Bishop of St. David's, claimed that when he was twelve (probably around the beginning of the twelfth century), he ran away because he "had had more than enough of the harsh discipline and frequent blows meted out by his teacher." He was approached by two tiny men, who offered to take him to a "land where all is playtime and pleasure." They traveled "through a dark underground tunnel ... into a most attractive country, where there were lovely rivers and meadows, and delightful woodlands and plains." Due to its being underground, this kingdom was "rather dark," without benefit of sun, moon, or stars. The people of this kingdom were, like his guides, tiny. They rode on horses no bigger than greyhounds. They were vegetarians; they did drink and cook with milk, but they ate no meat or fish. They delighted in pudding-like desserts spiced with saffron. They frequently made trips to the human world. They spoke a language resembling ancient Greek. They "had no wish for public worship." Elidyr was introduced to the king and to his son, with whom he became good friends. The two boys often played ball together. Elidyr was permitted to come and go whenever he pleased. He told only his mother of the other kingdom. As gold was plentiful there, she asked him to bring her a present of gold the next time he visited. He stole the golden ball that he and his friend always played with. Two guards followed him and retrieved the ball. Because of his crime, and although he felt great remorse, he was never permitted to return to the other kingdom.

"[W]hen he came to where the underground passage had been there was no entry to be found." Gerald relates, "In the process of time [Elidyr] became a priest. The years passed and he became an old man; but whenever David II, Bishop of St. David's, questioned him about what had happened, he would burst into tears as he told the story. He still remembered the language of the little folk." This tale is, in my view, extremely significant in linking the fairies to elements of the earth-centered worldview.

We are reminded that other non-demonic beings beyond the Biblical God, angels, and saints exist. We encounter in this narrative recognition of other worlds, of multidimensional reality. We encounter the notion that these other worlds are not chiefly transcendental, but rather immanent, existing upon our own earth; that is to say, they argue not for transcendence but instead for an invisible immanence, or perhaps we should say, a *selectively invisible immanence*. We are made aware that these realms are reached via wormhole-like portals that connect our world to those of other beings. We are told of deep bonds that can be shared between human and other beings. We learn that beings of other realms possess food customs (such as the fairies' vegetarianism), languages, ethics, and traditions (or, lack thereof) differing from our own. It is suggested that innocence, trustworthiness, and respect for the possessions of others may play roles in our admission into other realms. We sense that the priest's longing for the other realm – bursting into tears each time he tells the story – is not completely satisfied by his life as a Christian, a worldview hostile toward fairies.

Olaus Magnus (1490-1558) observed that in the sixteenth century, many persons continued to believe in and observe companies of fairies playing music and dancing; and Keith Thomas notes in *Religion and the Decline of Magic* (1971), "In Elizabethan Wales there were said to be swarms of soothsayers and enchanters who claimed to walk with the fairies on Tuesday and Thursday nights."

Late in the sixteenth or early in the seventeenth century, a Scottish lord of the Duffus family was allegedly carried off by fairies as "he was walking abroad in the fields near to his own house." He was "found the next day at Paris in the French King's cellar, with a silver cup in his hand." The King interrogated him as to how he had happened to be in the cellar. He explained that he had been walking when he had been suddenly lifted up by a whirlwind. As this was occurring, he heard "voices crying 'Horse and Hattock!'" He was then carried to the cellar, where he and a troop of fairies had drunk heartily, whereupon he fell into a deep sleep. He had awakened to find himself alone except for those who escorted him to the king's throne room. A strange goblet had been found in his hand, which the King, after hearing his tale, returned to him; into the nineteenth century, it was known as the 'fairy cup.'

Unfortunately, there were those who exploited the belief in fairies. In the early seventeenth century, John and Alice West, conned gullible individuals by accepting large sums of money from them, convincing them that the fairies would tell them where treasure was buried, and they would deliver it to the client. Indeed, the Wests even managed to convince some that they were the very King and Queen of fairies. They were tried, convicted, and imprisoned in 1613. Nevertheless, belief in fairies persisted.

William Temple claimed that belief in fairies had dwindled dramatically during the seventeenth century; yet Elias Ashmole (1617-1692) reported that in that century, "a piper in Lichfield that was entertained by the Fairies, and had oftentimes seen them;" he claimed to know "which houses of the town [stood on] Fairy-ground." Ashmole was primarily known as a Royalist who was keenly interested in antiquities, especially in magical practice, and who kept extensive journals and collected objects of interest to Classicists, folklorists, and occultists. The Ashmolean Collection is now housed at Oxford. Ashmole was familiar with a "cavernous place" at Frensham in Surrey, where people would ask the fairies for pewter wares to use at wedding celebrations; they were permitted to borrow these, but if they failed to return them after the celebrations, "they should never be supplied anymore."

One seventeenth-century Englishman claimed that the "ground opened, and he was brought into strange places underground where they used musical instruments, viols, and lute, such ... as Mr. Thomas the Rhymer did play on."

Sometime during the mid-seventeenth century, the butler of a gentleman was sent on an errand when he encountered a band of fairies. A mysterious stranger, who turned out to be the ghost of a libertine, warned him not to join in feasting or dancing with the fairies. They were quite insistent, however, and did manage to raise him into the air temporarily in an effort to kidnap him. This event was allegedly witnessed and verified by the Earl of Orrery, Robert Boyle (1627-1691), a Christian zealot as well as a celebrated natural philosopher and chemist responsible for Boyle's law (pertaining to the compression and expansion of a gas at constant temperature).

Anne Jeffries (1626- after 1696) of St. Teath, Cornwall, claimed that when she was nineteen, she was sitting in the garden when she was visited by six fairies dressed in green. She became terribly frightened and ill. She could no longer eat the food her family ate. The fairies, who continued visiting her, fed her on "fairy bread." Her health returned. Her siblings observed her dancing among the trees, although only one apparently also saw the fairies, and at least one of her siblings tasted the fairy bread, while another handled a silver cup belonging to them. Jeffries was given medicines by the fairies which were considered as being "of invaluable efficacy" in healing others. Unfortunately, some individuals did not believe Jeffries' account, considering her mad or a criminal; thus, at some point after she told others of her meetings with the fairies, she was jailed. Thankfully, however, she later married and lived until at least the age of seventy.

The Reverend John Horsley, in his *Materials for the History of Northumberland* (1729-1730), insisted that by the early eighteenth century, "stories of fairies seem now to be much worn both out of date and out of credit." Yet the folklorist Michael Aislabie Denham, writing in the nineteenth century, determined Horsley's assessment – and, presumably, the others' as well – to be decidedly premature: "This is, however, incorrect, so far as regards country people, long after Horsley's time." In the *Statistical Account of Scotland,* John Sinclair, perhaps a more astute and less partisan observer, reported that in 1730, "the lower class ... firmly believed in ghosts, hobgoblins, fairies, elves, witches, and wizards. These ghosts and spirits appeared to them at night. They used many charms and incantations to preserve themselves, their cattle and houses."

Martin Martin, a native of the Isle of Skye, in *A Description of the Western Islands of Scotland* (1695, 1703), further described beings "that appeared in the shape of women, horses, swine, cats, and some like fiery balls, which would follow men in the fields." Of course, while such beliefs may have concentrated in the rural working class, it was not only that class that continued to hold them; moreover, although Scotland was certainly a hub of earth-centered concepts and practices during this time period, such traditions were also common in many other parts of Europe. Thomas Pennant (1726-1798), in reporting continuing Scottish "belief in specters," pointed toward the ancient and extremely common association of fairies and the dead. He describes a Scottish seer, an elderly, poor farmer whom he encounters as sharing with him an incident in which he was "raised suddenly into the air, and conveyed over a wall into an adjacent cornfield." There, he "found himself surrounded by a crowd of men and women, many of whom he knew to have been dead some years, and who appeared to him skimming over the tops of the unbended corn, and mingling together like bees going to a hive." These beings or ghosts, however, spoke an "unknown language and with a hollow sound." They began shoving him "to and fro," as if dancing roughly with him. He was then approached by a "female sprite," a fairy, who told him she would protect him and that no harm would come to him. He then found himself at his own dwelling, his hair having been "all tied in double knots," an action frequently undertaken by fairies and kindred beings.

In the late eighteenth century, in southern France, a young army captain named Eugene Garriggia, from a noble family, went hunting in the forest of Cailhavel, in the Languedoc-Roussillon region. In the forest, at the bank of a stream, he noticed a beautiful young woman with whom he instantly fell in love. He later described her as being dressed very simply but as having very refined manners. She invited Garriggia to her nearby cottage, where she "spread a table, and placed before her guest, a true huntsman's repast, consisting of milk, brown bread, chestnuts, and eggs." When the young man returned home, he told his uncle and father of the beautiful young woman. His uncle, who was in the process of arranging a marriage for his nephew, was not pleased. When the uncle asked persons living in the vicinity of the forest about the young woman, no one had heard of her. The uncle, determined to find her, went to the forest; he found her at home and insisted that she should surrender any designs she might have on his nephew, who was to wed a noblewoman in an arranged marriage. When she replied that she would not do as he said, but would abide only by the wishes of his nephew, then the uncle insisted on seeing proof of her noble ancestry. She said she would show such evidence only to the nephew. She then gazed at the unclr and said, "Love will smoothe way all obstacles." The uncle returned home infuriated and reported his experience to the young man's father. Later, when Eugene's father went to retrieve his son for supper, he was not in his quarters. His father and uncle decided that he must have left for the forest. When his elders reached the forest, Eugene was not to be found – nor was the young woman, nor, most mysteriously, was her cottage. A massive search turned up nothing. Locals remarked that it seemed almost as if the young woman had "fallen from the clouds," to which she had now returned. As for Eugene Garriggia, "all trace [of him] was lost."

Also in the late eighteenth century, the Scottish minister Lachlan Shaw, in *History of the Province of Moray* (or *Murray*, 1775) – we have already encountered this area in speaking of the Moray Firth above, in regard to reverence of the deities Nicneven and Shony – in reporting the persisting belief in fairies, noted that some persons believed that they were a latter-day manifestation of ancient priestesses. They typically appeared in groves as beautiful young women with disheveled hair, clad in green. Francis Grose (*c*. 1731-1791), in *The Antiquities of England and Wales* (1783), recounted that in Ireland, fairies were known to enjoy baking. Occasionally they would leave oat cakes called "bannocks" on the roads for travelers. Should a traveler not accept the cake and eat it, the fairy considered this a great offense, and he or she was sure to be punished. However, also in the late eighteenth century, scientific theories were increasingly being put forth regarding the existence of fairy rings; these were not circles created by fairies dancing but rather tracks of animals (dancing in circles?) or else the effect of lightning.

In 1806/1810, Dr. Patrick Graham described the fairies of Perthshire, Scotland in *Sketches of Perthshire* as "the people of peace." He reported that their influence was greatest at noon and midnight, especially on Fridays. They were composed of extremely light matter, somewhat denser than air; their voices sounded like whistling, very high-pitched; they were of both sexes; and they were mortal. In 1822, in his *Description of the Shetland Islands*, Samuel Hibbert described a "good man in the Island of Unst, who had an earthen-pot containing an unguent of infallible power" which he had received from the fairies.

Around 1830, a young man of Nether Buckie, a town on the Moray Firth coast of Scotland, was "sent by his father for a chappin of ale and did not return for a year." On the young man's return, the locals were convinced that he had spent the year "living with the fairies." Somewhat later, an old shoemaker of Tomintoul – which, also in northeastern Scotland, lies on the northern slopes of the Cairngorm Mountains – "confessed [that] he had [had] some dalliances with a *lanan shi* [i.e., a Sidhe, a fairy woman] in his younger days." Still later in the nineteenth century, also in northeastern Scotland, in Banffshire, yet again in the vicinity of Moray Firth, a woman asserted that she had received a cure for a certain illness from a wisewoman who had in turn learned it during an eight-year, underground sojourn with the fairies. When the woman who asserted this was asked if the wisewoman had told her anything else of the fairies, she responded that it "wasna safe to be talking o' the gude folk," for "maybe they wad be spiriting her awa' next."

Dr. Delogne, a folklorist and doctor, reported that Jean-Baptiste Duseur (b. *c.* 1825) said in 1913 that he had once known a woman from Vresse, Belgium who had assisted a fairy woman in childbirth. As payment, the fairy gave her two sheaths of wheat, which turned into gold when the woman returned home. In early twentieth-century Romania, in the region of Clisura Dunãrii, a driver for folklorist Marcu Beza told him that he had personally known a young man who had been abducted by the fairies. "The fairies came and wafted him into the air. A long time the boy was borne thus," he continued, "carried along as if by the wind, with eyes closed, not seeing where he went. And, believe me, the lad did not get off unharmed. After some days he passed away for ever."

In 1964, Stewart Sanderson wrote in "A Prospect of Fairyland," published in the journal *Folklore*: "I myself have met, for instance, a lady whose uncle was king of the fairies in a particular district of Inverness-shire. I even know a minister of the Church of Scotland…who…has seen fairies; and finally I was delighted to learn in 1957 that…a fairy and a brownie had…taken up residence in Edinburgh."

Jacques Vallée, in what is admittedly a wildly speculative treatise, *Passport to Magonia: From Folklore to Flying Saucers* (1969), nevertheless may have a point when he describes the realm of Fairy and other non-human realms as "tangential universes." He writes: "In Nithsdale [in Scotland] a fairy rewards the kindness of a young mother, to whom she had committed her babe to suckle, by taking her on a visit to Fairyland. A door opened in a green hillside, disclosing a porch which the nurse and her conductor entered. There the lady dropped three drops of a precious dew on the nurse's left eyelid, and they were admitted to a beautiful land."

Vallée suggests that the ability to perceive that which might be described as selectively invisible immanence depends in part on the other being's willingness to share knowledge of the realm with a human and also with the use of a tangible substance, in this case a "precious," "green dew," perhaps some sort of herbal concoction. Emphasis is placed on perception, on the ability to perceive that which the untrained or unaided human eye normally does not perceive, as Blake and Huxley would argue. Emphasis is also placed on nurturing bonds between humans and non-humans.

Another element dealt with in other fairy narratives indicates the relativity of time. As in "Rip Van Winkle," *Alice in Wonderland*, and the film versions of *The Wizard of Oz* and *Lost Horizon*, humans who journey into other realms may return much older on reentry into the ordinary realm after only a day has passed on earth; or they may return the same age, on the same day, after having spent a long time in the other world; or they may return the same age as when they departed on their journey, years having passed both in the human realm and in the other world; or they may experience some other altered relationship between themselves and time. The relativity of time described in fairy narratives has been, to a certain extent, supported by the theory of relativity and other contemporary concepts in physics, as, to a certain extent, the notion of multidimensional reality has been supported by Michio Kaku's (and others') conception of hyperspace and Brian Greene's description of string theory.

In *Daemonologie* (1597), King James VI/I insists that the Fairy Queen is the current avatar of Artemis/Diana, as frequently conflated with Hecate, and the object of a cult. "That kind," he observes, "the Gentiles ... called Diana, and her wandering court, [which] amongst us [is] called the Phairie [i.e., Fairy, or Faerie]." According to King James, the cult is widespread. In 1438, 1499, and 1556, and on other occasions, alleged English witches had been accused of consorting with fairies.

The King reports that the fairies are ruled by a "King and Queen of Phairie," who possess a "jolly court" with whom they ride and feast "like natural men and women." He suggests that contact with the fairies is thought to be attained after votaries fall into a trance, not unlike a shamanic trance; in this state, votaries' "senses [are] dulled ... as [if] it were a sleep ... their bodies being senseless." He blames Catholics for not succeeding in stamping out, and the Devil for encouraging, belief in fairies. He describes those who honor the fairies as "sundry simple creatures" on the one hand, and as demonically possessed on the other. Like other witch-hunters, he insists that wisewomen and second-sighted men who communicate with fairies, as well as those who rely on such persons, should be "as severely...punished as *any other Witches* [italics mine], and rather the more" since they claim to be practicing the magical arts for beneficial purposes when, according to James, they are doing the work of the Devil.

Beza relates that in Romanian tradition, the moon is a beautiful maiden and the sister and/or spouse of the sun; she is the goddess Ileana Sânziana. She is associated with the fairies, sometimes identified as their queen, and she is celebrated during the winter festivities. Beza is convinced that Ileana is synonymous with Diana. It is, of course, conceivable that in some times and places, the cult of the Goddess(es) and of the fairies, if either or both existed – and ample evidence suggests that they did – that they were not always linked to each other.

In 1576, Bessie Dunlop of Dalry in Ayrshire, Scotland was allegedly visited by a fairy or ghost named Thom Reid, who instructed her in the art of healing. Reid was described as a man dressed in grey, wearing a black hat and carrying a wand, probably made of willow. At least one occasion they met occurred on the morning after an indigenous, earth-based festival, that of Imbolc/Candlemas. Although Dunlop encountered twelve companions of his who were fairies, she refused to go with them to the Elfin court where she was supposed to continue her tutelage. Nevertheless, Thom Reid instructed her in the art of herbal healing, and she healed quite a number of people; one remedy he recommended consisted of an herbal powder to be stirred into ale, comprised of ginger, cloves, anise, and licorice. In spite of beneficently assisting others, she was executed for witchcraft, burned alive on Castle Hill in Edinburgh, on November 8, 1576.

In 1586, Alison Peirsoun of Byrehill, Scotland was indicted on charges of witchcraft. She claimed to have met with the fairies, the "good neighbors" and the "Queen of Elfland." Like Dunlop, she was given instruction in herbal medicine and healed many. She gathered herbs with the fairies and was taught by the ghost or spirit of her cousin or paternal uncle, William Sympsoun. One of those she cured was Patrick Adamson (1537-1592), the Archbishop of Saint Andrews, who then repented and had her arrested, after which she was burnt alive.

A highly organized fairy cult may have flourished in the late sixteenth century in Sicily, particularly around 1588, as Gustav Henningsen indicates in " 'The Ladies from the Outside': An Archaic Pattern of the Witches' Sabbath." Known as the *donni di fuora*, the "women from outside," the cult appears to have been comprised primarily, as its name indicates, of women, with a minority of male members. A majority of members appear to have been poor or working-class, with professions including farm-laborers, fishermen, shoemakers, laundresses, spinners, and prostitutes. There were a number of groups (covens?) of *donni di fuora*, with each group comprised of five to thirty-three members (surely thirty-five classifies as a cult; recall that according to the New Testament, two or three is enough). These groups included the Companies of the Mother, the Noble, Palermo, the Poor, Ragusa, the Romans, and the Table and Distaff. It is conceivable, from certain associations occurring within Sicilian witch trials, that the "Romans" may have included, or else been named after, the Romani (or, pejoratively, Gypsies). The *donni di fuora* venerated fairies and allegedly joined with them in rites.

The fairies were led by the Queen of the Fairies, whom they called by that name as well as "the Instructress," "the Woman of Grace," "the Greek Lady," "the Gloved Lady," "Lady Zabella" ("The Wise Sibyl"), "La Matrona," and "Mandatta." Of these, I find the last two especially intriguing. "La Matrona" can, of course, mean "the Matron," "the Mother," but in this context, it may also signify both "the Mother Goddess" and "the Midwife." "Mandatta" might mean "Lady of the Mandate," i.e., "She Who Hands Down the Law," but beyond this, the name Mandatta is a mysterious one, being found in the ancient Indian epic *Ramayana*, wherein it refers to a legendary king. This might seem utterly disconnected from our present context, except for an equally mysterious remark made by a spiritual descendant of the Sicilian wisewomen interviewed by Henningsen in 1985. During the interview, Signora M. told Henningsen that every autumn she traveled to India in spirit, where a great "feast [was] given especially in her honor." In some groups, the Fairy Queen appears to have been associated with the Queen of Sheba. Female fairies are described as beautiful women except for occasionally having "cats' paws," "horses' hooves," or "pig tails." They typically, although not always, dressed in black or white. Fairies, as well as mortal women, of the Company of Palermo may have worn garments of red, pink, and gold, with white or red and white shoes and with headdresses.

The Fairy King seems to have been second in command, perhaps more of a consort than a father figure. He is depicted as "red" or as dressed in red. Other than the King, at least one other male fairy appears to have taken part in the rites, a musician who plays the lute while they dance.

The Queen and King sat on thrones, explaining to practitioners that they were to worship them as they might the Biblical God and the Virgin Mary. If practitioners committed themselves to the fairies, then they were promised beauty and prosperity, among other things. Because the fairies loved small children dearly, they often blessed them "so that [they] should be[come] rich."

The fact that women explained that they had been chosen on different occasions to hold the office of the Fairy Queen suggests that they may have in some sense believed themselves to be embodied, perhaps "possessed," by the Queen, as deities and similar beings embody human worshippers in Vodou and other African-diasporic religions/traditions. Most groups convened on Tuesday, Thursday, and Saturday evenings, holding a great celebration in March in the forest. Benevento, underneath a walnut tree, was a prime location for gatherings. At least some practitioners were alleged to travel "in spirit," astrally or in trance, rather than physically to meetings.

Gatherings included singing, dancing, feasting, and lovemaking, accompanied by music of lute and tambourine. They also involved traveling to the houses of others in spirit to find fine garments to wear to the gatherings and to bless the households with prosperity, much as the fairies do at the end of *A Midsummer Night's Dream.*

The fairies instructed practitioners in the art of healing, particularly of illnesses incurred by ignoring, offending, or injuring the fairies. Those who did so were comparable to Spanish and Mexican *curanderas* and were described as possessing "sweet blood." The ability to heal brought in a bit of extra money to the mostly poor practitioners. Some practitioners were also instructed by the fairies in lace-making, reminiscent of the veneration of Richella.

One of the most well known alleged practitioners of the fairy cult is Andro Man, a native of Tarbrugh, Rathven, Scotland, tried and executed in 1597. Man allegedly first encountered the Queen of Elfland in or near 1538, when he was a boy. As he was gathering water from the family well, she approached him, telling him that one day she would teach him many things. He met her again about twenty-five years later. At this time, he also encountered the male being Christsonday, as well as the ghost of Thomas the Rhymer, who had shared an intimate relationship with the Fairy Queen. They celebrated in Elfland, especially at Halloween. At this time also, he and the Queen allegedly commenced a thirty-two year intimate relationship.

Marcu Beza suggests that such divine-mortal relationships may be traced back to antiquity and are exemplified by such sacred marriages as that between the goddess Fortuna and the legendary or historical King Servius Tellius (c. 550 BCE?) and that between Dionysus and the wife of the Archon of Athens.

Returning to Andro Man, the Fairy Queen taught him to cure numerous illnesses including epilepsy, utilizing chants, including "If thou wilt live, live! If thou wilt die, die!," and ritual paraphernalia including salt and black wool. During their three-decade relationship, they allegedly had a number of children, who would've been born beginning around 1567 and possibly as late as years just preceding his trial.

John Stewart, tried for sorcery in 1613, "declared that after two meetings with the King of the Fairies, each at Hallowe'en, he had been accustomed to join these people every Saturday night at seven o'clock and spend the night with them in fairy hills." Numerous others were alleged to convene with fairies, including Katherine Carey, Elspeth Reoch, Katherine Jonesdochter, and Isobel Haldane, who were instructed by the fairies in the art of healing; Isobel Sinclair, who was bestowed with the gift of second sight by them; and Janet Drever, who allegedly lived with the fairies for twenty-five years.

In his 1822 *Description of the Shetland Islands*, Scottish geologist and antiquary Samuel Hibbert reported a link in his own day between witches and fairies:

Several Shetlanders, among whom are *warlocks and witches* [italics mine], have enjoyed a communion with the *guidfolk*, and, by a *special indulgence* [italics mine], have been transported in the air, whenever occasion served, from one island to another. In their visits to Trolhouland, ...they have been allowed to enter the interior of the hill at one side, and to come out of it at the other; and, in this subterraneous journey, have been dazzled with the splendour exhibited within the recesses through which they have passed.[66]

Just as some scholars continue to doubt the historical reality of a cult of Diana or of cults of local goddesses or female beings, so some continue to doubt the historicity of a cult or cults of fairy. Nevertheless, highly respected scholars including Hans Peter Broedel and Éva Pócs argue that such cults may have indeed existed.

In the late nineteenth and early twentieth centuries, a system of belief in fairies, including ways in which mortals might please or demonstrate respect toward them in order to their occasional vengefulness on being slighted, persisted in Ireland, the Isle of Man, and elsewhere. One might anger the fairies by doing such things as casting dirty water out of the house without paying attention to where it might fall or putting garbage on one of their residences or "playground[s]." One might please them by greeting them in the morning and evening, by carrying heavy objects for them, and by sweeping the hearth and lighting a new fire therein when retiring to bed "so that the fairies can warm themselves there." Those who venerated the fairies were often rewarded with gifts. "Fairy doctors" continued to be employed to heal others, including healing victims of "fairy darts" (in earlier times called "elf-shot") resulting from offending the fairies. Edgar L. Wakeman reported that fairy doctors were "still popular" on the Isle of Man in 1892 and that they were especially "well liked by the peasantry." Fairy doctors' instruments, kept in "elf-bags," included coins and/or pieces of silver, pieces of copper, "polished white quartz pebbles," and "fairy darts," flintstone arrowheads believed to have been deployed by fairies.

Invoking Fairies

Fairies were invoked by practitioners of magic, some of whom may have belonged to a fairy cult. In a spell having as its aim the securing of the fairy Sibylla/Sibylia as a servant, as Puck serves Oberon in *A Midsummer Night's Dream* and Ariel serves Prospero in *The Tempest*, the magician commences by obtaining the promise of a condemned man, who promises that, upon his death, his spirit will serve the magician, in exchange for prayers pleading for the criminal's admission into heaven. The dead man's spirit serves the magician by bringing to him the "fairie Sibylia." The magician's invocation of Sibylia clearly demonstrates the intermingling of Christian and pagan elements: "I conjure thee, Sibylia, O gentle virgin of fairies, by the mercy of the Holy Ghost ... and by all the angels of Jupiter and Venus ... and by the king and queen of fairies ... I conjure thee, Sibylia, by the blood that ran out of the side of our Lord Jesus Christ crucified."

In another spell, the magician conjures not only Sibylia but also her sisters, Milia and Achilia, together comprising a trinity reminiscent of the Parcae, the Norns, and other divine female triads. It is possible that the pair Milia-Achilia may signify, at least in part, the yarrow plant *Achillea millefolium*. This herb, sometimes possessing beautiful red or lilac flowers, was typically gathered at midsummer, in the sign of Cancer. It is named after the hero Achilles and is governed by Aphrodite/Venus, sometimes nicknamed "eyebrow of Venus." We have already noted that Sibylia was sometimes conflated with Venus. In Germanic tradition, yarrow was sacred to the goddess Freyja and to Thor. Although yarrow is best known for its medicinal properties, it has also been used in amatory divination and magic, hence a link to the previously mentioned spell; in the "British Isles maidens cut the yarrow at moonlight with a black-handled knife, placed it under their beds," and prayed: "Thou pretty herb of Venus' tree,/ Thy true name it is Yarrow:/ Now who my bosom friend must be,/ Pray tell me tomorrow." This spell, which has as its aim the acquisition of a ring conferring invisibility and the consequent discovery of hidden treasure, reiterates the magical hybridity of the former invocation: "I conjure you, three sisters of fairies, Milia, Achilia, Sibylia, by the Father, by the Son, and by the Holy Ghost."

Another spell is likewise peppered with Christian (and possibly also other non-pagan) names and figures. This rite should be undertaken at the time of the new moon, at 9 p.m. (or possibly 4 a.m.; it is not quite clear whether Scot, by "the hour of 4," refers to 4 o'clock or to the fourth hour of the night), when sun and moon are conjunct (thus, the new moon) in Cancer, Sagittarius, or Pisces. When Sun and Moon are conjunct, the masculine and feminine principles unite. When this occurs in Cancer, however, the feminine principle, associated with nurturance, fertility, sensuality, and intuition, predominates and attracts. In the *Picatrix*, an Arabic manual, primarily concerning astrology, composed in the tenth century, we are told that when the moon is increasing in Cancer, Pisces, and Sagittarius (as well as in Taurus), magical works are rendered especially potent, and that one should "make images of love and delight" during this period. The magician performing the work to Sibylia draws two magic circles in chalk on the floor, four feet apart (notice the deployment of the number 4 in this rite). He and his apprentice stand inside the other circle. His apprentice holds a crystal, aimed toward the second circle. He also draws a ritual diagram which resembles both a lyre and a bearded, horned figure (could this be the "Lord of the Wild," or "Horned One," possibly conceived of here as companion to Sybilia?). Inside this diagram, he draws three small crosses, under which he writes the words "Sorthie, Sorthia, Sorthios." He pins this diagram to his chest. He then evokes a certain being "N.," to search for and bring back with him/her the "fairie Sibylia," so that he "may talk with her in those matters that shall be to her honor and glory." He compares her to the Virgin Mary and asks the angels and beings of Venus and Jupiter to assist him and "N." in bringing her into manifestation. On her arrival, he asks that she appear to him in the circle near his and his apprentice's own, "in the forme and shape of a beautiful woman in a bright and vesture white and garnished most fair." That is to say, that she manifest as a beautiful mortal woman. When she does so, he joins in lovemaking ("copulation") with her, recalling the ancient rite of ruler or warrior engaging in *hieros gamos* with a priestess of the Goddess.

In yet another Renaissance spell, Sibylia is once more invoked together with Milia and Achilia. In this spell, the three fairies are envisioned as beautiful women dressed "in white vestures." The magician deploys this spell to ask them to provide him with the "ring of invisibility, by which [he] may go invisible at [his] own will and pleasure." His desire for a ring that provides invisibility suggests an association of the three fairies with the Germanic Nibelungen in their depiction as an ancient dwarf- or fairy-like people, as in the transformation of the dwarf Alberich to the Fairy King Oberon.

In 1646, Elias Ashmole and William Lilly (1602-1681) successfully invoked the Fairy Queen. Lilly, the author of *Christian Astrology* (1647), is now considered the father of horary astrology. Lilly was condemned by Puritans and others who felt that astrology should be prohibited. Because he supported Cromwell, however, he was more protected than others who practiced the art. Moreover, Lilly's Christianity did not prevent him from constructing a syncretic spirituality/ enspirited materiality incorporating belief in fairies and the practice of magic. Thought to be a gifted prophet, Lilly was nicknamed "Merlin" by his supporters. Collaborating with Lilly, Ashmole sought to entreat fairies and other beings to appear. They used a crystal to conjure them. Before the arrival of the fairies, powerful winds arose. After three or four invocations, the Queen of the Fairies made an appearance in Hurst Wood, a property belonging to Lilly. Ashmole advised others wishing to commune with fairies not to keep them too long, for "they will grow unruly and troublesome, perhaps dangerous."

The Fairy Feast

In Persian earth-centered, hybrid ritual, *parîs* were celebrated with feasts, perhaps the most well known one variously known as *Sufra-Sabzî*, meaning "the table spread on the greensward" or "a colorful carpet placed on the green for a special guest," and as *Ziyâfat-I Dukhtâr-i Shah-I Pariyân*, "the Feast for the Daughter of the Fairy King." These feasts were especially held on certain occasions such as when someone was "suffering from sickness or misfortune." It was often thought that persons suffered because they had ignored or abandoned the *parîs*). In order to determine whether or not this was the reason for the illness or ill luck, a special rite needed to be undertaken; Nicholson (1930) writes:

> The priestesses of the rite, – certain old women acquainted with the proper ceremonies...are [alone] permitted to celebrate it, and nothing can be done till their consent has been obtained. The rite is performed in the following manner :– One of these old women...[takes] with a mirror, a cup of water, a piece of sugar-cane, ...some frankincense, ...and the egg of a black hen. ...[S]he deposits [these things] at sunset in a [special] spot, ...chants certain invocations to the Daughter of the Fairy King and departs, after having lighted a fire and thrown into it some seeds of rue.[67]

Performance of this ritual would make it clear if the illness or misfortune had resulted from an offense against the *parîs*. If so, the elder women would tell the sufferer, "Your only remedy is to give an entertainment to the Daughter of the Fairy King, in the hope that she will eat salt with you and pardon your offence." This feast included the sacrifice of two birds (one a pigeon) and a black sheep which were then cooked in sesame oil, vegetables and fruits, and an array of desserts, as well as roses, incense, and music. The woman assuming the role of priestess would then invoke the *parîs* and invite "them to the feast." She would then bid the sufferer to repeat after her a prayer like the following:

Hail to thee, O Daughter of the Fairy King, and to you, O people who are better than we. By this bread and salt which ye have eaten and by this welcome which ye have accepted, I adjure and beseech you to pardon the fault of a poor ignorant wretch who is crying for mercy. Do ye in your majesty forgive me and close your eyes to whatsoever sin ye have seen me commit against you. Make me sound and well again very soon! Grant my wish and heal my pain![68]

It is conceivable that such feasts for the *parîs* may have, via cross-pollination during the Middle Ages, have inspired or influenced similar practices undertaken by Europeans.

In England, Scotland, France, Germany, and elsewhere, it became customary to offer the fairies a simple meal, typically some sort of porridge and milk, in the hope that they would grant the practitioner prosperity, health, or another thing she or he desired. A somewhat more elaborate offering was the "fairy feast." This practice, documented from the ninth century onward, was especially performed at New Year's, on Epiphany/Twelfth Night, at the spring and fall equinoxes, during the final stage of a woman's pregnancy, and upon the birth of children. A table of food and drink (including three loaves of bread, three pots of milk, three vessels of wine, and meat, cheese, and eggs) employing the household's best dishware, especially three knives (as the fairies often manifested as a triad), and an offering of three gifts was set up and left for the fairies, who arrived late at night, when the household slept. These feasts offered to fairies were sometimes called "Tables of Fortune," inferring that such offerings to fairies might bring good fortune to those mortals who did so.

In an effort to halt this practice, Church authorities insisted that no vessels be left uncovered, no food left out, when the household retired for the night. Gulielmus Alvernus (Guillaume d'Auvergne), Bishop of Paris, reported in *De universo creaturarum* (*On the Universe of Created Things*) that certain persons of early-to-mid thirteenth century France believed that the *bonae dominae*, the "good women" or fairies, visited their houses; for this reason, they "set out food and drink for them." During that century, the cult of the fairies seems to have reached a sort of pinnacle. At this time, they came to be increasingly associated with other sacred or supernatural beings including dwarves and nightmare spirits, and Church authorities escalated their campaign to demonize fairies. The fairies of Germany had often shared their feast with Frau Perchta; in certain locales, Perchta and the fairies had meshed as the Perchten. Church authorities insisted that if the same feast continued to be held, it must be offered not to the fairies but the Virgin Mary, Christ, or the Biblical God. Many did so, but it appears that in general, the primary compromise that Christianized pagans were willing to make was to continue offering sacrifices to the dead, as on the Eve of All Soul's, as the dead were often associated with the fairies, a compromise that was viewed as very "iffy" by the Church.

Numerous persons, however, continued to feast the fairies in fifteenth-century France and elsewhere. Thomas of Haselbach (*c.* 1420-1464), a professor of theology at the University of Vienna, Austria, the Dominican priest Jean Herolt (d. *c.* 1468), and many others documented and condemned the persistent practice of offering banquets to the fairies.

Within the Sicilian fairy cult described above, the fairy feast, or *tabula*, was sometimes connected to healing rites. When it became obvious that a person had become ill due to ignoring, insulting, or injuring the fairies, then wisewomen like Antonia Pallagona (fl. 1600) would, on a Tuesday, Thursday, or Saturday night, "decorate the sick person's room and set out a table with jugs of water and wine, and with sweetmeats, five loaves, five napkins, and a honey-cake, a cup, and other eating utensils. [And then she] covered the sick person's bed with a red cloth and perfumed the whole room [with sweet-smelling incense]." Then the wisewoman would wait for the fairies to arrive. When they did, she would shake a tambourine over the body of the sick person, then feed the fairies (who could not be seen by any non-initiates who might be in the room) and ask them how to heal the person.

John Aubrey claimed that when he was a boy (circa 1630),

> our country people would talk much of them: they were wont to please the Fairies, that they might do them no shrewd turns, by sweeping clean the hearth, and setting by it a dish whereon was set a mess of milk sopped with white bread: and did set their shoes by the fire, and many times on the morrow they should find a threepence in one of them.... Mrs. Markey of Hereford ... told me, that her mother did use that custom...[69]

Around twenty years later, Presbyterian church authorities stepped up persecution of those Scots who continued to venerate fairies; but in spite of such persecution, many continued to make offerings of "bread, butter, cheese, milk, eggs, fish, [and] fowl" to the fairies in Aberdeenshire and elsewhere in northeast Scotland.

In the nineteenth century, in the French Pyrenees and elsewhere in France, a simple meal was prepared for the fairies or "white ladies" on New Year's Eve. On a linen tablecloth, a loaf of bread, cups of water and wine, and silverware were placed. A candle burned in the middle of the table. All the members of the household then left the room so the fairies might eat in peace. After they had done so, the others reentered the room. Whatever bread remained was dipped into the water and wine and then distributed to the family and servants – a sort of non-Christian communion. It was believed that households who remembered the fairies would be blessed, while those who neglected them would be cursed. Also in the nineteenth century, as early folklorist Anna Bray (1790-1883) relates, women in Devon and the surrounding area, while not offering a feast per se, would place basins of water by the chimney nooks in the evening for thirsty pixies. In return, it was believed, thankful pixies sometimes deposited sixpence into the basins. Bray related that one woman had erred in telling others of a gift the pixies had left her; the pixies, offended by her betraying what they deemed a secret, never visited her house again.

Although in 1903, Sheila Macdonald reported that it was "generally agreed...that nobody sees [fairies] these days, because, as one old woman told me, there is so much Gospel preached nowadays," she nevertheless wrote of the now-invisible fairies: "Though no longer visible to our wise eyes, they are most emphatically there! If not, why does the milkmaid always spill a little drop of each milking as an offering for the little folks? Why does the housewife leave a little meal on her baking-board for the fairies?"

Haymakers in North Devon, England, as late as 1930, remembered to "throw a crumb or two of their lunch and a drop of cider on the ground" to the fairies. Intriguingly, this practice is performed today by practitioners of African-diasporic religions/traditions to the god of the crossroads and to ancestors. In early twentieth-century Greece, feasts for the Fates continued to mirror those offered to the fairies.

Occasionally it was the fairies who feasted the mortals, in exchange for something they desired. In the early nineteenth century, some ploughmen believed that fairies so coveted the soil that attached itself to the goad, an implement for guiding livestock pulling a plough, that if offered it, that they, the fairies, would prepare a meal of bannock and collop (mincemeat) for the ploughman and leave it for him at "the end of the fourth furrow" in exchange for a "*spurtle*" of earth from his "*gad end*."

Before leaving the fairies (for now), I would like to point out that within this brief exploration, we have observed references to Diana and other divinities, to Christianity, and to other sacred and cultural traditions. One of the most cherished bits of sacred wisdom I've received was from my Greek-American friend Peter Limnios; he once said to me at Café Flore, "Don't forget when you're thinking or writing about ancient Greek religion that the people of one town or village may not only have orshipped a different collection of gods and goddesses but they may have also worshipped a particular god or goddess very differently than they did in the town down the road." It's my view that it's crucial to understand such diversity and complexity if we are ever going to make sense of the many, many different combinations of sacred, mythic, and folkloric elements that we find when we set out to explore paganism/s and witchcraft/s, as, for example, evidenced by confessions during witch trials. Emma Wilby has done a remarkable job of illuminating a very particular and significant case of sacred hybridity in the alleged practices of Isobel Gowdie; in *The Visions of Isobel Gowdie* (2010), she focuses on shamanistic and demonic elements but also points out fairy and Christian elements in Gowdie's confessions.

Elves, Dwarves, and Such

Both Claude Lecouteux, in *Les Nains et les elfes au moyen age* (1988), and Jean Claude Bologne, in *Du Flambeau au bûcher* (1993), acknowledge the difficulty of determining the precise origin of dwarves and elves. It is conceivable that they commenced as pagan deities and, in part due to Christianization, were demoted. Lecouteux, acknowledging this, suggests that elves and dwarves may also and perhaps more significantly be linked to the figure of the genius, daemon, or tutelary spirit. However, as popular notions of dwarves and elves seem to have interwoven Mediterranean, Celtic, Germanic, and other traditions, they may represent a dramatic innovation in terms of personae allied with the earth-centered worldview. As in the case of divinities whose cults emerged or at least dramatically intensified in the Middle Ages and thereafter, whatever may or may not have constituted their ancient origins, it is the medieval and post-medieval presence of elves, dwarves, fairies, and kindred beings that brought them a significant place in the study of non-Christian folklore, mythology, and spirituality/enspirited materiality, indicating, once more, an evolution in paganism in a Europe that was becoming increasingly Christianized.

Lecouteux observes that elves tend to be perceived in more affirmative terms than dwarves. "Elf" from *alb-*, meaning white, connoted, in the Middle Ages, a beneficent, beautiful being. Elves are often given names. Names have been very significant in earth-centered traditions, indicating that one shares a relationship with a certain being, frequently the kind of relationship one shares with a guardian angel. Elves are especially linked to certain Germanic deities, namely, Njörð, Freyr, and Freyja, with Freyr and Freyja being envisioned as the lord and lady of the elves. Elves are thought to possess powers of divination and magic. Where divination is concerned, an elf named Dáinn was sometimes claimed to have fashioned the runes. The magic practiced by elves is known as *aelfsiden*, which has been linked to *seiðr*. Alaric Hall, in his brilliant study *Elves in Anglo-Saxon England* (2007), suggests that the term *"ylfig"* may signify a type of possession or trance state, an altered or shamanic state of consciousness, into which elves — as well as, perhaps, their devotees — fall, prior to prophesying. In this context, Hall suggests a possible association of elves and gender diversity by way of an association with *seiðr*.

In Lecouteux's view, a significant material sign of the elves' association with divination and magic is the mandrake, a plant resembling a human body that has been used in magic for millennia. One of its names is *alraun*, "secret of the elf." This term is related to *albrûna*, which refers to certain women diviners. Lecouteux observes that "all operations concerning this plant are performed on Friday, in German, Freitag, that's to say, "Freyja's Day [although others would say it pertains to Frigg, another goddess associated with fertility]; this goddess is the sister of Freyr, who is lord of the elves."

Many elves live in Asgard, a home of the gods, in a region called Alfheim(r).

The elves who dwell there are known as the Liósálfar, the "elves of light;" as such, they are linked to the sun as well as to clarity and enlightenment. There are also, however, sinister elves; they are known as the Döckalfar. They possess dangerous elf-arrows that cause 'elf-shot' and often bring illness or death to livestock and humans. In certain places, elves were thought to take part in the Wild Hunt, and as such, were characterized as the Milites Herlikini.

Lecouteux insists that "the elves occupied a significant place in pagan beliefs; they were at the heart of Germanic paganism." For this reason, the Church was determined to extirpate them. Because elves were so highly revered, Church authorities attacked them much more vehemently than they attacked dwarves, who did not share a widespread cult, since the latter were often considered to be "dangerous and malefic." Nevertheless, belief in elves continued (at least) into the sixteenth century. An item of material culture associated with the elves or fairies and "preserved in Edenhall, Cumberland" is the so-called "Luck of Edenhall," a goblet said to have been presented to Henry I (1068-1135, r. 1100-1135) by a lord of Colchester, seized at an elfin banquet by a member of the Musgrave family or else one of their servants. Continuing veneration of elves is also evidenced by a Germanic charm meant to protect horses from the disease of morve; the charm, placed in the horse's stall or on its body, includes the invocation "Albo, Albuo, Alubo," all of these words signifying an elf or elves. Also indicative of belief in elves is the nicknaming of the pentacle or pentagram, employed in magical undertakings, the "foot of the elf."

Dwarves (also called by other names, including "trows" in the Shetland Islands of Scotland and *Erdmännlein* in Germany) have been described as "partak[ing] of the nature of [both] men and spirits" in possessing "material bodies" but also the means "of making themselves invisible."

They are believed to possess "magic powers, [and] they [have been] linked to a cult of the dead, to rites of fecundity, [and] to the fabrication of weapons or sacred objects." In the sixteenth century, they were linked to the Lares, household gods of the Romans. According to Lecouteux, their possession of magic powers, as with elves, links them to the Vanir deities of the Germanic pantheon. Beyond this, dwarves share other associations with the Vanir: both are linked to wealth and to the mineral realm. Dwarves also share associations with the trickster god Loki, in being linked to artisanship and metamorphosis. As the craftsmen of the Germanic gods, Lecouteux relates, they fashion Mjöllnir, the hammer of Thor; Gungnir, the spear of Odin; Skiðbladnir, the boat of Freyr; and Brísingamen, the necklace of Freyja. The most celebrated of all dwarves is Oberon (or/also, Auberon, Alberich); perhaps because of the increasingly negative depiction of dwarves, he eventually metamorphoses into the Fairy Prince (or, King). He appears to have emerged very late in the Middle Ages, making an appearance in the thirteenth-century French work *Huon de Bordeaux*. In times past, persons who believed in elves and dwarves typically made offerings to them in the hope that they would treat them kindly and bring them prosperity. The winter feast of *álfablót*, celebrated by Germanic peoples, honored the elves as well as the ancestral dead. On certain occasions it appears that bulls were sacrificed to elves. Burchard of Worms' (d. 1025) *Corrector* indicates that offerings continued to be made to elves, dwarves, and kindred beings in the eleventh century. Persons suspected of making such offerings were queried: "Hast thou made little boys' size bows and boys' shoes, and cast them into thy storeroom or thy barn so that satyrs or goblins [*pilosi*, "hairy ones"] might sport with them, in order that they might bring to thee the goods of others so that thou shouldst become richer?"

The *Penitential* of Bartholomew Iscanus indicates that such practices continued into the late twelfth century, in condemning the practice of "cast[ing] into a granary or storehouse a bow or any such thing for the devils which they call fauns to play with, that they may bring more [grain]." In Christianized Sweden, traditional healers like the *klok gubbe* ("healer"), including the *klok gumma* ("wisewoman"), continued to offer hair and clothing of ill persons to the elves at places where three roads met (*tre-wäga-mot*) so that the elves might assist them in deciphering how to heal a certain illness by determining whether its origin lay in earth, air, water, or (presumably) fire.

Dwarves have tended to be perceived,

as mentioned above, as somewhat dangerous and frequently given to malefic actions. A pairing of elves and dwarves employing the theory of correspondences, with elves corresponding to water, the sun, daytime, and goodness, linked dwarves to stones, the moon, nighttime, and malignity. Thus, dwarves have not shared as affirmative a reputation or as widespread a cult as elves, and this has made it easier to demonize them. Bologne relates that the forces of "Christianization used against [dwarves] the same weapons that were used against fairies. They were first identified with certain Roman deities and were then assimilated together with these as members of a pantheon of demons."

Exemplary of this process is a French name given to certain dwarves: *lutin*. The term *lutin*, Bologne explains, "returns us directly to Neptune [via *luton- nuton*]." Lecouteux credits "above all, Christianization" with the demonization of dwarves. During the twelfth century, Church authorities, unable to Christianize them, undertook "diabolization" of dwarves, referring to *lutins* as 'demons.' Centuries later, Catholics, when they admitted the existence of dwarves, described them as fallen angels. Increasingly, a pairing of elves and dwarves with 'good' and 'bad' angels or 'consciences' arose. Dwarves came to be associated with the demonic beings called *incubi*, male demons that were believed to have sexual intercourse with women while they slept. Further, dwarves came to be linked to defiant pagans or heathens in Christianized Europe; and because, prior to baptism, infants were considered pagan/heathen, dwarves became the tutelary patrons of unbaptized children.

Despite demonization, beliefs surrounding dwarves experienced a kind of evolution in the sixteenth century; although their sinister character was enhanced, to a certain extent, they were also awarded greater respect once more, due to their association with mines. This shift in perception may have been due in part to the work of Georgius Agricola (a.k.a. Georg Bauer, 1494-1555), a German classicist, humanist, and scientist, the "father of mineralogy," regarded as among first scientists to stress empiricism. Among his most significant works were: *De re metallica libri XII* (1556, published posthumously), focusing on the arts of mining and smelting; and *De natura fossilium* (1546), a paleontology textbook. Spending several years exploring German mines, Agricola noted that several types of dwarflike beings or creatures were believed to haunt mines, including: Annebergius, a destructive, demonic being who appeared in the likeness of a horse and who killed more than a dozen miners with his breath at the Rosenkrantz mine at Anneberg in Saxony; Snebergius, a fierce yet occasionally helpful being who might reveal the location of silver to miners; and kobolds (from the Greek *kobaloi*), variously identified with or associated with elves, dwarves, hobgoblins, or trolls, trickster-like, often jovial beings who appear to assist miners but who may or may not be actually doing so. Dwarf-like kobolds were, incidentally, not only thought to inhabit mines; Germans of the sixteenth century observed them elsewhere as well. Johann Weyer (1516-1588), in *De praestigiis daemonium* (*On the Illusions of the Demons*, 1563), describes them as jovial "little men of the mountains," akin to the kindly (as opposed to the sinister) trolls of Scandinavia, typically twenty-seven inches in height, also called *Gütlein* because of their generally beneficent character. In 1803, François Joseph Michel Noël wrote of them: "These spirits...lived in secret parts of houses, and even in cracks in the wood. One offered them the most delicate dishes to eat. When they decided to set up house in a dwelling, they would notify the head of the household beforehand."

The witchmonger Weyer also writes of kindly dwarves or dwarflike beings who visit people's houses during the night who are thought to assist in various chores. Comparing these to the Lares, the Roman household deities, he notes, "As a boy, I witnessed this phenomenon on several occasions, quite in fear, along with my brothers Arnold and Matthew, in the house of my parents." German beliefs were imported to England when Elizabeth I (r.1558-1603) hired German miners to work in Cornish mines. Lewes Lavater (1527-1586), chief pastor of the Calvinist church of Zurich, observes in *Of Ghostes and Spirites Walking by Nyght* (1572):

Pione[e]rs or diggers for metal do affirm, that in many mines, there appear strange shapes and spirits, who are appareled like unto other laborers in the pit. These wander up and down in caves and underminings, and seem to bestir themselves in all kinds of labor, as to dig after the vein, to carry together ore, to put it into baskets, and to turn the winding wheel to draw it up ... They very seldom hurt the laborers ... except they provoke them by laughing and railing at them ... . These are especially haunting in pits, where metal most aboundeth.[70]

Near the end of the sixteenth century, Einar Gudmund, an Icelandic Christian pastor, giving voice to a hybrid pagano-Christian system, asserted of dwarves: "I am firmly of [the] opinion that these beings are creatures of God, consisting, like human beings, of a body and a rational soul; that they are of different sexes, and capable of producing children, and subject to all human affections ... and that they possess cattle, and other effects." He also believed that humans and dwarves were capable of mating and giving birth to hybrid children.

In the late eighteenth century, some Scots believed that dwarves inhabited coal mines in Whitehaven. During this period, they were typically depicted as dressing in green. Belief in dwarves continued into the early nineteenth century, with Samuel Hibbert relating that a woman living on Yell Island in the Shetlands who had died at a hundred years of age "some years ago" had reported encountering dwarves, especially dwarf children, on several occasions, including one who called himself "Trippa's son."

John Sargent (d. 1831), in *The Mine: A Dramatic Poem* (1785), alludes to a dwarf mythos and to a Queen of dwarves, who is the patron of miners:

To us our Queen, who, in the central earth,
:
Enormous solitude, has given these
Her subterranean realms; bids us dwell here,
In the abyss of darkness, and exert

Immortal alchemy.[71]

Belief in dwarves and dwarf-like beings inhabiting or laboring in mines, including the knockers of Wales, the buccas and spriggans (or, spriggians, also called "spirits") of Cornwall, and the Wichtlein of Germany, persisted in the nineteenth century. In 1835, Samuel Reynolds Hole, in *Thaumaturgia, or Elucidations of the Marvellous*, reported that the "spriggians are still believed to delude benighted travelers, to discover hidden treasure, to influence the weather, and to raise the winds." Cornish miners of the mid- to- late nineteenth century continued to observe "little imps or demons underground. Their presence [was] considered favorable; they indicate[d] the presence of lodes." In 1931, the English folklorist Arthur Robinson Wright, noting that the "older Cornish miners [had] not forgotten the 'knockers'…and the 'spriggans," drew his readers' attention to two very interesting accounts circa 1926:

…the most remarkable news from a mining district came in April 1926, when a "little, brown, man-like creature" was seen and handled in the Poolway Colliery of the Forest of Dean, but lost on the pit bank. A similar creature was found in a house at Coleford (Glos), crawling, but uttering no sound, in a coal scuttle. The "little man" was carried out and emptied into the drive of the house, and could not be found the next morning.[72]

The "little, brown, man-like creature" brings to mind the brownie. In seventeenth-century Scotland, some farmers offered milk to brownies by pouring it in the holes of certain "browny-stones," in exchange for which brownies would bring them "favorable harvests or other forms of good luck." Hole, in *Thaumaturgia*, recounted that in 1835, "The inhabitants of Shetland and the Isles pour libations of milk or beer through a hold-stone, in honour of the spirit Brownie…[T]he Cornish and the Devonians on the border of Cornwall, invoke to this day the spirit of Brownie, on the swarming of their bees."

Beings of Household, Farm, and Countryside

Many persons of the Middle Ages and later epochs persisted in believing in the existence of and venerating other beings resonating with elves and dwarves, including the Katerman (a feline being similar to "Puss in Boots"); Rumplestilt (akin to "Rumplestiltskin"); the dobie; the barghest; the *gruagach*; *ludki*; *kaukai*; *saiwo* people; and trolls. The dobie is a "household sprite or apparition supposed to haunt certain premises or localities," belief in whom also persisted in the seventeenth and eighteenth centuries. The barghest was especially thought to inhabit Swaledale in north Yorkshire. A mischievous, sometimes even malicious being with horns, teeth, claws, and fiery eyes, the barghest often takes the form of a menacing black dog who howls upon the death of prominent persons. Its existence was fearfully acknowledged in the seventeenth, eighteenth, and nineteenth centuries.

Many Wends acknowledged the existence of *ludki*, or 'little people,' who loved in

Lusatia, a Wendish region of northeastern Germany. *Ludki* are described as wearing wide-brimmed hats or red caps. They are expert musicians and craftspersons who long ago taught humans how to build houses. They also possess the gift of prophecy. Jan Máchal reports that the *ludki* "were pagans" who left the villages when the Christians came because, although they loved music, they couldn't stand the sound of bells. From that time on, they lived on mountains and in mines.

Lithuanians were no strangers to the *kaukai*, whose name suggests both "spirit" and "bear." They are also called *barstukai*. *Kaukai* are thought to be transformed souls of the dead, particularly deceased children. They are guardians of the dead and shapeshifters who may have originated in shamanism. According to some sources, they are ruled by a deity named Puskaitis. In recent times, they have been depicted as wearing colorful, tattered garments, as dwelling beneath elderberry bushes, traveling in groups, and as sojourning in barns, rewarding humans who are kind to them, hindering those who are not. They sometimes assist in doing household chores and promoting abundance of grain. Those who care for them offer them midnight feasts of bread, butter, cheese, and meat in barns. Certain place-names indicate sites of their veneration; these include Kaukaliskis, Kaukenai, and Kaukas Hill at Jogvilai in the Ukmergë district of Lithuania. Certain roads are also said to be traveled by *kaukai*. Veneration of *kaukai* persisted into at least the twentieth century.

Erich Johan Jessen-Schardebell (1705-1783) discovered unflinching belief in elf-, dwarf- or fairy-like beings among the Sámi of the eighteenth century. These chthonic beings were generally referred to as *saiwo* people, *saiwo* indicating both a subterranean location and magical energy. Saiwo, the name of the land which they inhabit, also includes *saiwo* plants, animals (including domesticated ones), and water. *Saiwo* people are believed to be "happier than humans on earth." They are "a noble and rich people well versed in witchcraft and magic." Their "livestock [are] ... far more beautiful than [those] of the Lapps." Sámi sometimes visited the *saiwo* people, dancing, singing, feasting, and enjoying tobacco, liquor, and "other treats" with them. They formed bonds with them based on exchange: Sámi would make offerings and sacrifices to the *saiwo* people, in exchange for protection, prosperity, and instruction in the divinatory and magical arts. Closely related to the *saiwo* people are the *kadnihah* of the Lule Sámi of Norway and the Pite Sámi of Sweden, "a kind of people living underground" who dress in red attire and who have waist-length hair "which resembles green linen." Also akin to the *saiwo* people are the chthonic *maahiset* of Finland and the *underboniga*, the "undergroundlings," of Westerbotten, a province of Sweden. Continuing belief in all of these was documented in the eighteenth as well as in the nineteenth century.

Swedes persisted in speaking of encounters with trolls in the seventeenth century. In 1660 (or, according to another source, 1671), Peter Rahm reported that he and his wife were sitting in their farmhouse one evening when a troll appeared at their door. He had a swarthy complexion and was dressed in grey. He asked if the farmer's wife, skilled at midwifery, could help him by delivering his wife's baby. Her husband was concerned for her, but said a prayer and let her go. "She seemed to be borne along by the wind." When she had finished delivering the troll's baby, she was returned to her home in the same manner. In *A Traveller in the Northern Countries* (1708), it was reported that numerous Icelanders not only believed in trolls but were served by them.

Wends also venerated the *dziwje zony*. These were the 'Wild Women of the Woods.' They were typically depicted as having long, flowing red hair. They lived in the depths of the forest, often underground. They were particularly skilled in herbal medicine and magic. They loved to sing and dance, and their wild dancing was thought to bring storms. Mortals typically observed them at noon and at sunset, and especially on Midsummer Eve. They brought bountiful harvests to those who venerated them. Although they are considered divinities or similar beings, their description likens them to witches and cunning women.

Nineteenth-century Scottish Highlanders shared their world with glaistigs. They typically appeared as thin, greyish-skinned women with blonde hair reaching to their feet, dressed in green. They lived on farms and loved milk. When farmers offered them milk, they were kind to them; when they did not, they howled and cursed their cows so that they would cease producing milk. They were linked to certain families, as, for example, the MacCleans and MacDougalls. The glaistig of Glen Duror of Appin, in Argyll was still alive, it was said, in 1870. She was described as having a face like a "grey stone overgrown with lichen." At this time, the owner of the farm on which she lived made offerings to her on the Clach na Glaistig (the Glaistig's Stone). "But there came to the farmhouse in the course of time," Alasdair Alpin MacGregor relates in *The Peat-Fire Flame: Folk-Tales and Traditions of the Highlands and Islands* (1937, 1947), "a new tenant who omitted to supply this offering, with the result that ... there was no more milk in [his cows'] udders."

Among Slavs, a generic name for household non-human beings is *did* (or, *didko*). Domovoi, or Dzed, the "Old Man" or "Grandfather," is an ancestral being who guards the home. A shapeshifter, Domovoi sometimes appears as a very hairy man or as one covered with fur; however, he may also assume the form of a bale of hay. Sometimes he may be heard whispering, groaning, or weeping, especially when a member of the family dies. He was honored in some Slavic homes into the twentieth century. Demonstrating an uncanny resonance with reverence of the Yorùbá *orishá* Eshú (or, Eleggúa), "[s]mall statues [of Domovoi] were made of clay or stone ... [and] placed in niches near doors ... they generally represented an old man." Those who knew and respected him offered him part of their evening meal, salted bread and milk, and occasionally, the sacrifice of a cock, with whose blood they marked the corners of house. In return for acknowledging his presence, Domovoi protected the household, helped with the spinning, and assisted in caring for the livestock.

Slavs knew many other beings of

household and farm, many of whom they venerated into the twentieth century. These included: Bannik, a patron of the family bathhouse, depicted as bald, bearded, furry, and clawed, and as carrying bundles of leaves, who loves to bathe and divines the future if enough water is left in the tub for him; Dvorovoy, a being who guards the stable and cattle and who is offered bread, wool, and glittering objects for doing so; Kikimora, a female household being who lives behind the oven, can help or hinder with household tasks, guards poultry, despises laziness, and is offered fern tea; Ovinnik, a guardian of the barn who often assumes the form of a disheveled black cat; Pasichnyk, who protects bees; Plon, a guardian of grain; and Polevik (or, Polovyk), a guardian of crops who is sometimes depicted as having black skin and green hair, can assume form of whirlwind, assists in harvesting, disapproves of working at noontime, and is offered eggs and cockerels.

Lithuanians and Old Prussians venerated a number of beings of home and farm, including: Apydeme, a female household being; Aspelinie, a female patron of the hearth; Dimstipatis, a patron of the farmstead to whom pigs and roosters were sacrificed; and Aitvaras, a household god and shapeshifter who assumes the form of a rooster, cat, or dragon, who likes to steal butter, grain, and money in order to give it to his master or mistress, and who is offered scrambled eggs. Western Lithuanians probably knew him as Pukys, a name reminiscent of Puck's; his veneration persisted into the twentieth century.

Familiars

In the names of "familiars" – sometimes called "imps," "poppets," or "puckrels" – of the sixteenth and later centuries, we find one of the most obvious examples of pagan-based, non-Christian and hybrid pagan-Christian innovation. Familiars were indeed sometimes linked to mandrake-poppets and to other sorts of poppets.

"Familiars" are alternately described as animals possessing magical and medicinal powers, as animals embodied by divinities or similar beings, or as spirits who can assume the forms of various animals – the latter two more Platonic and likely later conceptions. They include dogs, cats, toads, mice, hedgehogs, horses, stags, and others. Familiars are reminiscent of the *exotikó* of Greek tradition. They are most often associated with witches and witchcraft.

Names of familiars have included: Amie, Ball, Besse, Bonne, Browning, Crowe, Dandy, Dick(e), Elimanzer, Elva, Fancy, Fillie, Gibbe, Gille, Ginnie, Greedigut, Grissell, Hercules, Hoult, Inges, Jack(e), Jarmara, Jeso, Jolybois ("Charming Wood"), Jone, Leird, Lightfoot, Lunch, Maistre Persil ("Master Parsley"), Makeshift, Mamet, Mawde, Mercurie, Minny, Ned, Nicholas, Panu, Philip, Pigen, Pretty, Prickeare, Red Riever, Robert the Rule, Robin, Rug, Rutterkin, Sack and Sugar, Saute-buisson ("Jump[ing the] Hedge"), Sotheons, Suckin, Tewhit, Tib(b), Toad, Tyffin, Tyttey, Tzum Walt Vliegen ("Off to the Woods"), Verd Joly ("Charming Green"), Verdelet ("Greenish"), and Vinegar Tom.

A couple of names, Hercules and Mercurie, signal the persistence and transformation of Classical divinities and, in regard to the latter, the possible influence of alchemy and/or astrology. Robin, of course, reminds us of Robin Goodfellow/Puck. I find the name "Mamet" or "Mommet" especially intriguing. This is a medieval European term for Mohammed. I also find Maistre Persil to be an intriguing name, one that links familiars to the realm of plants. Parsley was thought to have numerous healing and magical or transformative uses, including the power to grant, when mixed with "rainwater collected immediately after a thunderstorm," to ensure good eyesight in newborns; and, when eaten with pig's brains, to promote "greater mental agility" in adults. Parsley, like asparagus, does not like to be transplanted. If someone transplants it, or so it was believed in Devon into the early twentieth century, then either she or he or someone in their family is "sure for to die." Enid M. Porter notes in "Some Folk Beliefs of the Fens:" "Parsley was widely grown and was sown annually with a certain amount of ritual…[T]he sower [of parsley] was obliged to work at night, taking his bearing from the Pole Star and the Plough."

Another familiar's name, Rutterkin, appears in a lyric attributed to the poet John Skelton (*c*.1460-1529) and the composer William Cornysh (1465-1523). This lyric indicates how the alleged witch Joan Flower and her daughters may have perceived the exceedingly Puckish familiar in the early seventeenth century:

Rutterkin is come unto our town,
In a cloak without coat or gown,
Save a ragged hood to cover his crown.
Hoyda, hoyda, jolly Rutterkin!
Rutterkin can speak no English.
His tongue runneth all on buttered fish
Besmeared with grease about his dish.
Hoyda, hoyda, jolly Rutterkin!
Rutterkin shall bring you all good luck,
A stoup of beer up at a pluck,
Till his brain be wise as a duck.
Hoyda, hoyda, jolly Rutterkin!
When Rutterkin from board will rise,
He will piss a gallon-pot full at twice,
And the over plus under the table of
    the new guise.
Hoyda, hoyda, jolly Rutterkin![73]

The name which intrigues me the most, however, is that of Sotheons. Although Barbara Rosen is content to say that "Sotheons" is a mistranslation of a manuscript that reads "*herculus* sothe *hons* [i.e., John] or *Jack*," I am not so sure. Doing some digging, I have learned that the name "Sotheon" refers to Sirius, with "Soth-" signifying the dog-star and "-*theon*" signifying "the gods." Sotheon also appears to be a male counterpart to the goddess Sothis. Further, Sotheon appears to be linked to Dionysus/Bacchus in his hypostasis as Iacchus, a "light-bearing star of nocturnal mysteries;" and further still, to the god Sarapis. Indeed, one finds the name "Dionysotheonis" in the *Oxyrhynchus Papyri* of Roman Egypt; it appears to have served as a personal name to a man living in the city of Oxyrhynchus (now, El Bahnasa). What strikes me as especially uncanny is that "Sotheon" is found as a rare surname in northwest England and Wales. Even more intriguing, one Rebecca Sotheon, born circa 1770, appears to be an ancestor of *Great Gatsby* author F. Scott Fitzgerald.

Some names of familiars, like Robin and Maistre Persil, were also names given to the Devil and/or the deity or similar being who presided over gatherings held by alleged witches. Tibb appears as a male being or incarnation of the Devil in the case of the so-called "Pendleton Witches."

Occasionally familiars are found in pairs or couples, such as Hercules and Mercurie, mentioned above, and the couple "John" and "Impe," a black male familiar paired with a white female familiar.

Familiars were, for persons alleged to be witches, similar to beings evoked by learned practitioners of ceremonial or ritual magic, such as the *parhedros* beings evoked by practitioners of Hellenistic magic, *jinns* evoked in medieval Cairo by magicians possessing magical lamps, or beings like Ariel (or, Uriel) evoked by Renaissance mages, in that they were called upon to serve the practitioner in works of divination and magic.

In an account centering on a man from Nuremberg named Paul Creuz that links dwarves to familiars, we learn how he conjured two dwarves that ultimately became familiars who assisted him in his practice. Creuz conjured the dwarves by mixing milk and honey with the blood of a black pullet. "After that he…saw two tiny dwarfs that came up out of the ground and sat down at the table and ate…Then he asked them questions, to which they replied, and after several such occasions they got so friendly with him that they moved as guests into his house."

Familiars were often given to practitioners by those who had previously housed them, reflecting a kind of lineal bond. They were typically housed in boxes, bottles, or clay pots containing beds of wool or cotton. One alleged witch housed one familiar in a "wicker bottle," one in a "leather bottle," and a third in a "wool pack." These containers were sometimes placed near the beds of practitioners. Intriguingly, in *Oriental Magic*, Idries Shah cites an invocation which includes: Commander of the *jinn* and men! Come, or I will imprison thee in a metal flask!" In 1523, the Inquisitor Don Alfonso Manriquez "gave orders to arrest 'any person [who] made or caused to be made…phials of glass or other vessels to contain some being who should reply to his inquiries and aid his projects.'" Familiars were fed milk, bread, wheat, barley, oats, blood (including human blood), and sometimes chicken.

On occasion, familiars allegedly embodied or "possessed" persons, such as was the case with Louise Maillet of Burgundy in the final years of the sixteenth century.

Of course, as in most instances of pagan innovation, there may also be found a continuance of, or else conspicuous likeness to, ancient and/or indigenous concepts and practices. Familiars are, for example, reminiscent of the *hamingja* or *fylgia* souls or aspects of soul in Germanic spirituality/ enspirited materiality, which may manifest as animals, as well as of animal beings called *nagual* in Nahuatl by the Nahuas (Mexicas/Aztecs), and other indigenous beings.

Although it was once considered controversial, present-day scholarship is confirming a very old notion that puts forth that the emergence and conception of European fairies were inspired or influenced by Arabian belief in the *jinns*, known in the West as "genies." Like fairies, *jinns* are often called by euphemistic names, including "the concealed ones," "those people over there," and "those better than ourselves." R. A. Nicholson (1930) describes *jinns* as "familiar spirit[s]" who are reminiscent of both humans and angels but who constitute another species; who share an intimate bond with humankind; and who "can assume any shape they please; they are often seen in the form of animals, especially snakes." It is conceivable that cross-pollination occurring in the Middle Ages and Renaissance between Europeans and peoples of the Middle East may be at least partly responsible for the rise of familiars, signifying pagan-based innovation. In this context, it is worth noting that in Arabian folklore, witches are sometimes said to ride not on brooms but on earthenware jars, including wine jars.

In regard to their being housed in boxes, pots, etc., familiars of the Renaissance and thereafter bear resemblance to beings and dwelling-places found in antiquity and in Indian, African, and other cultures. Vessels thought to house the souls of the dead may have been used by ancient Greeks. As Jane Harrison relates in *Prolegomena to the Study of Greek Religion*, "the *pithos* was a grave-jar, that from such grave-jars souls escaped and to them necessarily returned."

Spirit pots called *dhabu* are used by certain tribal peoples in India to contact their deities. In the late nineteenth century, Henry Whitehead described a ceremony honoring Kurumbaiamma (probably meaning "Coconut Mother Goddess"), a local goddess of the state of Tamil Nadu in southern India. In this ceremony, the goddess' energy or force was invoked into a clay pot (*karagam*) in which coconut, oleander flowers, and water are placed, these ingredients shielded by a bunch of mango leaves, and the pot ornamented with bamboo, a lime, and a small silver umbrella. The pot is then offered rice. Whitehead writes:["D]uring the festival [the pot] is treated exactly like the goddess. It is taken round in procession on the head of a *pujari* [i.e., local priest] to the sound of tom-toms and pipes; offerings of fruit and flowers are made to it; a lamb is sacrificed before it, and it is worshipped with the orthodox prostrations." Marcu Beza has described a Romanian ceremony performed in the early twentieth century that is reminiscent of this one; it centers on a vessel called a *gãleata*. This vessel, like the Indian one, is filled with water from fountains /well"}] and is "beautifully ornamented with flowers." As with the Indian vessel, offerings are made to it, primarily silver coins. Like the Indian vessel, it is carried in procession, accompanied by young women singing songs about beauty and marriage. On the night following the procession, it is "put to sleep" and "guarded by young men with drawn wooden swords." Although the name of the divinity of the vessel is not – or is no longer – named, it is highly likely that the term *gãleata*, "helmet," is meant to suggest Pallas Athena/Minerva or a local hypostasis of this goddess, and possibly also the ancient Syrian Queen Zenobia's transition from warrior to matron, and that the vessel in some way marks the transition in the young women's lives from virginity and chastity, of which Minerva is patron, to marriage and fertility, of which Aphrodite/Venus is patron.

Although the phenomenon of keeping familiars fades dramatically after the seventeenth century, it did not die out (has not died out?) completely. For instance, in July, 1813, it was reported in the *Monthly Magazine* that a woman living in Staffordshire, England had become very upset with her husband for killing a toad. It seems that she had been housing him in a pot in her garden and had intended on the following "Sunday to [take] the sacrament, for the purpose of getting some of the bread to feed him with, and make him thereby a valuable familiar spirit to her."

James Rennell Rodd, in *The Customs and Lore of Modern Greece* (1892), draws our attention to a Greek belief at that time in "local genii," one of which was "attached to every house." He describes them as having "thin voice[s]" and as manifesting in the forms of dogs, cats, pigs, and snakes. He explains that these beings were respected and were offered food and beverage (typically milk). We learn of a woman (unfortunately unnamed) in Mark R. Taylor's "Norfolk Folklore" (1929) who was born circa 1820-1825, who lived in the vicinity of Attleborough, and who was alleged to practice witchcraft. She kept three familiars "to do her bidding, – called Pug, Lightfoot, and Bluebell." Around 1890, a local farmer and horse breeder, wishing to mock her, named three of his Hackney horses after her familiars. Although men who worked for him cautioned him not to do so, he did so in spite of their warning. It came as no surprise to the workers – and most probably as no surprise to the alleged witch – when the horse "Bluebell was killed accidentally, Lightfoot turned out [to be] a kicker, and Pug went lame." In 1915, according to folklorist A. R. Wright, the *St. Albans Diocesan Gazette*

> gave an account of a reputed witch in Essex, recently dead, whose ghost was laid to rest in the traditional manner. A lady told the exerciser that before [the alleged witch's] death, a neighbour had called [on her] and [had] found [the witch] feeding her *niggets*, those creepy-crawling things that witches keep all over them."[74]

A brief article in the *London Times* (September 3, 1915) has this to say about this report: "Mr. V. surmises that a nigget is a kind of familiar spirit. Fancy such things going on forty miles from London."

The Mandrake Being

The mandrake (or, mandragora) is a plant belonging to the nightshade (Solanaceae) family. It has been difficult to decide where to speak of it, and I admit that my choice in placing it here has been somewhat arbitrary. It might also be discussed under various other topics including plants, materia deployed in healing and magic, even under divinities, especially divinities whose cults catapulted in the Middle Ages and thereafter. However, despite these multiple possibilities, it is my view that the mandrake, in its relationship to, and use by, practitioners, most closely resembles a familiar.

The mandrake has been used in magic and healing since antiquity. Egyptians used the mandrake in potion form to inspire sleep, joy, and love. The Greeks allegedly learned of the mandrake and its uses by way of the Egyptians.

Pythagoras is said to have given the name "Anthropomorphon" to the mandrake. Charles Dickens, Jr. wrote in "A Little More Plant Lore" in 1885: "[T]he Germans have long regarded the [mandrake] plant as something uncanny. Other names which they have for it are *Zauberwurzel*, or Sorcerer's Root, and *Hexenmännchen*, or Witch's Mannikin." They also call it *Galgemännlein*, because it is thought to spring up at the site where someone has been hanged. In Iceland, the mandrake was known as *thjofarót*, "Thieves' Root," because it was thought to be born from the froth of the mouths of hanged thieves. Because of its power to inspire and enhance eroticism, Muslim Arabs referred to it as *tuphac el shaitan*, the "Devil's Apple."

The mandrake has for millennia been associated with female divinities. The physician, botanist, and pharmacologist Dioscorides (*c.* 40-90 CE) was said to have been bestowed with a mandrake by Euresis, the goddess or nymph of discovery and exploration. The mandrake has been called the "Apple of Love" and as such corresponds to the goddess Aphrodite/Venus. Lecouteux observes that "all operations concerning this plant are performed on Friday, in German, Freitag, that's to say, "Freyja's [or Frigga's] Day." In medieval and post-medieval Germanic lore, associations of Venus, Freyja, Hörsel, other female divinities, and the mandrake converged. In a medieval manuscript we find: "Friday is a holy day and Mistress Venus' own day in the Hörselberg where the mandrakes live." In the nineteenth and early twentieth centuries in Romania and Moldavia, the mandrake, primarily associated with passionate love, was linked to a feminine divinity or other being euphemistically called the "Great Lady," the "High Lady," the "Powerful Lady," "(Most Honored) Empress (of Herbs)," "Good Mother," "Our Mother," "your Holiness," or the "Lady of the Forest." This divinity may have been the Romanian goddess Ileana Sânziana.

In Germanic lore, the mandrake has also been linked to elves. One of its names is *Alraun*, "secret of the elf" or the "All-Wise One," which not only links the mandrake to a "goddess who meets you at the crossways" but also to a "helpful elf." Likewise, another name for the plant is *Erdmann*, or "earth-man," which can also refer to a dwarf and possibly also to a male counterpart of the goddess Erde. This name holds special significance for me because I have ancestors who lived in Lithuania Minor in the eighteenth and nineteenth centuries who were named Erdmut ("Earth-Mother") and Erdmon(s). In nineteenth-century Texas, one of my ancestors' names transformed (sadly) from Erdmon to Edward; my grandmother was called "Mutta."

The mandrake has also been linked to wisewomen and/or "witches" for millennia. Germanics associated the mandrake with Albrûna (called Aurinia in Latin), a "sorceress with elf-like power," who may have lived in the early first century CE. In turn, the plant came to be associated with medieval and post-medieval women who practiced divination, including rune casting.

Undoubtedly one of the most powerful poppets, a type of sacred art object resembling a doll that is used in healing and magic, is that made from mandrake root. The mandrake is considered a living being and is thought to scream or shriek when it is removed from the ground. Thus, when we speak of the mandrake as a "poppet," we need to bear in mind that in no way are we suggesting that such a poppet is a non-living object, a thing. As a plant, the mandrake poppet already possesses life-force. In the process of ritualizing and "humanizing" the plant, it acquires even greater life-force and either begins to express a more human-like or elf-like energy or else draws such a being into its form. In other words, the mandrake becomes increasingly like a familiar. In the past, some persons believed that the mandrake possessed a human heart.

In the sixteenth and seventeenth centuries, learned men like the musician and botanist Fabio Colonna (1567-1650) and others described the mandrake as a "man in blossom." Francis Bacon (1561-1626) described "witches" as "mak[ing] an ugly image" from the mandrake, "giving it the form of a face at the top of the root, and leaving those strings to make a broad beard down to the foot." Shakespeare, in the final years of the sixteenth century, has his character Falstaff, in *The Second Part of Henry the Fourth*, describe the character Shallow as a mandrake poppet:

When 'a [i.e., he] was naked, he was for all the world like a
fork'd redish [i.e., radish], with a head fantastically carv'd upon it
with a knife.
...[T]he whores call'd him mandrake.[75]

Jews, Greeks and perhaps other ancient peoples ritualized the collecting of mandrakes, fashioning a rite that would persist for millennia. The plant was chanted to, danced around, and then ritually unearthed – sometimes with a sword in the direction of the West. Because the mandrake "shrieks so dismally" when she (less often, he) is removed from the ground, it can kill a human being who tries to do so. Thus, in some places, the practitioner must deploy a dog to fetch the mandrake, while he or she plugs his/her ears. Unfortunately, the dog is typically sacrificed in order for the mandrake to be obtained.

In Romania, a group of wisewomen typically picks the mandrake. In Christianized Romania, this activity usually takes place between Easter and Ascension Day. Mircea Eliade describes the ritual as commencing when a group of "old wisewomen" gathered together "eggs,…a cake made from puff paste, stuffed cabbage, brandy, [and] wine." They then went to the forest and located a mandrake, which they ritually tied with a red ribbon. Then they took the eggs and other items to the place where the mandrake grew and placed the items around it as an offering. Then the women "embrace[d] and caress[ed] one another," and took the mandrake home. If the intent concerns love magic, the women may perform the rite in the nude, "exchange passionate words of endearment," "caress and embrace one another," "lie one on top of the other, mimicking [?] the sexual act," "dance naked around the mandragora," and invoke, praise, and plead with the mandrake to find a spouse for them within a month. In Moldavia, the invocation goes as follows:

Lady Mandragora, with honey I will anoint you,
with wine I will sprinkle you,
with sugar I will sweeten you,
with bread I will feed you.[76]

Due to Christianization, this invocation also includes mention of the Virgin Mary, but she appears in the context of encountering a woman named Ileana, who is a goddess of the moon and winter, who reigns as the Fairy Queen, and who has been compared to Artemis/Diana. In this context, Ileana seems to refer both to the mandrake and the woman or person whose life it is to ameliorate: Be still, Ileana, cry no more,/...with cold water I will wash you/...your heart will be at peace." When this part of the rite has concluded, the mandrake is bathed with wine and then secretly carried to one of the women's homes.

As a living, human-like being, the mandrake lies in a state resembling sleep or suspended animation until called upon to do a practitioner's bidding. As such a being, the mandrake was "washed with red wine, wrapt in silk red and white, laid in a casket, bathed every Friday, and clothed in a new little white smock every new moon." The German writer Johann von Rist (1607-1667) described seeing a mandrake poppet that was at that time over a century old. It was kept in a small coffin, "on which was a cloth bearing a picture of a thief on the gallows, and a mandrake growing underneath." Alternatively, the mandrake was sometimes kept in a cupboard or, like some familiars, in a bottle. Like a familiar, the mandrake poppet was fed, typically milk and biscuits.

The mandrake or mandrake poppet is thought to hold the power to confer prosperity and wisdom; arrange and bless marriages; promote fertility and cure barrenness; prevent nightmares; prevent illness in humans and animals (in Cambridgeshire, England, "mandrake root was widely used as a cure [for] sick horses"); cause cows "to give more milk;" promote "business affairs;" improve the weather; remove obstacles and enemies; and double any offerings of money given to her/him. The mandrake, in being linked to kobolds, was also thought to be able to locate subterranean treasures, a belief that persisted into the late nineteenth century. The mandrake, as a magical or divine being, was also thought to hold the power of shapeshifting, including transforming into spiders, scorpions, and apes.

Thanks to the linguist Simeon Mangiuca (1831-1890), Eliade relates an account of a healing rite undertaken by a wisewoman wishing to cure a man of a fever, with the assistance of the mandrake. The wisewoman takes the sick man to the forest at twilight. To the mandrake she presents a glass of honey, a cake, red thread, and a silver coin, and a new shirt that the patient has brought, a "spread" reminiscent of the "fairy feast." Then the wisewoman bows before the mandrake and greets her as "Mandragora, good lady and good mother." She praises her as she "who touches the heavens with [her] head,/whose roots go deep underground,/and whose dress floats in the wind." She names her Queen of Sky and Storms, and Queen of Flowers. As the wisewoman invokes her, she bends her forehead "to the ground," asking Mandragora to grant her and her beloveds strength and health. She then bows to the mandrake, and she and the patient sleep near it in the forest.

The mandrake or mandrake poppet was often passed down from mother to daughter, or father to son, or else within families, with the human-mandrake relationship mirroring one of parental guardianship and speaking to the notion of lineage.

In 1603, Margaret Ragum Bouchery, the "wife of a Moor, was hung as a witch" for having "kept and fed daily a mandrake fiend." In 1630, three women were executed in Hamburg, Germany for keeping mandrake poppets. In the late eighteenth century, the use of mandrakes became so popular that con-artists tried to push off carved carrots, parsnips, and bryony as mandrakes to naïve customers. At that time, to be "accused of possessing the mandrake" was tantamount to being called a witch.

A poppet similar to that made of mandrake was sometimes created from bryony root. In an account found in *Secrets du petit Albert* (1718), one allegedly influenced by Romani (Gypsy) practice, a peasant practitioner, after receiving a bryony root from a Romani, buried it again the following spring, on a Monday when the Moon was conjunct Venus, in a grave, sprinkling it with milk in which three mice had been sacrificed. A month later, when he disinterred it, the root had become much more human-like. He kept it in an oven surrounded by vervain and wrapped in a dead man's shroud. The root-being brought him luck and prosperity. Charles Dickens, Jr. notes that poppets of mandrake root were still being sold in France, particularly at portside markets, in 1810. As we have seen, the deployment of mandrakes in healing and magic persisted into the twentieth century.[77]

Chapter 10
The Goodman's Brood
Demonic Beings and Practices

O you, wisest and handsomest of Angels, God betrayed by fate, deprived of praises, Satan, take pity on my long misery! - Baudelaire, "The Litanies of Satan"

In or near 1582, Elizabeth Sowtherns, a.k.a. Old Demdyke, allegedly encountered "a spirit or Devil in the shape of a boy, the one half of his coat black, and the other brown, who [told her that] if she would give him her soul, she should have anything that she would request. Whereupon [she] demanded his name, and the spirit answered, his name was Tibb."

Present-day Wiccans tend to argue that in such a text as the above, the Devil refers to a horned male god whom Christians, as dualistic monotheists, must identify with Satan. Moreover, they insist, often for ethical and/or political reasons, that Devil worship or Satanism and witchcraft are worlds apart; or that, as many scholars of witchcraft argue, that Satanism is nothing more than Christian fantasy. Thus, for example, the notion of a "Satanic witch," such as we encounter in *Rosemary's Baby*, or such as promoted by the twentieth-century Satanic high priest Anton LaVey (1930-1997) in *The Satanic Witch* and elsewhere, is either an oxymoron or – although a popular fictive type – an historical impossibility. As I see it, however, there is evidence that in some contexts "the Devil" may represent a pagan horned god; Christian fantasy; a being identified by Christians who exists just as the Biblical God exists; or a being that emerges from an innovative, pagano-Christian, hybridizing approach to the sacred; that reverence of the Devil may be an historical fact; that reverence of the Devil and/or Satanism may mean different things to different people dwelling in differing times and places; that reverence of the Devil may, like certain manifestations of the being himself (or herself), form a part of spiritually hybrid traditions; and that unlike present-day Wicca, witchcraft may at times overlap with reverence of the Devil.

Women of Brittany offered buckwheat in the early seventeenth century to a deity or similar being whose name is lost to us in order that she or he might provide them with prosperous crops; Father Michel Le Nobletz referred to this deity, not surprisingly, as "the Devil." His name for this deity may be a generic designation for *any* pagan deity; on the other hand, at this time, in this instance, it is conceivable, based on quite a significant amount of evidence emerging from seventeenth- through early nineteenth-century European sources, perhaps especially from Scotland, that the Bretagne women may have in fact referred to and conceived of the deity as "the Devil." This does not mean, however, that the "Devil" envisioned by many persons matched the "Devil" of the Christian Bible. To the contrary, it is reasonable to suspect – as present-day Wiccans might – that this deity/being represents a mask worn by one of the many gods of pagan antiquity, or else the eventual, spiritually-hybrid conflation of the Celtic gods Cernunnos and Belenus, the Classical Pan or Faunus, and the Germanic/Anglo-Saxon Woden [Odin], most of whom possess horns on their heads or wear horned helmets. Drawing upon Arawn, the Cymric god of the underworld, Annwn, he is described as extremely tall, as having dark skin and/or dark hair, as carrying a hunting pole, and with a horn slung over his shoulder. In *The Visions of Isobel Gowdie*, Emma Wilby refers to this manifestation as the "folkloric Devil" as opposed to the "theological Devil."

The Devil, in the context of witch trials, is often depicted as a man dressed in black or as one possessing dark or black skin. As for a "man in black," when the Devil's attire is given a color, well over 50% of the time, it is described as black; whereas, about 15% of the time, it's described as green or blue. He is frequently described as a musician; especially in more recent centuries, as a fiddle-player. He is also a dancer and lord of the dance.

Entire texts have been written on the Devil and his alleged cults, including several of the world's greatest works of literature and music – Marlowe's *Doctor Faustus*, Goethe's *Faust*, the operas *Faust* by Charles Gounod and *Mefistofele* by Arrigo Boito, *The Damnation of Faust* by Hector Berlioz, and others. Even if we assume that Christians misconstrued those who revered Diana and other beings as Devil-worshippers, and even if many of those who honored the Devil as a mask of an ancient deity with "folkloric" qualities, this does not negate the possibility that there have for millennia been those who have revered the Devil per se – Satan, Mephistopheles, Lucifer, and so on. I think it is wise to acknowledge the probable existence of Devil worship, Satanism, or Luciferianism in the same way that we acknowledge the manifold Christian heresies of the Middle Ages. In *Witchcraft in the Middle Ages*, Jeffrey Burton Russell draws our attention to cults existing in Germany, including the twelfth-century Luciferans and thirteenth-century antinomian groups, who revered the Devil. The former revered the Devil in his manifestation as Belphegor, a "pagan god of love and fertility appearing in the Old Testament," as well as, presumably, in his manifestation as Lucifer. They allegedly kissed their priest on his buttocks and on Christmas Eve held a ceremony mocking the birth of Christ. This suggests that parody, satire, the carnivalesque, or even what today we might call "camp" contributed to the makeup of their rites. They believed that since all things are a reflection of God, then the Devil must also be a reflection of, or the equivalent of, God. Antinomians of the thirteenth century, "by arguing that all action was virtuous and that Satan was God, advanced the cause of rebellion, libertinism, and Satanism. ...[They] were in a sense witches themselves."

Pripegal

Pripegal, alleged to be of Wendish origin, is a deity reminiscent of both Wilby's "theological" and "folkloric" Devil. Some of what has been written about Pripegal and his cult is most probably the product of Christian fantasy, but at least some of what's been written indicates the emergence of an actual cult defiantly opposed to Christianization. Near 1110, Aldegott, the bishop of Mainz and Magdeburg, Germany, reported that his diocese had been vandalized by bands of "fanatics," Wendish pagans who "profaned Christian churches and destroyed altars, taking the faithful" and "cutting off their feet and hands and crying, 'Where is their God now?'" and sacrificing them to "demons," i.e., to pagan deities. He claimed that in their ceremonies, they exclaimed, "It is our Pripegal who wants the sacrifices. Christ is vanquished. The victory belongs to Pripegal. Let us rejoice!" They proclaimed the "Days of Joy" to celebrate what would prove to be an exceedingly brief victory against Christianity.

The French anthropologist Sigismond Zaborowski-Moindron (1851-1928) suggested that Pripegal may have been linked to the practice of cremation, as his name signifies "burning" (*prepjekac*), and the conjoint practice of funeral feasting (*tryzna*), which were forbidden by Christians. Alternatively, Louis Paul Marie Léger, in *La mythologie slave* (1901), thought that his name might signify "the glorious one" (*pribychval*). Pripegal may have also been a phallic deity. In our context, what seems highly significant is that Pripegal, possibly a descendant of Czernabog or another Slavic deity, appears to have emerged in or near the early twelfth century in response to the Christianization of the Slavs; thus, Pripegal's cult, perhaps especially in its defiant dimension, clearly represents an example of pagan innovation – a pagan innovation that wanted no part of Christianity or a sacred hybridity combining paganism and Christianity.

Pripegal is experiencing a sort of revival today in various countries including Croatia, the Czech Republic, Hungary, Poland, and Slovakia, primarily a pop-cultural one linked to Heavy Metal music and its culture. In this milieu, he is quite sinister and is associated with ghosts, werewolves, and vampires. His name has been taken by a 'Pagan black metal' band, and he is honored by a kindred band, Ancestral Volkhves, in "Oh Pripegal, We Invoke Thee."

Most often, however, it appears that "the Devil" revered by medieval and post-medieval Europeans conforms more to Wilby's "folkloric" than her "theological" Devil; it also appears that this "Devil" is to some extent a product of pagan or pagano-Christian innovation.

The Devil's Grandmother and Female Relations

When I was a child, whenever it would rain when the sun was shining, my grandmother would look up at the heavens, point, and say, "The Devil is beating his wife." She said this very nonchalantly, although quite seriously. She usually smiled, although I knew she wasn't joking. Even as a child, I remember being troubled by this. I was not troubled on learning that the Devil had a wife; that seemed only natural. At my young age, I knew that beating one's wife was nothing to smile about. So what in the world could her smile be about? Somehow, perhaps because English was sometimes difficult for her, I think that she heard the word "beat" as some other word, something more like "frig" or "frick" – that was as close as she ever came to saying the "F-word." Considering that she had a fondness for Italians and even told me that some of our ancestors had lived in Italy, it's conceivable that she'd heard the old Italian expression for this event, *"Quando piove e c'è il sole, sono le streghe che fanno l'amore!"*, that is, "When it rains and the sun is shining, the witches are making love!" Many years later, I learned that both of these expressions were once commonplace, as were many others alluding to the Devil's grandmother, mother, or wife – "Inseparable, like the Devil and his Mother;" "You can go to the Devil and his Grandmother;" "The Devil brought me to you, and his mother brought you to me." When a soup is too thick, the "Devil's Grandmother can dance on it;" when a whirlwind occurs, "The Devil's dancing with his Grandmother." "What the Devil and his Dame shall I do now?" Herod asks in a fourteenth-century Mystery play. In *Othello*, Bianca cries, "Let the devil and his dam haunt you!" When in *The Comedy of Errors*, Antipholus of Syracuse remarks of a courtesan, "It is the devil," Dromio of Syracuse replies, "Nay, she is worse, she is the devil's dam." I am reminded of an old Italian expression: "If you are the Devil, I am his Mother."

So it seems that the Devil, unlike the Biblical God, has often been thought to have a grandmother, a mother, and a wife, as well as a daughter or numerous daughters. They often appear to represent the power behind the throne. In the trials of Joan Wilimot, William Barton, Marjorie Ritchie, and other alleged witches, we learn that the "Devil" appeared to them in the form of a woman.

The "Devil's Grandmother" – in German, des Teufels Großmutter, in Italian, Nonna del Diavolo, in transliterated Russian, D'yavola Babushki – appears to be a hypernym, an umbrella term, embracing a number of ancient and not-so-ancient female beings; the same is true for the Devil's Mother, Wife, and Daughter. Indeed, these figures are often identical or transferable. For this reason, in an effort to simplify, I will henceforth refer to them in the singular. Goddesses with which she is identified include Diana, Hecate, Minerva, Bellona, Ceridwen, Frigga, Valkyries, Eostre, Holda (or Holle), Frau Werra, Fru Fricke, La Befana, and Baba Yaga, not to mention the Abrahamic Lilith, most of whom have been associated with witchcraft. As Fauna Fatua, the wife or sister of Faunus/Pan, she, like her male counterpart, is a horned deity.

However, she also appears to have become a hybrid being in her own right. She often wears a dark-hued, hooded cloak, typically green (the color most associated with fairies), but sometimes red or blue. She is sometimes considered the "Queen of the Witches," the *Hexenkönigen*. As such, she is especially celebrated on Walpurgisnacht/Beltane.

She is often depicted as a death-wielding divinity, a patron of hunting and of animals, and a shapeshifter (often transforming into a hare). She has been depicted as a goddess reigning over the seasons. In her unfathomable past may be a connection to the depths of the sea, as Alphons Barb suggests in "Antaura, the Mermaid and the Devil's Grandmother," as the Biblical *tehom*[a] or the Sumerian Tiamat, the very face of the deep.

Fragmentary evidence suggests that at some unknown point, perhaps somewhat prior to the thirteenth century, her nickname of "the Devil's Grandmother" may have come to be accepted by nominally or somewhat Christianized communities who believed in her existence. Moreover, if pagan-based, duotheistic rites took place in post-ancient Wales, it is conceivable that she and her male counterpart were both revered with sacrifices and such.

In her manifestation as the Devil's Daughter, she persists primarily in fairy tales. Like the Devil's Grandmother, she often ends up assisting the hero. In Christian folklore, the Devil sometimes has seven daughters, who represent the Seven Deadly Sins. Witches are also sometimes deemed "the daughters of the Devil," as are women deemed overly aggressive by men, in the past sometimes called "termagants." A popular curse goes, "May you marry the Devil's daughter, and may the old folks come and live with you!" In *Grose's Classical Dictionary of the Vulgar Tongue* (1823), one finds: "It is said that one who has a termagant for his wife, that he has married the Devil's daughter."

Termagent
We could just chalk up this connection of the Devil's Daughter with "uppity" women to patriarchal sexism; the term "termagant," however, suggests that more than meets the eye may be going on here. This term, which typically refers, as in Bailey's *Universal Etymological English Dictionary* (1775), to a "ranting, lusty, bold woman" and which is found in Chaucer, Shakespeare, etc., derives from the transliterated term for a deity thought by medieval Europeans to have been worshipped by Muslims alongside Muhammad, or else a deity who continued to be worshipped by certain peoples after they had converted to Islam and when they were no longer supposed to be worshipping the deity. M. A. Richardson observes in *The Borderer's Table Book* (1846):

Termagant was a Saracenic deity worshipped by the Turks, before, and for some time after, the introduction of Mahomedanism. In an old Norman MS. romance preserved in the Bodleian library, but of which the title is destroyed, the names of Tervagan (i. e., Termagant) and Mahun [i. e., Mohammad] are placed in juxtaposition. The same thing occurs in *Le Roman de Roncevaux*. The old English writers frequently make their monsters swear by Termagant, as Chaucer does in his "Rime of Sire Thopas"…

In the British islands, long after the Gods of Scandinavia had ceased to be worshipped, the inhabitants, though they were converted to Christianity, believed the old deities to exist as evil spirits; and so it was in the east—for many years after the introduction of the Mahometan [i.e., Muslim] faith, its professors firmly believed, that the old gods of their country, (of whom Termagant was one of the chief,) had an existence as evil spirits. This superstitious notion was embraced by the Crusaders, who added to it the belief, that such evil spirits were worshipped by the Mahometans, and aided them in the battle field!...The origin of the word Termagant as applied now to a scolding woman, may be easily deduced from the above remarks...[78]

Although a number of scholars have sought to discover the deity to which the transliterated "Termagant" refers, they seem to have gotten farther and farther away from its mysterious meaning, to which the earliest scholars, who suggested that it might mean "thrice great," together with Ugo Foscoli's 1819 suggestion that it might refer to a Saracenic/Arabian equivalent of the goddess Diana, in her manifestation as Diana Trivia (that is, as Diana, Selene, Hecate). This is particularly intriguing in light of the fact that Diana and (or, as) the Fairy Queen were (was) sometimes referred to as the "Wife of Mohammed," an appellation which would've clearly been extremely offensive to religious Muslims. It occurs to me that if we combine the data thus far, we have something like "thrice great" "bold" female divinity resembling Diana Trivia. This suggests to me that what we might have here is a reference to the trinity of goddesses Al-Uzza, Al-Lat, and (Al-)Manat (corresponding roughly to the Maiden, Mother, and Crone), whose reverence persisted alongside that of Muhammad long after it had been forbidden on pain of death. Taken together, this data would suggest that a medieval European conception of a Saraceni/Arabian triple goddess – drawing upon a phrase signifying "x 3 [roughly, *theroth maraut*]— fairies [*jinniyah*]" – may have contributed to the construction of the archetypal figure of the "Devil's daughter," with *Ther- ma-dj—ah* becoming "Termagant."

Lilith

Although Lilith evolved in Biblical, especially Jewish, folklore, which is beyond the bounds of this book, I am very briefly considering her here because of her pagan Assyrian-Babylonian roots as Lilîtu and Lamashtu, because of her association with other pagan female beings, and because of her association with witchcraft and with pagano-Abrahamic spirituality. Described from the Middle Ages onward as the first, unruly wife of Adam – a tale revisited and reinterpreted by feminists – Lilith is primarily viewed as a combination siren-vampire-horned goddess. Stunningly beautiful except for avian claws for feet, she wears a horned headdress, dwells, bird-like, in a tree, has avian claws for feet, and is surrounded by predatory animals, including owls and lions. Amulets protecting mothers and infants against Lilith's aggression were worn in antiquity, the Middle Ages, and persisted into the eighteenth century and thereafter; as R. J. Z. Werblowsky notes, "To this day [*c*. 1984] there are circles where no woman in childbed would do without the protection of an anti-Lilith amulet, especially in the cradle of the newborn."

Lamia

Lilith was sometimes conflated with Lamia, especially in late medieval and Renaissance literature and visual art depicting witches and witchcraft. Lamia, a Libyan princess, was, according to some, the child of a mortal African woman and Poseidon. Lamia was changed into a demoness of the Greeks when the jealous Hera punished her rather than her husband Zeus, who sought to seduce Lamia. Over the centuries, Lamia was feared by many, and prayers, amulets, and such were used to keep her at bay. It's important to note that Lamia, like other beings, can appear as a singular entity or as possessing many hypostases. Some Greeks continued to believe in her existence into the twentieth century. In a Greek text published in 1904, Lamia is described as follows:

> The *lámnia* [i.e., Lamia] is a tall woman with a beautiful body. That's why when people want to point out that a girl is lissome and graceful, they say that she has the body of a *lámnia* or that she walks like a *lámnia*. She has one great defect, however. Her feet are not two human ones, but three or more, and of different sorts. The one may be of copper, the other a donkey's, the other a cow's or a goat's…[79]

Lamia may manifest as singular or plural. Especially when she manifests in triplicate, she is/they are called not only lamiae but also "masques." Especially in multiple manifestation, Lamiae are linked to *strigae*, roughly, "witches", as they were during the period of the witch trials.

Lamia also came to be called the "Queen of the Shore," "Queen of the Sea," and "Queen of the Nereids;" as such, she is depicted as a "beautiful creature, half-woman, half-fish" who drowns those who "swim at midday."

Gello

Lilith and Lamia are in turn linked to the Greek demoness Gello. Gello's name suggests that she may have originated in the Babylonian demoness Gyllou, akin to or synonymous with Lilîtu. A vivid portrait of Gello is painted by Sarah Iles Johnston in her marvelous book *Restless Dead: Encounters Between the Living and the Dead in Ancient Greece*. Gello, she relates, is a "demonic creature" who, euphemistically said to be "fond of children," "the soul of a dead virgin who wander[s] around in the world of the living." Indeed, Gello makes la Llorona look like Snow White. Dying prematurely, Gello "lives" to cause "trouble for the living." She kills virgins and pregnant women, "thwarts reproduction," and haunts and kills children. Like Lamia, she is associated with the sea, and as a demonstration of her power of metamorphosis, she sometimes manifests as a fish. When chased by humans wishing to repel her, she has been known to "jump into the ocean." Gello can manifest singly or as a group.

Although in Christianized Greece, she came to be conflated with, or else displaced by, Satan, belief in Gello as herself – in spite of the Orthodox Church's denial of her existence – spans just under three thousand years. A Byzantine tale recounts how, in the form of a fly, or, according to another version, as a bit of dirt or a grain of millet ("Gello" can mean a "sheaf of grain"), she hitched a ride on St. Sisinnius' horse. In the past, Gello was among the "demonic" beings exorcized by Greek Orthodox priests. The seventeenth-century Greek scholar Leo Allatios (*c.* 1586-1669), a scholar trained in theology and medicine, and author of *De Graecorum hodie quorundam opinationibus* (1645), believed in the existence of Gello, explaining that Gello can kill someone by poisoning them with her touch and that, akin to the traditional vampire, she sucks the blood of children. Johnston notes that in the twentieth century, "*gelloudes* still haunt[ed] parts of the Greek countryside;" and Charles Stewart relates that they were often held responsible for "[m]iscarriages, infant mortality, and devastating childhood illnesses." She also brings migraines, which are believed to originate in the "depths of the ocean." Stewart also notes that like the *Kallikantzaroi*, human women who are destined to become *Gelloudes* are thought to be born either on one of the forty days leading up to Christmas or on Christmas Day itself; also reflecting Christian influence, it is said that persons who most often encounter *Gelloudes* are those who have not been "properly baptized."

Striga, or Strix

Sometimes identified with Gello, compared to the Eumenides and Furies, and nicknamed the "bird of the night," the *striga* or *strix* (or, stryx) is a hybrid owl-, vulture-, or bat-woman being, similar to La Lechuza in Mexican folklore. She is alternately depicted as a vampiric being who sucks the blood of infants (and/or others) and as an *amma* (a term known in many languages), that is, a mother, grandmother, or nursemaid or wet-nurse who suckles infants because she loves them. She bears an uncanny resemblance to the Yorùbá Ajé.

At some as yet undatable point, the *striga* came to be seen not only as a non-human being but also as a mortal witch; we will discuss this figure when we look at ritual specialists.

As a non-human being, however, the *striga* continued to be an object of belief in the early twentieth century, although primarily as a demoness, in Italy (as *strega*) and elsewhere: "one of the evil powers of a *striga* (*strega* in Italian) is supposed to be the power to suck the blood of people, especially of children."

Vrykolakas

The *vrykolakas*, predominantly conceived as male, anciently, and in some places still, resembling the African/African-diasporic *zombi*, has, particularly due to Slavic influence on Greek culture, become in other places much more like the vampire, transforming from an "animated corpse which can leave his grave" to a sinister "devil" who sucks blood and tortures and slays humans. The *vrykolakas* is thought to be able to leave his (/her?) grave "every day except Saturday." The *vrykolakas* "destroys [others] with his gaze…alone" or else with his foul breath. In the seventeenth century, as Allatios demonstrates, belief in the *vrykolakas* persisted. In the twentieth century, Greek Americans living in Massachusetts and elsewhere continued to believe in the existence of *vrykolakoi*, although more so in its ancient manifestation as a zombi-like figure. D. Demetracopoulou Lee relates that in 1934, informants in the Boston area "were always ready to tell about *vrykolakes* who were known to their friends and relatives."

Helen Mcbrune

In the late sixteenth century, in Ayrshire, Scotland, Jonet Hunter, Patrick Lowrie, Katherine M[c]Teir, and Margaret Duncane – who were tried in 1605 – were said to have assembled at "Hallow-evin," that is, on Samhain or Halloween, on Loudoun Hill and to have there revered a "devilish Sprite" who "called herself Helen Mcbrune." Helen instructed devotees in primarily destructive magic and bestowed Patrick with a magic belt to which was attached a hand, perhaps that of a corpse, the fingers of which were likened to the "claw[s] of the Devil." It is conceivable that the being's Gaelic name was Liannan Mac Braoin, as "Liannan" is the Scottish Gaelic form of "Helen" and as "Mac Braoin" is the old Gaelic form of Mcbrune, Mac Breen, Mac Brewne, and Mac Breane (Irish, O'Braoin). If this is the case, then it might suggest that the being was a hypostasis of the Liannan Shith, of whom Yeats writes: "This spirit seeks the love of men. ...Her lovers waste away, for she lives on their life. ... [In exchange,] she gives inspiration ...and is indeed the Gaelic muse... [She] carrie[s her lovers] away to other worlds."

In particular, this might be a manifestation of the Liannan Shith bearing, like the banshee patrons of particular families, a protective relationship to the Mac Braoin family of Ossory; and/or the "Mcbrune" might be meant to signify a being also linked to *braoin*, "moisture." This is, however, speculation. What is known is that Loudoun Hill and the environs, in East Ayrshire, had been settled since the Iron Age; was held sacred by the Druids, in regard to sacred stones, a grove of oaks, and temples thought to have once been found there; and had later been settled by Romans.

Dame Dark and Malen

In nineteenth-century (and perhaps earlier) West Sussex, England, the Devil was accompanied by Dame Dark. Dame Dark appears to be related to Mother Midnight, a figure who appears in the Elizabethan comedy *Wily Beguiled* (or, *Wylie Beguylie*, 1566/7), as a pseudonym of the mad poet Christopher Smart, and as a character in Defoe's *Moll Flanders*? In *Wily*, Mother Midnight appears in connection with Robin Goodfellow, and in *Moll*, according to Robert A. Erickson (1979), she represents "omniscient power which gives life and takes it away," "powers assigned to the Greek Fates," a "Witch," one who "possess[es] uncanny powers of prophecy," one of "Satan's ministers," and "the old woman of the night." In turn, I'm reminded of an Algerian *jinn* called "Mother of the Night." She takes devastates the flocks and herds of those who disrespect her but grants prosperity to those who remember her and who wear amulets sacred to her.

One of this figure's most significant hypostases is as the Welsh being called Malen (or, Malt y nos; also, Bela, Mam y Drwg, Matilda of the Night, the Old Hag, Y Wrach). Some have deemed this being an avatar of the Celtic goddess Ceridwen; as such, she is envisaged as a "goddess of nature, but also goddess of death as well as of the renewal of life," the fashioner of a "mystical vessel...into which it was only necessary to look to discern the future." Others have deemed her to be an avatar of the goddess Andraste. Andraste is an Iceni goddess of battle. Unfortunately, little is known about her. Her name may signify "inviolate," "unbroken," "unconquered," and/or "victory." She appears to have demanded the sacrifice of prisoners of war and at times of women. She appears to have been associated with a form of divination focusing on the movements of hares, considered her sacred animal. It is possible that hounds and bears were also sacred to her. She may have possessed groves or shrines in the vicinity of Pevensey in East Sussex and Colchester; the Forest of Andred (Andredsweald) was especially sacred to her. Llanandras Church in Presteigne, Wales may have been built on a site sacred to her: "Presteigne was celebrated as a place of British worship to Andras...The Christians changed the name of Andras to St. Andrew." Her most well-known devotee was Boudica, Queen of the Iceni (d. 60/61 CE), who led the fight against Roman invaders. Prior to battle, Boudica released a hare for purposes of divination and prayed to Andraste, "I thank thee, Andraste,1 and call upon thee, who are a woman, being myself also a woman that rules...I supplicate and pray thee for victory and salvation." Over the centuries, as a result of Christianization, she apparently, as Andras, came to be called Malen and/or the "Devil's Grandmother." The expression *"chwareu yr Andras"* means to "play the [female] Devil." Malen may also have gathered into herself some of the archetypal force of the Roman goddesses Bellona and Minerva. It is possible that Malen may reflect the sinister and/or "masculine" aspect of a sort of "Double Woman" Moon Goddess whose beneficent and/or "feminine" face may be that of the goddess Arianrhod. As Malen, she is, like Llyr's daughter Bronwen, considered a *gwrvorwyn*, an amazon, a "man-maid, or virago."

As a latter-day incarnation of Andraste, Malen's spouse is the Devil, himself, in this particular context, being a hypostatis of the god Arawn. Less often, she is partnered with Lugh. She rides on a horse and it's been suggested that she may occasionally manifest as a horse or as a woman possessing a horse's head. She may also manifest as a reptile. Her primary companions are the Cron Annwn, luminescent white dogs with red ears (or, alternatively, black dogs with red eyes), also known as the "Wish," "Wisked," "Yell," or "Yesh Hounds."

Her hounds also link her to witches; in the mid-nineteenth century, an informant told James Motley: "The wish, or wisked hounds, as they are called, a name probably connected with the Anglo-Saxon *wicca*, or witch, are under the guidance of that mysterious being." Indeed, Motley speaks of her as a "powerful witch." Together, they fly through the air, reminiscent of the Wild Hunt, announcing, like the Irish banshee, that death is imminent. They typically travel during Beltane (when the flight is referred to as "Malen's March"), midsummer, and on nights when the fog is thick. They are said to haunt cemeteries, the Vale of Taff, Rhondda Valley, the Vale of Neath, and St. Donat's Castle in Wales.

She searches for lost souls, especially that of the fifteenth-century pirate Colyn

Dolphyn; and she cares for the souls of infants who die before being baptized, suggesting, as elsewhere, that babies are pagan until formally Christianized. After the thirteenth century, she acquired certain attributes of a Norman noblewoman who allegedly lived in Wales during that time who boldly announced that when she died, she wanted no part of heaven unless one could hunt there.

The Goodman's Croft

In Scotland, Ireland, and Wales, farmers left a certain portion of their land uncultivated, dedicating it to a deity or similar being variously referred to as Black Donald, Clootie, Goodman, the Halie Man, Auld Hornie, Mahoun (a contemptuous name for Mohammad), Old Eric, Robert or Robin (these two linked to Robert Artisson, Puck and/or Robin Goodfellow), Auld Sandy, or simply, the Devil (or, Diel). It is noteworthy that in 1892, Henry Frederic Reddall, in *Fact, Fancy, and Fable*, penned: "The heathen deities were degraded by the Christian Church...and Pan...was transformed into his Satanic majesty, and called Old (Scotch, "Auld") Hornie."

Due to the predominance of the Goodman in northern Scotland and the location of the now lost great temple of Odin/Woden at Goodmanham in Northumbria, the Goodman may to some extent have been a latter-day incarnation of the Germanic god. It does not take a genius to realize that names such as Auld Hornie, the Halie Man, Clootie, Auld Sandy, and Black Donald signify pagan or spiritually hybrid innovation. Auld Hornie appears to have been especially linked to the Beltane ritual fire. It is noteworthy that the name "Old Hornie" continued to be used by persons living in Kentucky in the early to mid-twentieth century. Auld Clootie, suggesting "cloven feet," was the name given to the Horned God by John Douglas, the piper, and eight women who were tried for witchcraft, strangled, and burned in Scotland in May, 1659. Auld Clootie enjoyed certain airs; most pleasing to him were "Kilt thy coat, Maggie, and come away with me" and "Hulie the bed will fa'." Auld Sandy appears to have been associated in Banffshire with the phenomenon of crop circles, "flattened and twisted crop[s]." In the Christianized Central Balkans, we find names for the Devil including "Filip, Kralj,...Matek, Maticek, Pogan, Premuš, and Silnjak."

The portion of land devoted to the Devil was referred to variously as the "Gudeman's [or, Goodman's] croft," the "Devil's croft," "Goodman's Faul," "Goodman's Ground," the "Black Faulie," or the "Gi'en Rig." It is noteworthy that "croft" is in this context occasionally spelled "craft." Dedication to "the Devil" rather than to Christ or even a Christian saint during this period of intense, rapidly increasing Protestant-ization of Scotland suggests that doing so may have signified a defiant act of resistance on the part of rurals struggling against Christian and specifically Presbyterian hegemony. The Goodman's croft was not only left untilled; it was forbidden even to disturb the land by chopping trees that grew from it or moving stones that lay upon it. Cultivation of this land "would bring misfortune, particularly in the form of cattle diseases."

This piece of land was sometimes

triangular in shape and typically bounded by stones or a stone wall. One of the most well known of these crofts is at Killiesmont, near Keith in Banffshire; it is known as Helliman's Rig. It lies atop a mound with a view of – not surprisingly – Moray. A large stone peeks out of the earth; it appears to have had nine cups carved within it, perhaps for offerings. Many years ago, an urn containing ashes was found here, together with many other small stones which appeared to have been purposely placed there. Evidence of fires having been lit there also surfaced. This collection of evidence suggested that Helliman's Rig had been the sacred site of an "ancient religion," a "seat of worship, where sacrifice was offered and the divine blessing invoked upon the cattle and produce of the land.

It has been suggested that farmers often knew where to section off "Devil's crofts" because these sites were known to have been dedicated to ceremonies to ancient deities, and because they were sometimes the sites of holed stones or other things linked to ancient reverence. One finds in the *Transactions* of the Gaelic Society of Inverness for 1897:

The green patches called "the guidman's croft," which our ancestors never disturbed with spade or ploughshare, were…sacred to spirits, fairies, or pagan gods, and so passed over as by right of inheritance to the more modern devil. This is all the more certain, as beneficent gods were favourable to agriculture the world over, and the fairy knowe and guidman's croft were left untilled…from reverence…[80]

One of the main charges leveled against the Scottish male witch Andro Man, who lived in the parish of Rathven (not surprisingly, in the vicinity of Moray Firth) in the late sixteenth century, was that he had "met and measured divers pieces of land called wards to" a non-Christian "spirit," the Hynd Knight, with the interrogating Christians presuming this being to be the Devil. Andro Man had apparently created a Goodman's croft by way of bounding an area of land with four stones. By doing so, he was, it was thought, able to protect neighboring cattle and crops from diseases and such. It appears that this area was also thought to be a prime location for conducting rites. For example, the alleged Scottish witch Jonet Wischert, in the final years of the sixteenth century, performed a fertility rite involving nudity and the casting of stones on the site. What is more, Andro Man was charged with creating several Goodman's crofts in the area of Moray, possibly for the Innes and Caddell families.

This practice of setting land aside for the Goodman's croft demonstrates reverence of a hybrid being whose origins may well be pagan rather than simply invertedly Christian; speaks to an earth-centered practice for which there is a great deal of evidence; reflects an agrarian, rather domestic relationship to the deity or similar being, much as one finds in the reverence of Holda and other divinities; and speaks to the possible connection of the continuation of pagan and syncretic/hybrid traditions to acts of resistance.

In 1594, the Kirk of Scotland, in Session 11, ordained that if, in believing that a certain "parcell of ground [should be] dedicated to the devill, under the name of the Goodman's Croft," he would be thenceforth made to farm that piece of land under threat of his entire property being confiscated by the king as punish-ment for committing such disobedience.

Despite such prohibitions, the practice persisted into the seventeenth and eighteenth centuries. As Joseph McPherson states in *Primitive Beliefs in the North East of Scotland*, "[I]n the period referred to in the Church records, it appears as if it were essential there should be a Goodman's croft on every estate."

In 1602, some men from Clackmarras were questioned and condemned by the local church governing body, the Kirk Session, because they had "reserved a peise [of] land to the deuill callit the Gudmanis." That same year, incidentally, John Nauchtie of Elgin was called in by the Kirk Session because he had dared to perform "agricultural operations on Sunday." He responded defiantly that "the devil had as great power as God, and they who served him were in as good case as they who served God." In the following year, a church elder reported that tenant farmers he knew had set aside a Goodman's croft "for the welfare of the cattle." In 1646, church leaders accused William Siefwright and George Stronach of practicing sorcery because they had set aside land for a Goodman's croft; they were punished by being forced to work the land. When, in 1650, Norman Leslie and James Tuicks acknowledged that they had promised to let the Goodman's portion of their land lie fallow, the congregational Kirk session condemned their actions as "impious" and referred them to the Presbytery, a religious court, which "ordered the land to be labored." Near the beginning of the nineteenth century, a tenant farmer used the notion of the Goodman's croft to curse the landowner who was throwing him off the land he had worked. When he was ploughing the land for the last time, he "drove his plough with all the earth it could carry off the farm and unyoked it on a neighboring farm." He appears to have deposited the earth on the Goodman's croft of the neighboring farm. In this way, the "outgoing tenant took away the luck," and presumably the farm would go to ruin. This incident suggests that tenant farmers may have played a significant part in the continuation of this practice, as well as that they may, as persons having little economic or other powers, have called upon the Goodman (etc.) when seeking justice – which in turn suggests that the Goodman's croft and practices allied with it may have signified acts of sacred (and other) resistance. According to Sir James Young, the practice of setting aside a Goodman's croft persisted in the vicinity of Edinburgh into the mid-nineteenth century. During this period, apparently in order to bring less unwanted attention to the traditional practices of farmers, the croft came to be called "The Owd Lad's Bit."

It is noteworthy that with the exception of the possible usage of the Goodman's croft to bring harm to the unjust, its raison-d'être, and the allied reverence of a being who might be the Devil, is life-affirming and beneficial rather than malefic. In relation to the continued practice of the Goodman's croft, "hell-fire clubs," wherein which the Devil appears to have been "celebrated ... in all sincerity to propitiate a Higher Power," allegedly persisted in Scotland and elsewhere into the nineteenth century (and perhaps into more recent times). Of Scotspersons who revered the Goodman (etc.), Joseph McPherson makes what I consider to be a very astute observation: "They were really at heart nature worshippers ... . The very name by which the devil was called shows he was not the terror he was later represented to be ... . In the olden time there was something of familiarity, if not indeed of affection, in the way the devil was regarded."

Sources

Full bibliography will appear in vol. 5.

Sources for the Introduction

1 : Block quotations: Rio, *Arbre philosophal*, 70.
2 Filotas, *Pagan Survivals*, p. 79.
3 Kamborian, "Children," 131.
4 Dendy, *Philosophy*, 429.
5 James, *Varieties of Religious*, 571.
6 Markale, *Aujourd'hui*, 16.
7 Wood-Martin, *Elder Faiths*, 1: 343.
8 Owen, *Skeptics of the Italian*, 58-59.
9 Beza, "Pagan Remnants," 394.
10 Other main sources for the Introduction: Ali, and Rehman, *Indigenous Peoples*, 10; Allen, Alther, Brown, Piercy, et. al., "What I Do," 23; Anon., *Rehearsall both Straung*, 35; Arnold, "Gramsci and Peasant," 31-32, 41; Aubrey, *Three Prose Works* (*Remaines of Gentilisme*), 149-150; Bagulia, *Encyclopedia of Human*, 270; Belmont, "Mythic Elements," in *Mythologies*, 2: 735; Benoist, *On Being a Pagan*, 164; Berend, *Christianization and the Rise*, 33; Bernard de Montfaucon, *Supplement to 'Antiquity,'* vol. 1, pp. 62-64; Brenneman, Jr., "Serpents, Cows, and Ladies," 342; Brewer, *Wordsworth Dictionary*, 403; Brewster, "Ozark Superstition," 76; Bromley, *Teaching New Religious*, 34; Casebolt, and Niekro, "Some UUs Are More," 235, 238, 239; Chatterjee, "Nation and its Peasants," 22; Christ, in Gross, Christ, Burford, Wadud, Chireau, Sered, Simmer-Brown, West, Goldenberg, and Shapiro, "Roundtable: Feminist Theology," 81; Cirlot, *Dictionary of Symbols*, 60, 271, 306, 340; Classen, "Sweet Colors," 723; Coleman, *Tribal Talk*, 25; Davies, *Europe: A History*, 19-20, 25; Davies, *Grimoires: À History*, 211; Derbyshire, "Archaeologists Uncover Headless" (website); Dergachev, *About Scepters* (in Russian), 460-461, 464; Dodson, *Sacred Spaces*, 15, 37, 162, 169, 175; Domosh, and Jordan-Bychkov, *Human Mosaic*, 227; ECER, ed., European Congress (website); Farnell, "Do You See," x; Filotas, *Pagan Survivals*, 41; Fletcher, and LaFlesche, *Omaha Tribe*, 597l; Foltz, "Review of *Voices from the Pagan*," 56; Foucault, "Nietzsche, Genealogy," 139-140; Foucault, "Two Lectures," 80-85; Gatens-Robinson, "Finding our Feminist Ways," 221; Geertz, "Thick Description," 18; Ginzburg, *Ecstasies: Deciphering the Witches'*, 15, 20-21, 139-140, 235; Glover, *Life and Letters*; Gramsci, *Selections from the Prison*, 54-55; Greiner, *Visualizing Human Geography*, 131; Gross, "Is the Goddess," 111; Hakutani, *Postmodernity and Cross Culturalism*, 9; Hallowell, *Culture and Experience*, 177; Horner, *Future Israel*, 95; Horsley, "Further Reflections," 95; Hutton, "Paganism in the Lost Centuries," 137; Hutton, *Pagan Religions*, 289-292, 295, 297, 298, 324, 339, 341; Hutton, *Stations of the Sun*, 218, 370, 410-420; Japtok, "Introduction," *Postcolonial Perspectives*, xxvi; Johnson, *Dictionary of the English*, no page number; Jolly, "Medieval Magic," 11-12; Jones, and Pennick, *History of Pagan*, 1; Jones, "Pagan Theologies," 34; Julian, *Works*; Keen,

Pelican History, 9; Keita, "Politics of Criticism," 339; Kinney, *Inner West*, 6-7; Kurin, Structure of Blessedness, 323; Lançon, *Rome in Late Antiquity*, 87; Lea, *Materials Toward*, 3: 1489-1490; Levi, "On Microhistory," 99, 102; Li, *Voices Rising*, 87; Long, "Goddess Movement," 312; Long, "Indigenous People," 179; Luckhurst, "Knowledge, Belief," 199; Macey, *Penguin Dictionary of Critical*, 163, 186, 236; Maes-Jelinek, *Labyrinth of Universality*, 483, 485, 487, 490, 493; Maffie, "We Eat of the Earth," 23; Magliocco, *Witching Culture*, 186; Mannhardt, *Letto-Preussische Götterlehre*, 611-612; Mather, *On Witchcraft*, 43-44, 62, 71, 129-130; Matthews, and Matthews, *Walkers Between*, 25, 38, 77, 134-138, 142, 181; McNeill, *History of Western*, 672; "Medieval Sourcebook" (website); Meskell, *Object Worlds*, 4; Mitchell, *Witchcraft and Magic*, 26; Momigliano, *On Pagans*, 21; Montrose, "New Historicisms," 399; Murray, "Missionaries and Magic," 100; Myers, "Other Nature," 8; Nerval, *Oeuvres complètes*, 2:1160; Ottmann, "Spiritual Materiality," 37-41; Paden, "Comparative Religion," 208, 213, 219, 221-223; Pandey, "Voices From the Edge," 282-284, 292-293; Paper, *Deities are Many*, 13-14, 105-106; Pearson, "Wicca, Paganism," 189-191; Pérez, *Chicana Art* (Tomás Ybarra-Frausto cited), 24; Pinar, "Lingering Note," 65; Plant, *Healing the Wounds*, 113; Poole, *Lancashire Witches*, 124-125; Rio, *Arbre philosophal*, 13, 176-177; Roper, "Introduction," *Charms, Charmers*, xv; Ruddick, *Maternal Thinking*, 82-83; Russell, "Witchcraft, Genealogy, Foucault," 121, 124; Ruth, "Bodies and Souls," 160; Rybakov, *Kievan Rus'*, 158-162; Schaff, *Theological Propædeutic*, 36; Schmidt-Haberkamp, "Writing-Back," 246; Semali, and Kincheloe, "Introduction," *What Is Indigenous*, 25-33, 42-43; Seznec, "Survival of the Ancient," 203; Skedros, Canons of the Councils, 296; Smith, "Athapaskan Way," 412, 413, 416, 419, 420, 425; Smith, *Decolonizing Methodologies*, 7; Starhawk, "Power, Authority, and Mystery," 73; Sukla, "Preface," *Art and Experience*, ix; Summers, *History of Witchcraft*, 431; Tarnas, *Passion of the Western*, xiii-xiv, 2; Tegg, ed., *London Encyclopaedia*, 8:635; Thin, "Why Anthropology Can Ill Afford," 28; Thomson, *Illustrations of the History*, 1: 30; Trinkauske, *Seeing the Swarming*, 1-11, 13, 19-20; Trombley, *Hellenic Religion*,1: ix-x; Turner, Avicebron, *Catholic Encyclopedia*, vol. 2 (website); Unitarian Universalist Association of Congregations, Paganism (website); Vico, *New Science*, 98-99, 144, 220; Walker, "Spirit Matters," 10; Wentersdorf, " 'Beowulf': The Paganism," 104-105; Werblowsky, "Polytheism," 11: 7315-7319; Wesley, "Extract of a Letter," 673; West, *Indo-European Poetry*, various; Weyer, *Histoires, disputes*, 1: Book II: p. 229; Whyte, "Beheaded Vikings Mass Grave" (website); Williams, *America's Religions*, 467; Winterbourne, *When the Norns* ,27, 120; Wood-Martin, *Elder Faiths*, 1: 341-353; York, *Pagan Theology*, 14, 67. See also: Ashcroft, Griffiths, and Tiffin, *Empire Writes*; Athanassiadi and Frede, *Pagan Monotheism*; Blain, Ezzy, and Harvey, eds., *Researching Paganisms*; Booth, *Secret History*; Cavalli-Sforza, *Genes, Peoples, and Languages*; Cavalli-Sforza, *Great Human Diasporas*; Chuvin, *Chronicle of the Last*; Dowden, *European Paganism*; Fox, *Pagans and*

Christians; Fuentes Guerra and Schwegler, *Lengua y ritos*; Gibbon, *Anthropological Archaeology*, Harrison, *Prologomena to the Study*; Kahn, *Pythagoras*; Lahar, "Ecofeminist Theory;" Murdoch, *Last Pagan*; Olanyin, *Scars of Conquest*; Pike, *Earthly Bodies*; Sertima, *African Presence*; Smith, R., *Julian's Gods*; Snowden, *Blacks in Antiquity*; Strmiska, ed., *Modern Paganism*; Terdiman, *Discourse/Counter-discourse*; Trungpa, *Cutting Through Spiritual*.

Sources for Chapter 1:

11. Symmachus, *Prefect and Emperor*, 41.
12. Shakespeare, *Midsummer Night's Dream*, *Riverside Shakespeare*, pp. 271, III: 2: 379-382.
13. This ballad is found in Friedman, *Viking*, 39-41.
14. Other main sources for Chapter 1: Adam of Bremen, *History of the Archbishops*, Book 2, sec. lxii (60), pp. 97-98 and Book 4, sec. xxvi (26), pp. 207; Assmann, "Monotheism and Polytheism," 17, 23-27; Augustine, *Confessions, The City* (1952 ed.), Book XVIII.12, p. 478; Berman, *Reenchantment of the World*, 62-63l; Bernard de Montfaucon, *L'antiquité expliquée*, 1: 110-111; Blázquez, "Iberian," *Enc. Rel.* 6: 547, 549; Blázquez, *Religiones en la España*, 35-36, 42-44, 59-62, 83-87; Boase, "Penitents of Love," 825; Bohm, *Wholeness and the Implicate*, 177, 189, 192; Bologne, *Flambeau au bûcher*, 69-70; Brand, *Observations on the Popular*, 1: 365; Calhoun, "Detective and the Witch," 308, 311; Carmichael, *Cultural History*, 25-29; Constantelos, "Byzantine and Ancient Greek" (website); Cosentino, ed., *Sacred Arts*; Coulton, *Medieval Panorama*, 107-108; Crawford, *Plague and Pestilence*, 151-152; Davies, *How to Build*, 109-110; Diderot, and Le Rond d'Alembert, "Myrionime," "Panthées," *Encyclopédie ou dictionnaire raisonné* (website); Dyer, *Folk-Lore of Shakespeare*, 83; Epton, *Spanish Fiestas*, 4-5; Farmer, *Oxford Dictionary of Saints*, 385-386; Fedotov, *Russian Religious Mind*, 8; Foley, "Part II: Interpretive Essay," 91; Frye, "Reforms of Chosroes Anushirvan"; Geffcken, *Last Days*, 227, 232; Grimm, *Teutonic Mythology*, 1: 285; 334-335; 2: 760; 3: 951-952; 4: 1323, 1325, 1332; Irwin, "Dreams, Theory, 238-239; Labriolle, *Réaction Païenne*, 483, 485; Lanciani, *Golden Days*, part 11, p. 82; Lee, *Enchanted Woods*, 198 ("No visible presence could have come up to the sense of her invisible immanence); McCartney, "Greek and Roman Weather Lore," 10; McNeill, and Gamer, *Medieval Handbooks*, 349; Mitich, "Orobanche: The Broomrapes" (website); Nerval, *Cagliostro, Les Illuminés*, 1: 317; Nicocini, *Ancient Spaniards*, 66-67; North, "Rome," in *Religions of the Ancient*, 230-231; Owen, ed., *Geoponika*, vol. 1, Book 2, chapter 42, p. 88; Book 7, chap. 31, p. 242; Paper, *Deities are Many*, 13, 14, 19-57, 59-68, 70-72, 78-95, 105-107, 125; Pitts, "Holographic Paradigm," 87; Pompeo Sarnelli, *Lettere ecclesiastiche*, 30; Price, *Viking Way*, 244-246; Riasanovsky, *History of Russia*, 38; Scot, *Discoverie of Witchcraft*, 24, 232; Scott, *Minstrelsy of the Scottish*, 2: 327; Seznec, "Survival of the Ancient," 203-204; Smith, and Cheetham, *Dictionary of Christian Antiquities* 1541; Thiers, *Traité des superstitions*, 152, 153; Trombley, "Paganism," 345-348; Trombley, *Hellenic Religion*, 1: 157-158, 170, 308; Wenzel, "Medieval Mystery Cult," 89-107;

Werblowsky, "Polytheism," 11: 7316-7318; White, *History of the Warfare*, 2:72; Wood-Martin, *Elder Faiths*, 1: 381. See also: Green, *Corpus of Religious Material*, especially 262-307; Henig, Martin, *Religion in Roman*; Merrell, "Borges' Tropological Avatars," 57; Rose, "Folklore of *Geoponica*," 66; Saint-Martin, *L'Auvergne: Des Monstres*, 111, 123, 125-126, 131; Sauer, *Archaeology of Religious*, 71; Societé de mythologie française, *France Mythologique*, 58; Spooner, "Cloud Ships," 323; Ziegler, *Histoire Secrète*, 9.

Sources for Chapter 2

15. Julian, "Letter to a Priest," Works, vol. 2: section 299, p. 323.
16. Columella, *On Agriculture*, vol. III, Book 10, p. 23, ll. 190-198.
17. Hull, *Folklore of the British*, 84, citing British Museum Manuscript Harley, 1585, ff. 12v-13r.
18. Apuleius, *Golden Ass* (Graves, trans.), 268-269, 271.
19. Nicolls, *Dreamer in Paris*, 188-194.
20. Lilly, "Nature of Venus" (website). See also Trottein, *Enfants de Vénus*, 61, referring to the fifteenth-century *Planetenbuch*.
21. Lemprière, *Bibliotheca Classica*, vol. 1 (no pagination; see under "Dionysia").
22 Brand, *Observations on the Popular*, 2: 137.
23. Chambers, and Chambers, *Book of Days* (website).
24. Other main sources for Chapter 2: Andrews, *Dictionary of Nature Myths*, 134; Apuleius, *Golden Ass* (Graves, trans.), 271; Aubade, "Isis romantique," 154; Augustine, *Confessions, The City* (1952 ed.), Book XVIII.12, p. 478; Bacconnière-Salverte, *Essai sur la magie*, 1: 262; Baltrušaitis, *Quête d'Isis*, 267-271; Begg, *Cult of the Black Virgin*, 64-66; Behringer, *Shaman of Oberstdorf*, 51-52; Birnbaum, *Black Madonnas*; Birnbaum, *Dark Mother*; Blázquez, *Imagen y mito*, 340, 433, 462; Blunt, *Vestiges of Ancient*, 89; Bricault, *Isis, Dame*, 172-173; Cohn, *Europe's Inner Demons*, 227; Corsu, *Isis: Mythe et mystères*, 256-257, 267-270; De Sivry, and Champagnac, *Dictionnaire*, 1142; Déal, *Dissertation sur les Parisii*, 19, 70-76, 114; Diderot, and Le Rond d'Alembert, "Isis," *Encyclopédie ou dictionnaire raisonné* (website); Diop, *African Origin*, 113-114; Douce, *Illustrations of Shakespeare*, 238-241; Dowden, *European Paganism*, 73; Enright, "Goddess Who Weaves," 59, 64-65, 68-70; Faber, *Origin of Pagan*, 3: 7, 13, 22-35; Filotas, *Pagan Survivals*, 73, 75, 265-266; Garbáty, "Chaucer's Weaving Wife," 341, 344-345; Gasparro, "Cultes isiaques," 35-62; Geffcken, *Last Days*, 228; Gordon, *Racines sacrées de Paris*, 214; Görres, *La mystique divine*, 5: 65; Hart, *Dictionary of Egyptian*, 101; Jenkins, "Bronze Athena," 67: 31; Karlin-Hayter, "Emperor Alexander's," 589-590; Lanciani, *Pagan and Christian Rome*, 27, 31, 92-93, 240; Lemprière, *Bibliotheca Classica*, vol. 1 (no pagination; see under "Dionysia"); Lidaka, *Book of Angels*, in *Conjuring Spirits*, 33, 55-56, 73; List, "Holda and the Venusberg," 307-310; Luke, "African Presence," 225; Magdalen, "Bath of Leo," 99, 111-112; Magne, "Divinités païennes," 117, 142, 150; Mango, "Antique Statuary," *Dumbarton Oaks Papers*, 17: 62, 68; Martin, *Religion des Gaulois*, 2: 13, 135-138; Merivale, *Pan the Goat*, 64; Moore, "Distribution of Oriental," 123; Murray, *Witch-Cult in Western Europe*, 45, 242; Nerval,

"Cagliostro," in *Les Illuminés, Oeuvres Complètes*, 1: 317; Noël, *Dictionnaire de la fable*, 2: 397, 743-744; Ovid, *Fasti* (Boyle and Woodard trans.), 59-66, 210 n. 3.169-402 (esp. n. 3.169-170); Owen, ed., *Geoponika*, vol. I, Book 5, chap. 24, p. 167; Paris, *Légendes du Moyen Age*, 71-72, 94, 101; Pohlsander, *Helena: Empress*, 87; Rhys, *Reliquary*, 3; Rio, *Arbre philosophal*, 185-186; Rose, Folklore of *Geoponica*, 80-81; Russell, *Witchcraft in the Middle*, 191; Seznec, "Survival of the Ancient," 203-204; Smedley, "Belief in Supernatural...Fairies," 25; Stow, *Survey of London*, 183; Tacitus, *Germania of Tacitus*, 53-55; Thorpe, *Northern Mythology*, 1: 287, n. 1; Trombley, "Paganism in the Greek," 328, 346; Trottein, *Enfants de Vénus*, 42; Vëlius, *World Outlook*, 53, 169 (invocation/prayer recorded by Maciej Stryjkowski in mid- to late sixteenth-century Lithuania); Vendryes, and Unbegaun, *Religions des Celtes*, 3: 244; Walters, "Predominance of Women," 63-90; Weigall, *Paganism in Our Christianity*, 132-133; Witt, *Isis in the Ancient*, 274-280; Yeates, *Dreaming for the Witches*, 145, 169, 206; Ziegler, *Histoire Secrète*, 6-8. See also: Green, *Corpus of Religious Material*, especially 262-307; Henig, Martin, *Religion in Roman*; Merrell, "Borges' Tropological Avatars," 57; Rose, "Folklore of *Geoponica*," 66; Saint-Martin, *L'Auvergne: Des Monstres*, 111, 123, 125-126, 131; Sauer, *Archaeology of Religious*, 71; Societé de mythologie française, *France Mythologique*, 58; Spooner, "Cloud Ships," 323; Witt, *Isis in the Ancient*, 276-280; Ziegler, *Histoire Secrète*, 9.

Sources for Chapter 3

25. Giraldus Cambrensis, *Journey Through Wales*, Book II, Chapter 7, p. 187.
26. Quehl, *Die Religion der Thüringer*, 45.
27. Eckenstein, *Woman under Monasticism*, 31-32.
28. Macleod, and Mees, *Runic Amulets*, 32.
29. Taylor, *Words and Places*, 219.
30. Other main sources for Chapter 3: Balas, *Mother Goddess in Italian Renaissance*, vii, 16-17, 24-25, 28, 44, 81, 87, 97, 115-117, 149-152; Bernard Silvestris, *Cosmographia*, 67-75; Bertolotti, "Ox's Bones," 49, 64; Branston, *Lost Gods*, 41-42; Butler, *Chronological, Biographical*, 6, 9, 12, 85, 101, 141, 149, 179, 188, 314, 321, 466, 479; Cato, in Cato and Varro, *On Agriculture*, CXXXII, p. 113; Columella, *On Agriculture*, vol. I, Book 1, secs. 2-3, pp. 3 & 5; vol. III, Book 10, ll. 60-70, p. 11, ll. 200-210, p. 23; Davidson, *Pagan Scandinavia*, 30, 117; Davidson, "Thor's Hammer," 9; Déal, *Dissertation sur les Parisii*, 20; Dronke, "Bernard Silvestris, Natura," 16, 18-25; Fogel, *Beliefs and Superstitions*, 8-10; Gimbutas, *Balts*, 191-192; Gordon, *Encyclopedia of Myths*, 70, 129, 368-369, 444; Grimm, *Teutonic Mythology*, 1: 250-258, 286; 2: 456, 470, 883; 3: 925-927, 993 and n. 2; 4: 159, 1363, 1696; Grottanelli, "Archaic Forms," 22-25; Gundarsson, *Teutonic Magic*, 223-226; Hermannus Dalmata, [*Liber*] *De Essentiis*, 71, 73, 239; Jakobsdóttir, "Gunnloð and the Precious Mead," 27-57; Julian, "Hymn to the Mother of the Gods," in *Works*, 1: Oration V, section 166, p. 463; section 169, p. 473; sec. 174, p. 487 (for editorial note regarding Julian's equation of Christian practice with 'wandering in darkness,' see Oration IV, sec. 131, p. 355); Koch, *Celtic Culture*, 1: 287; Lancre, *On the Inconstancy*, 31, 52, 62-63, 67-69, 301, 303,

307, 313-314, 354, 500-501, 507; Larrington, *Hávamál*, *Poetic Edda*, stanza 105, ll. 1-2, p. 28; stanza 108, ll. 3-4, p. 29; stanza 111, ll. 3-5, p. 29; stanza 112, ll. 4-5, p. 29; stanzas 112-137, pp. 31-34; stanza 140, p. 34; stanzas 146-163, pp. 35-37; stanza 145, p. 35; Larrington, "*Himiskviða*," *Poetic Edda*, stanza 3, l. 3, p. 78; stanza 16, l. 1, p. 80; stanza 24, l. 5. p. 100; MacNeill, *Festival of Lughnasa*, 30, 150-151, 307, 413, 552, 567; Markale, *Celts*, 70, 262, 273; Meaney, *Anglo-Saxon Amulets*, 159; Mitchell, "Odin, Magic," 266-279; Mitchell, *Witchcraft and Magic*, 29; Motz, *Beauty and the Hag*, 123; North, *Heathen Gods*, 16-18, 21-24, 32, 257, 271, 324-325; Ortiz-Osés, *Mitos vascos*, 25-27, 39; Owen, ed., *Geoponika*, vol. II, Book 11, chapter 2, pp. 68-69; Paxson, "Sex, Status, and Seidh;" Perkins, *Thor the Wind-Raiser*, 45, 53; Radford, *Thomas Hardy and the Survivals*, 79; Ross, "Anchors in a Three-Decker World," 66; Ross, *Pagan Celtic Britain*, 176-184, figs. 90-96; Saint-Martin, *L'Auvergne: Des Monstres*, 131; Sébillot, *Folklore et Curiosités*, 15-16, 66-67; Siikala, *Mythic Images*, 237; Stewart, *Demons and the Devil*, 115, 160, 252; Tabor, "Thar-Cake," 337, 338; Thorpe, *Northern Mythology*, 2: 49-50; Trombley, *Hellenic Religion*, 1: 15, 22, 42-44, 157-158, 183 n. 391, 315; 2: 240; Trottein, *Enfants de Vénus*, 11-12, 42-46, 50 fig. 20, 61, 66, 104, 177, 203 (I should note, however, that Trottein occasionally contradicts herself, as in certain passages where, in a reductionist manner, she compartment-alizes Venus into goddess and planet [see, for example, pp. 12-13]. Other than these few passages, however, I regard the book as extremely well written and enlightening.); Vaitkevicius, *Studies into the Balts'*, 49; Varro, in Cato and Varro, *On Agriculture*, Book I, Chap. 1, secs. 4-7, p. 161; Chap. 2, sec. 1 p. 167; Book III, Chap. 1, p. 425; Walsh, *Curiosities* 298; Weigall, *Paganism in Our Christianity*, 133.

Sources for Chapter 4:
31. Tacitus, *Germania of Tacitus*, 52.
32. Jouet, *Religion et mythologie*, 109.
33. Other main sources for Chapter 4: Balys, "Lithuanian Mythology," *Funk and Wagnalls*, 633; Christiansen, *Northern Crusades*, 138; Dlugosz, *Annals of Jan Dlugosz*, 4, 6; Flowers, *Wendish Mythology*, 12, 24-26; Gordon, *Encyclopedia of Myths*, 636-637; Greimas, *Of Gods and Men*, 27, 86-89, 104, 127, 186; Herberger, Batfeld und das Burgfeld, LXXX, LXXXIX, XC, XCIII, (Roman numeral pagination); Ivanits, *Russian Folk Belief*, 17; Jouet, *Religion et mythologie*, 123; Kmietowicz, *Slavic Mythical Beliefs*, 203 204; Kravchenko, *World of the Russian*, 12, 20-21; Léger, *Mythologie slave*, 10, 56, 62, 123-124, 164-165, 173-174, 179; Máchal, "Slavic Mythology," 37-39, 50-51; Matossian, "Vestiges of the Cult," 120-123; Pócs, *Between the Living*, 52, 125, 130-131; Puhvel, "Baltic Pantheon," 10, 102-108; Rodd, *Customs and Lore*, 182; Rybakov, *Kievan Rus'*, 160-163; Simonov, *Essential Russian Mythology*, 14-15; Sirutis, "Laima," *Romuva* (website); Slovisha, "Slavic Pagan Kalendar" (website); S³upecki, *Slavonic Pagan Sanctuaries*, 25, 44-46, 140, 202-203; Vaitkevicius, "New Outlook" (website); Vëlius, *World Outlook*, 52, 57, 59; Wilibald von Schulenburg, *Wendisches Volksthum*, 45-46.

Sources for Chapter 5
34. Manning, *Daina*, 5.
35. This version of the tale is based primarily on the version given in Martinkus, *Eglé*, 35-39. (my translation); however, I have also referred to Zheleznova, *Tales*, 204-212 and to Zobarskas, *Lithuanian Folk*, 1-11.
36. Kuncaitis, "Chthonic and Indo-European."
37. Other main sources for Chapter 5: Balys, "Lithuanian Mythology," 633; Dundulienë, "Ancient Lithuanian Mythology;" Dundulienë, *Žalèiai*, 190; Elyjiw, "Ukrainian *Pysanky*," 11; Everson, "Tenacity in Religion;" Gimbutas, *Ancient Symbolism*. 24-25, 34-35, 46-47, 59; Gimbutas, *Language*, 318-321; Hubbs, *Mother Russia*, xi-xii; Kazitenas, "Amid Trees," 83; Kelly, *Goddess Embroideries*; Krivickas, "Relations between the Living," 4, 6; Landsbergis and Mills, *Green Linden*, 23; Lietuvos Automobiliø Klubas, *Lithuania: Guiding Facts*, 60-63; Martinkus, *Eglé*, 35, 60-104, 111, 121, 135-142, 146-155, 158-159, 165-166, 221, 243; Martinkus, *Eglé*, retellings # 11, 12, 13, 25, 29, 30, 34, 37, 40, 42, 43; Matossian, "Vestiges," 120-123; Milosz, *Collected Poems*, 383; Sliazas, "Elements," 91, 93; Tracz, "Tradition in Ukrainian Life," 14; Vaitkevicius, *Senosios Lietuvos*, 732; Vëlius, *World Outlook*, 127-128, 132.

Sources for Chapter 6:
38. Block quotations: Beza, *Paganism in Roumanian*, 29-30.
39. Beza, *Paganism in Roumanian*, 31.
40 Other main sources for Chapter 6: Araquistáin, "Some Survivals," 33; Beza, "Roumanian Legends," 356-357; Beza, *Paganism in Roumanian*, 16-35; Caro Baroja, *Los Vascos*, 194, 409; Caro Baroja, *World of the Witches*, 237-238; Contreras-Gil, "Zugarramurdi: El Pueblo" (website); Eliade, *Zalmoxis: The Vanishing*, 204, n. 1, 206, 212-219, 224; Fjellström, "Sacrifices," 50; Grimm, *Teutonic Mythology*, 4: 1342; Hamori, "Hungarian Mythology" (website); Holmberg, "Lapps," *Encyclopædia of Religion and Ethics*, 7: 799; Jighira, "Noaptea de Sanziene" (website); Læstadius, *Fragments of Lappish*, 73-77, 83-87, 90-93, 97, 99, 100; Lancre, *On the Inconstancy*, 303, 307, 313; Lönnrot, *Kalevala*, 12, 24, 52, 72, 80-84, 10-101, 167, 320, 386-389, 398, 402; Lundmark, "Rijkuo-Maja, Saami Shaman," 159; Magnus, *Historia de Gentibus*, vol. I, Book 4, p. 219; Magyar, "Ancient Magyar Rovás" (website); Ortiz-Osés, *Los mitos vascos*, 31-34, 37-45; Price, *Viking Way*, 247; Rydving, "Saami Responses," 104-105; Salo, *Ukko: The God of Thunder*, 24; Siikala, *Mythic Images*, 114, 161-163, 172, 176, 198, 203, 215, 235-239, 290, 338-339; Porteous, *Forest Folklore*, 108; Sisa, "Ancient Magyar World" (website); Solbakk, *Sámi People*, 100; Stef, "*Maramure*" (website); Winterbourne, *When the Norns*, 85.

Sources for Chapter 7:
41. Block quotations: Lankranza, as cited by Motz, *Beauty and the Hag*, 124.
42. Hull, *Folklore of the British*, 170-171.
43. Anon., 1817, "Account of the Stormy Petrel" 3 (5): 55.
44. Anon., 1889, "Whence the Name," 51.
45. Vyvyan (pseud.), "Mother Carey's Chickens," *Mirror of Literature* 19 (547):

306-307. See also Glascock, Superstitions of the Sea, *Cincinnati Miscellany* 2: 8.
46. Kerr, ed., *General History and Collection*, vol. 8, p. 46.
47. Kingsley, *Water-Babies*, 185.
48. Rudkin, *Origin of the German*, 9.
49. Gee, "Some Notes," 95-96. I have taken the liberty of modifying the translation very slightly.
50. Cheney, "Roman Festival," 205-206.
51. Conway, "Mystic Trees and Flowers," 718.
52. Wägner, Macdowall, and Anson, *Asgard and the Gods*, 115-116.
53. Wedgwood, and Atkinson, *Dictionary of English*, 234.
54. Wägner, Macdowall, and Anson, *Asgard and the Gods*, 114-115.
55. Noël, *Dictionnaire de la fable*, 1: 854.
56. Other main sources for Chapter 7: Anon., "Whence the Name," 51; Anson, *Asgard and the Gods*, 116: Baciu, "Tradiciones en zonas," 16-17; Barth, *Die Altteutsche Religion*, 117; Blind, "Freia-Holda, the Teutonic Goddess," 113 (1464): 805, 809; Busk, "Curiosities of Superstition," 422; Cattabiani, "Il volto segreto," 212, 216, 217; Centini, *Le schiavi di Diana*, 98, 119-121; Chesnel de la Charbouclais, *Dictionnaire des superstitions*, 697; Cromek, ed., *Remains of Nithdale*, 281; Davidson, "Scandinavian Folklore," 180; Dovidat, and Dovidat, eds., "Frau Holle Teich" (website); Duni, *Under the Devil's*, 28; Gee, "Some Notes," 95-97; Golban, martisorul in calendarul" (website); Gurevich, *Medieval Popular Culture*, 84; Holtzmann, *Deutsche Mythologie*, 139-140, 163-165, 307; Johns, *Baba Yaga*, 22-29, 54-58; Lecouteux, *Au-delà du merveilleux*, 172; Lund, *Tolv fragmenter*, 157-170; Manciocco, and Manciocco, *L'Incanto e l'Arcano*, 9, 13, 14, 19, 21-27, 146, 161-171; Mannhardt, *Germanische Mythen*, 268-295; McKenzie, "Antiquary Repertory," no. 3, vol. 78, pp. 344-352; Monaghan, *Red-Haired Girl*, 33; Motz, "Winter Goddess," 151-161; Motz, *Beauty and the Hag*, 78-79, 124-125; Rager, *Dictionnaire* 378, 452-453; Ross, *Pagan Celtic*, 63, 279, 281, 284, 292, 313, 436, 454; Rucsanda, "Tradition and Contemporaneity," 2 (51): 61-65; Rudwin, "Origin of the German" (article), 407; Thirlwall, "On Some Traditions," 201; Thorpe, *Northern Mythology*, 1: 278-279; Touati, "Des Striges antiques," 38-39; Tsurumi, "Development of Mother Goose," 30; Vanin, "Leggende Ladine; Wägner, Macdowall, and Anson, *Asgard and the Gods*, 104, 117-118; Zaunert, *Deutsche Natursagen*, 104-108.

Sources for Chapter 8:

57 Block quotations: Latimer, *Sixth Sermon* (website).
58. Mitchell, *Past in the Present*, 167.
59. Burton, *Our Summer in the Harz*, 181-182.
60. Ewbank, *Descriptive and Historical*, 399.
61. Latimer, *Sixth Sermon*.
62. Other main sources for Chapter 8: Barth, *Altteutsche Religion*, 117; Bertolotti, "Ox's Bones," 49, 54, 64; Burton, *Our Summer in the Harz*, 180-183; Cattabiani, "Il volto segreto," 212-217; Centini, *Le schiavi di Diana*, 118-119; Evans, "Rollright Stones," 45; Gimbutas, *Living Goddesses*, 29, 30; Grimm, *Teutonic Mythology*, 1: 26, 267-273, 285; 2: 478-483; 4: 1424-1426, 1545; Harrison, *Roots of Witchcraft*, 219;

Henderson, *Norse Influence*, 49, 101; Hope, *Midsummer Eve's Dream*, 75-78; Hutton, *Pagan Religions*, 289; Laroque, *Shakespeare's*, 145; Lubell, *Metamorphosis of Baubo*, 143; Lund, *Tolv fragmenter*, 167; Merivale, *Pan the Goat*, 16, 64-65, 73; Motz, *Beauty and the Hag*, 125; Motz, "Winter Goddess," 156-161; Pitcairn, *Ancient Criminal Trials*, 3: 606, 614; Quehl, *Religion der Thüringer*, 23-24; Ross, *Pagan Celtic*, 176-184, and figs. 90-96; Rucsanda, "Tradition and Contemporaneity," 2 (51): 65, 66; Spalding Club, *Miscellany*, 1: 120, 165, 170-174; Thorpe, *Northern Mythology*, 1: 277-290; Vigfusson, ed., *Cleasby's Icelandic-English Dictionary*; Vulpius, *Handwörterbuch der Mythologie*, 5-6, 97; Ward, *Women in Medieval*, 238-244; Weyer, *On Witchcraft*, 21-22.

Sources for Chapter 9

63: Lea, *History of the Inquisition*, 3: 382.
64. Scot, *Discoverie of Witchcraft*, 24.
65. Digby, *Mores Catholici*, 717.
66. Hibbert, *Description of the Shetland*, 447.
67. Nicholson, Some Notes, 356-357.
68. Nicholson, Some Notes, 355-358.
69. Aubrey, *Three Prose Works (Remaines of Gentilisme)*, 203.
70. Lavater, *Of Ghostes and Spirites*, 73-74.
71. As cited by Hunt, *Popular Romances*, 315.
72. Wright, *English Folklore*, 91.
73. Skelton, *Complete Poems*, 37. The lyric was later set to music by Peter Warlock.
74. Wright, *English Folklore*, 113.
75. Shakespeare, *2 Henry IV*, Riverside Shakespeare, 3: 2: ll. 310-316, p. 949.
76. Eliade, *Zalmoxis: The Vanishing*, 205-210, 214, 216, 224.
77. Other main sources for Chapter 9: Anon., *Critical Dissertation*, 7-14; Ashmole, *Autobiographical and Historical*, 1: 162; 3: 1115; Aubrey, *Three Prose Works (Remaines of Gentilisme)*, 204; Behringer, *Shaman of Oberstdorf*, 67; Beza, "Pagan Remnants," 389-391, 393; Bologne, *Flambeau au bûcher*, 88-90; Brand, *Observations on the Popular*, 1: xvi; 2: 478-489; Briggs, "Fairies and the Realms," 95; Caro Baroja, *World of the Witches*, 125-126; Conway, "Mystic Trees and Flowers," 705-70; Dalyell, *Darker Superstitions*, 534-541; Eliade, *Zalmoxis: The Vanishing*, 204, n. 1, 218-219; 212, 213, 217, 218, 219, 224; Flowers, *Wendish Mythology*, 11; Frazer, *Jacob and the Mandrakes*, 8; Gordon, *Encyclopedia of Myths*, 197-198; Henningsen, "Ladies from the Outside," 191-215; Hibbert, *Description of the Shetland*, 447; Hole, *Thaumaturgia*, 78; Hope, *Midsummer Eve's Dream*, 92; Hull, *Folklore of the British*, 99-100, 105; Kirk, *Secret Commonwealth*, 67-78; Kmietowicz, *Slavic Mythical Beliefs*, 164, 194-196, 202-203; Lamothe-Langon, *Evenings with Prince Cambacérés*, 1: 153-156; Lecouteux, *Au-delà du merveilleux*, 169-173; Lecouteux, *Nains et les elfes*, 14, 109, 111-118, 123-127, 149, 194; Mac Gregor, *Peat-Fire Flame*, 60-65, 219; Máchal, "Slavic Mythology," 30-37; Mackenzie, *Scottish Folk-lore*, 200-211; Map, *De Nugis Curialium*, 189; Markale, *Melusine, ou, L'androgyne*; Martin, *Religion des Gaulois*, 2: 189; Pitcairn, *Ancient Criminal Trials*, 51, 54, 57-58; Purkiss, *At the Bottom*, 7, 9-10, 143; Rodd, *Customs and Lore*, 169-170; Sanderson, "Prospect of Fairyland," 18; Scot, *Discoverie of Witchcraft*, 24, 232-237, 408; Scott, *Letters* 64; Scott, *Minstrelsy of the Scottish*, 2: 304, 320, 322; Seyed-Gohrab, "Magic in Classical Persian," 74; Thompson,

"Irish *Sí* Tradition," 360; Vallée, *Passport to Magonia*, 105-106; W.W., *True and Just*, 81, 105, 124; Westropp, "Study of the Folklore," 312-319; Weyer, *On Witchcraft*, 30-32.

Sources for Chapter 10:

78. Block quotations: Richardson, *Borderer's Table*, 22 n. 2.
79. Stewart, *Demons and the Devil*, 180-181, citing Nikólaos Polítis.
80. Gaelic Society of Inverness, Fauns and Fairies, 272.
81. Heckethorn, *Secret Societies*, 296.
82. Other main sources for Chapter 10: Blok, "Cavaliers du Bouc" (website); Davidson, "Untilled Field," 20-25; Erickson, "Moll's Fate," 84-86; Funck-Brentano, *Princes and Poisoners*, 216; Gander, *Niederlausitzer volkssagen*, 149; Gordon, *Book of the Chronicles*, 53; Hartnup, "On the Beliefs," 274, 280; Heckethorn, *Secret Societies*, 296; Hood, "Folk Culture;" Johnston, *Restless Dead*, 22, 28, 73, 165-166, 175, 209, 215; Lee, "Greek Accounts," 126-127; McPherson, *Primitive Beliefs*, 139; Meyrick, "On the State," 25; Motley, *Tales of the Cymry*, 60-61; Oliphant, "Story of the Strix: Ancient," 134-137, 143; Potts, *Wonderfull Discoverie*, 183; Rhys, *Lectures on the Origin*, 608-609; Russell, *Witchcraft in the Middle*, 129, 141-142; Scott, *Letters on Demonology*, 59; Stewart, *Demons and the Devil*, 173-174, 196, 287, n. 11; Trevelyan, *Folk-lore and Folk-stories*, 50, 52, 269; Tucker, *Blood Work*, 203; Werblowsky, "Commerce with the Supernaturals," 132; Wilby, *Visions of Isobel Gowdie*, 426.

Index

A

Abundance
　Prosperity 58, 73, 79, 117, 134, 138, 141, 156, 157, 158, 159, 188, 196, 223, 274, 279, 283, 287, 296, 297, 306
　Treasures 60, 89, 94, 155, 225, 228, 296
　Wealth 98, 108, 238
African and African-diasporic religions
　Ajé 305
　Eshú 288
　La Regla de Ocha 19, 117, 199, 206
　Orishá 52, 77, 134, 178, 201, 206, 288
　Osanyin 116
　Oshún 77
　Oyá 201
　Vodou 19, 117, 125, 192, 215, 274
　Yemayá 77, 199, 206
Altered states of consciousness
　Ecstasy 29, 58, 92, 131, 197
　Entheos 95
　Trance 85, 272, 274, 282
Ancestral spirits 6, 7, 30, 52, 91, 147, 183, 262, 265, 283, 291, 300
Animals
　Animal soul
　　Fylgia 194
　　Varden 194
　Bat 223, 305
　Bee 126, 140, 186, 190, 269, 286, 289
　　Beehives 237
　Black pullet 291
　Boar 160
　Bull 58, 59, 62, 79, 108, 240, 241
　Butterfly 149, 235, 251
　Cat 112, 113, 130, 162, 193, 220, 222, 251, 265, 269, 274, 289, 293
　Cattle 70, 102, 107, 125, 129, 135, 136, 139, 148, 152, 178, 189, 190, 191, 220, 227, 236, 265, 269, 285, 289, 304, 308, 309, 310
　Chicken 199, 200, 318
　Crow 109, 130
　Cuckoo 139, 146, 148, 152
　Deer 18, 58, 92, 191, 225, 251, 264
　Dog 102, 115, 130, 133, 178, 235, 286, 289, 290, 293, 295, 307
　Eel 190
　Falcon 112, 128, 194, 196
　Goat 58, 95, 121, 142, 174, 225, 241, 242, 250
　　Akelarre, the Field of the Goat 173
　Hare 140, 153, 302, 307
　Hedgehog 235
　Horse 107, 116, 117, 118, 119, 125, 128, 132, 134, 135, 136, 139, 141, 143, 147, 152, 174, 184, 194, 196, 220, 244, 249, 250, 251, 261, 266, 269, 274, 283, 284, 289, 293, 296, 304, 307
　Magpie 130, 235
　Mouse 92, 247, 289, 297
　Owl 130, 228, 305
　Partridge 175
　Ram 174
　Raven 109, 116, 118, 174, 177
　Reindeer 179, 180, 233
　Rooster 131, 138, 143, 289
　Serpent 68, 128, 136, 138, 139, 147, 148, 149, 150, 151, 152, 153, 155, 156, 157, 158, 159, 160, 161, 162, 167, 168, 169, 170, 171, 172, 188, 192, 197, 222, 235, 261, 262, 263, 292, 293
　　Agatho-daemon 156
　　žaltys 152, 155, 157, 158, 162, 172
　　Giviotis 157
　　Kneph 156
　　Krikštas 157
　　Miðgarðs-ormr 156
　　Natrix natrix 155
　　Ofnir 156
　　Ophidian deity 159
　　Ophidian reverence 158, 161
　　Ophites 161
　　Peena mahtes 157
　　Serpentine 146, 148, 151, 156, 159, 160, 161, 171, 172
　　Svâfnir 156
　　Zmij 156

Sheep 174
Stag 108, 215, 240, 249, 250
Toad 147, 148, 189, 235, 293
Wolf 11, 137, 140, 177, 191, 192, 197, 244

Arthurian legends
King Arthur 120, 259
Merlin 240, 277

Astrology
Zodiac 128

Avatar and hypostasis 60, 66, 82, 85, 93, 97, 99, 100, 105, 114, 115, 123, 186, 193, 196, 210, 214, 225, 226, 236, 237, 241, 261, 272, 290, 292, 306, 307

B

Beverages
Beer 63, 73, 139, 143, 145, 286, 290
Mead 66, 67, 121, 129, 316
Patxaran 175
Vodka 157, 158
Whiskey 157, 192
Wine 61, 72, 95, 96, 97, 134, 135, 181, 188, 215, 227, 238, 279, 280, 292, 295, 296

Boats and ships
Cloudship 205
Navigium Isidis 75, 78
Shipwreck 199
Skiðbladnir 205, 283
Tiger 201, 202, 203
Vindflot 205

Broom, staff, wand
Broom 126, 188, 194, 204, 212, 213, 223, 242
Rune-stave 122
Staff 98, 161, 195, 243, 248
Wand 168, 193, 195, 197, 223, 272

C

Celestial bodies
Great Bear 177
Milky Way 220, 230, 232
Moon 72, 73, 75, 85, 92, 100, 105, 109, 119, 127, 128, 129, 141, 147, 158, 174, 175, 177, 188, 195, 197, 208, 220, 228, 230, 231, 235, 245, 261, 264, 266, 272, 276, 277, 284, 296
North Star 177
Pleiades 127, 236
Sirius 290
Sun 61, 72, 73, 75, 78, 83, 107, 108, 127, 128, 129, 134, 136, 141, 143, 144, 146, 147, 151, 152, 155, 157, 158, 175, 177, 179, 182, 190, 191, 219, 220, 240, 264, 266, 272, 276, 282, 284, 300, 301

Chant, music, and dance
Charivari 251
Daina 142, 163, 164, 165
Dance 8, 21, 90, 95, 102, 117, 136, 139, 190, 195, 215, 231, 234, 242, 247, 249, 250, 263, 264, 265, 267, 268, 269, 270, 274, 287, 288, 296, 301
Erotic 136
Dithyramb 84
Drumming 18, 180, 248
Eduardas Balsys 172
Flute 177, 247
Isadora Duncan 8
Katzenmusik 251
M. K. Èiurlionis 172
Mikas Petrauskas 172
Minstrel 81
Ritual dance 193
Shamans drum 178
Singing 95, 102, 139, 140, 153, 176, 215, 234, 236, 248, 274, 287, 292
Tambourine 280
Trumpet 234

Christian Penitentials
Indiculus 110, 112, 116, 122
Iscanus 256, 283

Christianization
Baptism 132, 221, 284
Crusades 317
Deicide 59
Demonization 139, 212, 224, 233, 235, 241, 258, 284
Eradication 177
Inquisition 162, 171, 256, 320
Missionaries 46, 170
Penance 164
Shunning 40
Torture 32, 34

Church authorities
Aldegott 300
Auger II de Montfaucon 6
Augustine 27, 30, 56, 95, 315
Balsamon 241
Bede 66, 113, 122, 230

Berthold of Ratisbonne 256
Boniface (Winfred) 110
Briçonnet 77
Burchard 107, 111, 122, 218, 219, 283
Caesarius of Arles 85, 86
Don Alfonso Manriquez 291
Eligius 5, 60, 85, 86, 87, 110, 121, 122
Eustathios Kollas 103
Gregory III 110
Guibert 169
Gulielmus Alvernus 119, 187, 279
Isidore of Seville 87
Jan D³ugosz 132
Jerome of Prague 142, 169
Martin of Braga 87
Maximus, Bishop of Turin 184
Michel Le Nobletz 104, 298
Tikhon Zadonskij 137
William Jones 99
Zonaras 241
Church councils and synods
   Council of Nicaea 80
   Council of Salzburg 187
   Trullo 60, 86, 87, 95, 97, 241
Clans and families
   Flaherty 262
   Lee 54, 321
   Luxembourg 262
   MacHennessy 262
   Rohan 262
   Sassenaye 262
Crossroads and trivia
   Crossroads 167, 226, 243, 280, 294
   Trivia 122, 283
Cults of the Virgin Mary and the saints
   La Vierge au Lys 77
   Our Lady of Aglona 155
   Our Lady of Czestochowa 155
   Our Lady of the Snows 223
   Santa Maria Aracoeli 215
   St. Anne 206
   St. Elias 137
   St. Michael 92, 94, 102
   St. Ursula 76, 77, 113, 206, 223, 228
   St. Vitus 135, 169

D

Days of the week
   Monday 297
   Tuesday 128, 177, 267, 274, 279
   Wednesday 79, 115, 116, 128
   Thursday 78, 110, 117, 121, 123, 125, 131, 132, 212, 213, 228, 267, 274, 279
   Friday 15, 80, 81, 115, 131, 282, 294, 296
   Saturday 69, 262, 265, 274, 275, 279, 305
   Sunday 193, 261, 293, 310
Death and rebirth
   Burial 137, 208, 241
   Cremation 300
   Funeral rites 63, 136, 164, 300
   Metempsychosis 163
   Regeneration 130, 138, 153, 154, 155, 158, 160, 164, 168, 170, 190, 193, 234
   Reincarnation 12, 14, 67, 149, 164
   Transmigration 7
Deities, Baltic
   Andajas 137
   Aušra 141
   Autrimpus 138
   Diveriksas 137
   Ežernim 138
   Žemepatis 73, 138
   Žemyna 145
   Gabija 144, 151, 153, 155
   Giltine 138
   Laima 15, 139, 145, 151, 152, 155, 164, 165, 166, 167, 317
   Lytuvonis 138
   Medeina 137, 139, 140, 141, 151, 152, 153, 155, 165, 167, 170, 235
   Menulis 73, 138, 141, 235
   Nunadievis 137
   Occopirmus 138, 145
   Pagirniai 138, 141
   Patrimpas 138, 156, 159, 160
   Perkûnas 15, 56, 124, 131, 135, 137, 138, 139, 140, 141, 142, 143, 145, 147, 152, 154, 157, 159, 161, 165, 166, 169, 178, 179, 192, 234, 245
   Pilwite 138
   Ragana 151, 153, 154, 159, 171, 183, 234
   Saulë 73, 138, 141, 143, 144, 147, 151, 152, 155, 157, 158
   Teliavelis 137, 138, 142
   Veïu Mâte 144
   Vejopatis 138

Velnias 138, 152, 154, 159, 160, 161, 162, 165, 166, 167, 168
Warpintas 138
Zvoruna 137, 139, 140
Deities, Basque
Aker 173, 174
Basajaun 173, 174, 241
Jaungoikoa 173, 174, 241
Mari 173, 174, 175
Deities, Celtic and Celto-Roman
Andraste 197, 307
Arduinna 60, 208, 264
Arianrhod 307
Badb 109, 177, 189, 197
Belenus 79, 107, 299
Brigid 104, 107, 195
Cailleach 191, 192, 193, 195, 212, 252, 254, 255
Cernunnos 79, 105, 108, 187, 240, 243, 299
Danu 105, 107, 189, 258, 261
Epona 184
Lleu Llaw Gyffes 108
Lugh 108, 109, 307
Macha 109, 197
Matronae 261
Medb 67, 261
Mórrigan 109, 197
Mórrígán 259
Nemain 189, 196, 197
Rosmerta 72, 187
Sirona 72, 109
Sulis 87, 88, 206
Tuatha Dé Danaan 104, 105, 191, 258
Deities, Earth and/or Mother Goddess 6, 64, 65, 66, 68, 69, 72, 79, 92, 114, 128, 130, 139, 154, 179, 183, 191, 211, 214, 237, 255, 273, 292, 306
Anima Mundi 242
Žemyna 15, 63, 66, 70, 73, 145, 151, 153, 155, 168
Erce 66, 68, 217
Jorð 66
Nagy Asszony 177
Nature/Natura 67, 69, 74, 78, 89, 170, 177
Tellus 68, 69, 71
Terra Mater 68, 205
Deities, Egyptian
Isis 3, 57, 59, 63, 64, 71, 72, 74, 75, 76, 77, 78, 79, 93, 102, 105, 113, 115, 127, 205, 206, 207, 220, 225, 228, 254, 315, 316
Egyptian religion 15
Horus 71, 72, 74, 75
Isaic 206
Maat 220
Osiris 6, 71, 72, 74, 75, 176
Serapis 71, 206
Deities, Finno-Ugric
Kuutar 177
Louhi 177, 178
Mielliki 177, 178
Nagy Asszony 177
Nyyrikki 177, 178
Otavatar 177
Päivätär 177
Tähetär 177
Tapio 177, 178
Tellervo 177
Tuoni 177
Ukko 178
Ututyttö 177
Vellamo 177
Deities, Germanic
Aesir 113, 114
Biel 181, 240
Disir 219
Dísir 111, 125, 261
Freyja 64, 67, 76, 81, 88, 98, 112, 113, 116, 129, 130, 183, 187, 205, 212, 217, 218, 220, 228, 229, 230, 251, 276, 282, 283, 294
Freyr 56, 110, 112, 113, 114, 115, 116, 122, 146, 205, 282, 283
Frigga 81, 88, 113, 114, 115, 118, 122, 187, 205, 217, 228, 229, 294, 301
Iðun 230
Loki 118, 121, 283
Norns 14, 88, 111, 112, 134, 139, 219, 232, 259, 261, 276
Odin 56, 66, 80, 110, 111, 114, 115, 116, 117, 118, 119, 121, 122, 123, 124, 156, 184, 194, 196, 217, 221, 243, 283, 299, 308, 317
Ostara/Eostre 66, 113, 186, 221, 230, 231, 232, 252, 254, 255, 301
Sif 121

Thor 56, 110, 111, 114, 116, 117, 121, 122, 123, 124, 125, 131, 135, 141, 146, 169, 178, 179, 192, 217, 245, 276, 283, 316, 317

Trude, or Þhrúðr 125

Urðr 111

Valkyries 67, 88, 111, 112, 125, 126, 183, 194, 228, 264, 301

Vanir 113, 283

Deities, Greek and Roman

Apollo 57, 58, 59, 60, 62, 71, 72, 83, 84, 89, 98, 102, 107, 143, 145, 153, 182, 242

Artemis/Diana 7, 15, 57, 58, 59, 60, 61, 64, 71, 73, 74, 78, 85, 86, 90, 93, 97, 100, 105, 109, 110, 120, 127, 130, 140, 153, 169, 175, 181, 182, 183, 184, 185, 186, 187, 188, 191, 208, 209, 210, 211, 212, 213, 214, 215, 218, 219, 225, 227, 230, 235, 236, 238, 240, 251, 252, 253, 254, 255, 256, 257, 258, 260, 261, 262, 272, 275, 281, 296, 299, 301, 303, 319

Pan 15, 59, 60, 73, 84, 95, 97, 144, 145, 181, 241, 242, 243, 299, 301, 308, 315, 320

Amphitrite 72, 101, 102, 200

Antinous 102

Aphrodite/Venus 15, 33, 57, 58, 59, 61, 64, 72, 74, 78, 80, 81, 83, 91, 92, 102, 127, 130, 153, 181, 186, 206, 225, 229, 258, 262, 276, 293, 294

Ares/Mars 33, 57, 58, 60, 72, 86, 91

Asclepius 83, 138, 145, 156

Attis 58, 59, 92, 153

Baubo 55, 189, 207

Bellona 74, 78, 125, 194, 301, 307

Bendis 175, 188

Cupid 72

Cybele 58, 59, 60, 62, 71, 91, 92, 153, 184, 205, 210, 211, 213, 214, 218, 254

Demeter/Ceres 15, 55, 58, 59, 64, 65, 71, 74, 77, 78, 93, 94, 100, 102, 103, 127, 145, 154, 185, 186, 187, 236, 254

Dionysus/Bacchus 15, 55, 56, 57, 60, 61, 71, 72, 82, 84, 95, 96, 97, 102, 103, 136, 173, 184, 200, 203, 210, 244, 245, 275, 290

Eros 136

Eumenides 305

Flora 64, 72, 175, 261

Furies 145, 305

Gorgon 153, 159, 189

Hecate 74, 78, 83, 93, 100, 122, 130, 133, 154, 156, 167, 177, 185, 186, 194, 197, 225, 235, 238, 272, 301, 303

Helios 80, 83

Hephaestus/Vulcan 62, 136

Hera/Juno 57, 58, 64, 72, 76, 78, 97, 98, 181, 186, 200, 209, 210, 214, 215, 236, 258

Heracles/Hercules 97

Hermes/Mercury 55, 56, 59, 80, 98, 102, 115, 156, 178, 258

Hesperides 89

Hestia/Vesta 64, 72, 89, 107

Hyacinthus 153

Iris 131

Janus 60, 138

Maia 60, 64

Medusa 159

Minerva 16, 57, 64, 72, 76, 78, 87, 88, 89, 90, 91, 97, 107, 125, 181, 182, 206, 252, 254, 256, 292, 293, 301, 307

Mithra 59, 221

Moirae 98, 111, 258

Noctiluca 100, 183, 186

Oceanus 72, 244

Orpheus 185

Parcae 88, 98, 111, 187, 219, 258, 276

Persephone/Proserpina 56, 58, 73, 74, 78, 93, 100, 150, 154, 167, 174, 185, 186, 194, 238

Pomona 72

Poseidon/Neptune 15, 57, 59, 62, 65, 72, 101, 102, 135, 145, 200, 244, 284, 304

Priapus 102, 245

Prometheus 65

Robigus 72

Saturn 56, 58, 65, 80, 145, 245

Selene/Luna 71, 100, 175, 303

Silenus 95

Sylvanus 145

Tyche/Fortuna 15, 145, 187, 210, 232, 275

Zeus 59, 60, 71, 89, 102, 141, 178, 185, 192, 259, 304

Zeus/Jupiter 33, 212

Deities, Indigenous American

Huitzilopochtli 14
La Llorona 133, 226, 304
Deities, Mesopotamian
  Adonis 79, 80, 92, 153, 176
  Astarte 58, 79, 82, 100, 231
  Baal 15, 63, 79
  Jinn 291
  Tanit 58, 82, 100
Deities, Sami
  Baiwe 179
  Biegga Olmai 180
  Horagalles 179, 180, 233
  Jouksáhkká 179
  Junkare 180
  Máttaráhkká 179
  Sáráhkká 179
  Uksáhkká 179
Deities, Slavic
  Baba Yaga 127, 183, 212, 235, 236, 252, 301, 319
  Ciza 76, 83, 127, 128, 130
  Czernobog 137
  Dazhbog 127, 128, 129, 131, 136
  Dodola 233, 234, 252, 254
  Drăgaica 236, 237, 254, 255
  Dziewanna 127
  Ileana 296
  Ileana Sânziana 175, 176, 236, 272, 294
  Kalojan 175, 176
  Khors 127, 129, 131
  Kolyada 127
  Lada 129, 130, 147, 229
  Mat Syra Zemlia 66
  Mokosh 127, 130, 131, 235
  Morena 128, 130
  Pehtra Baba 127, 233, 234, 252, 255
  Perun 127, 132, 133, 135, 178, 192, 234, 245
  Pripoldnica 133, 235
  Püsterich 245, 247
  Radegast 134, 169
  Rod 133
  Rozhanytsi 133, 134
  Simargl 127, 129, 131
  Stribog 127, 129, 131
  Svantovit 134, 135
  Svarog 134, 135, 136
  Triglav 134, 135
  Yarilo 136, 137

  Zlota Baba 233, 234, 252, 255
Deities, witchcraft and/or Winter
  Aradia 20, 187
  Bensozia/Bizazia/Bona Socia 100, 127, 181, 183, 186, 188
  Berchta 205, 226, 229, 234
  Chlungeri 232, 252
  Fru Herke 217, 252, 254
  Gói 193, 194
  Gruagach 191, 254
  Gyre-Carline 194, 195, 197, 252, 254, 255
  Habundia 181, 183, 187, 188, 189, 225, 229, 245, 252, 254, 255, 259, 260, 264
  Herodias 90, 100, 181, 183, 184, 185, 186, 187, 196, 211, 214, 222, 229, 236, 252, 254
  Holda 56, 66, 81, 88, 91, 98, 113, 119, 121, 125, 127, 130, 181, 182, 183, 200, 209, 210, 212, 220, 222, 223, 224, 229, 232, 255, 309, 315, 319
  Hörsel 113, 220, 228, 252, 255, 294
  La Befana 184, 186, 209, 213, 215, 217, 252, 254, 301
  La Guenne 208, 252
  La Signora della Montagna 211, 252
  Lady Sibylla 256, 262
  Lilith 183, 301, 303, 304
  Madona Oriente 211, 252, 254, 255
  Nedela/Nedolya 127
  Nicneven 196, 197, 198, 252, 255, 270
  Perchta 98, 125, 181, 183, 186, 205, 209, 220, 225, 226, 227, 228, 232, 234, 252, 254, 255, 259, 279
  Pharaildis 121, 232, 252
  Phinzen 225, 228, 252, 254
  Pjatnica 127
  Richella 209, 210, 252, 254, 274
  Rupfa 229, 252, 254
  Sack Semper 225, 228, 252
  Saelde 219, 232, 252, 254
  Tante Arie 98, 209, 252, 254, 255
  Vénus de Quinipily 206, 252, 254
  Wanne Thekla 76, 115, 204, 206, 252, 254, 255
  Zobiana 211, 213, 252
Destiny and fate 67, 68, 98, 99, 108, 114, 129, 130, 133, 139, 156, 163, 164, 171, 187, 200, 219, 221, 228, 232, 238
  The Fates 61, 99, 111, 134, 179, 187, 258,

264, 280
Devil and kindred beings
  Beelzebub 79, 123
  Dame Dark 306
  Devils Grandmother 115, 219, 234, 300, 301, 302, 307
  Gello 304, 305
  Goodmans croft 308, 309, 310
  Helen Mcbrune 306
  Lucifer 139, 299
  Malen 306, 307
  Pripegal 300
  Striga/strix 86
  Vrykolakas 305
Divination
  Amatory divination 139, 276
  Astrology 80, 81, 82, 89, 277
  Runes 67, 112, 116, 177, 282
  Tarot 149
Drama
  Adam de la Halle 248, 249
  Ben Jonson
    Oberon, the Fairy Prince 283
  William Shakespeare
    Groundlings 8, 38, 203
    Macbeth 112, 197, 202, 203
    Midsummer Nights Dream 52, 261, 274, 276, 314
    Romeo and Juliet 261
    The Tempest 276
Dreams 10, 20, 55, 79, 89, 168, 204, 209, 237
  Nightmare 279

E

Earth-centered beliefs and practices
  Specific traditions
    Animism 13, 242
    Pantheism 176, 242
    Shamanism 13, 112, 116, 176, 178, 211, 214, 287
Earth-centered worldview 9, 15, 20, 21, 22, 28, 29, 35, 38, 39, 42, 44, 51, 54, 57, 64, 101, 104, 112, 151, 154, 160, 172, 242, 248, 258, 259, 267, 281
Elementals
  Elementals of earth
    Forest nymphs 137
    Genii loci 243
    Gnome 119, 159
    Landvættir 243
  Elementals of water
    Nickers 196, 244
Elves and dwarves
  Álfablót 283
  Dáinn 282
  Dwarves 111, 114, 116, 221, 225, 247, 262, 279, 281, 282, 283, 284, 285, 286, 291
  Elf Queen 221
  Elves 55, 67, 81, 111, 114, 205, 221, 243, 247, 250, 251, 262, 265, 269, 281, 282, 283, 284, 286, 294
  Erdmännlein 283
Embodiment, possession 41, 52, 56, 70, 116, 136, 153, 156, 160, 169, 186, 203, 230, 282, 283

F

Fairies 55, 61, 67, 90, 92, 104, 105, 109, 111, 115, 119, 127, 128, 167, 181, 183, 188, 189, 192, 198, 204, 208, 211, 219, 220, 236, 243, 247, 250, 256, 257, 258, 259, 260, 261, 262, 263, 264, 265, 266, 267, 268, 269, 270, 271, 272, 273, 274, 275, 276, 277, 278, 279, 280, 281, 282, 284, 292, 301, 303, 309
  Anne Jeffries 268
  Ariel 201, 203, 276, 291
  Arsile 261
  Dames Vertes 264
  Dominae bonae 260
  Donni di fuora 273
  Elidyr 266, 267
  Esterelle 208, 252, 254
  Eugene Garriggia 269, 270
  Fairy cult 206, 256, 260, 273, 274, 276, 279
  Fairy feast 256, 279, 296
  Fairy King 73, 261, 274, 277, 278
  Fairy Queen 53, 62, 67, 73, 81, 107, 175, 185, 193, 214, 220, 234, 250, 258, 259, 261, 262, 264, 272, 273, 274, 275, 277, 278, 296, 303
  Hansel and Gretel 235
  Invoking fairies 276
    Elias Ashmole and William Lilly 277
  Lanan shi 270
  Laumës 70, 151, 152, 167, 168, 261, 262

Mab 67
Magloire 261
Morgue 261
Nether Buckie 270
Nibelungen 277
Oberon 201, 261, 276, 277, 283
Paris 259, 260, 278
Queen Maeve/Mab 67, 259, 261
Salige 261
Sibylia 262, 264, 276, 277
Sleeping Beauty 229
Thom Reid 273
Titania 201, 258, 261, 264
Vily 261
Familiars
  Maistre Persil 289, 290, 291
  Rutterkin 289, 290
  Sotheons 289, 290
Fire
  Bonfires 93, 143, 231, 232
  Hearth 144, 152, 153, 179, 259, 275, 280, 289
  Veneration of fire 144
Flowers 297, 317, 319, 320
  Aconite 124
  Cowslip 226
  Daisy 147, 225
  Eglantine 90
  Perûnik flower (Iris germanica) 131
  Primrose 225
  Rose 15, 133, 149, 220, 227, 229, 249, 259
  Roses 129, 162, 186, 278
  Violet 90, 95
  Yarrow 112, 276
Folk figures and local divinities
  Aïa 213, 252, 254
  Aitvaras 289
  Žaltys 146, 147, 148, 149, 150, 151, 152, 153, 154, 155, 156, 158, 159, 160, 161, 162, 165, 166, 167, 168, 170, 171, 172
  Apydeme 289
  Aspelinie 289
  Barghest 286
  Bil 229, 230, 245
  Brava Part 209, 252, 254
  Brownie 286
  Buccas 286
  Christsonday 73, 249, 250, 274
  Davy Jones 199, 202, 204, 244

Dimstipatis 289
Dobie 286
Dvorovoy 289
Eglë 146, 147, 148, 149, 150, 151, 152, 153, 154, 155, 156, 158, 159, 160, 161, 162, 166, 167, 168, 170, 171, 172
Faun 283
Frau Werra 228, 233, 234, 252, 254, 301
Fru Gaue 217, 228, 252, 254
Glaistig 288
Green Man 108, 240, 245
Gruagach 190, 286
Harlequin 204
Harvest Queen 69, 93
Herne the Hunter 108, 240
Hjúki 230, 245
Hobgoblin 243
Jecha 229, 230, 254
John Barleycorn 108
Kaukai 159, 286, 287
Kikimora 289
Knockers 286
Kornmutter 128
Krodo 245
Lady Horiens 211
Leshy 240
Lord of the Forest 73, 108, 174, 240, 241
Ludki 286, 287
Maid Marian 248
Mélusine 262
Mermaid 192, 206, 262
Messerweible 128
Metal Man 250
Mither o the Sea 198, 252, 255
Mother Carey 198, 199, 200, 201, 202, 203, 252, 254, 255, 318
Mother Goose 98, 200, 225, 232, 319
Mourie 181, 241
Nymph 258
Ovinnik 289
Pasichnyk 289
Pied Piper 247
Polevik 289
Puck 108, 181, 201, 203, 240, 242, 243, 250, 255, 276, 289, 290, 308
Robert the Jackis 250
Robin Artisson 243
Robin Goodfellow 181, 242, 243, 250, 256, 264,

290, 306, 308
Robin Hood 19, 169, 181, 239, 242, 243, 248, 249, 250, 256, 264, 289, 291, 306, 308
Saiwo 287
Satyr 283
Scrat 251
Selkies 262
Senach 198
Sheela-na-gig 189, 190, 254
Shony 181, 243, 244, 255, 270
Spriggans 286
Trolls 225, 284, 285, 286, 287, 288
Vampire 86, 300, 305
Werewolf 111, 235, 251, 300

Foods
Bannock 281
Bread 63, 74, 76, 99, 134, 144, 145, 148, 153, 188, 209, 215, 217, 224, 227, 266, 268, 269, 278, 279, 280, 287, 288, 289, 291, 293, 296
Butter 280, 287, 289
Cake 69, 99, 124, 129, 135, 144, 190, 221, 225, 227, 231, 261, 262, 270
Feast 72, 95, 99, 109, 110, 124, 131, 135, 179, 180, 184, 188, 190, 193, 206, 210, 216, 227, 230, 249, 250, 272, 273, 278, 279, 280, 283
Gingerbread 124, 231, 262
Herring 227
Honey 99, 128, 134, 135, 139, 144, 156, 177, 186, 227, 261, 279, 291, 296
Thar-Cake 124, 317

Fruits
Apple 15, 83, 107, 143, 163, 207, 211, 222
Fruits 65, 71, 72, 95, 129, 145, 159, 165, 187, 215, 221, 222, 224, 278
Grapes 97, 127
Strawberries 114, 238

G

Gender diversity
"dressing and living as a woman" 116
Ceremonial cross-dressing or mixed gender attire 116, 215, 249
Hermaphrodite or intersex 251
Personae
Hynd Knight 251, 309
Jalkr 116

Junius 65, 71
Transgender metamorphosis 177

H

Healing 16, 43, 44, 68, 70, 72, 84, 107, 109, 128, 131, 138, 156, 157, 158, 163, 168, 175, 186, 189, 190, 207, 209, 210, 211, 221, 254, 261, 268, 272, 274, 275, 276, 279, 290, 293, 294, 295, 296, 297
Epilepsy 163, 275
Fever 104, 142, 296
Headache 87
Rheumatism 125, 207
Toothache 142
Herbal medicine
Basil 124, 176
Herbal medicine 84, 109, 211, 261, 273, 288
Herbs 294
Rue 94, 129, 147, 186, 278
Thyme 129
Heroes
Cú Chulainn 108
Hyperochus and Amadocus 61, 128
Hills and mountains
Aizkorri 174
Amboto 174
Brocken 223
Carlines Loup 194
Eryx 82
Gudenberg 169
Harz Mountains 120, 245
Harz mountains 223
Hills 67, 95, 137, 178, 228, 231, 241, 246, 264, 275
Hörselberg 81, 217, 220, 227, 228, 294
Monti Sibillini 82
Mountain 82, 91, 119, 134, 137, 174, 192, 193, 195, 208, 216, 217, 220, 221, 225, 227, 228, 243, 259, 263, 266
Muru 174

I

Incantation, invocation, praise-hymn
Incantation 7, 269
Invocation 6, 7, 64, 67, 68, 69, 71, 72, 78, 79, 80, 81, 83, 84, 86, 87, 100, 102, 109, 110, 116, 117, 126, 130, 133, 141, 142, 145, 198, 202, 233, 234, 250, 262, 276, 277, 278, 283, 291, 292, 296, 309

Invoke 71, 87, 95, 97, 117, 198, 278, 286, 296
Praise-hymn 81
Incense and perfume
Frankincense 278
Incense 57, 83, 168, 176, 278, 279
Perfume 20, 58, 81, 279
Indigeneity 6, 7, 8, 9, 10, 11, 12, 13, 15, 16, 17, 19, 20, 21, 36, 46, 49, 58, 61, 66, 69, 92, 100, 131, 206, 218, 238, 239, 254, 272, 291
Intermediaries 41, 98, 157, 159, 160, 201
Psychopomp 98, 105, 144, 211, 235

L

Literature, 19th century
Gérard de Nerval 16
Percy Bysshe Shelley 84, 242
Literature, 20th and 21st centuries
Gloria Anzaldúa 175
Literature, ancient
Apuleius 57, 74, 315
Athenaeus 185, 186
Homer 61
Literature, medieval
Mabinogion 240
Poetic Edda 66, 317
Roman de la Rose 91, 188
Tristan and Isolde 91
Love, sexuality, marriage
Amatory magic 91
Bride 71, 80, 96, 154, 160, 168
Courtesan 185, 238, 301
Eroticism 59, 80, 112, 113, 121, 130, 294
Groom 80, 168
Hieros gamos 67, 70, 114, 277
Love 15, 20, 47, 80, 81, 83, 85, 91, 96, 99, 113, 114, 121, 129, 136, 141, 147, 150, 159, 161, 167, 171, 175, 186, 196, 214, 229, 230, 231, 233, 248, 254, 261, 269, 277, 294, 295, 299, 301, 306
Lovemaking 231, 274, 277
Marriage 70, 89, 96, 97, 99, 113, 114, 126, 129, 130, 134, 135, 139, 148, 151, 157, 166, 167, 168, 171, 175, 177, 183, 203, 210, 237, 252, 254, 269, 270, 292, 293
Passionate lover 141
Prostitute 273
Wedding 31, 71, 80, 130, 152, 160, 210, 220, 237, 268

M

Magic
Charm 60, 79, 87, 92, 106, 112, 117, 118, 168, 282, 283
Curse 69, 133, 165, 167, 187, 203, 262, 302, 310
Galdr 112
Love magic 295
Magical flight 85, 194, 196, 203, 266, 307
Magical practice 20, 56, 251, 268
Rainmaking 131, 234
Seiðr 52, 66, 88, 112, 116, 195, 212, 251, 282
Materials used in pagan practices
Amulet 122, 303
Black wool 275
Bottle 291, 296
Cauldron 121
Chalice 161, 215
Dirt 304
Mandrake 81, 159, 175, 228, 261, 282, 289, 293, 294, 295, 296, 297
Menstrual blood 179
Mirror 98, 144, 242, 278, 280
Ointment 270
Pendant 122
Poppet 295, 296, 297
Powder 77, 273
Rags 146, 214
Salt 275
Shells 61
Talisman 146
Metamorphosis 8, 42, 56, 63, 105, 120, 128, 152, 153, 158, 174, 178, 190, 191, 215, 219, 223, 258, 262, 283, 304. *See also* See gender diversity
Shapeshifting 56, 130, 144, 174, 195, 243, 250, 251, 288, 289, 296, 302
Theriomorphic 177, 196, 210

O

Offerings and sacrifices
Barley 291
Birds 278
Blood 291
Bread 134, 291, 296
Bull 241

Cake 124, 144, 156, 185, 190, 270, 279, 295, 296
Candles 77, 134, 143, 174, 176, 202, 227, 260
Cheese 134
   Pecorino 215
   Ricotta 215
Chicken 291
Desserts 278
Eggs 295
Feast 278
Goat 174
Honey 134
Jugs of water and wine 279
Milk 278, 291
Money 174
Oats 291
Pigeon 278
Porridge 278
Red ribbon 295
Roses 278
Sacrifice 278
Salt 134
Sheep 107, 130, 131, 143, 148, 174, 192, 238, 278
Sugar 296
Sweetmeats 279
Tables of Fortune 279
Wheat 291
Wine 134, 296
Otherworlds and afterlife locations
   Avalon 83, 259
   Fairy realm 52
   Magonia 271, 321
   Phairie 272
   Tuonela 177
   Valhalla 115, 118, 125

P

Pagan rebellion
   Erick Clauesson 117
   Magyars 176, 177
Paganism and the pagan worldview
   Pasaulëþiûra 154, 160, 168, 170, 171
Painters
   Bentveughels 96
   Luca Signorelli 8
Philosophers and related
   Apollonius of Tyana 98
   Giordano Bruno 30
   Leo Allatios 305
   Marsilio Ficino 30
   Pico della Mirandola 242
   Plato 8, 27, 30, 31
   Platonic Academy 59
   Pythagoras 294
   Symmachus 50, 314
Procreation, pregnancy, childbirth
   Childbirth 18, 63, 79, 85, 130, 134, 139, 154, 157, 160, 177, 179, 189, 232, 254, 260, 261, 271, 285
   Pregnancy 97, 139, 179, 187, 192, 208, 221, 222, 237, 279, 304
Psychic abilities
   Clairvoyance 264
   Telepathy 232

R

Rainbow 139
Ritual specialists
   Brujas 173, 174, 175
   Druid 104, 169, 306
   Estries 189
   Haegtesse 234
   Hechiceras 173
   Klok gumma 283
   Pagan priest 171, 246
   Persons
      Isobel Gowdie 197, 281, 299, 321
      Alice Kyteler 243
      Alison Peirsoun 258, 273
      Anders Paulsen 180
      Andro Man 73, 250, 251, 274, 275, 309
      Antonia Pallagona 279
      Aurinia 294
      Bessie Dunlop 272
      Circe 83, 93, 167, 201
      Demetrios of Sparta 62
      Janet McGillichoan 197
      Joan Flower 290
      John Dee 203
      Jonet Wischert 309
      Margaret Ragum Bouchery 297
      Mause and Jenny Barry 194
      Medea 83, 93, 166, 235
      North Berwick witches 203
      Prospero 201, 276

Ragnhild Tregagås 126
　　　Sibillia Zanni 211
　　　Thom Reid 273
　　　Tiresias 116, 192, 235
　　　Veleda 111, 219, 230
　　　Walburg 184
　　Priestess 7, 52, 56, 58, 66, 82, 92, 104, 111, 141, 153, 171, 173, 186, 192, 195, 208, 211, 219, 223, 230, 231, 232, 260, 270, 277, 278
　　Pythoness/pythonissa 188
　　Ragana 148
　　Shaman 235
　　Sorceress 85, 91, 148, 166, 167, 212, 259, 294
　　Streghe 301
　　Strigae 186
　　Stryx 189
　　Tietäjä 178
　　Wisewomen 7, 55, 175, 222, 231, 264, 272, 273, 279, 294, 295
　　Witch - Passim
Rulers and nobles
　　Charlemagne 86, 110, 169
　　Childebert I 75
　　Clovis I 75
　　Constantine the Great 80
　　Empress Helena 80, 316
　　Gediminas 138
　　Henry VIII 249
　　James VI/ I 272
　　Julian "the Apostate" 16, 33, 61, 65, 78, 127, 137, 315, 316
　　King Cnut 6
　　Queen Elizabeth I 42
　　Queen of Sheba 274
　　Vladimir the Greaat 16, 127, 131

S

Sacred hybridity 10, 19, 34, 35, 40, 53, 56, 77, 80, 110, 172, 206, 281, 300
　　Pagano-Christian 8, 35, 88, 118, 182, 249, 261, 285, 298, 300
Societies and communities
　　Companies of the Mother 273
　　Donni di fuora 273
　　Hell-fire clubs 310
　　Palermo 273
　　Philike Hetairia 94
　　Ragusa 273
　　Table and Distaff 273
　　The Noble 273
　　The Poor 273
　　The Romans 273
Soul 53, 68, 98, 115, 119, 152, 157, 160, 163, 164, 165, 166, 167, 184, 194, 199, 200, 211, 221, 225, 228, 253, 261, 304
Siela 163, 164
Stones, gemstones, metals
　　Amber (fossilized resin) 159
　　Metals
　　　Bronze 90, 96, 141
　　　Copper 15, 122, 141, 143, 276, 304
　　　Gold 81, 90, 95, 99, 100, 112, 121, 134, 135, 161, 174, 178, 186, 187, 213, 223, 224, 225, 226, 227, 233, 234, 266, 271, 274
　　　Iron 60, 76, 94, 98, 121, 142, 148, 154, 177, 195, 240, 243, 250
　　　Silver 81, 90, 128, 131, 134, 135, 141, 143, 178, 215, 220, 266, 267, 268, 276, 284, 292, 296
　　Named stones
　　　Externsteine 221, 231
　　Quartz 276
　　Sacred stones 44, 106, 129, 140, 150, 174, 204, 231, 232, 250, 306
　　Types of stone structures
　　　Dolmen 70, 174, 208
　　　Megalith 190
　　　Menhir 131

T

Tasks and professions
　　Baker 153, 209, 234
　　Beekeeper 140
　　Blacksmith 154, 174, 241
　　Farmer 61, 92, 141, 142, 143, 144, 150, 178, 187, 217, 219, 220, 222, 224, 238, 273, 286, 288, 308, 309, 310
　　Fisher folk 83, 138, 177, 198, 244, 273
　　Gamester 82
　　Goatherd 175
　　Laundress 273
　　Midwife 85, 127, 149, 179, 288
　　Milkmaid 280
　　Miller 174, 241

Miner 284, 285, 286
Shepherd 60, 174, 175, 238, 241, 242, 248
Shoemaker 270, 273
Spinner 88, 99, 124, 125, 130, 131, 139, 148, 152, 154, 177, 179, 183, 195, 196, 205, 210, 217, 221, 225, 228, 233, 234, 235, 245, 254, 266, 273, 288
   Distaff 148, 214, 229
Vintner 96, 97, 221
Weaver 87, 88, 92, 139, 152, 177, 183, 205, 210, 235, 254

Theisms
  Duotheism 71, 73, 248, 302
  Henotheism 52
  Monotheism 15, 16, 21, 43, 50, 51, 52, 53, 55, 56, 132
  Polytheism 5, 6, 7, 14, 21, 50, 51, 52, 53, 55, 56, 57, 71, 73, 181

Theoretical concepts
  Absolutism 24, 37, 42
  Alternative ways of knowing 37
  Archaeomythology 154
  Archetypal perspective 31, 87, 105, 116, 131, 139, 150, 154, 214, 251, 258, 303, 307
  Bricolage 56, 248
  Buried knowledges 43, 44
  Cartesian paradigm 28, 29, 42
  Christocentrism 14, 27, 35, 36, 39
  Counterdiscourse 8, 45
  Enspirited materiality 18, 19, 66, 175, 277, 281, 291
  Fluidity 22
  Hegemonic discourse 45
  Heterodox knowledge 154, 171
  Holistic perspective 10
  Holographic principle 54
  Implicate order 54, 55
  Invisible immanence 54, 55, 267, 271
  Liminality 235
  Material religion 146
  Multidimensional reality 15, 20, 41, 52, 53, 54, 55, 265, 267, 272
  Newtonian paradigm 28, 29
  Quantum theory 41, 55
  String theory 272
  Subaltern theory 38, 39
  Subjugated knowledges 43, 44, 45
  Theory of correspondences 15, 56, 102, 105, 145, 147, 284
  Unsanctioned narratives 44
  Vernacular theory 38, 147, 157, 159, 189, 263

Trees
  Alder 162, 179
  Ash 116, 164, 166, 167, 190
  Beech 231
  Birch 129, 149, 152, 162, 163, 164, 165, 167, 180, 235, 241, 261
  Chestnut 202, 215, 269
  Cornel 164, 168
  Fir tree 168
  Hazel 241
  Irminsul 122
  Juniper 163, 164, 169
  Linden 113, 139, 140, 152, 153, 163, 164, 165
  Maple 162, 163, 164, 165
  Oak 70, 107, 131, 135, 138, 140, 141, 142, 153, 163, 164, 165, 166, 167, 168, 169, 170, 222, 240, 241
  Pine 145, 151, 163, 164, 168, 169, 208, 215
  Poplar 167, 168
  Sacred grove 140
  Sacred groves 145, 162, 169
    Fochloch 169
    Hare Churches (Kiškio bažnyèia) 140
    North Karelia 177
    Romuva 137, 138, 150, 165, 317
    Savo 177
    Teutoburg Forest 231
    šventa giria 169
  Spruce 151, 152, 153, 163, 164, 168, 169
  Walnut 274
  Willow 160, 162, 167, 241, 272
  World-tree 156, 166, 167
  Yggdrasil 156, 169

V

Vegetables
  Beet 147
  Corn 73, 93, 113, 136, 139, 159, 178, 217, 269

W

War, warriors, weapons
  Axe 141, 142, 143, 147, 169
  Battle 27, 28, 61, 91, 109, 110, 112, 115, 125, 141, 190, 194, 196, 226, 228, 303, 307

Berserkr 197
Helmet 125, 156, 299
Shield 125, 156
Spear 85, 97, 108, 116, 137, 188, 240, 283
Sword 91, 98, 134, 135, 156, 292, 295
Ulfserkr 197
War 14, 80, 86, 87, 108, 109, 131, 134, 135, 136, 156, 165, 197, 221, 231, 235, 307
Warrior 58, 61, 67, 91, 112, 115, 125, 137, 140, 141, 142, 156, 176, 189, 192, 197, 277, 292
Warriorship 97

Water, bodies of water, and water rites
Baptism 58
Eżerai 138
Fountain 6, 47, 220, 292
Sauna 160, 178
Sea 198
Werra River 234

Wheel of the Year
Autumn
Harvest rites 217
Samhain (Halloween) 22, 168, 198, 222, 241, 243, 244, 250, 264, 274, 306
Fall equinox 279
Spring
Beltane 79, 107, 122, 190, 248, 250, 264, 301, 307, 308
Floralia 122
Spring equinox 123, 130, 136, 144, 146, 147, 152, 158, 167, 198, 213, 234, 237, 238, 248, 279, 297
Velykos 158
Walpurgisnacht 301
Summer
Lughnasa/Lammas 106, 108, 193
Semik 136
Summer solstice 128, 129, 136, 143, 158, 160, 167, 176, 237
Winter
Bacchanalia 95
Carnival 92, 205, 228, 229, 236
Harvest rites 93
Imbolc/Candlemas 143, 195, 244, 272
Matronalia 97
Solstice 95, 119, 122, 136, 176, 177, 183, 184, 217, 222, 233, 237
Twelfth Night 187, 213, 279
Wild Hunt 115, 118, 119, 120, 184, 194, 217, 222, 223, 226, 233, 282, 307
Yule 230

www.ingramcontent.com/pod-product-compliance
Lightning Source LLC
Chambersburg PA
CBHW080407230426
43662CB00016B/2341